PRO TOOLS® LE 7 IGNITE!

Second Edition

The Visual Guide for New Users

Andy Hagerman

COURSE TECHNOLOGY
CENGAGE Learning™

COURSE TECHNOLOGY
CENGAGE Learning™

Pro Tools LE 7 Ignite!, Second Edition
Andy Hagerman

Publisher and General Manager,
Course Technology PTR: Stacy L. Hiquet

Associate Director of Marketing: Sarah Panella

Manager of Editorial Services: Heather Talbot

Marketing Manager: Mark Hughes

Executive Editor: Mark Garvey

Project Editor/Copy Editor: Cathleen D. Small

Technical Reviewer: Brent Heber

PTR Editorial Services Coordinator: Erin Johnson

Interior Layout: Shawn Morningstar

Cover Designer: Mike Tanamachi

CD-ROM Producer: Brandon Penticuff

Indexer: Sherry Massey

Proofreader: Kim V. Benbow

For product information and technology assistance, contact us at

Cengage Learning Customer & Sales Support, 1-800-354-9706

For permission to use material from this text or product, submit all requests online at **cengage.com/permissions**

Further permissions questions can be emailed to **permissionrequest@cengage.com**

Library of Congress Control Number: 2007938247
ISBN-13: 978-1-59863-479-2
ISBN-10: 1-59863-479-8

Course Technology
25 Thomson Place
Boston, MA 02210
USA

Cengage Learning is a leading provider of customized learning solutions with office locations around the globe, including Singapore, the United Kingdom, Australia, Mexico, Brazil, and Japan. Locate your local office at: **international.cengage.com/region**

Cengage Learning products are represented in Canada by Nelson Education, Ltd.

For your lifelong learning solutions, visit **courseptr.com**
Visit our corporate website at **cengage.com**

Printed in the United States of America
1 2 3 4 5 6 7 11 10 09 08

This book is dedicated to Junko Hagerman,
the love and the light of my life.

Acknowledgments

Though the creation of a book is a long and sometimes difficult journey, the right companions along the way can make the whole process fun. This book has certainly been a pleasure to bring to you, due to the teamwork and contributions of some of the best in the business. The team at Cengage has been a joy to work with, with particular thanks going to Cathleen Small and Mark Garvey for their excellent editing and coordination. Brent Heber lent his massive expertise as technical editor, making sure that the information we bring to you is accurate and comprehensive. Not only are these folks all aces at what they do, I'm happy to count them as friends as well.

There are other people who, though not directly involved with the creation of this book, have helped immensely. Thanks go to the great staff at Digidesign—the company's success in our industry is due in no small part to the skill, devotion, and downright passion of their people. Thanks to Dave Oxenreider and Brian Smithers for their unwavering faith and support (and for helping "release my inner geek," as Brian would put it). Finally, and most importantly, thanks to my family (my wife, Junko, and daughter, Sachiko) for their love.

About the Author

Andy Hagerman has been a professional musician for the majority of his 42 years, beginning with formal musical training as a classical tuba player (yes, tuba). During his years at Northwestern University (working toward a bachelor's degree) in the early 1980s, music technology began to take off with the introduction of MIDI, and Andy was immediately hooked. As music and audio technology has advanced over the years, he has worked to keep up with this evolution, constantly amazed at the creative doorways that have opened as a result.

In addition to being a performing musician around the world (including at Disneyland, Walt Disney World, and Tokyo Disney Sea), Hagerman has channeled his love of music technology toward compositional pursuits. Particularly active in the planetarium field, he has composed original music for clients ranging from the American Museum of Natural History to Caterpillar Tractors. He's also had the privilege of teaching others the art and craft of digital audio in a number of ways, including as a lecturer at Full Sail, a college in Central Florida.

These days, Andy is busy working and playing in Tokyo, Japan. He works with musicians and educators throughout the growing Asia Pacific region, is an active composer with Singularity Arts (www.singularityarts.com), and continues to create music for a variety of uses.

Contents

Introduction

First off, congratulations on becoming a Pro Tools user, and welcome! I suppose such sentiments are on Page 1 of virtually every user's guide and manual, but this time is a little different. When Digidesign says that their powerful Digital Audio Workstation (DAW) is the industry standard (for good reason), you can believe it. Indeed, you'll find the full Pro Tools product line, from the Mbox2 Mini all the way up to high-end HD systems, hard at work in every facet of audio and musical production. It's a serious, professional product, and your decision to buy it (and learn it) is a step in the right direction.

Speaking of steps, remember the old saying, "A journey of a thousand miles begins with a single step?" That's where this book comes in. Gaining a solid fundamental understanding of the basics will ensure that your journey starts off well prepared and heads in the right direction. In this book, you'll learn the basic techniques of creating, recording, editing, and mixing digital audio and MIDI (*Musical Instrument Digital Interface*). You'll learn to harness the power of Pro Tools' impressive array of tools, from software effects to virtual instruments, to create mixes that are automated and edited with some of the best tools in the business.

This is my third *Pro Tools Ignite!* book, the first being about version 6 of the software, and the second being about Pro Tools 7 (based upon version 7.1). This third *Ignite!* book stands on the shoulders of the previous titles and adds some of the very exciting new features that were introduced in Pro Tools LE 7.3 and 7.4. Even though Pro Tools has been a world leader for some time, I think you'll find that some of the newest features are particularly exciting for LE users, especially for the musically creative. These new tools, combined with the solid foundation of the Pro Tools DAW in general, open the door to inspiring possibilities indeed.

If you're out to create and produce audio, Pro Tools is an obvious choice, and *Pro Tools LE 7 Ignite!* will be your companion during those critical first steps down the road to success and fun!

Who Should Read This Book

This book is geared toward beginners with little or no experience in working with a DAW. You'll find that the book's highly graphical and plainly worded style makes it easy to follow. Further, once you're finished with the chapters and exercises, it will be a valuable reference later on as well. Nearly every step in the processes discussed is accompanied by clear illustrations, so you won't have to spend your time hunting around the screen for tools and menus. (What fun is *that*?)

Don't worry if you're not a formally trained musician or if you haven't really dealt with digital audio before. The beauty of Pro Tools and computer music in general is that even untrained (but creative) musicians can enjoy great success in this kind of environment. In fact, many of the new features in Pro Tools make it even easier and more fun to be creative than in previous versions! Of course, any general music or audio knowledge you bring to the table is an added advantage, but it is certainly not a requirement for this book.

Now, with that being said, Pro Tools is a *deep* program, and even those of us who have been using it for years are still finding new tidbits now and then. For that reason, I can't dedicate the limited space I have in this book to covering basic computer operations. That means it's up to you to understand the most basic processes of your particular platform (either a Mac running OS X or a PC running Windows XP). Don't worry too much, though—the general computer knowledge required to use Pro Tools is pretty basic, and if you can locate, launch, and close programs already, you're probably in fine shape.

How to Use This Book

Music in general is a progressive process, and from creation to performance it's the result of many small steps taken in order. A solid mastery of Pro Tools works much the same way. The book is laid out to mirror the creative process, from setup through the recording process, editing, mixing, and putting on the final touches. Additionally, the first sections of the book will also include a bit of information about the nature of DAWs in general, so that you understand the logic of these devices and can work most efficiently. If you're just beginning with DAWs, you'll find this information valuable in the long run.

Because the book is arranged sequentially according to the production process, you'll be able to follow it from the very start of a project through its completion. If you're interested in some areas more than others though (which is pretty common with more experienced users), feel free to read the book out of order and just concentrate on specific sections first—this book will work that way as well.

You'll find that most of this book is laid out in a tutorial-style format; there are even tutorial files you can download and use side by side with the book's examples. Of course, you can also use this book as a point reference source as well, using the clear, illustrated style of this format to your advantage as you locate specific functions.

Last but not least, you'll note that peppered throughout this book are a number of Notes. Take a look at these to find additional ways to increase your efficiency, additional information on key functions, and even warnings that point out common pitfalls and how to avoid them.

NOTE

Speaking of notes, there's no time like the present to start!

If you've already got some experience with a previous version of Pro Tools, you might be particularly interested in checking out what's new in the software. This book has been updated to show the latest features as of Pro Tools LE v.7.4, which includes updated screenshots, shortcuts, and other general information throughout the text.

Additionally, you'll find sections dedicated to features introduced in version 7.3 or 7.4. Section titles will call attention to features added in these later versions.

Finally, a Little History...

Pro Tools systems can be broken down into two families: HD and LE. HD systems are derived from a hardware-based architecture, which means that there are PCI cards with chips dedicated to the tasks of running Pro Tools functions. This means two things: First, it is a reliable, scalable, powerful system—an obvious advantage for professional facilities. Second, it costs more (and it can be a *lot* more).

LE systems aren't hardware-based; they're host-based, which simply means that the host computer (meaning the computer that you're using to run the software) is charged with all the tasks of running Pro Tools, from recording and playback to effects and automation. This allows an LE system to be a good deal more economical than its HD counterpart. Of course, since your computer's CPU is doing *everything*, you won't get the same kind of power from an LE system, and there are a few features that are reserved for HD systems only.

The good news—and it's great news, really—is that the software environments in HD and LE are nearly identical. This means you can take advantage of one of the most powerful and well-developed user interfaces on the market. What's more, if and when it becomes time for you to upgrade to HD, you'll already know the software.

In recent history, Digidesign introduced the Pro Tools LE version 7 series (for PC and Mac), which incorporated some real advancements, especially for LE users. Among the advancements are:

- A new, cleaner user interface and a well-designed reorganization of menus and tools
- Additional editing power, including region looping and Region Groups
- New MIDI features, such as dedicated Instrument tracks, previewing options, and new MIDI editing tools
- New free plug-ins, such as Dynamics III and EQ III Band-Pass Filter

Digidesign followed up on the successful release of Pro Tools LE 7 with Pro Tools LE 7.3, which added even *more* good stuff, such as:

- New organizational tools, such as variable track heights, track colors, and customizable Window Configurations
- Powerful new editing tools, such as Region Groups and region looping
- A greatly enhanced new mixing environment, which allows you to do more than you ever could before—and all without stopping playback

Now we've got Pro Tools LE 7.4, which adds a few more great tools to the mix, including:

- Elastic Audio
- A greatly improved file-browsing environment
- New flexibility in setting up your session's fundamental processing, which will enable you to get maximum power out of your system when you need it most

If a lot of this sounds like Greek right now, don't worry—we'll cover it in the chapters to come. Ready? Let's go!

1 Welcome to Pro Tools LE 7

Congratulations, and welcome to the world of Pro Tools! Through the more than 20 years of Digidesign's history, Pro Tools has established itself at the forefront of the DAW (*Digital Audio Workstation*) community, and version 7.x (including versions 7.1, 7.3, and 7.4) provides a new level of power and creativity. As a result, Pro Tools 7 can be found in virtually every level of the audio industry, from music production for CDs to surround sound for theatrical soundtracks. Now, armed with Pro Tools LE's powerful array of functions and features, you'll be able to tap into this world of digital audio for yourself to realize your own creative vision. Welcome to the party!

The first step in the process is to set up your system and master the basic functioning of Pro Tools. In this chapter, we'll discuss the structure, function, and most basic operations of Pro Tools LE 7, and you'll learn how to:

- Identify and assemble the hardware and software components of a Pro Tools LE system and understand their functions
- Organize sessions and data in Pro Tools
- Use Pro Tools' most basic functions
- Create, open, play, and close a session

What Makes Up a Pro Tools System?

Digidesign's Pro Tools systems fall into one of two families—LE or HD. Pro Tools LE, which we'll discuss in this book, is a *host-based* type of DAW, which means that the overall system completely relies upon the processing power of your computer's CPU (the *host*) for operations such as mixing and effects processing. HD systems, on the other hand, have dedicated PCI hardware cards added to the computer, which take care of those kinds of functions.

HD systems, because of their added processing horsepower and greater flexibility, tend to be more commonly found in professional recording studios, whereas LE systems have found their niche in the growing number of home and project studios worldwide. It bears mentioning that both types of systems are certainly pro-level in their own right, and the broad compatibility of Pro Tools allows you to begin projects in LE-based home studios, and then complete them in more powerful HD-powered studios with ease!

Let's talk about your new Pro Tools LE system. LE systems, regardless of their specific configurations, all rely on a few key components.

The Heart of Your DAW: The Computer

The host computer is the cornerstone of your Pro Tools LE system. Your computer, particularly your computer's CPU (*Central Processing Unit*), will be called upon to do everything from mixing and automation to effects processing, so the more speed your CPU has, the more powerful your Pro Tools software will be. The host computer can be either a PC (running Windows XP, Vista Business, or Vista Ultimate) or a Mac (with OS X).

In addition to CPU speed, your computer's RAM (*Random Access Memory*) plays a role in how your digital audio workstation will perform. It probably comes as no surprise to hear that the more RAM your computer has, the better. Your RAM will allow your Pro Tools session to run more real-time effects and will make for an overall more powerful DAW.

Ideally, your DAW computer should be dedicated solely to music-related tasks. Other applications running on your system can steal from your computer's overall efficiency when running Pro Tools. The task of recording and playing digital audio can be very demanding on your computer's CPU, and other programs, interrupting the steady stream of data to and from your hard drive, can cause major problems. Of course, having such a dedicated computer can be impractical for many users; in that case, you should avoid resource-sapping applications (particularly games) and limit the number of programs active during your Pro Tools sessions.

Pro Tools Audio Interface

Your Pro Tools audio interface (which you purchased with your system) is the doorway for audio going to and coming from your computer. Generally speaking, your computer will connect directly to the audio interface, and your various audio devices (mixing boards, keyboards, or microphones) will connect to the interface's available audio inputs. To listen to your session, you should connect the audio outputs of your interface to an amplifier, and from there to monitor speakers. Following is a brief rundown of the audio interfaces available for Pro Tools LE systems and their key features.

Mbox 2 Micro

The Mbox 2 Micro is Digidesign's newest addition to the LE family, and already it's making a big splash. The real attractiveness of this particular interface is its size—it's roughly the size of a USB flash drive, which allows Pro Tools users to work virtually anywhere (in combination with a laptop).

There's one limitation that you should be aware of with the Micro, however, and that lies in its I/O complement: There are *no* inputs on the Mbox 2 Micro (which one might reasonably expect given its compact size), so you won't be able to use it for typical recording purposes. However, if you're looking to take a previously recorded session on the road, or you are only concerned with composing with virtual instruments and pre-made bits of audio, this is an interface worth looking at. Here's what you'll get:

- USB connection to the host computer, which also powers the unit. An extension USB cable is included. (You'll want to use this if your USB ports are very close together.)
- Two channels of analog output, combined in a ⅛-inch stereo jack. This jack can be connected to either headphones or monitor speakers, and has a volume control on the interface.
- Support for up to 24-bit/48-kHz digital audio.

Mbox 2 Mini

What makes the Mbox 2 Mini so great is its balance of power and portability. It has just enough I/O to take care of the basics, and with its size and USB bus power, it is a perfect travel companion to a laptop. Here are some of the notable features of the Mbox 2 Mini:

- USB connection to the host computer, which also powers the unit.
- Two analog inputs/outputs, including one XLR connection (usually used for a microphone, and including switchable phantom power), and two ¼" connections that can be used for line-level signals or instruments.
- A sturdy metal chassis. This might not sound like a particularly special feature, but if you're going to use the Mbox 2 Mini when traveling, you'll really appreciate the more robust housing. The housing also includes a Kensington security lock so you can cable the interface to your desk and so on.
- Headphone outputs.
- Support for up to 24-bit/48-kHz digital audio.

Mbox 2

The Mbox 2 is a nifty little interface that delivers a lot for its modest price. Though it doesn't have the number of inputs and outputs of other Pro Tools interfaces, its portability is a very attractive feature for many users. The core features of the Mbox 2 interface include the following:

- USB connection to the host computer, which powers the unit in addition to transferring audio information

- Two analog inputs/outputs (Mic, Line, or DI instrument level), plus one stereo S/PDIF input/output, all of which can be used simultaneously
- Two microphone preamps with switchable phantom power for condenser mics
- Headphone outputs
- Supports up to 24-bit/48-kHz digital audio
- MIDI In and Out ports

What about My Mbox?

The Mbox 2, as you might guess from the name, is the next generation of the original Mbox (which has been an immensely popular LE interface). Do you have one of those original Mboxes? Not to worry—they will work just fine with Pro Tools LE 7!

Mbox 2 Pro

The Mbox 2 Pro is the most advanced member of the Mbox 2 family. Though this interface is a bit bigger than the Mbox 2, it will give you higher audio quality and more inputs and outputs. Take a look at the features:

- IEEE 1394 (FireWire) connection to the host computer. If you use a 6-pin connection to the host computer, the Mbox 2 Pro can receive power from the computer. (Be careful, though—the Mbox 2 Pro requires a good bit of power and can deplete a laptop battery quickly in some cases!)
- Six analog inputs/eight analog outputs, including two XLR connections (for microphones) and two instrument connections conveniently located on the front of the interface.
- A phono preamp for turntable connections.
- Switchable phantom power for condenser microphones.
- MIDI In and Out ports. (These support MIDI Time Stamping (MTS) for greater accuracy.)
- Two headphone outputs with independent volume control.
- BNC word clock connections.
- Support for up to 24-bit/96-kHz digital audio.

Digi 003

Just as the Mbox 2 family is the next generation of the original Mbox, the new Digi 003 is the evolution of a previous device called the Digi 002. The new 003 (also commonly referred to as the *003 Factory*) interface is the flagship of the LE hardware line, and it features not only expanded I/O, but a very cool mixer-style control surface. The core features of the Digi 003 interface include the following:

- IEEE 1394 (FireWire) connection to the host computer
- Eight analog inputs/outputs, one stereo S/PDIF digital input/output, and eight channels of ADAT optical input/output
- Built-in control surface, including eight touch-sensitive motorized faders, and rotary encoders (a fancy term for "knobs") for controlling pans, plug-ins, and so on
- MIDI I/O
- Four microphone preamps, with switchable phantom power
- Headphone outputs
- BNC word clock connections
- Support for up to 24-bit/96-kHz digital audio

As I mentioned, the 003 is the newer version of the 002. Among numerous small improvements, there are a few particularly notable differences between the two:

- The 002 features a standalone digital mixer mode, whereas the 003 can function as a standalone MIDI controller mode.
- The 002 has a single headphone jack located in the upper-right corner of the control surface. Though this was convenient enough, it resulted in the headphone cable laying over the control surface. The 003 has improved this by giving you *two* headphone jacks and moving them to the very front of the control surface.
- The 003 adds a dedicated jog/shuttle wheel. This is very useful for navigation and playback.

Digi 003 Rack

The Digi 003 is available in two versions. In addition to the full-blown 003 Factory discussed previously, there's the rackmount version, called the *Digi 003 Rack*, which is a two-rack space module sporting the same I/O complement as the 002, but without the control surface component.

> **Where Can I Learn More?**
>
> If you want to learn more about the specifications of any Pro Tools hardware, the Digidesign website (www.digidesign.com) is a great place to start. From the Digidesign home page, click on the Products link (located in the upper-left area of the page), and then click the Pro Tools LE and M-Powered button to view a list of the current Pro Tools LE line. Incidentally, from the Products page, you can explore the entire Digidesign range of products, from the highest-end ICON system to the most basic plug-in.

Hard Drive(s)

Just as traditional tape-based recording studios rely on magnetic tape as a recording and storage medium, Pro Tools relies on hard drives for the recording and playback of its digital audio. The drives can use SCSI, IDE/ATA, Serial ATA, or even FireWire connections.

It is important to remember two factors when choosing a hard drive for Pro Tools—size and speed. First, a larger-capacity drive will allow you to store more audio data. This can translate into more minutes of audio that you can store, higher-quality digital audio, or both. A fast drive will allow for more efficient transfer of data (also called *throughput*) when you are recording and/or playing back audio. A faster drive can also translate into higher track counts and more reliability when working with complex sessions.

Using a Second Hard Drive

Adding a second drive dedicated to the storage of your Pro Tools sessions will increase your Pro Tools system's performance greatly.

You'll still want to install the Pro Tools application on your computer's system drive, but when you create your sessions (something we'll get into later in this chapter), put them on your "audio" drive. That way, you'll have one hard drive occupied with the nominal tasks of your computer and another separate drive (with its own read/write head) dealing only with your Pro Tools session and audio.

Will Partitioning My Drive Do the Trick?

Partitioning a single hard drive may give the outward appearance of creating a second drive, but in reality there is still only one physical hardware device. Although partitioning can be a convenient way of organizing your data, it *doesn't* add another physical drive with its own read/write head, so it won't help Pro Tools with the real-time tasks of recording and playing back digital audio.

New with Pro Tools LE 7.3: HFS+ Disk Support

If you're like me, you spend a lot of time working on both PCs and Mac computers. In the past, it's meant that my Mac-formatted (HFS+) drives were useless on a PC, but those days are over now! Pro Tools LE 7.3 introduced an HFS+ Disk Support option in Pro Tools' installation process. Just click the appropriate check box when you install Pro Tools, and your PC will be able to read and write to Mac-formatted drives (regardless of whether Pro Tools is running).

Though it's quite a handy feature, there's one caveat: If you're using a Mac-formatted drive, you'll want to have all of your session's related files (a concept we'll talk about later in this chapter) also on Mac-formatted drives. Recording and playback of a single session using a combination of both PC- and Mac-formatted discs is not recommended.

A Great Resource: Digidesign's Compatibility Documents

You might have noticed that though I've talked about desirable qualities of a powerful DAW system, I haven't mentioned many specific details about what kind of hardware you should be using (things such as minimum CPU speed and RAM requirements, for example). I apologize if I seem evasive on the subject, but the truth of the matter is that the ever-changing landscape of computer-based products changes and grows so rapidly that any specs I quote here might well change over time. Don't despair, though—Digidesign has provided the help you need for constructing a system that's completely up to date!

Digidesign keeps an up-to-date list of compatible hardware on its website. To get to the compatibility pages, just click the Support link located at the top-center area of the Digidesign website (www.digidesign.com), and you'll find loads of useful technical information at your fingertips. Since we're dealing with LE systems in this book, just click the drop-down menu below the Pro Tools LE image, and you can search information based upon the interface you're interested in (for example, MBox 2 Mini) or the software version you want (for example, Pro Tools 7.4 Mac). No matter which route you choose, you will find a comprehensive list of minimum system requirements and information.

To view more compatibility information and alerts, you can also take a look at the Quick Links section on the right-hand side of the Support home page. Click the Compatibility Information link, and you'll be able to see more information. In particular, take a look at the Compatibility Grid section at the bottom of the page—it's a quick and easy way to find compatibility between operating systems and Pro Tools software versions.

A Word about Installation

When it comes to installing your Pro Tools software, I've got good news and bad news. First the bad news: Because installation can vary from interface to interface and system to system, the installation procedure is another topic that's tough to describe in a book like this. Not only are there many different configurations possible (with different audio interfaces, computers, and so on), but Digidesign is constantly upgrading and tweaking their products. Bottom line: The details of installation are constantly subject to change.

The good news is that, again, Digidesign has got you covered. The documentation you received with your Pro Tools LE software and hardware is the first place to look for information on installation. In the ever-changing world of computers, though, even that documentation could be slightly out of date. Once again, the Digidesign website is an invaluable resource for the latest software version updates and information on installation and troubleshooting.

If you go to the Support page of the Digidesign website (where you went to check out the compatibility documentation earlier in this chapter), you can search information on your specific LE software version by choosing it from the drop-down menu below the Pro Tools LE image. In particular, I'd recommend checking out the Download section to make sure that you've got the latest version for your system. The FAQ and Tech Docs sections are also useful for hunting down all sorts of other relevant information.

The documentation that came with your Pro Tools hardware, combined with a little Net surfing (if needed), should allow you to successfully install and configure your Pro Tools LE system. Once that's finished, you're ready to move on.

A Word about Pro Tools M-Powered

About a year ago, Avid Technology (Digidesign's parent company) acquired a company named M-Audio, which has been a leader in the home studio market. Since welcoming M-Audio to the family, Digidesign and M-Audio have been in close cooperation, which has resulted in a brand-new version of Pro Tools—Pro Tools M-Powered—which can run on M-Audio interfaces!

The list of supported M-Audio interfaces is impressive and growing all the time. To get a completely up-to-date list, take a look at www.m-audio.com/products/en_us/ProToolsMPowered-main.html to see all the different kinds of devices available. For many users, the different options (for example, a combined keyboard/MIDI interface/audio interface like the Ozonic) are quite attractive. But what about the software?

The good news is that the Pro Tools M-Powered software (which is *not* included with the interface—it must be purchased separately) is nearly identical to Digidesign's Pro Tools LE. There are a few differences that do bear mentioning, however:

- Digidesign's high-end Ethernet control surfaces won't work with Pro Tools M-Powered.
- Avid video hardware doesn't work with Pro Tools M-Powered.
- Pro Tools M-Powered does not support DV Toolkit (a Digidesign bundle product for producing audio in sync with video material).
- Pro Tools M-Powered doesn't support DigiTranslator (which provides file interchange between Pro Tools and other media production applications, such as Avid systems, Logic Audio, and others).

As you can see, these differences between Pro Tools LE and Pro Tools M-Powered are really not great hardships for many beginning Pro Tools users. In fact, if you've got Pro Tools M-Powered, you'll be able to use the vast majority of this book as a production resource, with little concern about these small differences.

Understanding Sessions and Files

Now you've got your system set up, and Pro Tools is installed. Before you get any deeper into the world of Pro Tools, you should take a moment to understand the general principals behind this powerful digital audio workstation. An understanding of Pro Tools' functioning and how its different elements work together will serve you well as you continue to grow in this environment.

Pro Tools Is a Pointer-Based Application

It's common to refer to a cursor as a *pointer*, but when you're discussing a pointer-based application such as Pro Tools, you're referring to the way the program deals with digital audio data.

In Pro Tools' case, this pointer-based structure can be broken down to three interdependent elements—session files, folders, and audio files. In this situation the term "pointer" refers to the way your Pro Tools session file will access (or "point" to) other files on your hard drive as your session plays.

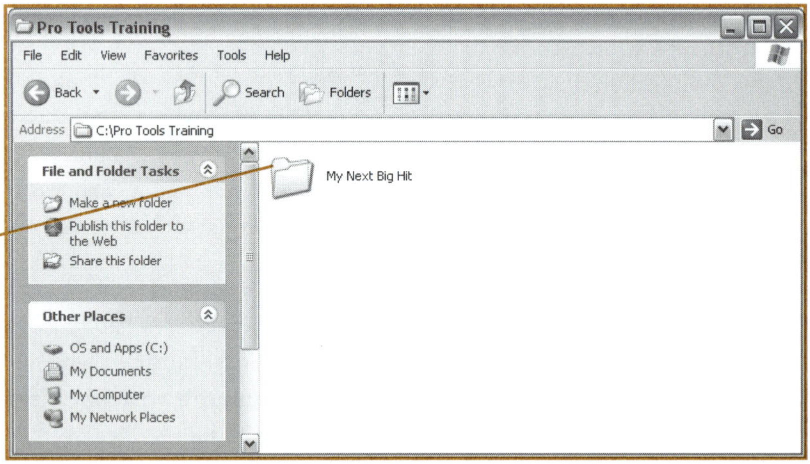

A session folder is created when you create a new session; it contains the following items (as needed):

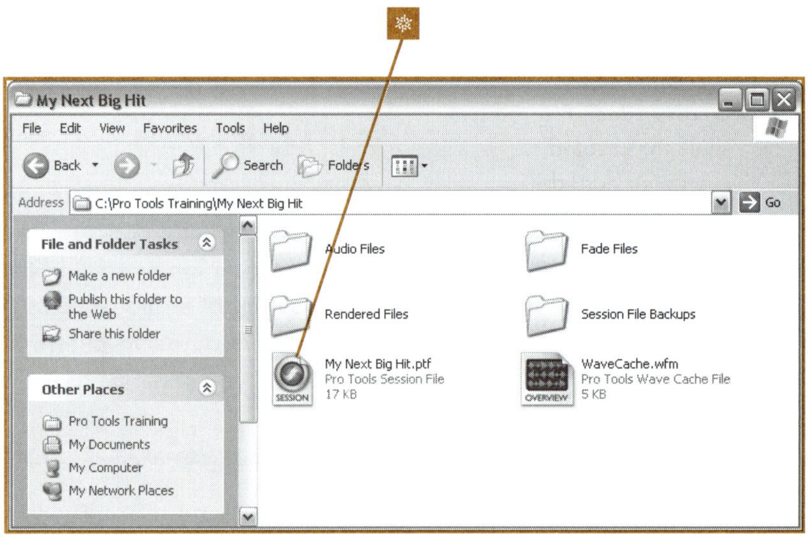

- **Session file.** The session file is at the top of the Pro Tools hierarchy. This is the file created by Pro Tools when you create a new session, and it's the file you open to return to a session you already created. Although this file is relatively small, it is the master of all your session elements. Session files have the .ptf extension and contain the following elements of your session:
  - The names, types, and arrangement of all tracks in your session
  - All MIDI data
  - Essential settings, such as inputs and outputs
  - All edits and automation data

Sessions and Audio

It might sound as if all you need is a session file, but that's not quite true. Although the session file contains all the important aspects of a project (and more), it doesn't in itself contain any audio. Instead, the session file refers (or points) to audio files located elsewhere on your hard drive.

Audio Files subfolder. As soon as audio is recorded, it is stored in an Audio Files subfolder in the session folder. Different takes are stored in this folder as individual audio files. When you play a session, Pro Tools calls upon, or points to, the audio files in this folder.

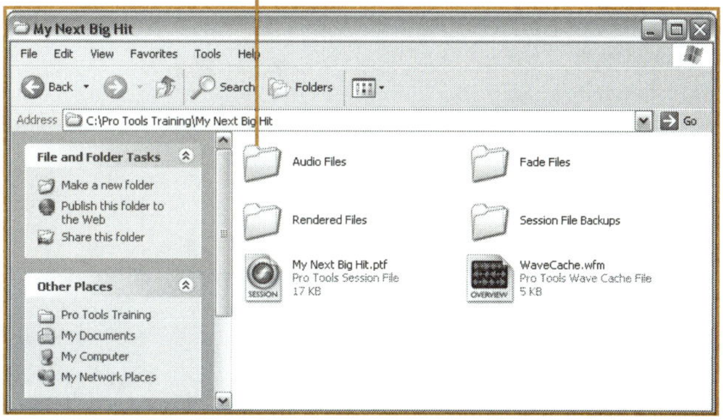

Fade Files subfolder. When you start creating fades (including fade-ins, fade-outs, and crossfades), Pro Tools renders the created fades to files on your hard drive. Audio files are again created, but they're not stored in the Audio Files folder. Instead, they're stored in a folder named Fade Files. It's important to keep in mind that even though fades are audio files, they are significantly different in function from the audio files you record or import into your session (in ways that you'll learn about later); thus, they are stored separately.

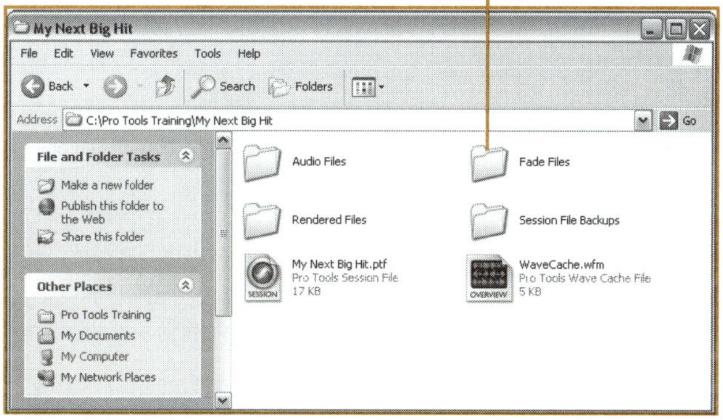

How Do Audio Files Get Their Names?

When you record audio in Pro Tools, the name of the file created follows the name of the track on which it is recorded. For example, if you record onto a mono (one-channel) Audio track named Bass, the files created by Pro Tools in the Audio Files folder will be named Bass.01, Bass.02, and so on as you record takes on this track. In the case of stereo Audio tracks, two mono files (one for the left side and one for the right) are created. If you record onto a stereo Audio track named Stereo Piano, two files named Stereo Piano_01.l and Stereo Piano_01.r will be created.

- **Region groups.** This is brand new in version 7. As the name suggests, Pro Tools now allows you to select multiple regions and link them together in a single Region Group. Digital audio and MIDI can be grouped together, and this new feature promises to make editing much faster and easier. You'll learn more about Region Groups later, but for now just know that groups you create are stored in this folder. (If you don't create any Region Groups in a given session, a folder won't be created.)

- **Rendered files.** One of the new features in Pro Tools LE 7.4 is called *Elastic Audio*. This is a very cool new addition indeed, and one you'll learn about in Chapter 10, "Moving to the Next Level: Tips and Tricks." For now, though, all you need to know is that when you're working with Elastic Audio, you have the option of "rendering" your elasticized audio to an audio file—and when you do, it will be stored in this folder.

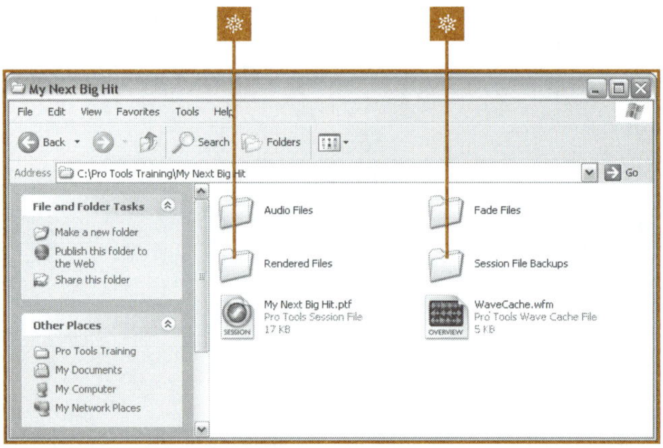

- **Session file backups.** Depending upon your preference settings, Pro Tools can automatically create backups of your sessions and store them in this folder. By default, a new session backup is created every 5 minutes, and the folder keeps the last 10 backup files. This is highly recommended, particularly for new users to Pro Tools, and can help you recover quickly if you encounter technical trouble.

If you start using video files and/or creating custom plug-in settings, Pro Tools may create additional subfolders as needed:

- **Plug-In Settings subfolder.** In Pro Tools you have the option of using plug-ins, which are programs designed to work within the Pro Tools environment and function as virtual effects. (You'll learn more about plug-ins in Chapter 8, "Basic Mixing.") When you create specific plug-in presets, you can save them in this session subfolder.
- **Video Files subfolder.** When your session calls for a video track, you can save it in this session subfolder.

What about the WaveCache?

There's one more file you'll often find in your session folder that we haven't talked about yet. It's a small file named WaveCache, and it stores all the waveform overviews for any audio in your session. *Waveform overview* is a fancy way of describing the visual representation of audio waves that you might see on an Audio track. This small file is automatically created and updated, so there's nothing you need to worry about with it!

Regions versus Files

Given the fact that Pro Tools records audio to individual files on your hard drive, how do you later access these files? When audio is recorded to an Audio track (or even MIDI data to a MIDI track), Pro Tools creates an object or region in the Edit window. In the case of Audio tracks, these regions refer (or *point*) to files on your hard drive, triggering them to sound as your session plays.

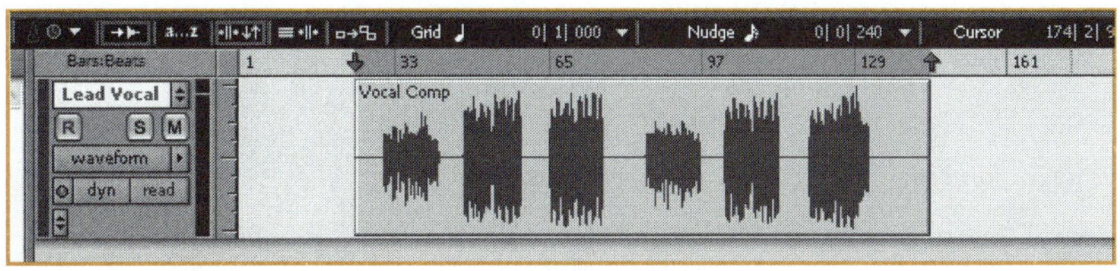

Here's a close-up of Pro Tools' Edit window. There's one Audio track in this session, and only one region on that track. That region is referring to a file named Vocal Comp.

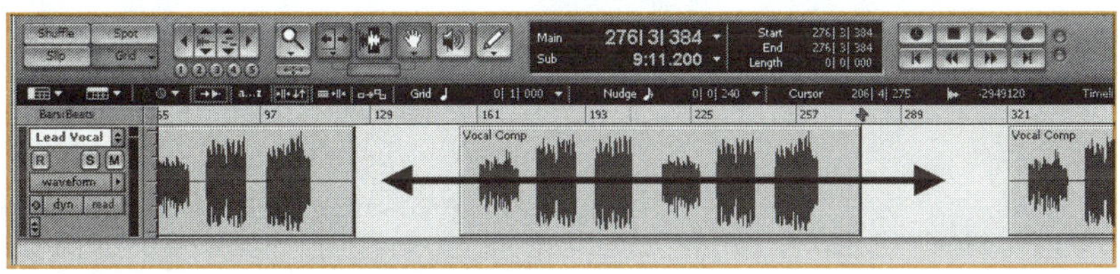

Working with regions has many advantages. One of the first you'll discover is that you have the ability to move them earlier or later on the session's Timeline, allowing you to precisely position the regions in time. An environment in which you have the ability to manipulate elements independently on the Timeline is commonly known as *nonlinear*. In addition to moving regions to different locations in time, you have the option of moving them to other similar tracks. (In other words, you can move a region on a mono Audio track to another mono Audio track, and so on.)

Nondestructive Editing

Another great advantage of using regions is that you can nondestructively trim the audio that's being used in your session (meaning that no audio *data* is being lost, so you can always undo what you've done).

In this example, assume that the region named Vocal Comp is playing an audio file of the same name in the Audio Files subfolder. What if you don't want to use the whole song in your session? No problem—you can adjust the start or end boundary of that region, effectively taking the unwanted bit of audio out of your session.

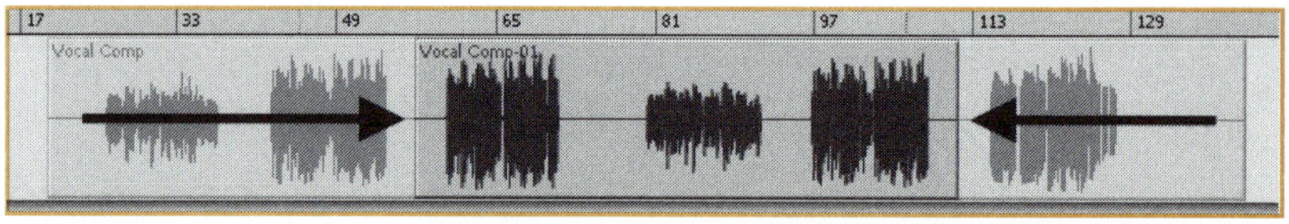

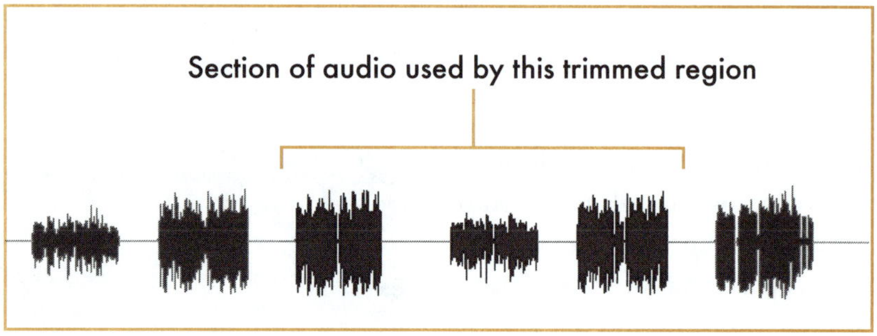

Does this mean that you've changed the file on your hard drive? No! You've changed only the region that is pointing to that file, so only a portion of that file will be heard in the session. Don't worry; because you haven't changed the audio file (only the region that is pointing to it), you can always drag the region boundaries back out if you change your mind later!

In addition to being able to trim data, there are other situations in which nondestructive editing can aid you in your production work, and you'll discover them as this book proceeds. The bottom line is that a nonlinear pointer-based environment coupled with nondestructive recording and editing gives an educated Pro Tools user a huge amount of flexibility and power and the ability to undo changes and operations when needed.

Basic Pro Tools Operation

The end of the beginning: You've set up your system efficiently, taken some time to understand the way Pro Tools works, and now, based on that understanding, you're ready to start working. The last step before you dive deeper into Pro Tools is to open a preexisting session:

The Chapter 1 Tutorial Session

At this stage, you might not have a preexisting Pro Tools session to work with, but that's not a problem. Just insert the CD included in this book and copy the folder named Chapter 1 Session to your hard drive.

When you open your session, you may see a few message boxes, including a Missing Files dialog box. It's not a big problem—it simply means that one or more of the audio files that Pro Tools is expecting to find is not easily located. However, it is something you'll have to fix before moving on. Please take a look at the "Setting Up Your Session" PDF document, also included on the book's CD.

Opening a Session When Pro Tools Is Running

Suppose you've already launched the Pro Tools application. Here's how to open a session:

1. Click on File. The File menu will appear.
2. Click on Open Session. The Choose a Session dialog box will open.

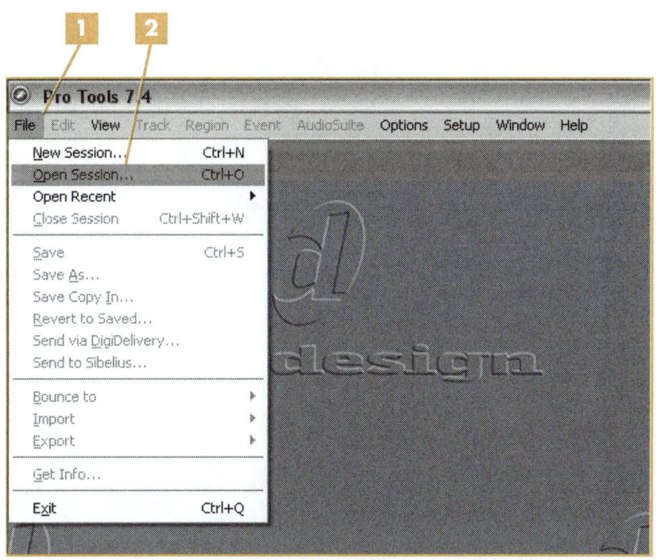

Your First Shortcut

As I mentioned earlier, Pro Tools includes shortcut keys that enable you to work more efficiently. The shortcuts for New Session and Open Session (Ctrl+N and Ctrl+O, respectively, in Windows, and ⌘+N and ⌘+O, respectively, on a Mac) are very useful—and easy to remember as well!

3. **Select** the **drive** that contains the audio session. The drive will be selected, and the folders on that drive will appear.
4. **Click** on the **folder** that contains the session folder. The folder will be selected, and the contents of that folder will be displayed.

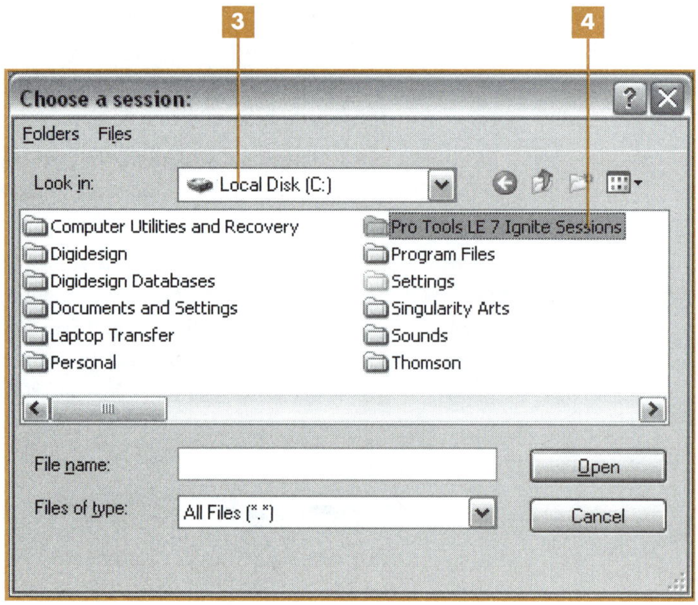

5. **Click** on the **subfolder** that contains the session file. The contents of the subfolder will be displayed.

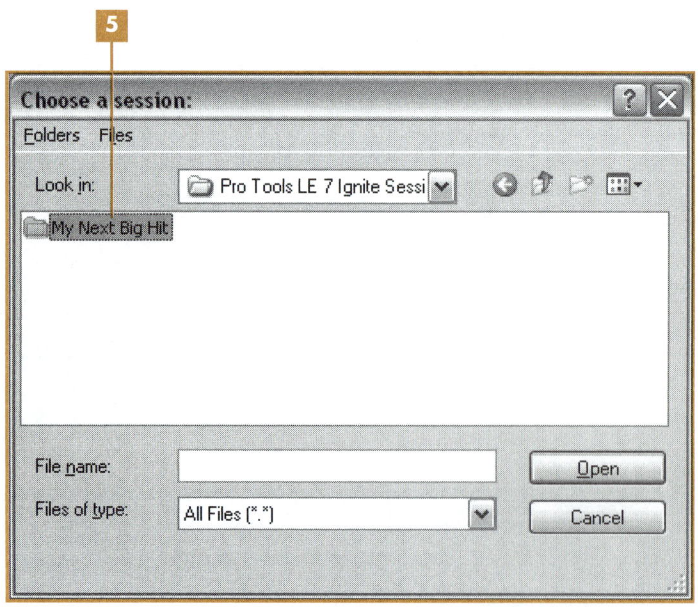

6 Click on the desired session file. The file will be selected.

7 Click on Open. The session will be loaded into Pro Tools.

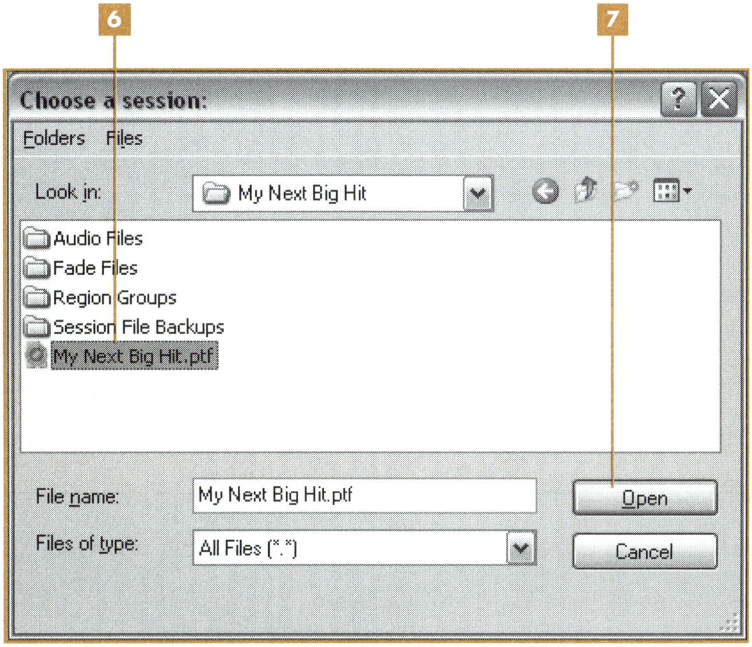

New in Pro Tools 7.3—Open Recent Sessions

The ability to select a recently opened file from a list is fairly common in the software world, and most users will be familiar with this idea from other applications. The Open Recent item can be found immediately below the Open Session menu item. Simply click Open Recent, and you will see a list of up to 10 of your most recently opened sessions.

Opening a Session When Pro Tools Is Not Yet Launched

In this case, suppose Pro Tools is not yet launched. To open a session, follow these steps:

1. **Select** the **hard drive** that contains your session. On a PC, this will involve using My Computer or Windows Explorer. On a Mac, you can use the Finder or simply click on the hard drive icon on your desktop.

2. **Open** any **folders** that contain your session folder. The contents of the folder will be displayed.

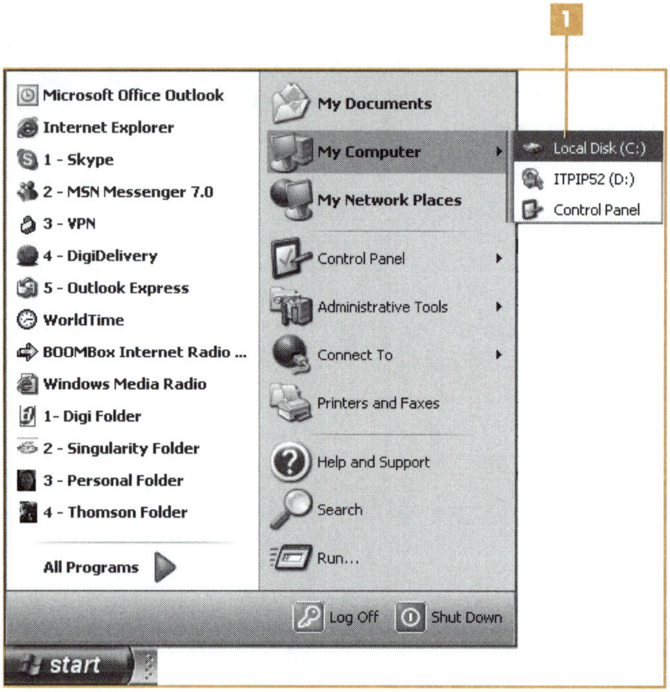

3. **Open** the **folder** that contains the session file. The contents of the folder will be displayed.

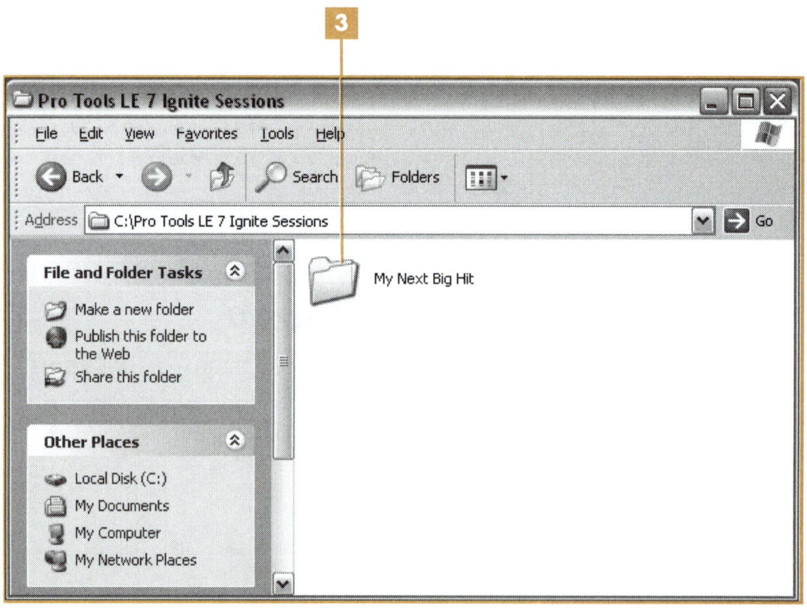

4 Double-click on the desired session file (in this case, My Next Big Hit). Pro Tools will launch automatically, and the session will be loaded.

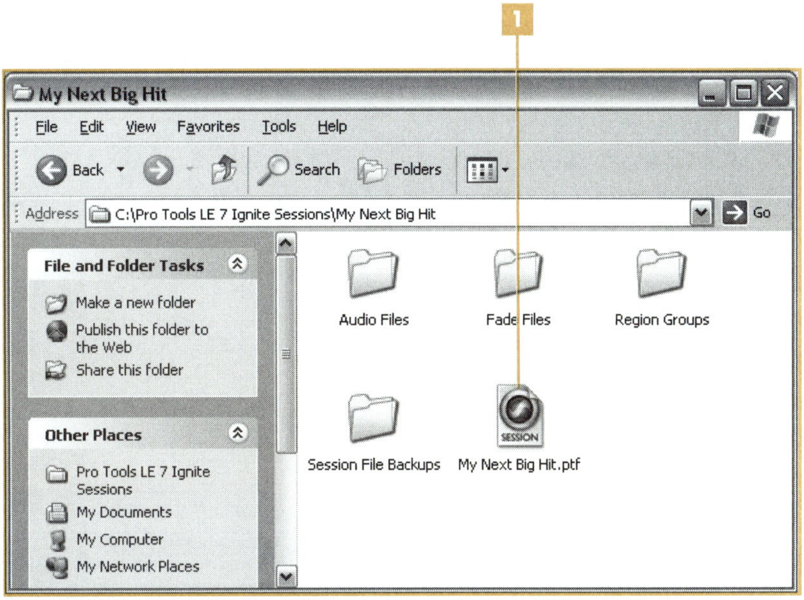

Creating a New Session

Now that you've got your system put together and everything's installed, you can create a new session (as opposed to opening a preexisting session, as you did in the previous section of this chapter). Our earlier discussion of how Pro Tools works will come in handy here. In addition to these previous concepts, you'll have to start thinking about how you can best set up your new session and maximize your computer's resources.

Starting the Process

After you've launched Pro Tools, you'll see the program's basic array of drop-down menus. Here's where the important process of creating a session begins!

1 Click on File. The File menu will appear, containing a list of Pro Tools' basic functions. Because there is no session open at this time, only the New Session and Open Session options will be available; the rest will be grayed out.

2 Click on New Session. The Name the Session dialog box will open.

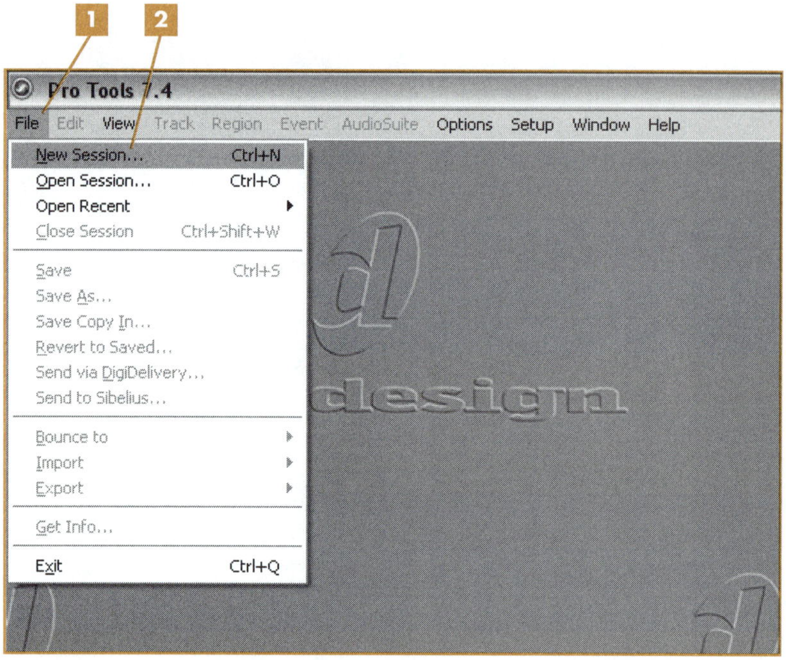

More Shortcuts!

As you explore Pro Tools further, you'll notice that there are many functions that have shortcut keys associated with them. These shortcut key combinations are displayed to the right of the (such at the shortcut for creating a new session—Ctrl+N (PC) or +N (Mac)—shown in the previous image). Although there are far too many shortcuts to learn all at once, learning the combinations for popular functions, such as opening or creating a session, can help you work more efficiently.

Choosing the Name and Place

Two of the most important skills you can learn as a DAW user are file management and documentation. Though these are fairly simple and straightforward tasks, you shouldn't underestimate their importance. The last thing you want is to misplace a session and waste valuable time trying to find it—or worse, inadvertently delete a session because it was in the wrong place!

Knowing where your sessions reside and what kinds of resources they use is critical, especially when you have multiple projects in the works!

1. The first thing you have to choose is the name of your session. Type the name in the File Name text box.

2. Click on the Save In down arrow to reveal the Navigation window.

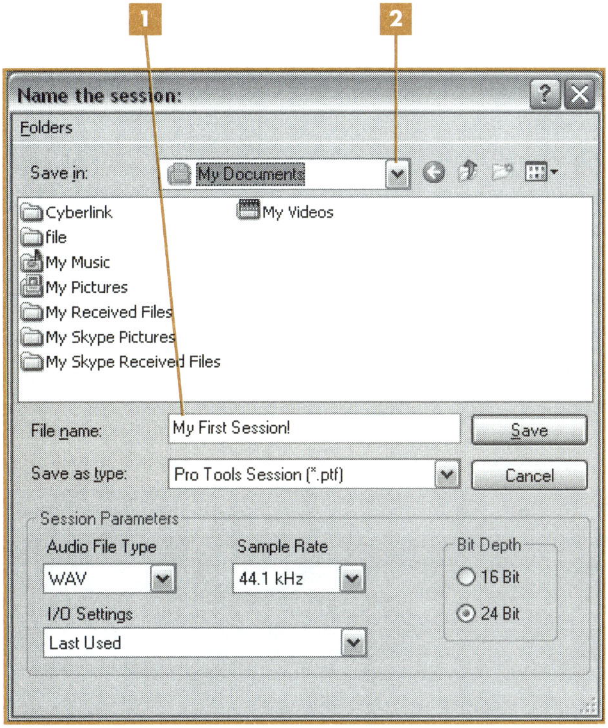

Where to Create Your Session

According to this screen, this new session will be created in the My Documents folder. This means that the session will be created on your system's hard drive. As I mentioned earlier, this is not the best place to keep your session. Choose a location on your audio hard drive instead.

3. According to your operating system, navigate to the desired drive. (If you have a hard drive devoted to digital audio, go to that drive.)

4. Next, you might want to create a new folder for your session. Create a new folder according to the normal conventions of your operating system.

5 Type a name for your new folder, and then enter that folder according to the conventions of your operating system. I created a new folder called Pro Tools Training Sessions. Depending on the name of the folder you created, your screen should look something like mine does here.

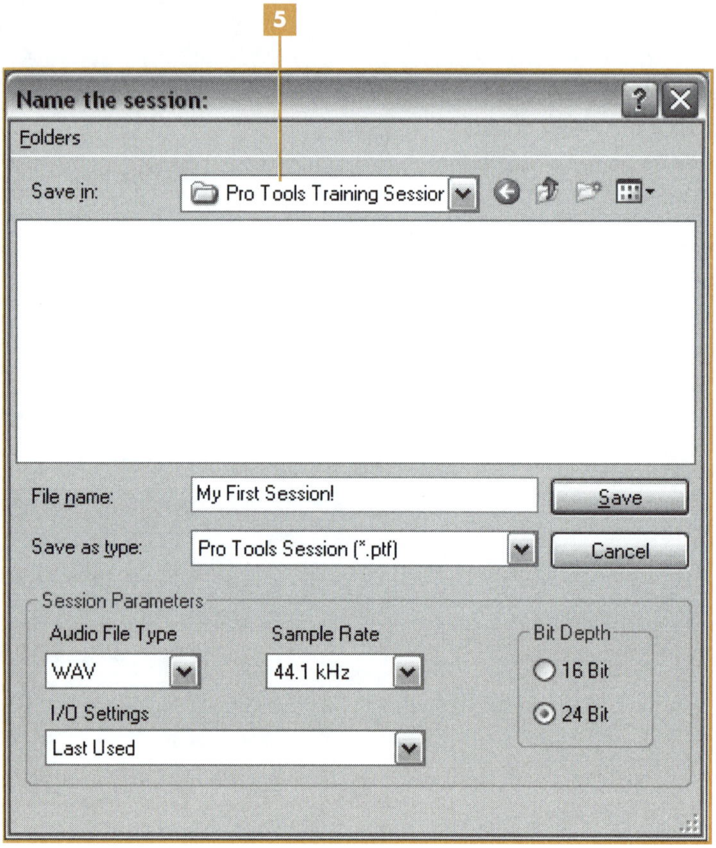

Choosing Session Parameters

You've named your new session and assigned it to a specific location on a hard drive. Now that you've done this, your next task is to choose your session parameters, which will determine other important aspects of your session.

Choosing a File Format

Pro Tools' default file format is BWF (.WAV), or Broadcast Wave, and this generally works for most applications. If you are planning to share files between Mac and Windows systems, this is the preferred file format.

1. Click on the Audio File Type down arrow. A drop-down menu will appear. Choose a file type from the following options:
   - **WAV.** A WAV file is a Windows standard file. This is a good format choice for session files that will be used in Windows XP systems.
   - **AIFF.** This is the standard audio file format for Macs.

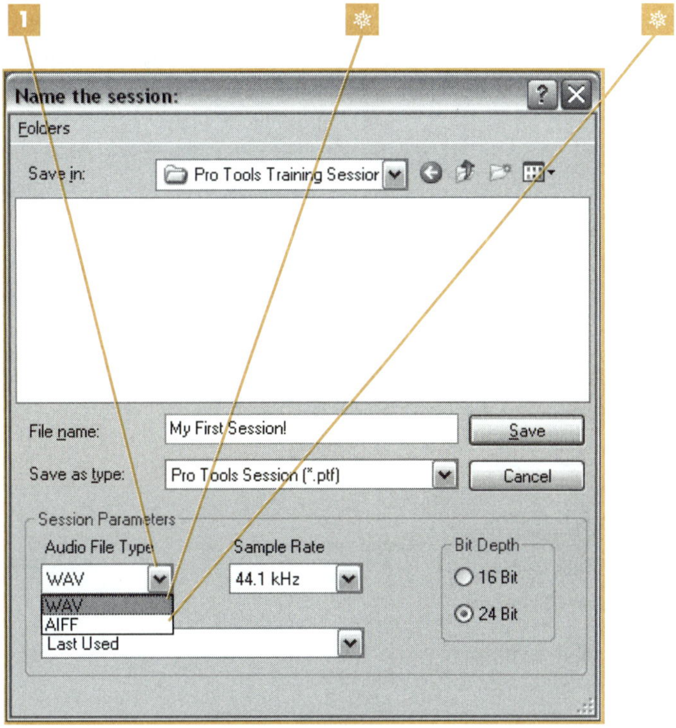

2. Click on the Sample Rate down arrow. A menu will appear, determined by the sample rates supported by your audio interface.
3. Select a sample rate for your session.
4. Select either 16 Bit or 24 Bit audio as the bit depth for your session. The option will be selected.

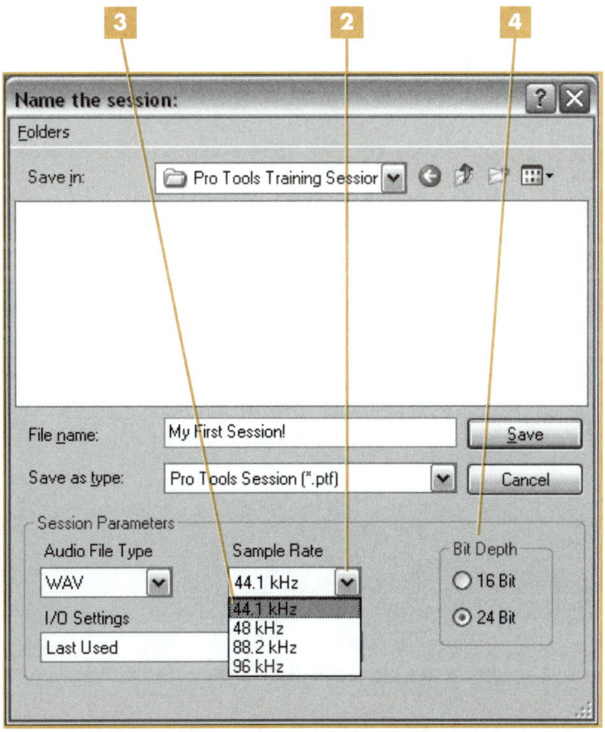

What about Importing Audio?

Once selected, the sample rate and bit depth will become the overall sample rate and bit depth for all audio in this session. This means that any audio you import into the session (a process we'll go through in Chapter 3, "Getting Started with Audio") will either have to match these specs or be converted to match the session (something that Pro Tools does automatically when conversion is needed).

5 Click on the I/O Settings down arrow. The I/O Settings drop-down menu will appear.

6 Select your I/O (Input/Output) settings for this session. For now, choose Stereo Mix. The option will be selected.

7 You've made all the choices you need to create a new session! Click on Save. Pro Tools will begin to build your session.

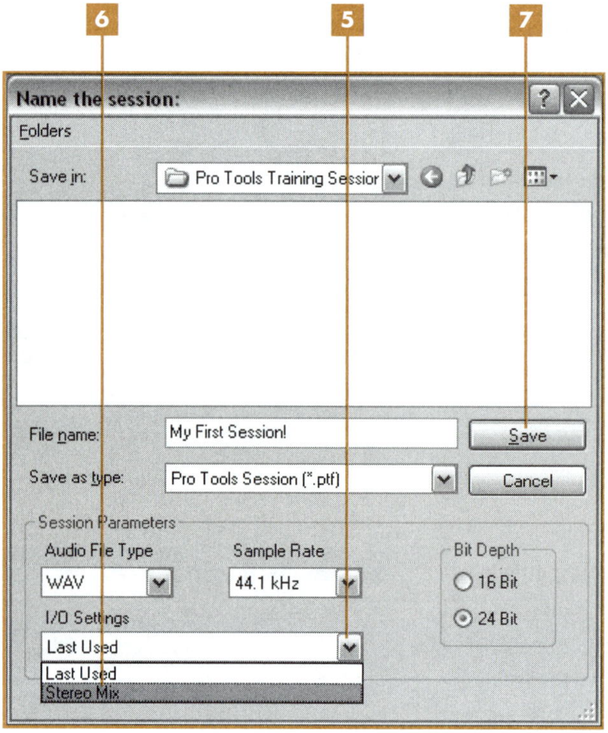

Where Can I Learn More about I/O Settings?

Your I/O settings determine the assignments and names of inputs, outputs, inserts, and busses. Don't worry if this doesn't make a lot of sense now—you'll learn more about how to make the most of your I/O settings in Chapter 3.

Playing a Session

Let's assume that you've got Pro Tools running and you've opened up a preexisting session (for example, the online session that I referred to earlier). Wondering how to play it? No problem!

The transport section in the upper-right area of a window that Pro Tools calls the *Edit window* (which you'll learn more about in the next chapters) will help you with basic play and record operations. It looks very much like the same controls you would find on almost any media player—let's take a look at the basic ones:

> **How to Get to the Edit Window**
>
> If you're not seeing any transport-style controls at the top of your Pro Tools window, you've probably opened your session into the other main window (called the *Mix window*, which looks very similar to a mixing console). Getting to the Edit window is very easy—just go to the Window drop-down menu at the top of the Pro Tools window, and choose the Edit menu item.

- The Stop button—you guessed it—stops playback.
- The Play button will play back your session from the current position.
- The Return to Zero button takes you directly to the beginning of your session.
- Rewind quickly moves your playback point earlier in your session.
- Fast Forward quickly moves your playback point later in your session.
- The Go to End button takes you directly to the end of your session.

Finishing Up

Now that you've got the very basics down, it is time to think about winding things up. This is a crucial stage, and it's important to do the job correctly.

Saving Your Work

There are a number of ways to save your work, each with its own specific advantages.

Save

This is a pretty standard feature and as straightforward as they come:

1. Click on File. The File menu will appear.
2. Click on Save. Your work will be saved, and you can continue to work on the saved session.

Save As

If you use the Save command, the previous version of the session will be overwritten with the new one. What if you don't want to overwrite the old session? That's where Save As comes into play.

1 Click on File. The File menu will appear.

2 Click Save As. The Save Session As dialog box will open.

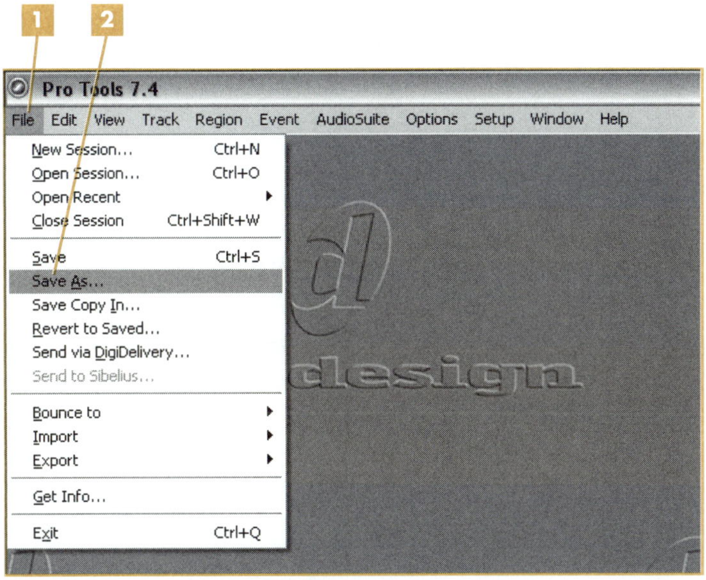

3 Type a different name for your session in the File Name text box to avoid overwriting the original session.

4 Click on Save. The new version of the session will be saved with the name you specified in Step 3. You are all set at this point to continue work on the newly saved session.

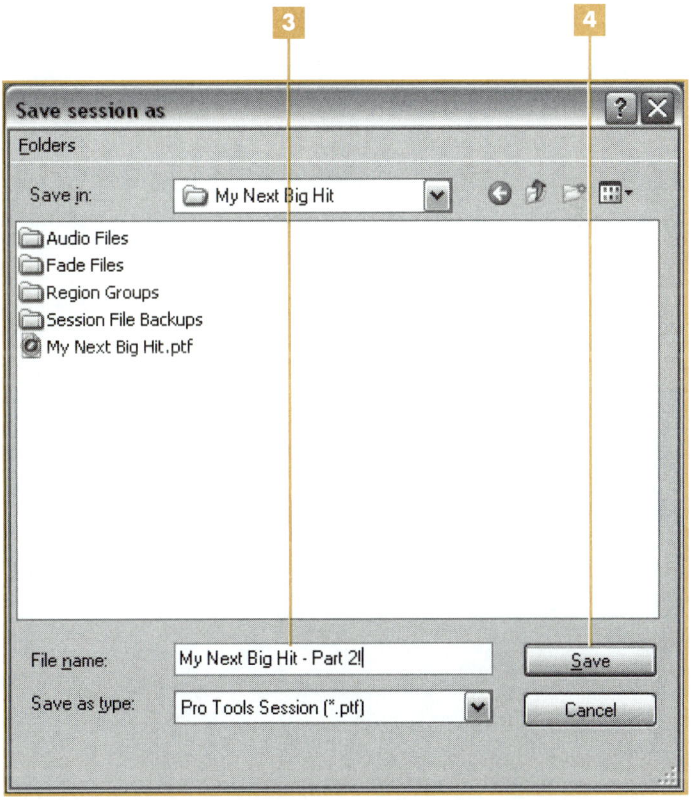

Where Do I Save the New "Save As" Session File?

It's important to note that both the original session file and the new version of the file can reside in the same session folder and can access the same source audio files.

Save Copy In

If you want to save your session with a different name *and* create a new folder, complete with all the dependent audio files, the Save Copy In feature is for you! This is commonly a part of the final archiving process when a project is complete (which you'll learn more about later).

1. Click on File. The File menu will appear.
2. Click on Save Copy In. The Save Copy of Session In dialog box will open.

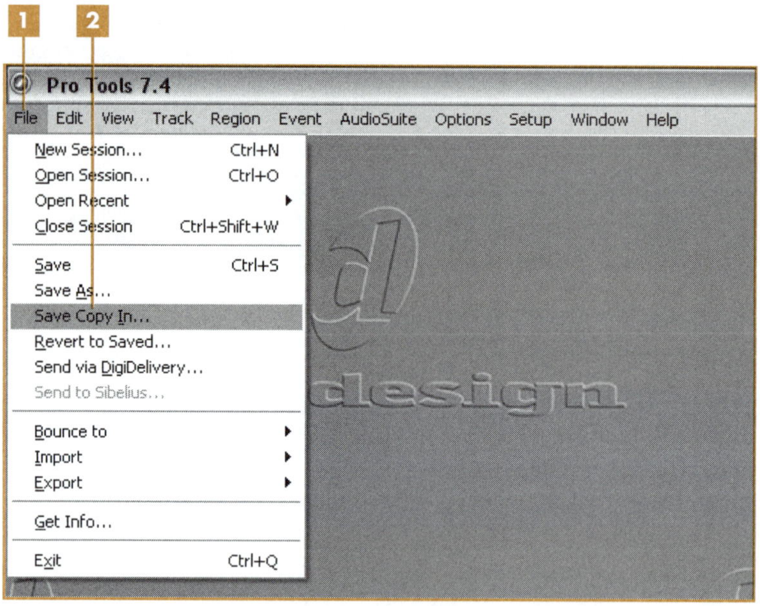

3. In the File Name text box, type a descriptive session name that is different from the original session name.

4. Select a location for your session from the Save In menu. This section is identical to the related sections in the dialog boxes when you choose Save or Save As. This time a new folder will be created for your new session, though.

5. If you want to create your session folder *within* another folder, click on the New Folder button.

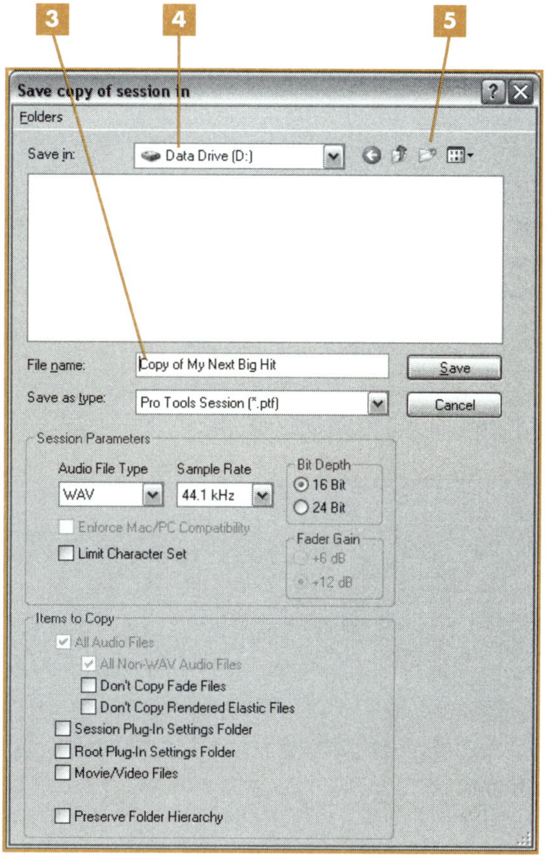

Save Copy In also gives you the option to resave all of the elements of your session (audio files, fade files, and so on), which gives you a whole new dimension of flexibility. Here are some things to consider:

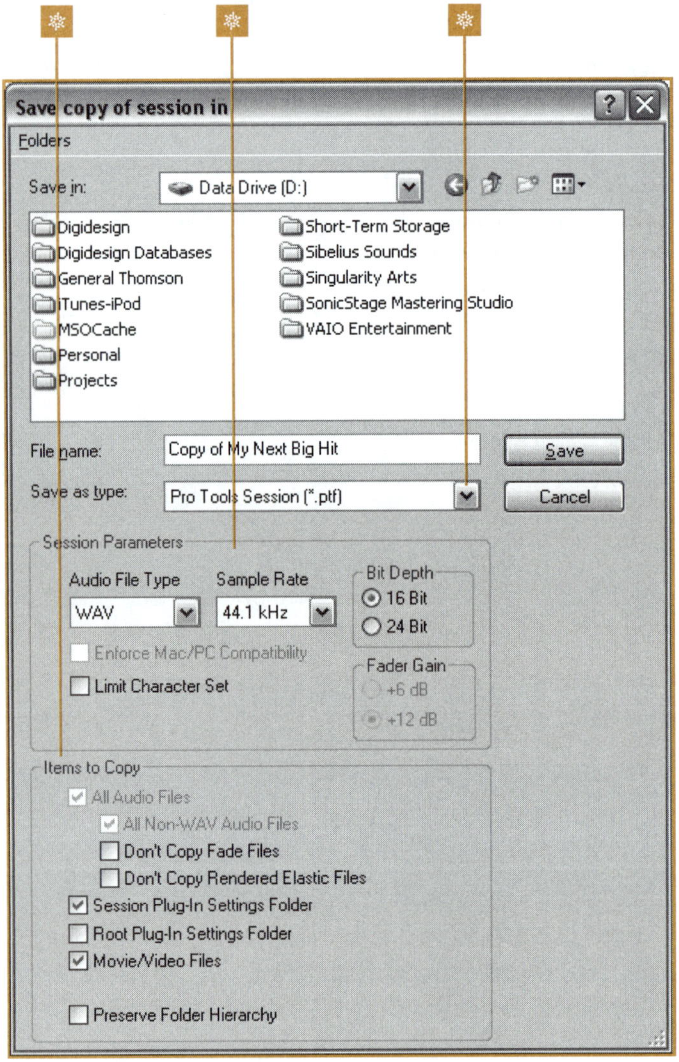

- **Save As Type menu.** This drop-down menu contains options for previous versions of Pro Tools. You might select one of these other formats if you intend to open this session in an older version of Pro Tools.
- **Session Parameters section.** These are the same options you saw when you initially created your session. You can select different file types, sample rates, and/or bit depths for your session. Pro Tools will automatically convert audio files as needed in your new session's Audio Files folder.
- **Items to Copy section.** You can choose the elements of your original session that you want to copy over to your new session folder. Click to select the boxes that represent aspects of your old session that you want to create in your new session folder.

The Importance of Backing Up Your Work!

Backing up (or *archiving*) your work is a tremendously important part of production. It might not be terribly exciting, but you'll be glad you established good file-saving habits if something unexpected happens!

Save Copy In is particularly suited to archiving because it makes copies of your original session in a separate (and hopefully safe) place. Additionally, this process intelligently gathers all the elements your session needs (assuming you selected them in the Items to Copy section) and saves them in one central location. Bottom line: When you're backing up your session (for example, making a CD-ROM of your work for long-term storage), Save Copy In is a very smart way to go!

New Feature: Preserve Folder Hierarchy

Sometimes (particularly in sessions with higher track counts) you'll want to record audio to multiple hard drives at once (something we'll discuss in Chapter 4, "Recording Audio"). By default, the Save Copy In feature will gather all your session's audio files into a single new Audio Files folder. Many times this is desirable, but you might want to keep these audio files separate so that you can move them back to their original drives at a later time. In that case, click the Preserve Folder Hierarchy check box (at the bottom of the Save Copy of Session In dialog box). Checking this box will create separate Audio Files folders within your new session folder, each placed within folders named for your audio drives. For example, instead of a single subfolder named Audio Files in your session, as you've seen earlier in this chapter, you'll have sessions such as Audio Drive 1/Audio Files, Audio Drive 2/Audio Files, and so on.

Closing Your Session

The last basic procedure you have to complete is to close down your session.

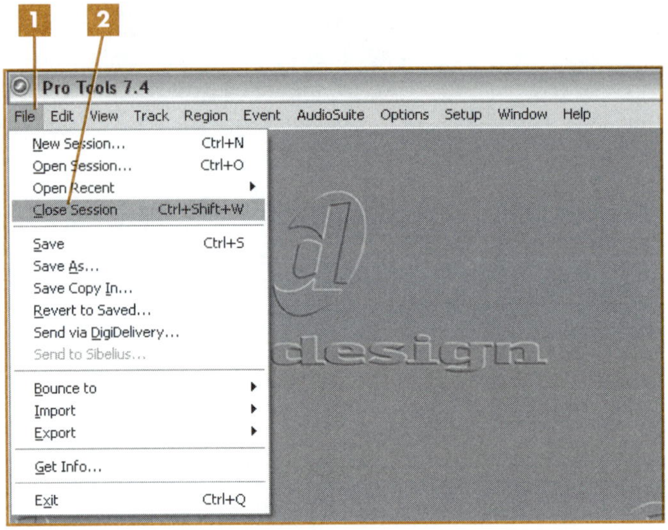

1. Click on File. The File menu will appear.
2. Click on Close Session. Pro Tools will shut down the current session and make itself ready for the next step.

Do You Want to Save Your Changes?

Before your session closes completely, a message box might prompt you to save your changes. This message box appears when you make *any* changes to your session and then try to quit Pro Tools before saving those changes. You can choose Save or Don't Save and move on.

Quitting Pro Tools

Actually quitting Pro Tools varies slightly depending upon the operating system you use:

1a If you're using Pro Tools on a PC, closing the software is exactly the same as the process in virtually every other program you've used in Windows. Simply click on the File menu and select Exit.

OR

1b For Mac users, quitting Pro Tools is also just like quitting any other program. Click on the Pro Tools menu and select Quit Pro Tools.

That's it!

2 Getting Around in Pro Tools

You've taken the time to install and set up your Pro Tools system. You've gone the extra mile and learned how Pro Tools "thinks" regarding sessions and files. You've even reached the point of creating, opening, and playing session files. Now, before you go to the next level of using Pro Tools, it's time to get better acquainted with the layout of the Pro Tools environment.

Think of this chapter as a brief primer in the Pro Tools way of getting the job done. Based upon the general architecture discussed in this chapter, you'll be able to more efficiently navigate through the operations and features we'll go through later.

Some more experienced computer-based producers will immediately see similarities between Pro Tools LE and other well-designed DAWs, but it will be a good use of your time to learn the proper names and layouts of these new workspaces. There are a number of windows in Pro Tools, many with specific functions, and you'll find that getting acquainted with the most common ones will really pay off later. In this chapter, you'll learn how to:

- Recognize the main sections of the Edit window and how to customize them
- Recognize the basic layout and functions of the Mix window
- Access other useful windows, such as the Big Counter, System Usage windows, Playback Engine window, and Workspace Browser

The Edit, Mix, and Transport Windows

When you open a session, it will display any number of window configurations. These configurations will reflect the windows that were displayed the last time you saved that session. Generally speaking, one of Pro Tools' two main windows, the Edit window or the Mix window, will be shown. It's important to know what each of these two windows does and how to navigate between them. There's one more window that's crucial for Pro Tools operation, called the Transport window. (You used a smaller version of that window when you played a session in Chapter 1.) Let's take a quick look at the general layout of these important windows.

A Quick Way to Change Windows

You'll be making the switch between the Edit and Mix windows often, so doing this as quickly as possible will be very useful. The shortcut to toggle between the Mix and Edit windows is Ctrl+=(equals key) for Windows or ⌘+= for the Mac. You'll move between these windows a lot, and this shortcut will help you do it quicker!

Working with the Edit Window

If there's a primary window in Pro Tools, it's the Edit window. This workspace is packed with useful tools and information about your Pro Tools session!

The Track Area

To follow along, just open the session named Chapter 2 Session, which is included on your book's disc. (Remember, you'll have to copy the session files to your computer's hard drive first.)

When you begin a new session from scratch, the Track area will be an empty white field. Any kind of track you create (Audio, Aux, MIDI, or Master Fader) will appear in this area as a horizontal row. Here, for example, there are five Audio tracks, four stereo and one mono (the bass track). As discussed in Chapter 1, the colored blocks are called *regions*.

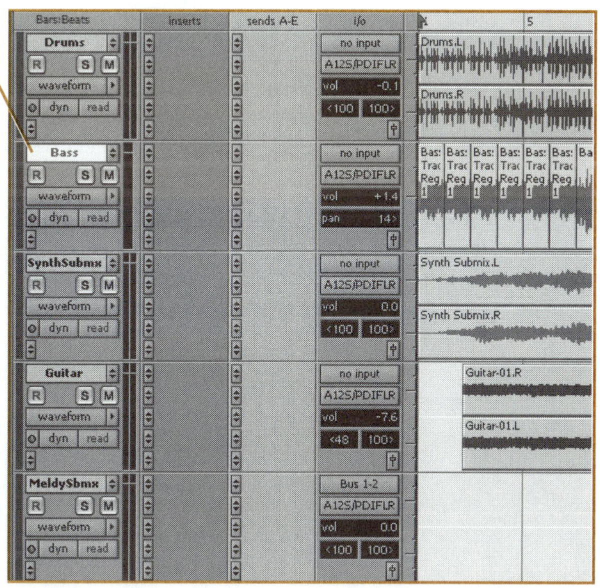

For each track there is a specific track name (located in the upper-left corner of each track strip). When you need to select a track, you can do so by clicking on the track name button. Tracks that are selected will be highlighted (in this case, the bass track is selected). Each track strip shows a lot of information besides regions and track names; you'll get into that in Chapter 3, "Getting Started with Audio."

The Track Show/Hide and Edit Groups Areas

Immediately to the right of the Track area, you'll notice two vertical cells—the Show/Hide Tracks area and the Edit Groups area. The Show/Hide Tracks area can be divided into two main parts.

- **Tracks list.** All the tracks in your session, whether visible or hidden, are listed in this area. Shown tracks are highlighted in this list.
- **Tracks List button.** In addition to being a heading for this list, you can click on this button to view a list of options related to displaying and hiding each of the tracks in your session.

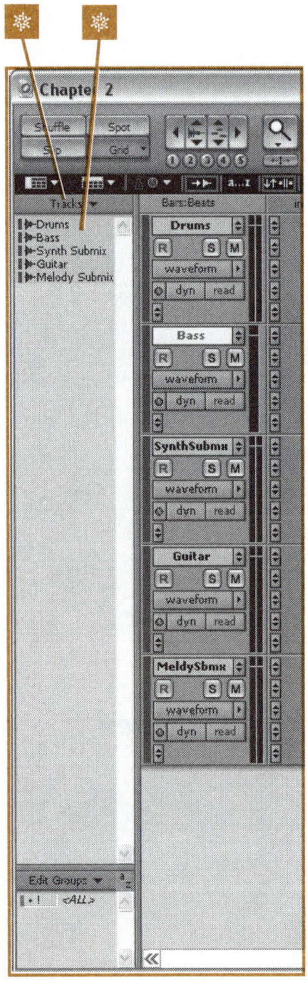

Will Hidden Tracks Be Heard?

All active and unmuted tracks, whether they are shown or hidden, will sound during playback. The ability to hide or show tracks is simply a feature to help you manage your editing and mixing desktop. (But it's a feature for which you'll be grateful when your tracks start adding up!)

An *Edit Group* is a user-definable selection of tracks that can be edited as one. As with the Tracks area, the Edit Groups area can also be divided into two main parts.

- Edit Groups list. As you create edit groups, they'll show up here. As with the Tracks list, active groups will be highlighted.
- Edit Groups button. Like the Tracks List button, you'll see a list of group-related functions when you click on the button at the top of the Edit Groups list.

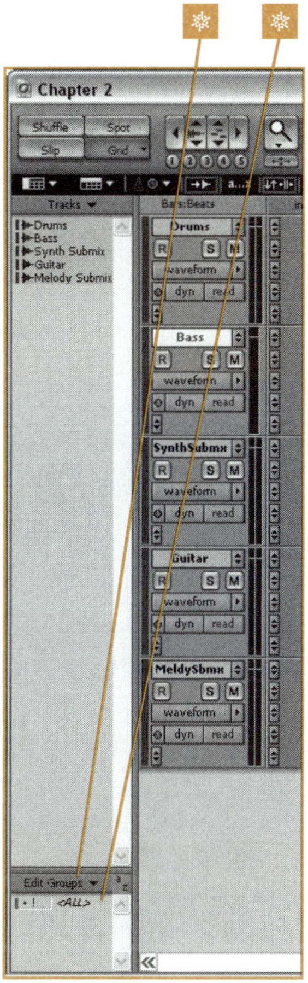

The Ever-Present "All" Group

When you create a new session, you'll notice that there's already a group (named "All") shown in this list, even though you didn't create it. The All group is created automatically when a session is created. Clicking on the word "All" will toggle between selecting and deselecting all the tracks in your session. (We'll cover the creation and use of additional Edit Groups in Chapter 6, "...And More Editing.")

The Regions Lists

Just to the right of the Tracks area, you'll find another vertical area. This is the storage area for regions that are or will be used in your session.

What Happened to the MIDI Regions List?

Those of you who are familiar with Pro Tools version 6 or earlier will note that this area is just a little bit different. Earlier versions of Pro Tools had a dedicated Audio Regions list and a MIDI Regions list. With version 7, the two lists have merged into a more powerful and manageable single list.

- Regions list. This is a complete collection of all the regions (audio and MIDI) in your session, regardless of whether they're being used actively in a track. From here you can drag and drop regions onto the appropriate tracks.
- Regions List button. At the top of the Regions list, you'll find the Regions List button. In addition to serving as a heading for this area, it will display a drop-down menu of region-related functions when you click on it.

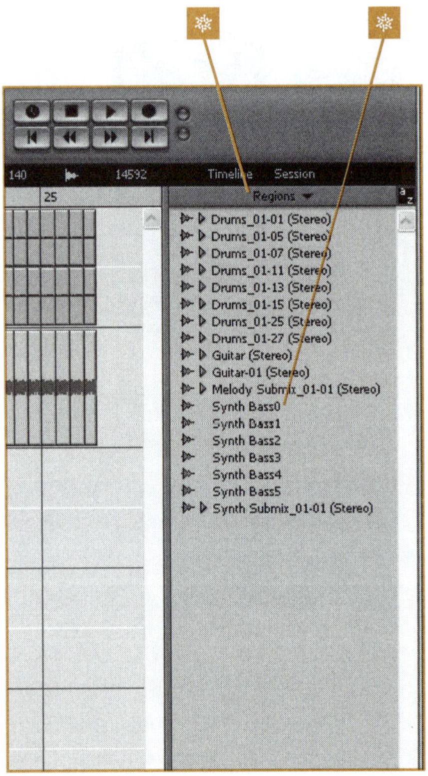

What's MIDI?

You might notice that we've been mentioning a thing called MIDI (*Musical Instrument Digital Interface*). We'll go into MIDI and how to use it in Pro Tools in Chapter 7, "Using MIDI."

The Rulers and Tools Areas

The Rulers area allows you to view the passage of time in your session in a number of different ways. Different scales, such as minutes and seconds or bars and beats, will be useful to you depending upon the kind of work you are doing in Pro Tools. Any combination of the following ruler types can be shown:

a Timeline ruler types (Bars:Beats, Min:Secs, or Samples)

b Conductor ruler types (Tempo, Meter, Key, or Markers)

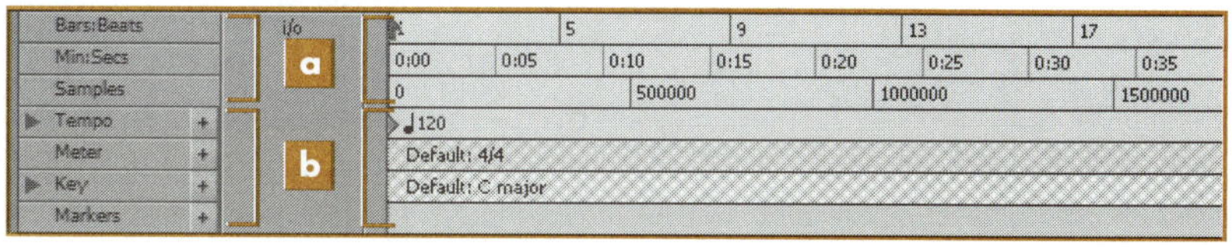

The Timeline itself can be displayed simultaneously in many time scales, with each visible ruler's type displayed to the left of the Timeline.

The Edit Tools area can be broken down into a number of functional areas:

a Edit modes

b Zoom tools

c Basic Edit tools

Last but certainly not least, the location and selection displays can give you location information.

d The Main and Sub time scales will tell you exactly where you are in your session. (The Sub time scale will allow you to see the same time location as the Main time scale, but in a different format.)

e The selection area will tell you the beginning, end, and duration of your selection. (The format for this section is based upon the format that you've chosen for the Main time scale.)

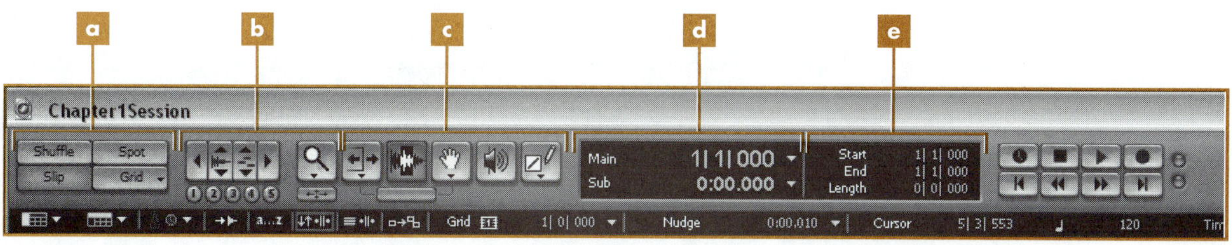

Customizing the Edit Window

Now that you've identified the overall layout of the Edit window, the following sections describe a few ways to set up the window to make working easier in any given circumstance.

Viewing Menus

As you learned earlier, the tops of each of the four Edit window lists serve not only as identifiers, but also as buttons that will reveal drop-down menus of operations specific to that area if you click on them. For example, here's how you can show the Tracks list's drop-down menu:

* Click on the Tracks List button. The Track Show/Hide pop-up menu will appear. The menu will allow you to control which tracks will be shown and which will be hidden. You'll find that the menu is very easy to navigate and understand, and has a degree of flexibility as well (as shown in the Show Only submenu).

Here's what you'll get when you click on the Edit Groups List button.

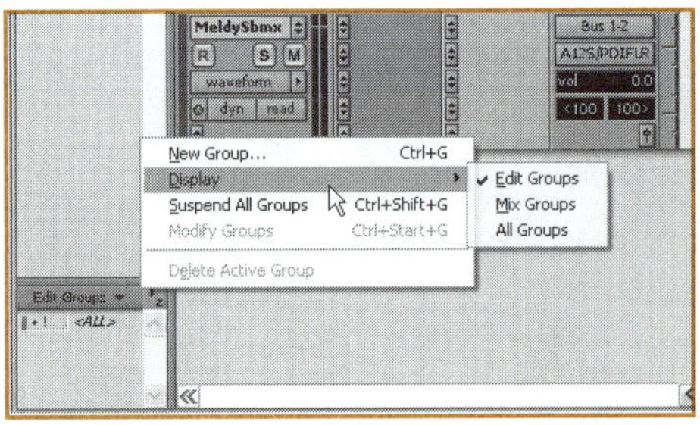

And the Regions List button.

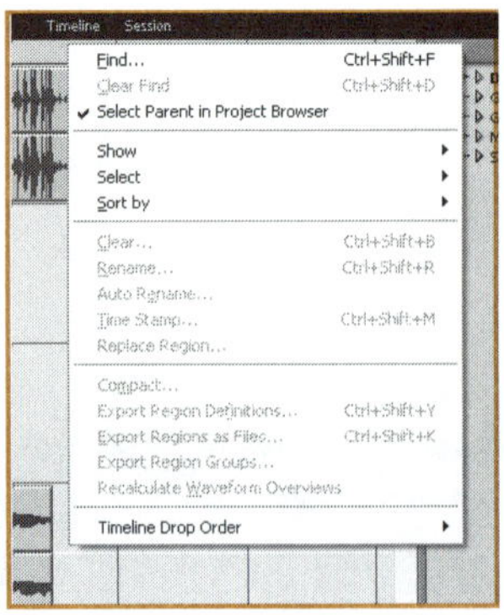

Adjusting List Size

You can customize your desktop in other ways as well. For example, if your session calls for more groups than tracks, you might want to give a little more room to the Edit Groups list on your desktop.

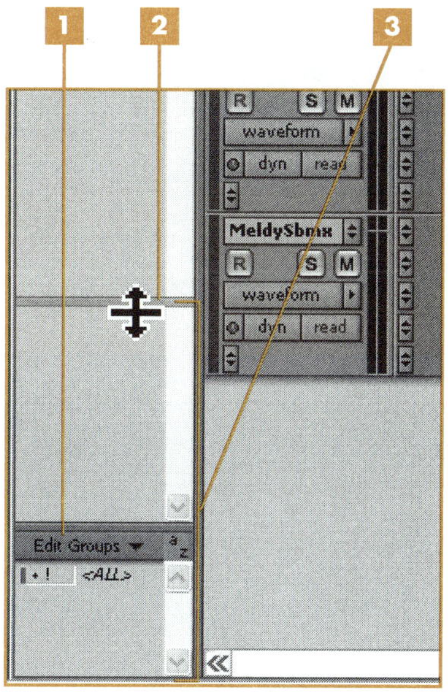

1. Move your cursor to the boundary between the Tracks list and the Edit Groups list. The cursor will change from the usual arrow into a double-arrow cursor (which you've no doubt seen when resizing areas in other programs as well).
2. Click and drag the boundary up or down as needed. As you drag, you'll see a light-grey line marking the movement of the boundary.
3. Release the mouse button. The boundary will be "dropped," and the lists will be reorganized.

Resizing the Lists

You can similarly adjust any of the boundaries (horizontal or vertical) for the Tracks list, Edit Groups list, and Regions list. Be careful, though—adjusting the vertical edges of these areas can affect how much area you have on your screen for tracks.

Hiding Lists

In addition to adjusting the sizes of these lists, you can hide them entirely when you're not using them.

1 Click on the arrows at the inner-bottom corners of either (or both) vertical section. The columns will be hidden immediately, and more of your Edit window will be usable by your Track area.

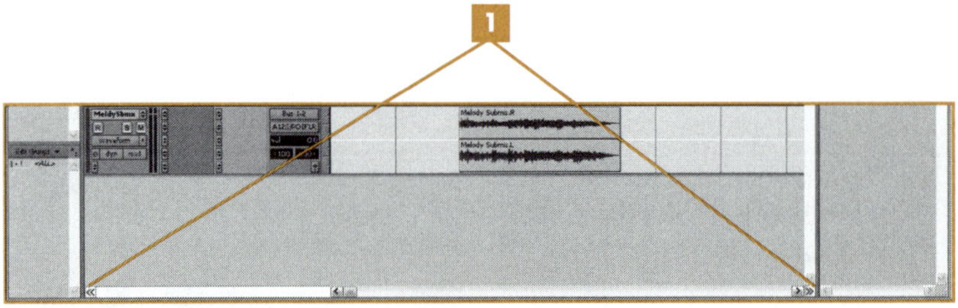

2 Not seeing your lists? That means that they're currently hidden. Click again on the arrows in the lower corner(s) of the Edit window. The sections will reappear immediately.

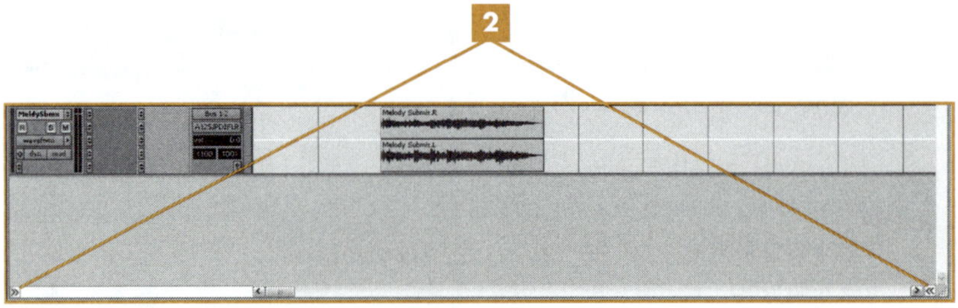

What Will I See When I Open a Session?

Remember, the window arrangements that appear when you open a session are the same as they were in the session when you last saved it. It can be a bit surprising to open a session and see no Region areas in your Edit window. Don't worry, though—you can always follow the previously mentioned steps to display the lists.

Displaying Track Columns

There are a number of columns in the Edit window's Track area that provide track-specific information on things such as inputs, outputs, inserts, sends, and comments. We'll go into each of these in due course, but for now, here's how to show or hide them:

1. Click on the View menu. The View menu will appear.
2. Click on Edit Window. A submenu of the available columns that can be shown in the Track area will appear. Checked columns are currently displayed.
3. Click on any column to check or uncheck it.
4. To quickly get to the Edit Window View menu, you can also click the Edit Window View Selector icon.

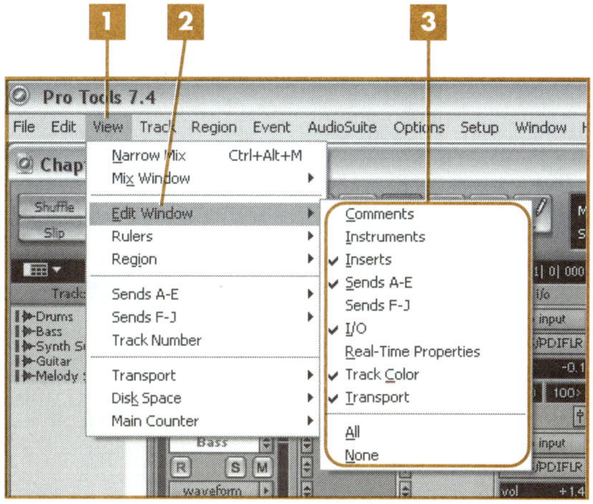

Two Ways to Do the Same Thing—Almost!

The view lists are *nearly* identical, whether you use the View menu or the Edit Window View Selector icon, with the following exception: The View menu's list includes the ability to show or hide the transport controls in the upper-right area of the Edit window.

Totally Extreme Viewing, Dude!

In addition to selecting columns individually, you can select All or None to show or hide all columns, respectively.

Displaying Rulers

You can also choose which rulers are to be shown.

1. Click on View. The View menu will appear.
2. Click on Rulers. A list of the available time scales you can show in the Rulers area will appear. Checked scales are currently displayed.

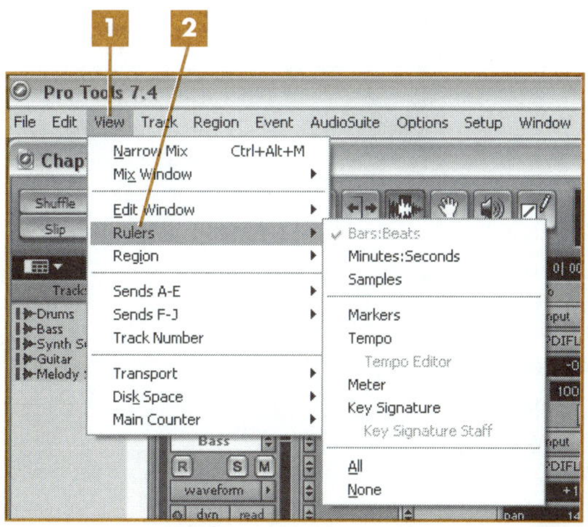

3 There's another way to get to the same list: Click the Ruler View selector to show the Ruler View Shows submenu.

Adjusting Track Heights

In Pro Tools, you have the ability to change the height of each track individually. This can come in handy, particularly when you have many tracks in your session and you want to see them all, or when you really want to do some microsurgery on one track in particular. Here's how:

1a Click the Track Height Selector button on the desired track. The Track Height drop-down menu will appear.

OR

1b Between each track's columns (I/O, Inserts, Sends, Comments) and the Region area is a small vertical area showing the amplitude scale. Click in this area. The Track Height drop-down menu will appear.

2 Select the desired track height. The track will change immediately to match your height choice.

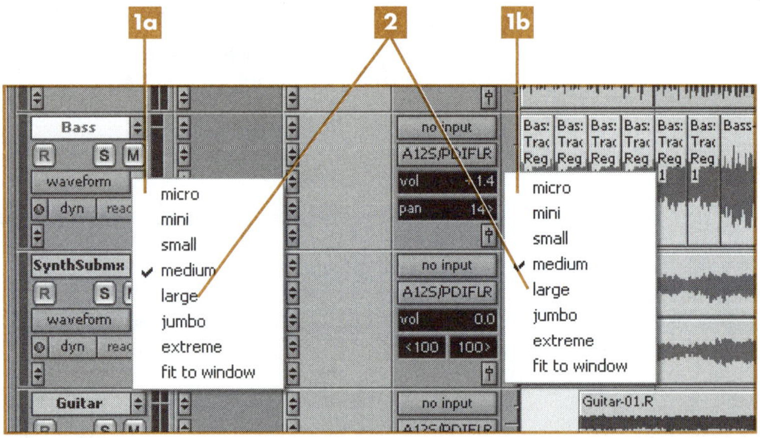

Changing the Track Height for Different Track Types

You can change the height of any Pro Tools track (including MIDI and Aux tracks, which you'll explore in later chapters). However, the thin vertical area for other types of tracks looks a little different than the amplitude scale of an Audio track. MIDI tracks, for example, show a keyboard-like display. In any case, clicking in this area will bring up the same Track Height menu.

With Pro Tools 7.3, you now have the ability to change track heights even more easily. Simply move your cursor to the bottom of the desired track, in the columns area. You'll see you cursor turn into the familiar double arrow shown here. Once you see this cursor icon, just click and drag up or down to decrease or increase that track's size (by the same size increments that you saw in the lists shown earlier).

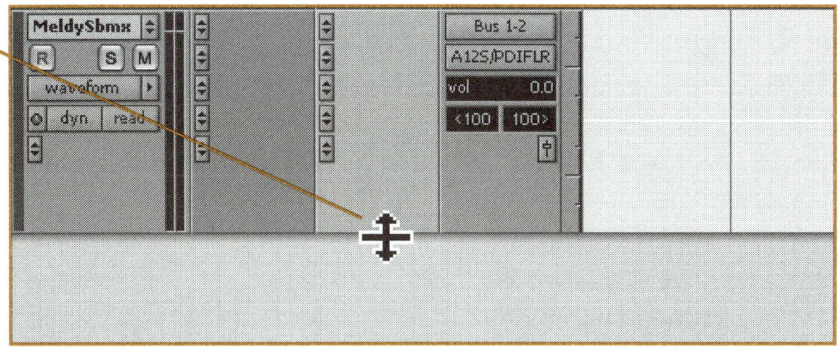

Smoothly Changing Track Heights

You can resize a track smoothly (without it snapping to the standard height increments) by holding down the Ctrl key (PC) or Key (Mac) while you drag your mouse.

Making Global Changes

Here's another useful shortcut: Hold the Option key (Mac) or the Alt key (PC) while you change the height of any one track, and the heights of all shown tracks will change at once.

New: Custom Track Colors

This isn't exactly a new feature to version 7, as it was added to later versions of Pro Tools LE 6, but it has been taken to the next level with the current version of Pro Tools 7. Like other Edit window customizations, this won't change the *sound* of your music, but it can really help you control how it looks. Users of all levels will find this sort of control a powerful ally in organizing tracks, regions, and more!

1a From the Window menu, choose Color Palette. The Color Palette window will appear.

OR

1b Double-click the Track Color column (at the leftmost edge of the track you want to change). The Color Palette window will appear. Be aware that you will have to be *showing* the Track Color column to click on it. (Refer to the section on showing and hiding columns earlier in this chapter.)

2 Click the desired color box, and the selected track's color column will immediately change color coding to match.

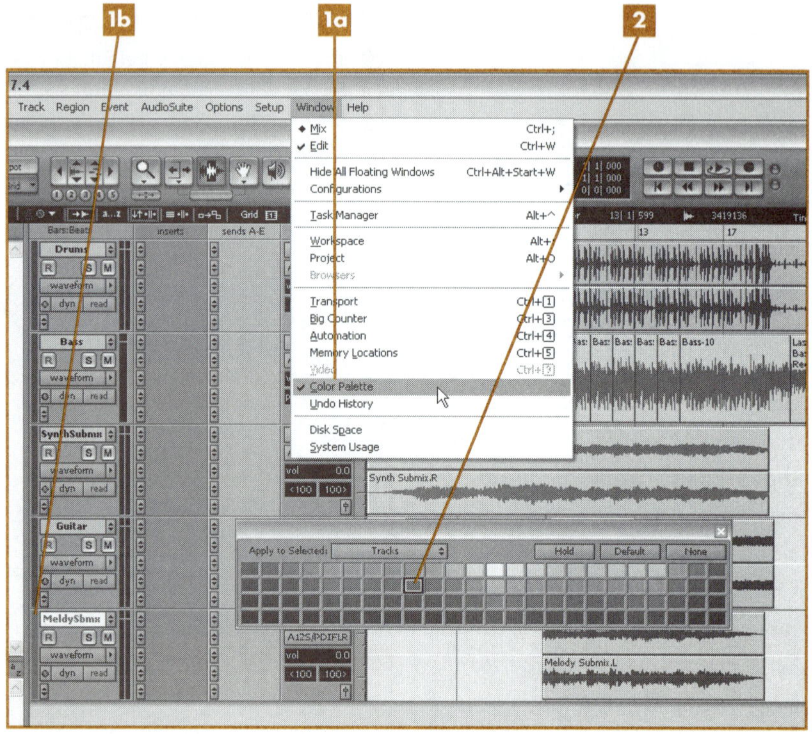

But wait, there's more!

1 Click the Apply to Selected drop-down menu (which will display "Tracks" when the window first appears). A menu will appear, as shown here.

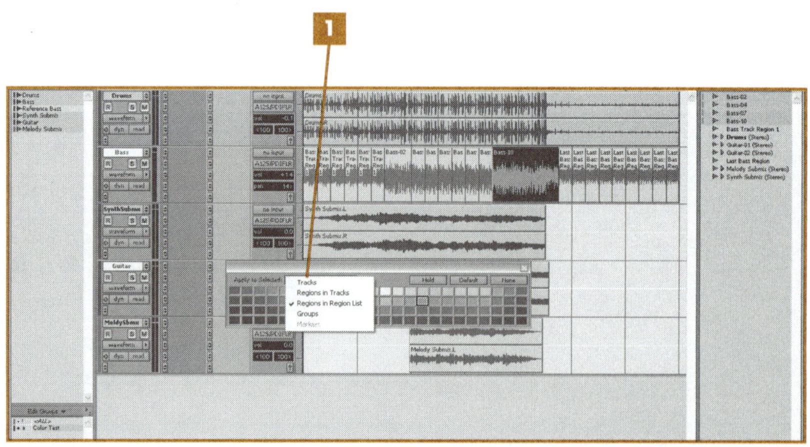

- **Regions in Tracks.** This will change the color of regions that have been selected in the Track area of the Edit window. In this case, the Bass 10 region will be recolored.

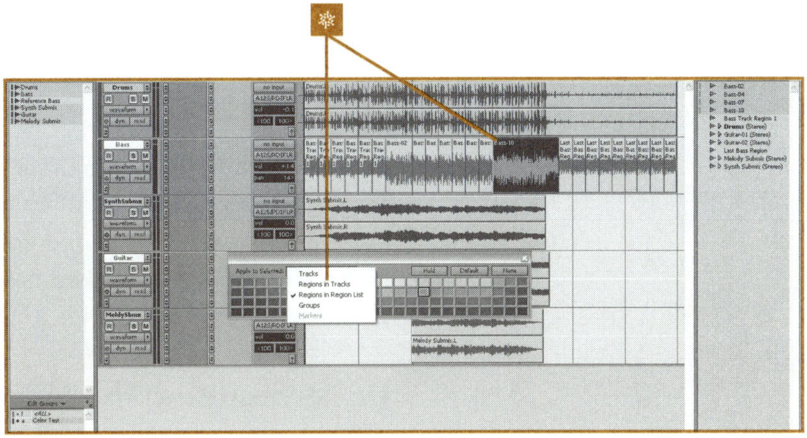

- **Regions in Region List.** Selecting this menu item will allow you to change selected regions in the Regions list area. In this case, Bass-02, 04, 07, and 10 will be recolored.

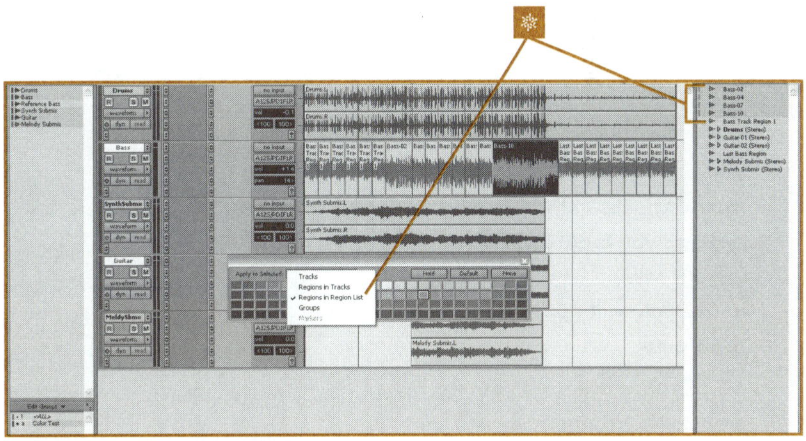

- **Groups.** This will allow you to recolor the color coding of selected groups. In this case, Edit Groups Color Test will be changed.
- **Markers.** Markers may also be color coded, which you'll learn more about in Chapter 6.

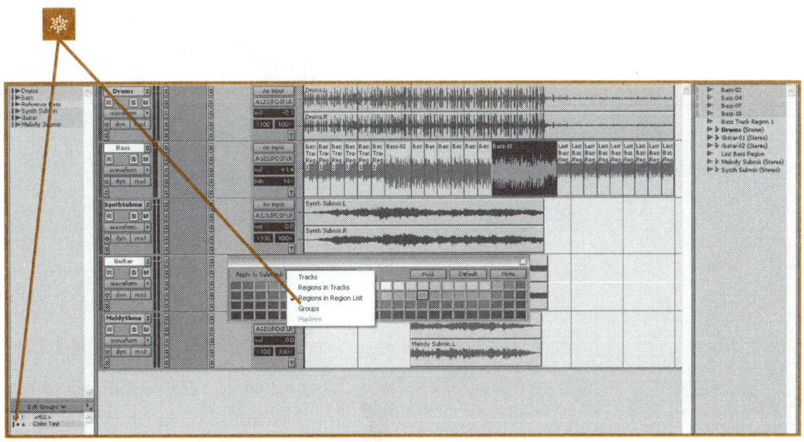

Working with the Mix Window

After the Edit window, the other primary window you'll use in Pro Tools is the Mix window. Although there's a good bit of common ground between the Mix and Edit windows, the layout and function of the Mix window is geared toward the mixing and automation phases of your production.

Understanding the Mix Window Layout

Most of the general layout of the Mix window is similar to the Edit window.

- **Tracks list.** This area functions similarly in both the Edit and Mix windows. In the Mix window, as you toggle each track in your session, channel strips to the right will appear and disappear.
- **Mix Groups area.** As you create mix groups, they will show up in this area.
- **Channel Strips area.** When you create any kind of track (Audio, Aux, Master Fader, MIDI, or Instrument), it will appear as a vertical strip.

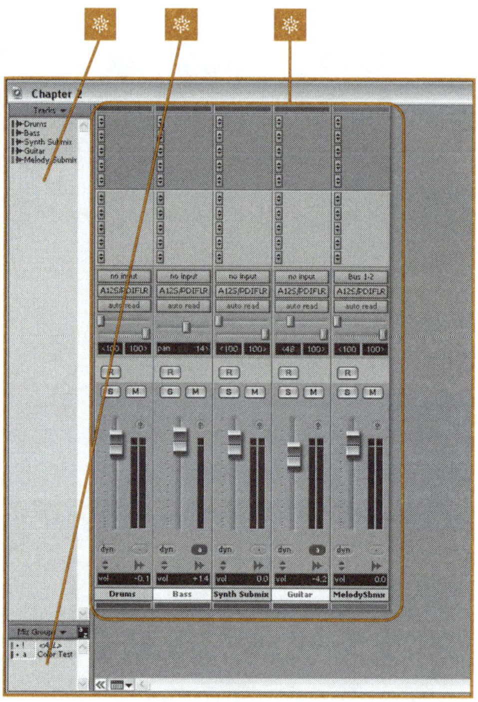

Customizing the Mix Window

Track Orders in the Edit and Mix Windows

Tracks that appear at the top of the Edit window will appear on the left side of the Mix window. As tracks descend in the Edit window, they move from left to right in the Mix window's Channel Strips area.

Track Show/Hide in the Edit and Mix Windows

There is a one-to-one correspondence between the tracks that are shown (or hidden) in the Edit and Mix windows. Also remember that whether a track is shown does not affect that track's audibility.

Tailoring your Mix window for maximum ease and efficiency will make mixing much easier. This section presents some of the most common customizations for the Mix window.

Hiding the Lists Column in the Mix Window

As in the Edit window, clicking on the double arrows in the corner of the Mix Groups area will hide both the Tracks list and Mix Groups sections. This will give you more space on your desktop for channel strips.

As with the Edit window, you can control the aspects of your mixer that are displayed.

1a Click the View menu, then choose Mix Window. The Mix Window submenu will appear.

OR

1b Click the Mix Window View Selector icon. The Mix View menu will appear.

2 Click on any element (Comments, Inserts, Sends, Track Color, or Instruments) to check or uncheck it.

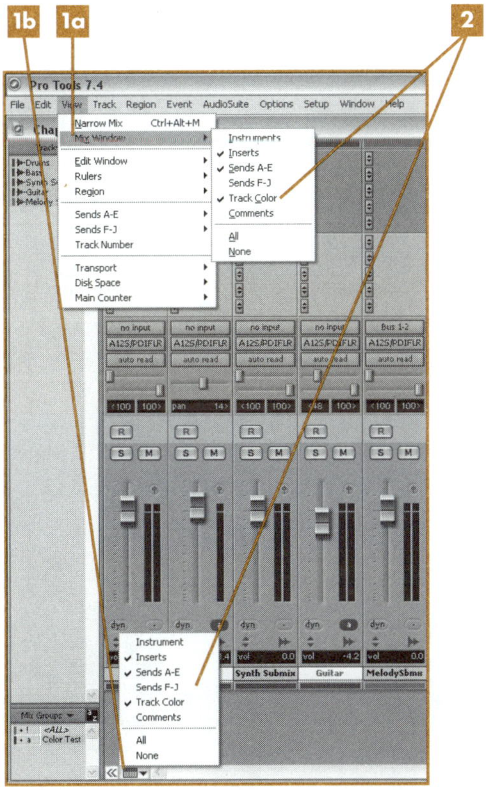

Showing All or Nothing!

In addition to selecting rows individually, you can select All or None to select all the rows or none of them, respectively.

Sends and Inserts

Sends and inserts are particularly useful in the mixing process, and the ability to show and hide them will be helpful as you tweak your mix. You'll learn more about mixing techniques in Chapter 8, "Basic Mixing."

Suppose you have a lot of tracks in your session, and you'd like to see as many of them as possible in the Mix window. Here's how to squeeze more tracks onto your limited desktop.

1. Click on View. The View menu will appear.
2. Select Narrow Mix. Technically, the Mix window itself won't narrow, but the individual channel strips will, allowing you to fit more tracks within a given space.

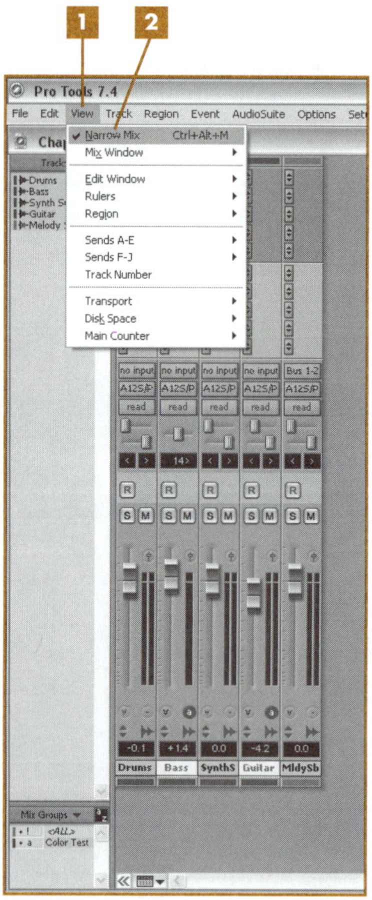

Last but not least, you might be wondering whether you can use track color coding in the Mix window as well as the Edit window. Absolutely, and you'll find that the colored areas (shown at the tops and bottoms of every track) will aid you greatly in organizing more complex mixes.

- Double-click on either of the color code areas of a given track to open the Color Palette window. From there, you can change the color coding of selected tracks just as you do in the Edit window.
- You can also click the Window drop-down menu to access the Color Palette window (again, just as we discussed earlier with the Edit window).

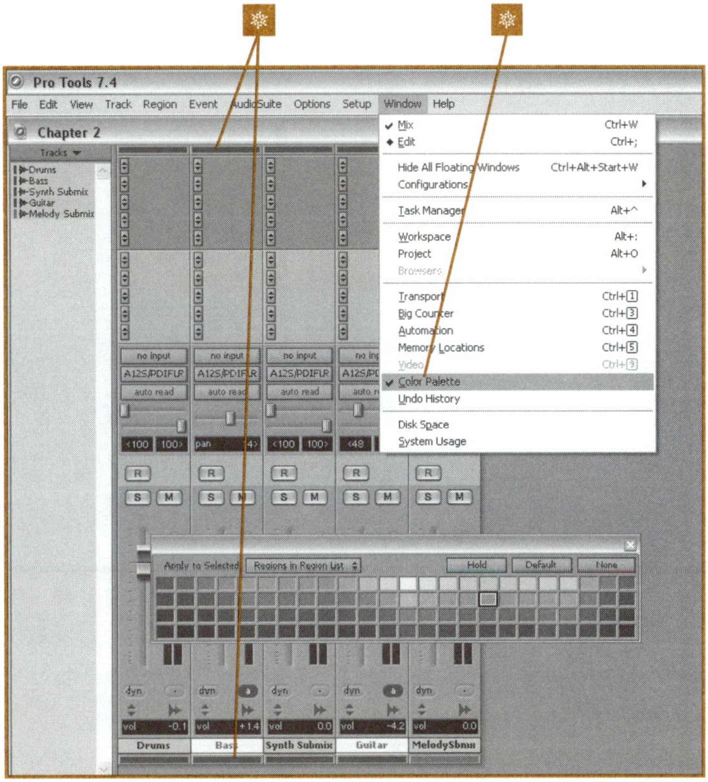

You can go one step further with track coloring in a way that works especially well in the Mix window. You can color the entire channel strip with one easy (but somewhat hidden) shortcut. Here's how:

- While holding down the Ctrl, Start (Windows), and Alt keys (PC), or Control, 🍎 (Apple), and Option keys (Mac), click in the colored tile section of the Color Palette window. Each track's color will be applied to the entire track!

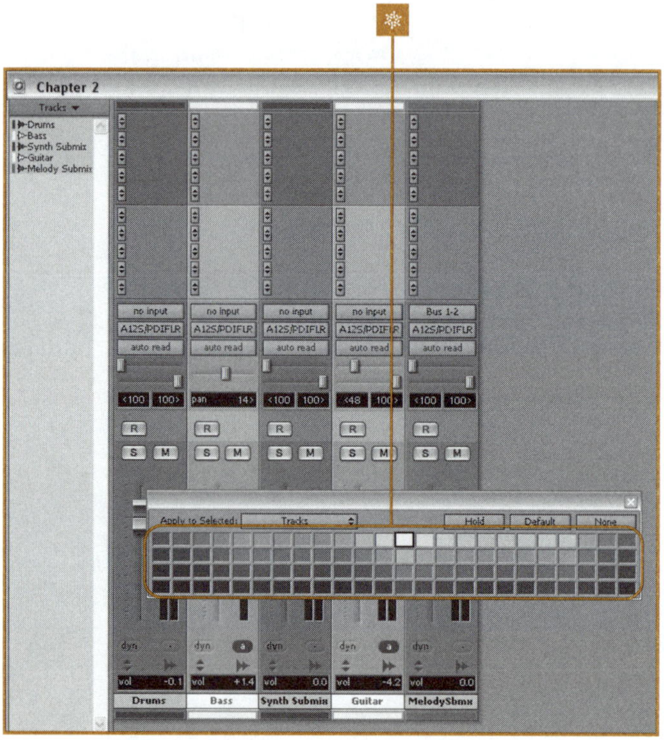

Color Coding and the Mix Window

Since the Mix window doesn't deal with specific regions, you will probably want to limit your color coding to tracks and groups in this window. Color changes made in this window will be applied to the Edit window as well.

The Transport Window

Yet another window, the Transport window, will be useful in playing your session.

1. Click on Window. The Window menu will appear.
2. Click on Transport. The Transport window will appear. Like the Edit and Mix windows, the Transport window has a number of functions, but for now we'll focus on just the basic transport controls:

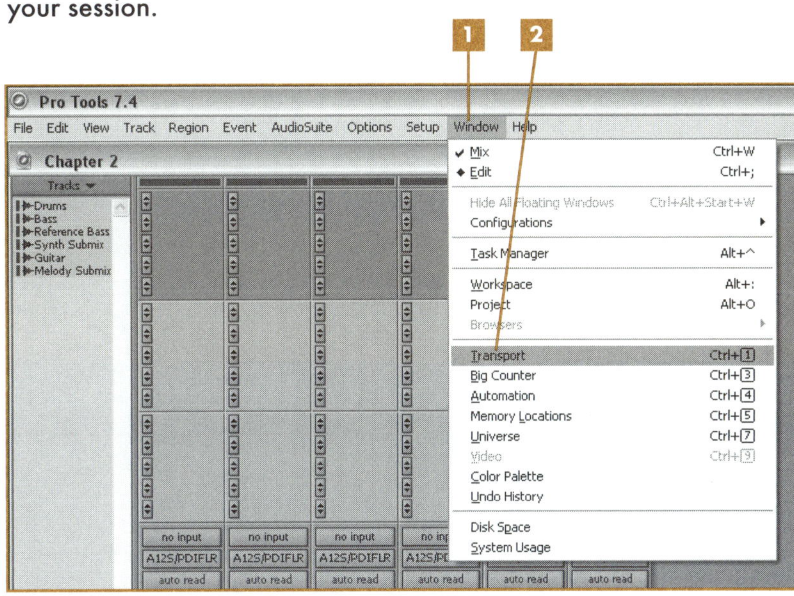

a. Go to Beginning
b. Rewind
c. Stop
d. Play
e. Fast Forward
f. Go to End
g. Record
h. Main Time Scale
i. Sub Time Scale (Think of this as a way to view the passage of time in a different format from the Main time scale—something we'll look at later in this chapter.)

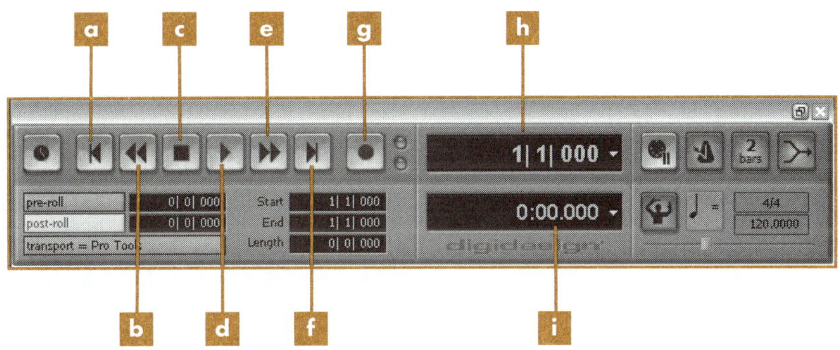

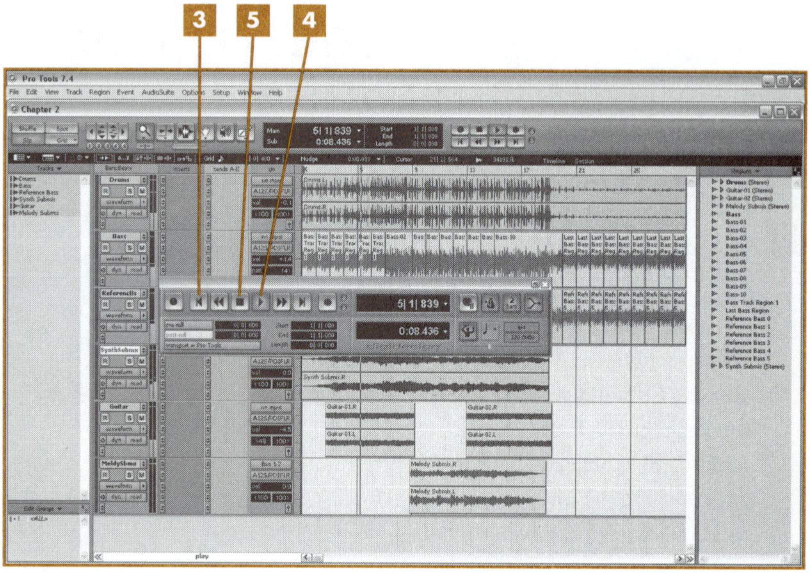

3. Click on the Go to Beginning button to make sure you're at the beginning of your session.
4. Click on the Play button. Your audio will begin playing, as shown in this illustration. You'll notice that a long vertical line travels from left to right in the Track area of the Edit window. This is called the Timeline insertion, and you'll notice that as it intersects with different regions, different audio will sound.
5. Click on the Stop button when you're finished. The playback will stop.

Customizing the Transport Window

The Transport window bears discussion, as does how to customize it. This window is especially useful when working in the Mix window, because the Mix window has no built-in transport controls:

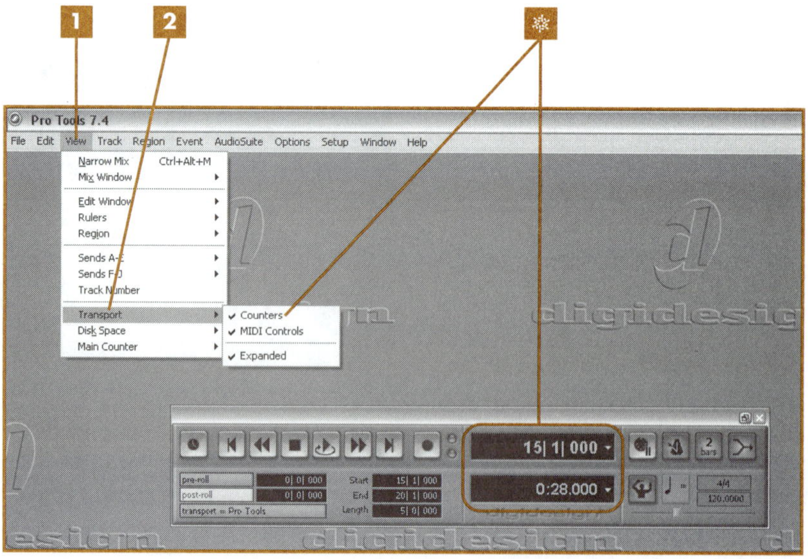

1. Click the View menu. The View menu will appear.
2. Click the Transport menu item. The Transport submenu will appear with the following options:
   - Counters. This option will add the main counter to the Transport window.

❋ **MIDI Controls**. This option will add basic MIDI controls to the Transport window (which will be discussed in detail in Chapter 7, "Using MIDI").

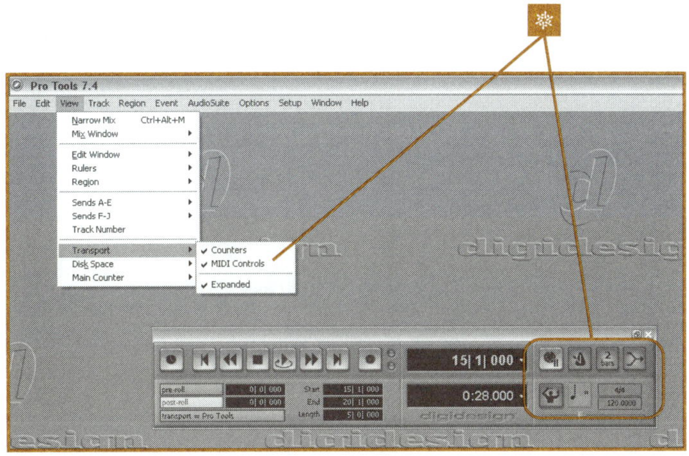

❋ **Expanded.** This option will add additional transport controls to the bottom half of the Transport window. In addition to functions such as pre-roll and post-roll, this option adds the sub location indicator below the main one and adds secondary MIDI controls below the primary ones.

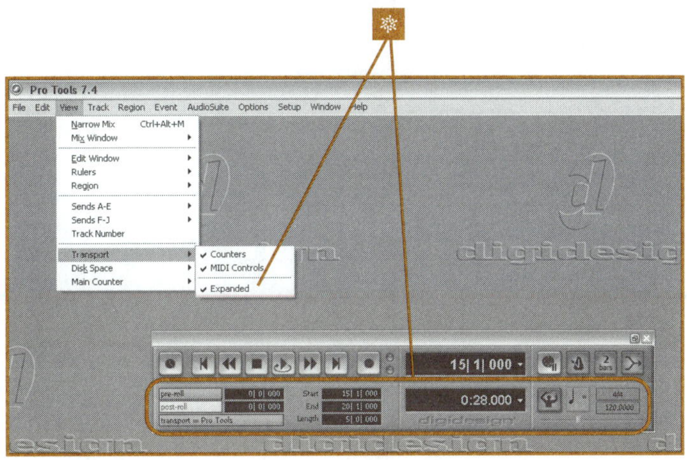

❋ Clicking on this icon will also show (or hide) the expanded features of the Transport window.

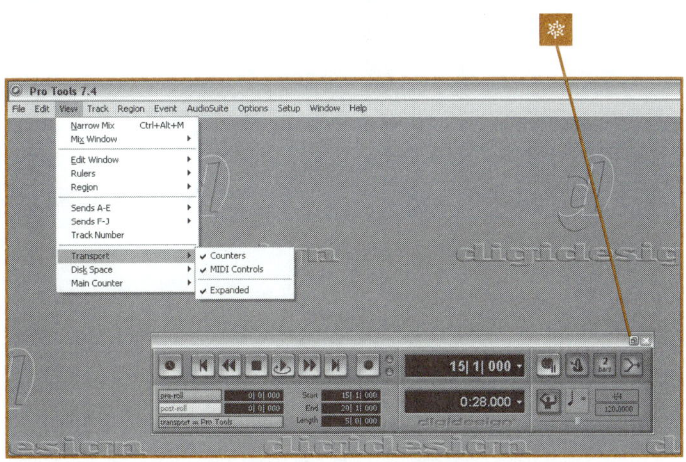

Other Useful Windows

Even though you'll spend the majority of your Pro Tools life working in the Edit and Mix windows, there are a number of other windows that serve specific purposes. These windows usually operate in conjunction with either the Edit or Mix window (whichever one you're using). You can access these secondary windows through the Windows menu, like so:

1. Click on Window. The Window menu will appear, displaying an assortment of choices.
2. Click on the window you want to display. The following list details some of the available windows.

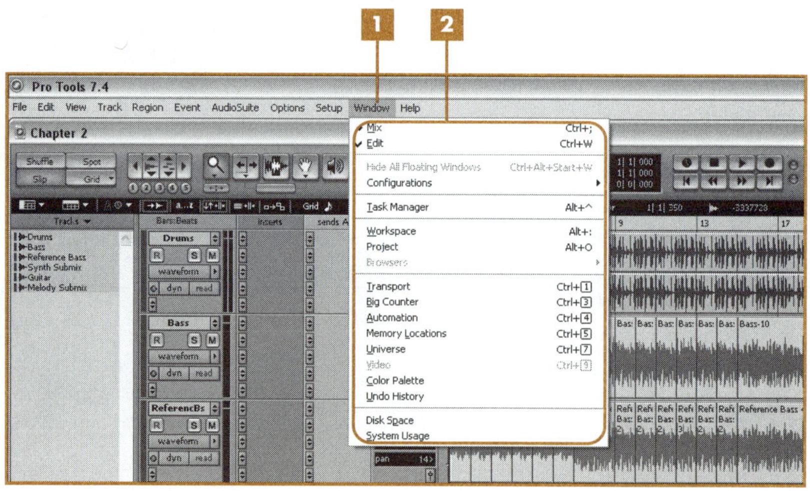

Getting Transport Control in the Mix Window

You've already worked with the Transport window. (Remember, the shortcut is Ctrl+1 (on your computer's numeric keypad) on the PC and ⌘+1 (on your computer's numeric keypad) on the Mac.) Like the Transport window, the windows discussed here will open on top of either the Edit or the Mix window.

Big Counter

- Big Counter. The Big Counter window is simply a larger display of your Main counter, but it really comes in handy when you want to watch your session's progress from across a room! The shortcut for the Big Counter window is Ctrl+3 (on your computer's numeric keypad) on a PC and ⌘+3 (on your computer's numeric keypad) on a Mac.

Automation Enable

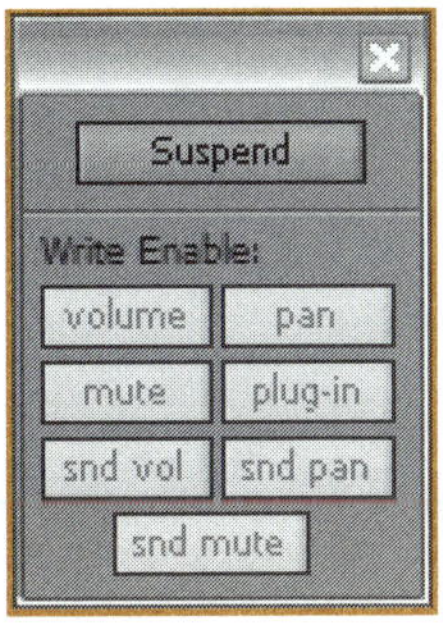

- Automation Enable. Automating Pro Tools is a topic you'll work with later in this book. Simply put, it's a way for you to make your mixes and effects more dynamic as your session plays. The Automation Enable window shown here allows you to enable or disable various aspects of your session for automation. The shortcut for the Automation Enable window is Ctrl+4 (on your computer's numeric keypad) on a PC and ⌘+4 (on your computer's numeric keypad) on a Mac.

Memory Locations

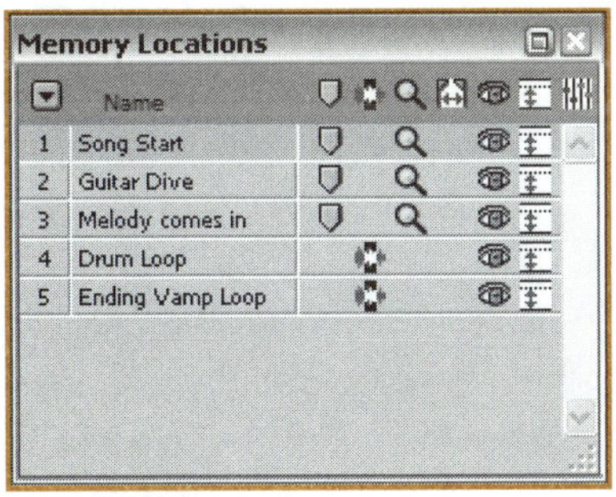

- Memory Locations. As you become more advanced, your sessions will naturally become more complex. You'll find that navigating around your intricate session will start taking more and more time and effort. Wouldn't it be great if there was a way to immediately jump to a specific location, or even a specific region of your session? That's exactly what memory locations are. As you'll learn later, memory locations are a powerful and flexible way to get from place to place instantly! For those of you who will use this feature frequently, you can open it by pressing Ctrl+5 (on your computer's numeric keypad) on a PC and ⌘+5 (on your computer's numeric keypad) on a Mac.

Tell Me More about Memory Locations!

You'll learn more about memory locations (and how to use them) in Chapter 6.

QuickTime Movie

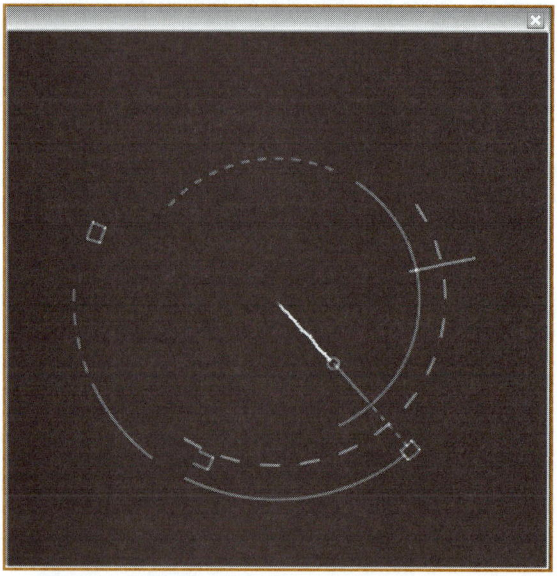

- QuickTime Movie. Though Pro Tools is an audio application, that doesn't mean that you can't work with video. And although your video editing options are limited, to be sure, importing video files into your session is easy, and viewing your movie as your session plays is as simple as choosing QuickTime Movie from the Window drop-down menu. You can also get to this window quickly by pressing Ctrl+9 on a PC or ⌘+9 on a Mac.

Session Setup

Those of you experienced with Pro Tools version 6 or earlier might remember that the Session Setup window, which *was* in the Window menu, has been removed! Not to worry; it just moved to another menu. Here's how to open the window:

1. Click on Setup. The Setup menu will appear, displaying an assortment of window choices.
2. Click on Session. The Session Setup window will appear.

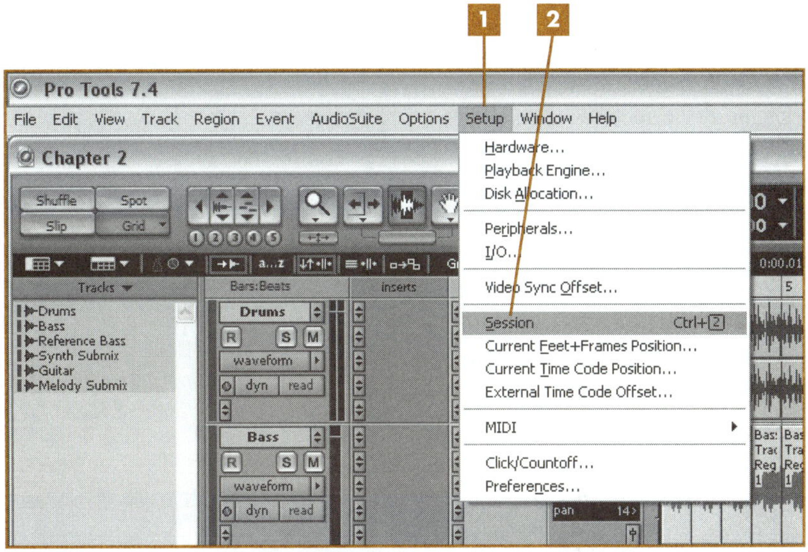

The Session Setup window displays useful information about your session's configurations. The shortcut for the Session Setup window is Ctrl+2 on a PC and ⌘+2 on a Mac.

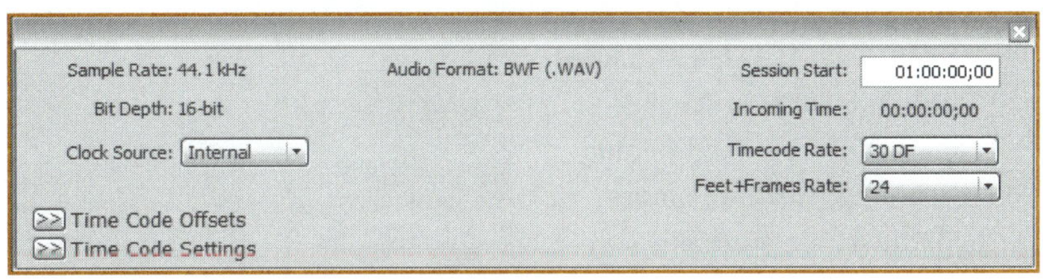

System Usage and Disk Space

Last but not least, these two windows will give you important information about how your system is doing. There are no shortcut keys for these windows (you'll have to open them from the Window menu), but they're critical windows nonetheless!

New in Pro Tools 7.4: Elastic Audio CPU Meter

Those of you familiar with previous versions of Pro Tools will notice that the System Usage window has changed just a bit. In previous versions, there was a single CPU meter, which showed RTAS plug-in activity in your session. Now, with the introduction of Elastic Audio (which we'll get into in Chapter 10, "Moving to the Next Level: Tips and Tricks"), there is a second meter that will tell you how hard your computer's CPU is working on Elastic Audio-related tasks.

* **System Usage.** As you learn more about how to efficiently use Pro Tools, you'll want to refer to the System Usage window from time to time to check on how your computer is dealing with the tasks associated with Pro Tools. This window gives a simple and efficient view of the workload for your system.

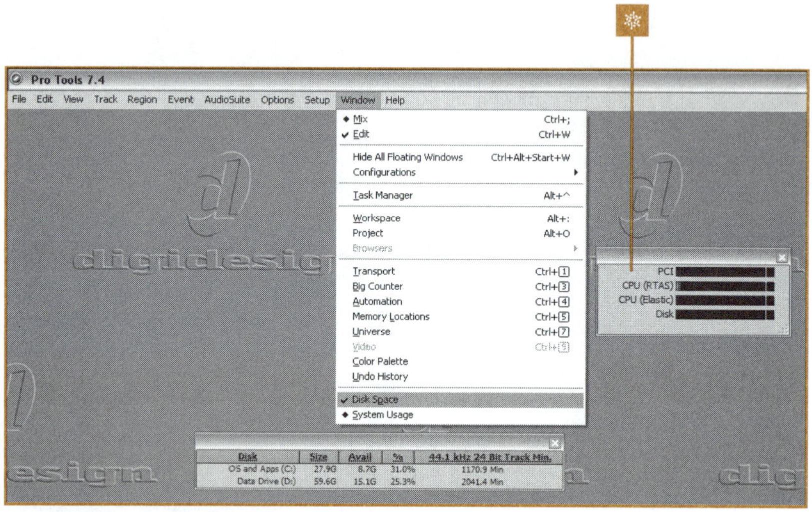

* **Disk Space.** The size of a hard drive in a DAW is like the amount of tape in an analog recording studio—the more you have, the more you can record. The Disk Space window will let you know how much free space you have for recording audio and how much time you have left to record (at a given sample rate and bit depth) on each of your computer's hard drives.

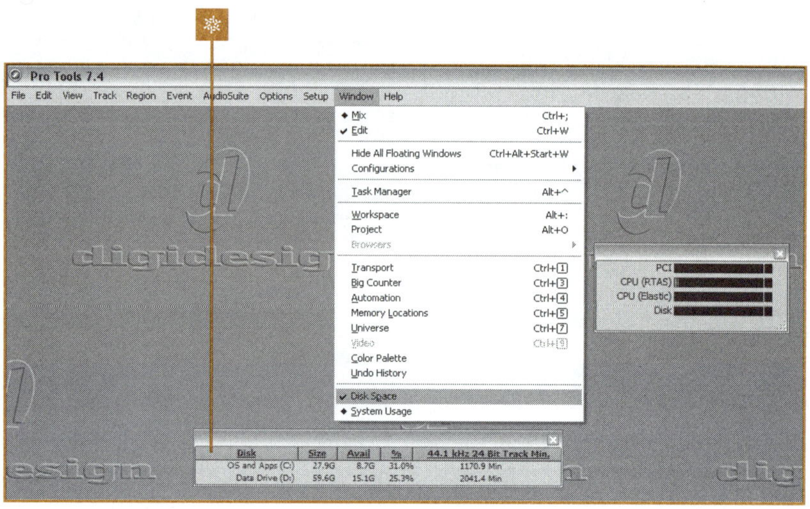

New Features

We've covered a lot of important introductory ground in this chapter, but if you'll indulge me, here are some quick and helpful new features for you to use!

Window Configurations

One of Pro Tools' most useful new features is the ability to recall specific arrangements of windows. With Window Configurations, you can quickly change the windows being displayed, as well as their size and positions. The process is as simple as it is useful:

1 Arrange your windows in any way that suits your workflow. In this case, I've chosen a simple arrangement of both the Edit and Mix windows.

2 The next step is to capture this arrangement of windows. From the Window menu, choose Configurations, and then New Configuration.

3 In the New Window Configuration window, you have the option of capturing the entire layout (including Mix, Edit, and Transport windows) or specific aspects of your desktop, as shown in the bottom radio button's drop-down menu. In this case, I'll choose the top radio button and type a descriptive name in the Name field.

4 Click OK. The New Window Configuration window will close, and your screen arrangement will be ready to be recalled at a moment's notice!

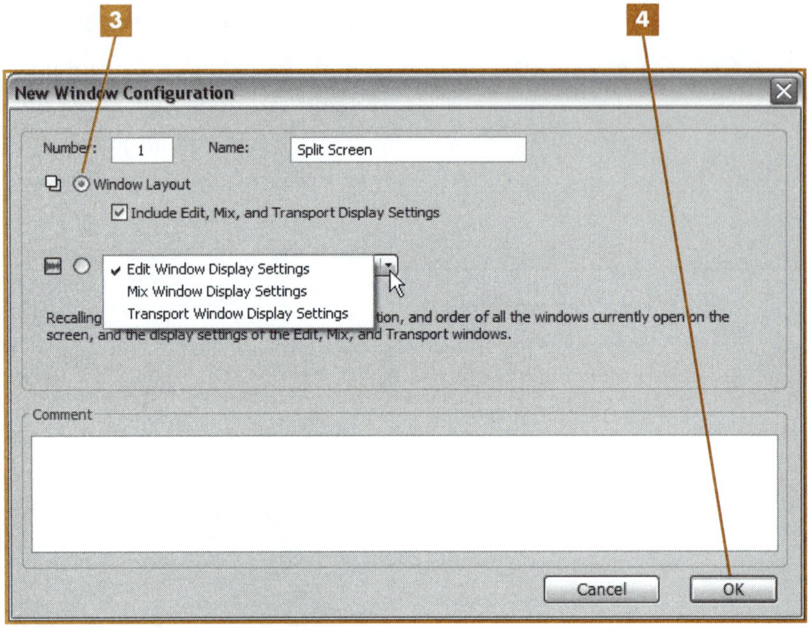

Recalling a Window Configuration is as easy as recalling its creation, and, as with most things in Pro Tools, there are a number of ways to do it:

1 From the Window menu, choose Configurations. You can select any created Window Configuration by choosing it at the bottom of the menu that is revealed.

2 There is also a convenient floating window that shows a list of your Window Configurations, similar to the Memory Locations window that you saw earlier in this chapter. Choose Window Configuration List to show this window.

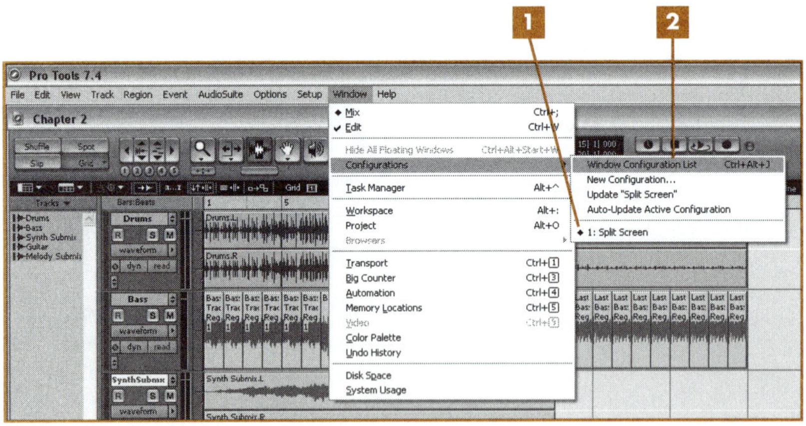

3 This window will not only show you a list, but it will also show you the aspects that are recalled with each configuration through the icons that are to the immediate right of the configuration name (Windows, Edit window, Mix window, Transport window, and Comments). Just click on the configuration that you want to recall.

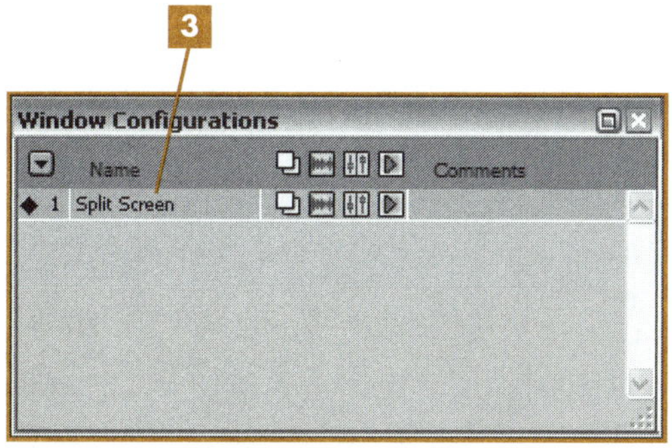

Window Configurations Shortcut

Here's a shortcut for recalling a Window Configuration, but be careful—the key order is important. First, press the period key on your numeric keypad, then press the number of the Window Configuration that you want to call up (again on your numeric keypad), then press the asterisk key (yet again on your numeric keypad).

Updating a Window Configuration

In the Window, Configurations submenu, you'll note that there is an Update "[configuration name]" option, which will allow you to change the named configuration to reflect the current window arrangement. Auto-Update Active Configuration will do this automatically.

Hiding Floating Windows

From time to time, your desktop may get a bit cluttered with floating windows of all kinds, which can get in the way of seeing the Edit and Mix windows clearly. There are two ways to quickly hide (and bring back) all floating windows in one fell swoop:

How to Hide All Your Floating Windows—Fast!

Press Ctrl+Alt+Start+W (PC) or ⌘+Option+Control+W (Mac) to hide or show all floating windows.

From the Window menu, choose Hide All Floating Windows. All floating windows will immediately disappear, and the menu item will be checked. Re-clicking Hide All Floating Windows (when it is checked) will reveal all hidden floating windows.

You'll find that this feature, though simple, is particularly useful when using plug-in effects and virtual instruments, and it will allow you to quickly alternate between windows.

Congratulations! You now have a fundamental understanding of what Pro Tools is and how it functions, which will help you be a more intelligent user as you delve deeper into this powerful environment. Now you're ready to begin actively using Pro Tools LE and making music!

3 Getting Started with Audio

Now that you have a solid basic understanding of what Pro Tools is and what it can do, it's time to start making things happen. The first step down this road to Pro Tools proficiency is to set up your session and start using audio. In this chapter, you'll learn how to:

- Configure Pro Tools to make the most of your computer system
- Set up and customize your inputs, outputs, inserts, and buses
- Create Audio, Aux Input, and Master Fader tracks
- Import audio into your session
- Play your session in different ways

Setup

Before you can move to the next step, you'll have to call upon knowledge that you gained in the first chapter and create a session on which you can work.

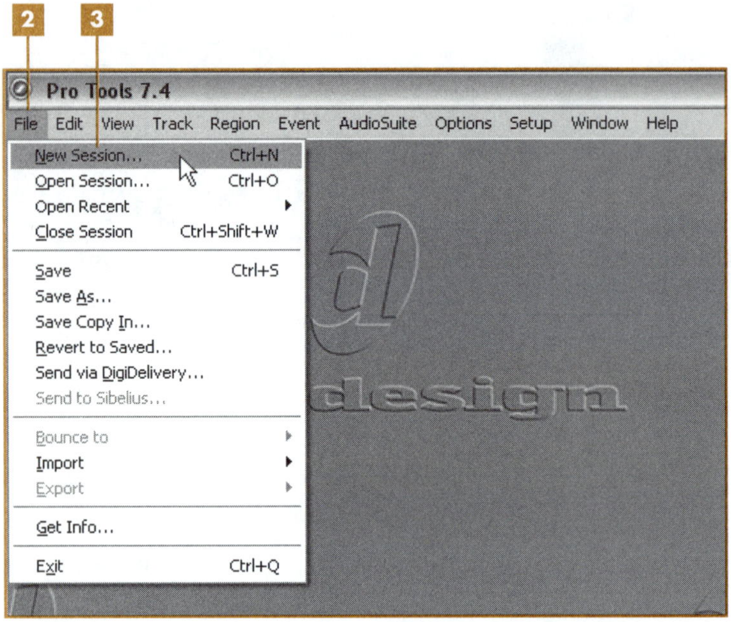

1. Launch Pro Tools.
2. Click on File. The File menu will appear.
3. Click on New Session. The Name the Session dialog box will open.

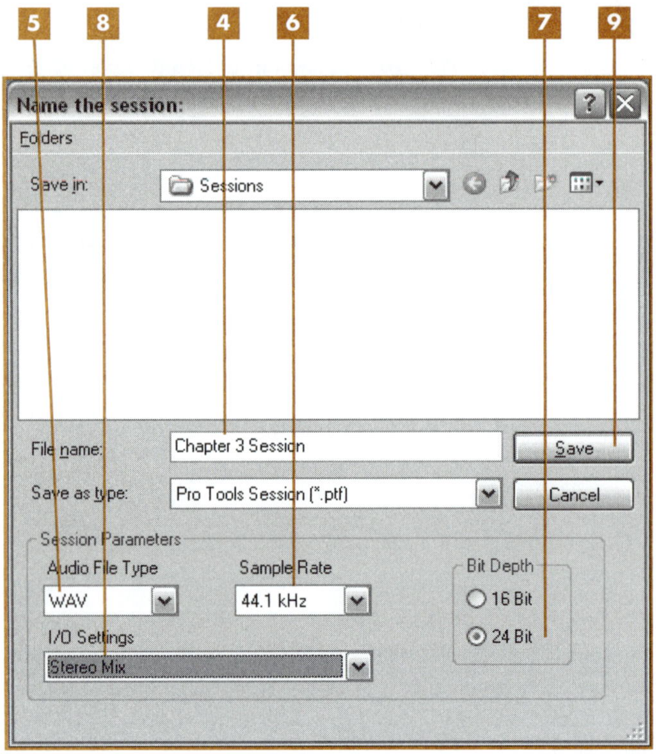

4. Type Chapter 3 Session in the File Name text box.
5. Select WAV from the Audio File Type menu. The option will be selected.
6. Select 44.1 kHz from the Sample Rate menu. The option will be selected.
7. Select the 24 Bit radio button in the Bit Depth area. The option will be selected.
8. Select Stereo Mix from the I/O Settings menu. The option will be selected.
9. Click on Save. Your session will be created and opened automatically.

The Playback Engine Window

Every DAW application has a certain amount of code devoted to the tasks of digital audio recording and playback. This bit of programming is so important that it has its own term—it's called the *audio engine*. Pro Tools' audio engine is appropriately called the *DAE*, or *Digidesign Audio Engine*. The DAE is at the very heart of Pro Tools' operations, and the quality of its construction is a big reason for Pro Tools' popularity.

Let's start this chapter by taking a look at the Playback Engine window, where you can choose settings for the DAE and make the most of your overall system. We'll start by locating the window:

1. Click on Setup. The Setup menu will appear.
2. Click on Playback Engine. The Playback Engine window will appear.

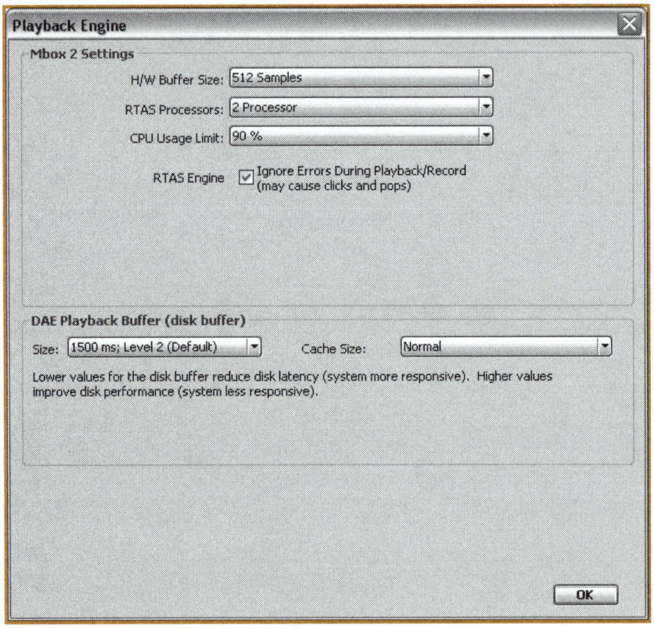

This window will give you a great deal of control over the DAE. You'll see that it's broken up into two major sections: The top area is devoted to your audio interface settings (in my case, the settings for my Mbox 2). The bottom area addresses the DAE Playback Buffer, which is devoted to the tasks of audio playback. Let's take these sections one by one:

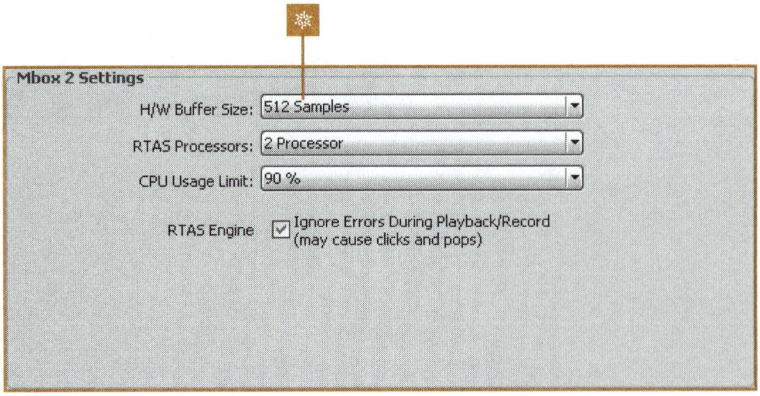

* The H/W Buffer Size (hardware buffer size) is particularly important with Pro Tools LE systems. With Pro Tools LE, your computer's CPU is responsible for all of the processes, including recording, playback, and plug-in effects. The hardware buffer will allow you to set aside some of your CPU's power to create a data buffer for these important tasks. Just click the arrow button at the right of the setting to reveal a drop-down list of options.

What's a Buffer?

You've probably heard the term *buffer* tossed about in the world of computers, but you might be a bit foggy on what exactly a buffer is and what it does. A buffer is a certain amount of computer memory (generally RAM memory is used due to its high speed) that a processor uses for short-term data storage during operations.

Though buffers are used in different ways for different kinds of applications, as a general rule buffers will allow a processor to work with more data in a more efficient way.

The Pros and Cons of Hardware Buffer Settings

Having a high hardware buffer setting will certainly enable you to have more simultaneous audio processes (such as plug-in effects, for example), but there's a catch: High buffer settings can also increase recording latency, or a delay between a signal going into Pro Tools and the audio heard out of the monitor speakers. High recording latency can be a real bother during LE recording sessions. (This delay can be very distracting to musicians when they are trying to hear their live performance through the headphones.)

Here's a good rule of thumb for you: Set your hardware buffer as low as possible when recording. (This may or may not be the first setting on the list, depending on your computer's power.) Set the buffer higher when the recording phase is finished, so you can take advantage of more plug-ins during the editing and mixing stages.

The RTAS Processors list (which you'll see if you click the arrow button to the right of the setting) will allow you to utilize any number of CPUs in a multi-processor system. If you have multiple CPUs, choosing to use them (as I've done in this image) will give you the option of launching more RTAS plug-ins. If other applications on your system (such as video editing applications) have high priority, or if your session has a great deal of mix automation, then consider using fewer CPUs to free up processing power.

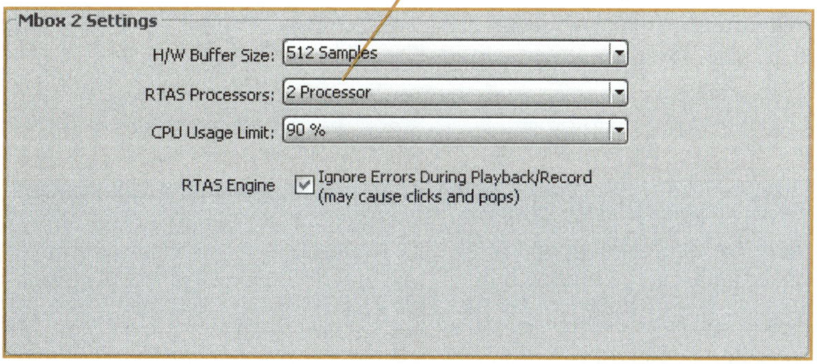

- The CPU Usage Limit allows you to set a cap on the amount of CPU power to be used by Pro Tools. When you click the arrow button indicated, you'll see a drop-down menu showing a series of percentages. A higher percentage (for example, the 90% shown here) will give Pro Tools more power, though it may rob power from other applications (again, such as a video editing application) that may also be running. A lower limit will restrict Pro Tools somewhat, but can also ensure adequate power for other applications.

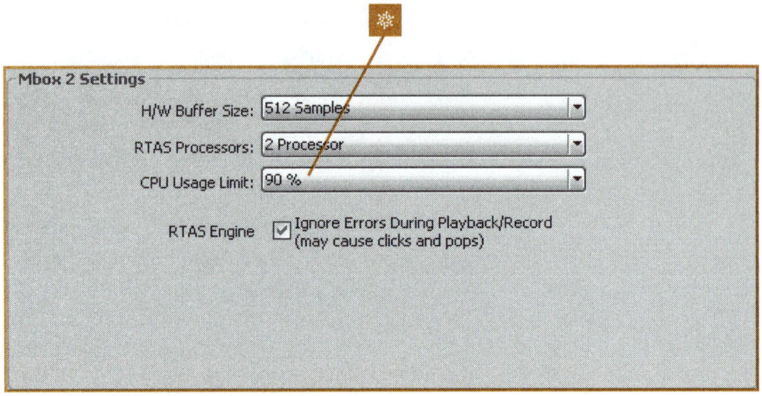

- One of the things I really like about the DAE is that it's a stickler for quality—if there are any errors in the playback or recording of your audio, the DAE will stop everything and tell you about the problem. I do find, however, that these messages (which will stop playback or recording) can get a bit bothersome when I'm working in a non-critical situation (for example, when I'm launching plug-ins during playback, just to see which effect suits my needs). In these situations, where a few clicks or pops are tolerable, check the RTAS Engine—Ignore Errors During Playback/Record box indicated here.

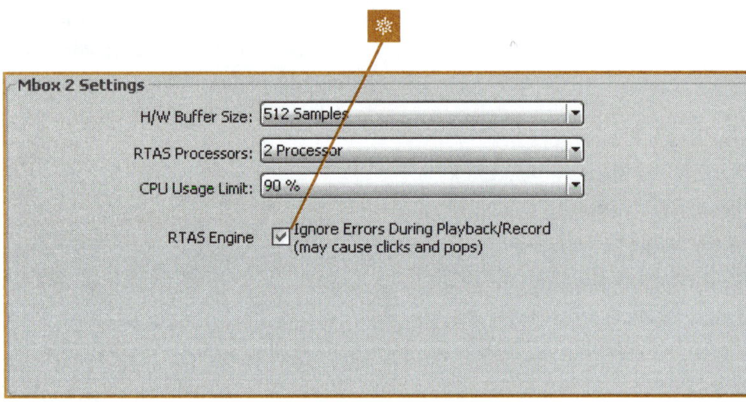

When *Not* to Ignore the Errors!

As a general rule, I only check Ignore Errors During Playback/Record when I'm experiencing problems. Just remember to *un*check the Ignore Errors During Playback/Record box when you're dealing with critical things such as final mixdowns—you certainly don't want to hear clicks and pops then!

Now let's take a look at the DAE Playback Buffer settings:

- The DAE Playback Buffer Size allows you to change (by clicking the arrow button to the right of the Size value) the storage capacity of the buffer. The default value (Level 2, or 1500 milliseconds) is fine for the vast majority of situations, but if you run into disk playback errors (errors telling you that your disk is too slow to continue playback of your session), you can choose a higher buffer setting to treat the symptom.
- The Cache Size is a new addition to Pro Tools 7.4, and it allows you to allocate memory specifically for Elastic Audio-related tasks. If you click the arrow to the right of the Cache Size setting, you'll be able to choose from three settings: Minimum (reduces memory use), Normal, and Large (improves performance).

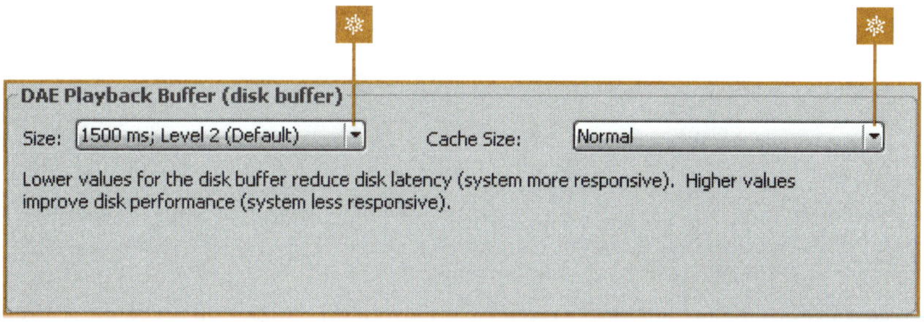

Will the DAE Playback Buffer Affect Recording?

As the Playback Engine window states, higher buffer settings may make Pro Tools less responsive. This should not be confused with recording latency—in fact, the changes you make to the DAE Playback Buffer won't affect recording latency one way or the other. The responsiveness that this window refers to is simply a very slight sluggishness with things such as transport controls.

Streaming Buffer Size Settings

If your system happens to be running the Structure software sampler, you will also see a Plug-In Streaming Buffer Size section, which will allow you to choose the amount of memory the DAE reserves for sample playback.

3 When you're finished, just click the OK button, and the window will close.

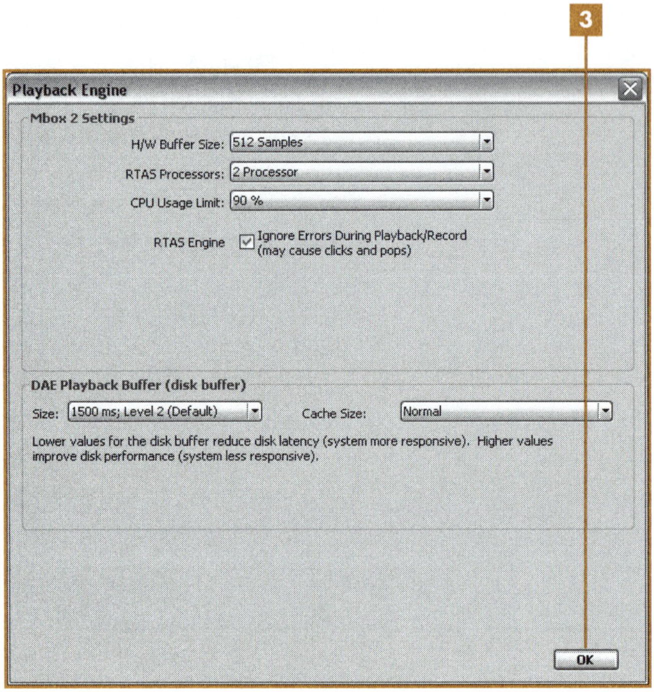

Customizing Your Session: I/O Setup

An understanding of Pro Tools' signal flow is critical to using this powerful DAW, and at the heart of signal flow is the I/O (Input/Output) Setup dialog box. Take a look.

Setting Up Inputs

When you created this session, you chose Stereo Mix as your I/O (Input/Output) setting. This I/O setting is Pro Tools' generic setup for stereo work, and although it works fine as is, you can customize it to match your own studio's setup and boost your productivity right from the start! You can start by taking a closer look at the input setup for your studio—in other words, the connections going into your audio interface, and from there to the Pro Tools software environment.

1 Click on Setup. The Setup menu will appear.

2 Click on I/O. The I/O Setup dialog box will open.

3 Click on the Input tab. The tab will move to the front.

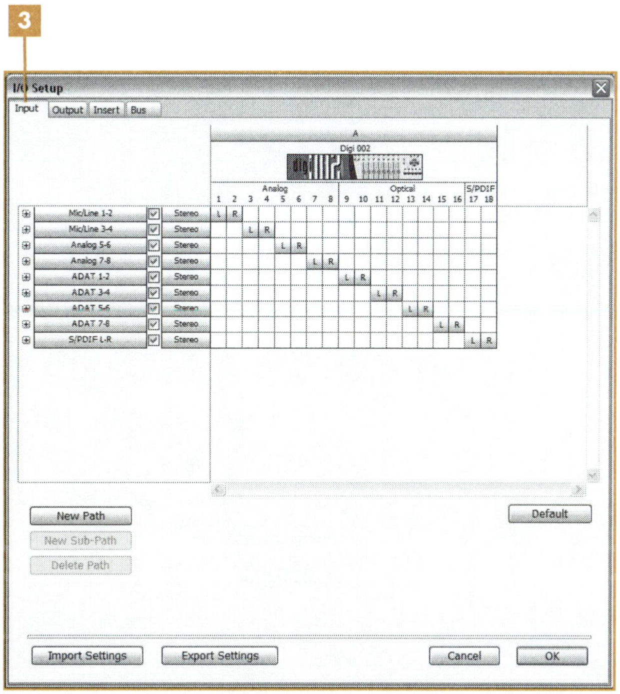

A Word about the Screenshots

The examples in this section show the windows you'll see if you have a Digi 002 system. If you have any other kind of interface, the window will look a little different (although the function will be the same). At the top of the window, you'll see your audio interface. Directly below the interface, you'll see a listing of all the available inputs for that interface.

Customizing Your Inputs

The grid area and the labels to the left represent paths, which allow you to assign inputs in the Pro Tools software to the physical inputs of your Pro Tools hardware. The dialog box currently displays a default input setup. You'll want to customize your inputs, and the easiest way to do that is to delete these paths and start from scratch. Here's how:

1. **Click** on the top **path name**. The name will be highlighted.
2. **Press** the **Shift key** and **click** on the remaining **path names** until all the paths are highlighted.
3. **Click** on **Delete Path**. All the input paths will disappear.

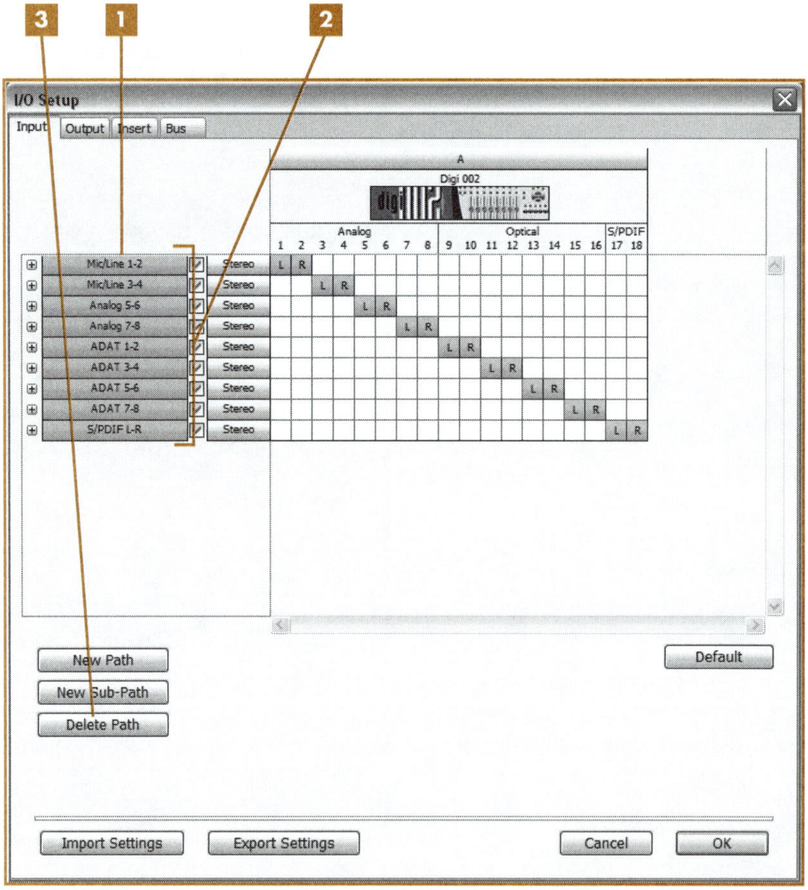

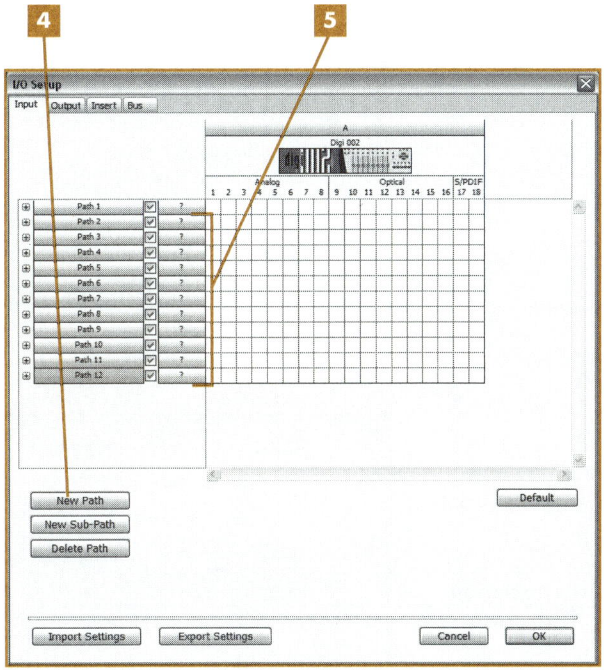

4 Click on New Path. A single new path will appear with the default name of Path 1.

5 Click on New Path 11 more times. Additional paths will be created, again with default names.

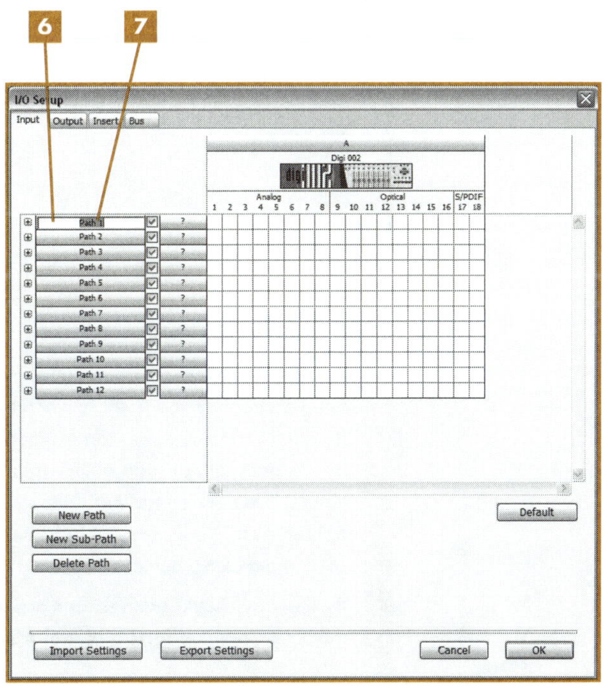

6 Although you've created input paths, they haven't been configured or assigned to physical inputs on your interface yet. That's your next job. Double-click on the top path name. The path name will be highlighted.

7 Type a descriptive name for this path.

8 Repeat Steps 6 and 7 for the other applicable default paths, naming each input descriptively.

How Should I Name My Inputs?

A good rule of thumb is to name your inputs for the devices that are connected to your system. As you list these devices, keep track of which inputs are coming from stereo sources and which are coming from mono sources—it'll come in handy later!

Configuring a Path as Stereo or Mono

Now you need to configure each path as either stereo or mono.

1. Click on the question mark (?) to the right of a path name. A path type pop-up menu will appear.
2. Choose a type for each path (stereo or mono). The type will be selected.

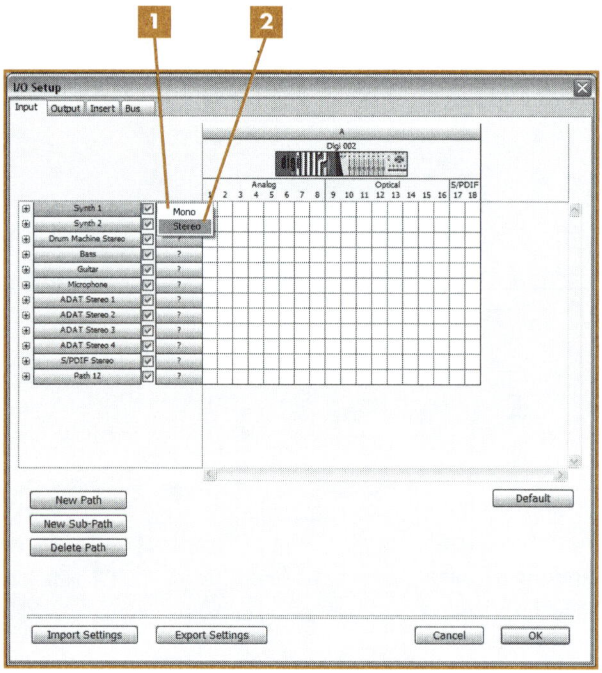

How I've Arranged My Inputs

In my system, I've set up my I/O Setup dialog box to reflect the devices that I might attach to my 002. The first two paths are reserved for two synthesizers (the first is stereo; the second is mono), then a drum machine (stereo), followed by the bass, guitar, and a microphone (all three mono). As for the ADAT inputs, I've divided the eight inputs into four pairs, then finally one stereo S/PDIF path. Your inputs should be set up according to your specific array of sound-making devices.

By the way, ADAT connections are used not only with ADATs, but also with any gear that supports a digital ADAT lightpipe connection.

Assigning Your Path

Now it's time to assign your path (in this case, Front Inputs) to specific inputs of your audio interface (in this case, Synth 1).

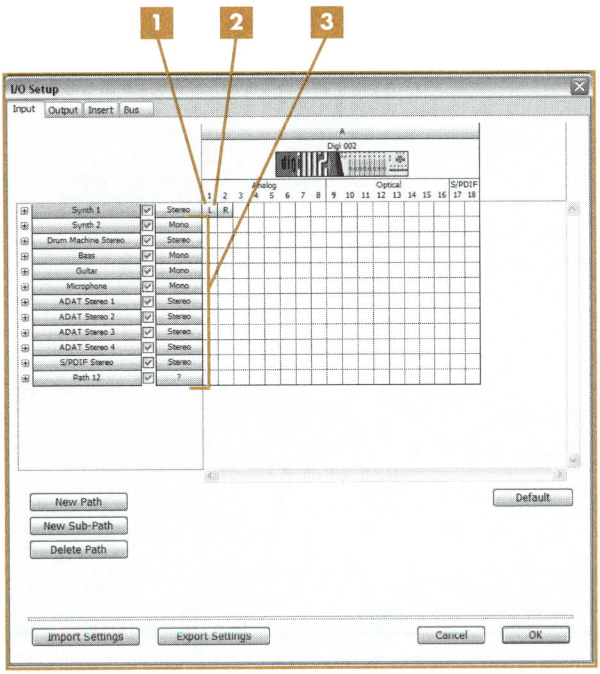

1. Move your cursor to the grid area in the top row. Your cursor will change from an arrow to a pencil.
2. Click in the square that matches the input you desire. Because this happens to be a stereo path, two blocks will appear, marked L and R (for left and right).
3. Repeat Step 2 for all your paths.

Assigning a Stereo Path

In the case of a stereo path, click on the square that is assigned to the left channel.

Setting Up Sub-Paths

You've set up your paths, and now it's time to think about sub-paths. *Sub-paths* are individual assignments within a path. For example, take a look at the first ADAT path—ADAT Stereo 1. If you have a stereo signal going into those two inputs, you're all set; however, if you want to use each input separately, you should consider setting up a couple of sub-paths within that stereo path.

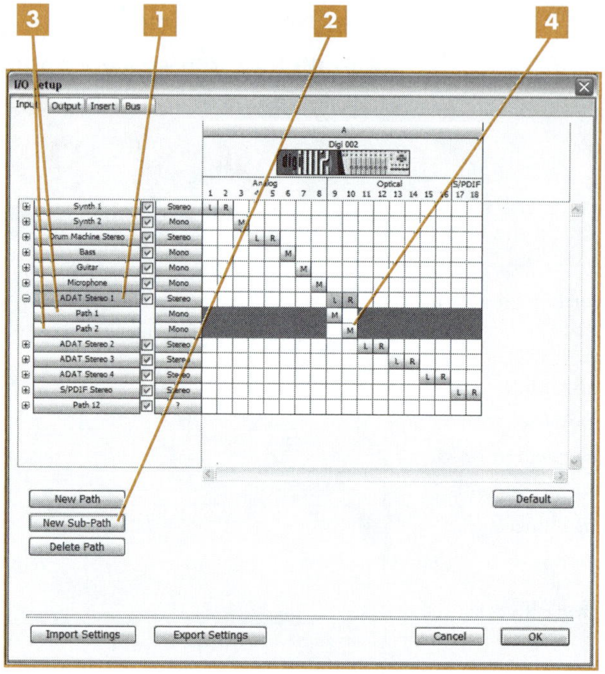

1. **Click** on the desired **stereo path name**. The name will be highlighted.
2. **Click twice** on **New Sub-Path**. Two sub-paths will be created below the first path, with default names (Path 1 and Path 2).
3. **Double-click** on each **sub-path** and **name it**, just like you did with the paths.
4. As you did with the paths, you need to assign a physical output to each sub-path. **Click** on the desired **grid square**. A block with an M (for mono) will appear.

Changing a Path's Input Assignment

Once you've created a path (or sub-path) and assigned a physical interface input to that path, you're all set. But what if you want to change the input of a specific path? For example, let's assume that the bass in my studio is actually plugged into Input 7, and the guitar is actually plugged into Input 6. Changing the inputs is extremely easy, and it is one of the real beauties of the I/O Setup dialog box:

1. **Click and hold** the **block** you want to change.
2. **Drag** the **block** until it is directly beneath the desired input. A hollow box will show where your input path will be redeposited.
3. **Release** the **mouse button**. The path's input block will be moved to the selected interface input.

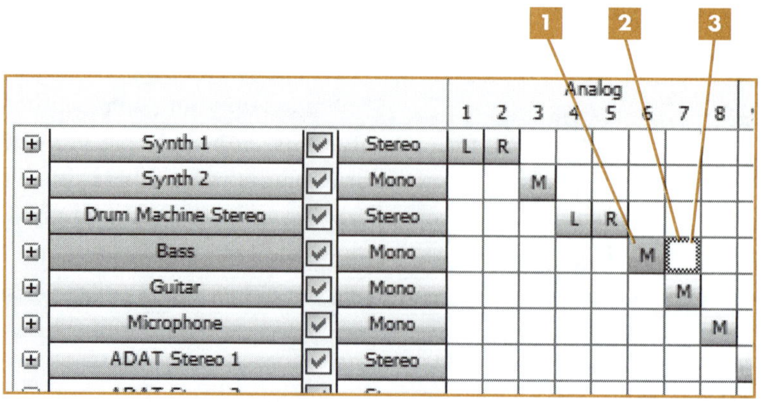

Setting Up Outputs

You've set up your system to deal with incoming audio—good job! The next step is to customize how audio exits your audio interface. For the examples shown in this section, we'll once again create a basic setup that happens to work in my studio—your setup will reflect your personal needs and I/O capabilities. The good news is that the Output tab of the I/O Setup dialog box is laid out similarly to the Input tab, so this should go a lot quicker!

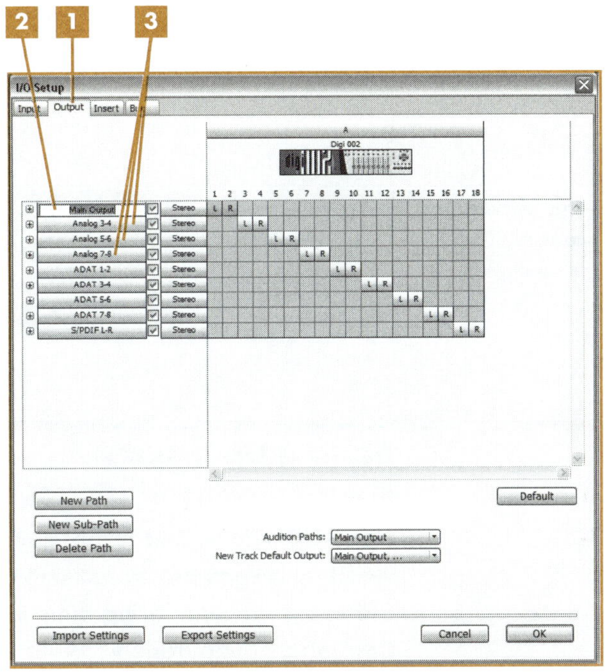

1. **Click** on the **Output tab** in the I/O Setup dialog box. The tab will move to the front.
2. **Double-click** on the first **output path name** and **type Main Output**. (This is the same method you used to name input paths.) The path will be renamed.
3. **Repeat Step 2** for the next three output paths (if your interface has them) and **rename** the **paths** as follows:
   - Drum Cue Mix
   - Bass Cue Mix
   - Guitar Cue Mix

General Rules for Outputs

This kind of setup is pretty common for stereo projects. In this case, you would typically use Main Output for your studio monitors. Use the Cue Mix outputs for individual headphone mixes for your recording musicians. Remember, though, that these are all line-level signals, and they will need amplification before they go to speakers. Also keep in mind that different interfaces have different numbers (and types) of outputs, so it's a good idea to check your interface's documentation for specific information.

4 Click on the plus sign (+) to the left of each path to show any existing sub-paths it contains. Because you simply renamed the paths that existed in the first place, each stereo path should have a couple of sub-paths, which will be automatically renamed as well.

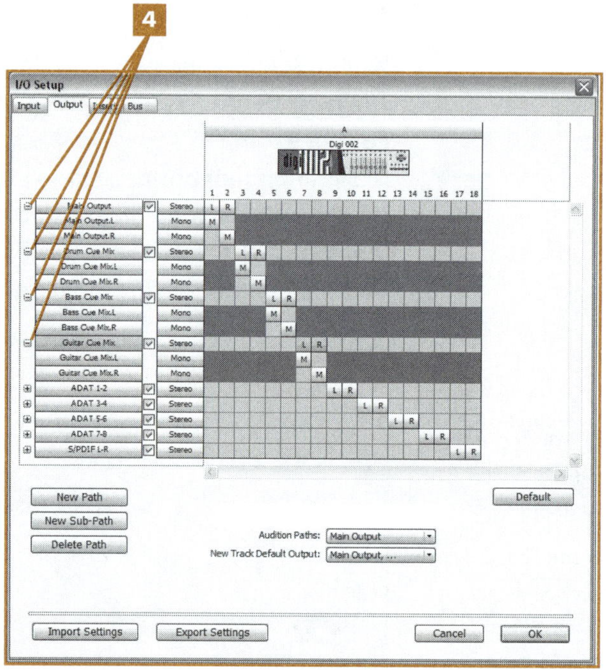

Paths, Sub-Paths, and Overlapping

When it comes to outputs in Pro Tools, main paths cannot overlap. (In other words, two active paths cannot both use the same physical output.) Sub-paths, on the other hand, *can* overlap.

Setting Up Inserts

In the world of DAWs, you'll be able to use software effects (reverbs, delays, and so on) called *plug-ins*. Does that mean you won't be able to use the rackmount effects you've got in your studio? Not at all—you can bring them into the Pro Tools environment through a configuration of your inputs and outputs called hardware or I/O inserts. You'll learn more about inserts and how to use them in Chapter 8, "Basic Mixing," when we talk about mixing.

One thing you need to know about hardware inserts now, though, is how to connect your gear. The rule is simple: Use the same number inputs for the insert that you used for the outputs. For example, if you have a rackmount stereo reverb unit that you want to use with Pro Tools, you have to use a pair of outputs (for example, #17 and #18) to send signal to the unit, and you have to use the same numbers (#17 and #18) on the input side to get audio from the reverb back to Pro Tools.

As we did when we configured our inputs, let's start by deleting everything, then building things up from scratch. Technically this isn't necessary, but it will make it easier to work with in the long run:

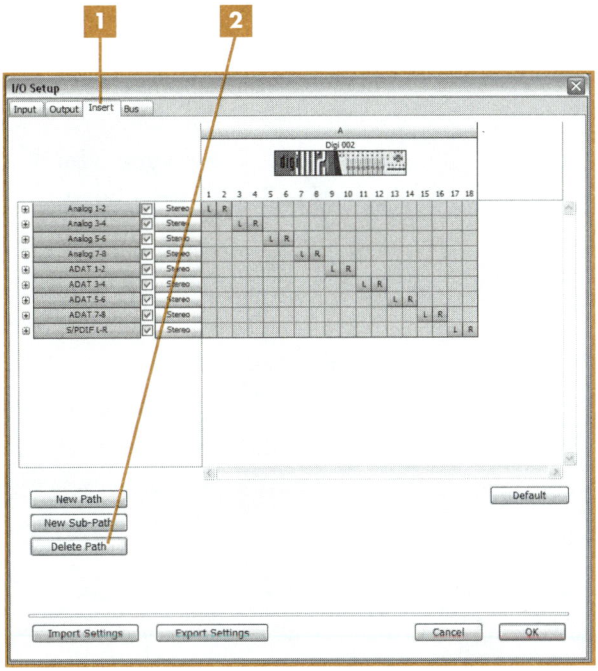

1. Click on the Insert tab in the I/O Setup dialog box. The tab will move to the front.
2. Click on every path name to select them, then click on Delete Path, just like you did with the inputs. The paths will be deleted.
3. Click on New Path to create a new path for each of your effects units (to the extent that your audio interface has the available physical inputs and outputs to connect effects units) and name each path the same way you did on the Input and Output tabs (and configure each as either stereo or mono).
4. Again, using the same method you used for setting up your inputs and outputs, assign each path to the inputs/outputs to which your effect is connected. In this case, my EQ is connected to I/O #17 and #18. As mentioned before, you are setting an input and output pair, with signal leaving your computer through an interface output and returning to the Pro Tools environment through the same numbered inputs.

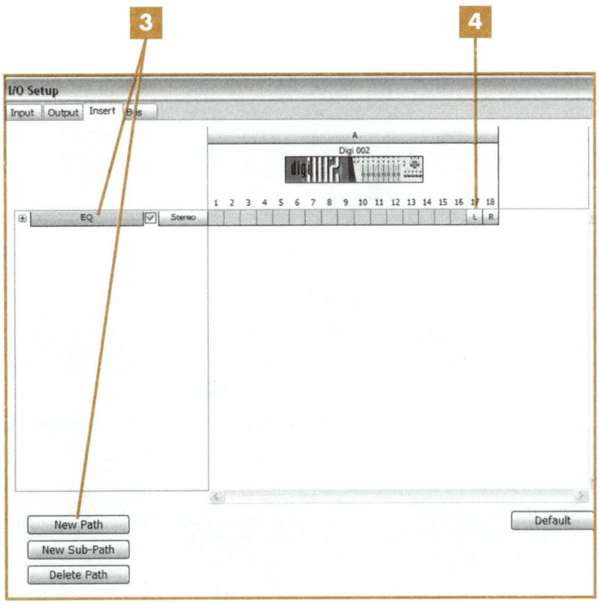

Setting Up Busses

Last but not least is the Bus tab. Busses are like virtual audio cables that you can use within the Pro Tools mixing environment. You'll use them for internal routing in Pro Tools, such as sending "dry" audio from an Audio track to a reverb on an Aux track. You have 32 of these virtual audio cables at your disposal, and unlike physical audio cables, they won't add noise to your mix! Don't worry if that sounds like Greek—you'll be doing this sort of thing in Chapter 8, using Pro Tools' trusty busses.

Often the default naming of the busses will suffice, and their generic names will suit their multipurpose functions. Sometimes, though, you might decide to name your busses more descriptively. Here's how:

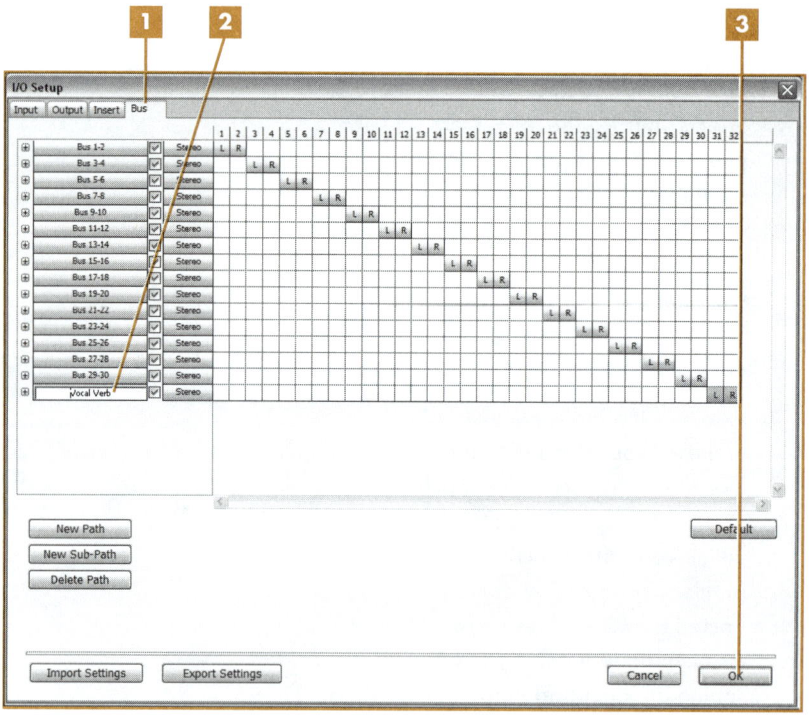

1. **Click** on the **Bus tab**. The tab will move to the front.
2. Because busses are so multi-functional, you really don't need to name them all. In this case, just name the last pair so you know to reserve it to use later for your vocals. **Double-click** on the last **path name** and **type Vocal Verb**. The path will be renamed.
3. **Click** on **OK**. The dialog box will close. You're finished!

Busses and Physical Inputs

Notice how this tab is different from the others. There aren't any references to your interface's physical inputs or outputs at the top of the window. That's because your busses are entirely a part of your Pro Tools software and not physical in any way!

Another thing you might have noticed about the previous image is that the window has been resized (just as you would resize any window in your operating system). Resizing the I/O window is another new feature in Pro Tools 7.

Managing Your I/O Settings

Now that you've created a tailor-made I/O setup, you'll want to save your I/O settings so that you can use these configurations in other sessions. Here's how.

Saving Your I/O Settings

To save your I/O settings, follow these steps:

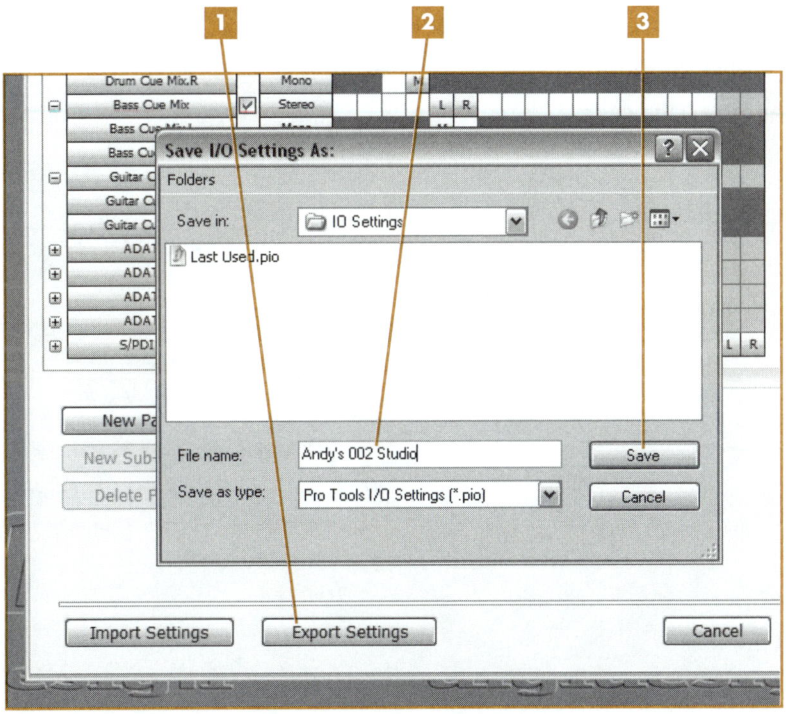

1. Click on Export Settings. The Save I/O Settings As dialog box will open.
2. Type a name for these settings in the File Name text box.

The Importance of Naming

Choose a descriptive name for your settings so you can recall them easily when you want to use them in another session.

3. Click on Save. Your settings will be saved to Pro Tools' default I/O location.

Recalling Your Settings

After you've customized and exported your I/O settings, you can always recall them. In this workflow example, you'll change your paths to their default names and then reload your previously saved settings. (Strictly speaking, you don't *have* to set your I/O settings to their default before importing, but for the purpose of this example, it makes the process easier.)

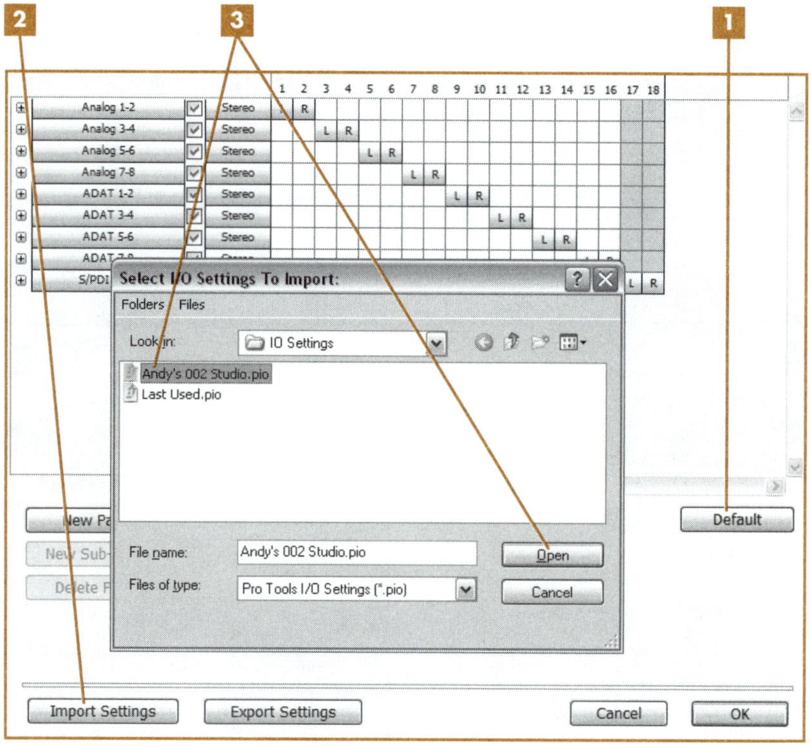

1. **Click** on the **Default button**. Your paths and labels will be reset to their most basic names and assignments for the displayed page.
2. To load previously saved I/O settings, **click** on the **Import Settings button**. The Select I/O Settings to Import dialog box will open.
3. **Select** the desired **I/O settings** and then **click** on **Open**. The I/O settings you selected will be loaded.

I/O Settings and New Sessions

There's another benefit to exporting your tweaked I/O settings: When you create a new session, your new setup will be an option in the I/O Settings drop-down menu.

Tracks

Whether you're looking at the Edit window or the Mix window, you'll notice that your new session opened without any tracks in it. It's up to you to create the tracks you'll need in your session.

Making Tracks

No matter what kind of track you want to create, you'll start by following the same first few steps.

1. Click on Track. The Track menu will appear.
2. Click on New. The New Tracks dialog box will open.

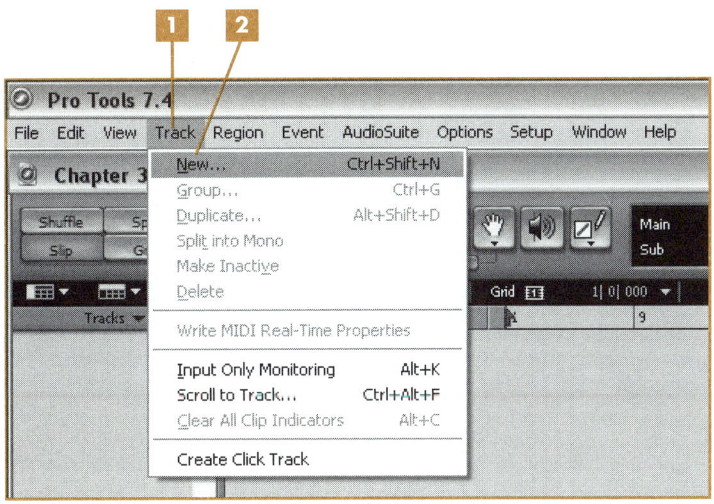

New Track Shortcut

Because you'll be making many tracks as you work more and more in Pro Tools, you might want to learn the shortcuts. Shift+Ctrl+N (PC) or Shift+⌘+N (Mac) will call up the New Tracks dialog box.

3 The dialog box is set up right now to create one mono Audio track. For this example, you want to create four tracks instead. Double-click in the Create field to highlight it (if it isn't already highlighted), and then type 4 for the number of tracks you want to create.

More about the New Tracks Dialog Box

The first drop-down menu (the Track Format menu) allows you to specify whether your track will be stereo or mono. The second drop-down menu allows you to select the kind of track you will create. You'll learn more later about the different types of tracks available in Pro Tools (such as Audio, Aux, MIDI, and Master Fader) and how to use them.

4 Click on the Create button. The New Tracks dialog box will close, and the tracks will be created in your session.

Now you can create a couple of stereo Audio tracks.

1 Open the New Tracks dialog box as you did in the previous section.

2 Type 2 in the Create field to create two tracks.

3 Click on the Track Format drop-down menu. The menu will appear.

4 Click on Stereo. The option will be selected.

5 Click on Create. Two stereo Audio tracks will be created, just as you specified.

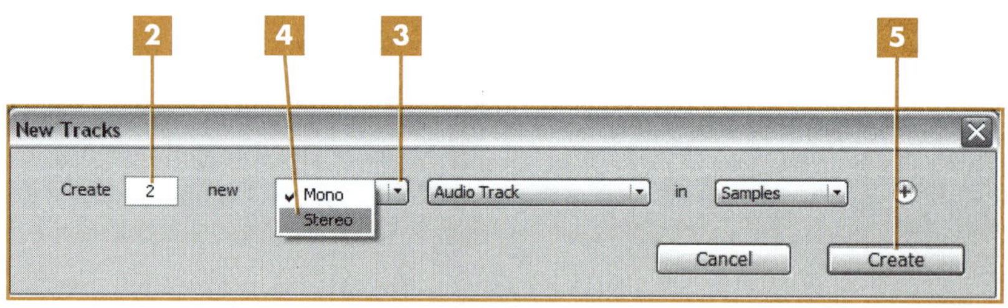

Creating an Auxiliary Input Track

An Auxiliary Input track (also commonly called an *Aux Input* or simply an *Aux track*) is similar to an Audio track in many respects, except it doesn't use any audio regions. Its main function is to serve as a means of routing audio from a source to a destination or as a place to process one or more audio signals with plug-in effects.

You'll learn how to use Aux tracks in Chapters 7 and 8, and you'll find that knowledge very handy, particularly when you get down to the business of mixing. To begin, let's start with the process of creating a couple of stereo Aux tracks, which is almost identical to creating Audio tracks.

1. Open the New Tracks dialog box as you did in the previous sections.
2. Type 2 in the Create field to create two tracks.
3. Click on Stereo in the Track Format drop-down menu to make these Aux tracks stereo. The option will be selected.
4. Click on the second drop-down menu. A list of all the different types of tracks that you can create in Pro Tools will appear.
5. Click on Aux Input. The option will be selected.
6. Click on Create. Two stereo Aux tracks will be created, just as you specified.

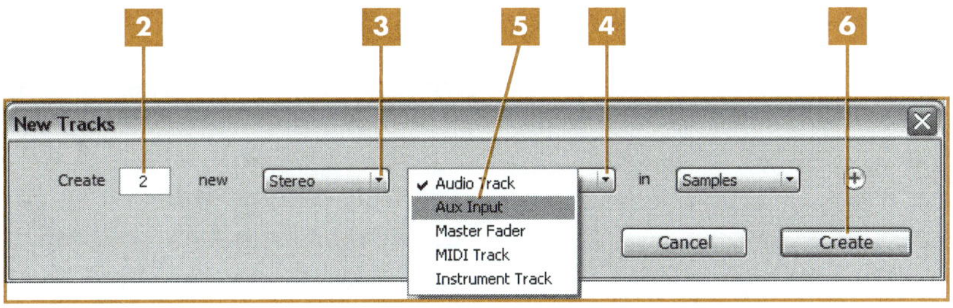

Master Faders, MIDI, and Instrument Tracks

As you probably noticed, there are three other types of tracks listed in the Track Type drop-down menu—Master Fader, MIDI, and Instrument tracks. Although you might not use these kinds of tracks in every session you create, they will be very useful when you need them.

If you've ever worked with a traditional mixing board, you know what Master Faders can do. These are the faders that control the overall volume of your entire mix after you have blended all the individual tracks. A Master Fader in Pro Tools does pretty much the same thing. Simply put, it is a fader that controls the overall volume of a given output path. It will also allow you to add plug-in effects to the entire mix at once. You'll learn about Master Fader tracks in Chapter 9, "Finishing Touches."

MIDI is not audio. Rather, it is a digital language that allows different musical devices to communicate, somewhat like a network. You can record (and then edit) MIDI data on a MIDI track in Pro Tools. When combined with Pro Tools' powerful set of audio features, this will open new creative doors! Related to MIDI, Pro Tools 7 has added a new kind of track, called an *Instrument track*, which will allow you to use MIDI and virtual instruments together in one convenient track. You'll learn about MIDI and Instrument tracks in Chapter 7, "Using MIDI."

The method of creating a Master Fader, MIDI, or Instrument track is almost identical to creating any other kind of track. The only difference is that you'll choose your type of track accordingly. Just for practice, try creating one new stereo Master Fader, using the steps outlined earlier. (Refer to the preceding image for your reference.)

Why Can't I Choose a Stereo or Mono MIDI Track?

When you choose to create a MIDI track, you'll notice that there is no stereo or mono option available. Don't worry, it's not a malfunction of Pro Tools—it's because MIDI isn't audio, so the terms *stereo* and *mono* don't really apply in this case.

Managing Your Tracks

This section contains a few techniques you can use to make the creation of tracks even easier, and to set tracks up for efficient use after they've been created.

Creating Multiple Tracks

In the previous sections of this chapter, you created different kinds of tracks one type at a time (mono Audio tracks, then stereo audio, Aux tracks, and so on). This was the way the job got done in earlier versions of Pro Tools, but in the last versions of Pro Tools, a neat little timesaver was added. Take a look:

1 If you've opened up the New Tracks dialog box, and you want to create more than one type of track in one path, simply click the plus (+) sign at the right end of the dialog box. A second row of track parameters will appear.

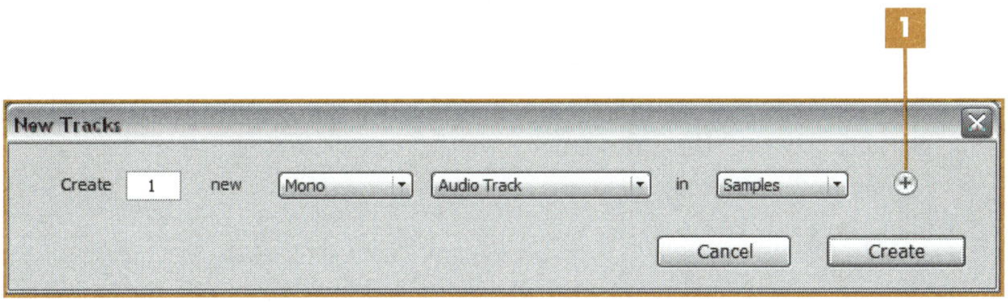

You can continue creating different kinds of tracks by repeatedly clicking the plus sign, as shown here.

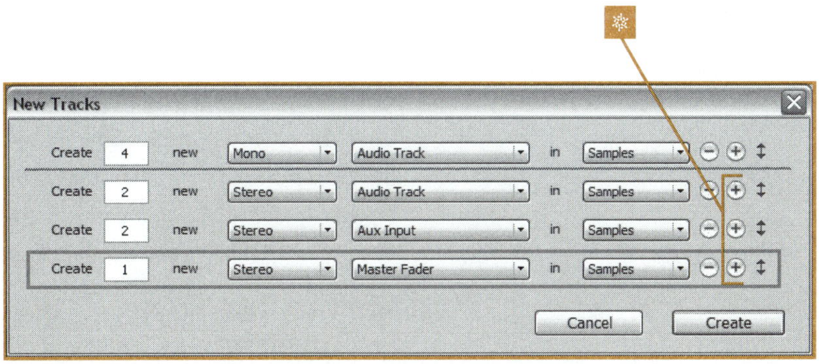

- Did you go one step too far, and do you now want to remove one of the rows? It's easy—just click the minus (-) sign to the left of the row you want to delete.

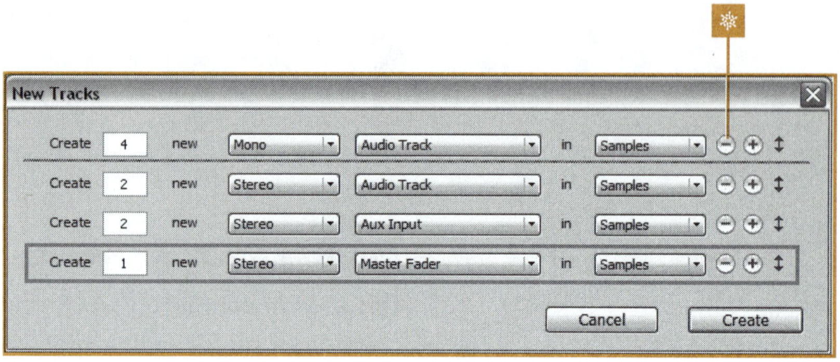

- The tracks shown here will be created in your session from top to bottom, just as shown in this dialog box. If you want to re-order the arrangement of tracks, just click and hold the double-arrow icon at the far right of the row that you want to move. A blue box will appear around that row (the Master Fader, in this case), indicating that it's ready to be moved. Still holding your mouse button down, drag the row up or down. A dashed line will appear, displaying where the track will be deposited when the mouse is released.

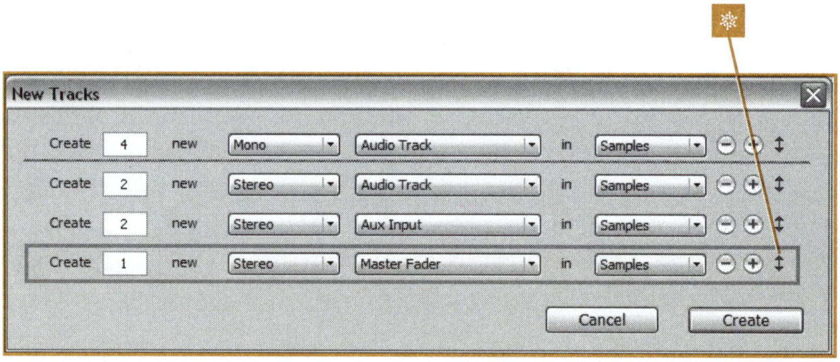

Naming Your Tracks

One of the most important (maybe *the* most important, depending on who you talk to) aspects of working in a DAW is documentation. Keeping track of your sessions, files, tracks, patches, and so on is absolutely critical, especially as your sessions become more complex.

When Pro Tools creates a new track, it assigns a generic name (such as Audio 1) as a default. Descriptively naming your tracks is a big part of session documentation—and the good news is, it's easy!

1. **Double-click** on the **name** of the track you want to rename. A dialog box will open.
2. **Type** a **name** for the track in the Name the Track field.
3. If you want to continue naming tracks, **click** on **Previous** to name the track above the current track, or **click** on **Next** to name the track below the current track.
4. When you're finished naming tracks, **click** on **OK**. The dialog box will close.

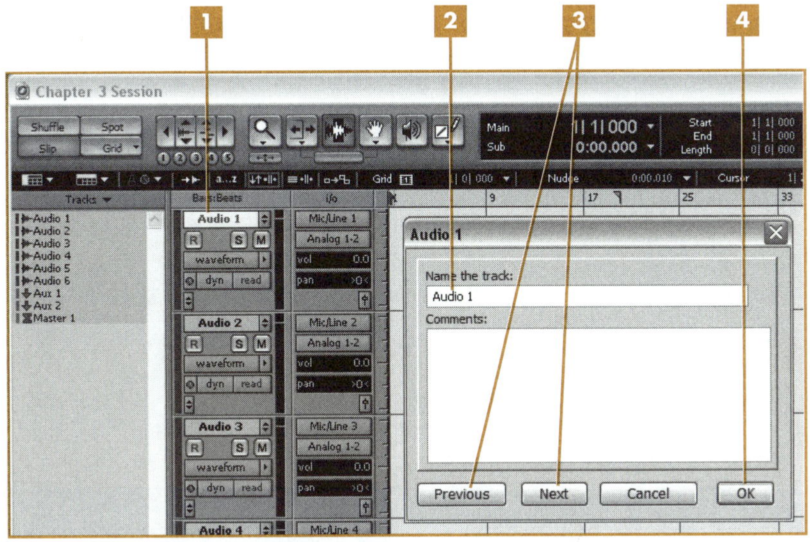

Naming Your Tracks for the Tutorial Session

If you've been following along with this chapter's examples, you should have four mono Audio tracks, two stereo Audio tracks, two stereo Aux tracks, and one stereo Master Fader. To keep the ball rolling, name each of the tracks as follows: Bass, Guitar, Vocal, Sax, Drums, Keyboards, Vocal Reverb Aux, Drum Reverb Aux, and Master Volume.

Moving Tracks

After you've assigned names to all your tracks, you might want to reorganize them so that related tracks are near each other. Although moving tracks around in the Edit or Mix window won't change how they play back in any way, a logical arrangement of tracks can make the entire production process much easier. There aren't any hard-and-fast rules on how to arrange your tracks—each session is unique, and you have to decide how to arrange your tracks so they make sense to you.

In this example, I want to move my Drums track to the top of my Edit window:

1. **Click and hold** on a **track name** in the Edit area of the Edit window. The track will be selected.
2. **Drag** the **track** up or down to the desired location. As you drag the track, a thin line will appear, indicating the position the track will assume when it is dropped in its new location.
3. **Release** the **mouse button** when you have the track at the desired location. The tracks in your session will be reorganized.

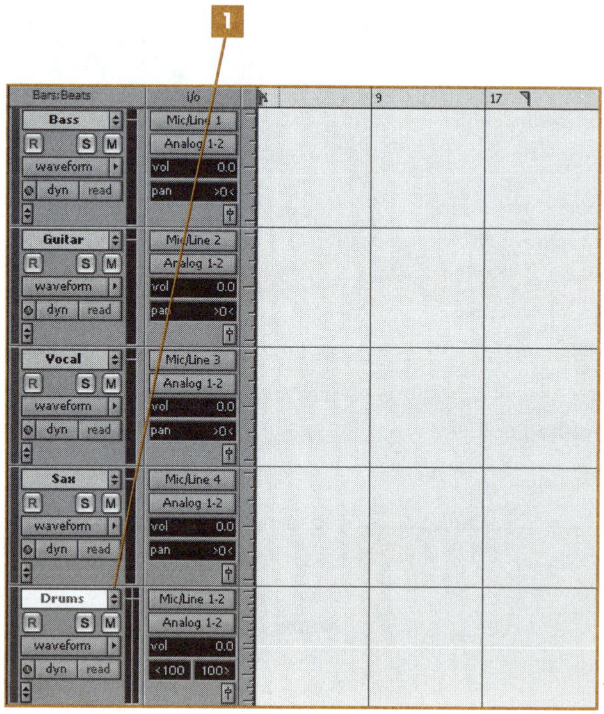

Another Way to Move Tracks

Here's another way to do it: Click and hold the track name in the Track Show/Hide list. A thin line will appear below the track name you have selected, indicating that it's ready to be moved. Drag the track up or down to the desired position. (The thin line will move, indicating where the track will be moved.) When you release the mouse button, your tracks will be reordered.

In the Mix window, you **click and hold** to drag any **track** to a new location. Of course, instead of dragging up or down, you drag left or right.

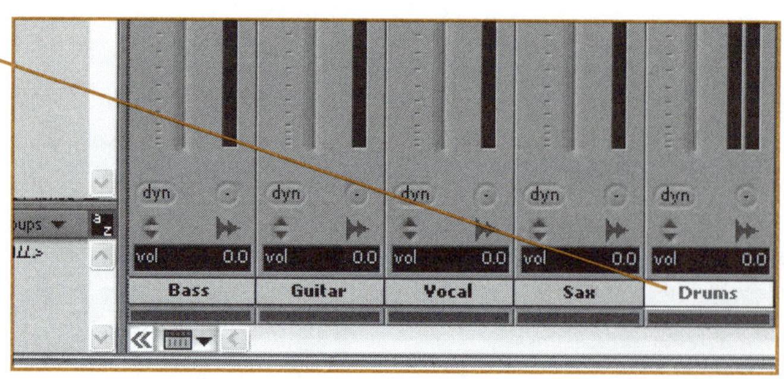

Track Orders in the Edit and Mix Windows

The Mix window reflects any rearrangement of tracks you make in the Edit window. Tracks are listed in the Edit window from top to bottom; in the Mix window, they're displayed from left to right.

Duplicating Tracks

From time to time, you'll want to do a little more than create a new blank track—you'll want to "clone" your track, making an exact copy (including any regions that are on the track). Here's how it's done:

1. Select the track(s) you want to duplicate by clicking the track name(s).

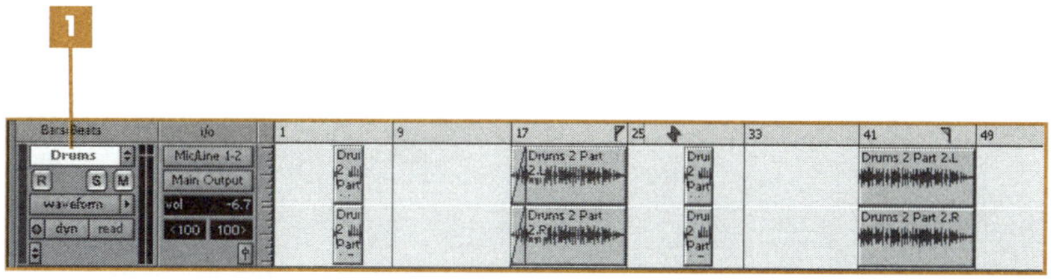

2. Click on Track. The Track menu will appear.
3. Click on Duplicate. The Duplicate Tracks dialog box will open.

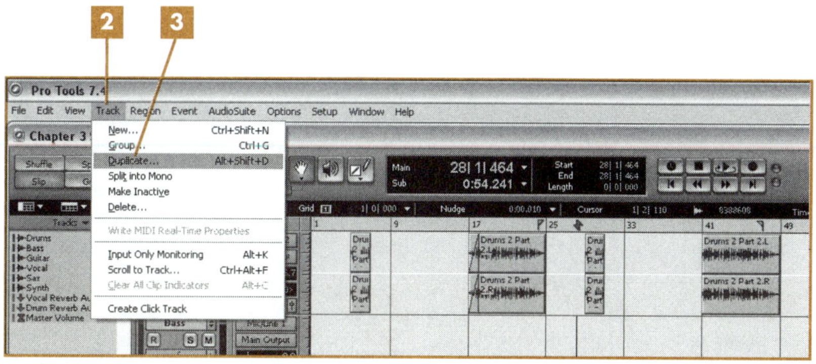

4. In the Number of Duplicates field, type the number of duplicates you want to make.
5. Choose the aspects of the track that you want to copy. At this point, these terms might have little meaning, though we'll explore them in later chapters. To make a complete duplication of the selected track(s), check all boxes in the Data to Duplicate section.

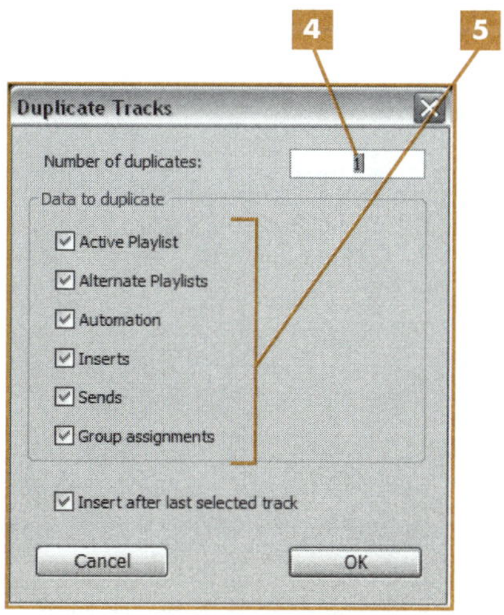

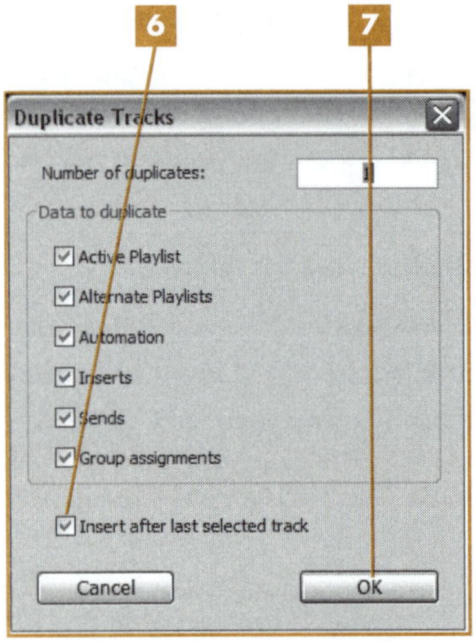

6. **Check** the **Insert after Last Selected Track check box** to have your new tracks created directly adjacent to your selected tracks. With the box unchecked, your new tracks will be created at the bottom of your Tracks list.

7. When you're finished, **click OK**. The duplicate track(s) will be created.

Deleting Tracks

Also from time to time, you'll want to delete tracks that you've created but are not using for one reason or another. Suppose you've created a duplicate track (as you have just done), and then you decide it was a bad idea! No worries—deleting tracks is even easier than creating tracks.

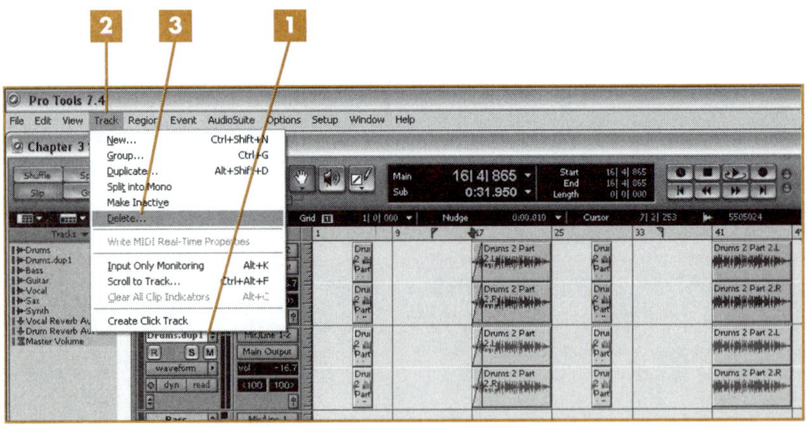

1. **Select** the **track(s)** you want to delete by clicking the track name(s).

2. **Click** on **Track**. The Track menu will appear.

3. **Click** on **Delete**. The track(s) will be deleted.

New in Pro Tools 7.3: Right-Click Power

If you have a mouse that has a right-click button (which is virtually all PC mice, and quite a few Mac mice as well), I've got some great news for you. Beginning with Pro Tools LE 7.3, Pro Tools has incorporated many common operations into right-click commands. This makes already easy jobs even easier.

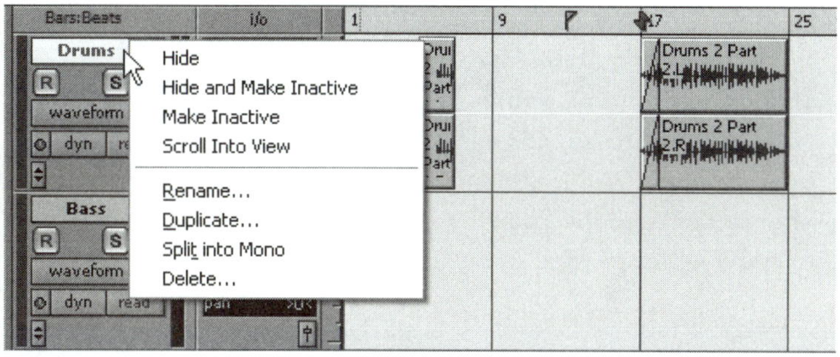

Track functions are a great example of this new functionality. Simply right-click on the desired track's name, and you'll see the list shown here. This list of common track-related operations includes many of the things we just covered, plus some that we'll cover in chapters to come.

Importing Audio

Although you can certainly record live audio in Pro Tools (it wouldn't be much of an audio workstation if you couldn't!), that's not the only way to get sounds into Pro Tools. Indeed, one of the great advantages of a computer-based DAW is that you can import digital audio files into a preexisting project, bypassing the recording process entirely!

Importing digital audio into Pro Tools is a fast and easy way to get a project started, and as with so many of Pro Tools' operations, there are a number of ways to do it.

Using Your Tutorial Sessions

The examples shown in the remainder of this chapter are using the Chapter 3 materials on the CD. In particular, you'll be using sessions and audio in the Chapter 3 Import Materials folder, which you should now copy to a specific location on your computer's hard drive, if you haven't done so already.

Choosing Where to Import Audio From

The first thing you need to do is locate the file you want to import into Pro Tools.

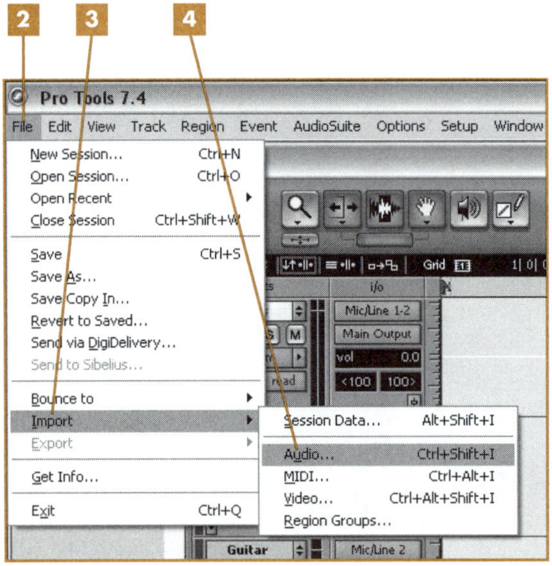

1 If you're looking at the Mix window in Pro Tools, you'll want to switch to the Edit window. From the Window menu choose Edit, and the Edit window will appear.

2 Click on the File menu.

3 Choose the Import menu item. A second menu will appear.

4 Choose Audio. The Import Audio dialog box will open.

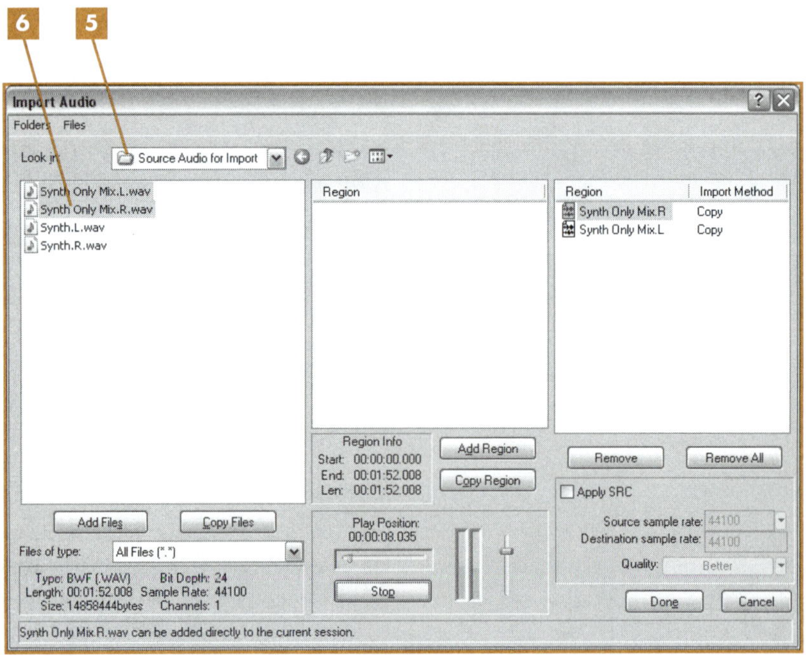

5 Now it's time to choose an audio file to import into your session. According to the conventions of your operating system, navigate to the folder that contains the audio you want to import. (If you downloaded the Import Materials folder, navigate to the Source Audio for Import subfolder.)

6 Click on the audio file(s) you want to import into your Pro Tools session. The file(s) will be selected. If you're working with the materials set up for this book, select the two Synth Only Mix files.

What Kind of File Am I Trying to Import?

The Import Audio dialog box gives you relevant information regarding the file you select in the lower-left corner of the window.

7 The box on the left shows audio in folders, but that audio has not actually been incorporated into your session as of yet. To do that, you'll need to add those files to the box on the right. Click the Copy Files button. The files will be added to the right box, as shown here.

8 To audition any single file before importing, select the desired audio file, then click on the Play button to preview your selected file. The file will begin to play.

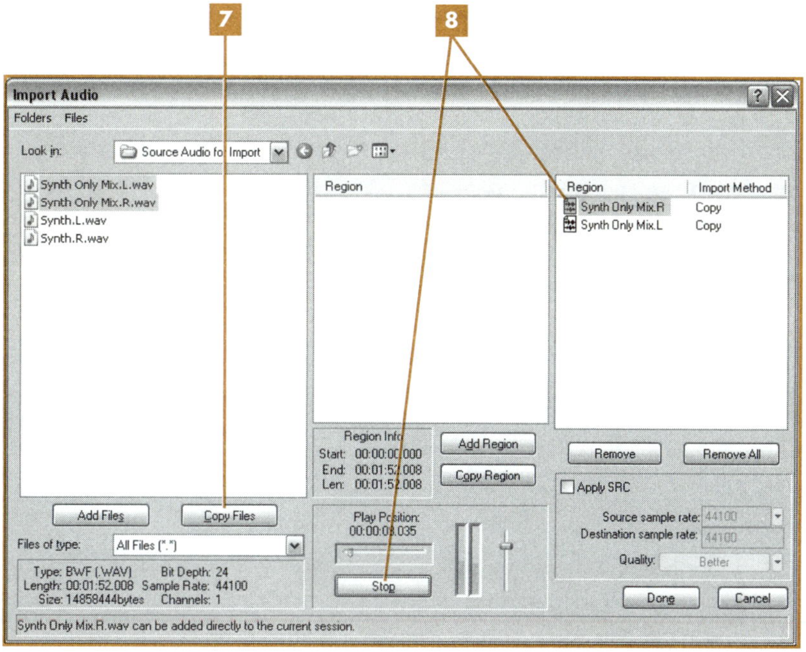

Adding Files versus Copying Files

You'll notice that there's an Add Files and a Copy Files button at the bottom of the leftmost box. Clicking Add Files will simply add the file to the Pro Tools session, and Pro Tools will play the audio file from its original location on your hard drive (which in this case is in the Source Audio for Input folder). Clicking Copy Files instead will actually make a copy of those files and place the copy in the session's own Audio Files folder.

When importing audio files with different sample rates or bit depths from your Pro Tools session, those files must be copied (and converted).

What If I Can't Hear Anything When I Try to Preview a File?

If you don't hear your selection, you might want to check the Audition setting in the I/O Setup dialog box. Review the "Managing Your I/O Settings" section earlier in this chapter for more information.

Before you proceed, you should notice a couple things:

- This file has .L listed before the file extension (in this case, it's a .wav file). This indicates that the file is the left half of a stereo track. The Synth Only Mix.R.wav file is listed right above this file. These two files together are elements of a stereo Audio track.

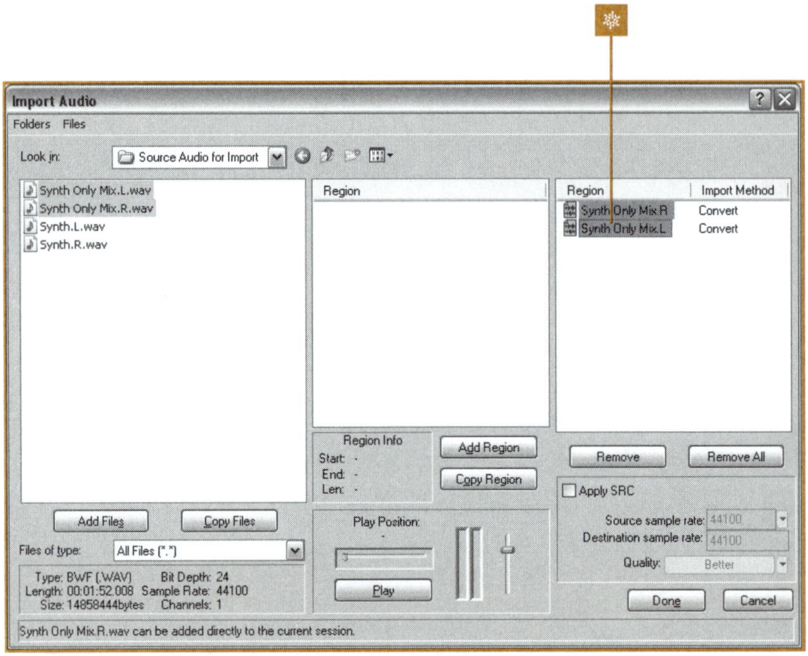

- Though Pro Tools can automatically convert sample rates and bit depths when necessary, checking the Apply SRC box will allow you to specify the source file's sample rate (even if it's different than the reported sample rate shown in the lower-left corner). You can also specify a conversion quality setting, which will override the Pro Tools default setting. Manual sample rate conversions like this are commonly done when converting between NTSC, Pal, and Film video sessions.

9. **Click** on **Done** when you're finished. The audio will be immediately incorporated into your session.

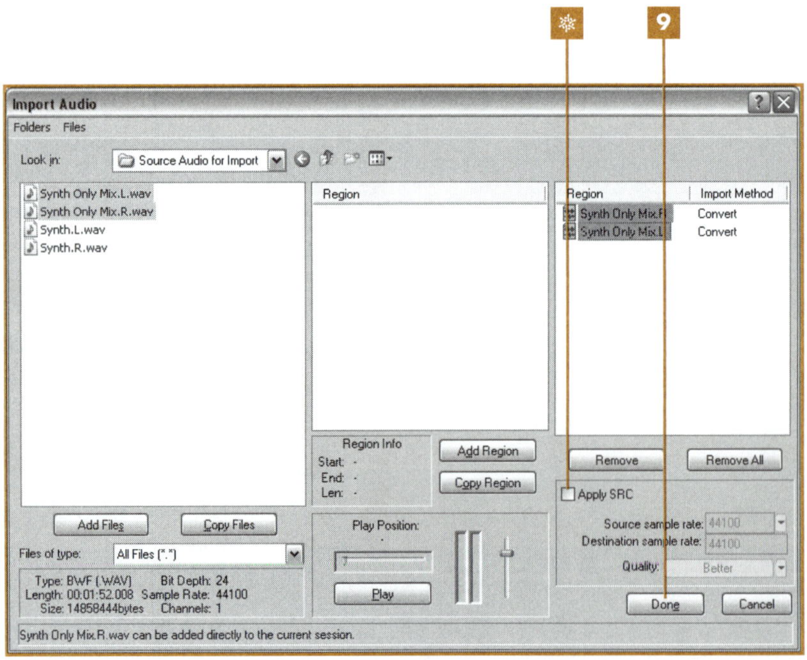

Choosing Where to Import Audio To

If you choose to copy the files, you'll import in the following manner:

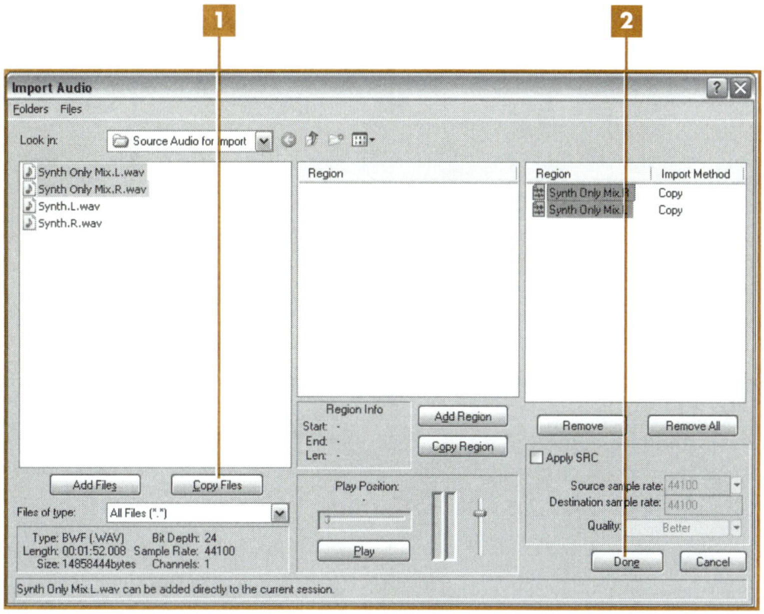

1. After selecting your file(s), click the Copy Files button. Again, the files will be shown in the rightmost box.
2. When you're finished selecting your files, click Done, as you did before. This time though, the audio won't be immediately shown in your session. Instead, you'll have to choose where copies of these files will be created.

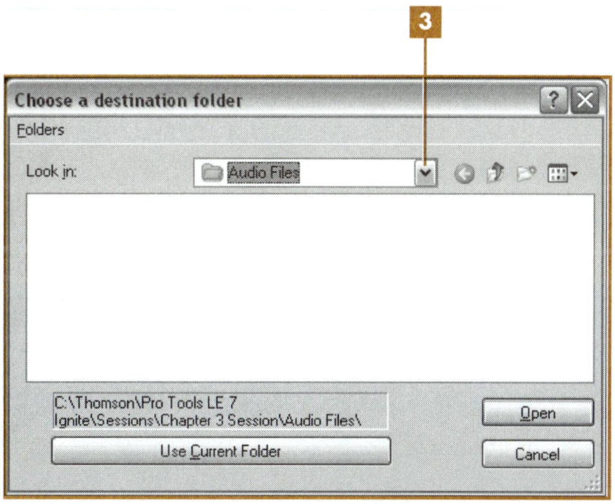

3. By default, Pro Tools will choose to copy the audio files to your session's Audio Files folder, as shown here, but you can choose to place that copy in any location on your hard drive. If you want to change the location of the copies, simply navigate to the desired location according to the conventions of your specific operating system.

Where Will My Files Be Stored?

The bottom-left corner of the Choose a Destination Folder dialog box will always show you where your copied files will be placed.

4a Click on Use Current Folder. The audio file will be copied to the folder and imported into your session.

OR

4b If you have subfolders shown in the window that you want to use for your copied audio, select the desired folder and click the Open button. Once inside the desired folder, click Use Current Folder, and your audio will be copied and imported. Once that's finished, the Audio Import Options dialog box will open.

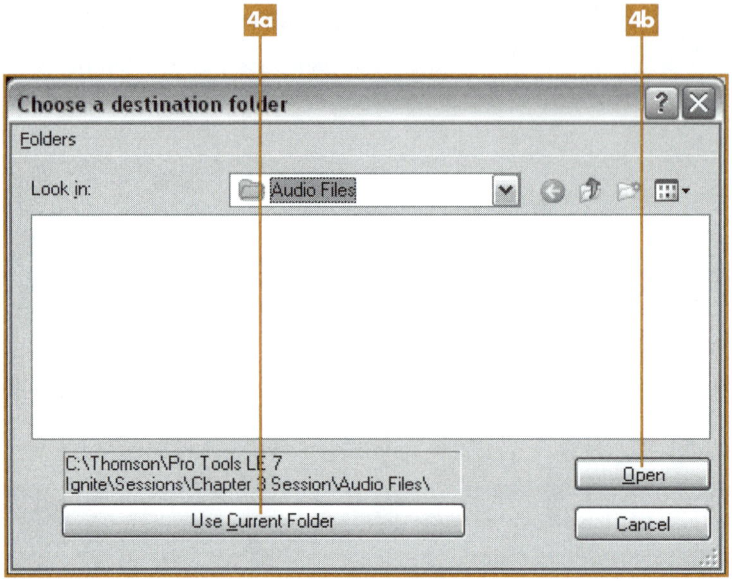

Watch Out!

Users commonly fall into a little trap during this last phase of importing. Often, they are tempted to open the folder, and then try to save the file in it. In this particular case, you just choose the folder itself, simply by highlighting it. The file will automatically be saved inside it.

Importing to the Regions List

The next window will allow you to import either to the Regions list only or to an Audio track as well. Let's first run through the steps involved in importing to the Regions list.

1 In the Audio Import Options dialog box that opens after the Choose a Destination Folder dialog box, click the Region List radio button.

2 **Click OK**, and your files will be imported into your session.

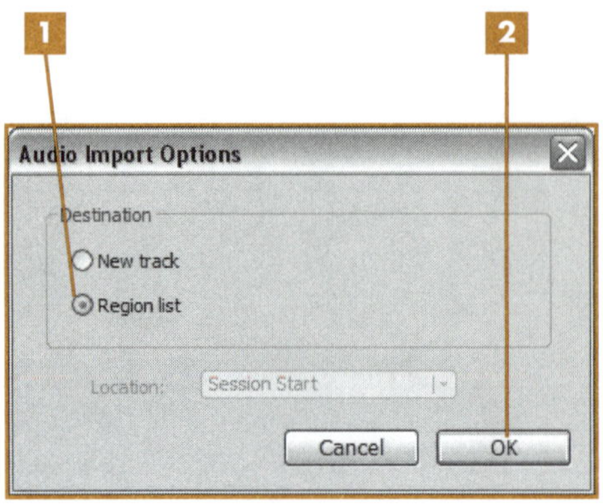

You'll notice that although the audio file is imported into the Regions list, there is no audio region visible on any of the tracks that you created. Don't worry—that's the way this method of importing is supposed to function. Later, you'll drag this audio file onto an Audio track and use it as a sounding element for your session.

Stereo Regions in the Regions List

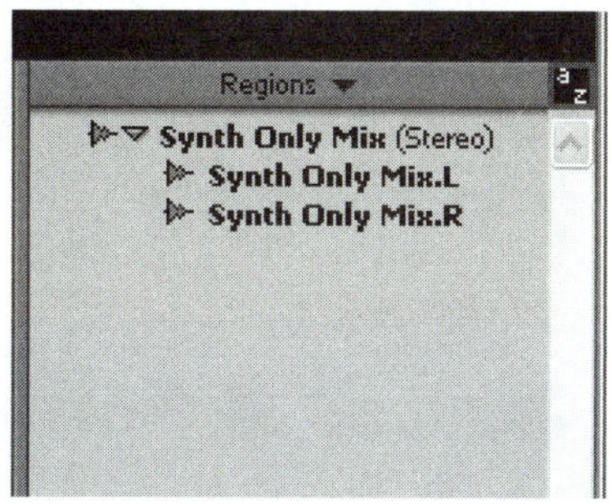

For every stereo region in your Regions list, you'll see a triangle by the region name. You can click on the triangle to reveal a list of the component mono audio files that make up that stereo audio region.

Importing Audio to a Track

Sometimes, instead of importing an audio file to the Regions list and using it later, you'll want to import audio directly into a track. Pro Tools can even make this easier by creating a new Audio track just for the audio you are importing, if you're so inclined. Just for practice, let's import the Synth audio into a brand-new Synth track. The steps for importing audio to a track are, for the most part, the same as importing to the Regions list.

1. Click on File. The File menu will appear.
2. Choose Import. A second drop-down menu will appear.
3. Choose Audio. The Import Audio dialog box will open.

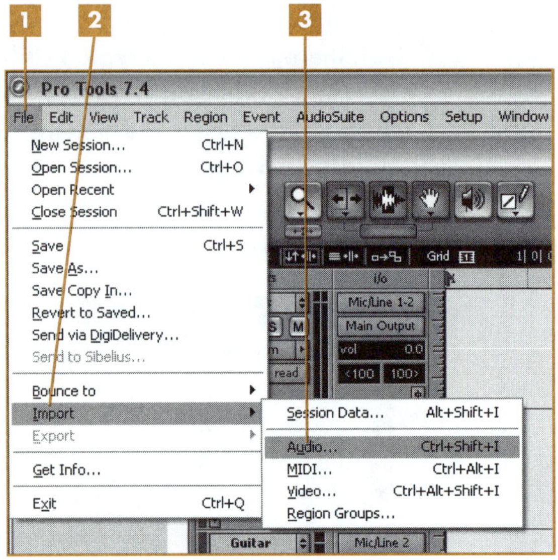

4. Select the audio file(s) to import into your session. If you're following the example shown here, you'll want to choose Synth.L and Synth.R.
5. Click the Add Files button (or the Copy Files button, if you prefer—if you choose to Copy Files, you will see the Choose a Destination Folder dialog box before you see the Audio Import Options dialog box).
6. Click on Done when you're finished making your choices. The Audio Import Options dialog box will open.

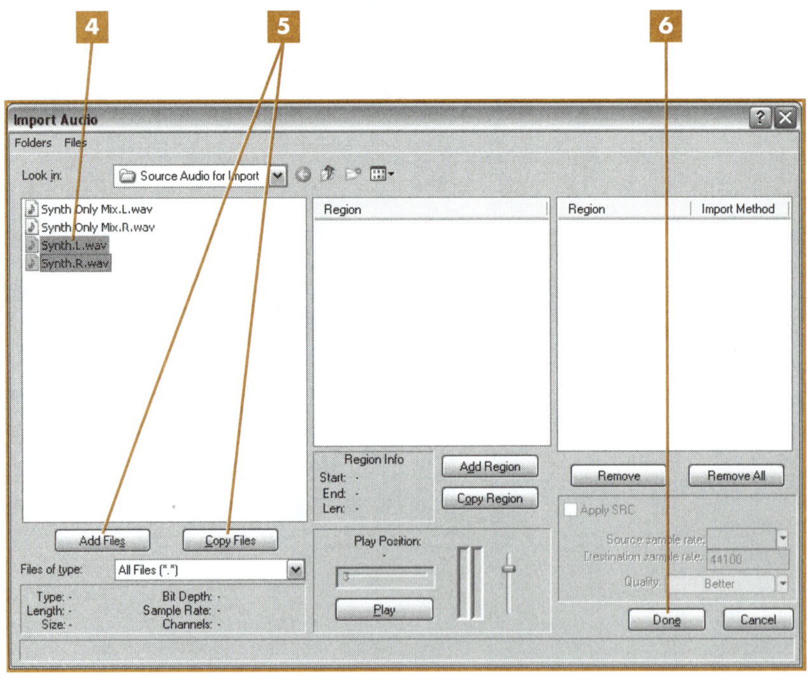

7 In the Audio Import Options dialog box, choose the New Track radio button. When you select this mode of operation, the Location drop-down menu will become available, and clicking the arrow button to the right of the menu (as shown in the graphic here) will give you a number of placement options.

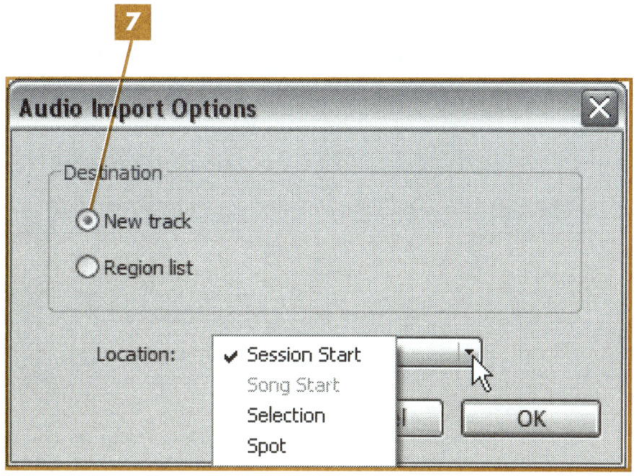

- Session Start. This will place the audio region at the very beginning of the track.
- Song Start. You can set your song to start at a place other than the beginning of a track (which we'll explore in Chapter 6, "...And More Editing"). If you have done this, the option to place your audio at the song start will become available.
- Selection. Choosing this option will place your audio at the beginning of any selected area. (You'll learn more about selecting an area in your session later in this chapter.)
- Spot. The term "Spot" (usually used in a video context) is used to describe the placement of audio at a specific point in time. Choosing this option will open the Spot dialog box, where you can type a specific time location for your audio. You'll learn more about Spot mode operations in Chapter 5, "Editing."

8 For the purposes of this exercise, choose the Session Start option.

9 Click OK. The dialog box will close, and your track will be created.

You'll notice that Pro Tools has done multiple operations with the click of a single button.

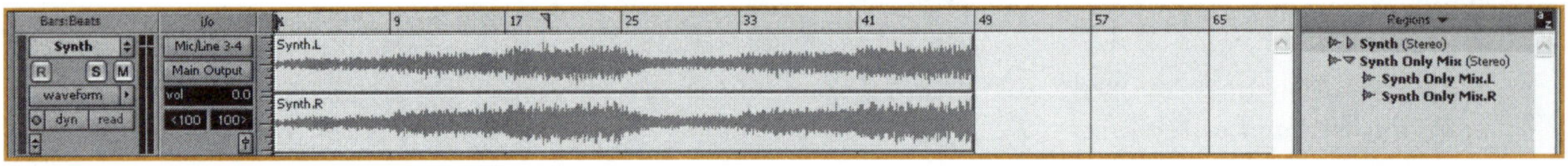

- Pro Tools has imported the desired region (in this case, Synth) into the Regions list. This means that the region is completely accessible in the session.
- Pro Tools has *also* created a brand-new track, named Synth (named for the audio file being imported). Since the files being imported had an "L" and "R" after them, Pro Tools recognized them as being left and right channels, and so incorporated them into a single stereo Audio track. Pretty cool, don't you think?

Importing Tracks

Importing audio to a track is certainly an easy way to get going with audio, but there is a limitation. The region that you import will be placed at the beginning of your session's Timeline, with no specific editing or mixing. But what if you want to import a tweaked-out track you created in another session? No problem—Pro Tools can import tracks from a previous session, preserving all edits, volume, panning, and so on, for you to use in your current session!

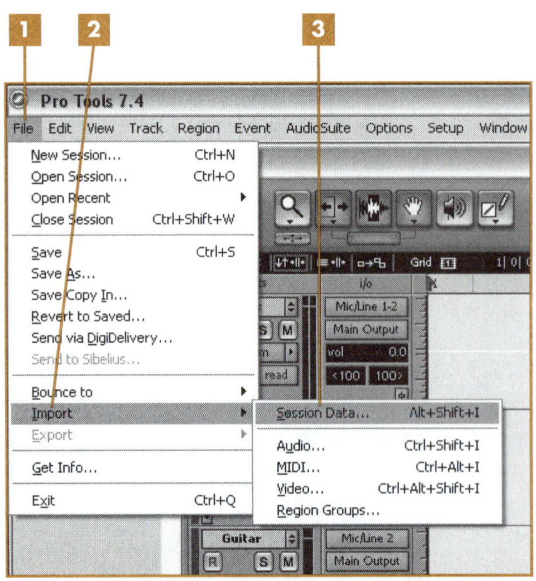

1. Click on File.
2. Choose Import. A second menu will appear.
3. Choose Session Data. The Choose a File to Import Session Data From dialog box will open.

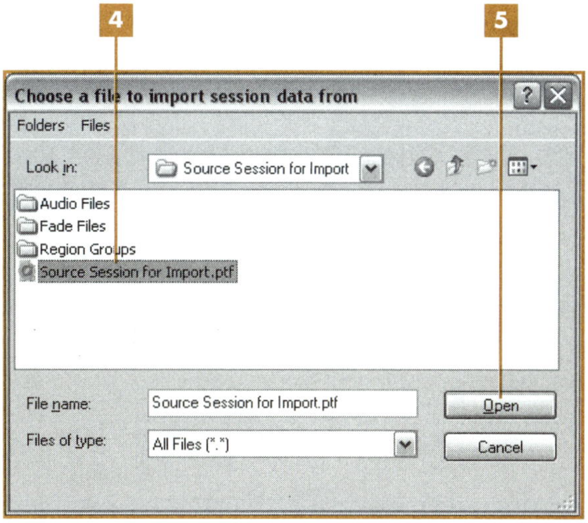

4 Navigate to the session from which you want to import a track. Remember, you're not importing just audio anymore, but rather an entire track. That track exists in the session file, which is why you're selecting a session file, not an audio file. If you're following the example shown here, you'll find a folder named Source Session for Import within the Import Materials folder. Select the session named Source Session for Import.

5 Click on Open. The Import Session Data dialog box will open.

6 Click on the Drums 1 (Stereo Audio) button. The Import menu will appear.

7 Choose New Track. The option will be selected.

8 It's possible to import more than one track at a time. Click on the Drums 2 (Stereo Audio) button and select Import As New Track. The option will be selected.

9 Before you leave this window, you should choose whether to simply add any audio files to your session, or copy that audio to your Audio Files folder. Click the Audio Media Options button. A drop-down menu will appear.

The Source Properties section of the Import Session Data dialog box provides a wealth of specific information regarding the session from which you'll be importing tracks. Of particular note are the Name, Audio Bit Depth(s), Audio Sample Rate(s), and Audio File Type(s) fields shown in the upper-left corner. The bottom of the dialog box contains a list of all tracks in this session.

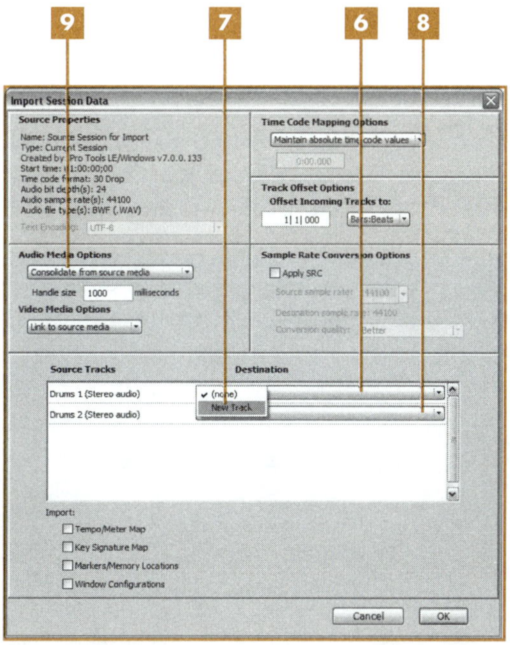

10 For our purposes, the Link to Source Media (Where Possible) and Copy from Source Media options are the most commonly used. Linking to source media will not make a copy, but rather will direct the session to refer to audio files in the original session. Copying from source media will copy the audio media to the session's Audio Files folder. In this case, choose Copy from Source Media.

11 When you're finished, click OK.

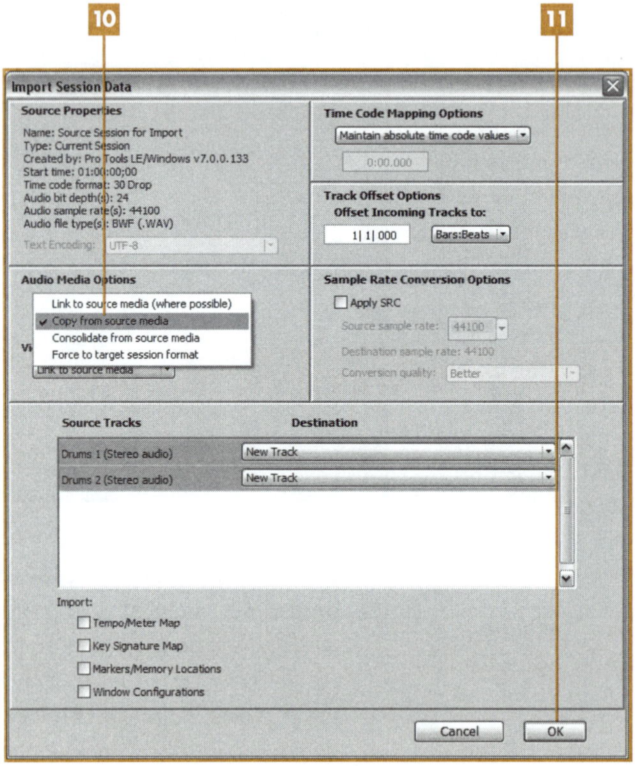

Again, you'll see that Pro Tools has done a number of operations with one user command.

- Two new tracks will be created in your session. The interesting thing you'll notice about both tracks is that you've imported a number of audio regions, and they are already arranged at specific times in your session.
- Note also that each separate region in each of the tracks is listed individually in the Regions list.

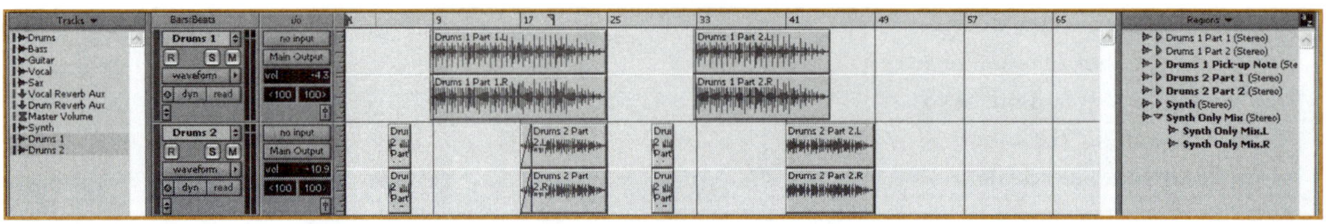

The Workspace

A nifty new feature was added to Pro Tools in version 6, called the Workspace window, and it has been improved upon over the more recent Pro Tools 7 versions. The Workspace Browser provides you with yet another way to import audio into your session, and it offers a few other useful tools as well.

1. Click on Window. The Window menu will appear.
2. Click on Workspace. The Workspace window will appear.

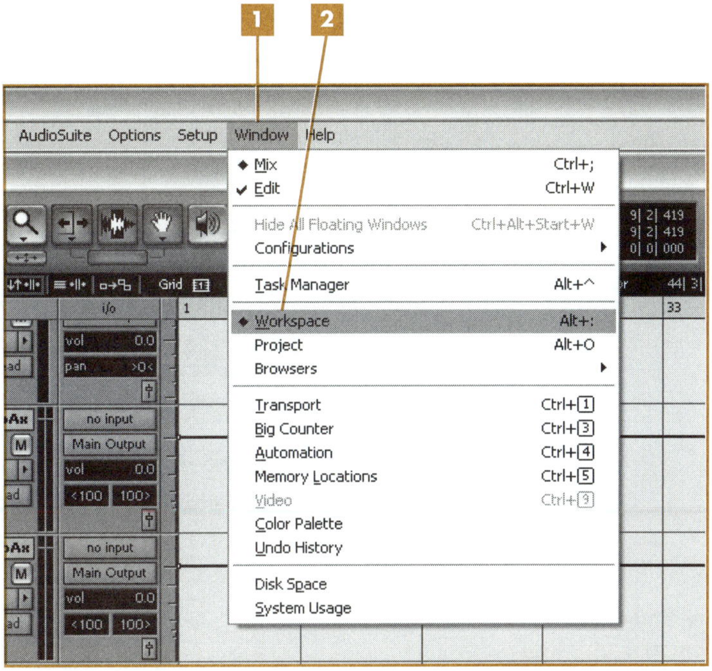

Searching for Audio Using the Workspace

You can easily search for audio using the Workspace window.

1. Click on the magnifying glass button. The Find section will appear.

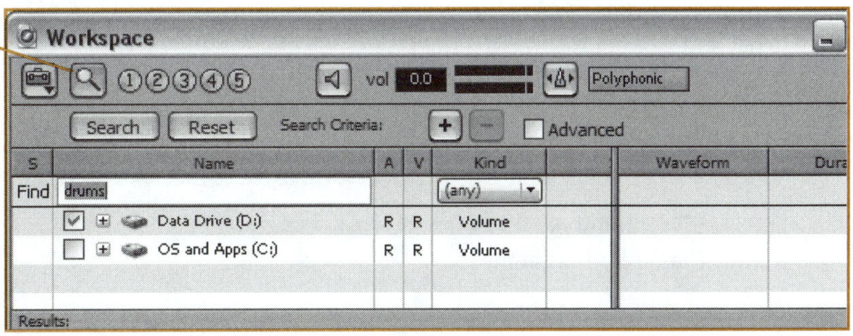

2 **Click** on the **check boxes** to select the drives you want to search. The drives will be selected.

3 **Type** the **name** of the file (or keyword) you want to find in the Find text box.

4 **Click** on **Search**. Matching results will appear in the bottom section of the Workspace window.

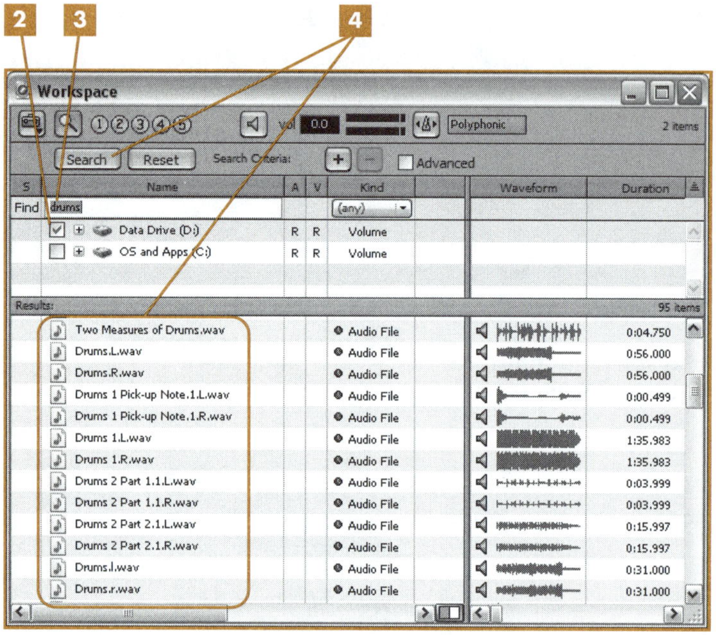

You can also navigate this window in a more traditional way, if you know where to look for a specific file. For this example, import audio yet again from the Chapter 1 session.

1 In the Find section, **double-click** on the **hard drive** where your audio file resides. A second browser window—called a *Volume Browser window*—will open. You will note that the Volume Browser's window heading is named for the hard drive that's being accessed.

2 **Navigate** through the **folders and subfolders** of your drive until you find the desired file.

3 **Double-click** on the **Audio Files folder**. The audio files in the folder will appear.

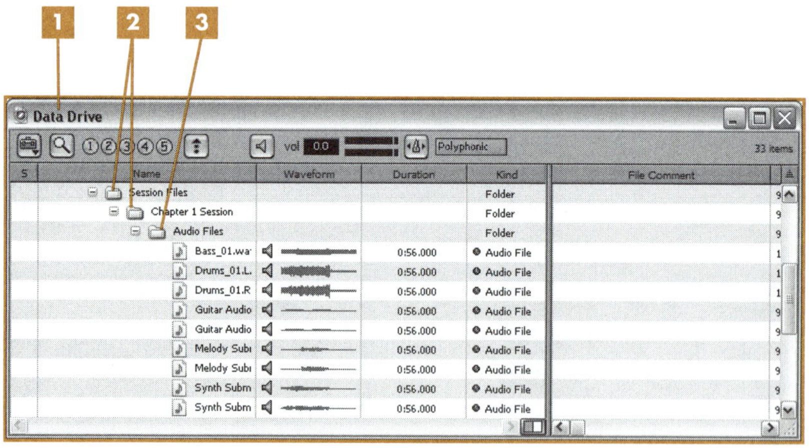

Be Careful!

Do *not* click on the session file. You're not importing a track this time; clicking on a session file will only cause Pro Tools to close the present session and open that session file. Don't worry too much, though—Pro Tools will double-check before doing this, and you can always choose to cancel the operation if you clicked on the session by mistake.

This window provides a few interesting features.

- The secondary window will give you additional information about each of the files (such as sample rate, bit depth, date created, and comments). Use the scroll bar at the bottom of this section to view different aspects of each file.

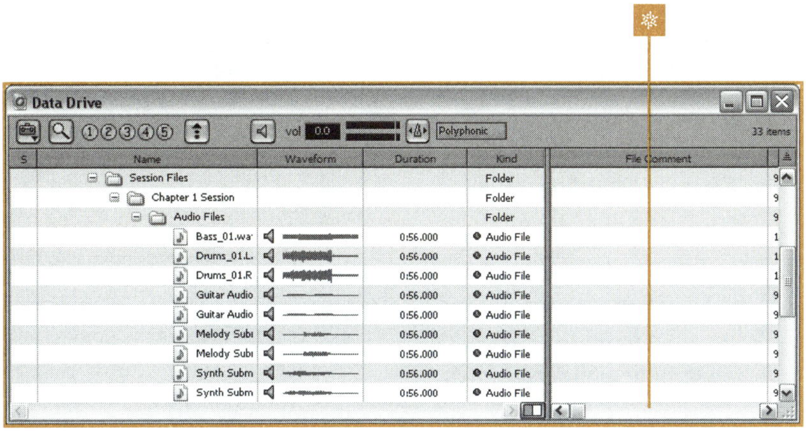

Making the Most of the Workspace Browser

You can make this section of the Workspace window a bit more functional by arranging the columns to suit your needs. Just drag and drop each column heading!

- You can audition each audio file by clicking the speaker icon to the right of each file name. The waveform display to the right of the speaker icon will give an indication of the file's characteristics. To stop playback, simply click on the speaker icon again.

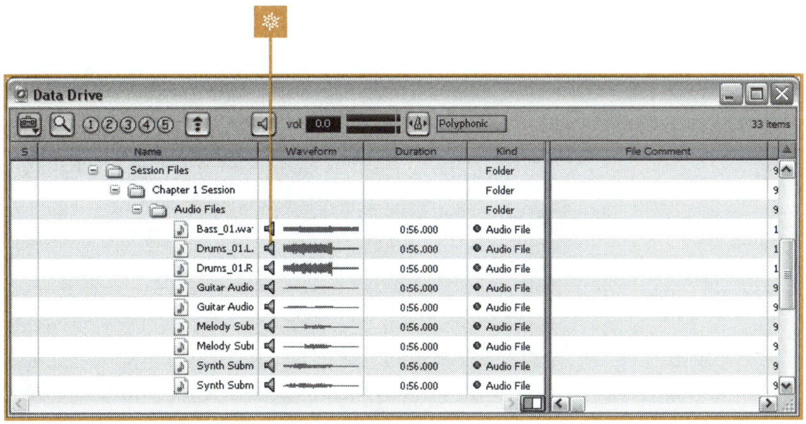

A Tip When Auditioning Long Files

If you're auditioning a particularly lengthy audio file, you can click at any point within the blue audio waveform to begin playback from that point.

4. Here's the cool part. Click and hold the file you want to import into your session. For our purposes, choose both the Drums_01.L.wav and Drums_01.R.wav files. (We'll be importing these to a stereo track.)
5. Drag the audio file into the Edit window onto the desired track. An outline of the region will appear in the Track area.
6. Release the mouse button to drop the file at the desired location. For this example, deposit the regions on the Drums track. The region will be deposited on the desired track at the desired point on your Timeline.

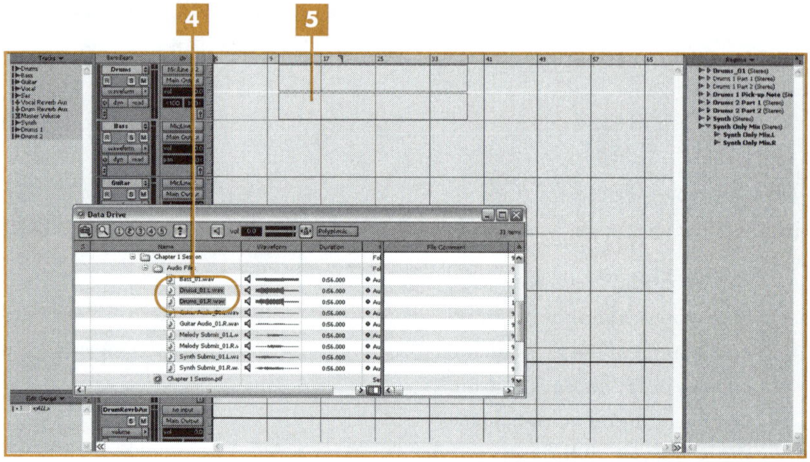

Again, you'll notice that adding a region to a track will automatically add an audio region to your Regions list.

More Ways to Import with the Workspace Browser

There are other ways to drag and drop from the Workspace window. For example, you can drag and drop from the Workspace window directly to the Regions list. (No region will be automatically deposited on any tracks.) Also, if you happen to drag files to an empty part of the Edit window (where there is no track), an appropriate track will be created, and the audio will be deposited at the point where you release the mouse! Finally (and this is a personal favorite of mine), if you drag the files directly to the Tracks list, a new track will be created, *and* the region will be deposited at the beginning of the track!

File Conversion

Did you notice that you didn't have to do any sample rate or bit depth conversion? Pro Tools automatically converts the file if it's necessary!

Preference: Automatically Copy Files on Import

Importing audio from the browsers is certainly very convenient, but there's one thing that you should be aware of when you do it. By default, Pro Tools will *refer* to audio files dragged in from a browser, which means that the audio will not automatically be copied into your Audio Files folder, but will be accessed from its original location. (In any cases in which sample rate or bit depth conversion is needed, files are *always* copied into your Audio Files folder.) Sometimes, especially for new Pro Tools users, this can lead to confusion about where your audio files actually are!

Pro Tools has a very important window called the *Preferences window,* which allows you to configure a wide variety of options. Let's take a quick look at this window, and look at a preference that will allow you to *always* copy files when you import them.

1. Click the Setup menu.
2. Choose the Preferences menu item. The Pro Tools LE Preferences dialog box will open.

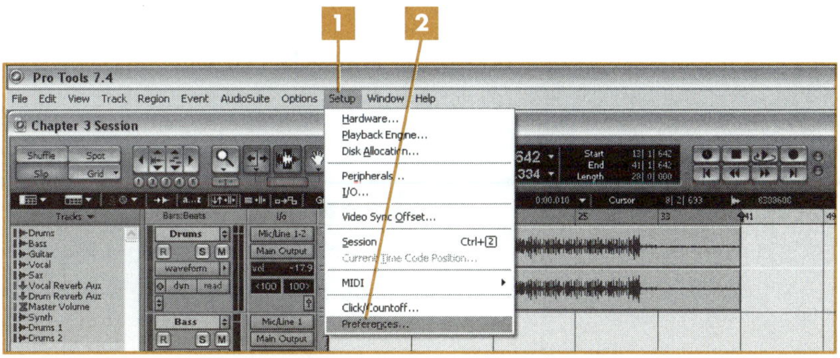

3 **Click** the **Processing tab**. The Processing preferences will be revealed.

4 **Click** the **Automatically Copy Files on Import option**. You're finished—now your dragged and dropped files will always be copied to your Audio Files folder, even if no file conversion is required.

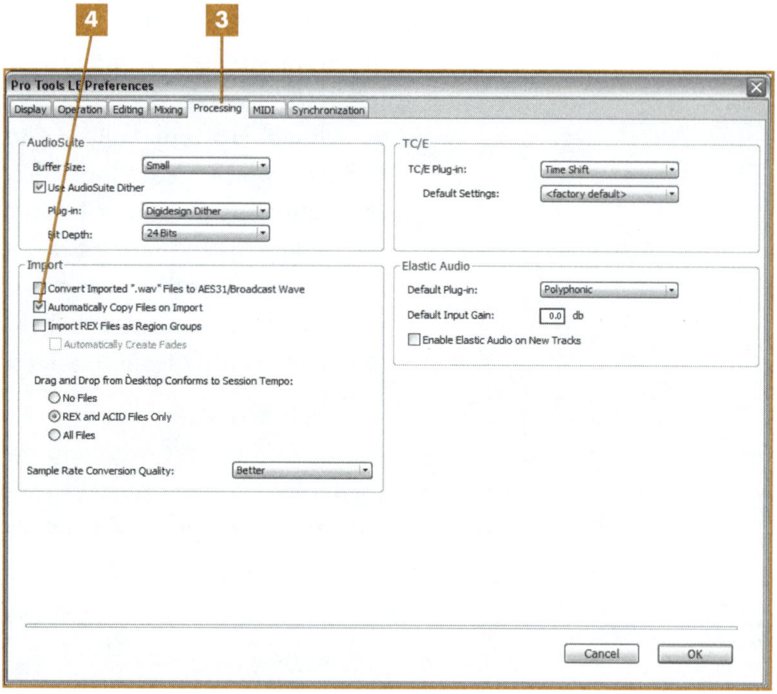

New Browser Features

Before we move on from the Pro Tools browser windows, there are a couple of notable new features to check out:

- **Loop Preview**. Click the Toolbox icon in the upper-left corner to reveal a list of useful browser-related options. At the bottom of the list, you'll see the Loop Preview menu item. Selecting this option (which will be shown by a check mark next to the item, as shown here) will automatically repeat the file when you preview it by clicking the Speaker icon. This is especially useful when you are previewing drum beats and other kinds of files that are typically repeated in a mix.

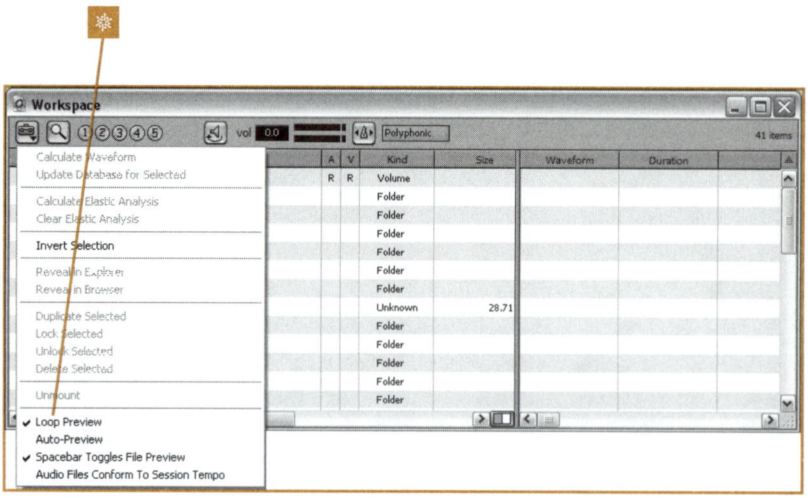

Auto-Preview. The Auto-Preview option will direct the browser to automatically play an audio file when it has been selected. This means that you won't have to click the Speaker icon to hear it, but it also means that files will always start playing as you select them, which can be a distraction for some users.

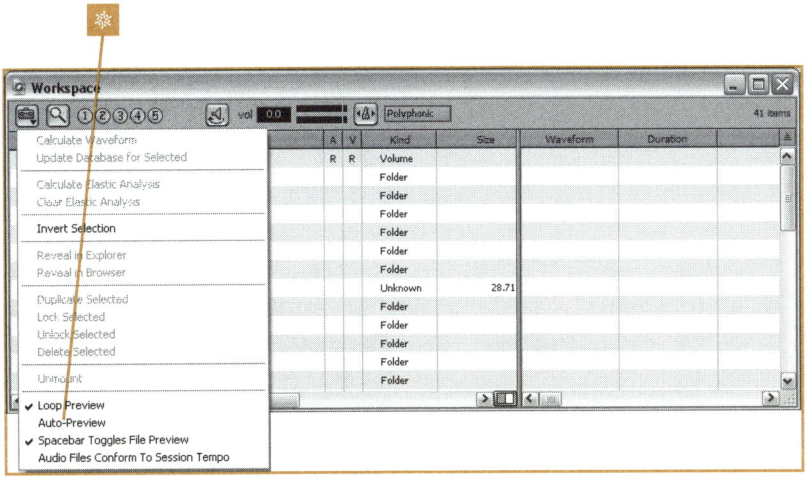

New in 7.4—Preview Volume Control. Longtime users are only too aware that in previous versions of Pro Tools, previewed files would play at their full volume. This was often a shock to the ears, and could potentially even damage speakers! Thankfully those days are over—simply click on the volume field indicated here, and a volume slider will be revealed. Just drag the slider up or down to increase or decrease the volume of the previewed audio.

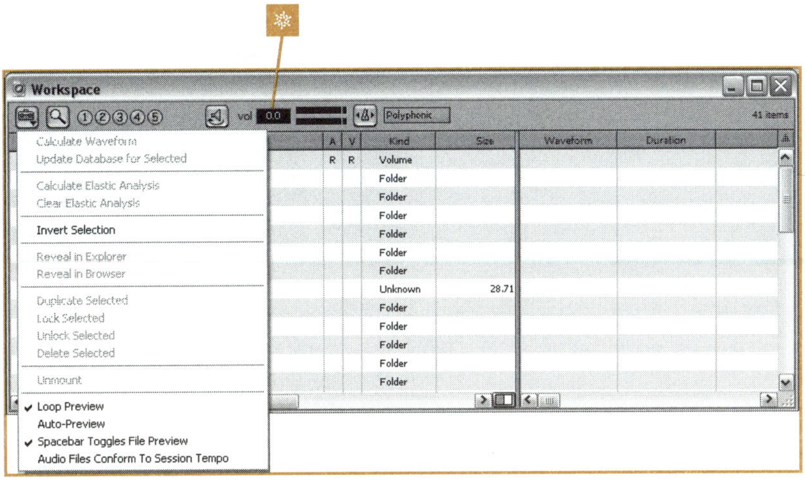

Making Selections and Playing Audio

Now that you've learned how to import audio into your session, you're ready to move to the next level of playback. Being able to play your session in a few different ways (in addition to being able to play it from the beginning of the session) will allow you to concentrate on specific parts of your project.

Selecting and Deleting Tracks

This next section will take some of the things that we discussed in the first chapter and put them into a more practical situation. You can start by moving your newly created tracks to the top of the Edit window.

1. Hold the Shift key and click the track names of the track(s) you want to move. In this case, I've selected the Synth, Drums 1, and Drums 2 tracks.
2. Just as you did when you moved a single track, click and drag the group of tracks to the desired location in your Edit window.

If you drag the tracks to the top of the window, your Edit window should look something like this.

If you've been following the exercise throughout this chapter, you'll notice that you have two imported drum tracks, plus the Drums track that you originally created. Let's delete that original track.

1. **Click** the **track name** of the track that you want to delete (in this case, the Drums track).
2. **Click** on **Track**. The Track menu will appear.
3. **Click Delete**. The track will be removed permanently.

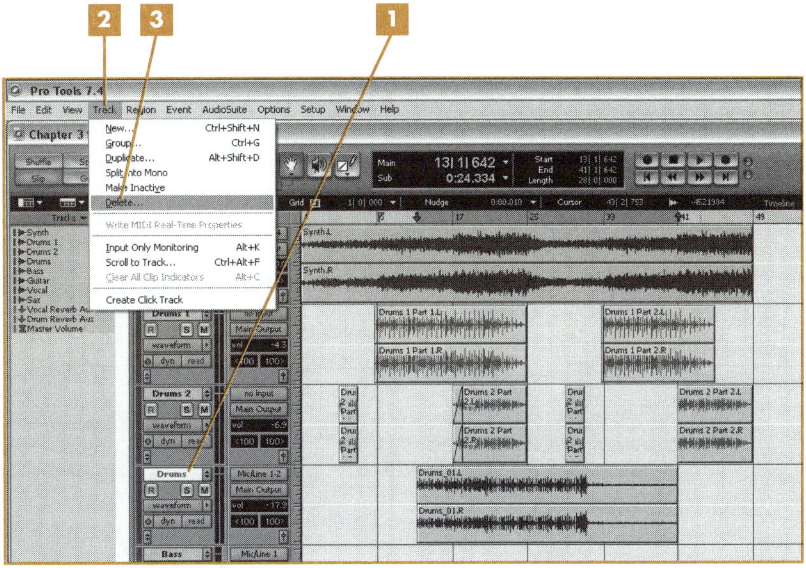

Muting and Soloing Tracks

Many readers probably already know what these terms mean, but here are some definitions for those who don't know what exactly *mute* and *solo* mean:

- **Mute.** Tracks that are muted will be inaudible.
- **Solo.** Tracks that are soloed will be heard, and any non-soloed tracks will be inaudible.

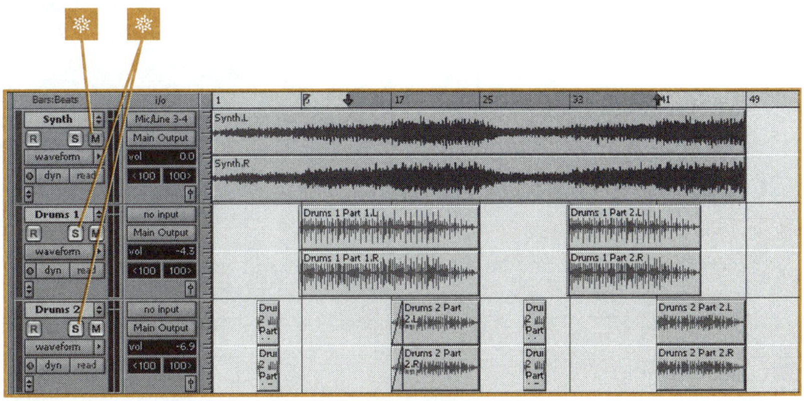

Soloing Multiple Tracks

Clicking the S button on multiple tracks will allow you to solo more than one track at a time.

Playing a Selection

Playing a selection may just be the easiest process of them all! First, start with a basic playback scenario.

1 Click on the Selector button. The Selector tool will be selected.

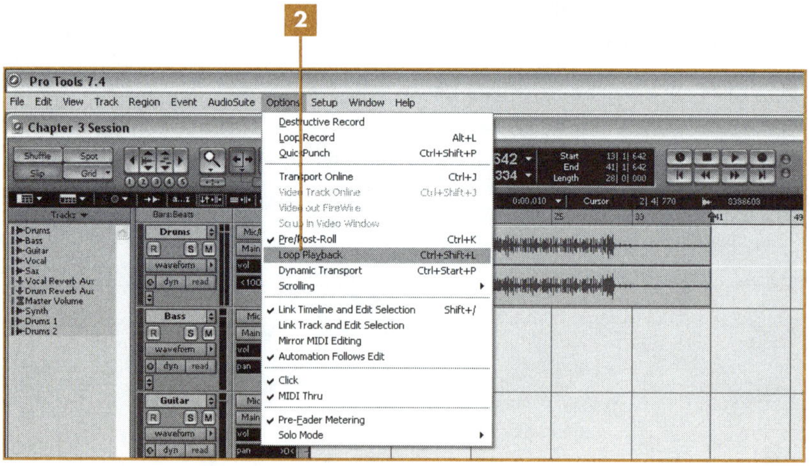

2 If there is a circular arrow in the Play button, deselect the Loop Playback option in the Options menu. The arrow in the Play button will disappear.

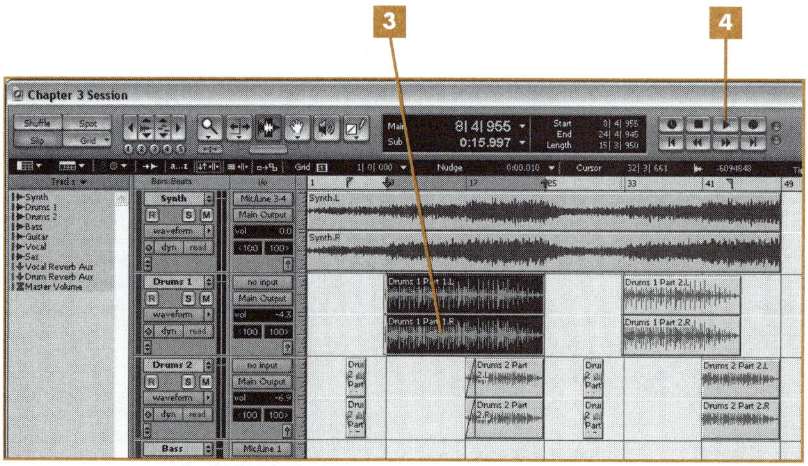

3 With the Selector tool chosen, click and drag over a section of any area in your session (or, to select an entire region, just double-click the region). The area you select will appear dark.

4 Click on the Play button to play the selection one time.

Edit and Timeline Selections

Note that the selection you make is also shown in the Timeline.

Here's Another Useful Shortcut

You can press the spacebar instead of clicking on the Play button to play the selection.

Here's another way to play a selection:

1. Click on Options. The Options menu will appear.
2. Select Loop Playback. The option will be selected.
3. Click on the Play button (or press the spacebar) to begin loop playback of your selection. The selection will repeat until you press the Stop button (or until you press the spacebar again).

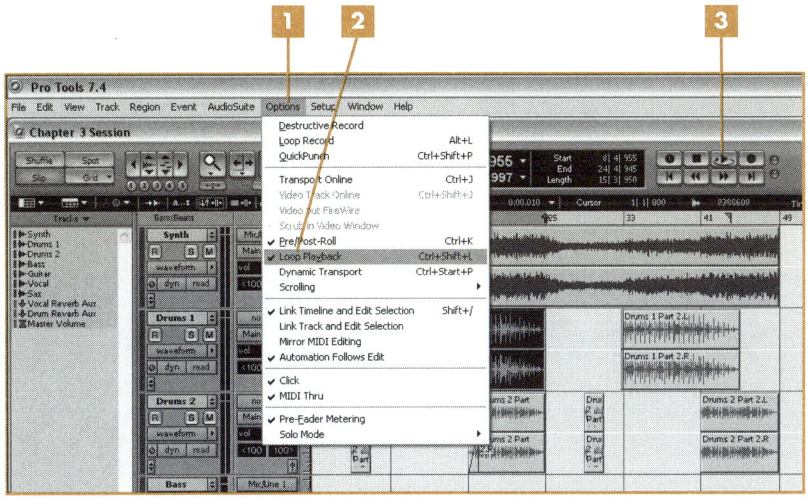

A Quick Way to Activate Loop Playback

In the Transport window, right-click on the Play button and choose Loop from the list shown.

Good work! Next up...recording!

4 Recording Audio

Everything we've talked about up to this point is crucial to being an informed Pro Tools user. Sooner or later, though, you'll want to move beyond simply importing audio and actually *record* an audio performance! No problem—this is a key area where Pro Tools shines, and the flexibility this software affords has helped it earn its place as a leader in the field. In this chapter, you'll learn how to:

- Set up a click track
- Make your first recording
- Use punch-in/punch-out recording and other recording options
- Make the most of your monitoring options

Getting Started: Signal Flow 101

You took a good first look at the Edit window in Chapters 1 and 2. Now it's time to take a closer look. First, though, you'll need to create a new session. (See Chapter 1 for a complete rundown of this process.)

If you don't have any musicians on hand to record, don't worry—we've got you covered. The disc that is included with this book is actually a *hybrid* disc, which means that it is a data disc *and* an audio CD.

Just pop the CD in a regular CD player, and you'll hear the following tracks:

1. Kick
2. Snare
3. Hi Hat 1
4. Hi Hat 2
5. Drum Stem
6. Bass
7. Blorp
8. Synth Pad 1
9. Synth Pad 2
10. Synth Pad 3

You can connect the line out of your CD player to line inputs of your Pro Tools interface.

1. After you launch the Pro Tools application, click on File. The File menu will appear.
2. Click on New Session. The Name the Session dialog box will open.

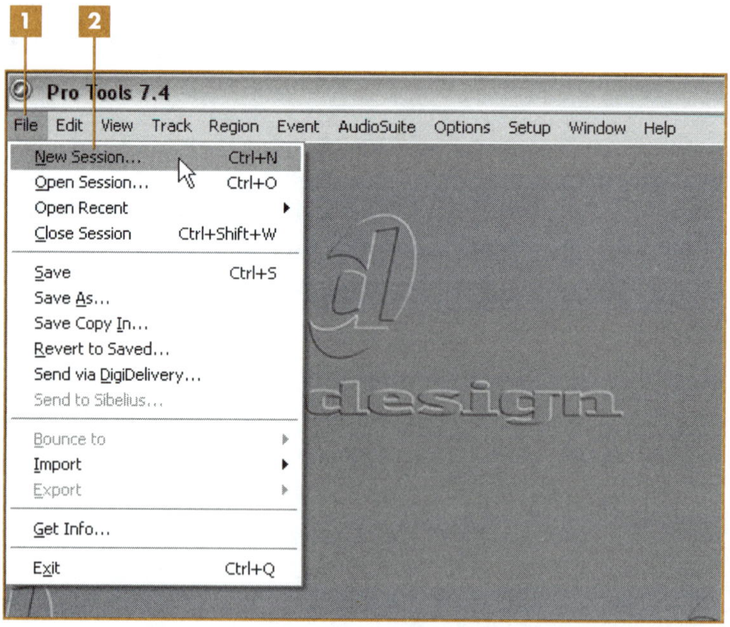

3 Choose your new session's name, location, and settings and then click on Save. Your new session will be created by Pro Tools.

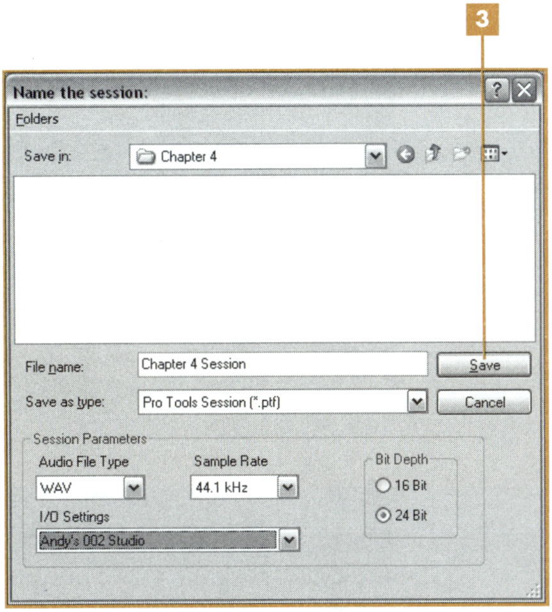

Should I Use the "Last Used" I/O Settings?

By default, Pro Tools' Name the Session dialog box opens with "Last Used" as an I/O setting. These are the settings that were last used by Pro Tools on this system. Of course, you might not know what settings you'll get, especially in a multi-user facility. Generally speaking, you'll want to specify an I/O setting of your own (like the I/O settings you created in Chapter 3).

If you're going to record audio, you need to create an Audio track on which to record.

1 Click on New in the Track menu. The New Tracks dialog box will open.

2 Click on Create. A single mono Audio track will be created.

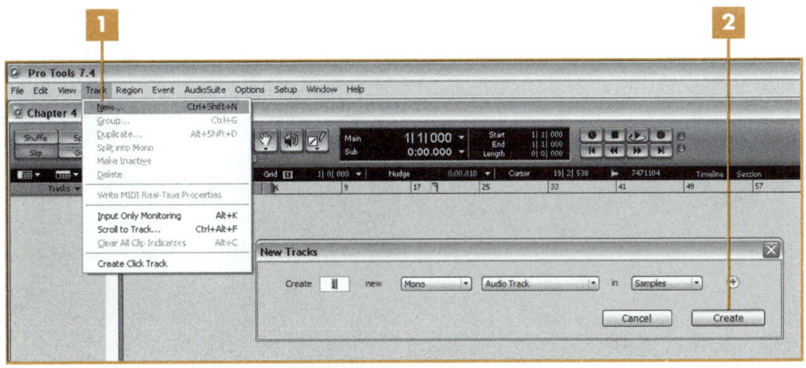

3 Double-click on the track name, and type a descriptive name for the track in the Name the Track text box.

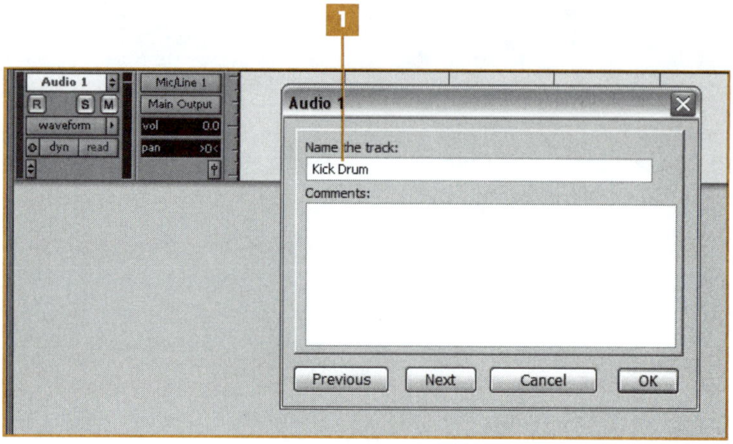

How I/O Settings Affect Your Session

It's time for the work you put into your I/O settings to start paying off. The configuration of the I/O Setup window (and any customizations you've made) will determine how your tracks receive and output audio.

Setting Up the Output

There is an output assignment button in the I/O column of each track. By default, each track will be assigned according to the Default Output setting in the I/O Setup dialog box. In a typical studio setup, this output will be connected to your studio monitors. If you want to change the output assignments, however, changing the output is easy—just follow these steps.

1 Click on the Main Output button for any track. An output drop-down menu will appear.

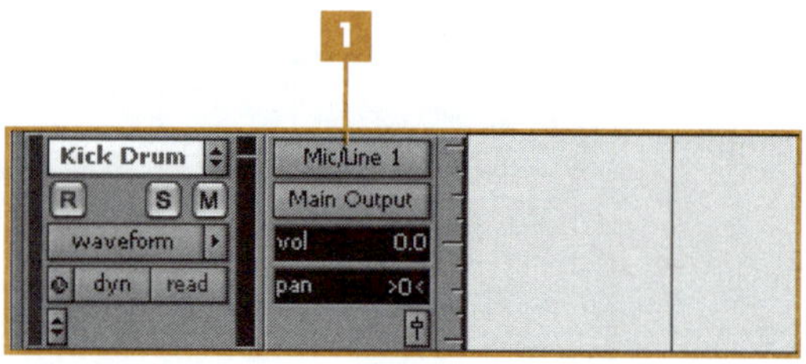

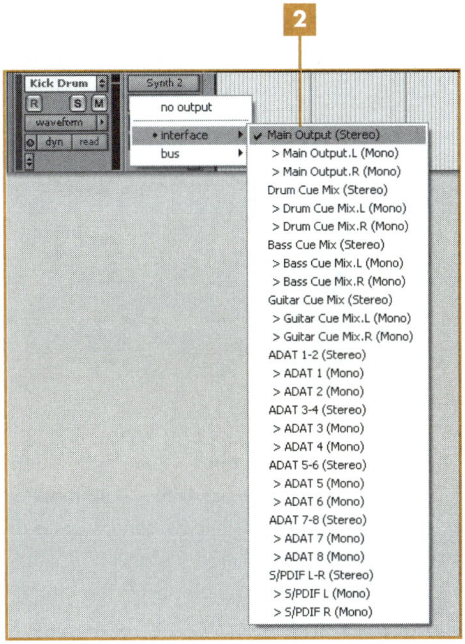

2 Click on Interface. A submenu will appear, from which you can select any output path or sub-path you created earlier in your I/O setup.

Setting Up the Input

The top button in the I/O column of each track shows the input of the track. You can click on the button to select an input.

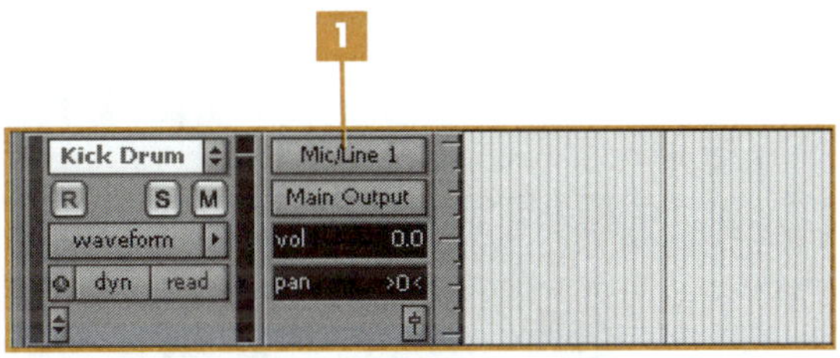

1 Click on the Input button. A drop-down menu will appear.

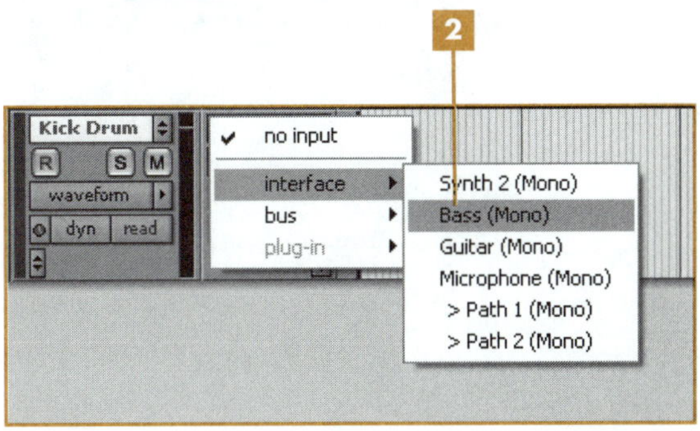

2 Click on the physical input or bus that your audio will be coming from (as specified in your I/O settings). The input will be selected.

Input Options

Since the track in this example is a mono track, only the mono input paths (and sub-paths) you created will be displayed.

New Feature: Right-Click Renaming

Here's another great new implementation in Pro Tools—the ability to rename inputs or outputs *without* going into the I/O window. Simply right-click on either the Input or the Output button (depending upon which one you want to rename), and you'll see the drop-down menu shown here. Choose Rename from the list. The Rename I/O window will appear, and the changes you make there will be reflected in the I/O window. *Note that this feature does not work with Master Fader outputs.*

Setting the Output Volume

The third field shows the volume of the track's output. You can adjust the volume by clicking in this field.

1. Click in the Volume field. A volume fader will appear.
2. Click and drag the fader to the volume level you desire, and then release the mouse button. The volume will be adjusted.

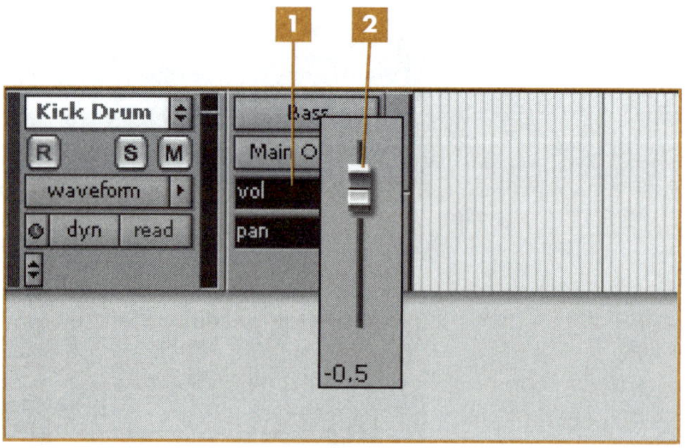

Setting the Output Pan

The fourth field shows the pan (the placement of the audio between the left and right speakers) of the track's output. You can adjust this setting by clicking in the field.

1 Click in the Pan field. A small slider will appear.

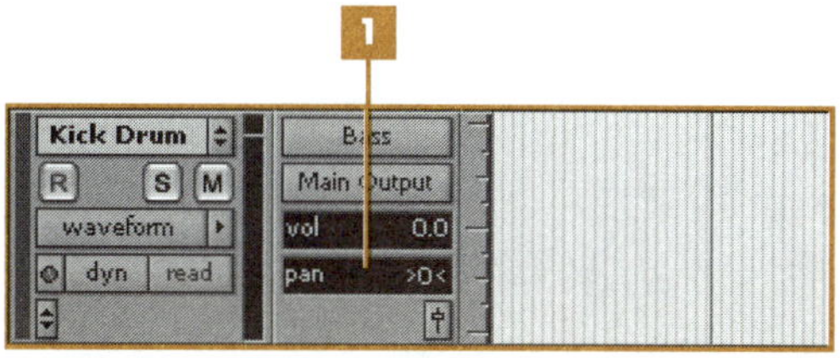

2 Click and drag the slider bar to the pan you desire, and then release the mouse button. The output pan will be set.

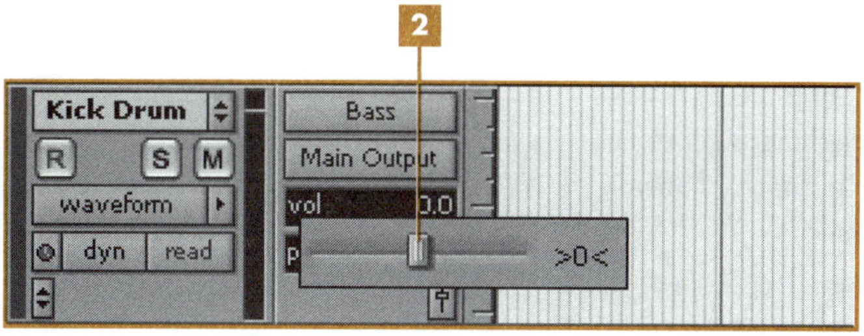

Recording Levels versus Track Output Levels

The output volume and output pan control the track's output only, not the input level. This means that to avoid clipping when recording, you'll want to bring down the level of your sound source (instrument, microphone, and so on) rather than the volume fader on the track.

Using an Output Window

There's another way to view and manipulate this essential track-related data. An Output window (also commonly called a *tear-away strip*) allows you to adjust many of your track's parameters within a single mixer-like format:

1 Click on the icon beneath the output pan display. (The icon looks like a tiny fader.) A track tear-away strip will appear. Note that much of the track-related data you've set up on the track is shown here as well:

- a Track name
- b Output View selector (which will allow you to quickly switch over to one of that track's sends—something we'll discuss in Chapter 8, "Basic Mixing")
- c Output Path selector
- d Pan knob
- e Volume fader, with a volume meter to its right
- f Mute button
- g Solo button

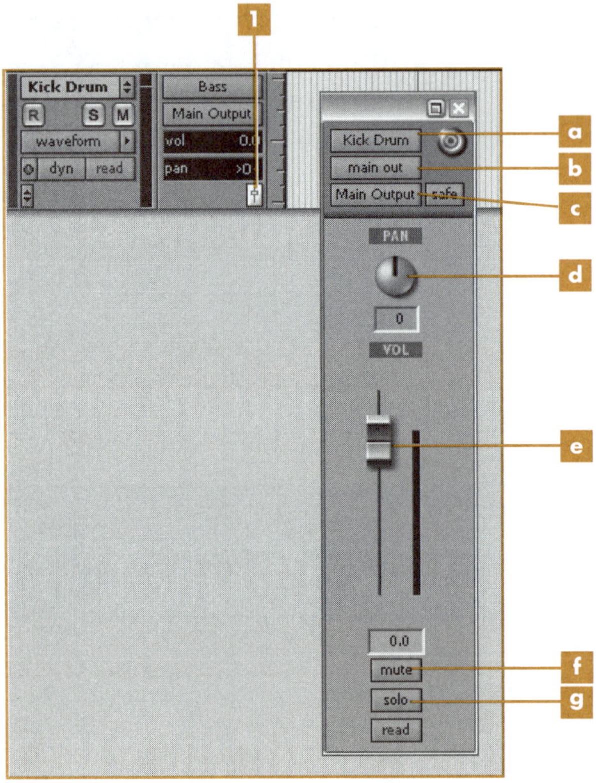

Quick Reset Shortcut

You can quickly reset your volume to unity (0.0) or your pan to center (0) by holding the Alt key (PC) or the Option key (Mac) while you click on the volume or pan controls in either the track or the tear-away strip.

Setting Up a Click Track

You might be wondering just what a click track is. Fair question—even though it's is a fairly common term, it's surprising how many musicians don't know what a click track is or what it's used for. The answer: A *click track* is an audible track in a multitrack environment that indicates the tempo of a song through a series of short tones (usually click sounds, hence the name). This is much the same way that a metronome helps a musician keep tempo in the practice room.

This feature is not specific to Pro Tools—indeed, click tracks have been used for decades, dating back to the earliest analog recording studios, when multiple musicians would all listen to the same click track on their headphones as they played, in order to stay in time with each other.

Although you certainly won't need a click track every time you work with Pro Tools, you'll find that click tracks are a convenient way to keep everything in sync as you add track upon track to a complex session. Especially suited to music-oriented work, click tracks are very common in studios worldwide, and the ability to work with them is considered an essential skill.

With the advent of Pro Tools version 7.3, creating a click track is very simple:

1. Click on Track. The Track menu will appear.
2. Choose the Create Click Track menu item. A click track will be created.

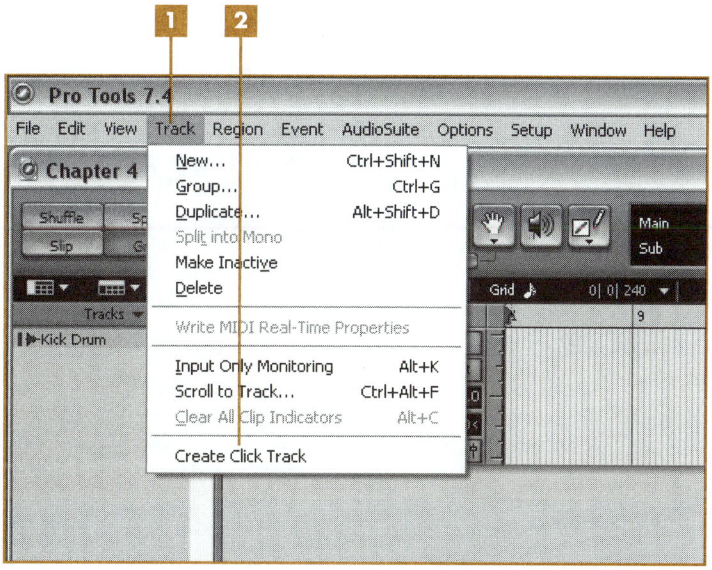

All you need to know is that you now have the ability to hear your click, but for the curious, here's what you've created: a mono Auxiliary Input track.

3 On this track, you'll see a small box in the Inserts column. This is a very simple virtual instrument plug-in called "Click." This primitive instrument has one simple job—to make "clicks" that follow the session's tempo. You have a few options at your disposal—just click the Insert button (on this track, it is the small box with the "C" on it, for "Click"). The Click plug-in window will open.

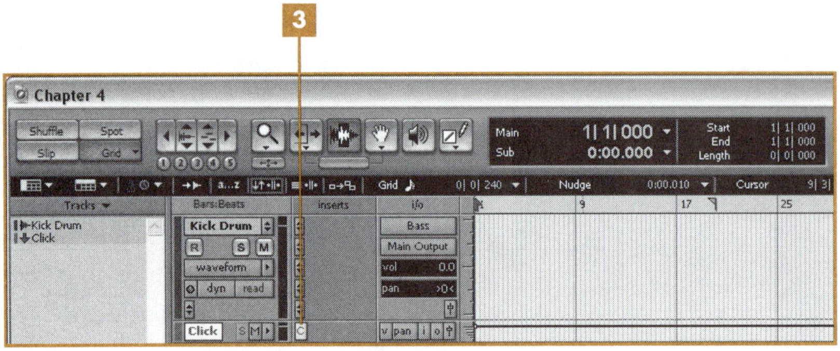

4a Adjust the Accented (for each measure's Beat 1) and Unaccented (for the other beats) sliders to get the best overall volume. You can change these values at any time in your session.

OR

4b Type a value in the Accented or Unaccented field to adjust the values manually. Press the Enter key when you're finished to confirm your entry.

5 Click on the plug-in preset name. A preset drop-down menu will appear, from which you can choose a tone for your click.

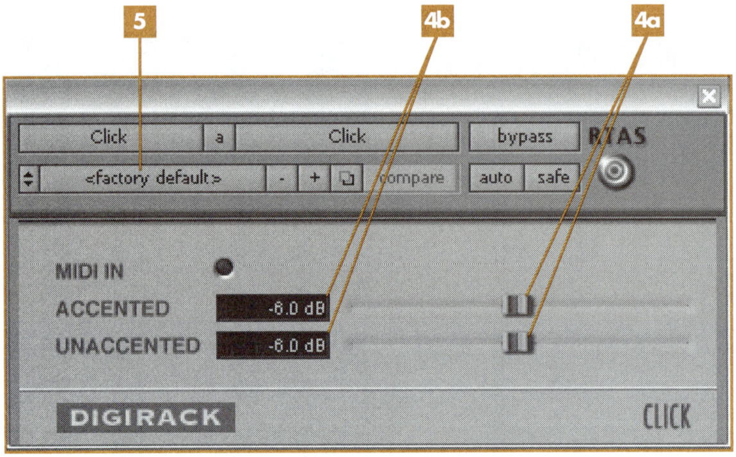

6. **Choose a tone** for your click track. The tone will be selected. Again, you can change this choice at any time in your session.
7. When you're finished, **click** on the **Close button**. The Click plug-in window will close.
8. If you want to change your settings as you work, **click** on the **Insert button** to reopen the Click plug-in window.

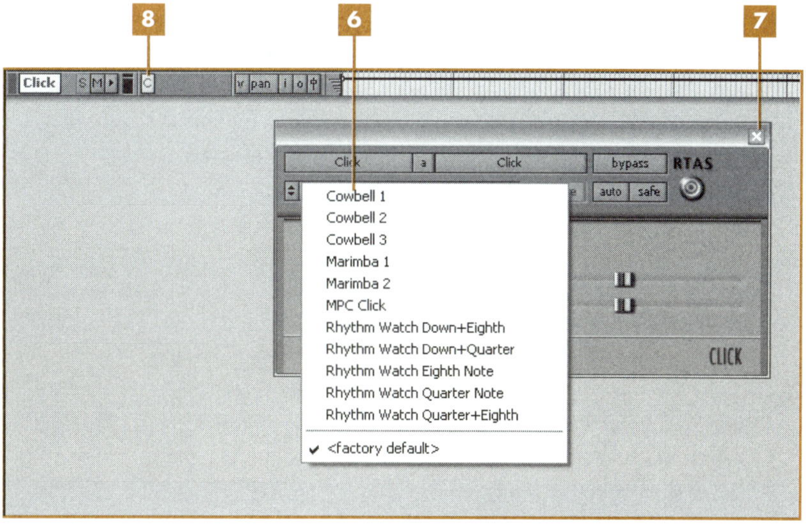

Setting Click and Tempo Options

The final thing you need to do is set up how your click track will behave.

1. **Click** on **Setup**. The Setup menu will appear.
2. **Choose Click/Countoff**. The Click/Countoff Options dialog box will open. This dialog box controls when the click will play.

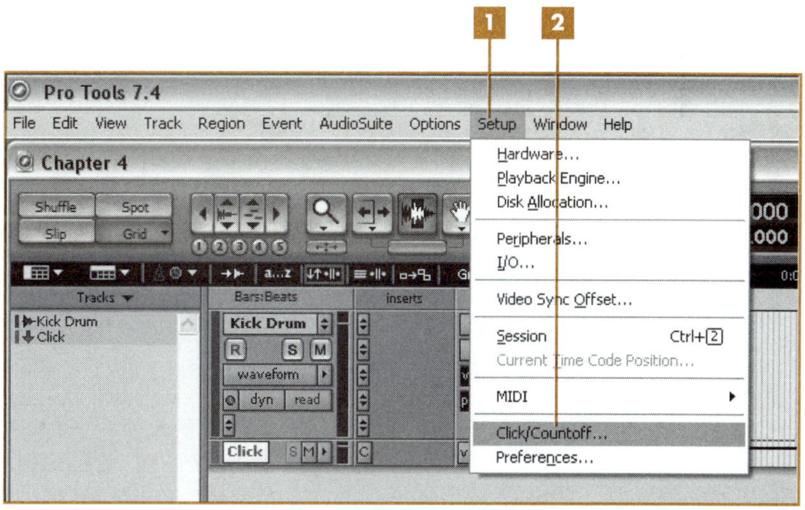

Click/Countoff Options Shortcut

Another way to access the Click/Countoff Options dialog box is to double-click on the Metronome icon in the Transport window.

You'll see that the Only During Record radio button is selected by default. This means that you'll hear the click when you're recording audio, but when you're playing back, the click won't be heard. Generally, this is a common way to use a click, so we'll leave this mode selected.

3 You have the option of sending click information to a MIDI synthesizer (which we'll discuss more in Chapter 7). In the case of using a MIDI synth for a click, you'll want to enter specific notes, velocities, and durations for the Accented and Unaccented fields according to the layout of your specific MIDI device. Because the Click plug-in isn't a MIDI synthesizer per se, you won't need to make any changes in this case.

4 Again, if you're using a MIDI synthesizer for your click source, you'll need to click on the Output menu and select a MIDI output port for your click information. The option will be selected.

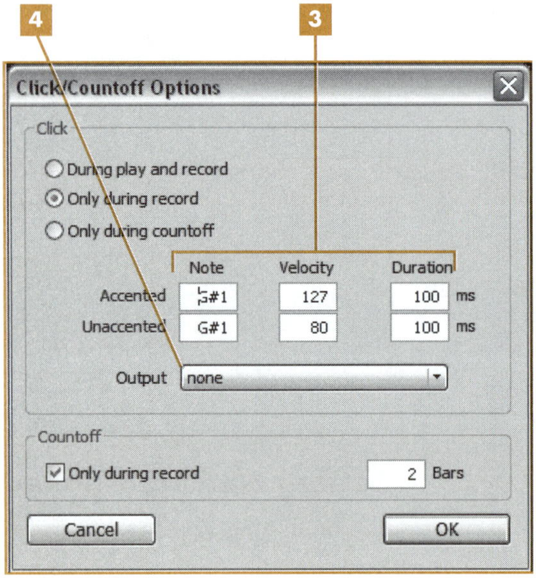

5 Select the Only During Record check box to ensure that your countoff will only be heard during recording. During regular playback, you won't be bothered with the countoff.

6 Enter the number of bars you want for your countoff in the Bars field. Two measures is a common setting.

7 Click on OK. The Click/Countoff Options dialog box will close.

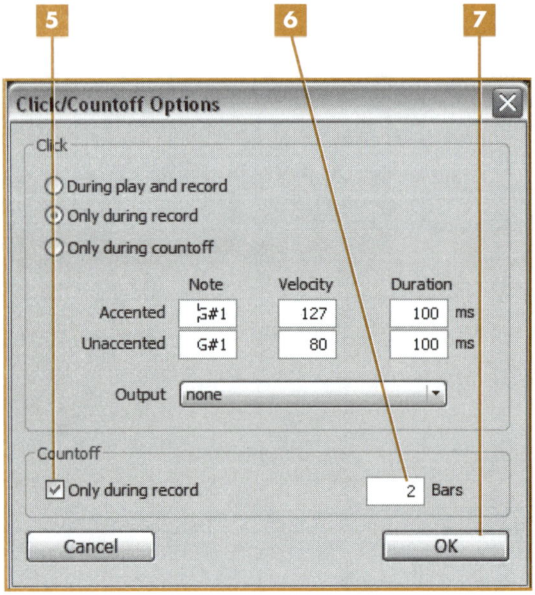

Click Plug-In Convenience!

If you're using the Click plug-in, you don't need to worry about assigning a MIDI output.

Now that the parameters of the click have been set up, you'll want to make sure that the click is actually enabled. There are two ways to do this.

1. Click on Options. The Options menu will appear.
2. Choose Click. The click will be enabled.

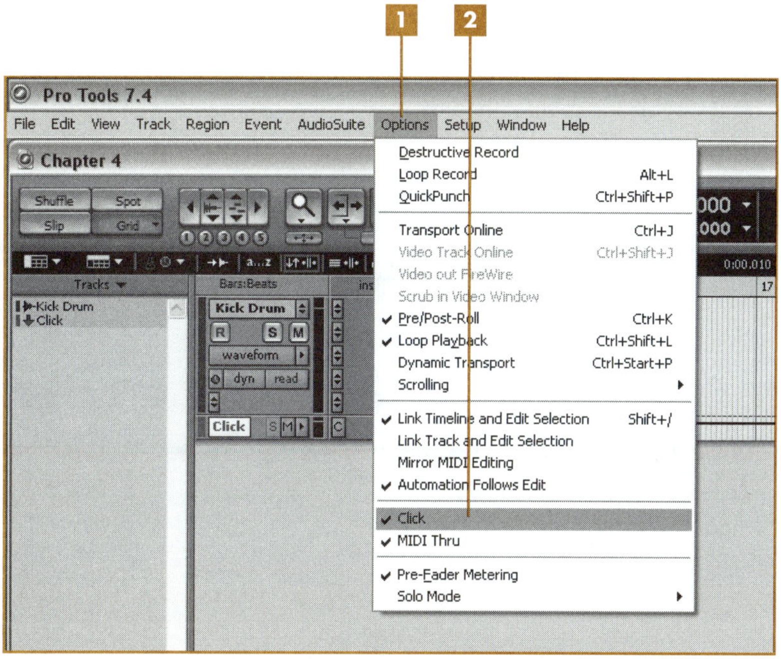

If you've followed these steps, you're all set, but as with many things in Pro Tools, there's more than one way to get the job done (to work with a variety of personal workflows). In the case of setting up a click, here's an alternative method for you to use in later sessions as you choose: You can enable the click (and the countoff) from the Transport window. (You can launch it from the Window menu.)

1 Click on the Metronome icon in the Transport window to activate the click, if it isn't already selected. The icon will be highlighted.

2 Click on the Countoff icon in the Transport window, if it isn't already selected. The icon will be highlighted. (Remember, you can disable the countoff at any time by deselecting this icon.)

3 For now, let's choose a static (unchanging) tempo. Deselect the Conductor icon. The tempo slider will appear solid now.

4a Use the tempo slider to set the desired tempo. The tempo value (shown in green in the lower-right corner) will change accordingly.

OR

4b Click the tempo value area, and type a tempo in the numeric tempo value field.

Another Way to Enter a Tempo

Here's an alternate way to enter a tempo that is particularly useful if you don't know the numeric tempo value you want: Just click the tempo numeric display to select it, and then press the T key on your computer keyboard in tempo. The numeric display will change to reflect the tempo of your taps. You can cycle through the beats as many times as you want until you settle upon the tempo you want to use.

5 **Double-click** on the **meter display** to change the meter. The Meter Change dialog box will open.

6 **Type** a **value** in the Meter field to select the meter you want to use.

7 **Type** a **location value** in the Location field to change meters throughout your music. The value in this field is displayed in bars | beats | ticks.

8 Now let's determine which kind of note will be the resolution of your click track. **Click** on the **Note icon**. The Note menu will appear.

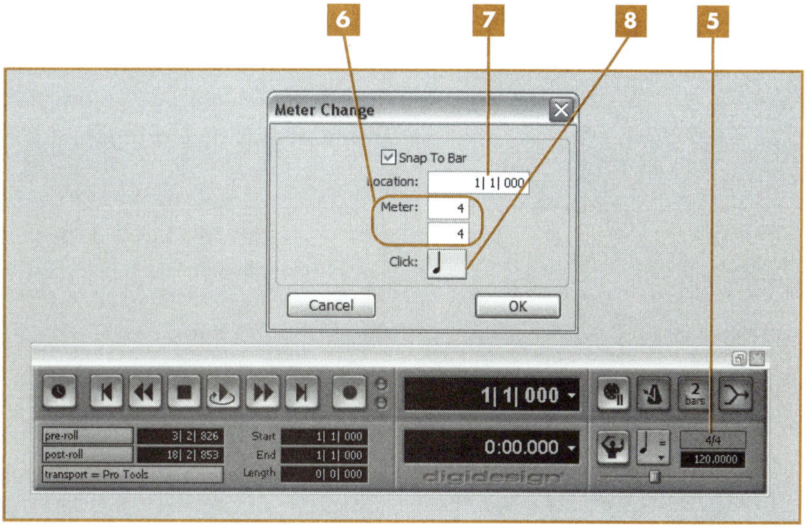

9 **Click** on the **note value** that matches the desired value of your click. The value will be selected.

10 **Click** on the **dot** if you want to use a dotted-note value for your click. The option will be selected.

11 **Click** on **OK**. Your meter changes will be applied, and the Meter Change dialog box will close.

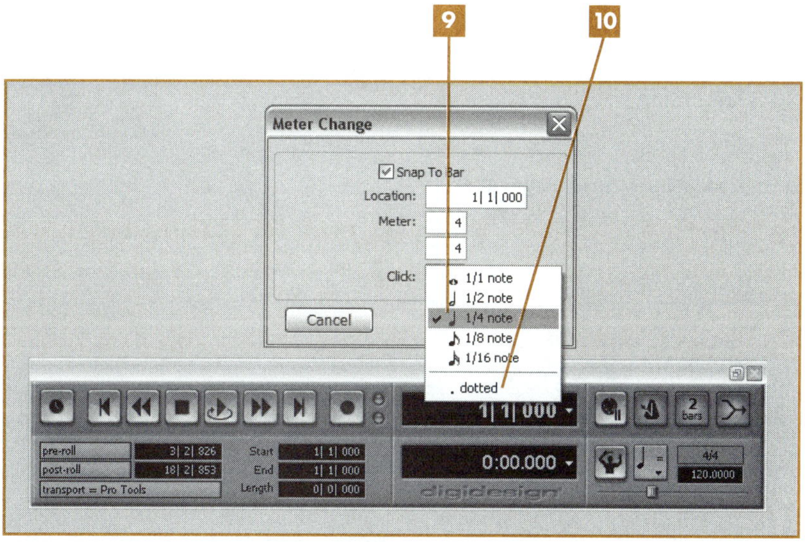

Basic Recording

You're all set—let's go! Now you're ready to record some audio from the outside world into the Pro Tools environment.

Tracks for Recording Practice

Here's where the included disc's audio CD tracks can help out. Just start playing the files, and you can record them into an available input on your audio interface. (Just make sure that you're familiar with the input assignments in your I/O Settings window.)

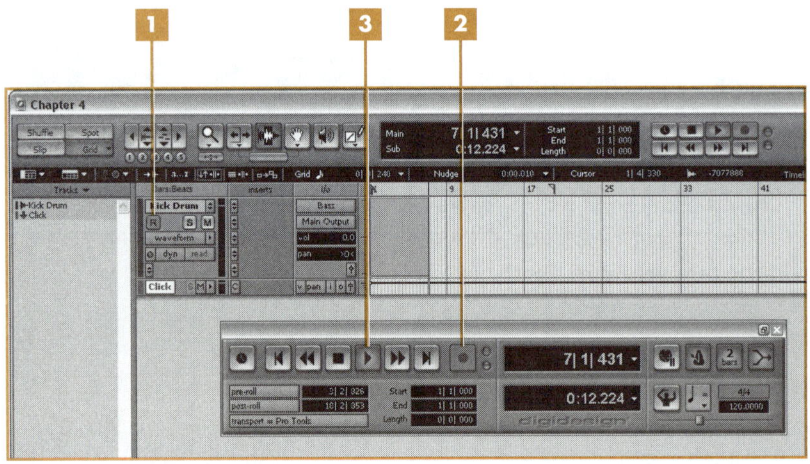

1. Click on the R button to arm the desired track for recording. The track will be armed.
2. Click on the Record button in the Transport window (or the Edit window's Transport section). The Record button will begin to flash.
3. Click on the Play button. Recording will begin.
4. Click on the Stop button when you want to stop your recording. An audio region will be created in your track.

   A new region will be shown in the track, and also will be listed in the Regions list.
5. Before you listen to your track, click the R button, and make sure the Record button is not highlighted and the track is not armed.
6. Click on the Play button. You will hear your newly created track.

Recording Shortcut

The shortcut for record/play is Ctrl+spacebar (PC) or ⌘+spacebar (Mac).

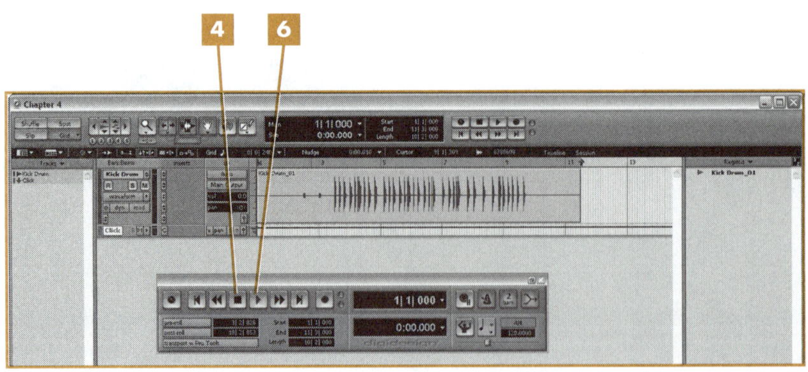

Other Recording Options

Congratulations! You've taken another important step down the road of Pro Tools use. Now let's explore some different ways to record audio that can come in useful when you need to accomplish specific goals.

Punching In and Punching Out

Suppose you recorded a perfect tape, except for that one measure! Not a problem when you're working with Pro Tools; you can specify a segment of your audio and replace it. Remember, too, that Pro Tools operates nondestructively, so you don't have to worry about losing your original take!

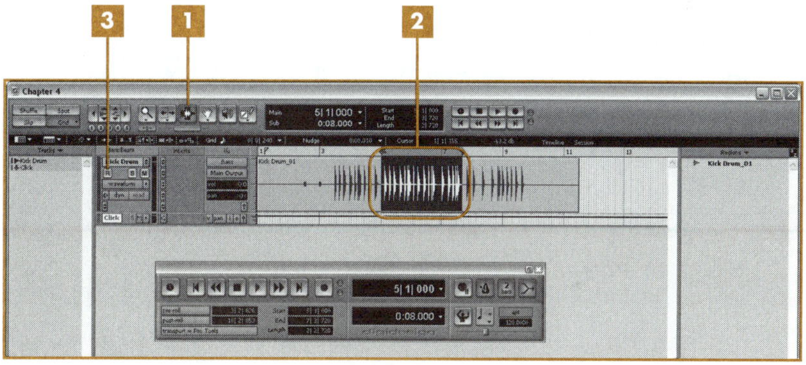

1. Click on the Selector tool. The tool will be highlighted.
2. Mark the area of audio upon which you want to re-record by clicking and dragging.
3. Click on the R button on the Audio track you want to re-record. The track will be armed for recording. You'll note that the selection in the Rulers area, which is usually bordered by blue arrows, is now bordered by red arrows.

Another Way to Make a Selection

While you're playing back your track, press the down arrow key to begin your selection and the up arrow key to end your selection.

4 If you want to hear a little bit of your original track before or after your punch in/out, you'll want to set up a pre-roll and/or a post-roll. Click on pre-roll. The option will be enabled.

5 Click inside the text box to the right of the pre-roll button and type the length of your pre-roll value.

6 Press Enter to confirm your entry. Bear in mind that the scale of this value follows the Main Counter display. A small green flag in the Rulers area will represent your enabled pre-roll.

7 Click on post-roll. The option will be enabled.

8 Click inside the text box to the right of the post-roll button and type the length of your post-roll value.

9 Press Enter to confirm your entry. Bear in mind that the scale of this value follows the Main Counter display. A small green flag in the Rulers area will represent your enabled post-roll.

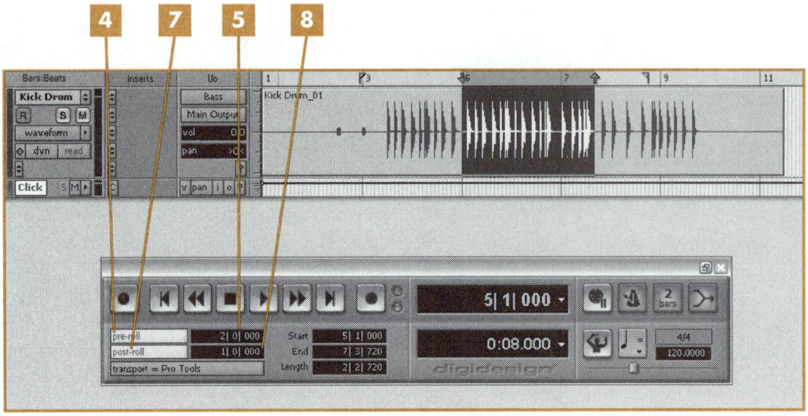

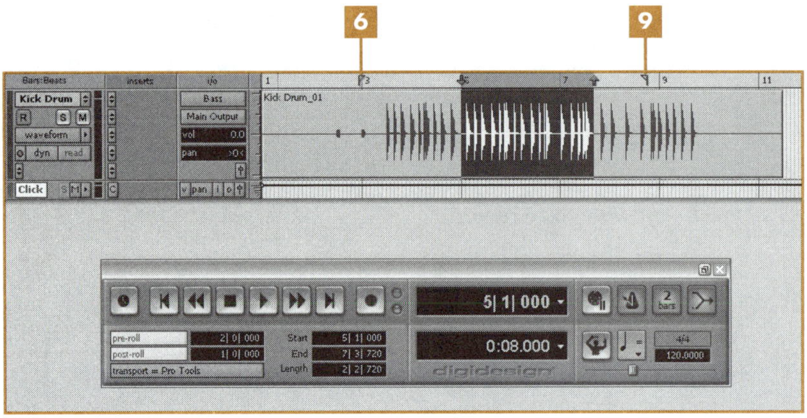

Making Changes

You can click and drag the arrows and flags on the Ruler Timeline to change your selection, pre-roll time, or post-roll time. You can also hold the Alt (PC) or Option (Mac) key and click before or after a selection to instantly move your pre- or post-roll to that location.

10 Click on the Record button.

11 Click on the Play button. Play will begin at the pre-roll location because you selected a pre-roll.

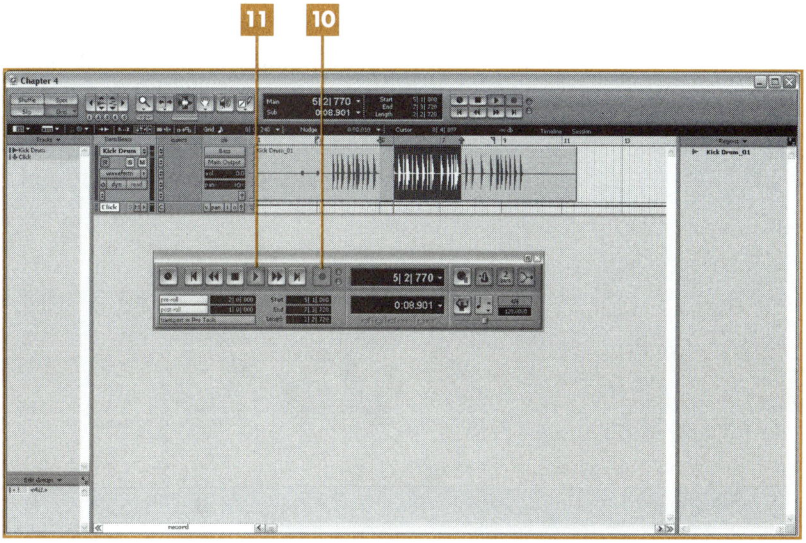

When the Timeline insertion reaches the selected area, Pro Tools will begin recording and will continue recording until the end of the selection. Pro Tools will then exit recording mode and continue playing for the post-roll duration. When the playline reaches the end of the post-roll duration, it will stop playing.

Here's what you'll end up with:

- Your original region has been split into two other regions.
- Both regions now appear in the Regions list. However, these regions are not shown in bold text because they are only incomplete parts of a whole file.
- Your punch has been recorded as a new region. For this example, I've recorded silence for visual effect.
- Your punch region appears in bold text because it is a whole file region, which means that it represents an entire file in your Audio Files folder.

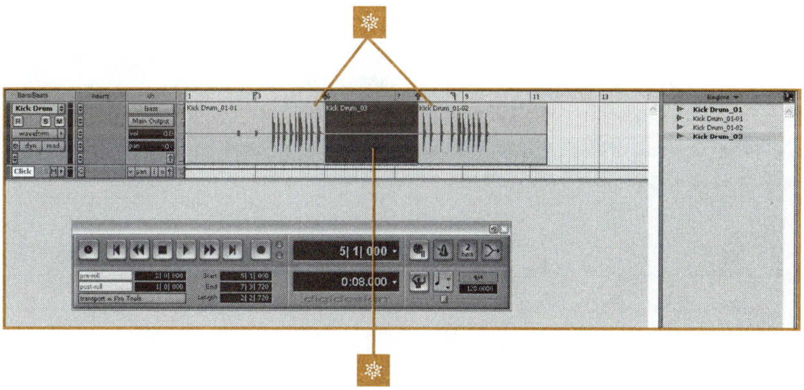

QuickPunch Recording

The main limitation of basic punch-in and punch-out is that it's a one-shot thing. So what if you want to make a single pass, but you want to punch in and out more than once? QuickPunch is for you! There are a couple ways to get into QuickPunch mode.

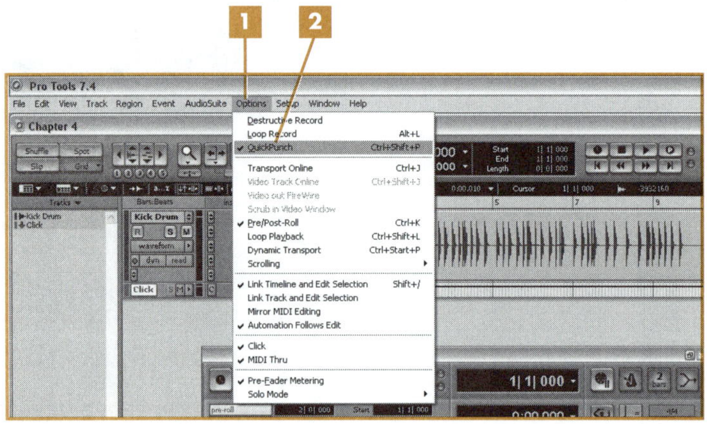

1. **Click** on **Options**. The Options menu will appear.
2. **Click** on **QuickPunch**. The QuickPunch feature will be enabled, indicated by a letter P displayed on the Record button.

QuickPunch Shortcut

Here's another way to access QuickPunch mode: Right-click on the Record button to reveal a list of the various recording modes.

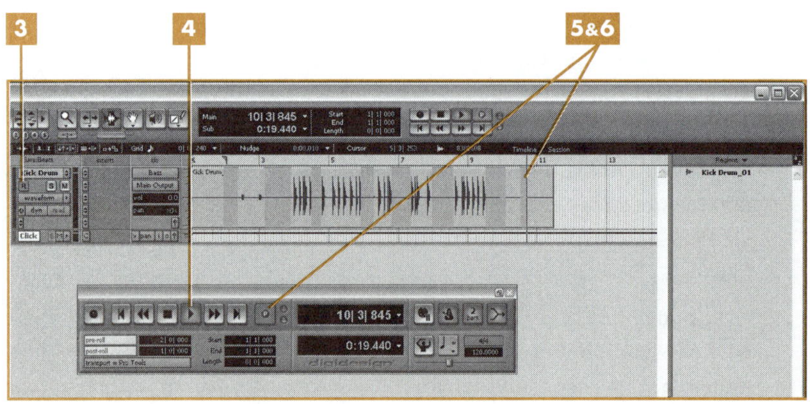

3. **Click** on the **R button** on the Audio track you want to re-record.
4. **Click** on the **Play button** at a point prior to when you want to record new audio. (In this case, I'm starting from the beginning of the session.) Your session will play as normal.
5. **Click** on the **Record button** when you want to begin recording. Recording will start.
6. **Click** on the **Record button** again when you want to stop recording. Recording will stop. To toggle recording, simply press the Record button.

Another QuickPunch Shortcut

Here's another way to punch in and punch out in QuickPunch mode: During playback, press Ctrl+spacebar (PC) or ⌘+spacebar (Mac).

Here's what you'll end up with:

- New regions will be created in your track to reflect each time you engaged and disengaged recording.
- As you might expect, new regions will also be added to the Regions list. The regions created in the track are not whole file regions, though a whole file region is also created in your Regions list. We'll discuss whole file regions in the next section.

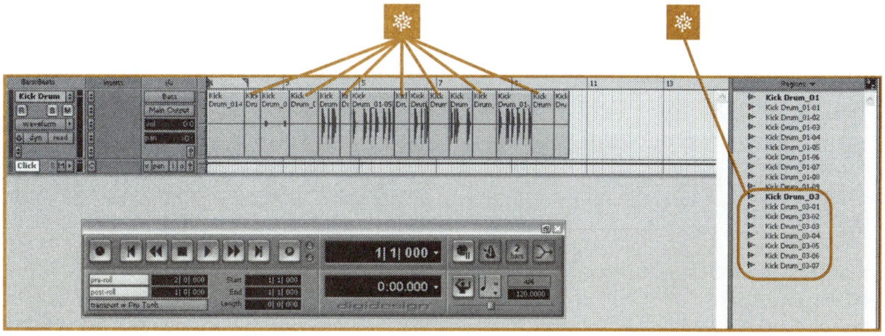

Loop Recording

Suppose you want to record several passes of a certain section (a guitar solo, for example), and then pick the best one. You'll want to use Pro Tools' Loop Record function.

1. Click on Options. The Options menu will appear.
2. Click on Loop Record. The Loop Record feature will be enabled (as indicated by a looped arrow around the Record button icon).

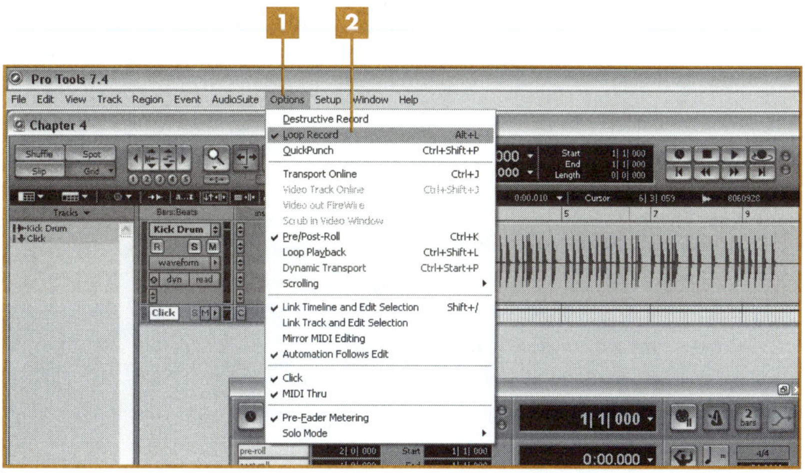

Loop Recording Shortcut

Again, you can alternatively right-click the Record button and choose Loop from the list that will appear.

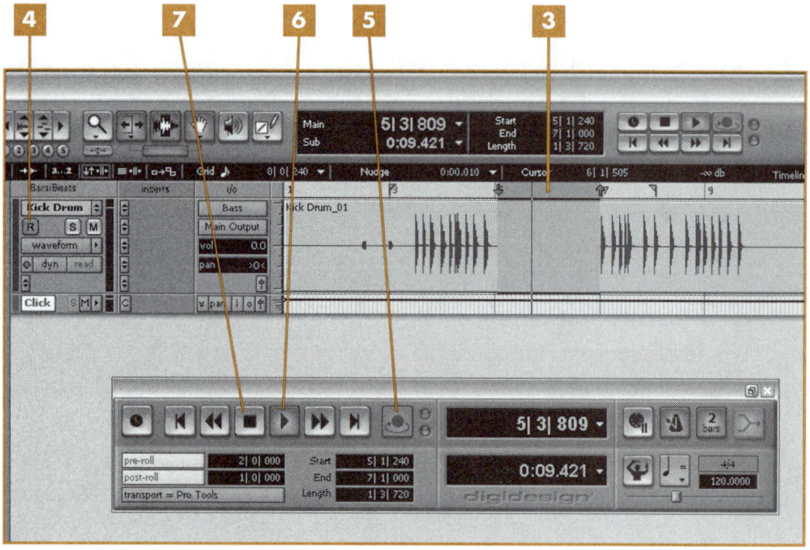

3 Use the Selector tool to select the section you want to loop. The area will be selected.

4 Click on the R button on the Audio track you want to re-record.

5 Click on the Record button.

6 Click on the Play button. Playback will begin at the pre-roll position (if pre-roll is enabled). When the selection is reached, Pro Tools will begin recording audio. At the end of the selection, recording will begin again from the beginning of the selection (even if pre-roll is enabled).

7 When you have enough takes, click on the Stop button. The latest take will appear in the selected area.

Whole File Regions and Loop Recording

In the Audio Regions list, notice that there is a whole file region (in **bold** text) that contains all the takes in sequence. Although it is not specifically used in the track, it represents the parent file in which all the individual takes reside. Below the whole file region are individual "takes" numbered sequentially in the order in which they were recorded.

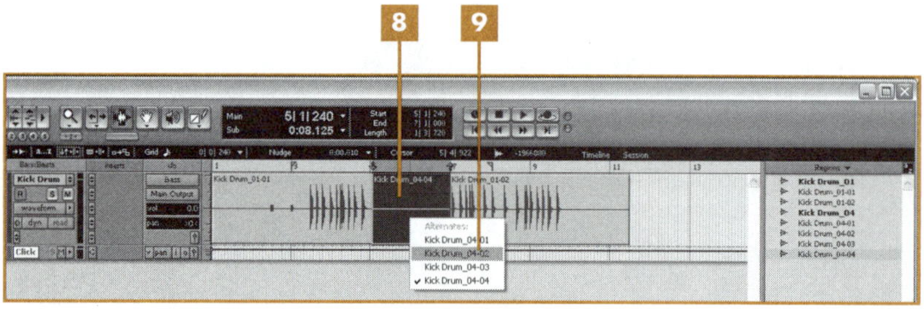

8 With the Selector tool chosen, Ctrl-click (PC) or ⌘-click (Mac) inside the region to reveal a drop-down menu that displays all the regions that match the same start time as the current region—in this case, all of your takes.

9 Click on the take you want to use. The take will be selected, and the region will be replaced. This is a great way to audition different takes to find just the right one!

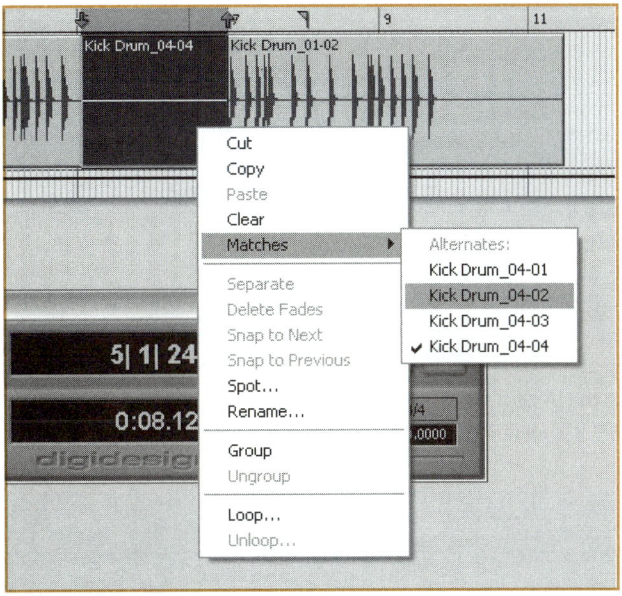

New Feature: Right-Click for Matching Takes

Just when you thought there couldn't *possibly* be more uses for that right mouse button, here's another one (and it's a good one at that!): If you right-click on your loop-recorded region, you'll see a menu of common region-related functions (many of which we'll get into later in this book). If you choose Matches, as shown here, you will see the matching takes list, and you can choose your favorite from here. This method has the advantage of not being shortcut-dependent, and it works with any of the edit tools chosen.

For the Brave: Destructive Recording

Thus far, you've only seen nondestructive recording modes, meaning that you never actually erase any audio in the process of punching in, punching out, or looping, and you can always undo your recording pass with no loss. This is a huge advantage over working with tape, and it was one of the initial attractions to DAWs in general. You can, however, record directly into an audio file that you created earlier. Be careful, though; there's no way to undo what you've done if you make a mistake!

1 Click on Options. The Options menu will appear.

2 Click on Destructive Record. The Destructive Record feature will be enabled. Destructive Record mode is indicated by a D on the red Record button.

3 Use the Selector tool to select the section of the Audio track that you want to overwrite. The area will be selected.

4 Click on the R button on the Audio track you want to re-record.

5 Click on the Record button.

6 Click on the Play button.

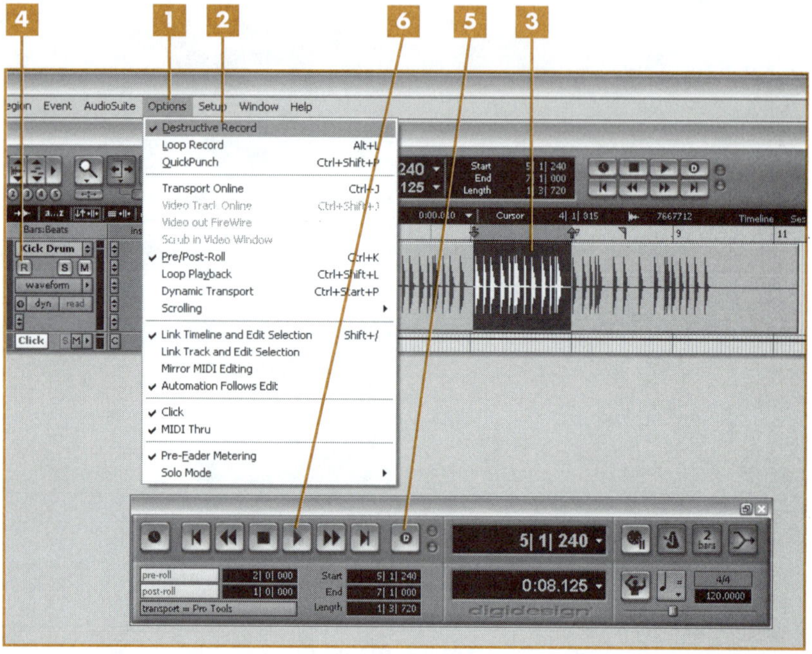

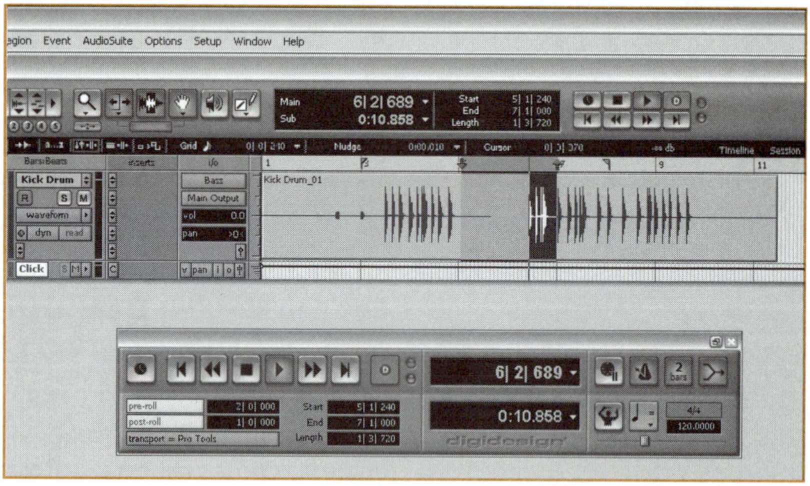

At this point, the process works exactly the same as basic punching in and punching out. Your session will begin playing at the pre-roll position (if you've enabled pre-roll), and then it will automatically begin recording at your selected area. It will stop recording at the end of your selection and play for the post-roll amount (if enabled).

The real difference between destructive recording and the other modes becomes apparent when the dust has settled.

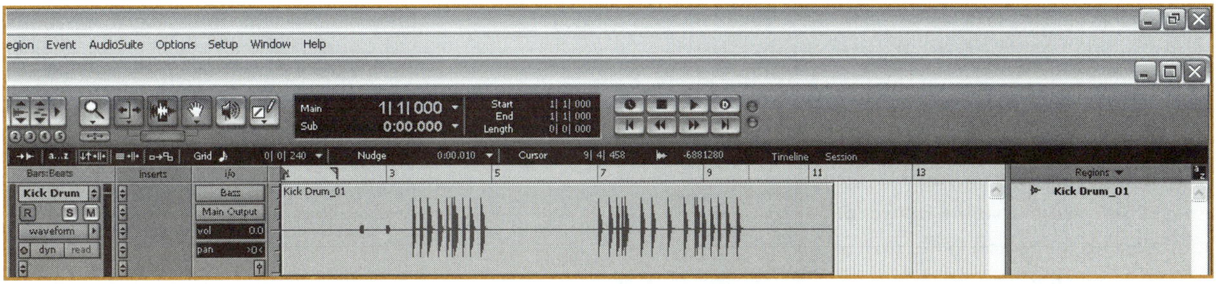

The important distinction between destructive recording and other modes is that no new regions have been created—in the track itself or in the Regions list. What you've done is permanently change the file you originally recorded!

Tips, Tricks, and Troubleshooting

Fantastic! You're on your way to running a great tracking session! This section includes a few final thoughts to call on when you need them.

Naming Tracks and Files

One very important thing to remember when it comes to good file management practices: The names of the regions that you record will follow the names of the tracks on which you're recording them. That means a track named Drums, for example, would yield recording passes named Drums_01, Drums_02, and so on.

That being said, the rule of thumb is to name your tracks *before* you record audio to them. However, if you forget to do this or if you ever want to change the name of a region after that region has been created, it's easy to do.

1 Double-click on the region you want to rename (either in the Regions list or in the track with the Grabber tool selected). The Name dialog box will open.

2 Type the new name for the region in the Name the Region text box.

3a If the region is a whole file region, you have the option of naming the region in the session only or changing the name of the region *and* the file name as it appears on your hard drive. Click on the Name Region Only radio button (which will leave the audio file name unchanged)

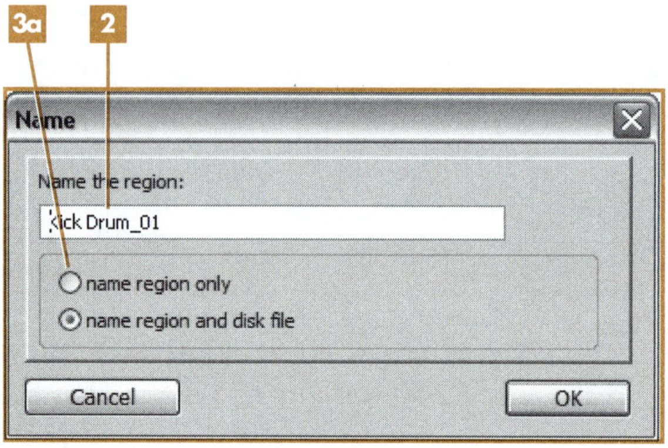

OR

3b Click the Name Region and Disk File radio button, if available. (This option will only be open to you if you're naming a whole file region.)

4 Click on OK. The Name dialog box will close, and the region will be renamed.

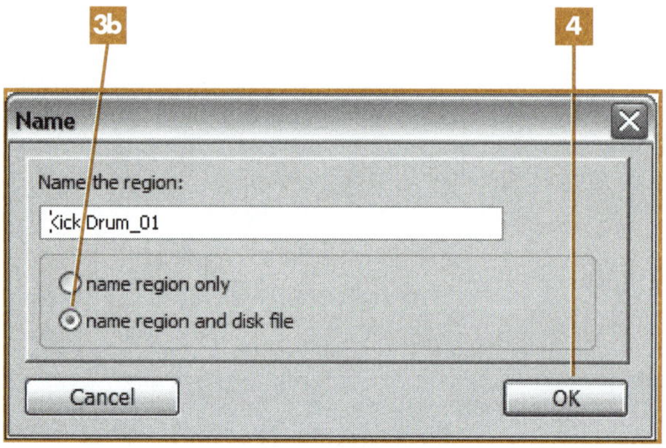

Understanding the Monitor Modes

In addition to all the different modes of recording that you've learned about, there are two monitor modes that affect how you hear your audio during the recording process. The two modes, called *Auto Input Monitoring* and *Input Only Monitoring*, will be useful in different situations.

1 Click on Track. The Track menu will appear.

The monitor mode that you're *not* in will be shown as an option in this menu.

2a Select Auto Input Monitoring if you want to hear what you previously recorded right up to your punch-in point. Pro Tools will behave as if it is in playback mode during pre-roll and post-roll periods, and it will automatically switch over to monitoring your input only during the selected overdub area.

A green light to the right of the transport controls (in the Edit window or the Transport window) will not be illuminated when you're in Auto Input Monitoring mode.

OR

2b Select Input Only Monitoring if you don't want to hear what you've already recorded during a punch-in/punch-out situation. Pro Tools will still only record during the selected area, but for the pre-roll and post-roll durations, you'll hear the live input rather than the previously recorded audio on the track.

A green light to the right of the transport controls (in the Edit window or the Transport window) will illuminate to signal that you're in this mode.

Low Latency Monitoring—and a Trick!

When you are recording, you might notice a bit of delay (called *latency*) between the time a note is played and the time it is heard through monitors or headphones. The bad news is that this is the normal functioning of host-based DAWs in general, a byproduct of the conversion of analog and digital audio. The good news is that there's a solution to this problem in Pro Tools, called *low latency monitoring*. This monitoring mode minimizes the process of running audio through the host computer's CPU, reducing the delay you hear.

1. Click on Options. The Options menu will appear.
2. Click on Low Latency Monitoring. The good news is that your latency problem just got a lot better.

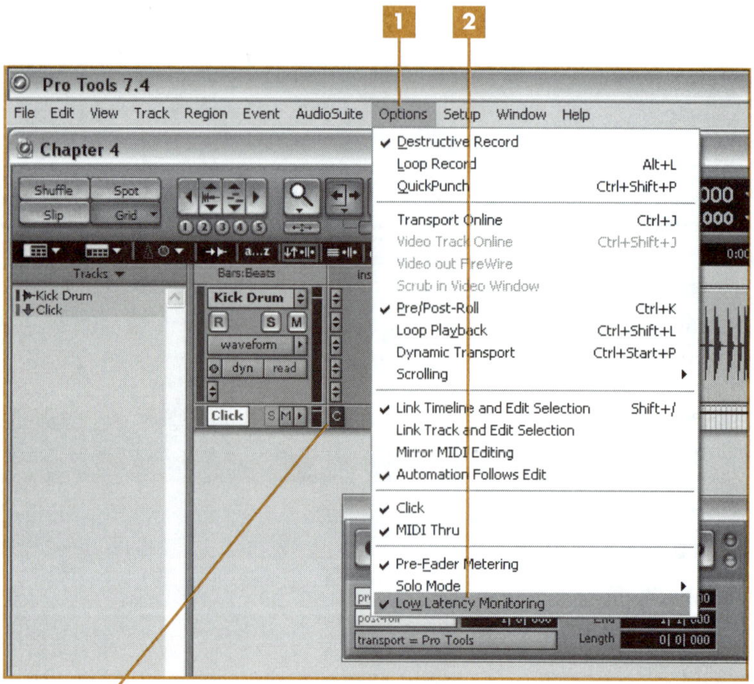

The bad news (you knew there'd be some, right?) is that the Click plug-in has turned dark, indicating that the plug-in has become inactive. This is the price of low latency monitoring—plug-ins become inactive. Does that mean you have lost the use of your click? Yes and no—read on!

Because the Click plug-in won't work in this mode, you need to figure out another way to hear it. The solution to this problem is to *bounce*—in other words, record—from one track to another. Because this bounce is internal (entirely within the Pro Tools environment), you can use a bus to make this transfer. I'll go deeper into the application of such concepts in Chapter 8, but for now let's just solve the problem!

1. First, make sure that you're not in Low Latency Monitoring mode (indicated by no check by the menu item).
2. Click on the click track's output selector (which is represented by the small button with an "o" on it, since the track is currently at the "mini" track height). The output menu will appear.
3. Choose an unused mono bus. In a session, already-used busses appear in bold text.

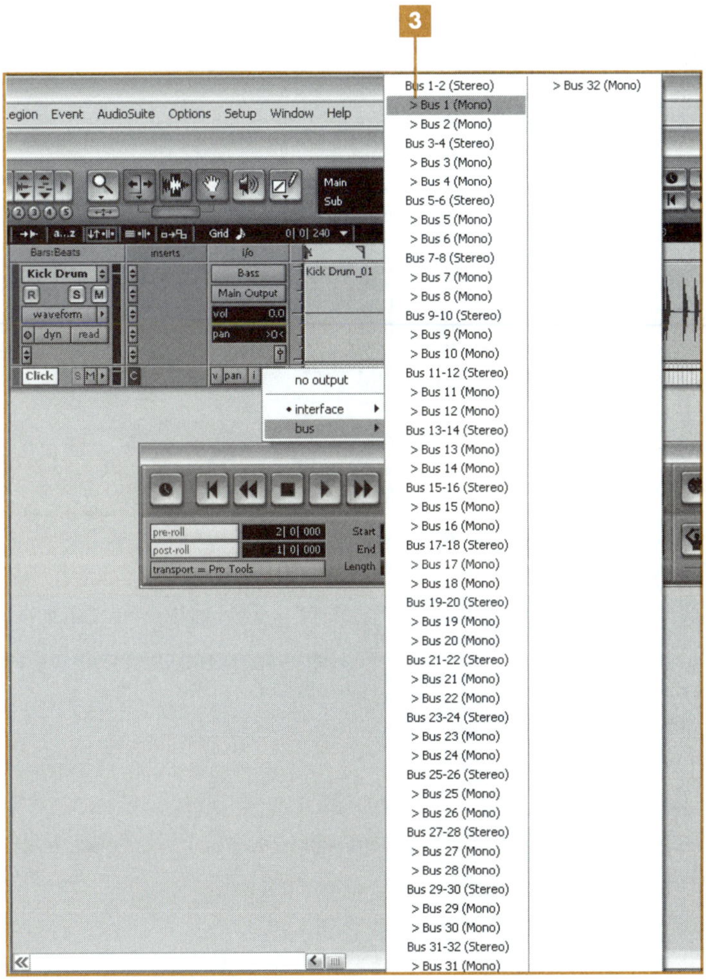

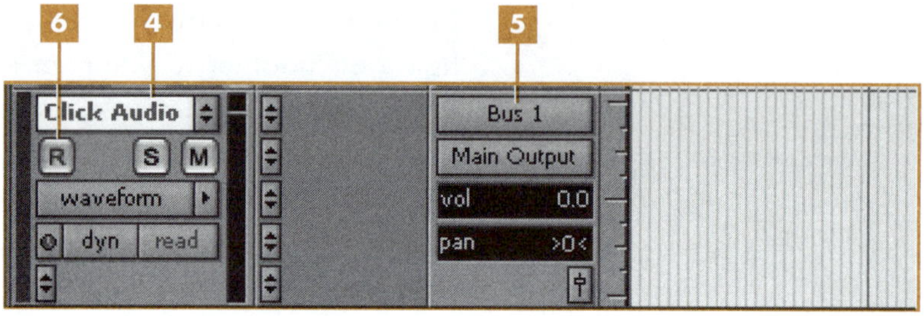

4. Create a mono Audio track and name it descriptively.

5. Now you need to set the input so you can record from the click track. Click on the track's Input button. A pop-up menu will appear. Choose the same bus you selected for the Click track's output. The bus will be selected.

6. Click on the R button. The track will be armed for recording.

Take Care!

Make sure you deselect the R button on any other armed tracks in your session, or you'll be recording on them as well!

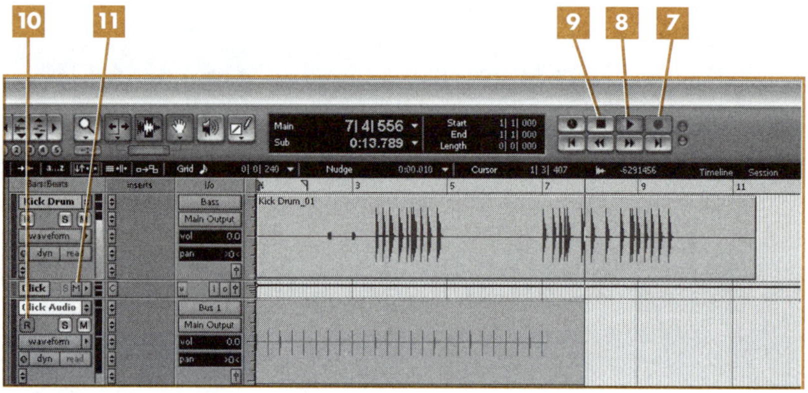

7. Click on the Record button.

8. Click on the Play button. Recording will begin on the Audio track. Whereas the Click plug-in creates the click in real time, the click track will be recorded as audio on the Audio track.

9. Click on the Stop button when you've recorded enough of the click. The recording will stop.

10. Click on the R button again. The click Audio track will be disarmed.

11. Mute the click Aux track. The track will be muted.

An Option with the Click Aux Track

Alternatively, you can delete the click Aux track entirely. You don't need it anymore!

You will now hear your click even when you're in low latency mode!

Mbox 2 Mini and MBox 2 "No Latency" Operation

If you're working with an Mbox audio interface, you'll notice that Pro Tools doesn't give you a low latency monitoring option. Does that mean you're out of luck? No way! The solution lies in the Mbox's Mix knob, which is second from the bottom on the front of your Mbox, or the third knob from the headphone output of the Mbox 2. When the knob is all the way to the input side (the furthest counterclockwise), you'll monitor signal coming directly into the interface only, and you won't hear the Pro Tools software at all. When the Mix knob is set all the way to playback (fully clockwise), you'll only hear audio coming from Pro Tools. Here's how to eliminate the latency problem using the Mbox's Mix knob:

1. Set the Mix knob to twelve o'clock as a starting point, giving you an even balance between input and playback.
2. Record arm the Audio track on which you want to record. Now if you play, you should hear a doubled signal. (The earlier signal is from the input side of the mix; the latent [delayed] signal is coming from the Pro Tools software, routed through the playback side of the mix.)
3. Mute the track on which you want to record. You can still record onto the track, but you won't hear that annoying delayed signal.
4. Adjust the Mix knob to get the desired balance between your live input and the Pro Tools software playback.
5. Record as normal.
6. When you're finished recording, you can change your mix to playback so you won't be distracted by any audio going into your Mbox or Mbox 2.

Next step—editing!

What about the Click Track?

This is an elegantly simple solution to a significant problem with DAWs. You'll even be able to use your Click plug-in!

A Setup for Mixing Practice

Included with this chapter's download materials are a number of audio files that together can be played back as a complete mix. If you record all these files into your session (from a burned CD, MP3 player, or your computer soundcard's output), you'll be able to use it in Chapter 8, when you learn about mixing.

5 Editing

Production can be broken down into a number of phases—tracking (recording), editing, mixing, and mastering, to name but a few. Because it's a computer-based workstation, Pro Tools perhaps shines brightest in the editing phase. In its nonlinear environment, you can accomplish in seconds what used to take minutes or hours with a tape-based system. And of course, there is always the Undo function if you make a mistake. Even better news, Pro Tools 7 has introduced a number of impressive new editing features that will make your work even more fun! In this chapter, you'll learn how to:

- Take full advantage of the functions of the Edit window
- Use Pro Tools' edit modes to their greatest advantage
- Work with Pro Tools' basic editing features
- Use processes such as cut, copy, and paste to create your own arrangements

Understanding the Edit Window

You took a good first look at the Edit window in the previous chapters, and now it's time for a closer examination of this powerful window. For the purposes of this chapter, I'll be reconstructing a song from rough elements, so if you want to follow the screenshots, just copy the Chapter 5 Session data from the included disc.

Using the Tools of the Trade

Some of Pro Tools' most useful tools are located in the top row of the Edit window.

- In the upper-left corner are the four edit modes—Shuffle, Spot, Slip, and Grid. The mode you choose will determine the manner in which regions can be moved in time in your session. You'll learn more about these modes in the section, "Moving Regions on the Timeline: The Edit Modes," later in this chapter.

- Moving to the right, you'll see the first of the zoom tools. These will allow you to zero in on a very brief section of your session (useful for fine editing) or zoom out to view longer sections in your project. You can also zoom in or out using other methods, which will enable you to view your regions in different ways. I'll discuss this more in the next section of this chapter.

- These are the most popular editing tools in the Pro Tools arsenal. From left to right, the tools are Zoom, Trim, Selector, Grabber, Scrub, and Pencil. These tools operate directly on specific regions within your session.

- Last but not least are the location displays. To the left you'll see a Main and a Sub display. Both of these displays show you exactly where you are in your session. To the right there are the Start, End, and Length displays, which show you the beginning, end, and duration of your selections.

Navigating

Before you can do anything else, you need to know the basics of how to get around. You'll find that the Selector tool is well suited to this task. Along with this tool, you need to use the location displays so you know where you are.

1. Click on the Selector tool. The tool will be selected.
2. Click on the arrow to the right of the Main time display. A drop-down menu will appear.

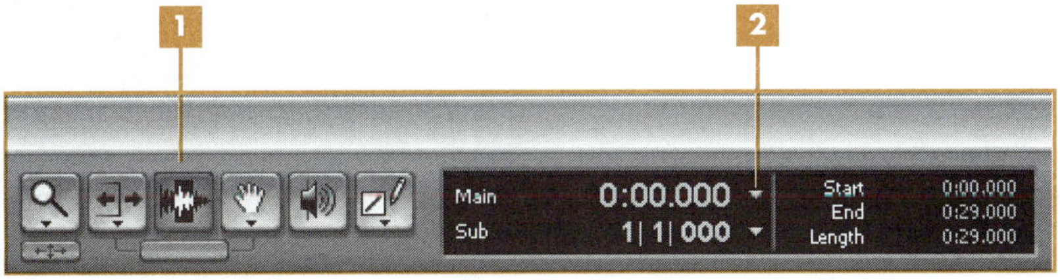

3. Choose the desired scale with which you wish to navigate through your session. For the purposes of this example, choose Bars:Beats. The time scale of the Main display will change to reflect your selection.

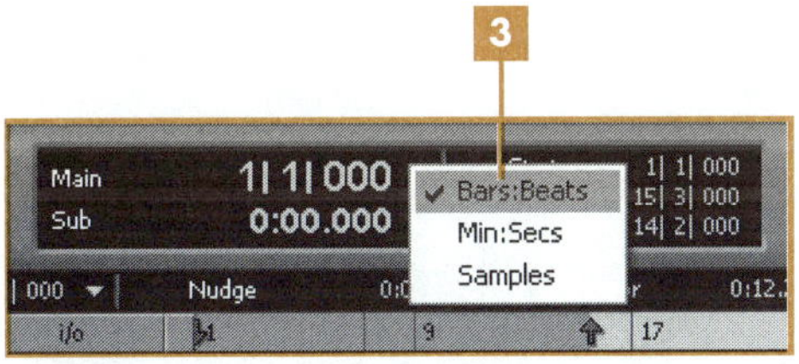

Selection Display Scale

The scale of the selection display (to the right of the Main and Sub location displays) will change to match the Main display's scale. For example, if you change the scale to Bars:Beats, the Main time display will count your session as it plays in bars and beats. When you make a selection, that selection will also be shown in bars and beats.

4 **Click** on the **arrow** to the right of the Sub time display. A drop-down menu will appear.

5 **Choose** any **time scale** for this display. You might want to choose a different scale than the one in the Main display; that way, you can view your session in two different ways simultaneously.

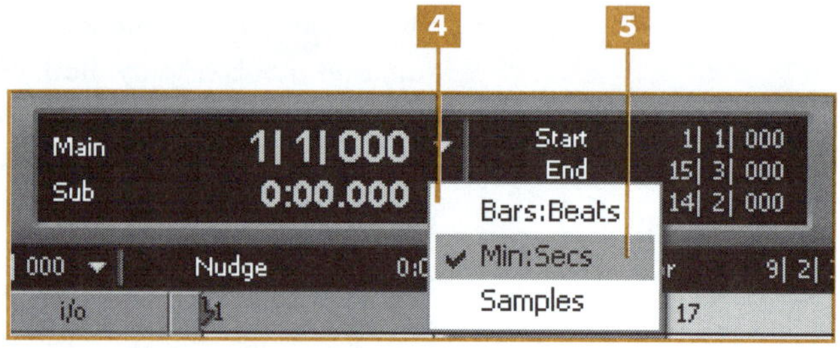

6 **Click** anywhere in the session's **Edit area**. A small line (called the *Timeline insertion*) will appear where you clicked. Also, a small blue figure will appear at this location in your Rulers area.

In the Main and Sub time displays, your Timeline insertion's location is precisely displayed.

Also, the selection display will show the Timeline insertion location. Because you've selected only a single location, the Start and End values are identical, and the Length value is zero.

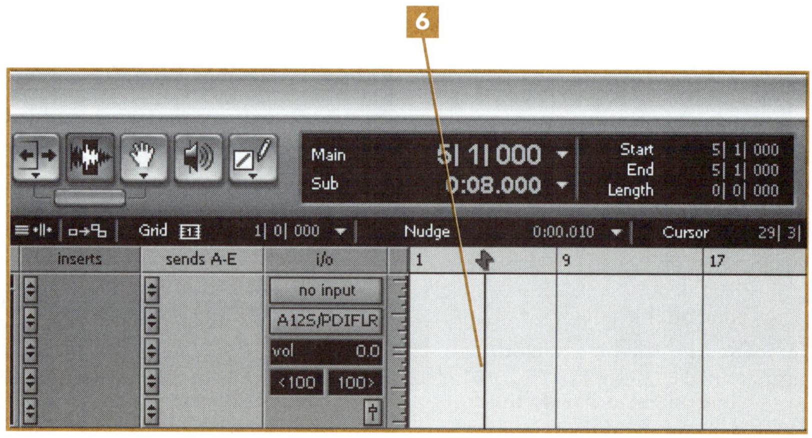

Now, try to make a different kind of selection.

1 **Click and drag** in the **Track area** to make a selection with a length greater than zero. The wider your selection, the more time you've selected.

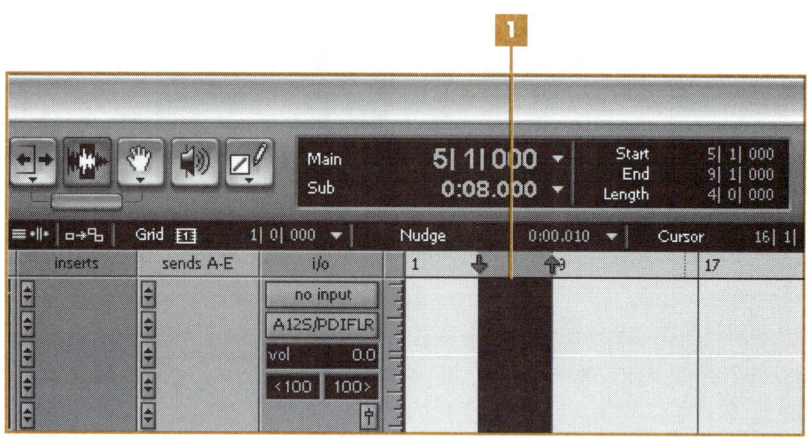

In addition to the selection you make in the Track area, a selection is made in the Rulers area. This time, however, the blue figure has split apart into a down arrow (indicating the beginning of the selection) and an up arrow (indicating the end).

The Main and Sub time displays will show the start of your selection.

The selection display will show the start, end, and length of your selection.

Here are a couple more ways to get around, this time using the Tab key.

1. Still using the Selector tool, click on a track with a number of regions, before any (or all) regions. A Timeline insertion will appear where you click.
2. Press the Tab key. The Timeline insertion will move to the next region boundary (the start or end of a region.)

   Each time you press the Tab key, the Timeline insertion will move to the next region boundary.

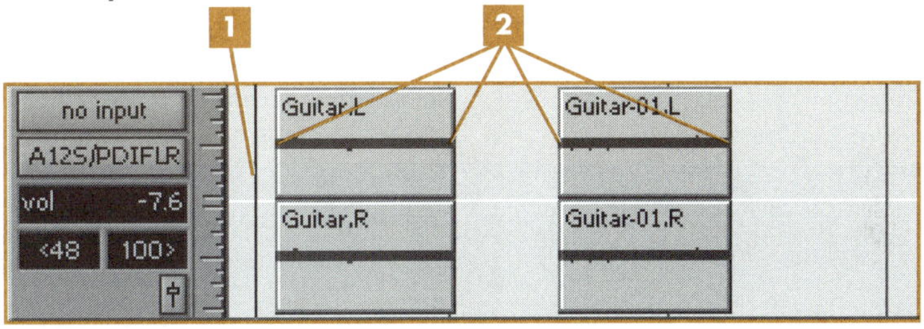

Modifying the Tab Key Behavior

Here's a twist on using the Tab key: Hold the Alt key (PC) or the Option key (Mac) while you press the Tab key to move the Timeline insertion to the previous region boundary.

Here's another way to use the Tab key.

1. Click on the Tab to Transients button. The option will be selected.
2. Click once on a region with audio to move the Timeline insertion. The Timeline insertion will be moved.
3. Press the Tab key. This time, instead of moving to region boundaries, the Timeline insertion will jump from transient to transient.

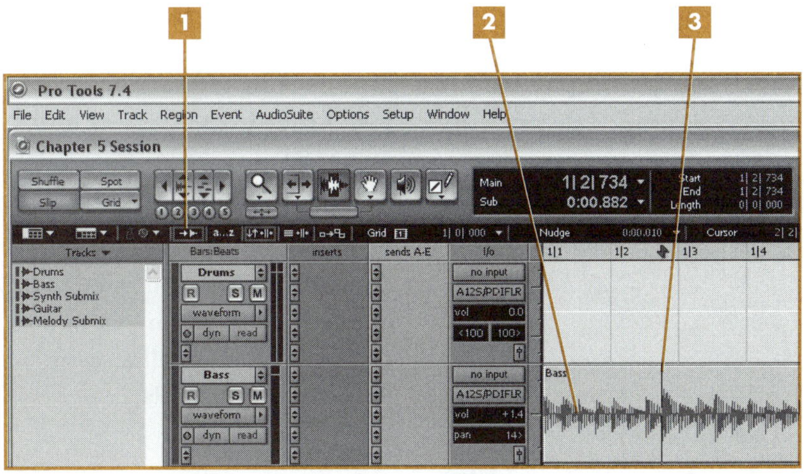

Modifying Tab to Transient

Again, the Alt key (PC) or the Option key (Mac) will move the Timeline insertion backward in time, this time to the *previous* transient peak.

So What the Heck *Is* a Transient, Anyway?

Simply put, a transient is the initial high-energy peak at the beginning of a waveform, such as one caused by the percussive action of a pick or hammer hitting a string or a drumstick hitting the head of a drum. Different types of instruments have different kinds of transients, but they tend to be good visual cues when editing, indicating the beginnings of notes (or words, in the case of a spoken track).

New Feature: Mouse-Based Scrolling

If you have a mouse equipped with a scroll wheel, you've got some additional navigation power at your disposal. You'll find that your scroll wheel will help you scroll up and down through your shown tracks. (This will only work when you have more shown tracks than can be seen at once in your Edit window.) Holding down the Shift key will allow you to scroll horizontally along the Timeline. Bear in mind that this horizontal scrolling will *not* move the Timeline insertion.

From time to time (such as when you're working with transients), you'll want to get a closer look at the audio. That's where zooming comes in!

Zooming

Sometimes when you're editing, you'll want to get a close look at your audio. When you're finished, you might want to get an overview of your entire session. To do this, you need to know how to use the zoom tools.

1. Click on the left zoom arrow to zoom out. Each time you click on this button, your view will encompass a greater span of time.
2. Click on the right zoom arrow to zoom in. Each time you click on this button, you will gain a finer view of your session.

Zooming Behavior

You will notice that your zooming centers on your Timeline insertion's location.

Zooming Shortcuts

You might use these shortcuts more than any others covered in this book: On PCs, it's Ctrl+] (right bracket) to zoom in and Ctrl+[(left bracket) to zoom out. On Macs, ⌘+] will zoom in, and ⌘+[will zoom out.

1. Click on the Zoom tool. The tool will be selected.
2. Click and drag on a track to select an area. The area will be selected.
3. Release the mouse button. The view will zoom in on the selected area.

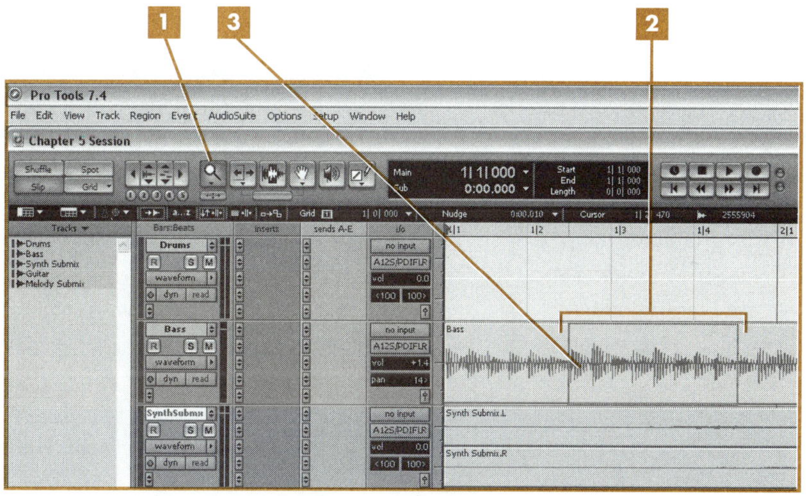

Here's another way to zoom in on a specific section.

New Feature: Scroll Wheel Zooming

Here's even more scroll wheel power: If you hold down the Alt key (PC) or the Option key (Mac), you'll be able to smoothly zoom in and out, centered on the Timeline insertion point. Scrolling "up" will zoom you in, and scrolling "down" will zoom you out. This is a very handy new addition, and you'll find that this new mouse power will speed up your editing processes!

Moving Regions on the Timeline: The Edit Modes

Pro Tools has four basic edit modes that determine how regions behave in your session. Each mode is unique, and soon you will get a feeling for which mode is best suited to a given task. For the purposes of illustration, we'll work with the drum track of this session.

Using Slip Mode

When you need it, Slip mode gives you the most freedom of motion with your regions.

1. Click on the Slip mode button. The mode will be selected.
2. Click and hold a region in the Regions list. The region will be selected.
3. Drag the region onto a track. You will see an outline of the region, indicating where it will be placed when you release the mouse button.

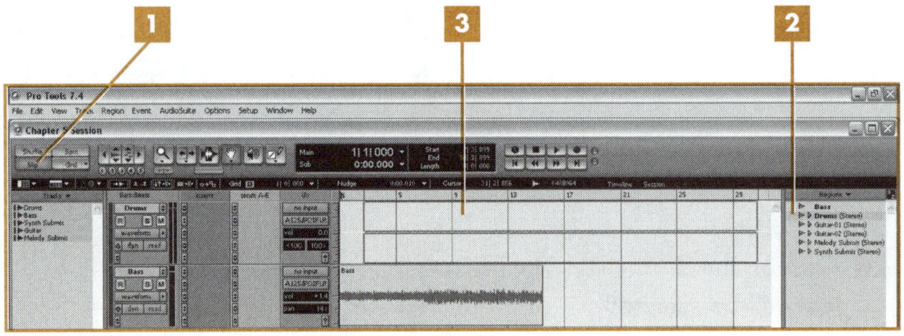

> **Some Rules on Moving Regions**
>
> It is important to remember that when you're working with mono regions, you can only drop them onto mono tracks. On the other hand, when you drag stereo regions onto the Timeline, they can occupy a single stereo track or two mono tracks.

Using Grid Mode

Sometimes it is convenient to have your regions snap to predetermined increments or grids. This can be particularly useful when you're working on a music-based project, when it's important to have your regions align themselves to bars and beats. Pro Tools actually gives you *two* ways of doing this sort of grid-based work, which we'll cover now.

Let's take a look at Grid mode in a typical music context. First (if you haven't done so already), you should set up your Main location display and Grid value so you can maximize the effectiveness of this mode.

If You're Using the Tutorial Session

If you're following the chapter, you should have a selected region on your drum track that you deposited while using Slip mode. Let's get that region out of there before we move on. Since the region is probably still selected, all you have to do is press the Delete key to remove it. (Note that the region is still present in the Regions list, so you're not losing anything.)

1. **Click** on the **Main down arrow** and **change** the **Main location display** to Bars:Beats. The scale will be shown in Bars|Beats|Ticks. Note that the selection display will also change scale.
2. **Click** on the **Grid Value arrow.** The Grid menu will appear.
3. **Select** the **desired scale** of your grid. Because we're working with music, Bars:Beats is the one for this example. The option will be selected.
4. **Choose** the **desired resolution** for your grid. For our purposes here, 1 bar will do the trick. The option will be selected.

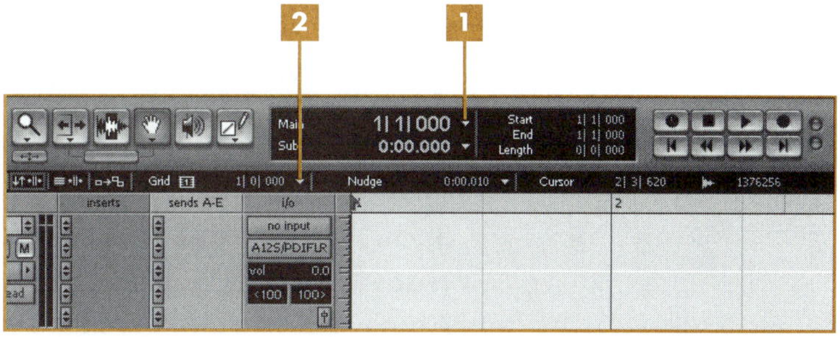

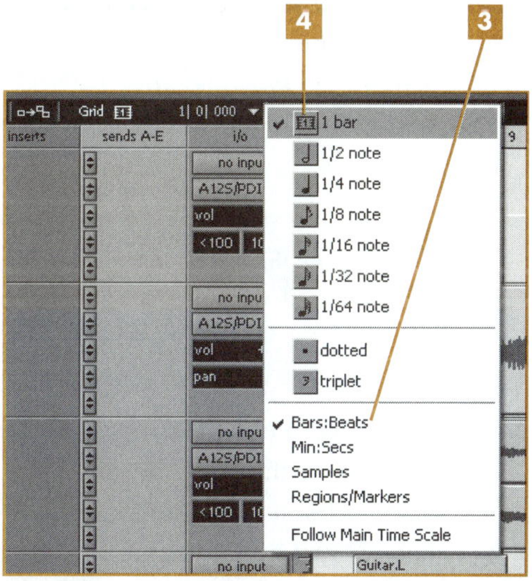

Bars:Beats Grid Increments

Because this scale is musical, you will see grid resolutions such as bars, half notes, quarter notes, and so on.

Showing the Grid Value

Notice that the Grid indicator to the left of the drop-down menu will change to match your choice.

5 **Click** on **Grid**. The mode will be selected.

6 **Drag** a **region** from the Regions list onto the Track area. The region will snap from bar to bar as you drag it.

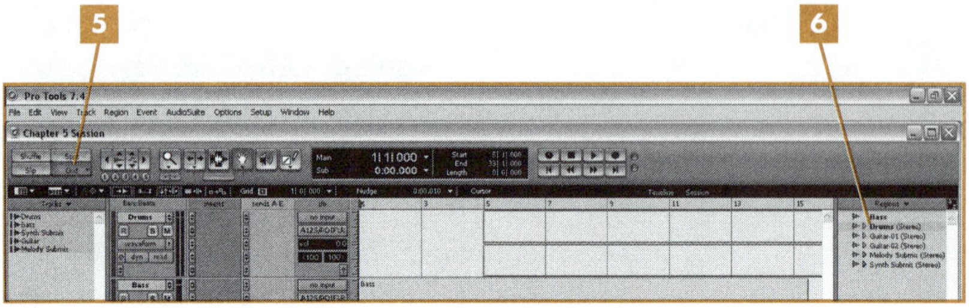

As you drag the region, you'll notice that the selection display will reflect the beginning, end, and duration of the region. Because you're in Grid mode and your grid resolution is 1 bar, the start value will always change in one-measure increments.

Relative Grid Mode

The previous workflow example outlined the default Grid mode of operation, otherwise known as *Absolute Grid mode*. You'll know if you're in Absolute Grid mode if your Grid mode button simply reads "Grid" and is blue when selected. As you saw just now, Absolute Grid mode will snap regions to the nearest grid line.

There's a second Grid mode available to you, called *Relative Grid mode*. This mode won't move regions *to* the nearest grid line, but rather will move regions *by* grid increments. Here's a hypothetical situation that shows the operation of Relative Grid mode.

Taking a Break from the Tutorial Session File

Because this is a hypothetical example, this isn't based upon the Chapter 5 session files. Don't worry too much about following these steps by the letter—we'll pick up with the Chapter 5 session when we discuss Shuffle mode.

You have a couple of drum tracks, named Kick and Snare, with the kick on Beats 1 and 3. (Since the kick regions are right on the grid lines, Absolute Grid mode might well have been used.) Using Slip mode, you have dragged a single snare region onto the track and placed it a little to the right of the Beat 2 grid line (if you look at the Main time counter on the following graphic, you'll see that the region has been placed at 1|2|078) to give the beat a bit of a groove.

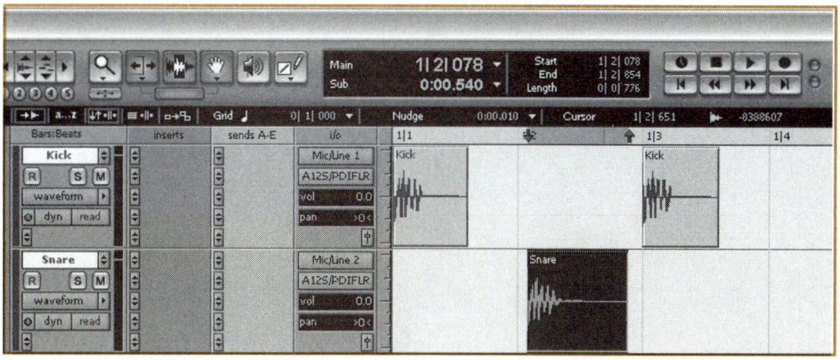

Now, you want to move that region to the fourth beat, but you also want to keep that same laidback feel and keep that distance from the grid line. Relative Grid mode will allow you to do this.

1. Click and hold the Grid mode button. The Grid mode menu will appear.
2. Choose Relative Grid from the menu shown. The Grid mode button will now be shown in purple and will read Rel Grid.

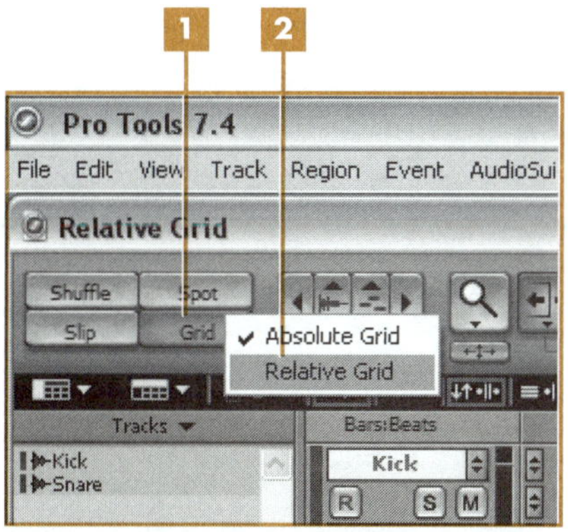

3. With Relative Grid mode selected, click and drag the region to its new position. You'll see that the region will be placed consistently *relative* to the nearest grid line.

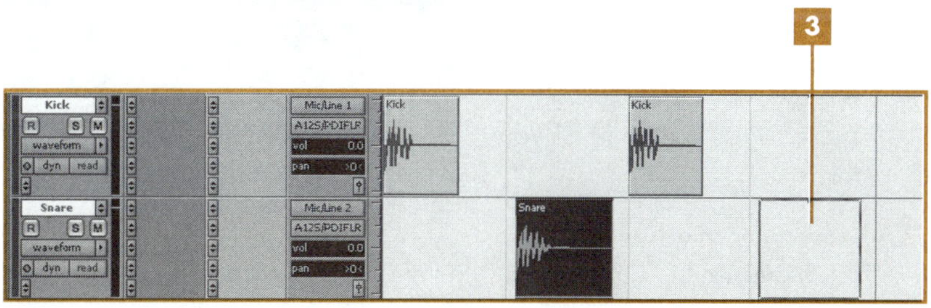

Using Shuffle Mode

Shuffle mode operates in a much different way than either Slip or Grid mode. In this mode, regions move end to end with each other. When you see how this mode works, you'll see how it can be useful for stitching together verses, choruses, and so on into a seamless final product!

Setting Things Up

Again, you should go ahead and delete the region that you've dragged onto the drum track while you worked with Grid mode—just hit the Delete key (assuming that the region is still selected). Also, you might want to zoom out a bit to see this mode in its best light.

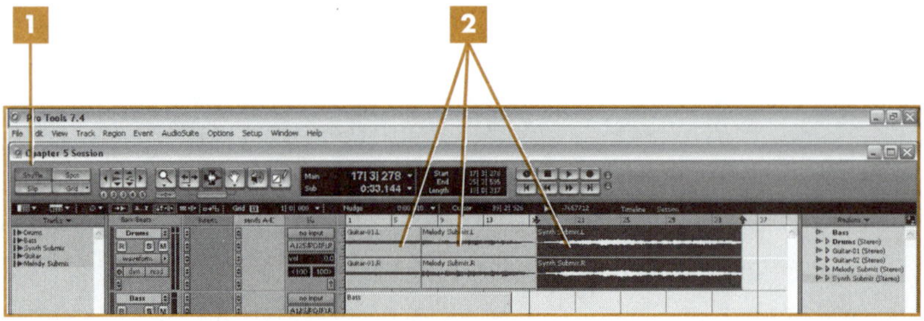

1 Click on Shuffle. The mode will be selected.

2 One by one, drag and drop various regions from the Regions list onto a single track. For the purposes of this demonstration, try dragging Guitar first, then Melody Submix, and finally Synth Submix. Wherever you drop these regions, they will snap end to end with the previous region, starting with the first region, which automatically snaps to the beginning of your track.

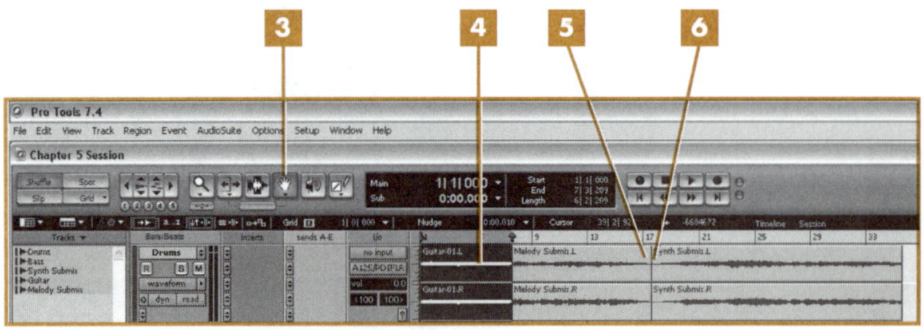

3 Now you can actually "shuffle" the regions a bit. Click on the Grabber tool. The tool will be selected.

4 Click and hold on a region. The region will be selected.

5 Drag the region over another region on the track.

6 When a dark line appears at the beginning of the preceding region, release the mouse button to drop the region. The regions will be reorganized.

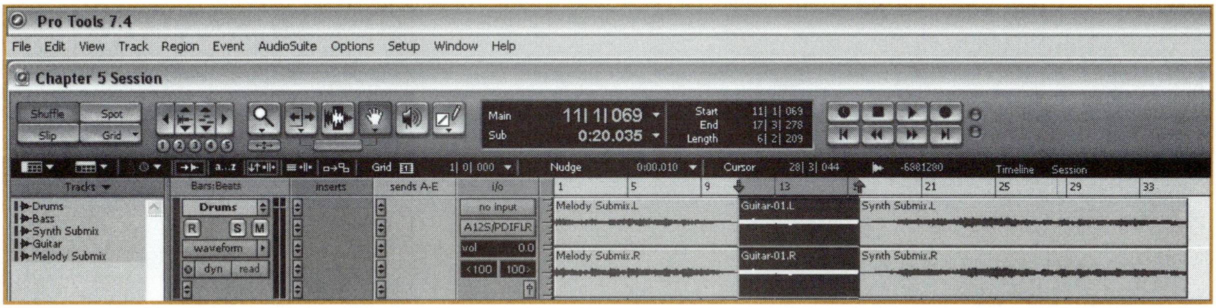

Note that all regions remain end to end, despite the fact that they have been moved. Of course, you can move more than one region at a time. In fact, you can shuffle regions forward and backward at will and create new arrangements of these regions, while keeping all the regions snugly end to end.

New Feature: Shuffle Lock

In some cases, users want to make sure that they *can't* enter Shuffle mode. If that fits with your workflow, it's easy to lock yourself out of Shuffle mode: While you're in any mode *other* than Shuffle mode, Ctrl-click (PC) or -click (Mac) on the Shuffle mode button. A small lock icon will appear in the lower-left corner of the Shuffle mode button. To unlock Shuffle mode, simply Ctrl-click (PC) or -click (Mac) on the Shuffle mode button again.

Using Spot Mode

You can use Spot mode when you want to assign a region to a specific numeric value. This is of particular use when you're assigning audio regions to sync with visual events in video production (also known as *spotting*). Although this mode lacks the freedom of motion of the other modes (by design), it is a quick way to place a region at a specific location.

Setting Things Up (Again)

Once more, you'll want to clear the drum track for this section. This time, though, you'll have to clear all your regions, and here's a quick way to do it: With the Selector tool, triple-click anywhere in the track you want to clear. All the regions in that track will be selected, and you can now remove them by pressing the Delete key.

1 **Click** on the **Spot button**.

2 **Select** a **region** and **drag it** onto an appropriate track.

3 **Release** the **mouse button** to drop the region on the track. The Spot Dialog box will open.

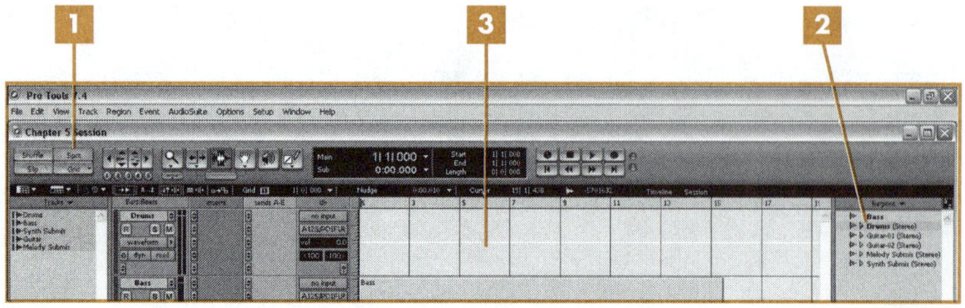

4 **Click** on the **Time Scale button** and **select** the **time scale** you want to use in positioning your region. (You can choose Bars:Beats, Min:Secs, or Samples.) The time scale will be selected.

5 You can choose to place your region's start, end, sync point (something we'll discuss in Chapter 10, "Moving to the Next Level: Tips and Tricks"), or even the duration. However, very often, you're most concerned about the start of the region, so let's try moving the region's beginning to a specific point in time. **Type** exactly **where you want your region to start** in the Start field.

6 **Click** on **OK**. The region will be placed on the track at the specified location.

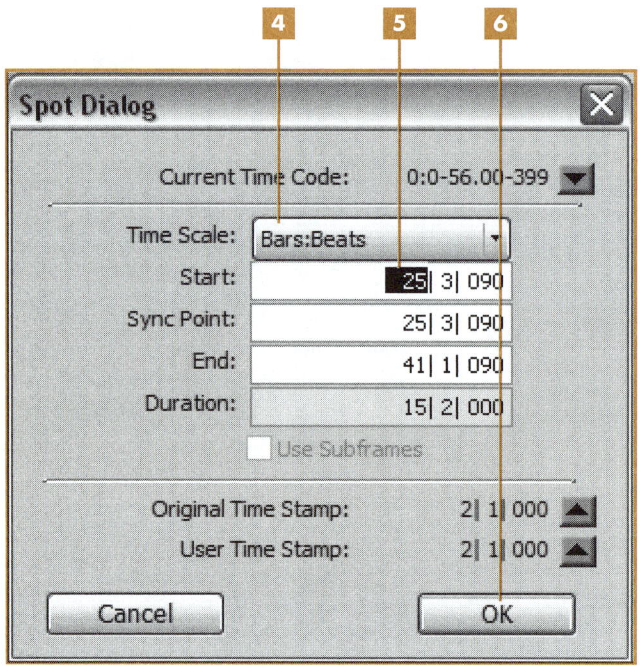

Basic Tool Functions

The three major edit tools you'll use when editing are the Trim, Selector, and Grabber tools. We touched on some of these functions earlier, but let's go just a little deeper before you start putting them into action. We'll take them on one at a time, from left to right.

Understanding the Trim Tool

The first tool to look at is the Trim tool. Its basic function is to change the leftmost or rightmost boundary of a given region.

> **Making Things Go a Bit More Smoothly**
>
> This tool can get a little tricky when you're working in Spot mode. Just for simplicity's sake, change your edit mode to Slip mode.

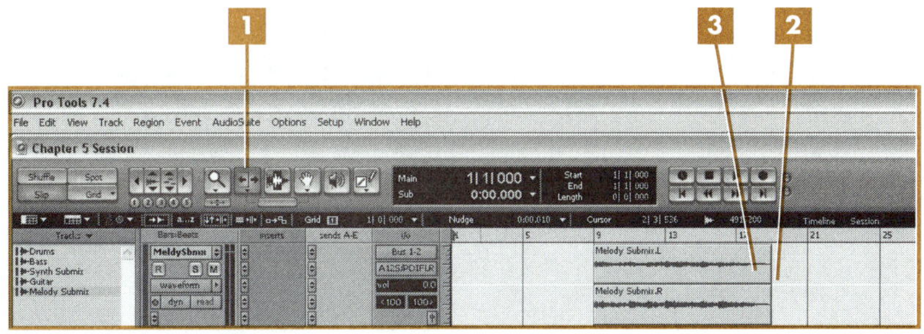

1. **Click** on the **Trim tool**. The tool will be selected.
2. **Position** your **cursor** at the beginning or end of a region. The cursor will take on the appearance of a bracket, indicating that you're using the Trim tool.
3. **Click and drag** the region's **edge**. The region boundary will change.

> **Some Notes on the Trim Tool**
>
> There are a few things to keep in mind when you're using the Trim tool:
>
> - Trimming a region is nondestructive. The fact that you're trimming the region only changes the part of the audio file you are choosing to use in your session.
> - Every time you use the Trim tool, a new region is created in the Regions list.
> - When you're in Grid mode, your trimming will snap to the current grid values.

Understanding the Selector Tool

You already used the Selector tool to select a segment of your session to play. You can do other things to selected areas in a session. For example, let's try removing several regions over a number of tracks.

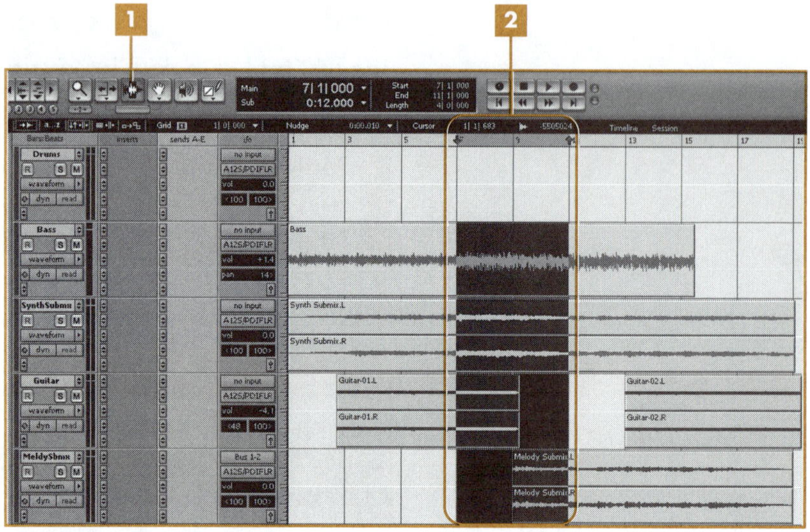

1 Click on the Selector tool. The tool will be selected.

2 Starting in one corner, click and drag a square area that includes regions you want to remove from your session. The regions will be selected.

3 Press the Delete key. The regions will be removed from your tracks.

The Power of a Nondestructive Environment

Remember that Pro Tools is a nondestructive DAW. The regions you clear from your tracks won't be removed from the Regions list or your hard drive. *Nondestructive* also means that you can easily undo what you've done (by choosing Undo from the Edit menu), which you should do *right now*!

New Feature: Link Track and Edit Selection

There's another way to easily make selections over a number of tracks or to move a selected area from one place to another. There's a new feature in Pro Tools 7, called Link Track and Edit Selection, which allows you to assign selections based upon track selections. In a nutshell, here's how it works:

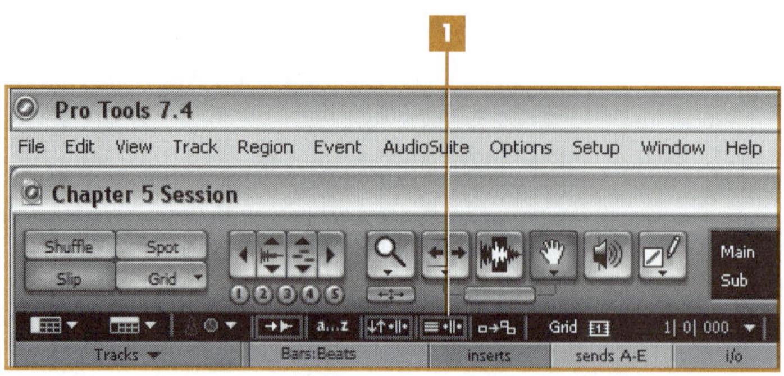

1 The first thing to do is to enable this feature. The Link Track and Edit Selection button is a small area just below the Trim tool. Just click it, and a blue box will be shown around the icon.

You'll notice the track that has a selected area is also selected.

2 To move the selected area to another track, simply click the desired track's name.

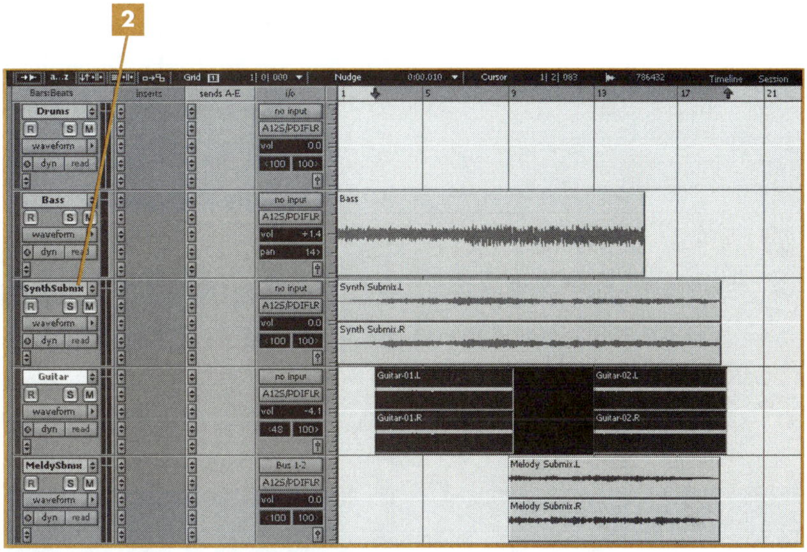

Here's what you get: The selection will be migrated immediately to the newly selected track.

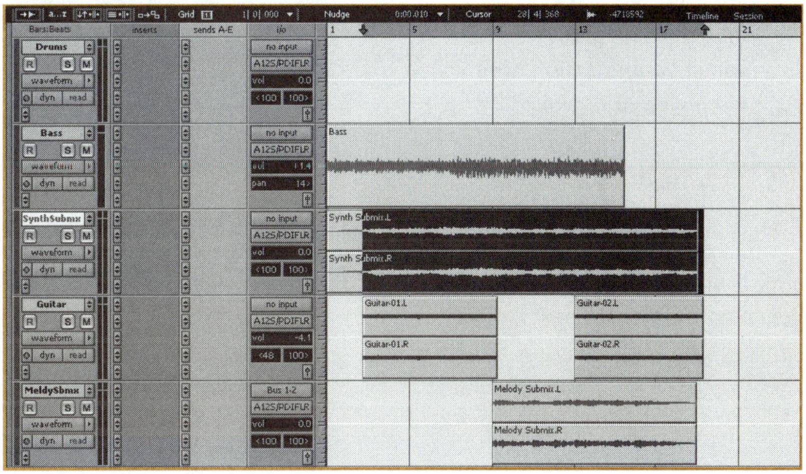

Selecting a Block of Tracks

If you want to select a block of tracks (and hence a selected area that spans those tracks), just hold down the Shift key when you click the tracks' names. If you want to add or remove selected tracks individually, just hold the Ctrl (PC) or (Mac) key while you click the track name.

Understanding the Grabber Tool

Finally, you get to the Grabber tool. You've used it before, but this section will show you how to move more than one region at a time.

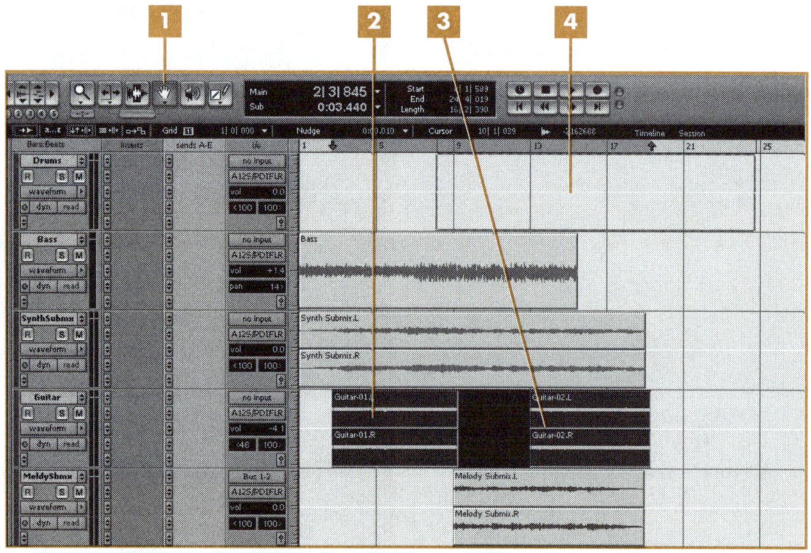

1. **Click** on the **Grabber tool**. The tool will be selected.
2. **Click** on a **single region**. The region will be highlighted.
3. **Press and hold** the **Shift key** and **click** on **additional regions**. The regions will be highlighted.
4. **Drag and drop** the **regions** you selected. Take care, though—all regions that fall within your selection area will be moved as a group!

Setting Things Up for the Next Section

Once more, please undo any changes you've made before progressing to the next section.

Grabbing a Block of Time

As you grab additional regions using the Grabber tool, a shaded area will appear. This area will include not only all the regions you directly selected, but also all regions that fall within that area.

Basic Editing Operations

Now you're going to combine a number of tools you've already learned to use with a few new tricks to re-create the bass line from the Chapter 1 session. In addition to tools from this chapter, you'll be drawing on some knowledge you picked up in earlier chapters. Put it all together, and you'll have a good idea of how to put together tracks of your own!

Capturing a Selection

Here's the situation: In this example, you have a reference track named Bass, which simply contains a single region. Your task is to reconstruct the Bass track from this single region.

1. Click on Grid. The Grid mode will be selected.
2. Click on the Selector tool. The tool will be selected.
3. Double-check the grid resolution to make sure it is 1 bar.
4. Select the first measure on the Virus Bass Audio track. The measure will be selected.

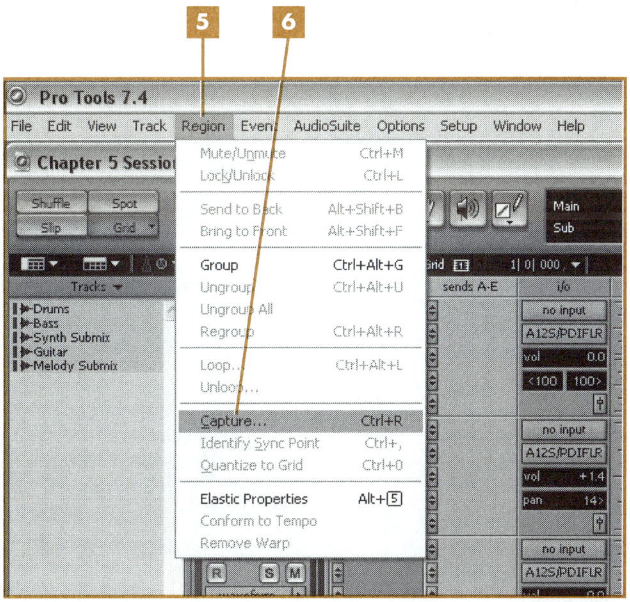

5. Click on Region. The Region menu will appear.
6. Click on Capture. The Name dialog box will open.

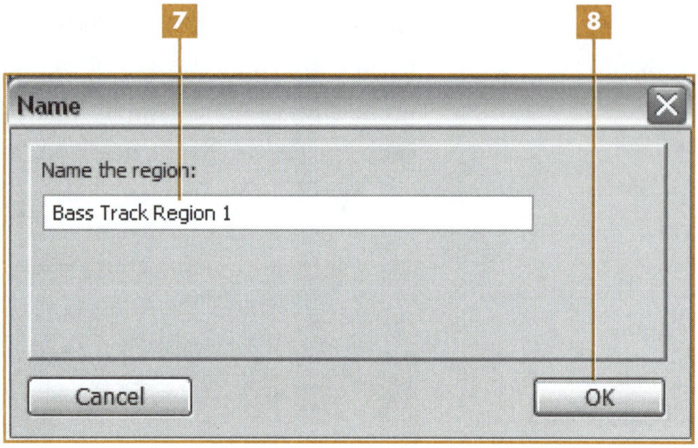

7 Type a descriptive name for the region you want to capture in the Name the Region text box.

8 Click on OK. The Name dialog box will close, and the new region and file that is a copy (or capture) of the area you selected will be created. You can see your newly created region in the Regions list (though it will not be placed on the track itself).

Separating a Region

Here's another way to create a region. This time, instead of capturing a selection, you're simply going to start chopping up your big region into smaller, more manageable regions. Visually, these two methods might appear quite similar, but by separating a region, you'll be creating a new region in the Regions list *and* in your track simultaneously.

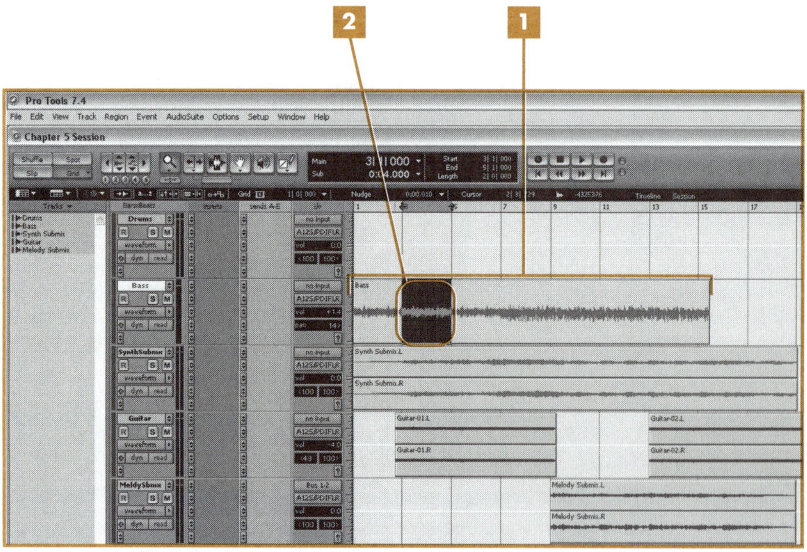

1 If you're working with the Chapter 5 session, double-click on the region named Bass to highlight it. Listen to the region alone to get an idea of how it sounds. You'll want to solo the track to hear it by itself. (See Chapter 3 for a refresher on how to solo a track.)

2 Select measures 3 through 5 on the Bass track. It's easy when you're in Grid mode with a whole-measure grid!

3. Click on Edit. The Edit menu will appear.
4. Click on Separate Region. Another menu will appear.
5. Choose the At Selection option. A new region will be created.

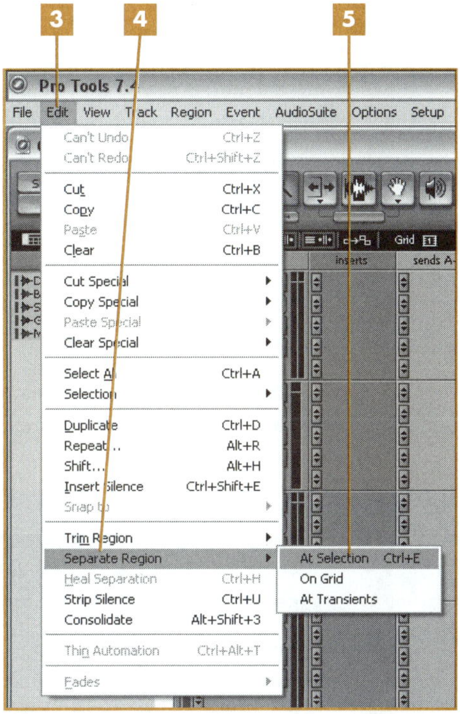

Auto-Naming Regions

At this point, Pro Tools might ask you to name your new region. You can disable or enable the Auto-Name feature by selecting the Setup menu, choosing Preferences, and then clicking on the Editing tab. You can select or deselect the Auto-Name Separated Regions field to enable or disable this feature, respectively.

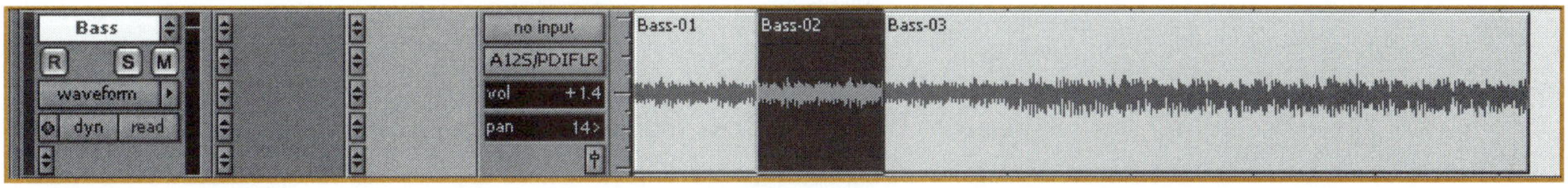

Your original region will be cut into three smaller regions. The region that matches your selection will be in the middle.

Constructing the Bass Track—Step One

If you're working with the Chapter 5 session and you're following the steps in this chapter, then you're well on your way to building the bass part from scratch. Good for you! Now you're ready to do some work on your own.

To get to the next step, you need to use either the Capture Region or Separate Region function to create the next three regions. To do so, follow these steps:

1. Import the Reference Bass track from the Reference Bass Track Session (in the Session 5 Import Materials subfolder). This will be your guide in rebuilding the bass track.
2. Listen to the region beginning at Measure 9 on the Reference Bass track. Find the section on the Bass track that matches it, and then capture or separate a region. Name this region Bass Part Reassembly 3 (if prompted for a name).
3. Repeat the same steps to create a new region that sounds like the one beginning at Measure 12 of the reference track, and name it Bass Part Reassembly 4 (if prompted for a name).
4. Finally, create a region that matches the region on the reference track that starts at Measure 15 and ends at Measure 20. (Keep in mind that this section is five measures long.) Name this region Bass Part Reassembly 5 (again, if prompted).

One last thing to keep in mind: Although capturing or separating will do the job as far as the session goes, there are differences in the way each function works. Capture will leave the original region intact on the Timeline and will create a new file in your Audio Files folder. Separating a region will alter the region in your track, and it won't create any new files in your session's Audio Files folder.

There are two different ways you can create the final region you need to build the Bass track—trim or crop.

Trimming a Region

There are two ways to trim a region. Because you're in Grid mode, trimming with the Trim tool is easy to do.

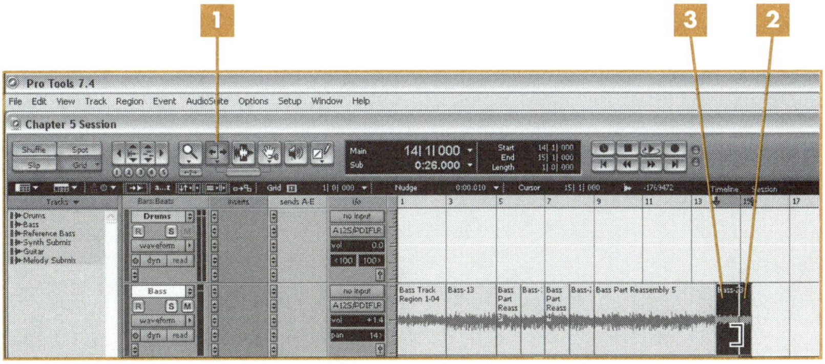

1. **Click** on the **Trim tool**. The tool will be selected.
2. **Click and hold** on the **region border** you want to change and **drag** the **boundary** to the desired location. As you drag, Pro Tools will indicate where the boundary is moving.
3. **Release** the **mouse button**. A new region will be created (but not a new audio file) with the new region boundary. For this exercise, you'll want the last region to be a one-bar audio region similar to the one shown here.
4. If necessary, **repeat Steps 1–3** for the other end of the region.

Here's another way to get the job done:

Getting Set for the Next Steps

Before you can re-edit this region to get the same results, you need to undo the trimming you just did. You can access the Undo function from the Edit menu, or you can use the shortcut keys (Ctrl+Z on a PC and ⌘+Z on a Mac).

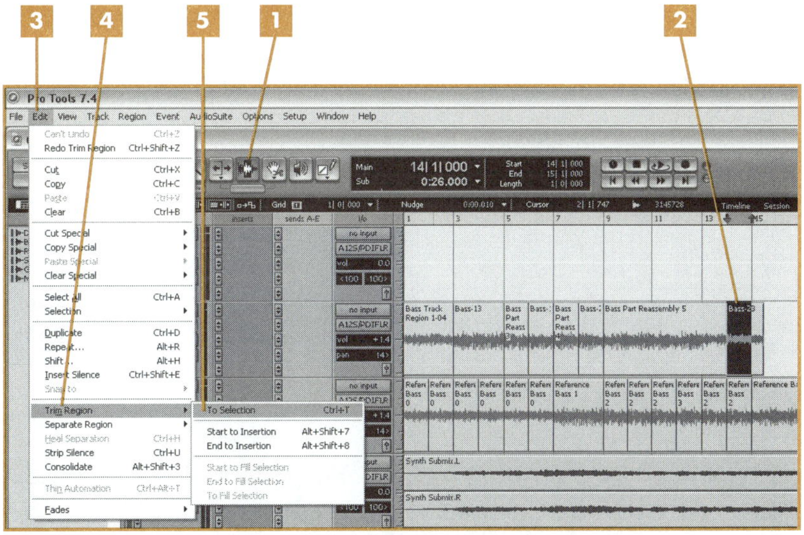

1. **Click** on the **Selector tool**. The tool will be selected.
2. **Select** the **area** of the audio region that you want to retain.
3. **Click** on **Edit**. The Edit menu will appear.
4. **Click** on **Trim Region**. The Trim submenu will appear.
5. Because you've made a selection (as opposed to setting a Timeline insertion point), the option you'll want to use is To Selection. **Click** on **To Selection**. The region will be trimmed to your selection.

Renaming a Region

When you're finished (with any of the edit processes we've discussed), you might want to rename the regions you have created. Here's how to rename any region:

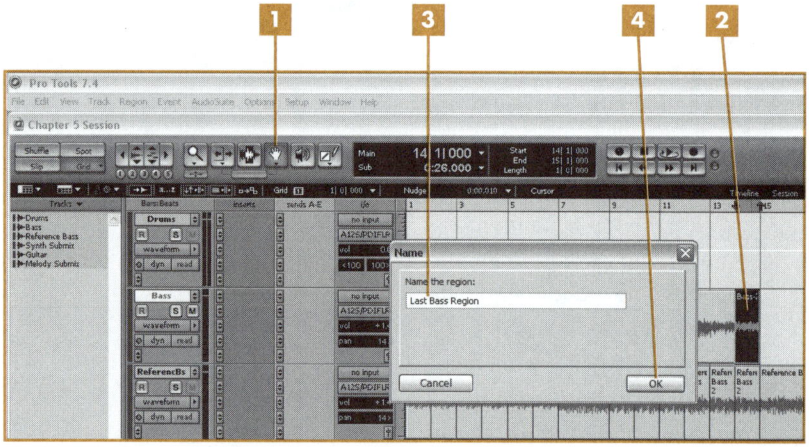

1. **Click** on the **Grabber tool**. The tool will be selected.
2. **Double-click** on the **region** you want to rename. The Name dialog box will open.
3. **Type** the **name** you want for the region in the Name the Region text box.
4. **Click** on **OK**. The Name dialog box will close, and the region will be renamed.

Assembling a Track

After you've created regions, the next step in the process is to organize them on the track. Of course, what you've already learned about the edit modes will aid you greatly in this process, but there are a couple additional tricks that can make the process even easier!

> **Constructing the Bass Track—Step Two**
>
> If you're following the examples shown here, you will want to select all remaining regions on the Bass track and remove them from the track, leaving a blank track on which to assemble your newly created regions.

Working in Shuffle mode makes the job easy!

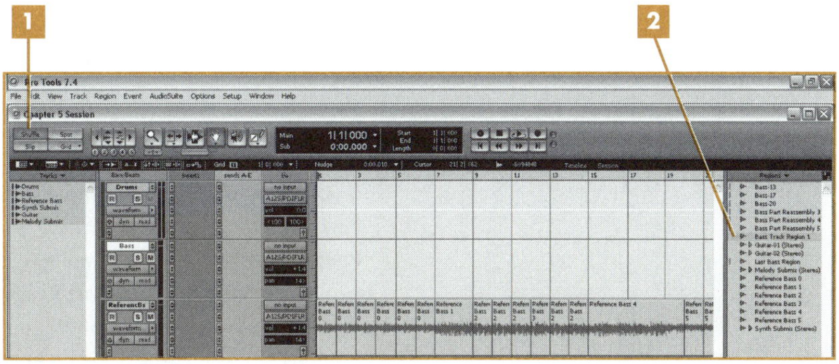

1 Click on Shuffle if you're not already in Shuffle mode.

2 One by one, drag regions onto the desired track in the order that you want them to be played back.

Constructing the Bass Track—Step Three

If you're following the example, drag Bass Track Region 1 onto the track six times, and then find the region that matches the region on the Reference track at Measure 7 (you'll have to use your ears!) and drag it onto the track once. Remember from earlier in this chapter that in Shuffle mode, it doesn't matter where you drop your regions—they'll automatically move to the edge of the preceding region.

Duplicating Regions

Of course, you *could* just drag the same region onto a track over and over and have a repeating loop, but that can get really boring very quickly. Here's another way to make a copy of a region or selection and place it after the original:

1 Drag and drop a single region onto a track, or otherwise select a region.

2 Click on Edit. The Edit menu will appear.

3 Click on Duplicate. The region will be copied immediately after the preceding selection.

Duplicate Shortcut

The shortcut for the Duplicate function is Ctrl+D on a PC and ⌘+D on a Mac.

Finishing Up the Bass Track

If you're following the example shown, you'll want to duplicate Bass Part Reassembly 3 (with manual renaming) two times, and then add Bass Part Reassembly 4 at Bar 12. Finally, you'll add Bass Part Reassembly 3 another two times, and then Bass Part Reassembly 5. Then you'll be ready to continue. If you have Auto-Naming enabled, you'll have to audition the regions in the Regions list [you can do this by holding down the Alt key (PC) or the Option key (Mac) and clicking and holding on the desired region's name], and really use your ears (which is a *great* way to practice!).

Repeating Regions

Repeating regions is similar to duplicating regions, but with a twist.

1. Drag and drop a single region onto a track or otherwise select a region. In this case, you'll want to place the Last Bass Region onto the end of your Bass track.
2. Click on Edit. The Edit menu will appear.
3. Click on Repeat. The Repeat dialog box will open.
4. Type the number of times you want the region to repeat in the Number of Repeats text box. (In this case, type 8.)
5. Click on OK. The selected region will be repeated the specified number of times, just as if you had used the Duplicate command a number of times.

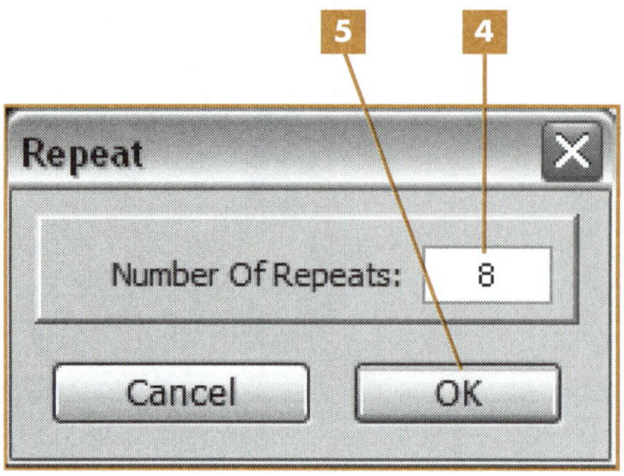

6 Solo both bass tracks (if you haven't already) and play them together. The tracks should sound identical. If they do, then you're finished! (If they don't, then it's time to take a close look at the reference track and the track you just created to find where they disagree, and then redo the necessary steps in this section.)

Working with Grids

Hopefully by now you're getting a good idea of the usefulness of working in Grid mode. However, using a grid as wide as a whole measure might not work for you in all situations. You can change the grid and see the possibilities.

If you've listened closely to the melody track, the timing seems a bit off. The good news is that the tempo isn't the problem—the notes have just been shifted—so we can still use the Grid mode, but we'll need to make a finer adjustment than a whole-measure grid can accomplish. Read on . . .

1 Click on the arrow next to the Grid value. The Grid menu will appear.

2 Select the scale (for example, Bars:Beats or Min:Secs) if you want to change the scale of your grid. If you want to continue in the same scale, click on the Grid value you want. To fix the melody track, you can choose an eighth-note value. The grid will immediately change in the Edit window.

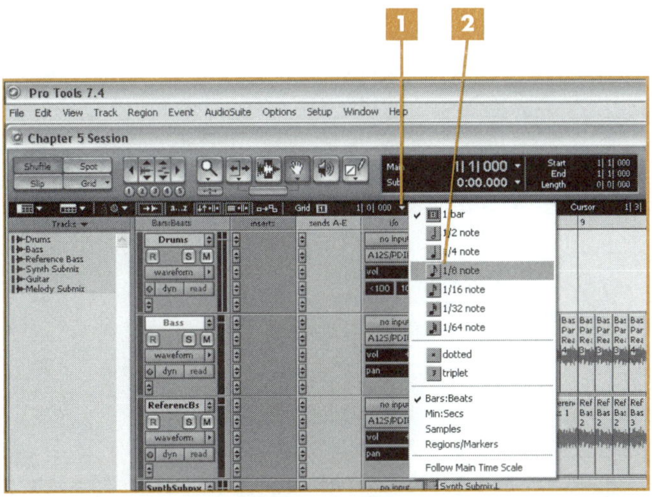

3. **Click** on **Grid** if you're not already in Grid mode.
4. **Drag** the **Melody Submix region** one eighth note earlier. As you drag the region in the track, the region will move in different increments and allow you to drop your region at different locations. This region will sound a *lot* better if it begins at 8|4|480.
5. **Drop** the **region** at the desired location. The location, as well as the start, end, and length of the selected region, will be shown in your location displays.

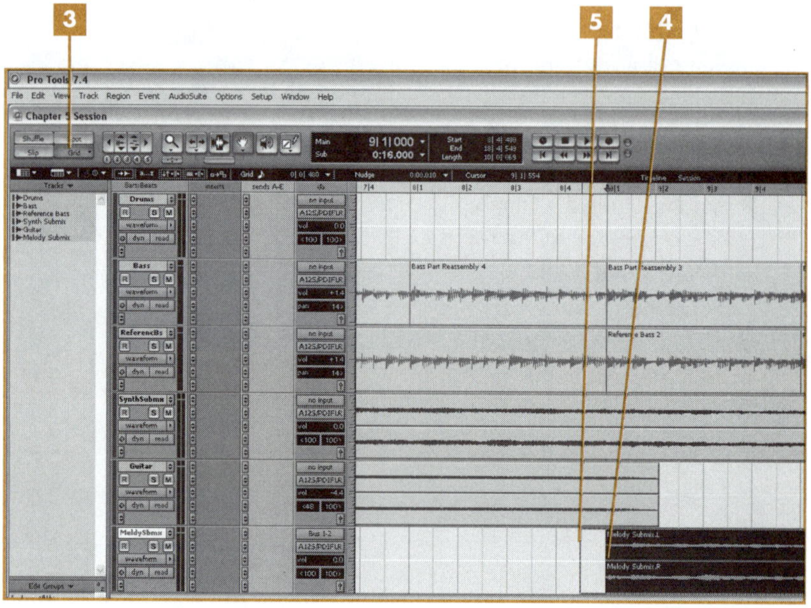

Cutting, Copying, and Pasting

Cut, copy, and paste are pretty tried-and-true staples of most audio software, and Pro Tools is certainly no exception. These processes are very straightforward and easy to use.

Copying a Region

Copying a region can be quite useful—and easy!

1. **Select** the **region** you want to copy.
2. **Click** on **Edit**. The Edit menu will appear.
3. **Click** on **Copy**. The region will be copied to the clipboard.

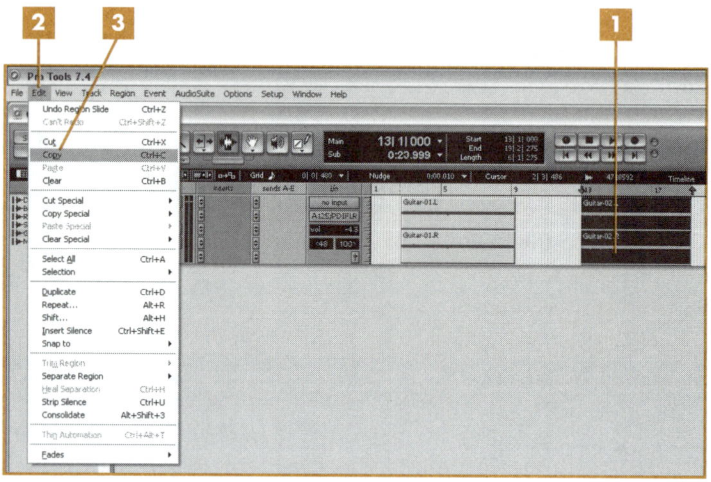

Selecting an Entire Region

One of the easiest ways to select a region is to double-click on it if you are using the Selector tool. You can also single-click on the region if you're using the Grabber tool.

Copy Shortcut

The shortcut for the Copy command is Ctrl+C on a PC and ⌘+C on a Mac.

Pasting a Region

A copied region means nothing until it's pasted to a new location. Here's how to do this:

1. Click on the Selector tool if it's not already selected. The tool will be selected.
2. Click in a track at the location where you want to paste the region you copied.
3. Click on Edit. The Edit menu will appear.
4. Click on Paste. The region will be pasted at the location you selected.

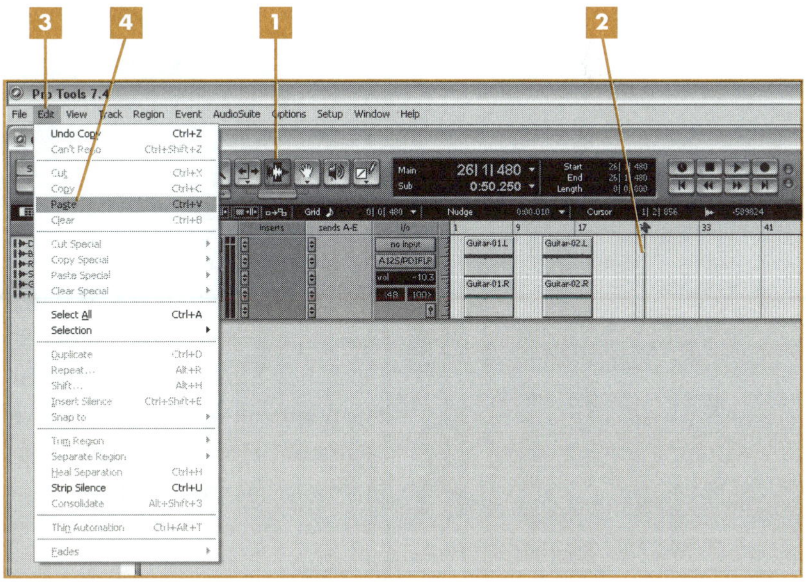

Paste Shortcut

The shortcut for the Paste command is Ctrl+V on a PC and ⌘+V on a Mac.

Cutting a Region

Because you're not going to use that region, go ahead and cut it.

1. **Select** the **region** you want to cut. The region will be selected.
2. **Click** on **Edit**. The Edit menu will appear.
3. **Click** on **Cut**. The region will be cut and placed on the clipboard.

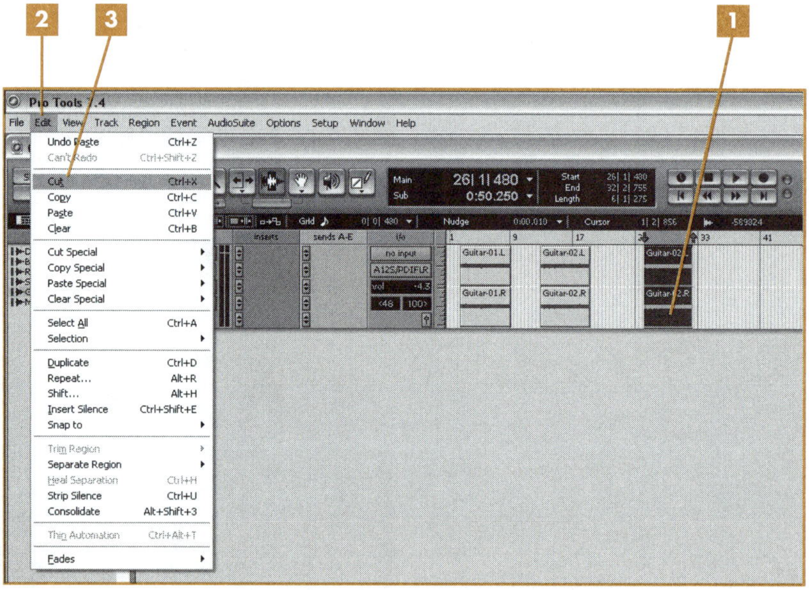

Cut Shortcut

The shortcut for the Cut command is Ctrl+X on a PC and ⌘+X on a Mac.

Working with Overlapping Regions

From time to time, you'll have occasion to move one region so that it partially blocks another region. This is absolutely not a problem—it happens all the time—but there are some things you should be aware of beforehand. First, you will only ever hear the region "in front," meaning that you won't hear both audio regions play together. Second, this sort of action is nondestructive, meaning that when you move the region "in front" out of the way, you'll see the region underneath unchanged.

Before we wrap up this chapter, let's take a look at how you can view and manipulate overlapped regions.

Now's a Good Time to Save Your Work

We're going to work with the Guitar track a little bit to show how overlapped regions work, but you don't want to keep this work. If your session sounds good (and it shouldn't sound too bad if you've been following this chapter), you should save your work before moving on with this section.

First, let's take a look at the standard behavior of overlapped regions:

- Drag a region over another region using the Grabber tool (in this case, the second of the Guitar regions over the first), and you'll notice that when you play back the track, only the region (and portions of regions) that are immediately visible will be heard.

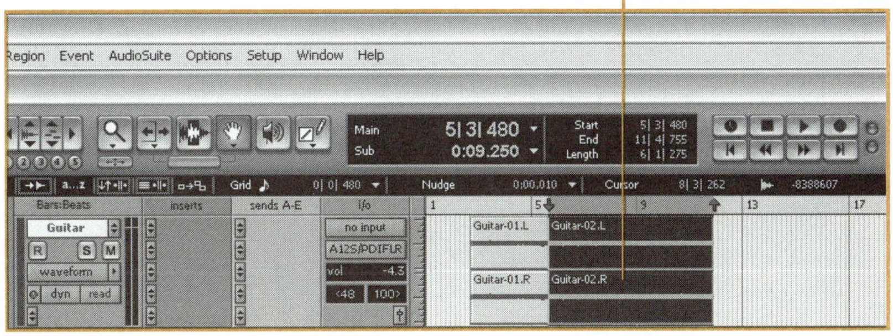

- Move the region on top out of the way, and you'll see that the region that has been partially blocked hasn't changed at all!

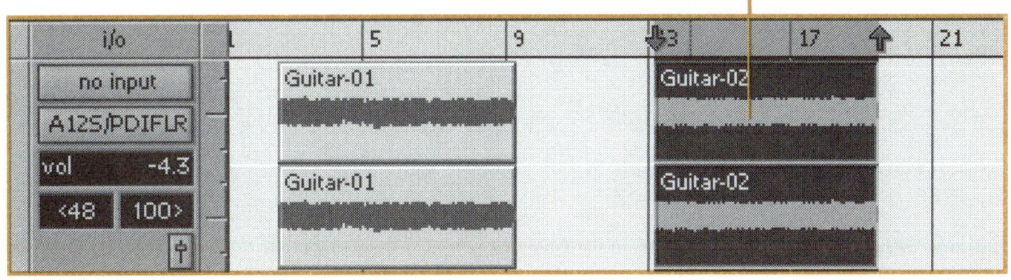

Overlapping Regions' Behavior

If only one region boundary overlaps another region, then you'll see the same nondestructive behavior that is shown above. If, however, a smaller region is dragged completely over a larger region and dropped (in other words, both region boundaries are overlapping), a hole will be left when that smaller region is moved away again. This is still fundamentally nondestructive, because you can use the Trim tool to reveal any material that is taken off the Timeline.

Often, it's hard to visually determine which regions are overlapping and which are simply next to each other. It would sure be easier if there were some sort of visual cue to show an overlap situation. No sooner said than done.

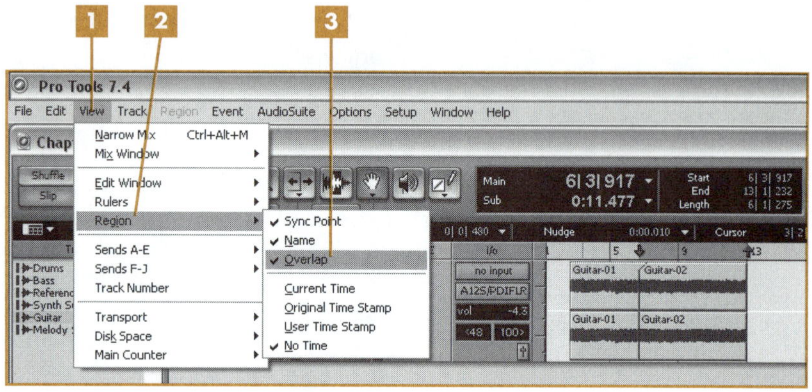

1. Click the View. The View menu will appear.
2. Click on Region. Another menu will appear.
3. This menu is a checklist of region-related aspects that can be shown or not shown. Click the Overlap menu item. (It will appear checked.)

Note that now you'll see a small bevel in the overlapping upper corner of a region that is covering another region.

But wait, there's more! What if you want to change the way the regions are overlapped *without* moving either of the regions?

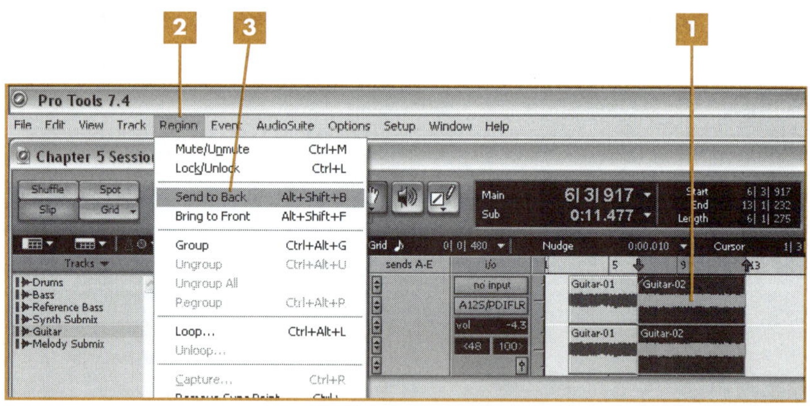

1. Select the region in front.
2. Click on Region. The Region menu will appear.
3. Click Send to Back. The region will be moved *behind* the first region and will be partially covered by it. Here again, you will not hear any audio except what is "in front," and there will be a beveled upper corner to indicate the overlap (though now it is in the first region, indicating that it is covering another region).

You can similarly choose a region that is in back and choose Bring to Front from the same menu. In either of these ways, the relationship between these two overlapping regions can be reversed, while leaving their timing untouched.

That's it for beginning editing! Now on to some of the more tweaky features!

6 . . . And More Editing

Although the editing power of a DAW ranks high in the production world, the editing process itself can sometimes be lacking in the way of glamour. A good editor knows that the job of editing essentially boils down to simple functions done many, many times. In the editor's world, patience is a virtue, and it is put to the test when you cut and paste, drag and drop, and perform like functions repeatedly. Indeed, it's not uncommon for a professional editing session to involve hundreds of individual editing operations!

The good news is that you already learned the basics of editing in Chapter 5 (cleverly named "Editing"). Now you're going to learn more efficient and flexible ways to work and expand upon the basic editing tools you've already begun to use. The idea behind these techniques is that the time you save with each editing function will add up, saving you a sizable amount of time by the end of the day. Better yet, by mastering these new processes, you'll not only save time, but you'll also become a better and more creative editor! In this chapter, you'll learn how to:

- Navigate your session with greater ease
- Use and customize the zoom tools
- Use the variations of the Trim and Grabber tools
- Boost your editing efficiency by using the Smart tool
- Put new region-based features (region looping, Region Groups) to use in your session

More Organization: Memory Locations

As your session gets more complex, organizing and navigating through the maze of regions and tracks will become more and more of an issue. Also, when you move on from the editing phase to the mixing phase, it will be a little more difficult to navigate through your session if you're only looking at the Mix window. You won't have the convenience of clicking on a specific time on a track and moving your Timeline insertion there (although you will still have the Transport window when you want it). The good news is that you can make navigation more than a little easier by setting up a few memory locations.

Memory locations are presets you can recall at the touch of a button, similar to the zoom presets you created in the last chapter. In this case though, you can recall specific selections, locations, zoom settings, and more!

Using the Tutorial Session

For this section, please use Chapter 6 (pt. 1), included on the disc that came with your book. Remember, you'll want to copy the folder to a location on your computer's hard drive before working on it.

Creating a Memory Location

Before you can use memory locations, you have to create them!

1. Click on Window. The Window menu will appear.
2. Click on Memory Locations. The Memory Locations window will appear.

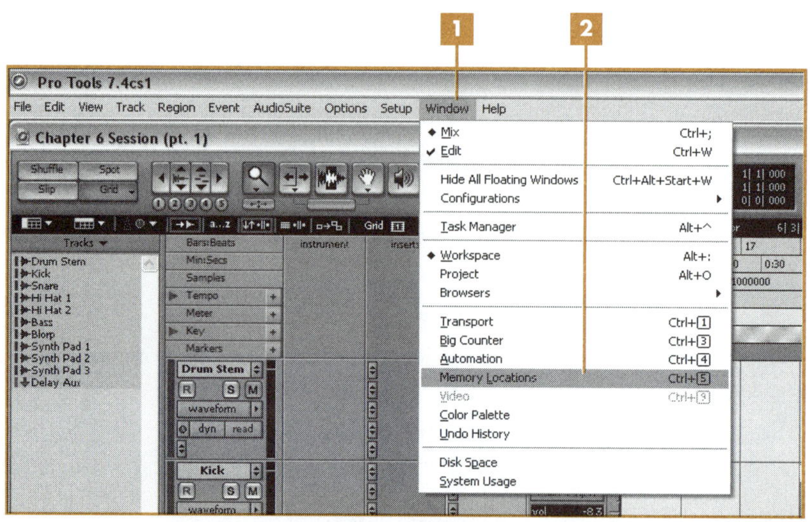

3 Using the Selector tool, place your Timeline insertion at a significant point in your session. In this case, I've placed it at the beginning of Measure 17, where the "blorp" starts. For this example, also set up any zoom levels, track show/hide settings, and track heights that you want to recall. (Refer to the next figure to see how I've set up my window, as a point of reference.)

4 Click on the Memory Location Menu button in the Memory Locations window. A menu will appear.

5 Click on New Memory Location. The New Memory Location dialog box will open, allowing you to set up your memory location.

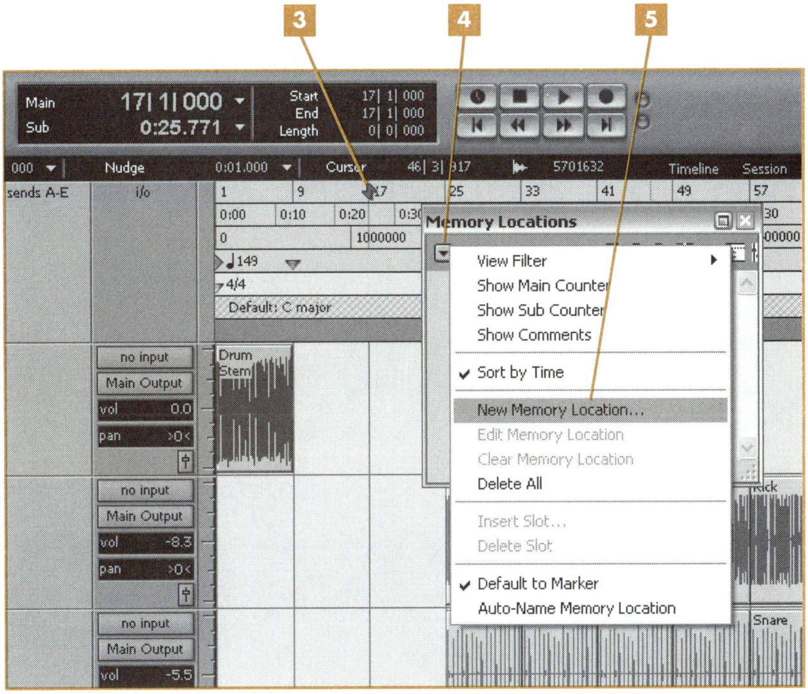

6 Select the time property that you want this memory location to recall. The choices are:

- Marker. The Timeline insertion will jump to a specific location when the memory location is chosen. This is the kind of memory location that I want for this example.
- Selection. A selected area will be recalled when the memory location is chosen.
- None. The Timeline insertion/selection will not change when the memory location is chosen.

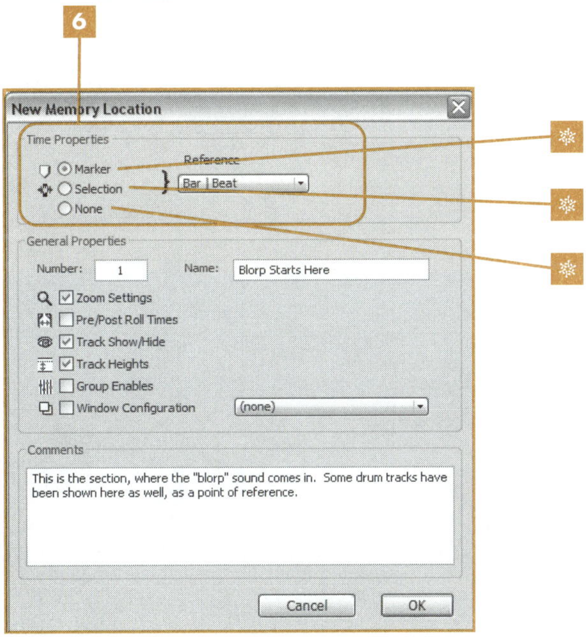

7 Type a descriptive name for this memory location in the Name text box.

8 Check the General Properties boxes that match the settings you want to be recalled with this memory location. The settings will be selected. In this case, when this memory location is recalled, the current zoom settings, track show/hide, and track heights will be recalled. Other characteristics, such as pre-/post-roll and group enables, will not change when you recall this memory location.

9 This is a newly added feature to Pro tools: Type a descriptive comment in the Comments field to describe or document what you've done.

10 Click on OK. Your memory location will be saved, and the New Memory Location dialog box will close.

11 Now try setting up another, different memory location. Select a different area (in this case I selected from Bar 65 to Bar 73), different zoom settings, track heights, and track show/hides, and this time enable a group.

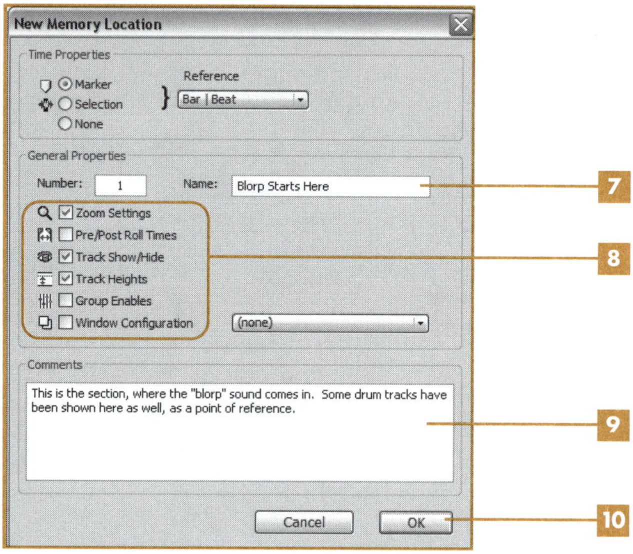

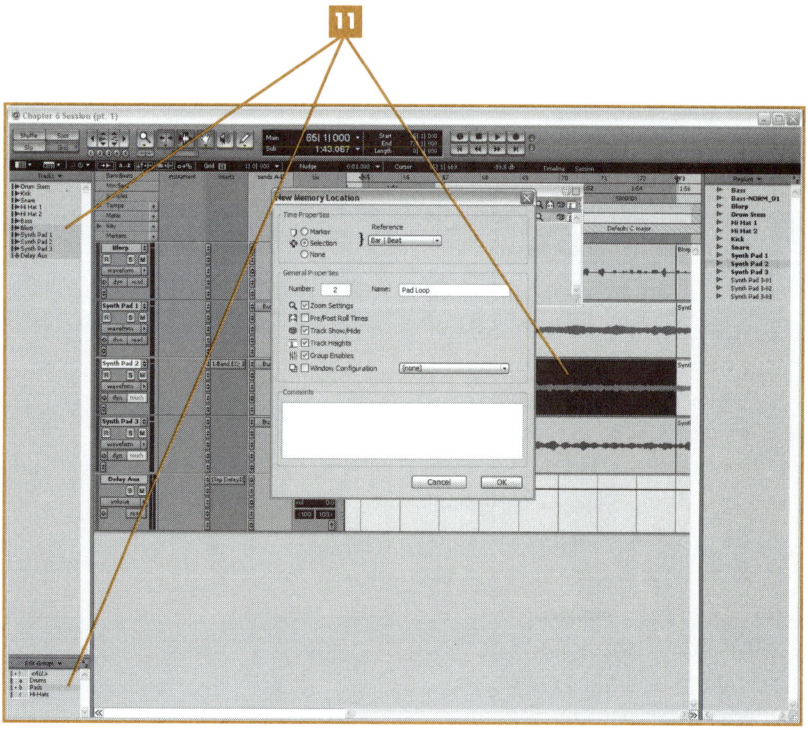

12 Create and set up a new memory location in the same way that you set up the first one (by clicking on the Memory Locations menu button, selecting Add Memory Location, and setting up the desired parameters of this new memory location). If you're following this example, choose the following settings:

- Selection Time Property. When this memory location is recalled, the selection will be as well.
- Zoom Settings selected.
- Track Show/Hide selected.
- Track Heights selected.
- Group Enables selected. This bit is different and will enable the currently enabled groups (in this case, Pads) when this memory location is recalled.

13 Click on OK when you're finished. The second memory location will be created, and the New Memory Location dialog box will close.

- By clicking on either memory location name, you will instantly recall its location on the time scale, as well as all included parameters, such as zoom settings and track show/hide.

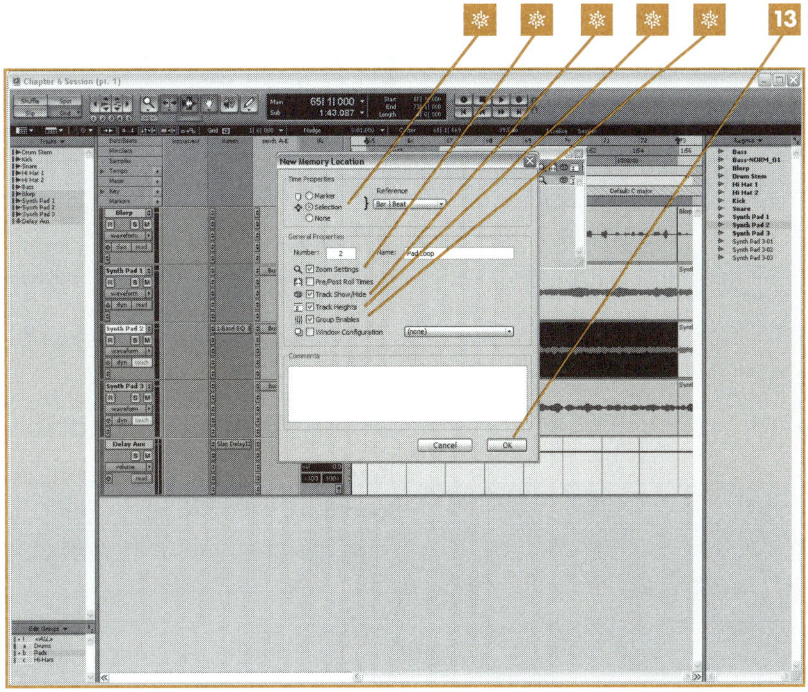

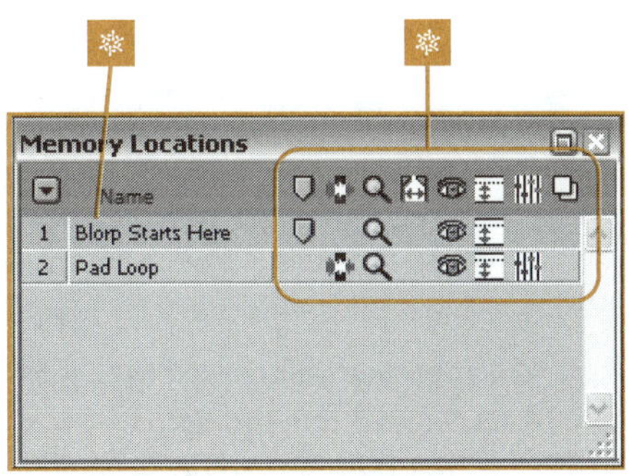

- If you forgot what parameters are enabled, just look to see what icons are included for each memory location. From left to right, the icons are Marker, Selection, Zoom, Pre-/Post-Roll, Track Show/Hide, Track Heights, Group Enables, and Window Configurations (something we'll talk about in just a few pages).

Memory Location Shortcut

You can recall any created memory location from your keyboard easily. On the Mac or PC, press the period key, then the number of the memory location you want to recall, and then the period key again.

Another Way to Create Memory Locations

You can also create memory locations as your session plays by pressing the Enter key on your computer keyboard's numeric keypad. After creating the memory locations on the fly, you can go back and edit them by right-clicking the desired memory location (PC), or double-clicking (Mac).

Using Memory Locations

Beyond this, there's no big mystery to creating and using memory locations; but before you jump into the Mix window, take a quick look at some of the other options open to you.

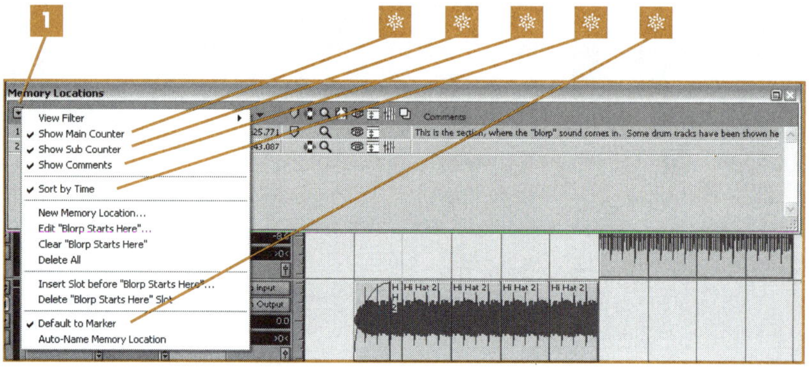

1. **Click** on the **Memory Location Menu button**. The menu will appear.

- When you select the Show Main Counter option, the location of each memory location in relation to the Main counter scale will be displayed (as shown at the top of the Edit window).
- When you select the Show Sub Counter option, the location of each memory location in relation to the Sub counter scale will be displayed (as shown at the top of the Edit window).
- When you select the Show Comments option, any comments you've entered for your memory locations will be shown.
- When you select the Sort by Time option, your memory locations will be sorted depending on how early or late they are in your session rather than by the order in which they were created.
- When you select the Default to Marker option, the Memory Location dialog box will be set to start off with the Marker option chosen.

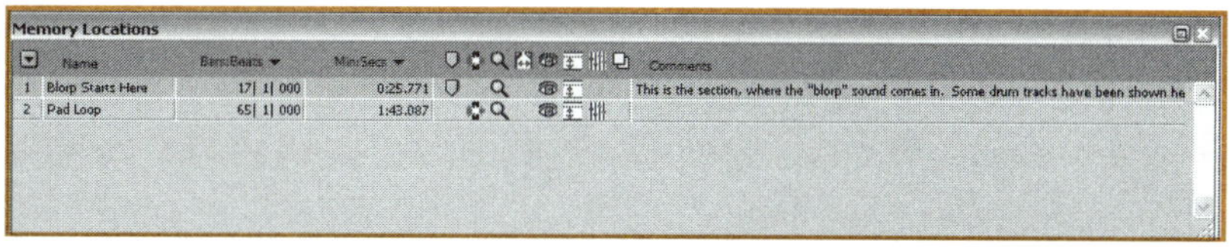

Here's what the window will look like when the two memory location counter options are selected, as well as the comments. Note the two new columns created, and their time scales reflect the currently selected Main and Sub counter scales. Each memory location's specific position is shown in these columns. Either or both of these two options can come in mighty handy, particularly when you're working in the Mix window, where it's harder to visualize your time position in your session.

New Feature: Inserting a Memory Location Slot

For those of you who have been using memory locations for some time already, you'll appreciate a subtle but useful new bit of functionality to the Memory Location window. The Insert Slot feature will allow you to create a new memory location *between* two other existing memory locations. Here's how it's done:

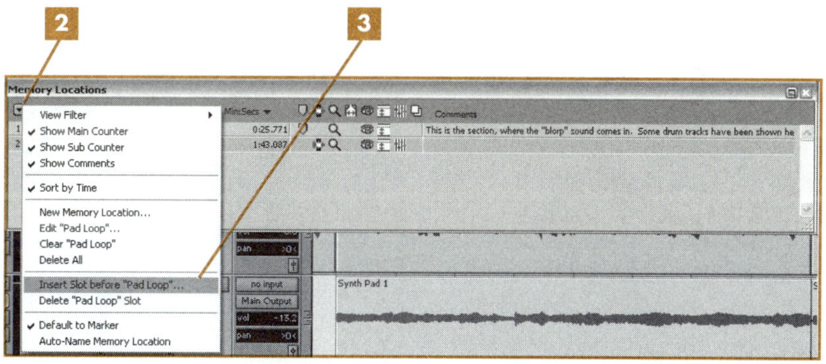

1. **Select** the **memory location** that you want to be *after* the new memory location. In this case, I've selected memory location #2, since I want to create a *new* slot #2 and move the existing slot to position #3.
2. After you set up your desired Memory Location settings (selections, zoom settings, track show/hide, and so on), **click** on the **Memory Location Menu button**. The menu will appear.
3. **Select Insert Slot before "[memory location name]"**. Once you click this menu item, the New Memory Location window will appear, and you'll be able to create the new memory location as usual. When you're finished, this new memory location will be inserted in the desired slot, and the appropriate existing memory locations will be moved to later slots.

New Feature: Window Configurations

In our Memory Location discussion, you may have noticed a property called Window Configuration, and wondered what the heck it is. Well, it's just what it sounds like—a recallable arrangement of windows that you can create to make your editing work go even more smoothly.

Creating a Window Configuration

Creating Window Configurations is even easier than creating memory locations. Here are the steps:

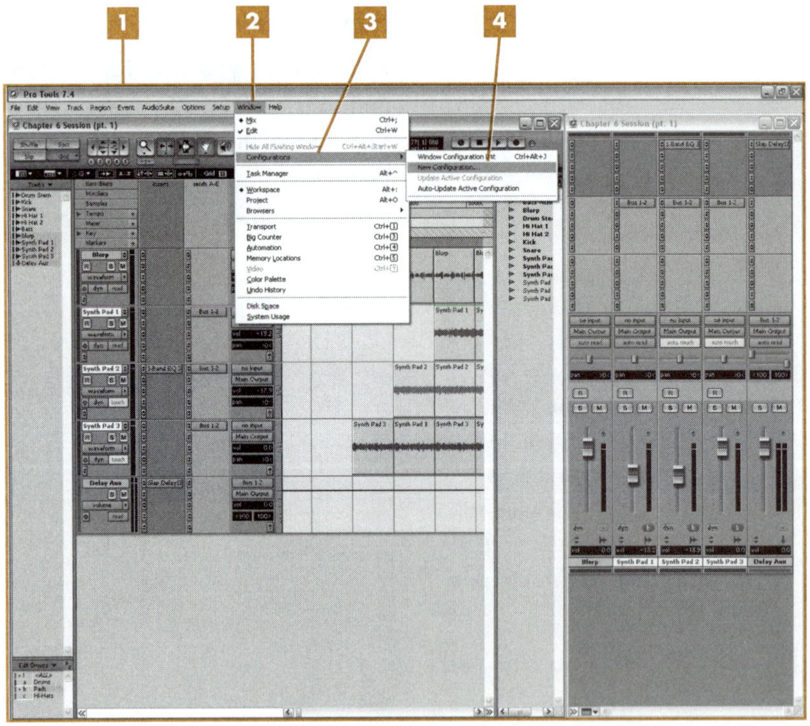

1. Arrange your windows in a desired configuration. For this example, I've resized and arranged my Edit and Mix windows so that I can see them both in a single monitor (a Window Configuration I use all the time, by the way).
2. Click the Window menu.
3. Click Configurations. A submenu will appear.
4. Because you want to create a new Window Configuration, click New Configuration. The New Window Configuration dialog box will open.

Now, you've got to choose what aspects of your layout you want to be able to recall. The choices are pretty simple:

- Clicking the Window Layout radio button will set up your Window Configuration to recall all the windows you see on your desktop, sized and positioned as they are right now.
- If you additionally check the Include Edit, Mix, and Transport Display Settings option, the view settings that you've chosen for these windows (things such as column show/hide settings) will also be recalled.
- The second main radio button will allow you to recall settings for only the Edit, Mix, or Transport windows. For example, if you *only* want to recall your ruler settings for the Edit window, you would click this radio button, and then select Edit Window Display Settings from the drop-down list to the right of the button. (Click on the arrow button to the right of the menu to reveal the options.)

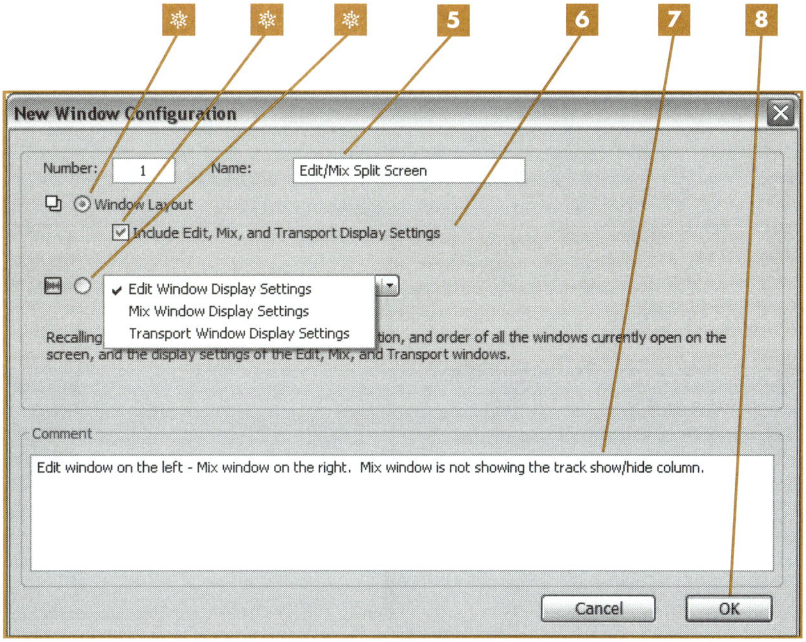

5. Type a name for your Window Configuration.
6. Choose the desired radio button. In this case, I want to recall the entire desktop, so I'll choose the first radio button.
7. This is an optional step, but a useful one: Type a description for your Window Configuration.
8. That's it—just click OK, and you're finished!

Recalling Window Configurations

Now that you've created your Window Configuration, you can recall it easily, much like a memory location. There are three main ways that you can do it:

1. Click the Window menu.
2. Choose the Configurations menu item. Again, a submenu will be shown.
3. At the bottom of the submenu, you'll see a list of all the session's windows locations. Just click the Window Configuration you want to recall.

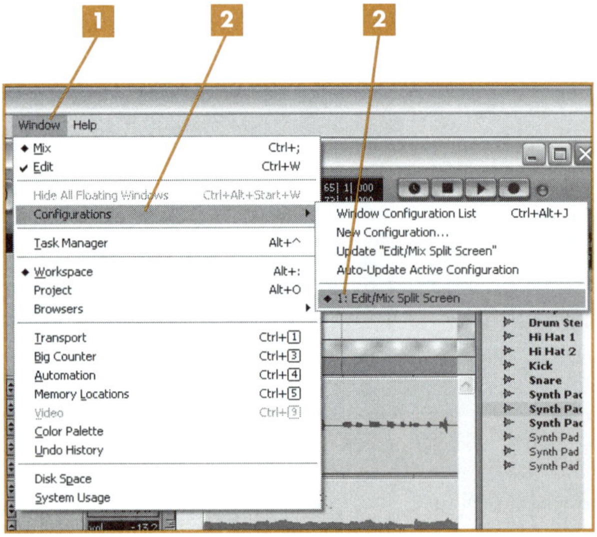

Here's another way:

1. Click the Window menu.
2. Choose the Configurations menu item. Again, a submenu will be shown.
3. Choose the Window Configuration List menu item. The Window Configurations window will appear.

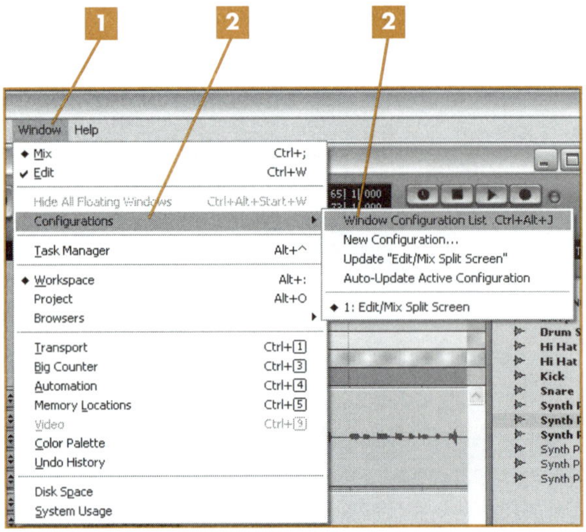

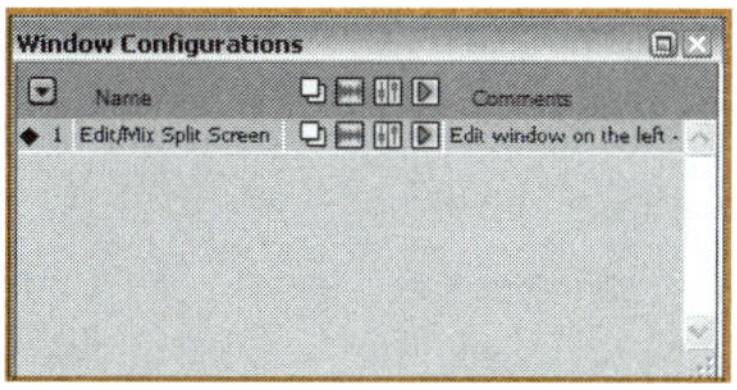

This window not only looks like the Memory Locations window, but it acts like it as well—just click the window location that you want to recall.

If that isn't easy enough, you can also recall a Window Configuration as a property of a memory location. Basically, this means that you can recall a Window Configuration just as you would recall zoom settings or a selected area! Here's how:

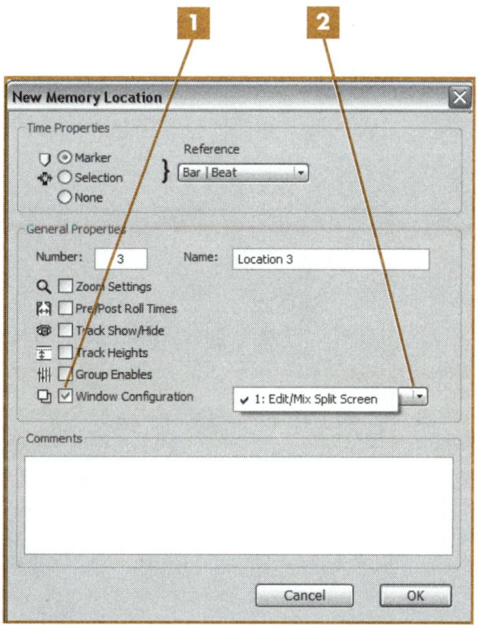

1. In the New Memory Location window, in the General Properties area, just click the Window Configuration item. This will recall a Window Configuration along with any other properties that you care to recall with any given memory location.
2. Which Window Configuration will be recalled? Any Window Configuration that you may have created can be recalled through a memory location. Just select the desired Window Configuration from the drop-down list to the right of the check box. (Click on the arrow button to the right of the menu to reveal a list of all the Window Configurations that you may have created in the session.)

Window Configuration Shortcut

Here's yet another way to recall a Window Configuration: On the Mac or PC, press the period key, then the number of the memory location you want to recall, and then the asterisk key.

Zoom

Zooming is not only one of the most basic things you'll do in any given editing session, it's also one of the most frequent things you'll do. Of course, the first step down the road of efficient zooming is to learn the shortcuts associated with basic zooming (refer to Chapter 5). The following sections will discuss other ways to zoom and how to use them.

Time to Change Tutorial Sessions!

For the remainder of this chapter, we'll take advantage of what you just learned about memory locations. Please download and use the Chapter 6 (pt. 2) session.

More Zoom Tools

Let's start from what you already know and work from there.

1 Click on the Zoom Out button. As you've seen before, your view of your session's Timeline will expand, and a longer duration will be shown in your Edit window. Note that all tracks, Audio and MIDI, are zoomed together.

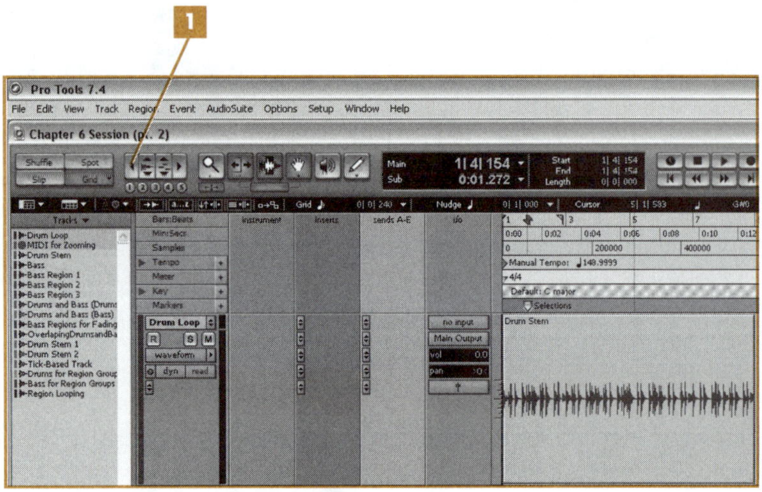

2 Click on the Zoom In button. Again, as you've seen before, your view will narrow in on a smaller slice of time with each successive click of the button. Again, you'll see that Audio and MIDI tracks are zoomed at the same rate. The Zoom In and Zoom Out buttons will allow you to zoom in on the time scale, and, although they won't affect the speed at which your session will play back, they will allow you to view your regions and data differently to suit different kinds of editing.

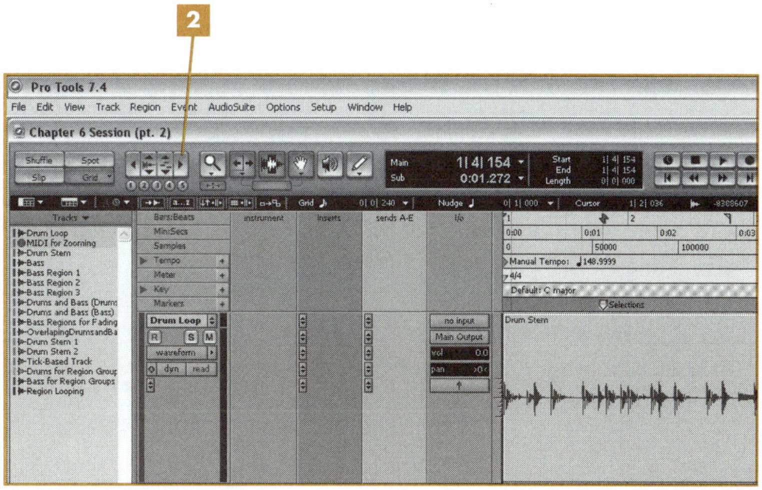

3 Click on the Audio Zoom Up button. With each click of this button your audio data will zoom up, allowing you to more clearly see low-level signals. Also, notice that all of your Audio tracks have zoomed up at the same time, but your MIDI data has remained unchanged.

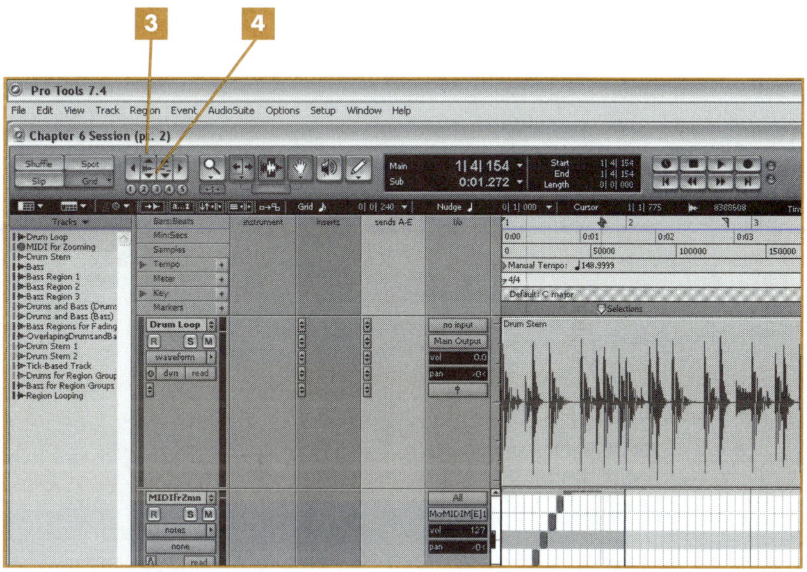

4 Click on the Audio Zoom Down button. The height of your audio waveforms will be reduced with each click of this button.

Vertical Zoom (Audio) Shortcut

Although this kind of vertical zooming is not quite as common as zooming in on the horizontal time scale, the shortcut keys are still useful to know. On the PC, it's Ctrl+Alt+] (right bracket) to zoom up and Ctrl+Alt+[(left bracket) to zoom down.

On the Mac, the shortcut is ⌘+Option+] (right bracket) to zoom up and ⌘+Option+[(left bracket) to zoom down.

5 Click on the MIDI Zoom Up button. With each click of this button, your MIDI data will zoom up, allowing you to more clearly see individual notes. Note that all your MIDI tracks have zoomed up at the same time, but your Audio tracks are unchanged when you click on this button.

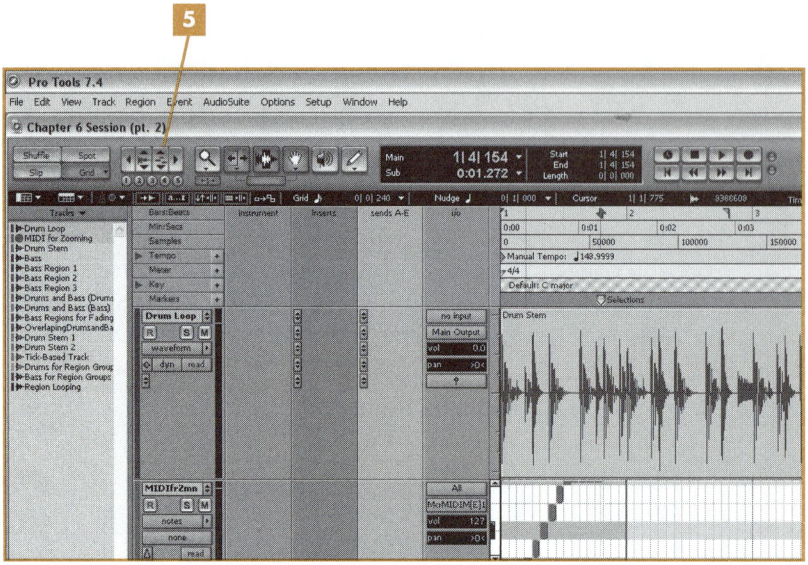

6 Click on the MIDI Zoom Down button. Your MIDI data will zoom down, allowing you to see a greater range of notes at one time in the Edit window.

As you zoom up or down, you will see less or more of the keyboard graphic on the left edge of each MIDI track. You can use this display as a reference point to see how broad (or narrow) of a tonal range you're viewing. Low pitches are displayed toward the bottom of each MIDI track, and high notes are toward the top. You can scroll up and down the MIDI note range by clicking on the up and down arrows at each end of the keyboard graphic.

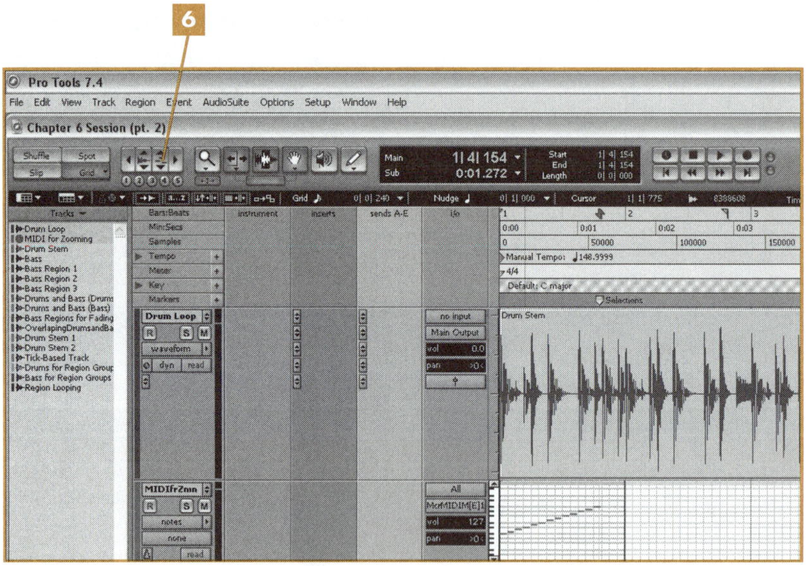

Vertical Zoom (MIDI) Shortcut

Here are the shortcuts for vertical zooming for MIDI data: On the PC, it's Ctrl+Shift+] (right bracket) to zoom up and Ctrl+Shift+[(left bracket) to zoom down. On the Mac, the shortcut for MIDI height zooming is ⌘+Shift+] (right bracket) to zoom up and ⌘+Shift+[(left bracket) to zoom down.

Zoom Presets

I'm going out on a limb with this comparison, but go with me on this. Take the average car radio. If you're a music lover, you probably use it quite a bit. On most car radios, there are a number of buttons (usually below the main display) that you can use to set the stations you listen to most often. Once you set them up, you can simply press an individual button and immediately jump to your favorite channel.

Many Pro Tools users find that, although they use all the zoom tools *a lot*, they tend to use certain zoom amounts more frequently than others. As on a car radio, you can set up your most common zoom presets and jump between them at the click of a single button. In fact, setting these presets is pretty similar to setting the presets on your car radio!

1 Click on either of the time (the vertical axis) zoom tools until you settle upon your most commonly used zoom setting.

2 Hold down the Ctrl key (PC) or the key (Mac) and click on the first Zoom Preset button. The button will flash briefly to let you know that the preset has been stored.

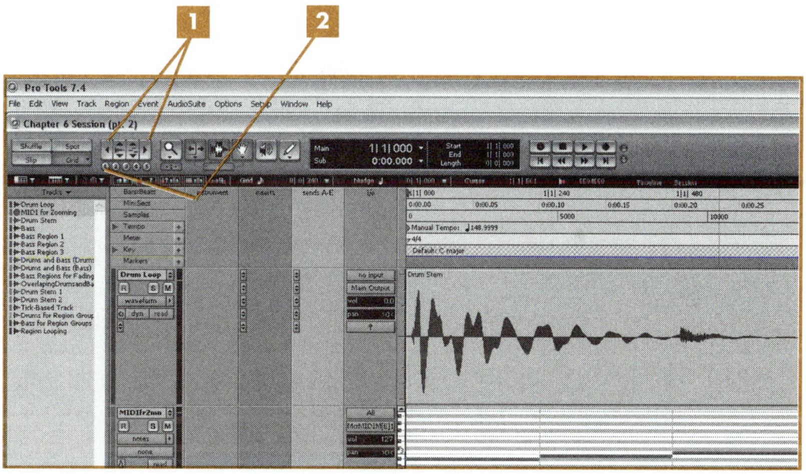

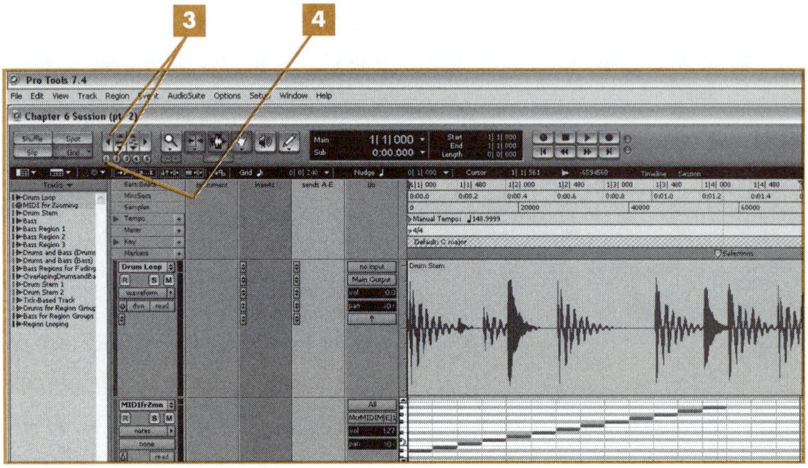

3 Repeat Steps 1 and 2 to set a preset for the second Zoom Preset button, using a different zoom level.

4 If you want to go back to your first zoom preset, click on the first Zoom Preset button. Your previously stored zoom preset will be immediately recalled.

From this point on, it's easy. Simply set the five presets for the five zoom settings you use the most. At that point, you can click on the Zoom Preset buttons to switch zoom settings, much as you would change favorite stations on your car radio.

Will Zoom Presets Recall Both Horizontal and Vertical Zoom Settings?

The Zoom Preset buttons will recall only the horizontal (time) zoom amount, not the vertical zoom levels for Audio and MIDI tracks.

Zoom Preset Shortcuts

The shortcuts to switch between your presets are pretty straightforward. Just hold the Start (Windows) button (PC) or the Control button (Mac) and press 1, 2, 3, 4, or 5 on your keyboard (above the alphabet section).

New Feature: Zoom Toggle

Over the last few versions of Pro Tools, Digidesign has added some new functionality to a feature called *zoom toggle*. Zoom toggle does just what its name would suggest—it allows you to quickly take a close-up look at a section and get back out to the previous zoom level. In truth, this feature has been a part of Pro Tools for some time, but with the new power that's behind it, it's very much like a brand-new feature!

Actually, using zoom toggle is very easy, using the Zoom Toggle button:

1. Using the Selector tool, make a selection of the audio or MIDI at which you want to take a closer look.
2. Click the Zoom Toggle button. The selection will zoom in according to the zoom toggle settings (which we will talk about in just a moment). The Zoom Toggle button will be shown with a blue color, to show that you are indeed zoomed in.
3. To zoom back out to your previous zoom level, just click the Zoom Toggle button again. You'll be zoomed back out, and the Zoom Toggle button will be displayed in its inactive grey color.

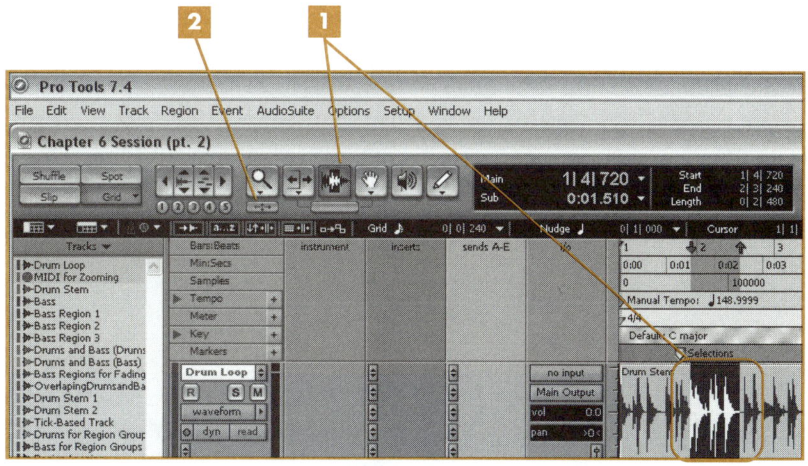

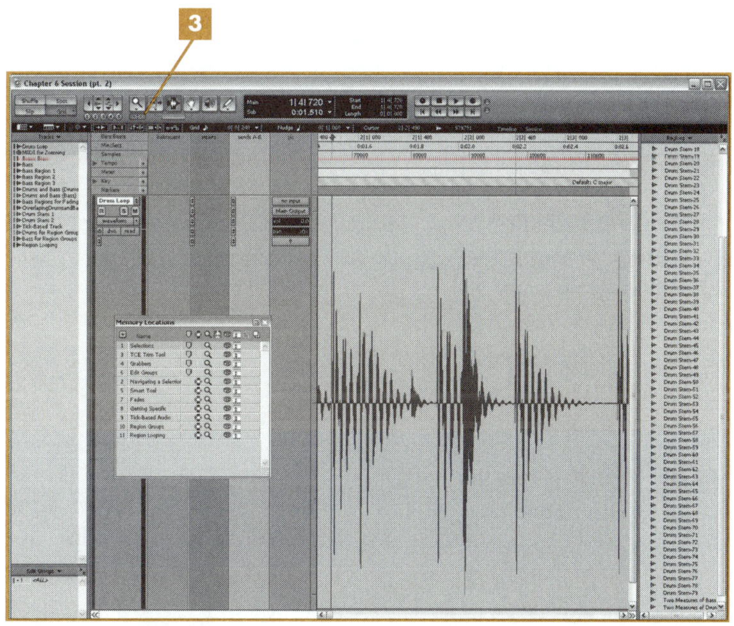

Zoom Toggle Shortcut

There is also a shortcut for zoom toggling: Just press Ctrl+E (PC) or ⌘+E (Mac).

What makes the zoom toggle function so interesting in these later versions of Pro Tools is the customization you can get through the setting of preferences. Here's how:

1. Click the Setup menu.
2. Choose the Preferences menu item. The Preferences window will appear:

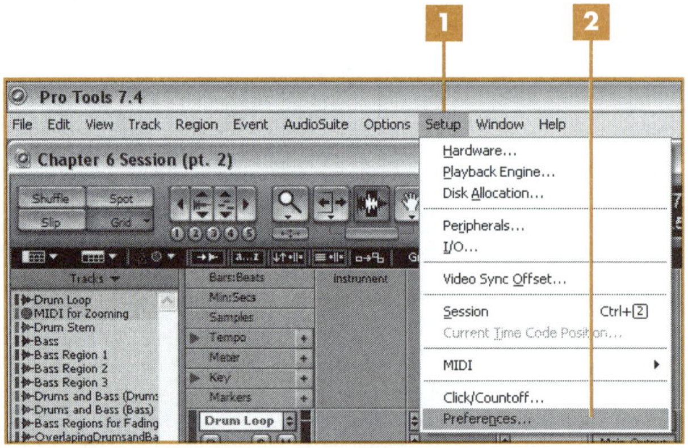

3. If your Preferences window isn't already showing the Editing page, click the Editing tab at the top of the Preferences window.

   The settings that you make here will determine just how the zoom toggle feature will behave when you engage it. The first set of choices you need to make is just how much you want to zoom in!

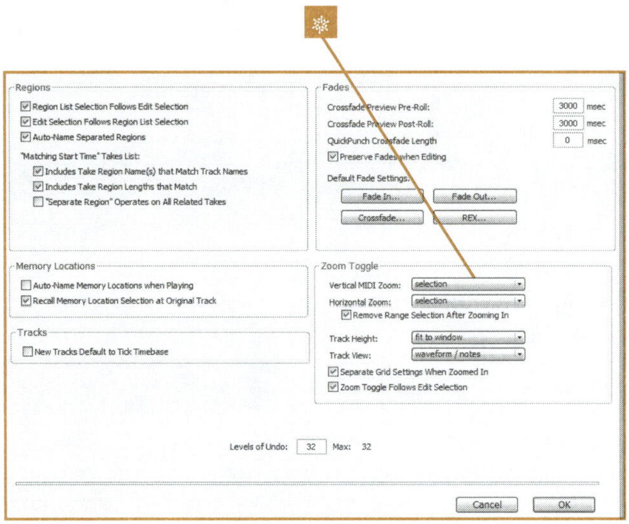

- The topic of MIDI is one that we'll be talking about later (in Chapter 7, "Using MIDI"), but for now it's sufficient to know that you can select individual notes in a way that is fundamentally different than the way you've made selections in Audio tracks. If you click the Vertical MIDI Zoom drop-down menu, you can control the zoom toggle behavior. You have two options in this list:
  - Selection. This option will allow you to zoom into only the note range that is currently selected in the Edit window.
  - Last Used. This option will recall the MIDI vertical zoom level that you used when zoom toggle was engaged. Practically speaking, this means that if you zoom toggle in, change your MIDI vertical zoom level, and then toggle out, the next time you engage zoom toggle, you will recall those last-used zoom settings.

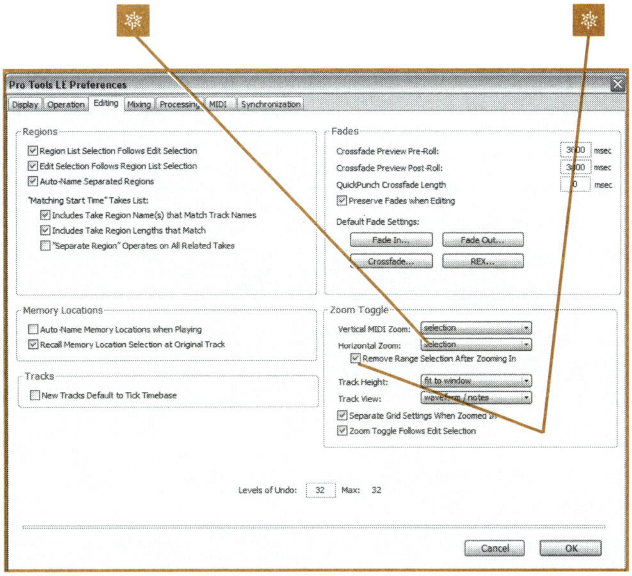

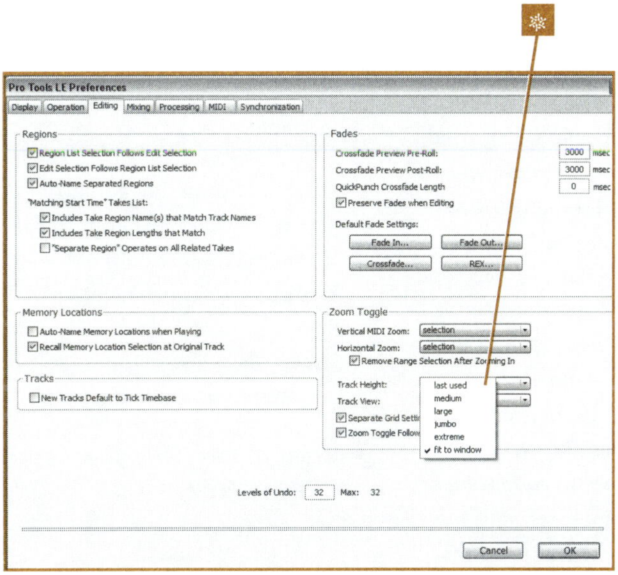

- The Horizontal Zoom setting that you choose will control how the zoom toggle tool deals with zooming in on the time axis. Here too, there are two options.
  - **Selection.** With this option, the selected area will be zoomed in on so that the selected area fills the Edit window.
  - **Last Used.** This option will recall the horizontal zoom level that you used when zoom toggle was last engaged.
- When the Remove Range Selection After Zooming In box is checked, as soon as you engage zoom toggle, your selected area will be removed so that you can quickly make a different selection.

  Sounds great, doesn't it? But wait—there's more!
- The Track Height drop-down menu will allow you to choose a track height that will be recalled when zoom toggle is engaged. Here's a little tip: When I engage zoom toggle, I want to look at *only* the material I've selected. The Fit to Window setting works particularly well for this sort of work.
- The Track View drop-down menu can allow you to change your track view as desired, even if your normal zoom mode is different. You can choose Waveform/Notes (waveform for Audio track, notes view for MIDI tracks), Warp/Notes (warp mode for Audio tracks, notes mode for MIDI tracks), Last Used (which will recall the format view that you used when you used zoom toggle last on that track), and No Change (which will make no view format change when you zoom toggle).

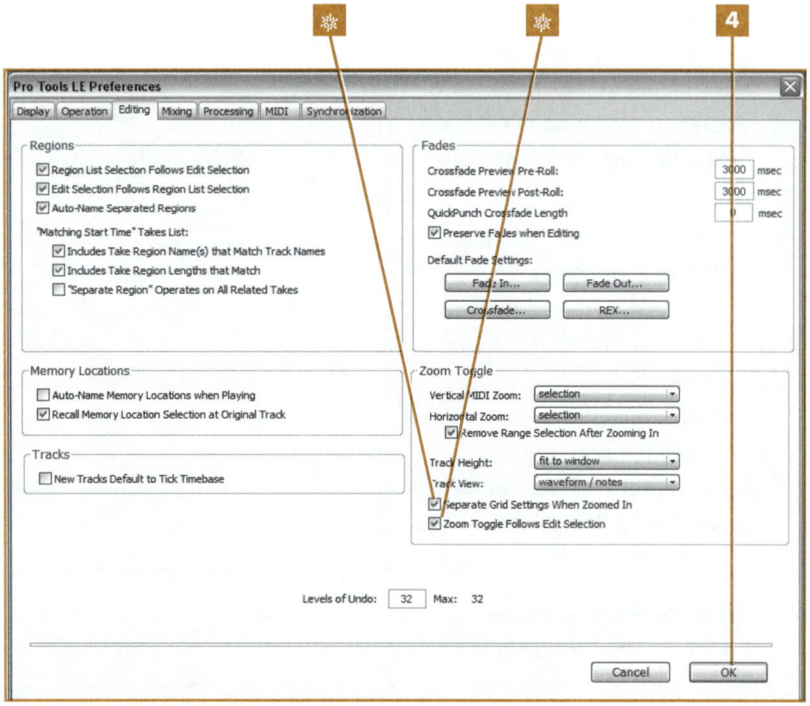

- If you check the Separate Grid Settings When Zoomed In box, it will allow you to choose two different zoom resolutions—one that you see when you're toggled in and one when you're in your normal mode.
- This last check box—Zoom Toggle Follows Edit Selection—is a new option in version 7.4 that needs a little explanation. What makes this feature just a little confusing is that it doesn't so much add functionality to zoom toggling, but rather it allows you to take some of that functionality *away*. In pre-7.4 versions of Pro Tools, when zoom toggle is engaged, aspects like track height will continually follow any tracks or regions that you have selected. For example, suppose you select a region on the top track in your session, and then turn on zoom toggle—your chosen zoom toggle settings will be recalled. Now, suppose you click a region on *another* track—now *that* track will change its track height to the zoom toggle level.

  This traditional functioning of the zoom toggle feature will be what you see when the Zoom Toggle Follows Edit Selection box is checked. Sometimes, you might not want to have your zoom toggle make these kinds of changes (admittedly, it can be a little distracting from time to time)—in these cases, just *un*-check this box. When this option is deselected, then zoom toggle will not continually follow your different selections as you make them.

4. Once you've made your desired selections, just click OK, and you're ready to rock!

More Ways to Work with Selections

After you get comfortable with these more flexible ways of zooming, you'll want to take a look at some different ways of making selections.

Setting Things Up

For this section, go to memory location #1—Selections. As you learned earlier in this chapter, you'll want to show your Memory Locations window (from the Window drop-down menu), then simply click on memory location #1.

Making Selections Using the Arrow Keys

In Chapter 3, you saw that the boundaries of your selection were represented in the Rulers area (above the tracks) by a down arrow and an up arrow, representing punch-in and punch-out points, respectively. Using the arrow keys is an easy way to make a selection as your session plays.

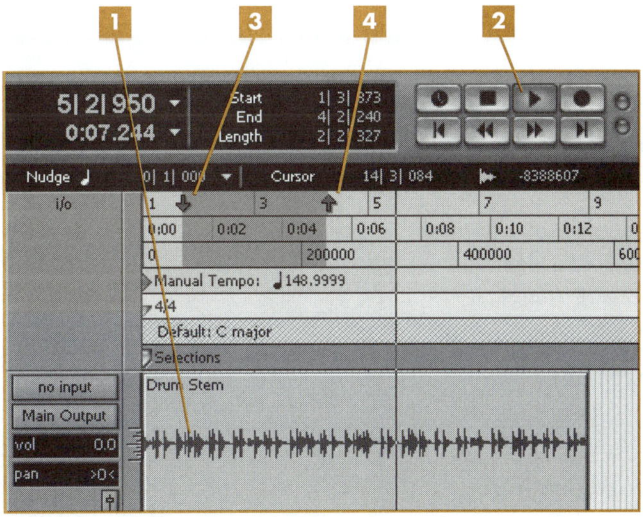

1. Choose a starting point, making sure that it is *before* the point where you want your selection to start. The starting point will be selected.
2. Start playback. (Remember, you can use the Start button on the Transport window or you can press the spacebar.)
3. As your session plays, press the down arrow key on your keyboard at the point where you want to begin your selection.
4. While your session is still playing, press the up arrow key on your keyboard when you want your selection to end.

Tweaking Your Selection

If you're a little late or early on a punch-in or punch-out, don't worry. You can adjust your selection by holding the Shift key while you drag either end with your mouse.

Hey, I Just Stopped Playback, and My Selection Disappeared!

If you find that you *lose* your selection when you stop playback, here's a quick fix (which we'll talk more about later in this section). Go to the Preferences window, then to the Operation tab. The first item on this page is called Timeline Insertion/Play Start Marker Follows Playback—make sure that this box is unchecked.

Making Selections Using the Return Key

You've already learned that pressing the Return key (Mac) or the Enter key (PC) will send you back to the beginning of the session. Here's how to use this function a little differently. This method will allow you to make a selection from the beginning of your session to a specified point.

1. Click on the Selector tool. The tool will be selected.
2. Click on the point on a desired track at which you want your selection to end. A flashing Timeline insertion will appear at the location you click.
3. Press and hold the Shift key and press the Return key. A selection will be made from the beginning of the session to the Timeline insertion that you created with the Selector tool.

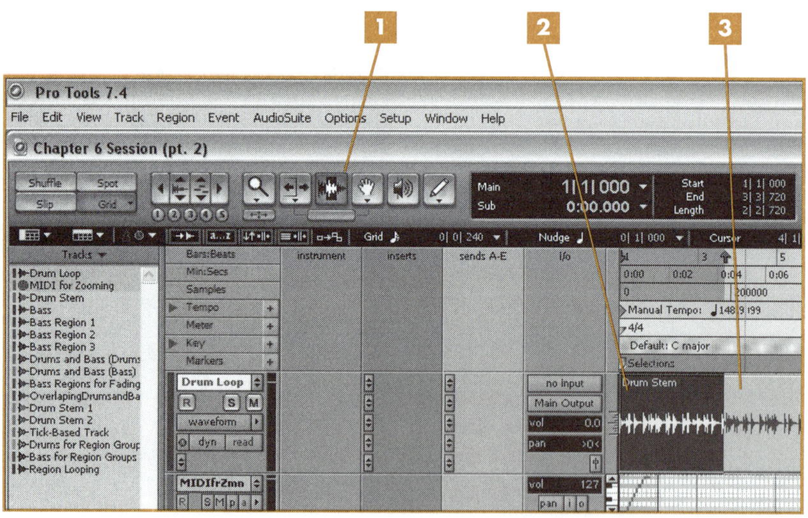

Here's a variation of that process that will allow you to make a selection from a specified point to the end of your session.

1. Click on the Selector tool if it's not already highlighted. The tool will be selected.
2. Click on the point on a desired track at which you want your selection to start.
3. Press and hold Control+Shift (PC) or Option+Shift (Mac), and press the Return key. A selection will be made from the Timeline insertion that you created with the Selector tool to the end of your session.

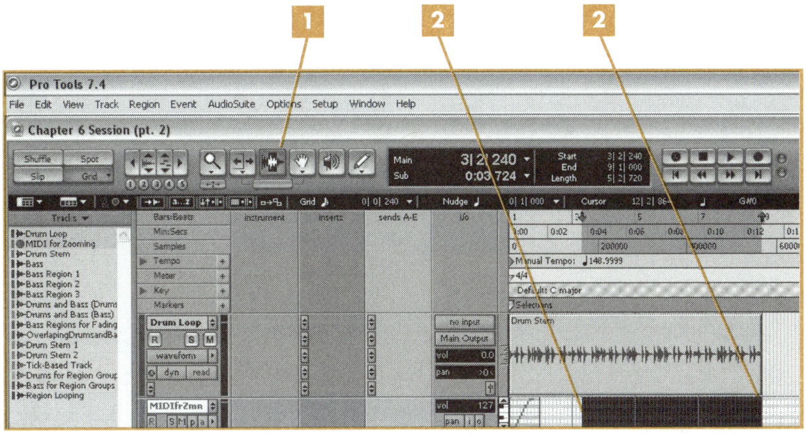

Making Selections Using Tab to Transient

The Tab to Transient function is cool for two reasons. First, it's a great concept, although by no means a unique one these days. Second, *it works*, a fact that certainly does distinguish it from similar features in competing software. That being said, the Tab to Transient feature is a great way to make certain kinds of selections, particularly for those of you who enjoy chopping up beats into loopable segments.

1. Click on the Tab to Transient tool. The tool will be selected.
2. Use the Selector tool to set a Timeline insertion a little before the transient you want to start with. The Timeline insertion will be set.
3. Press the Tab key. As you've seen before, the Timeline insertion will jump from transient to transient each time you hit the Tab key. Stop tabbing when you get to the transient that marks the desired beginning of your selection.

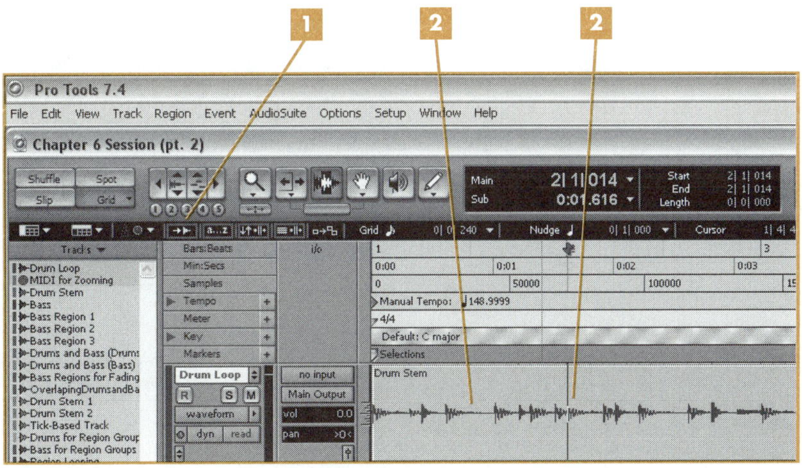

4 Press and hold the Shift key and press the Tab key. Again, the Timeline insertion will jump from transient to transient, but this time a selection will be made in the process.

5 When you reach the end of your desired selection, stop pressing the Tab key. You've now made a selection based upon Pro Tools' analysis of the transients, which will help you find the right start and end points quickly and accurately!

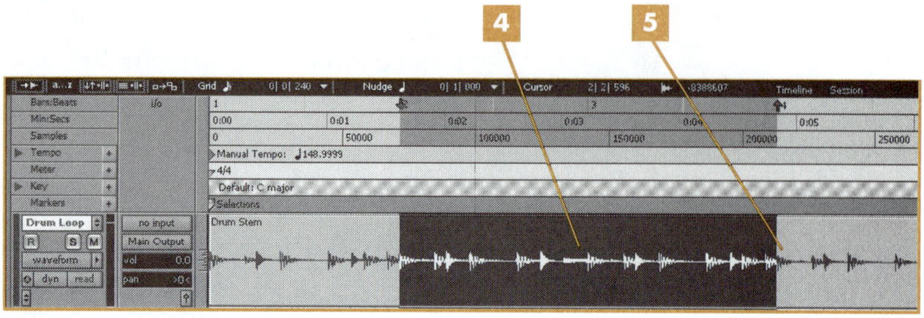

A Useful Preference: Timeline Insertion Follows Playback

Here's a scenario for you: Suppose you've selected a nice loopable selection. You wisely put yourself into Loop Playback mode and hear your selection in the proper context. Sounds great, doesn't it? Then you hit Stop, and the selection goes away! Is this a bug within Pro Tools? Nope—it's the effect of a preference named Timeline Insertion Follows Playback, which you can set in the software. You can either enable or disable this preference. Either mode has its uses, but it's important to understand this preference's functioning so you can know when to use it and when not to!

1 Click on Setup. The Setup menu will appear.

2 Click on Preferences. The Pro Tools LE Preferences dialog box will open.

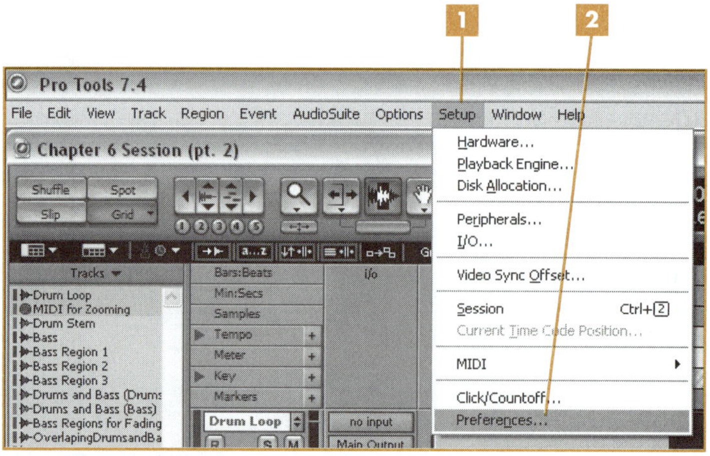

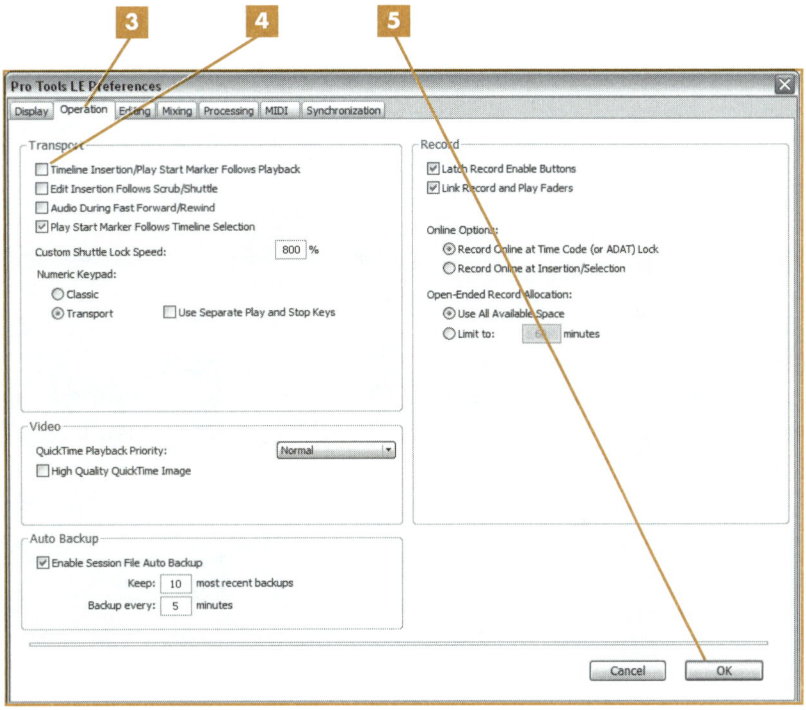

3 Click on the Operation tab. The tab will move to the front.

4 Select or deselect the Timeline Insertion Follows Playback check box. Here's what the options mean:

- Checked. Playback will begin wherever the Timeline insertion is set. When playback stops, the Timeline insertion will jump to the point where you stopped. When you start playback again, it will pick up where you left off. If you have made a selection, that selection will be lost when you hit Stop.
- Unchecked. Playback will begin wherever the Timeline insertion is set. When play-back stops in this mode, the Timeline insertion will stay where it was originally set. When you start playback again, it will start from the original position. If you have made a selection, that selec-tion will be maintained when you hit Stop, making this the ideal mode for editing loopable selections.

5 Click on OK when you've selected the desired prefer-ences. Your preferences will be set, and the dialog box will close.

Separate Regions Options

Once you've made your selection, you can separate your regions based upon that selection, as you've done already in Chapter 5. Hang on, though—there are two more new ways to use your selected area to separate your region.

For the purposes of this example, select the entire Drum Stem region shown in memory location 1.

Separate Region on Grid

As the name might suggest, this feature will chop up your region on every grid point. In this session, our grid value is sixteenth notes, so we will create new regions in sixteenth-note increments.

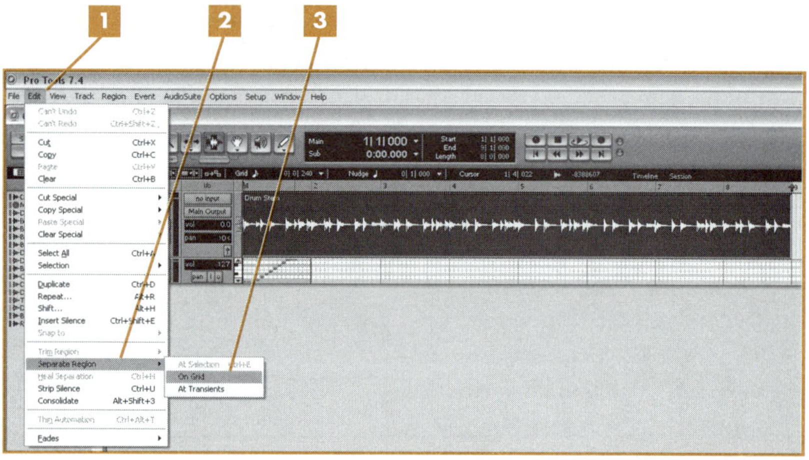

1. Click on Edit. The Edit menu will appear.
2. Click Separate Region. A secondary menu will appear.
3. Click on Grid. The Pre-Separate Amount dialog box will open.

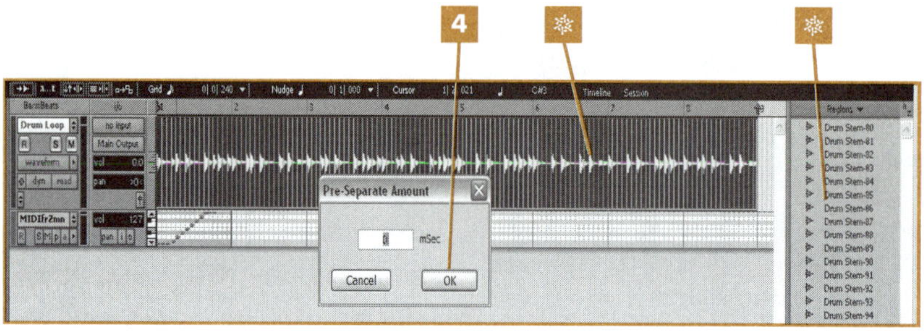

4. Setting any value above zero in the Pre-Separate Amount dialog box will shift the separations earlier. The greater the value, the farther ahead the separations. To separate regions exactly on the grid lines, choose zero. When you're finished, click OK.

- Your region will be separated regularly on every grid increment.
- New regions (in this case, *lots* of them) will be added to your Regions list.

Separate Region at Transients

A variation on the theme, this is a handy little feature that creates a new region boundary at each detected transient. Take a look.

1. Click on Edit. The Edit menu will appear.
2. Click Separate Region. A secondary menu will appear.
3. Click At Transients. The Pre-Separate Amount dialog box will open.

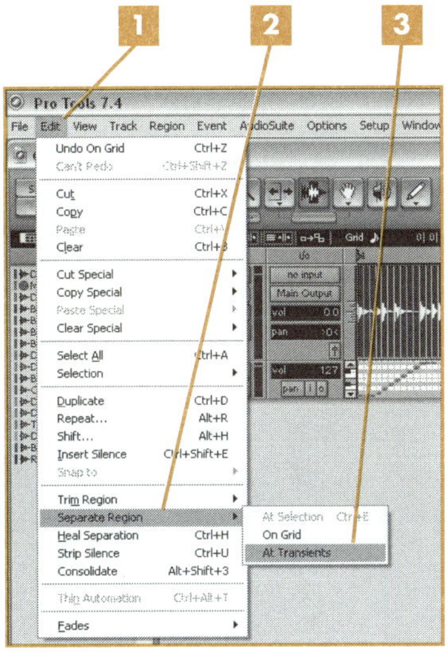

4. Setting any value above zero in the Pre-Separate Amount dialog box will shift the separations earlier. The greater the value, the farther ahead the separations. To separate regions exactly on the transients, choose zero. When you're finished, click OK.

- Your region will be separated regularly at every transient.
- As you saw when you separated on grid lines, new regions will be added to your Regions list.

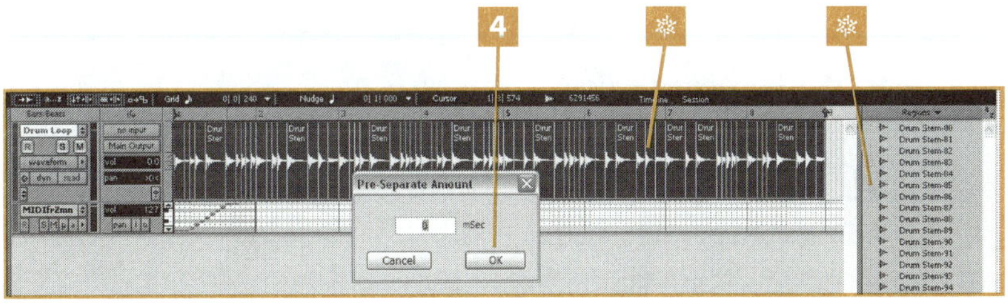

Navigating and Auditioning a Selection

When you make a selection, the most important parts are the beginning and the end. You'll be listening to the boundaries of your selection many times, just to make sure you've got everything you want and nothing you don't.

Setting Things Up

For this section, click the second memory location, Navigating a Selection. As you learned earlier in this chapter, just show your Memory Locations window (from the Window menu), then click on memory location #2.

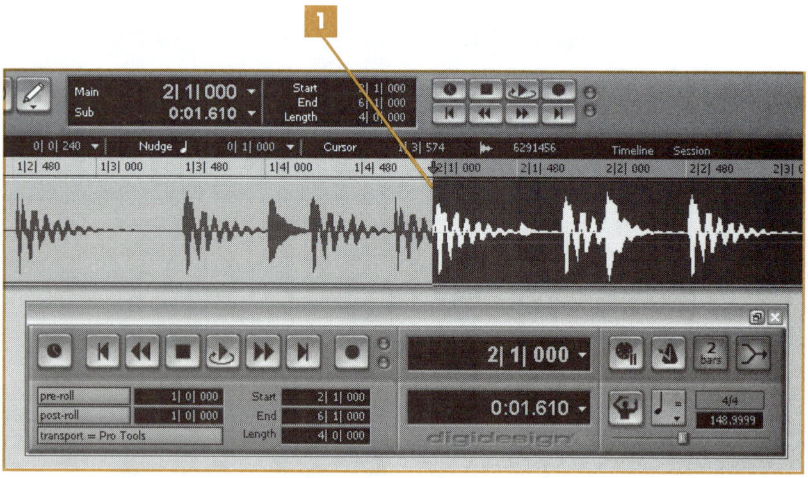

1. **Press** the **left arrow key**. The Timeline insertion (and the Edit window's focus) will move to the beginning of the selection, as shown in this image.
2. **Press** the **right arrow key**. The Timeline insertion will move to the end of the selection and center that boundary in your Edit window.
3. Now it's time to audition the boundaries of your selection. **Press and hold** the **Alt key** (PC) or the **Option key** (Mac) and **press** the **left arrow key**. Your audio will play up to the beginning of your selection by the pre-roll amount (even if pre-roll isn't highlighted). Since the pre-roll amount is set as one measure (in the lower-left of the Transport window), playback will start one measure before the beginning of the selection.
4. **Press and hold** the **Alt key** (PC) or the **Option key** (Mac) and **press** the **right arrow key**. Your audio will play up to the end of your selection by the pre-roll amount.
5. **Press and hold** the **Ctrl key** (PC) or the **key** (Mac) and **press** the **left arrow key**. Your audio will play from the beginning of your selection by the post-roll amount (even if post-roll isn't highlighted).
6. **Press and hold** the **Ctrl key** (PC) or the **key** (Mac) and **press** the **right arrow key**. Your audio will play from the end of your selection by the post-roll amount.

Beyond the Basics

You've already worked with the basic editing tools, and things such as trimming, selecting, and grabbing are starting to become familiar by now. Some of these tools have secondary layers to them, giving them added functionality. And then there's the Smart tool....

The TCE Trim Tool

First on the list is the TCE (Time Compress/Expand) Trim tool. This dandy little tool allows you to stretch or compress the duration of an audio region without changing the pitch!

Setting Things Up

To follow with this demonstration, go to memory location #3–TCE Trim Tool.

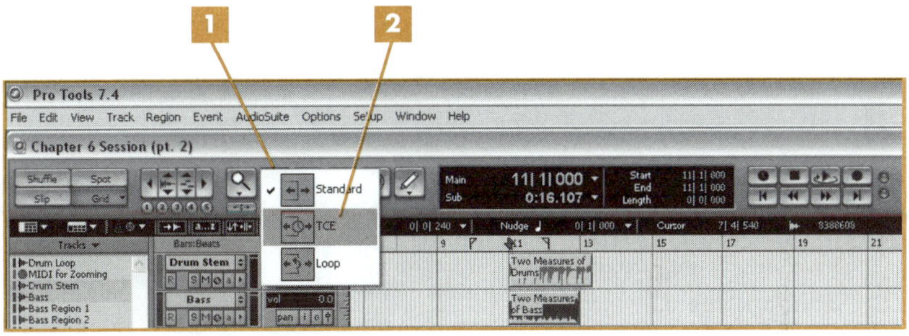

1. Click and hold the Trim tool button until the Trim tool options menu appears. The currently selected version of the Trim tool will be checked.
2. Click on TCE to change to the TCE Trim tool.

The icon for the Trim tool will change to reflect this different function. Make sure that it is highlighted. (If it isn't, just click on the icon.)

3. Click and hold either boundary of a region. In this example, I want to time-compress the top region so that it matches the bottom one, so I'm clicking on its right boundary and dragging left.

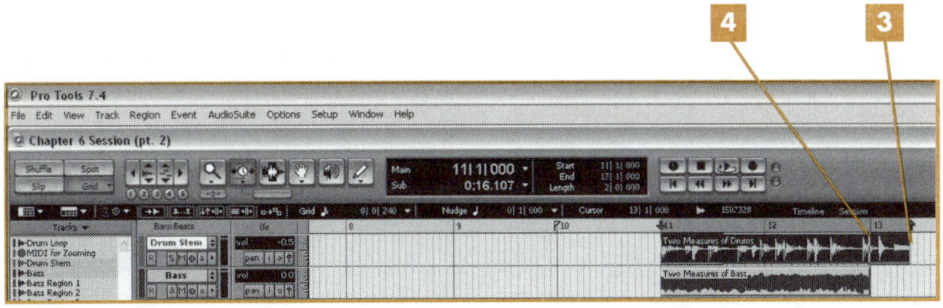

4. Drag the boundary in or out, as if you were using the regular Trim tool. When you release the mouse button, a new audio file will be created with a different duration than the original region, but without a different pitch.

Trim Tool Tip

The TCE Trim tool is really useful in Grid mode. Suppose you've imported a drum loop that doesn't match the tempo of the rest of your session. Just make sure your grids are a musical unit (such as quarter notes, for example) and use the TCE Trim tool. The edges of the region will snap to the nearest grid point when released, and you'll be perfectly in tempo!

The Object Grabber Tool

Up to this point, the Grabber tool that you have used has moved a block of *time* and all the regions that are contained within that block, hence the tool's name, *Time* Grabber. But what if you want to select more than one region without selecting all the regions between them? That's where the Object Grabber tool comes into play!

Setting Things Up

For this section, go to memory location #4—Grabbers.

1. Click and hold the Grabber tool button until the menu appears. The currently selected version of the Grabber tool will be checked.
2. Click on Object to change to the Object Grabber tool.

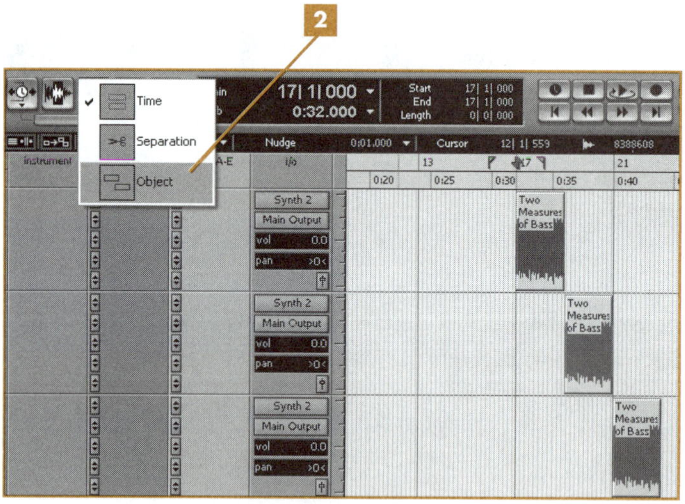

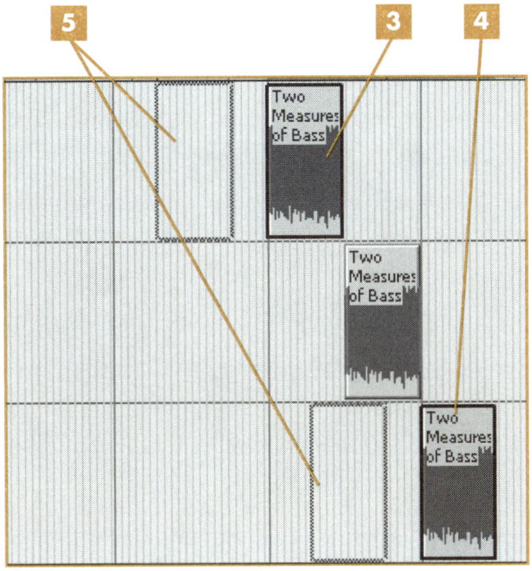

3. Click the first region that you want to select. You'll note that when you're using the Object Grabber, the region isn't highlighted, but rather a focus box is displayed around the edge of the region.
4. Holding the Shift key, click additional regions that you want to move. Note that only the regions (or "objects") that you click are selected, and not the time between them.
5. Drag and drop the regions that you want to move to the desired location. Note that you see an outline of where the regions will eventually be re-deposited.

The Separation Grabber Tool

The regular Grabber tool allows you to move regions around in your session. The Separation Grabber tool will let you take a selection from within a single region and move just that selection. This is a cool trick, but you have to go through a few steps first.

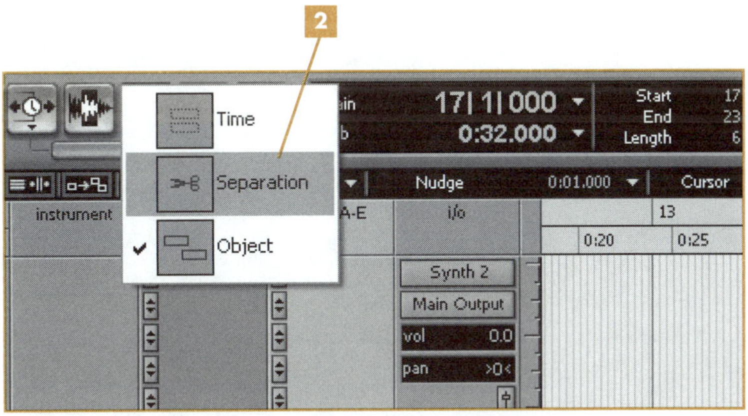

1. Click and hold the down arrow at the bottom of the Grabber button. A menu will appear. The currently selected version of the Grabber tool will be checked.
2. Click on Separation to change to the Separation Grabber tool.

3 Click on the Selector tool. (Have faith; we're going somewhere with this.)

4 Select the section of a region that you want to separate.

5 Click on the Separation Grabber tool.

6 Click and hold on your selection.

7 Drag and drop the selection to the desired destination.

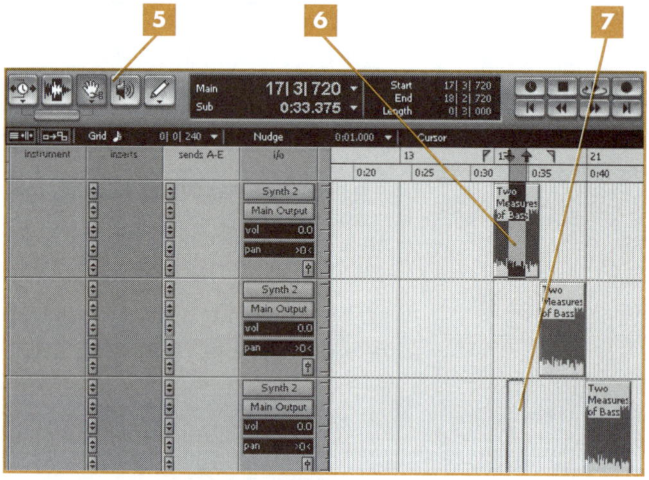

The selection will be removed from the source track and will become its own region, shown in the Regions list.

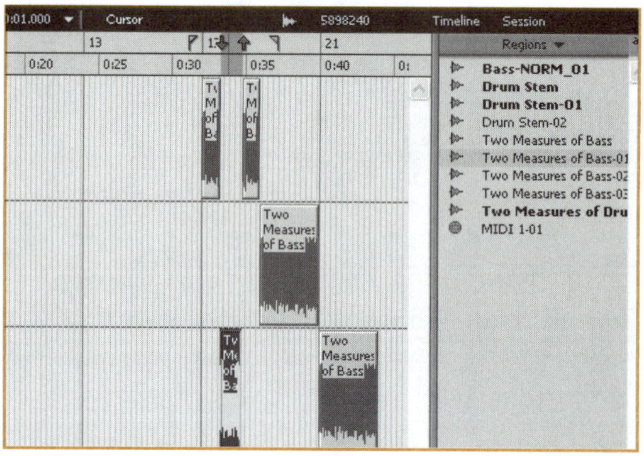

A Twist on the Separation Grabber

If you want to drag out a selection of a region but leave your source region unchanged, hold down the Alt key (PC) or the Option key (Mac) as you drag.

The Smart Tool

The Smart tool is a real timesaver, combining the use of many editing tools at once and adding some additional functionality for good measure. It might take you a while to get used to using the Smart tool, but once you've got it under your belt, you'll really start saving time.

The idea behind the function of the Smart tool is that when your cursor is in different places on a track, it will take on different tool behaviors.

Setting Things Up

For this part, go to memory location #5—Smart Tool.

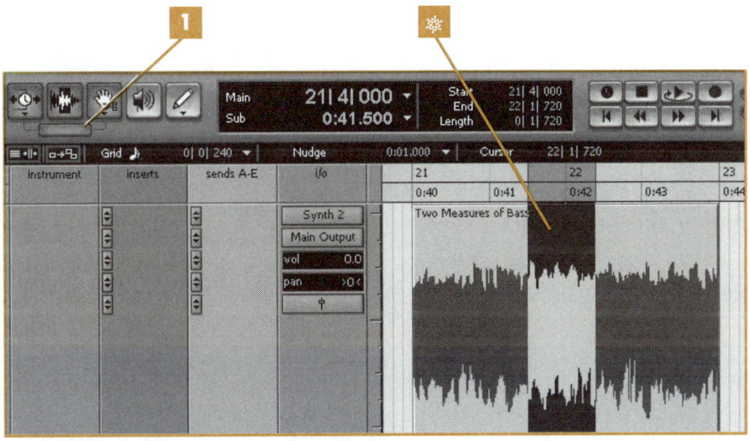

1. **Click** on the **Smart bar** below the three primary editing tools to activate the Smart tool. The button will be highlighted, and so will the three tools above it (Trim, Selector, and Grabber), which should give you a hint as to the Smart tool's function.

- When your cursor is in the upper half of a track, it will take on the function of the Selector tool.

When you move your cursor to the lower half of a track, the cursor will take on the behavior of the currently selected version of the current Grabber tool (in this case, the Separation Grabber).

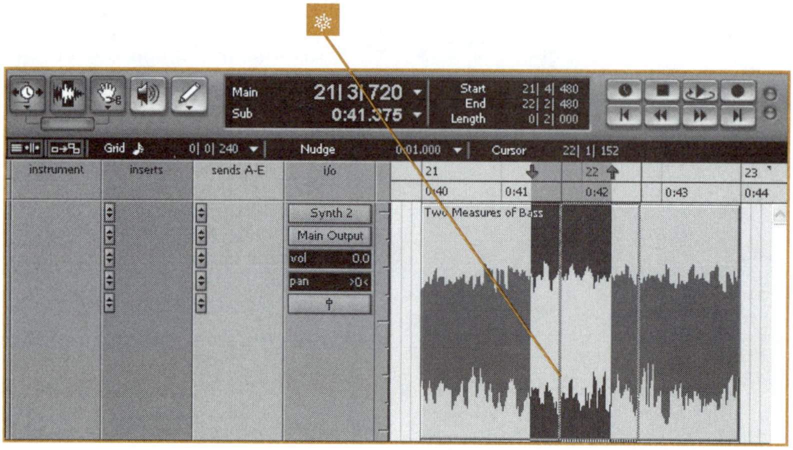

The Smart Tool and the Separation Grabber

The Smart tool works particularly well when you have the Separation Grabber tool selected, as we do in this particular situation. Just move your cursor to the top half of a track to make your selection, and then move your cursor to the bottom half of the track and drag the selection out!

When you move your cursor to either end of a region, the cursor will change its function to that of the currently selected version of the Trim tool (in this case, the TCE Trim Tool).

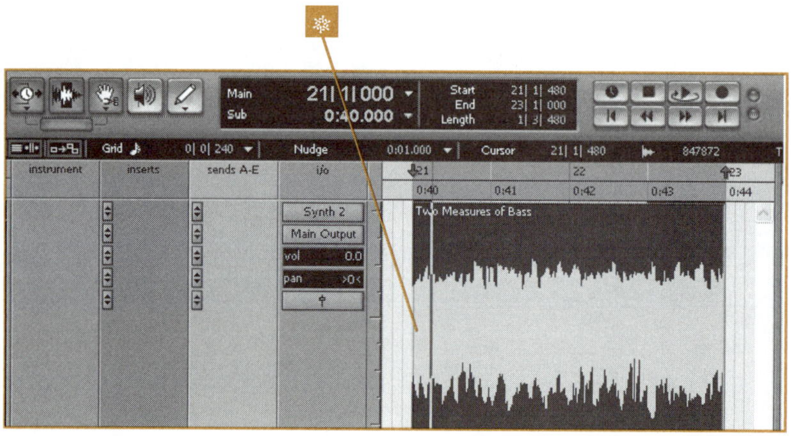

More Smart Tool Features

If you move your cursor to the corners, you'll notice that it will take on a different function, beyond that of the Trim, Selector, or Grabber tools. Be patient—you'll get to the answer in a couple of pages!

The Smart Tool and Track Heights

Because the position of the cursor within a track is so critical when you are working with the Smart tool, you should take special care with smaller track heights. (Mini height is particularly tricky.)

Edit Groups

Hopefully, you've found that these edit functions are powerful and easy to use. Now let's boost your effectiveness by being able to edit a number of tracks at the same time. The way to do this is through Edit Groups, and they're also powerful and easy!

Setting Things Up

For a simple, though effective, run-through of how an Edit Group works, go to memory location #6–Edit Groups.

Groups and Mixing

You'll notice that there are some features we'll pass over in this section. These are features that are more relevant to the process of mixing, so we'll cover those in Chapter 8, "Basic Mixing."

1. Holding the Shift key, select the tracks that you want to edit together. (In this case, choose both of the tracks displayed.)
2. Click the Edit Groups button. A pop-up menu will appear.
3. Select New Group from the menu. The Create Group dialog box will open.

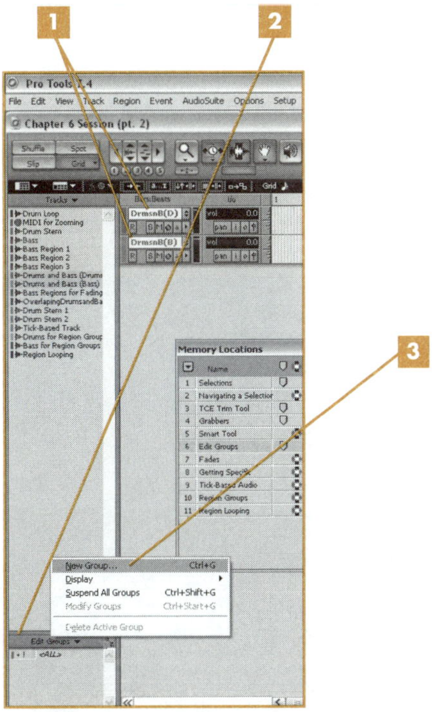

4 Type a descriptive name for your group in the Name text box.

5 You can choose to have your selected tracks available as a group only in the Edit window (an Edit Group), only in the Mix window (a Mix or fader group), or in both windows. Because we'll only be using these tracks as an editing exercise, choose Edit in the Type section.

❄ Initially, your track selection will determine the tracks that will be part of the Currently in Group area. If you want to add more tracks to your group, just select the desired tracks in the Available area, then click the Add button. Incidentally, if you want to remove a track from the group, just select the track in the Currently in Group area, and then click the Remove button.

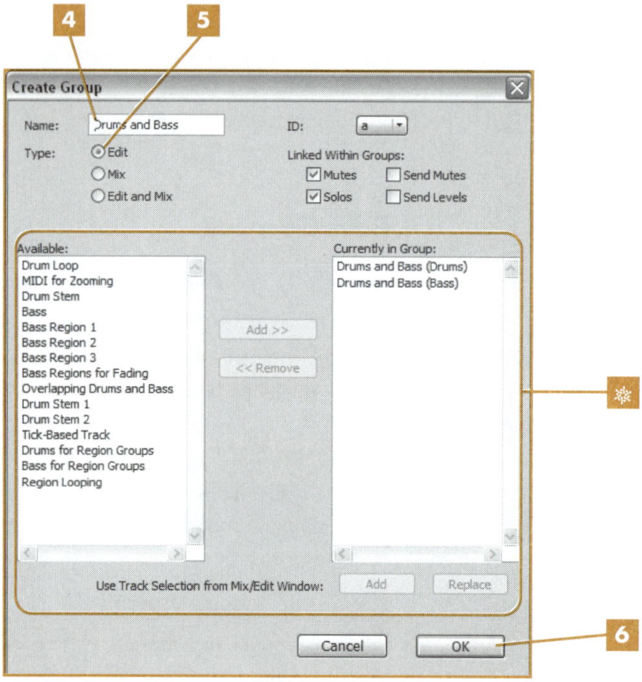

6 Click OK. The dialog box will close, and your group will be displayed in the Edit Groups list. Here's what you'll get:

❄ Your new Edit Group has been added to the Edit Groups list. By default, a newly created group is immediately made active, as shown by a light-blue shading on the group name. (Careful, it's hard to see sometimes!) To make the group *in*active, just click the group name to un-highlight it.

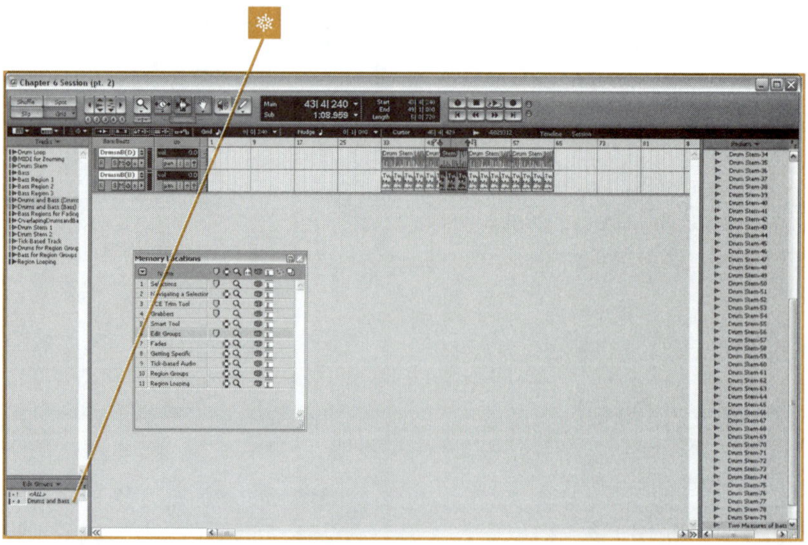

When you apply any edit tool to a member of an active Edit Group, you'll see that the tool is mirrored on all members of that group. This is particularly handy when you are assembling or tweaking tracks together (very commonly done for drum kits, string or horn sections, and multiple vocal tracks). Shown here, I've made a selection on one of the tracks, and that selection is made simultaneously on all members of this active Edit Group (named Drums and Bass).

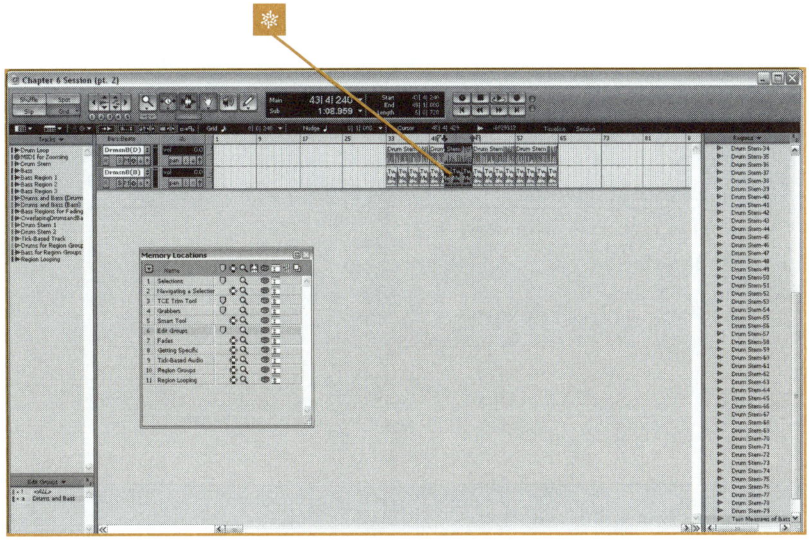

Creating and Customizing Fades

You can use fade-ins and fade-outs to soften the edges of a region. Additionally, you can create crossfades between regions to make a smooth transition from one region to another. Of course, this is nothing new in the world of DAWs, but Pro Tools makes fades easy to create and tweak. You can even use the Smart tool to create them!

Setting Things Up

For our discussion of fades, go to memory location #7—Fades.

Creating a Fade-In

Everybody has heard fade-ins in a mix, when a song starts from a silent beginning and gradually gets louder until it reaches its running volume. In Pro Tools, however, you can create a fade-in for an individual region *within* a mix. Here's how:

1. Using the Selector tool (or the Selector mode of the Smart tool), select the area of a region that you want to become a fade-in. The area will be selected.
2. Click on Edit. The Edit menu will appear.
3. Click on Fades. The Fades submenu will appear.
4. Click on Create. The Fades dialog box will open.

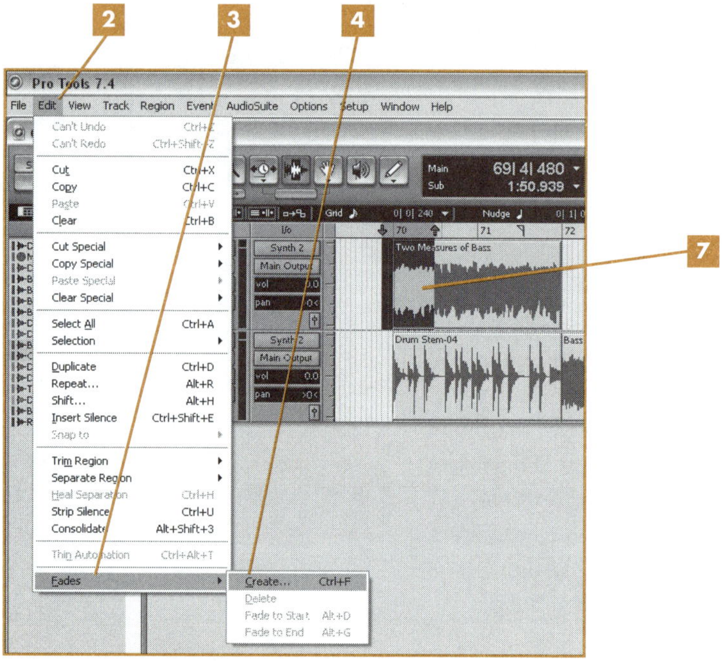

About Your Selection

It's important to make sure that your selection starts at or before the region boundary and ends where you want the fade-in to end.

5. Click on the Waveform Display button to show a graphic view of the audio you will be fading in. The waveform will be displayed.

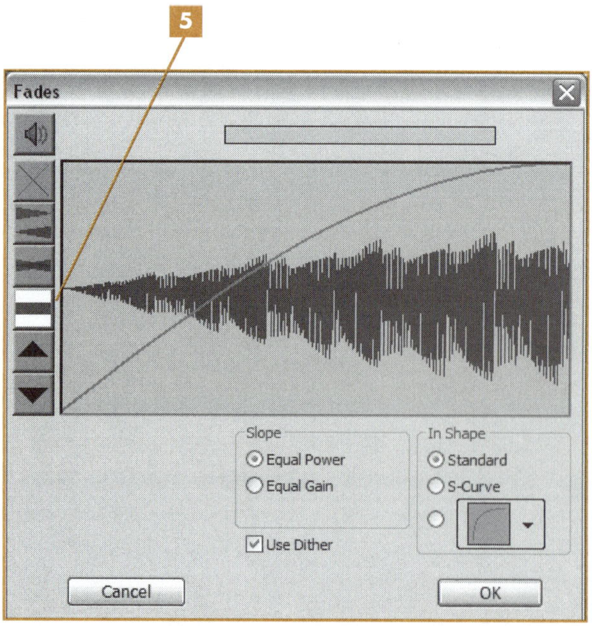

6a Click on the Standard radio button in the In Shape section to select a standard curve. The option will be selected.

OR

6b Click on the S-Curve radio button in the In Shape section to select an S curve, which rises quickly, evens out, and then rises again to full volume. The option will be selected.

OR

6c Click and drag the fade curve to change its shape. The contour of your fade-in will change along with the shape of the fade curve.

OR

6d Click on the Preset Curve Selection down arrow. A drop-down menu of additional fade-in curve presets will appear.

6e Click on the desired fade-in curve preset. The option will be selected.

6f Click the Preset Curve Selection radio button to use your preset shape.

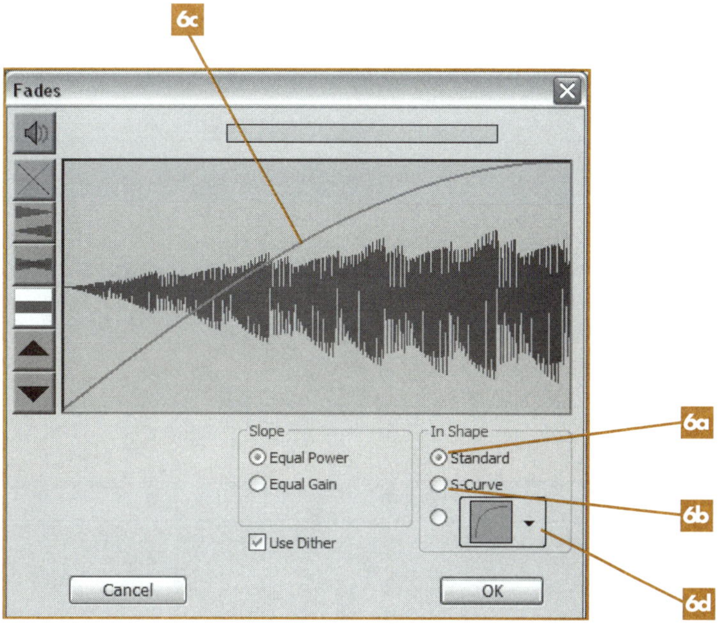

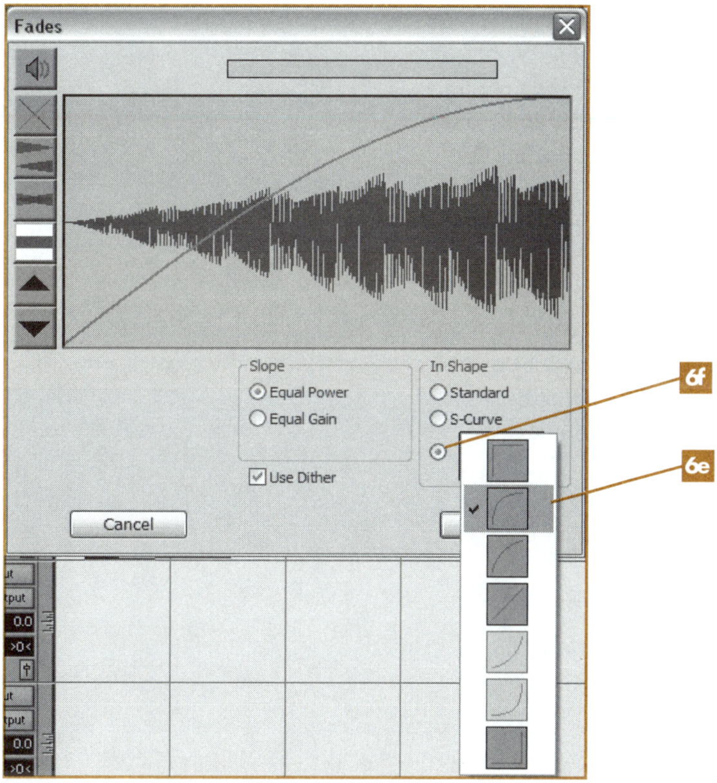

7 Click on OK. The Fades dialog box will close.

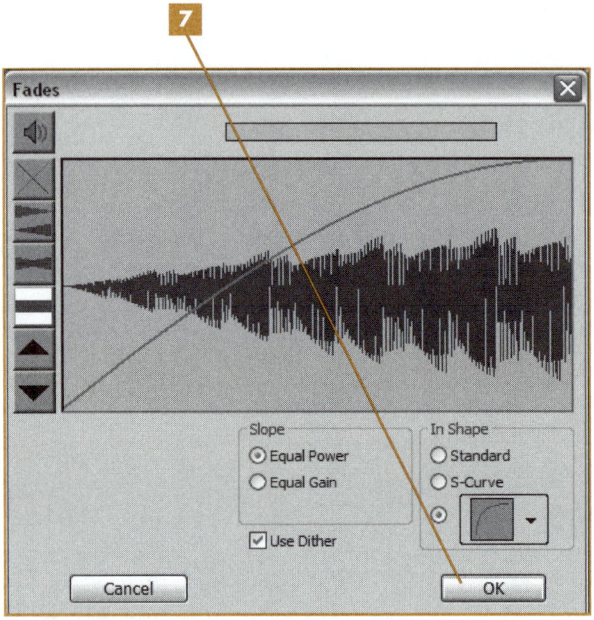

At the beginning of the region, you'll now see a fade region. This section is marked by an ascending diagonal line, indicating that it is a fade-in. This fade region represents a fade file located in the Fade Files subfolder. Although this is certainly a region (attached to another audio region) and an audio file, it will not be displayed in the Regions list.

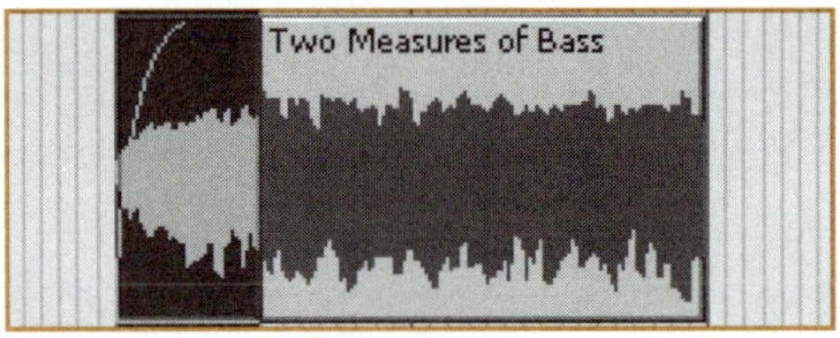

Creating a Fade-Out

After you've created a fade-in, creating a fade-out will be easy. It really is just a mirror image of the fade-in process.

1. Select the area of a region that you want to become a fade-out. Make sure your selection starts at the point that you want your fade-out to begin and ends at or after the region boundary.
2. Click on Edit. The Edit menu will appear.
3. Click on Fades. The Fades submenu will appear.
4. Click on Create. The Fades dialog box will open.

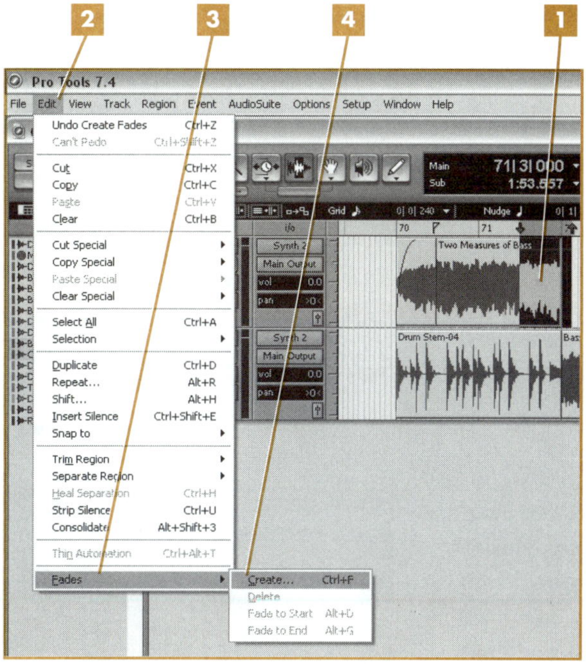

5. Use the options in the Fades dialog box to customize your fade-out, just as you did your fade-in. It still operates the same, just in the opposite direction!
6. Click on OK. The Fades dialog box will close.

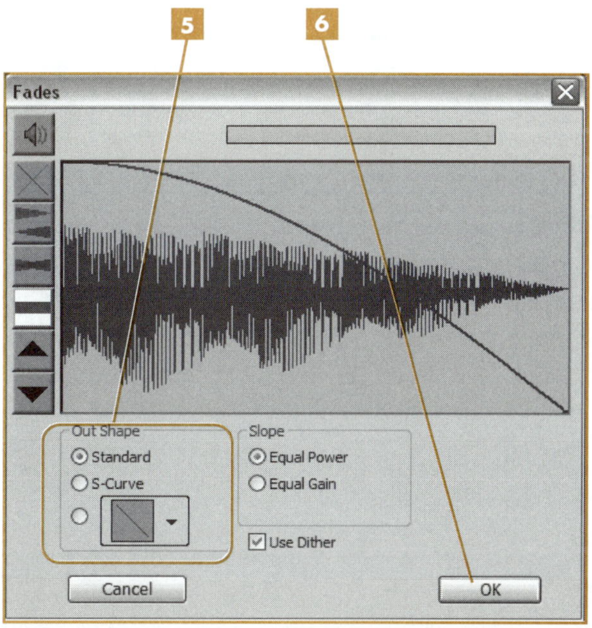

Fade-In or Fade-Out?

You've probably noticed that when you use these methods for creating fade-ins and fade-outs, Pro Tools automatically knows whether you want to create a fade-in or a fade-out. Here's something to be careful of when you create a fade-in or fade-out: If you don't select to the end (or beginning) of a region, Pro Tools will get confused about what you want to do. Even if you go to the Edit menu and select Fades, the Create option will be grayed out and unavailable.

Crossfades

Here's how to crossfade between two overlapping regions. (For those to whom "crossfade" is a new term, it's a simultaneous fading out of one sound, while another sound fades in, blending the transition from one sound to the other.)

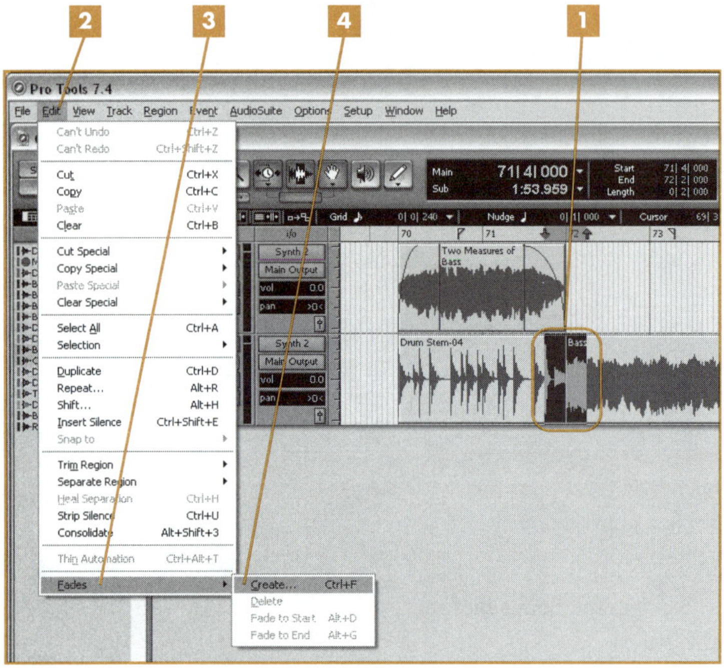

1. **Select** an **area** of two overlapping regions that you want to become a crossfade. In this example, I've made a track of overlapping bass and drum regions so that you can easily hear the transition from one region to another.
2. **Click** on **Edit**. The Edit menu will appear.
3. **Click** on **Fades**. The Fades submenu will appear.
4. **Click** on **Create**. The Fades dialog box will open.

5 **Set up** the **fade-in portion** of your crossfade the same way you would a standalone fade-in.

6 **Set up** the **fade-out portion** of the crossfade in the same way.

7 **Drag** the **crossing point** of your crossfade earlier or later, depending on your preference for this particular crossfade.

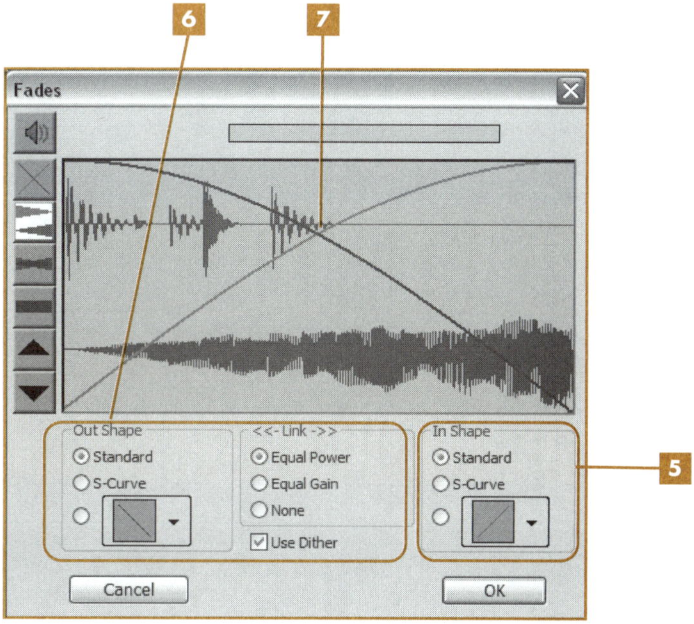

You'll notice that the fade-in and fade-out components of this crossfade are joined, and changes to either aspect will affect the other. Take a look at this linking.

1 **Click** on the **Equal Power radio button** in the Link area. The option will be selected. Use this option when you're crossfading audio that is not identical. These curves will compensate for the volume drop that can sometimes occur when significantly different waveforms are combined and is usually heard as a smooth transition between regions.

2 **Move** the **crossover point** from left to right. Notice that it remains at the same position, slightly above the middle of the dialog box.

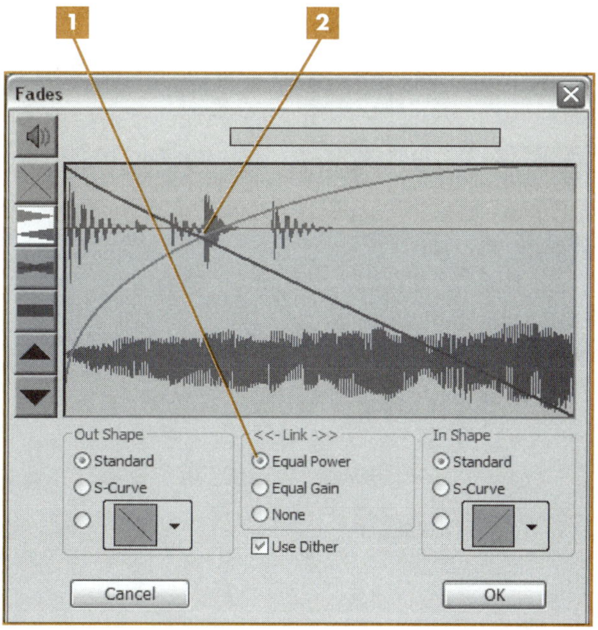

3 Click on the Equal Gain radio button. When you select this as a linking option, your crossover point will not be boosted in any way, although you can still move the crossover point from left to right (earlier to later). When you are crossfading identical or similar audio, this linking will give you the desired smooth transition from region to region.

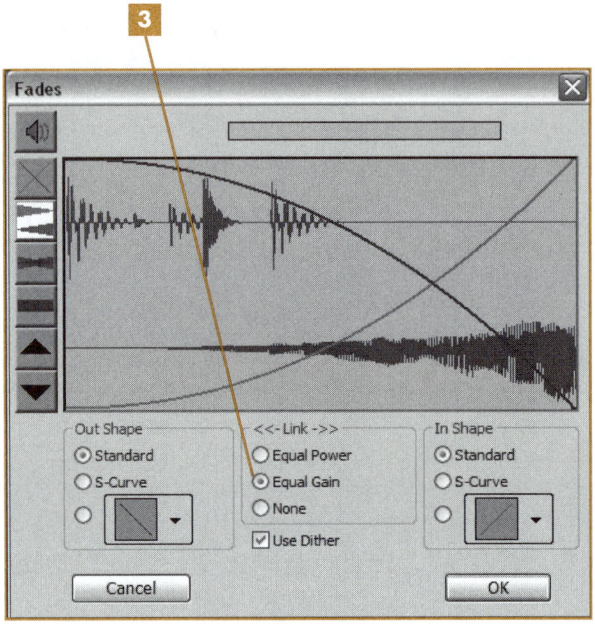

4 Click on the None radio button. This will change one half of a crossfade without changing the other half.

5 Click on the small black handle at the beginning or end of a fade curve. They're tricky to click on with your mouse, but once you do get them, you will be able to drag and drop them anywhere you want, and all other aspects of the crossfade will remain unchanged.

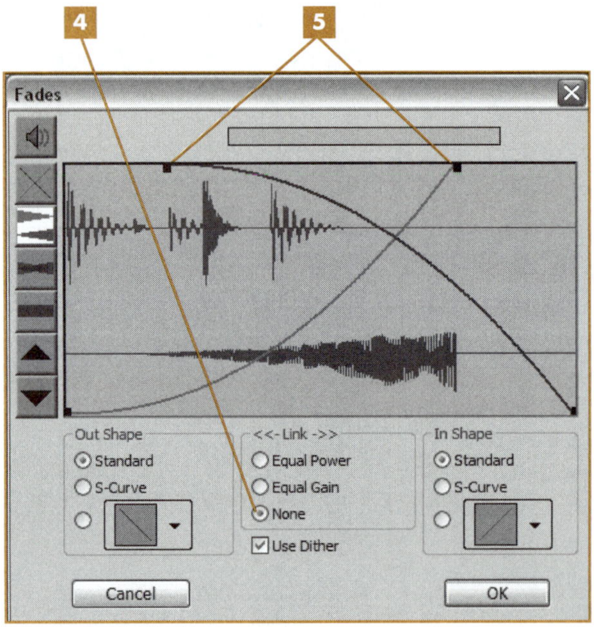

The Advantage of "None" Linking

Although the None link mode might not be the most commonly used mode of crossfading, it is often the mode of choice if you need a specific nonlinear transition.

Creating Fades Using the Smart Tool

In addition to the triple benefit of Trim, Select, and Grabber that you get with the Smart tool, you can also quickly create fade-ins, fade-outs, and even crossfades!

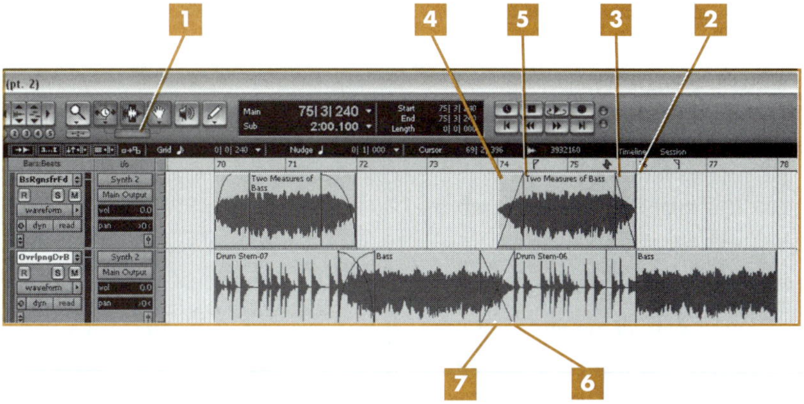

1. Click on the Smart bar to activate the Smart tool. The Smart tool will be selected.
2. Move your cursor to the upper-right corner of a region. The cursor will change to a small square with a diagonal line through it, which looks a bit like a fade-out region.
3. Click and drag your mouse pointer to the left and release the mouse button when you want your fade-out to start to create a fade-out region.
4. Move your cursor to the upper-left corner of a region to create a fade-in.
5. Click and drag your mouse pointer to create your fade-in the same way you created your fade-out (only in the opposite direction).
6. Move your cursor to the bottom corners of two adjacent regions. Now your cursor will be able to create a crossfade!
7. Click and drag your mouse left or right to create a crossfade centered on the regions' boundaries.

So how can you control the contours of your fades when you use the Smart tool to create them?

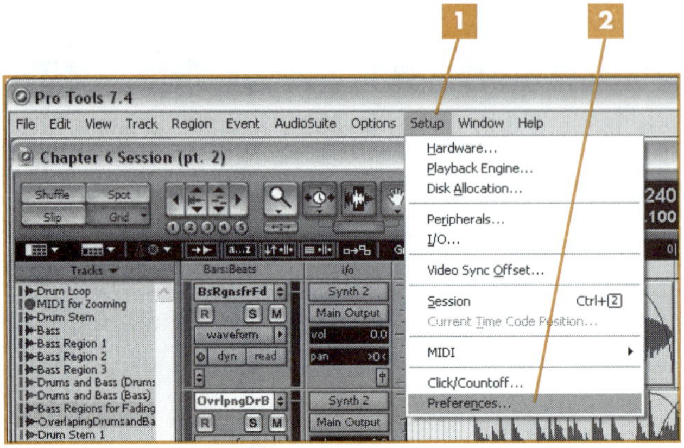

1. Click on Setup. The Setup menu will appear.
2. Click on Preferences. The Pro Tools LE Preferences dialog box will open.

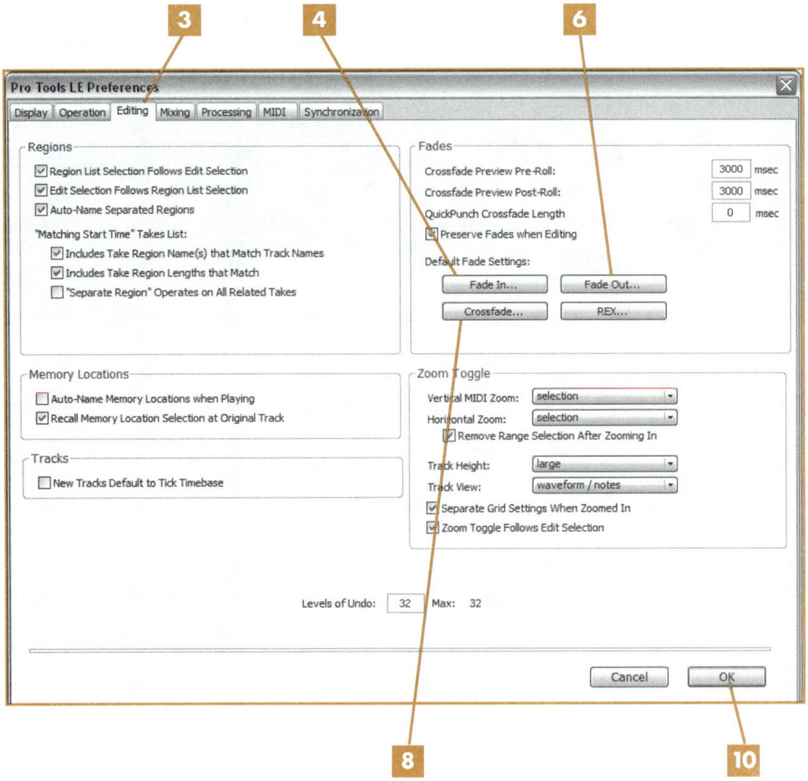

3. Click on the Editing tab. The tab will move to the front.
4. Click on the Fade In button. The familiar Fades dialog box will open.
5. Configure the fade-in curve as your default fade-in. (See "Creating and Customizing Fades" earlier in this chapter for details.)
6. Click on the Fade Out button. The Fades dialog box will open.
7. Configure the fade-out curve as your default fade-out.
8. Click on the Crossfade button. The Fades dialog box will open.
9. Configure the crossfade curve as your default crossfade.
10. Click on the OK button. Your settings will be saved, and the Preferences dialog box will close.

Guidelines for Default Fades

It's a good idea to set up your most commonly used fade-in, fade-out, and crossfade settings in the Preferences dialog box. Each time you create a fade using the Smart tool, the fade curve will be based upon these preferences.

Changing Fade Regions

Regardless of whether you used the Smart tool, if you create a fade and you later want to change its contour, double-click on the fade region with the Grabber tool. The Fades dialog box will open again so you can make your changes. Note that any changes you make in this dialog box will not affect your preferences.

New Fade Behaviors

Those of you who have used Pro Tools for some time will recall that there have been some things you simply couldn't do with fades, or with regions that contain fades. The good news is that with Pro Tools LE 7.4, essentially all of those limitations have been removed, and then some. Want to drag a region that has a fade? Not a problem. Want to drag or even separate a fade region? That can also be done, and the fade will simply re-render itself. Your rule of thumb these days can safely be that all the basic editing tools are fully functional with fade regions, except the Trim tool variations (the TCE Trim tool and the Loop Trim tool).

Getting Specific: Nudging Regions

Using the Nudge function, you can move regions (or region boundaries) by small incremental amounts, and you can get very specific with your locations. First, though, you'll have to set up your nudge amount.

1 Click on the Nudge value down arrow. The Nudge menu will appear.

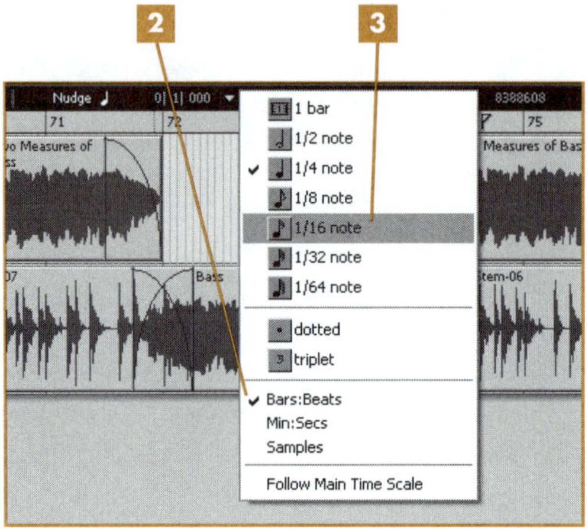

2. Select the scale by which you want to nudge your region. The scale will be selected.
3. Select the increment by which you want to nudge. The increment will be selected.
4. Select the region(s) you want to move.

5a. Press the + (plus) key. Your region will be moved later (to the right) by the nudge amount.

OR

5b. Press the – (minus) key. Your region will be moved earlier (to the left) by the nudge amount. The change in location might be visually imperceptible, so you'll want to keep an eye on your location display.

Nudging Shortcuts

Holding Alt+Shift (PC) or Option+Shift (Mac) while pressing the plus or minus key will nudge only the left boundary of the region. Holding Ctrl+Shift (PC) or ⌘+Shift (Mac) while pressing the plus or minus key will nudge only the right boundary. Neither of these variations on the Nudge feature will move your audio in time; they will only change the boundary.

Cool Editing Tools

Here are some great new additions to Pro Tools' editing arsenal!

Tick-Based Audio Tracks

Under most circumstances, you'll want your audio regions securely anchored to an absolute time location, right down to the sample. Conversely, it is pretty customary to have your MIDI data linked to your session's measures—bars, beats, and *ticks*. With Pro Tools, though, you have the option of assigning your audio regions to be locked to a tick-based location, which means that as you change your tempo, your regions will move accordingly.

If you go to memory location #9—Tick-Based Audio, you'll see a familiar-sounding drum part, separated at each transient. Basically, each drum hit has been separated. Let's see what can be done.

1 Click the Time Base Selector button. A list will appear.

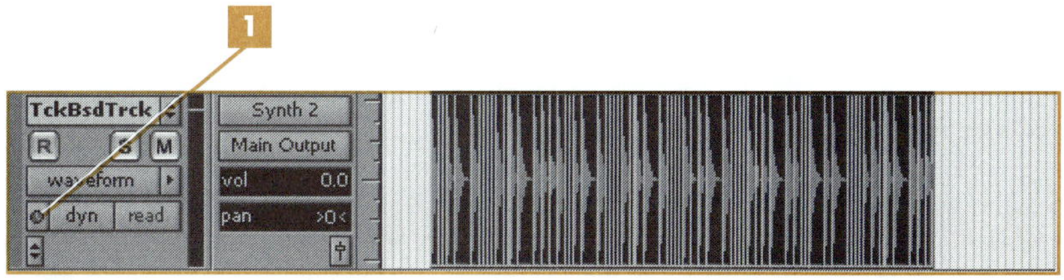

2 Choose the desired time scale for your track. In this case, click the Ticks option.

3 With this setting, all the regions on this track are assigned to tempo locations, which means if you change the tempo in your session, each individual region (in this case, each individual transient) will move accordingly. Drag the tempo slider, and see how your audio changes!

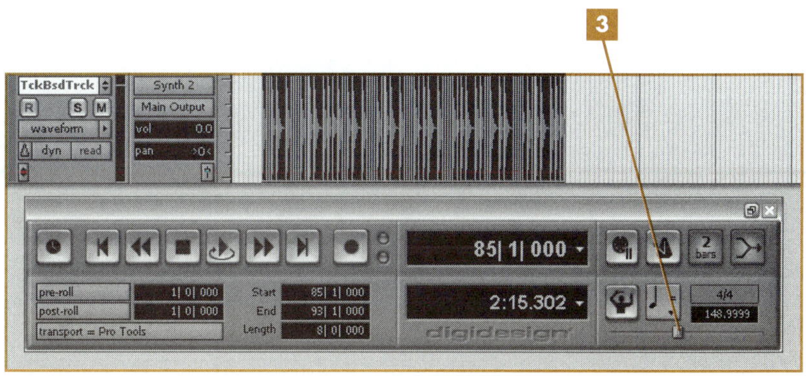

Link Edit and Track Selection

It's a simple enough feature, but definitely worth taking a look at!

Setting Things Up

For the purposes of this demonstration, show all the tracks of your session.

1. Click the Link Track and Edit Selection button.
2. Select the desired track.
3. Using the Selector tool, make a selection on the selected track.

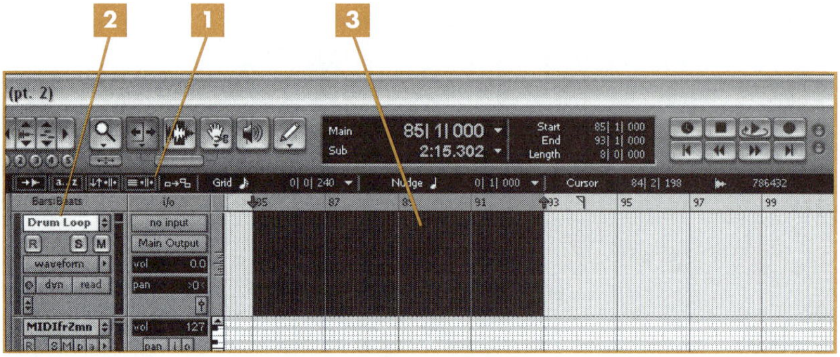

4. Now, select a different track. Note how the selection moves with your track selection.

Selecting a Block of Tracks

If you want to select multiple tracks, and thus make multiple selections, just hold down the Shift key as you select tracks.

Region Groups

Region Groups, a new feature in Pro Tools 7, are another way to link regions together so that they move and change as a single unit, even though they may span multiple tracks.

Setting Things Up

For this section, go to memory location #10—Region Groups.

1 Select the regions that you want to assign to your Region Group. In this memory location, your regions have been selected for you.

2 Click the Region menu.

3 Click Group. The regions will be joined into a single larger object.

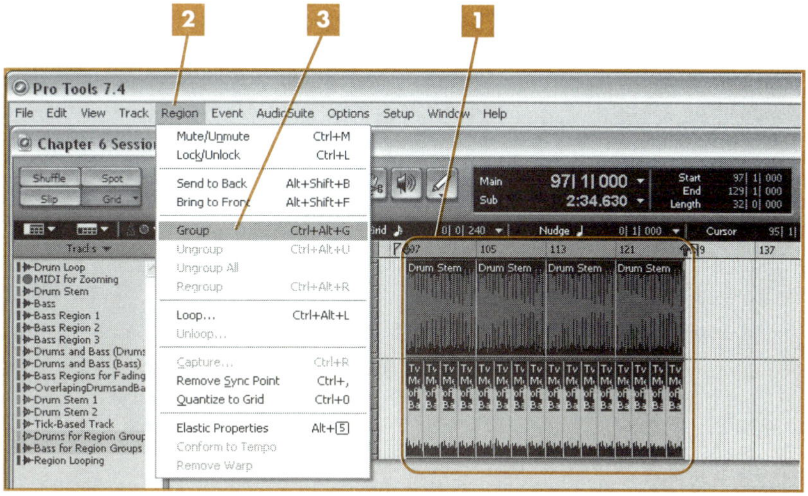

The Region Group will have its own name and will appear in the Regions list at the right edge of your Edit window. Better than that, though, you'll be able to apply edit processes in ways that were impossible before, such as creating a long fade over the entire Region Group—even one that contains many smaller regions—as shown here.

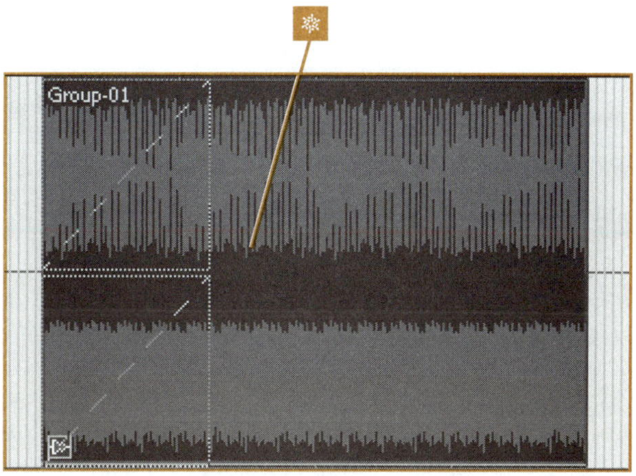

Region Looping

The ability to loop regions is another brand-new feature in Pro Tools 7 and will be a useful new feature for loop-based production. Here's how it works.

Setting Things Up

For this last section of the chapter, recall memory location #11—Region Looping.

1. **Select** the **region(s)** that you want to loop. In this memory location, your region has been selected for you.
2. **Click** the **Region menu**.
3. **Click Loop.** The Region Looping dialog box will open.

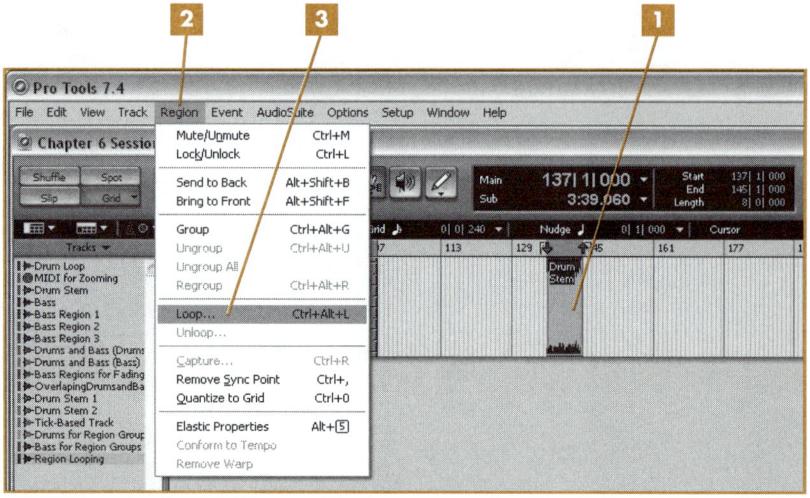

You have a number of choices when it comes to how you want your region to loop:

- Choose the number of repetitions you want your region to make.
- Specify a length of time (based upon the Main time scale) that you want to fill with these loops.
- Loop until the end of the session or until the next region (whichever comes first).

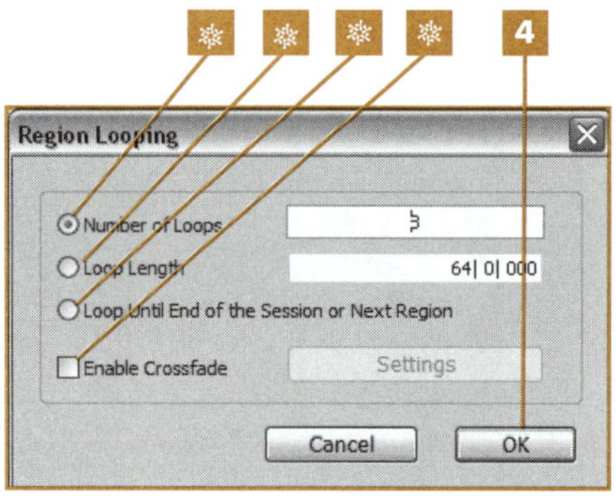

- Check the Enable Crossfade box to create crossfades between each loop iteration. When this option is selected, you can adjust the crossfade curve by clicking the Settings button. (The window looks exactly the same as the Crossfades dialog box you worked with earlier in this chapter.)

4. To commit your changes, just **click** the **OK button**.

In this example, I've chosen to repeat this region eight times, and here's the result. This series of looped regions, like Region Groups, functions in many ways like a single unit and can be moved and edited with great flexibility.

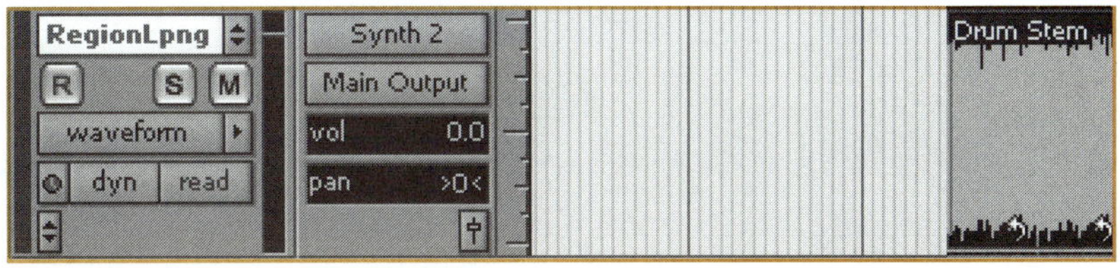

New Feature: Loop Trim Tool

As if region looping wasn't easy enough already, the Loop Trim tool will give you even more functionality in a couple of ways. First, you can use the Loop Trim tool to create just the right amount of looping.

1. Click and hold the Trim tool button until the Trim tool options menu appears. The currently selected version of the Trim tool will be checked.
2. Click on Loop to change to the Loop Trim tool.

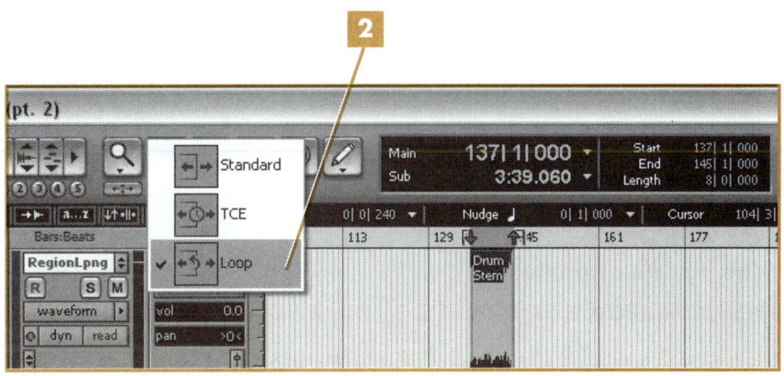

3. The rest is pretty simple: Just click and drag the desired region boundary (you can drag either the left or right boundary to loop forward or backward) when you see the Trim tool with the arrow icon, as shown in this image. As with other versions of the Trim tool, all you have to do is release the mouse, and you'll have your new looped region.

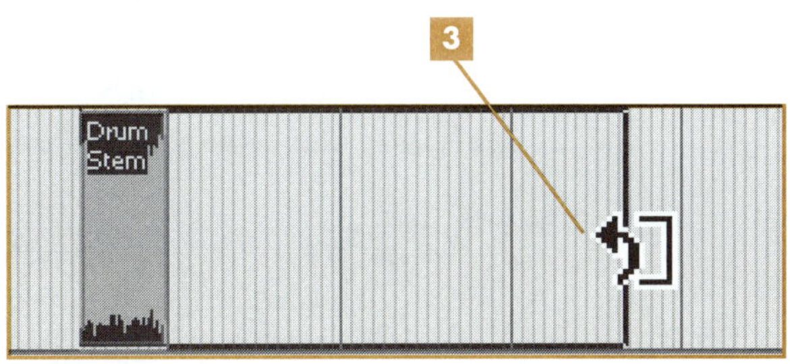

Here's what it looks like.

Now, there's something more about region looping that is particularly interesting: With the Trim tool, you can change the *individual* loop iterations without changing the total length of the looped section. Sound confusing? Take a look, and I think it'll become clear.

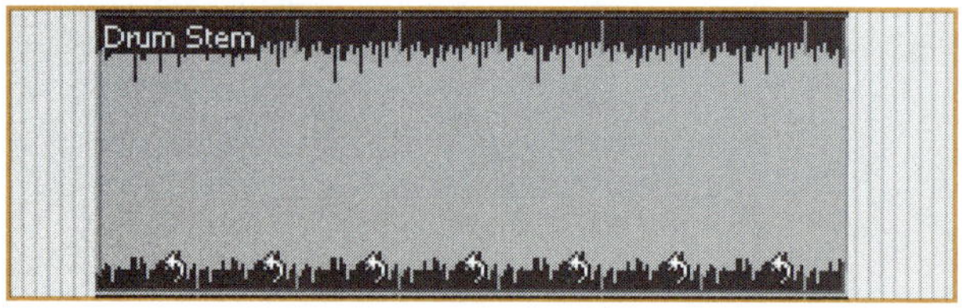

1. With the Trim tool selected (actually, *any* mode of the Trim tool will do the trick), move your cursor to a lower corner of any member region of your region loop object. The Trim tool will be displayed as a basic Trim tool, as shown here.
2. Adjust the boundary of the member region exactly as if you were trimming a normal region.

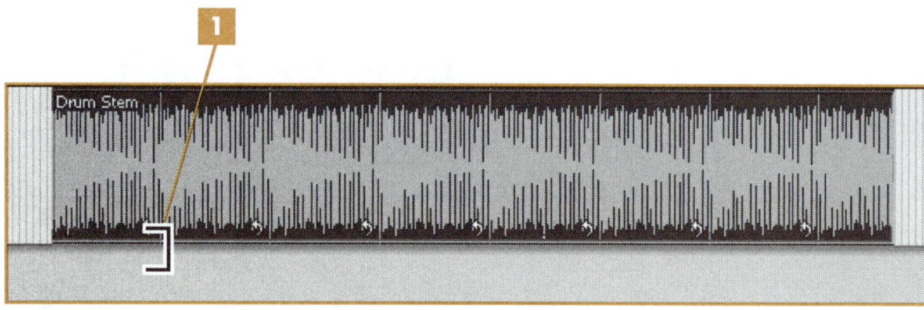

The difference comes in when you release your mouse—here's what you'll get. You'll notice that the overall length of the looped area is the same, but the length of each section within it has changed. This process can be particularly useful when you are dealing with drum beats, and can often yield interesting results!

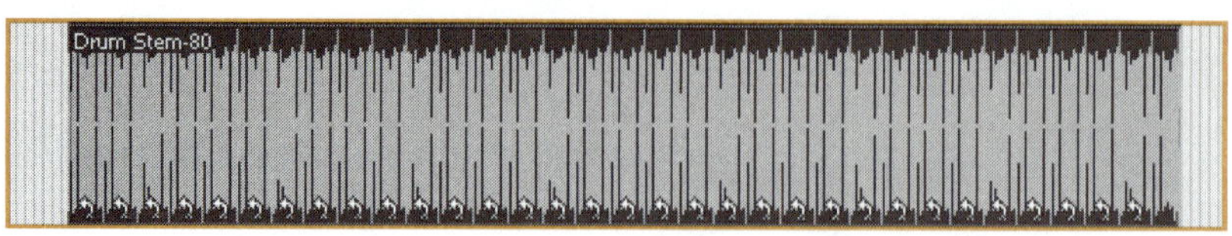

That's all for now. Next—MIDI!

7 Using MIDI

MIDI (*Musical Instrument Digital Interface*) is a language that allows keyboards, synthesizers, and other components to communicate with one another. Since its inception in the early 1980s, MIDI has proved to be an invaluable creative tool to musicians of all kinds, and it has changed the face of the music industry.

Not too long ago, music software worked with *either* audio or MIDI, but certainly not both. Thankfully, those days have changed, and there are a number of products, such as Pro Tools, that incorporate the creative power of MIDI and all the advantages of digital audio. Pro Tools LE 7 has made particularly impressive gains in its MIDI power lately, while remaining a solid audio workstation. In this chapter, you'll learn how to:

- Set up your MIDI studio
- Route MIDI and audio signals so you can work with synthesizers in Pro Tools
- Record and edit MIDI data
- Work with your MIDI data intelligently, including importing to and exporting from Pro Tools

> A mastery of MIDI is a study in itself, on which volumes of information have been written. It's virtually impossible to become MIDI-savvy after reading one chapter in a single book. Therefore, for the purposes of this book, I must assume a fundamental understanding of MIDI, and I'll focus on how to use MIDI in the Pro Tools environment. For a good book on the subject of MIDI, check out *MIDI Power! Second Edition: The Comprehensive Guide* (Thomson Course Technology PTR, 2005).

Xpand!

The exercise session for this chapter uses a plug-in called Xpand!—a virtual instrument that is powerful, useful, and best of all, *free*. Xpand! has been included with Pro Tools systems for quite some time now, so you probably have the disc. If you haven't installed it yet, now would be a good time. If you don't have a disc, don't fret—your local reseller should be able to help you.

Setting Up Your MIDI Studio

Just as you configured your audio inputs and outputs before you worked with audio, you'll want to configure your MIDI setup and identify your devices before getting down to work. Don't worry; it's easy!

1. Click on Setup. The Setup menu will appear.
2. Click on MIDI. A submenu will be displayed.
3. Choose MIDI Studio. The MIDI Studio Setup window will appear.

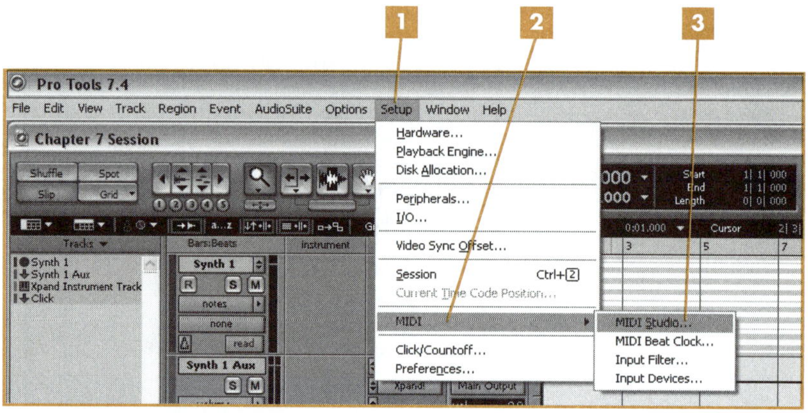

Adding a MIDI Device

Before you can record any kind of MIDI, you'll need to attach your external MIDI devices physically (of course). Once that's done, you'll need to set up Pro Tools to recognize that connection. Now you can add a synth to your setup.

PC and Mac MIDI Setups

Although the process of configuring your MIDI studio varies a bit between PC systems and Macs, the conceptual steps are similar. Due to the high percentage of PC users out there, and since the PC method is a tad less direct than the Mac method, we'll use the PC paradigm for these examples.

1. **Click** on the **Create button**. A new device, initially named New Instrument 1, will be created.
2. **Type** a descriptive **name** for your first device, then press Enter to confirm the name. The name New Instrument 1 will change to reflect your naming.
3. **Click** on the **Manufacturer button**. A menu will appear.

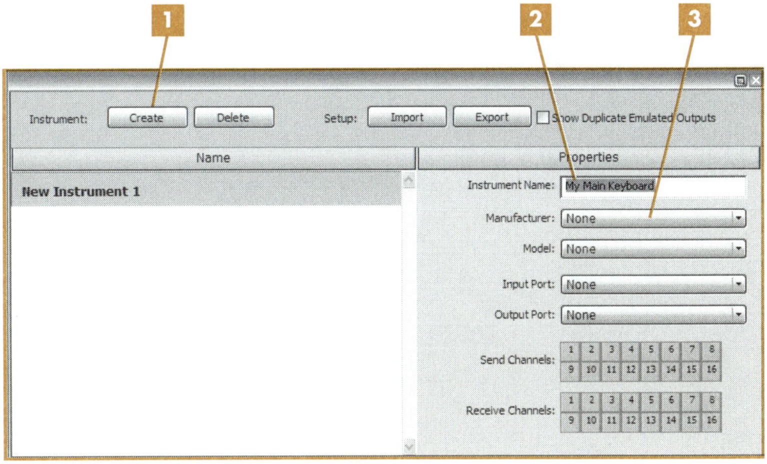

4. **Choose** the **manufacturer** that matches your device. The information will be added to the device description on the left side of the window.

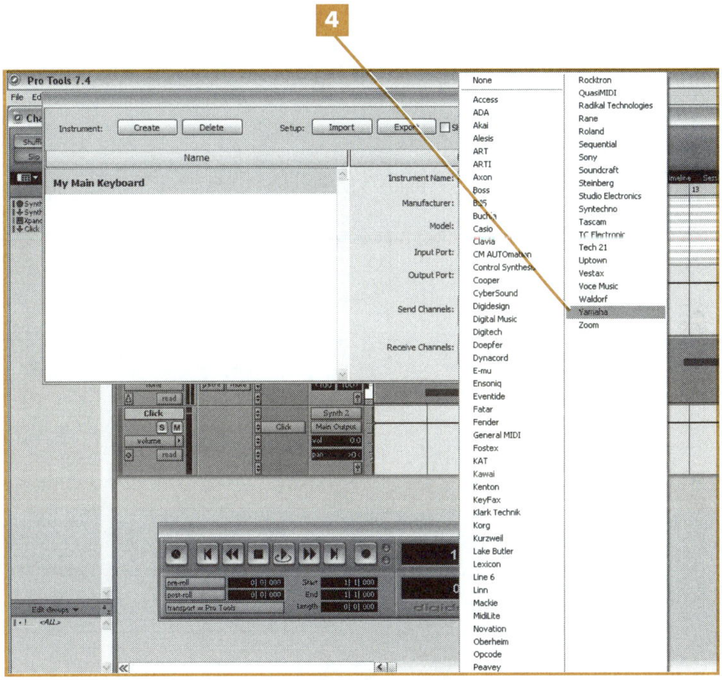

5 Now it's time to choose a model. Click on the Model button. A menu will appear.

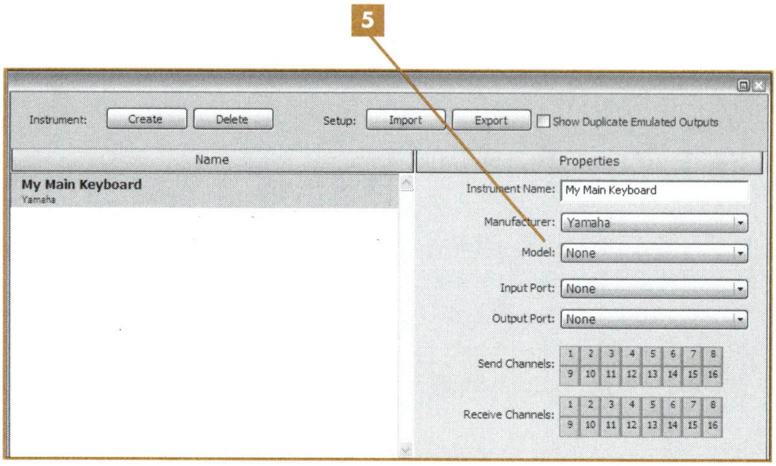

6 Choose the model that matches your device. The information will be added to the device description on the left side of the window.

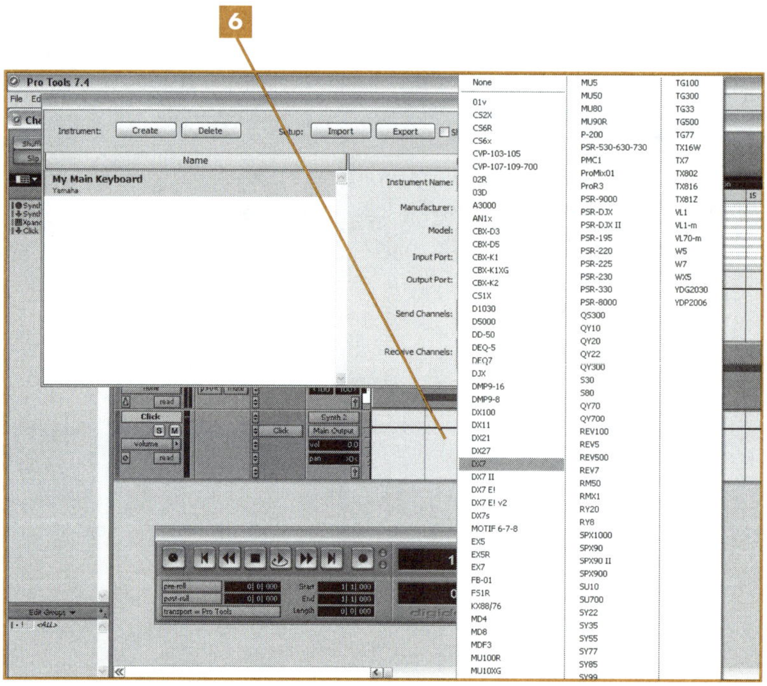

Connecting Your Gear

Let's assume that you've physically connected your MIDI gear in a traditional configuration—in other words, you've connected the output of your MIDI interface to the MIDI input of your device, and connected the MIDI output (*not* the Thru) of your device into an input on your MIDI interface. After you physically connect your MIDI cables to and from your MIDI interface and device, follow these steps.

1 Click the Input Port button. This will allow you to choose the MIDI In connection on your MIDI interface that is accepting data from this device. A menu will appear.

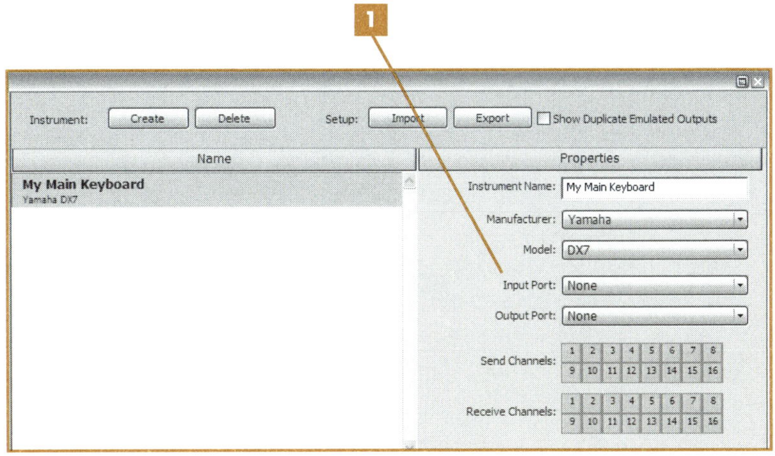

2 Choose the appropriate MIDI In port on your MIDI interface. If you're using a Digi 003, Digi 002 or Mbox 2 as a MIDI interface, there's only one MIDI In port, so it's an easy choice!

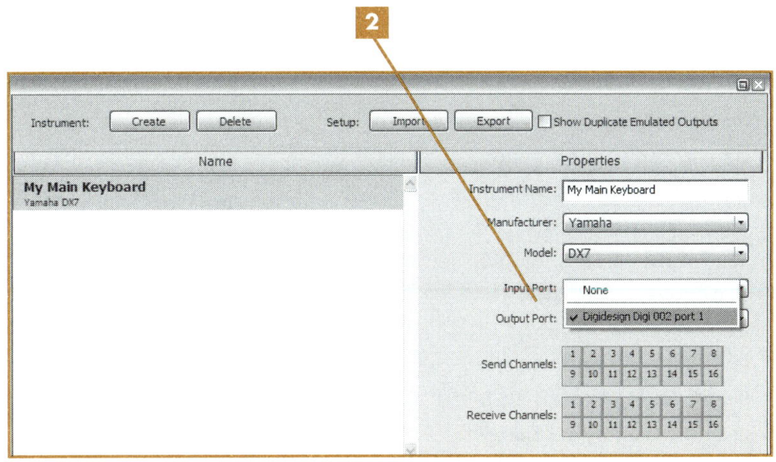

3 Now it's time to choose how you will *send* MIDI information to this device. Click the Output Port button. A menu will appear.

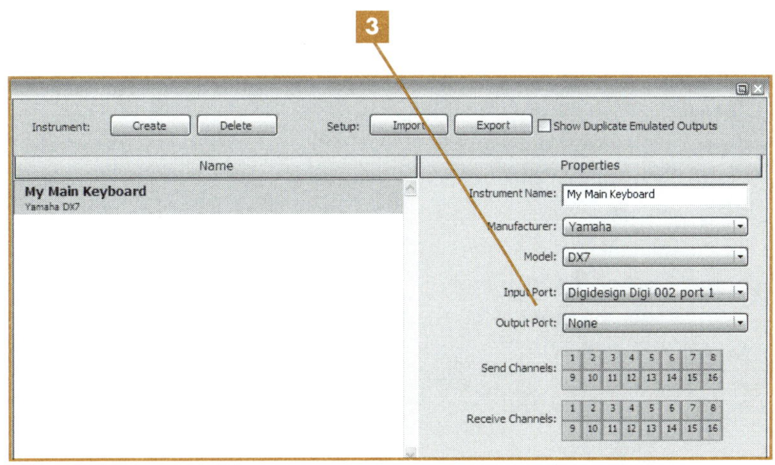

4 Choose the appropriate MIDI Out port on your MIDI interface.

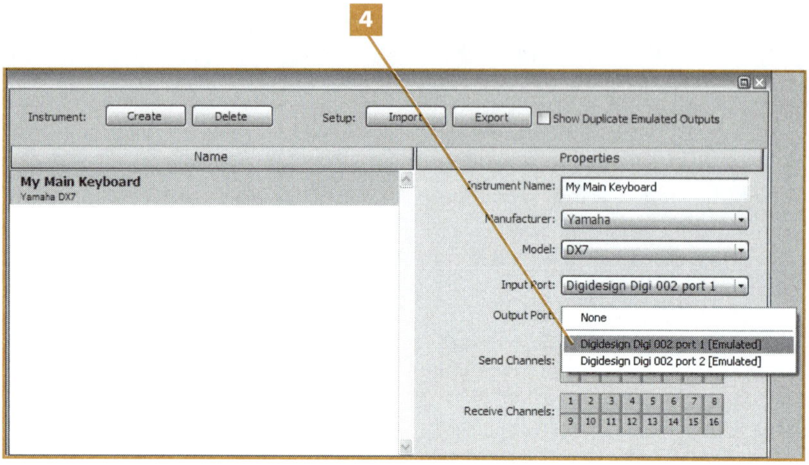

5 By default, a new device will be created with all Send Channels enabled, which means that the device can send data on all of the 16 available MIDI channels. Click any numbered box to un-highlight it and remove it from the set of channels that may be used by that device for MIDI transmission.

6 By default, a new device is created with all Receive Channels enabled, which means that the device can accept data on all of the 16 available MIDI channels. Click any numbered box to un-highlight it and remove it from the set of channels that may be used by that device for MIDI reception.

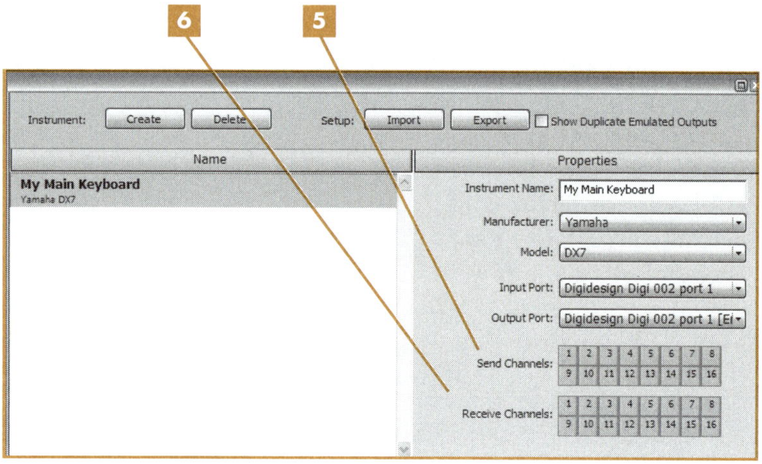

You can repeat this process to include all of the MIDI devices in your system. Before we leave this window, though, let's take a look at some of its other features.

- The Import button will allow you to open a MIDI setup file (called a DigiMIDIService Setup file, stored with a *.dms extension) that has been previously created. Be careful, though—this will overwrite your current settings.
- Want to store the setup you've got now for archiving or transporting to another system? Just click the Export button. You will be prompted to save a .dms file.

7 When you're finished, just close the window, and your settings will be applied to your system.

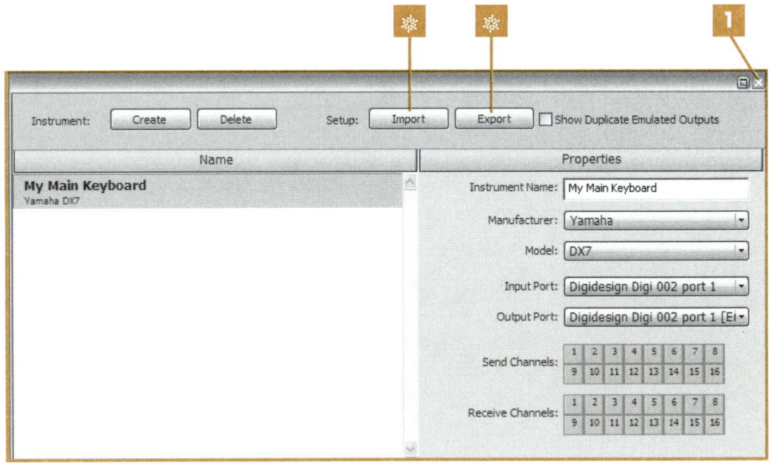

Signal Flow 201: MIDI versus Audio

Here's the important thing to remember about MIDI as opposed to audio: MIDI is *not* audio. MIDI isn't even audible—it's a digital language that allows musical hardware components to communicate with and control each other on a fundamental level. The common misconception that MIDI and audio are somehow related comes from the fact that the use of MIDI allows musical gear with MIDI connections to make sound.

Given that MIDI and digital audio are fundamentally different (although interdependent), it comes as no surprise that MIDI must have its own rules of signal flow. The good news about this is that you can manage both the MIDI signal path and the audio signal path simultaneously in one session.

Managing the MIDI Signal Path

The good news about MIDI data routing is that the look and feel of a MIDI track is similar to an Audio or Aux track.

1. **Create** a **MIDI track** and **name it** descriptively. (See Chapter 3 if you need a refresher on how to do this.)

   You'll notice that much of a MIDI track looks like an Audio track.

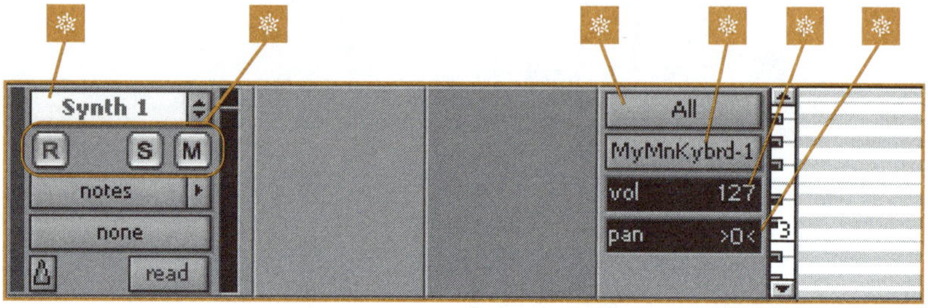

- Track name
- Record, Solo, and Mute buttons
- Input
- Output
- Volume
- Pan

2. **Click** on the **Input button**. The Input menu will appear, giving you a number of options for the input of the track. These options include the following:

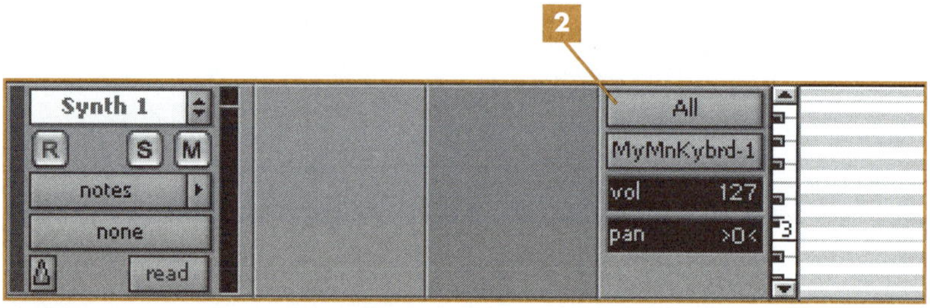

- Selecting All as an input will allow the track to accept MIDI data on any channel from any port. This is a particularly efficient way to work if you're a single user in a multi-keyboard studio. With All selected, you can move from MIDI instrument to MIDI instrument without having to change your input selection.
- Each input device you create in your MIDI setup will appear as an input option. You can specify a single device or even a specific MIDI channel as an input for your track. This is useful in multi-keyboard setups in which you have multiple musicians at one time. You can assign multiple tracks to accept input from only one MIDI port for each track; this way, you can isolate each musician's performance to a separate track even if all the musicians are playing simultaneously.

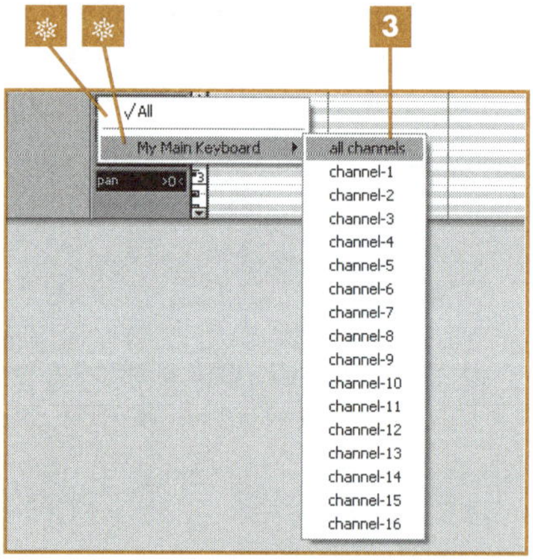

3. **Select** the **input** that matches the MIDI device you want to play. The input will be selected.

4 Click on the Output button. The Output menu will appear.

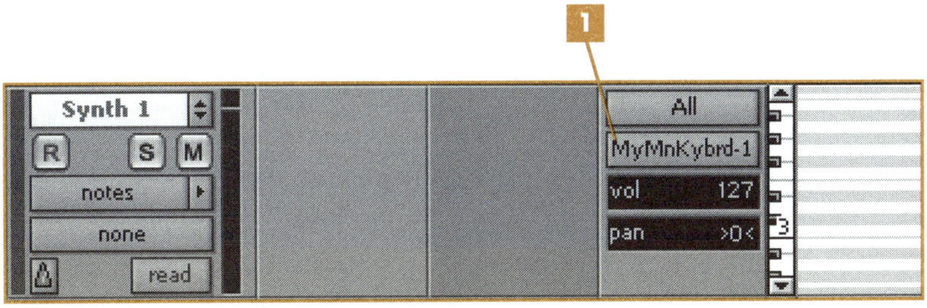

5 Click on the device and MIDI channel you want to sound when you play. The device and MIDI channel will be selected.

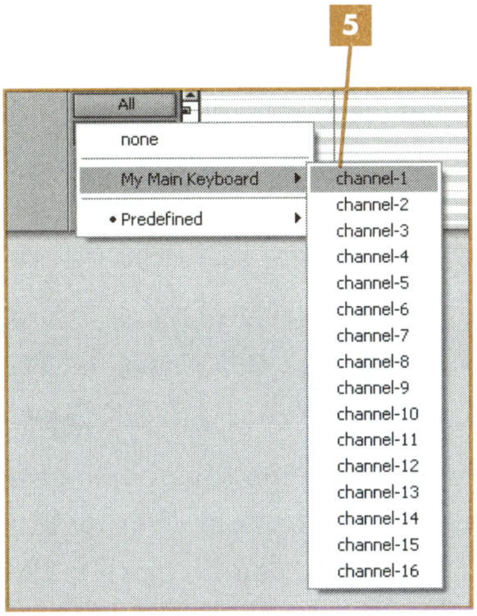

Using MIDI Controllers

The MIDI device that you physically play does *not* have to be the MIDI device that makes a sound. In this kind of situation, the device you actually play is commonly called a *MIDI controller* (not to be confused with controller data, such as modulation wheel or pitch bend).

6 Click on the Volume display area. A small fader box will appear.

7 Click and drag the slider on the fader box to adjust the volume to suit your mix. The MIDI volume will be adjusted.

8 Click in the Pan display area. A small slider box will appear.

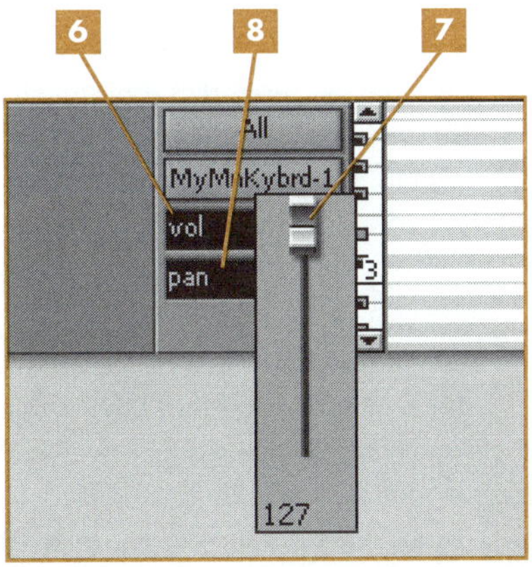

MIDI Volume Resolution

Note that this fader controls MIDI volume, which is why it has a maximum of 127. MIDI volume has a range of 128 steps, from 0–127.

9 **Click and drag** the **slider** on the box to adjust the pan value to your taste. The value will be adjusted.

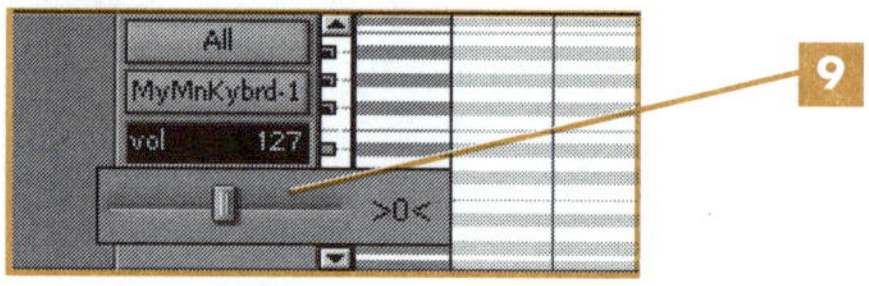

Now your MIDI track is set up to route MIDI data from the master device (controller) to the slave device. When you play your controlling instrument, you should see an indication on the slave device that it is receiving MIDI data. At this point, your slave device should respond to the MIDI data by making sound.

Setting Up an Aux Track to Monitor Your MIDI Gear

We discussed the idea of Aux tracks (or more formally Auxilliary Input tracks) back in Chapter 3. Essentially, they are tracks that you use when you need a track to handle an audio signal, but you *don't* need to record audio. In this case, we're going to use an Aux track to hear an external MIDI sound device through Pro Tools. First, connect the audio outputs of the slave device to the appropriate audio inputs of your Pro Tools interface, and then follow these steps.

Aux Tracks versus Audio Tracks

An Aux track is virtually identical to the Audio track above it. In fact, Audio tracks and Aux tracks are closely related. However, even though an Aux track is an *audible* track, it certainly isn't an Audio track. The main difference between the two is that an Audio track can play back regions in your session (as you've already seen), whereas an Aux track cannot. To play back audio regions, an Audio track uses voices. (A *voice* is loosely defined as a channel of audio going to or coming from your hard drive.) Mono Audio tracks use one voice, and stereo Audio tracks use two, up to a maximum of 32 active voices in a Pro Tools LE system.

The most significant difference between an Audio track and an Aux track is that an Aux track doesn't use a voice, which means you can't use audio regions on an Aux track. However, because an Aux track doesn't eat up one of your session's 32 voices, using an Aux track whenever possible (such as, for example, for monitoring an external MIDI device) will conserve resources so you can get the maximum performance out of your system.

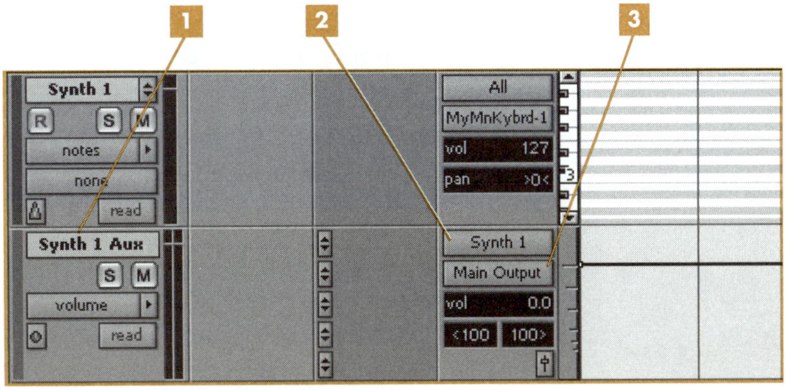

1. Create a new Aux track and name it descriptively. This track will allow you to hear your MIDI device.
2. Assign the input of this Aux track to match the *audio* inputs to which your MIDI slave device is attached.
3. Assign the output of this Aux track to the outputs attached to your monitor speakers.

At this point, you've completely configured your MIDI signal flow, as well as an audio signal routing that will allow you to listen to your gear. Now when you play your controller device, you should trigger your slave device (with MIDI data traveling through the MIDI track, and recordable on that track) and listen to the audio output of your slave device through an Aux track. (You can use the track's volume control to set the appropriate level.)

Using Virtual Instruments

The latest stage of plug-in evolution is virtual instruments. In a Pro Tools system, these plug-ins are RTAS (*Real Time AudioSuite*), which you'll work with more in the next chapter; but since these are MIDI-related, we'll discuss them here. Whereas most RTAS plug-ins are audio effects, virtual instruments don't process audio—they *make* audio! Think of them as the marriage between software plug-ins and MIDI synthesizers, taking advantage of both worlds. With virtual instruments, you not only have the power of a MIDI synth without the bulk of physical hardware, you also have the ability to automate its parameters just like any RTAS plug-in. (Don't worry; we'll talk about that in the next chapter.)

The secret to using virtual instruments is in the setup, which really is just a variation of a typical MIDI setup.

As with a typical MIDI setup, you can use two tracks to get MIDI data and audio data to work within Pro Tools—a MIDI track (for MIDI data) and an Aux track (for audio). In a traditional setup (which we discussed in the previous section), the Aux track would be used to route audio from an outside source into Pro Tools, and back out through an interface output. In this case, you still need the Aux track, even though there is no outside source involved.

1. Create a new Stereo Aux track.
2. Click on an Insert button. A menu will appear.
3. Select either multichannel or multimono plug-in. A submenu will appear.
4. Click Instrument. Another submenu will appear.
5. Click on a plug-in. In this case, I have chosen Xpand!, a virtual multichannel virtual instrument that is included with Pro Tools LE. The plug-in's window will appear.

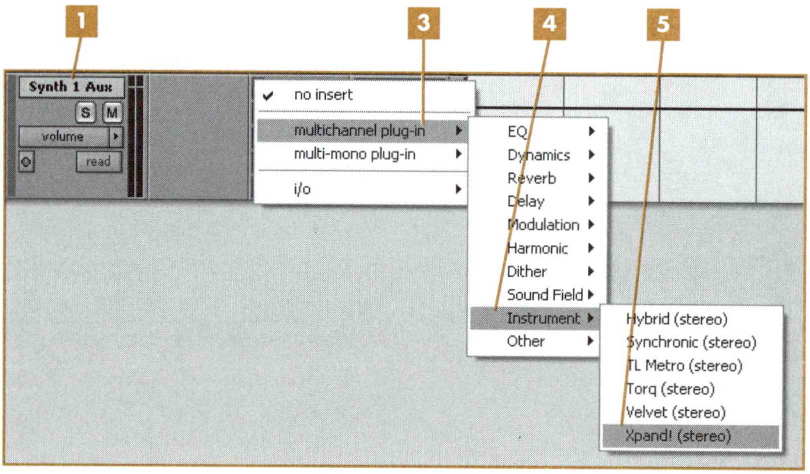

6. Now all you need to do is create a MIDI track (if you haven't already) and set up the output to be routed to your new virtual instrument. Fortunately, Pro Tools will automatically add the virtual instrument(s) to the list of outputs once the plug-in is instantiated. Click on the Output button of the MIDI track. An expanded menu will appear.

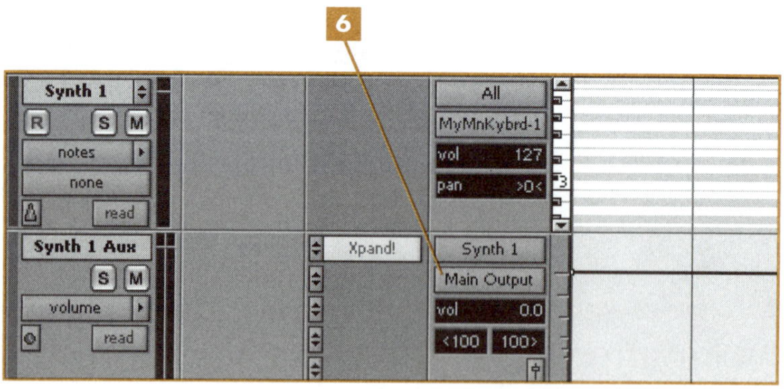

7 Select the instrument you want to control from the drop-down menu. Virtual instruments that have been launched in your session will appear on this list.

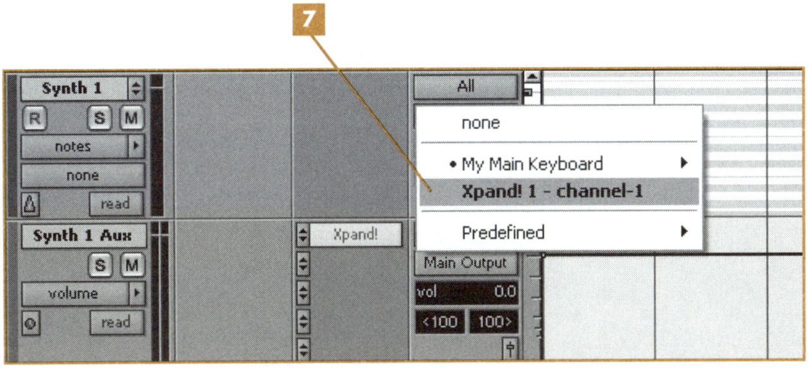

8 You're pretty much all set, but let's test the setup. Here's an easy way, even if you don't have a keyboard: First, bring up the volume level of the Aux track that holds your virtual instrument.

9 Click on any note of the "mini keyboard" to the left of your MIDI track's Timeline. If all is well, MIDI data will be created, the data will be sent to the virtual instrument, and the instrument will sound.

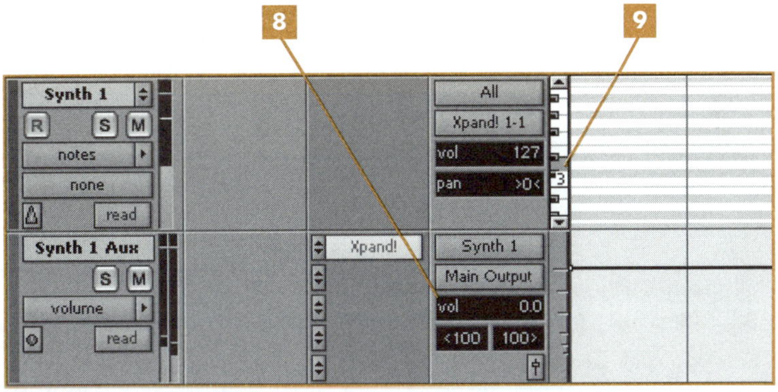

MIDI Metering

When you play a session that contains MIDI, you will see MIDI data being played in your MIDI track's level meters. Remember that what you're seeing is not audio, but rather control data being sent to the virtual instrument on your Aux Input track. The levels you see on the Aux track are the audible signal being routed to your monitor speakers.

Instrument Tracks

One of the most exciting new features in Pro Tools 7 is the addition of a brand-new type of track, called an Instrument track. This is a real timesaver for MIDI production because it combines the power of a MIDI track *and* an Aux track in one single strip. Let's delete the *two* tracks you just created in the previous virtual instrument scenario and redo the whole job within just one track. Check it out!

1 Click the Track menu. The menu will appear.

2 Click on New. The familiar New Tracks dialog box will appear.

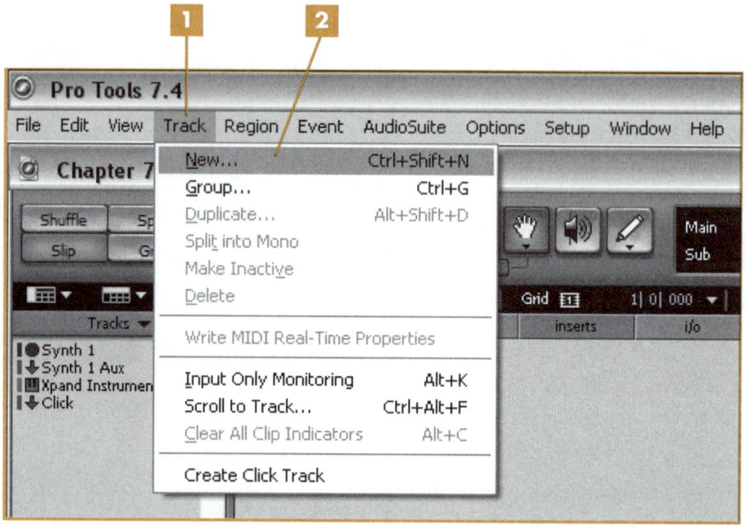

3 Click the Track Type button and select Instrument Track. When you click Create, a new track will be created.

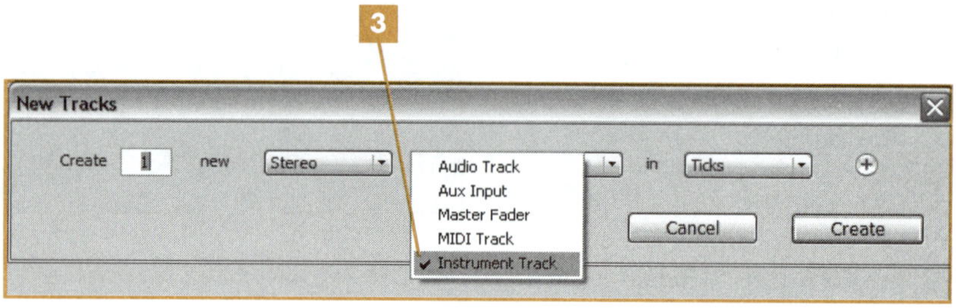

4 Name your track descriptively.

* Note that the section immediately below the track name is exactly the same as a MIDI track. You have all that functionality and more. Read on!

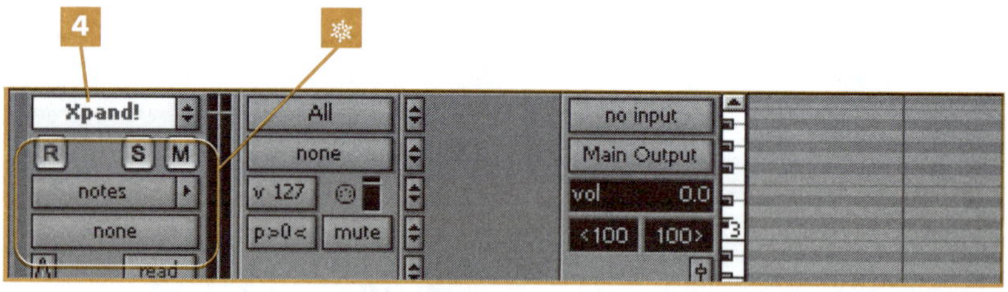

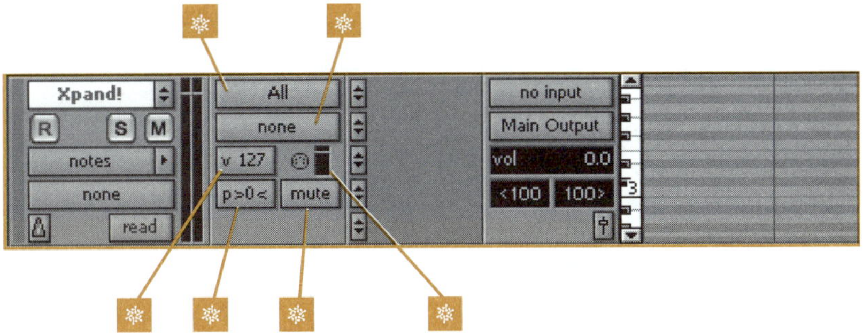

The Instrument column contains the functionality of a MIDI track's I/O column, plus some. . . .

- MIDI Input
- MIDI Output
- MIDI Volume
- MIDI Pan
- MIDI Mute
- MIDI Level Meter

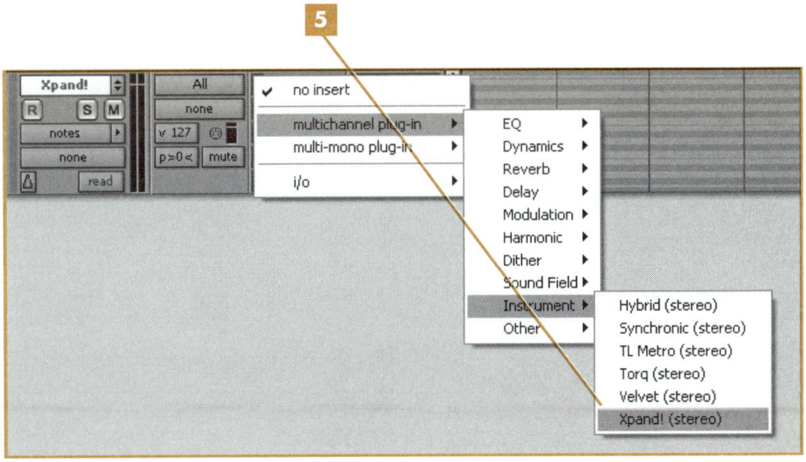

5 The Inserts column of an Instrument track functions like the inserts column of an Aux track. Just instantiate your virtual instrument plug-in on this track just as you did before with an Aux track. Your plug-in will launch, and the plug-in window will be displayed.

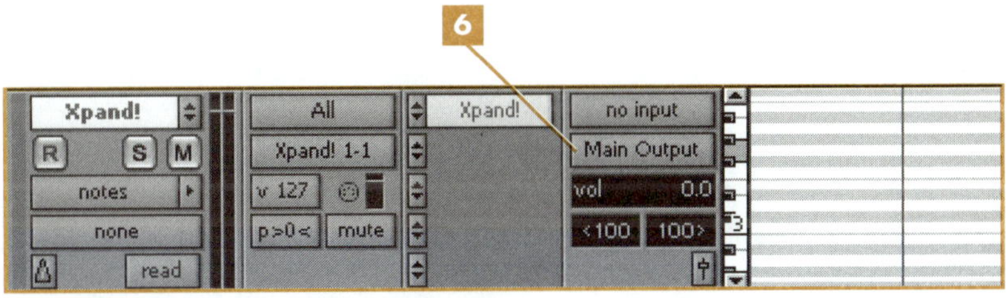

You'll notice that just as soon as your virtual instrument launched, the MIDI Output button of the Instrument track automatically changes to target the plug-in, just to make life easier for you. If you need to change that MIDI output, you can do it easily by clicking the MIDI Output button.

6 The I/O column of an Instrument track is just like the I/O column of an Aux track, and you'll use it the same way you did before. First, set the output of the track.

7 Last, but certainly not least, set your track's output level, or you won't hear anything!

8 Now, your track should look something like the example shown here. Click your mini keyboard to test your setup, as you did in the previous section of this chapter. Pretty cool!

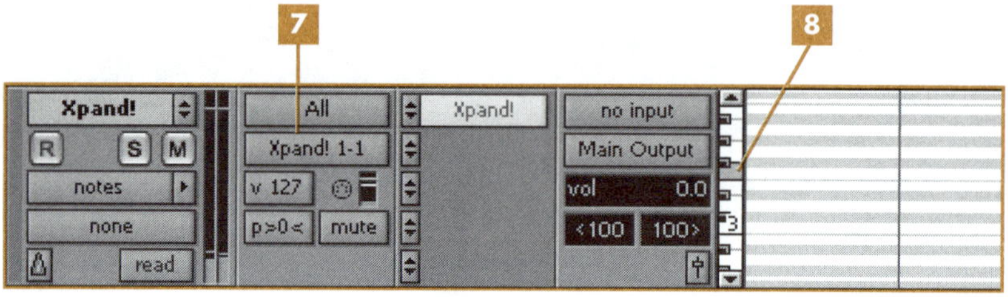

MIDI and Instrument Tracks in the Mix Window

The Mix window is uniquely suited to routing and combining individual signals in order to get a pleasing total "mix" that can be output to a pair of outputs (assuming that your mix is in stereo). We'll take a closer look at mixing in the next chapter, but let's take a look at how MIDI and Instrument tracks appear in this environment.

1 First, you need to make sure you're seeing the appropriate characteristics of each track strip in the Mix window. Click the View menu.

2 Choose the Mix Window menu item. A submenu will appear.

3 If the Instruments menu item isn't checked, click it now.

The following graphic shows an arrangement of a MIDI track followed by an Aux track, and lastly an Instrument track.

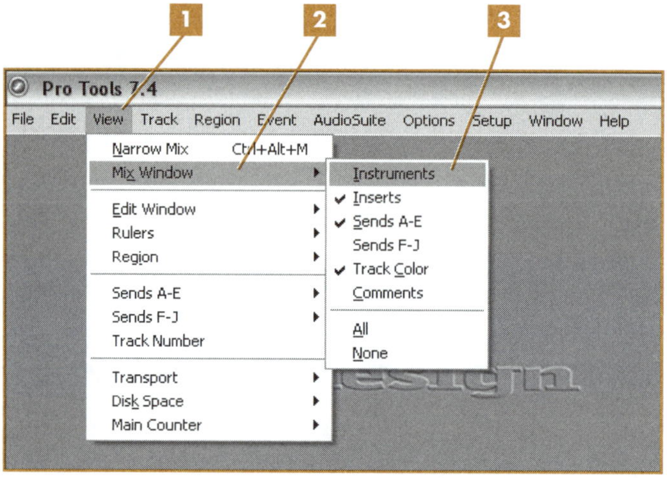

- The icons at the bottom right indicate the type of track (a MIDI plug for a MIDI track, an arrow for an Aux track, and a keyboard for an Instrument track).
- Note that the top section of an Instrument track offers the same functionality as the bottom section of a MIDI track (MIDI input, output, volume, and so on).

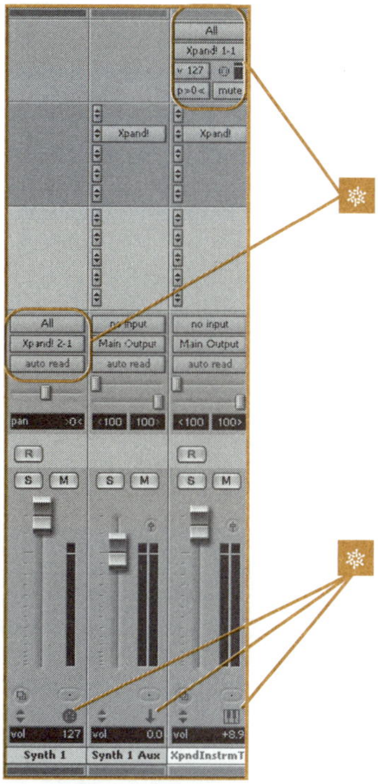

- The bottom sections of an Aux track and an Instrument track are identical, and it is here where you will set up your audio ins, outs, and more (which you'll learn about in the next chapter).
- All track strips allow the user to adjust positioning with pan controls, as well as record (when applicable), solo, mute, and volume controls.

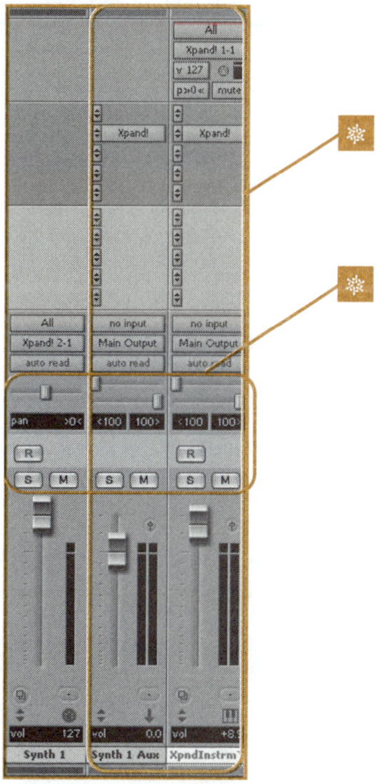

Recording MIDI

Recording MIDI is very similar to recording audio in many respects, but with some extra flexibility. The first step is to pick a sound that you want to use. Getting this done is slightly different depending upon whether you're using an external MIDI device or a Pro Tools virtual instrument plug-in—let's start with the external method:

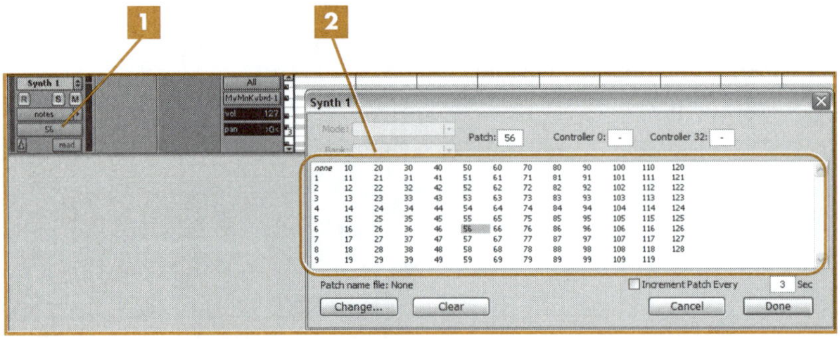

1. **Click** on the **Program Change button**. (Fortunately, it's in the same position on a MIDI *or* an Instrument track.) A dialog box containing a patch list for the MIDI device will open. Depending on the device, the patch list displayed will consist of numeric or text names.
2. **Click** on the **number of the patch** you want to use. The patch will be selected.

Increment Patch

Here's a useful feature: If you're searching for just the right sound, select the Increment Patch Every *n* Sec check box to cycle through all the sounds in this bank. You can specify the speed at which patches are changed (in seconds) by entering the value in the appropriate field.

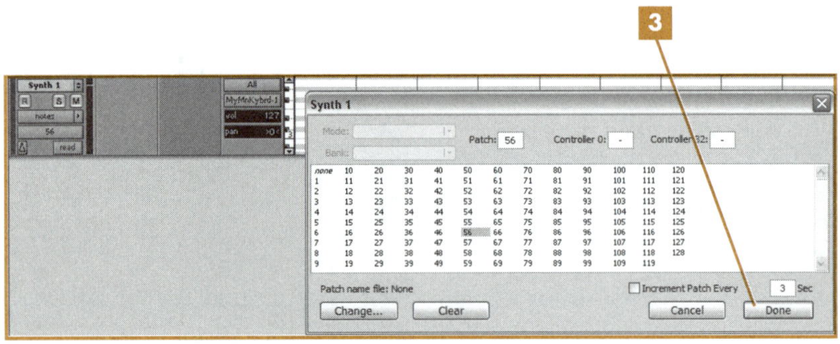

3. **Click** on **Done**. The dialog box will close. The program number or name will appear on the Program Change button.

If you're using a virtual instrument such as Xpand!, you'll need to choose a sound directly from the plug-in's window:

1. If your plug-in window isn't open already, you'll need to show it. Click on the virtual instrument's Insert button. The Insert button will be highlighted, and the plug-in window will open.
2. Click the Librarian Menu button (which will be displaying the current sound). A menu of available sounds will appear.
3. Choose the desired sound from the menu.

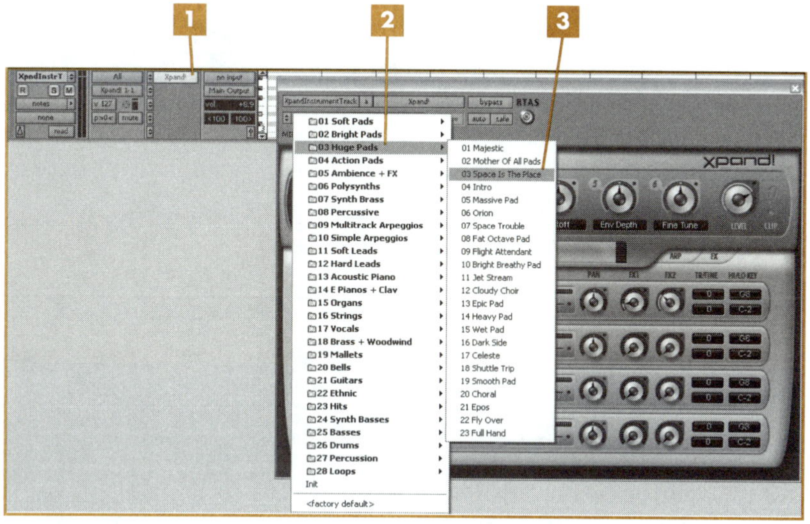

You can also see a program selector window similar to the one you would see by clicking a MIDI track's patch selector button:

1. Click the plug-in settings select button. The plug-in select window will open.
2. If your plug-in is organized into submenus (as is the case with Xpand!), click the Folder menu. The subfolder hierarchy will be displayed.
3. Select the desired subfolder from the list that is displayed. When you make your selection, the programs in that subfolder will be displayed in the window.
4. Select the desired sound.
5. When you've settled on the best sound, click Done.

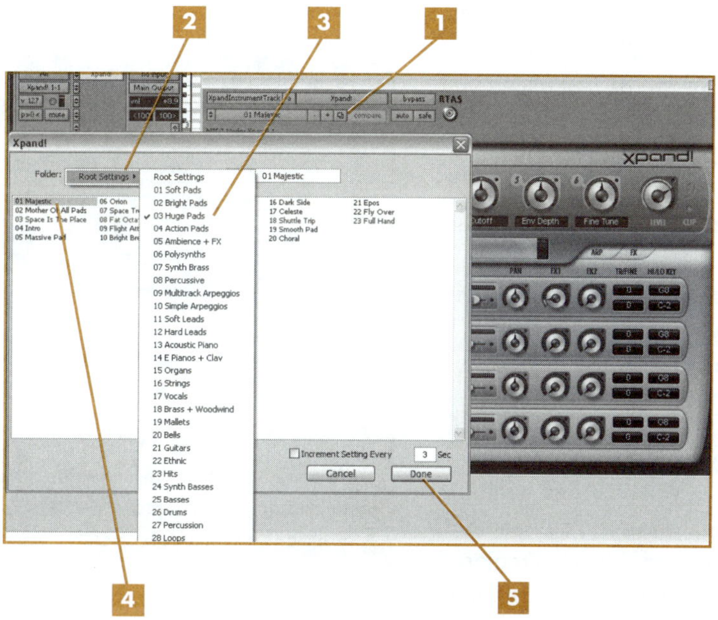

6 Before you start recording, you might want to set up a click track (which you learned about back in Chapter 4). Remember to click on the Metronome icon to enable your click.

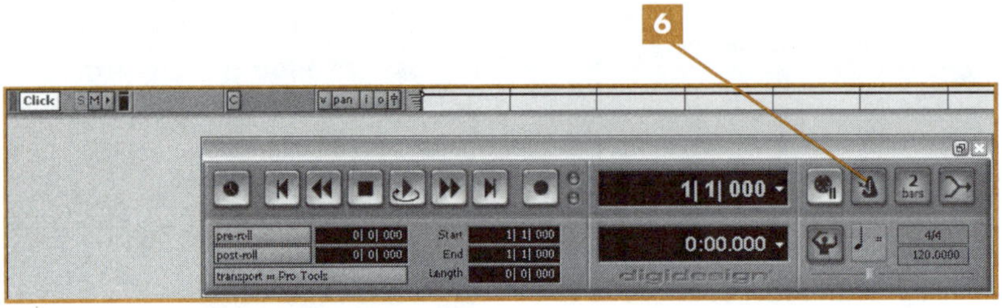

Now it's time to actually record the MIDI. The process of recording MIDI is nearly identical to recording audio.

7 Click on the track's R button to arm the recording.

8 Click on the Record button in the Transport window.

9 Click on the Play button. The recording process will begin. It operates the same as when you record audio, with pre-rolls, post-rolls, and so on.

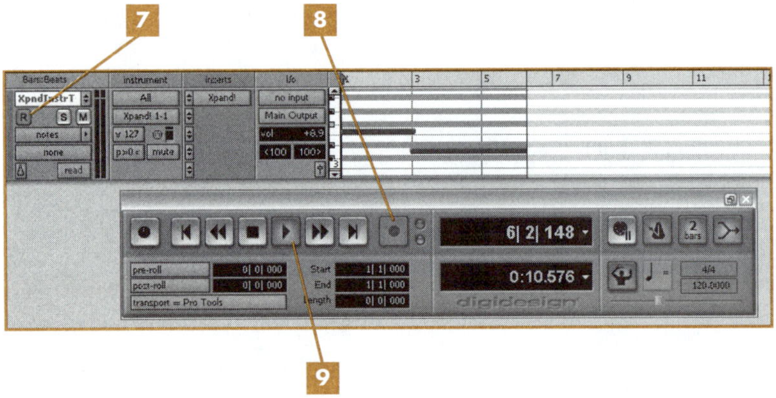

There's a nifty MIDI feature called Merge that allows you to record over a pre-recorded MIDI track and add to the data that's already there instead of erasing notes that you already played. It's an especially useful feature when you're working in Loop Playback mode.

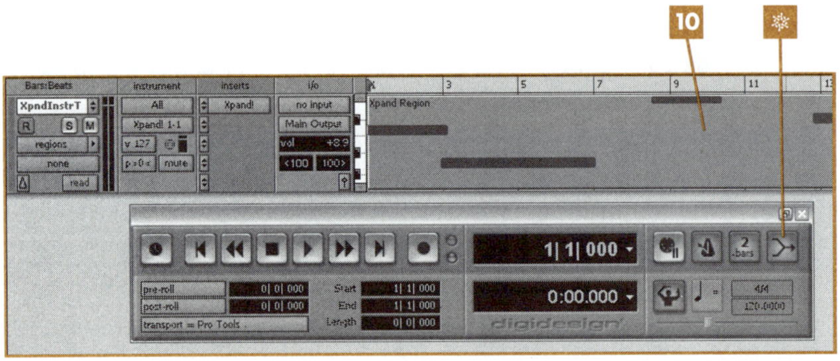

10 When you're finished, you'll have a region, as you did when you recorded audio. This time, however, you'll see MIDI note data within the region rather than audio waveforms!

Checking Your Work

To see a version of this chapter's processes (so far) in their completed form, just launch the Chapter 7 Session (pt. 1)-Finished session, which you'll find on your book's included disc.

Editing MIDI

There's a whole world of flexibility open to you when you work with MIDI. Operations that would be extremely difficult with digital audio, such as fixing one note in a chord, are easy with MIDI!

Setting Things Up

If you've recorded a few MIDI tracks in the previous sections, then you'll have some material with which to edit in this part. If not, just retrieve and launch the Chapter 7 (pt.2) session, which you'll find on your book's included disc.

Editing with Tools

There are many ways to edit MIDI data, and in a very real way you'll have a greater degree of control over specific notes than you might have with Audio tracks. To start with, you have all the region editing tools that you've come to know in the previous editing chapters. Selector, Grabber, and Trim (including the TCE Trim tool) will still work with MIDI regions in the same way that they've worked with audio regions. In the interest of expediency, we won't rehash these basic (but powerful) ways of working in the Edit window, but do take some time to reacquaint yourself with these tools when you get the opportunity.

The interesting thing about working with MIDI is that you have an extra level of control over your data. You can go beyond the relatively large region level and work with individual notes themselves. Even at this deeper level, you can still use the editing tools that are already familiar to you, though their behavior will be somewhat different. The first thing to do, though, is to change your Edit window's view so that you can actually *see* what you're working with—you need to look at your tracks in a different way:

1 Click on the Track View selector on the desired track. (In this example, I've chosen the Bass track.) The Track View menu will appear.

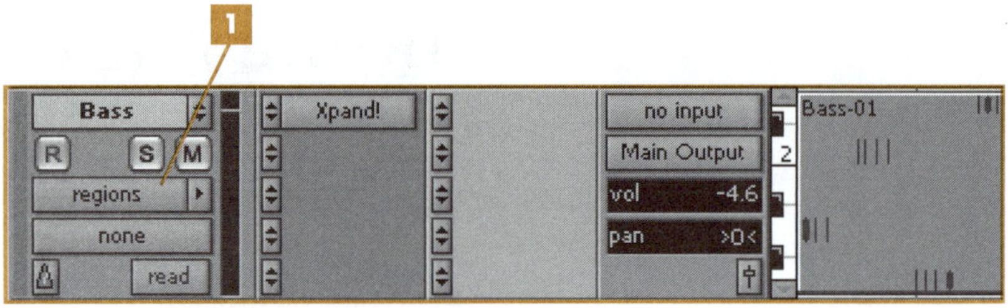

The menu includes options so you can control the kind of data you will view and manipulate. Because this is an Instrument track and contains MIDI data, the menu will display all editable aspects of MIDI in Pro Tools, including controllers and system-exclusive data.

2 In a Pro Tools workflow, you'll need to change your view to the sort of data you'll be working on. You'll be working on note data first, so click on Notes.

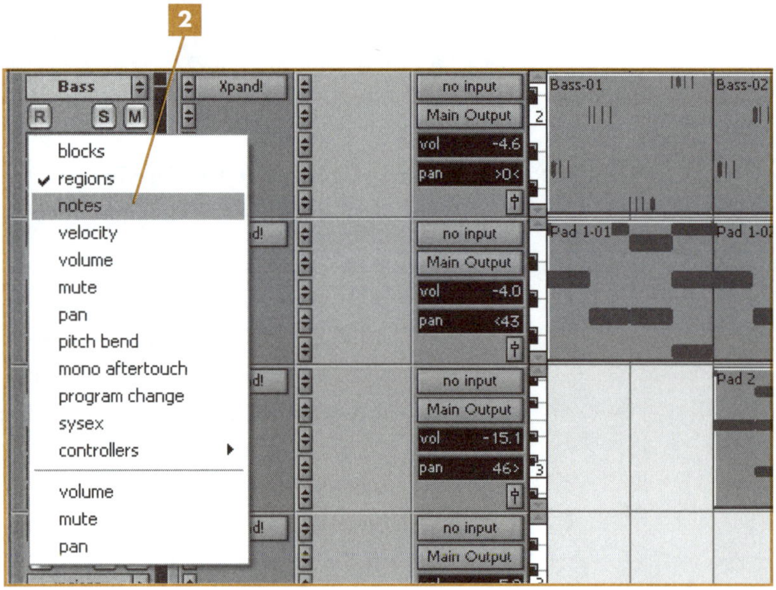

The familiar regions will fade somewhat, leaving only a series of small blocks. Each of these blocks represents a MIDI note.

On the left edge of the MIDI track's Timeline, you will notice a keyboard graphic. This graphic identifies the pitches of the MIDI notes in the track. Depending upon the kind of music part you're working with, the first thing you'll want to do is get your MIDI data into easy view. Here are a few ways to do it, some of which should look familiar.

- Use the horizontal zoom buttons to see more or less of your Timeline.
- Use the MIDI Zoom buttons to zoom *vertically* on your MIDI data. Note that your tracks' keyboard graphics will expand and contract accordingly, and that these adjustments do nothing to your Audio tracks.
- Click and drag the bottom edge of the desired track to change the track height to the desired level.
- Click on the arrow at either end of the keyboard graphic to scroll up and down the register of the track.

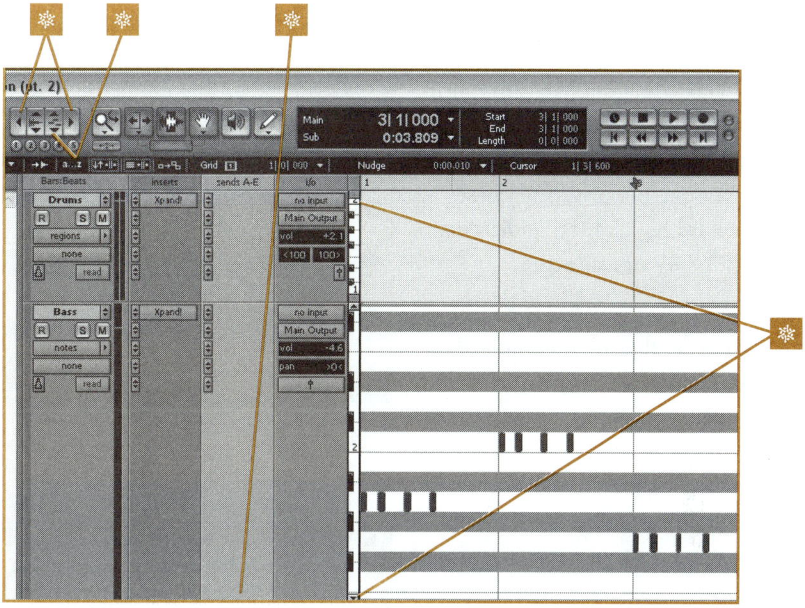

The Grabber Tool

One of the nicest things about Pro Tools is that the basic editing tools are easy to get to, and they're named well. The Grabber tool does just what it says—it allows you to grab objects in the Edit window and move them. In the case of MIDI note data, however, your "objects" are individual notes!

1. Click on the Grabber tool. The tool will be selected.
2. Click on a single note in your track. The note will be highlighted, indicating that it is selected.
3. Drag and drop the note to a different pitch or timing, as desired.

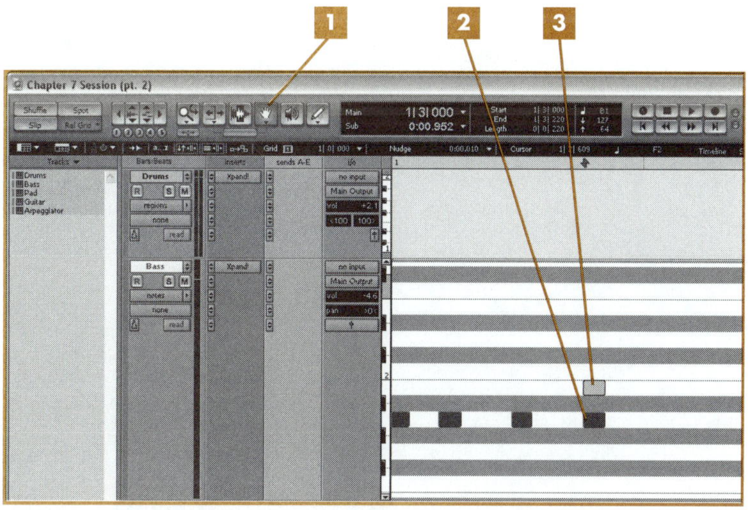

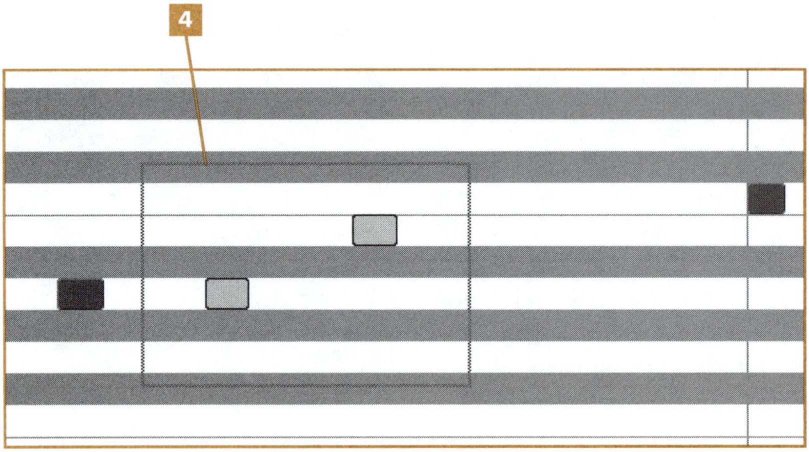

4 If you want to move more than one note at a time, drag a box around the notes you want to change. The group of notes will be highlighted, indicating that they are selected.

5 Drag and drop the group of notes in the same manner that you moved a single note.

Selecting a Single Pitch

Here's a quick way to select all the notes of a given pitch on a MIDI or Instrument track: Just click on the desired note on the mini keyboard at the left of your track. All the notes of that pitch will be selected. This is particularly useful when you are dealing with MIDI drum tracks (which typically use repeated notes of identical pitch)!

The Trim Tool

The Trim tool, the next of the primary edit tools, allows you to adjust the beginning and/or end of MIDI notes in much the same way you've changed region boundaries when working with audio.

Setting Things Up

If you're not in the Slip edit mode, now would be a good time to switch to it so that you can change your note length freely. Of course, each of the edit modes will work for you in different work situations, but in this case, slip will work the best.

1. **Click** on the **Trim tool**. The tool will be selected.
2. **Click** on **either end** of a single note in your track. The note will be highlighted, indicating that it is selected.
3. **Drag** the **end** of the note as desired. The duration of the note will be lengthened or shortened as appropriate.

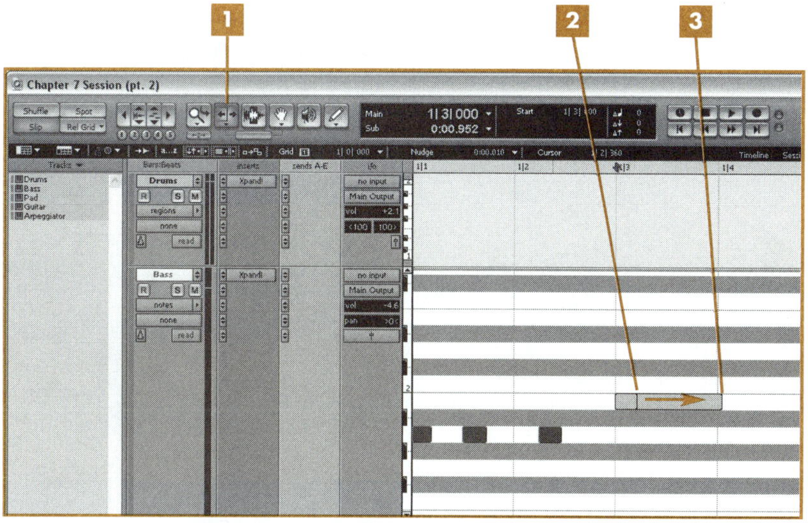

The Pencil Tool

The Pencil tool might just be the most useful of all the MIDI editing tools. For example, using the Pencil tool, you can create a MIDI note (or another type of MIDI data). In the Slip edit mode, you can create your data anywhere, but in this case, I want to create a quarter note right on Beat 4 of the first bar:

1. **Click** on the **Pencil tool**. The tool will be selected.
2. **Select Grid mode.**
3. **Set** the **grid** to 1/4 Note.
4. **Click** on any **open area** of your track. Wherever you click, a MIDI quarter note will be created.

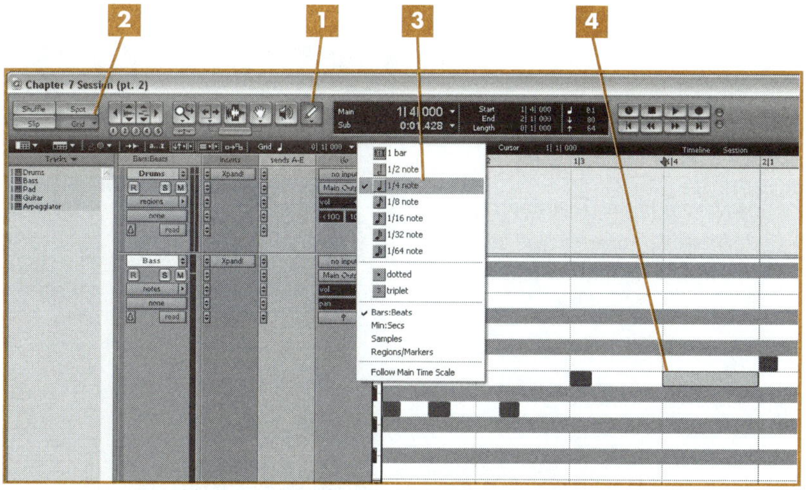

This mode works well if you want to write notes that have the same duration as your grid, but what if you wanted to write eighth notes, and still use a quarter-note grid? No problem—in fact, this is a great way to work with strings of notes. Take a look:

1 **Click and hold** the **Pencil tool icon**. The Pencil tool menu will appear.

2 **Click** on **Custom Note Duration**. A small button below the Pencil tool will appear.

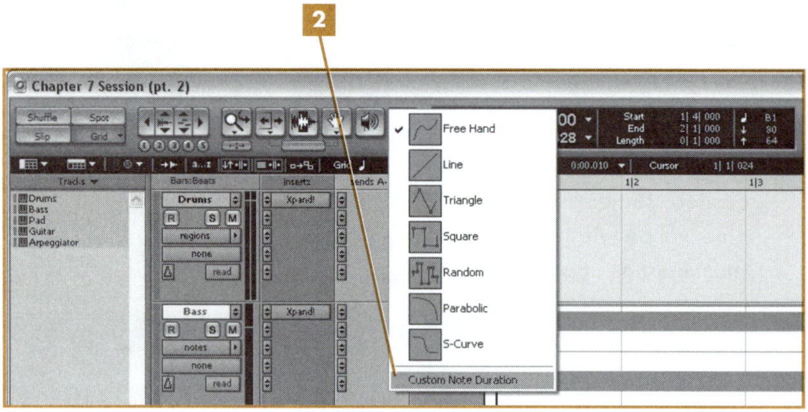

3 **Click** the **Custom Note Duration button**. A menu will appear.

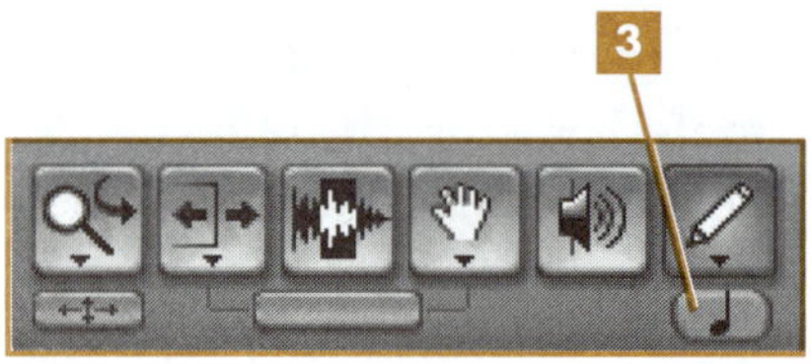

4 **Click** the desired **note value**. The value will be selected (in this case, an eighth note), and the menu will disappear. (The Custom Note Duration button's appearance will change to match your new choice.)

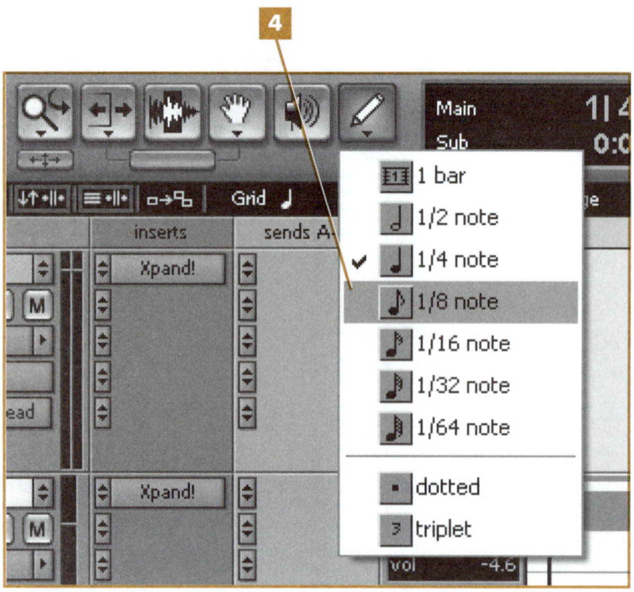

When you're not using Custom Note Duration with the Pencil tool, the length of your created notes will be identical to your grid value. By using Custom Note Duration, as you've just done, any note that you create with the Pencil tool will be an eighth note, regardless of whatever grid value you use.

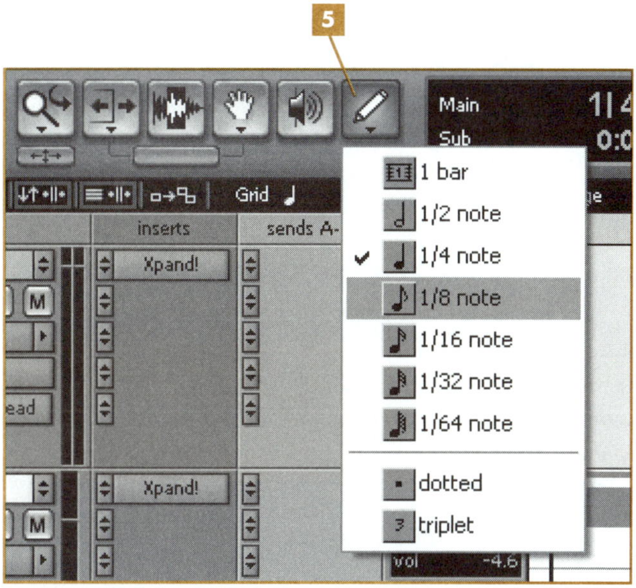

Now, let's take this process one step further and write a string of notes using this Custom Note value and this grid setting. In other words, we'll now create a string of eighth notes, with a new note beginning every quarter note.

5 Again, click and hold on the Pencil tool icon to reveal the Pencil tool menu.

6 To draw a string of notes, click the Line menu item.

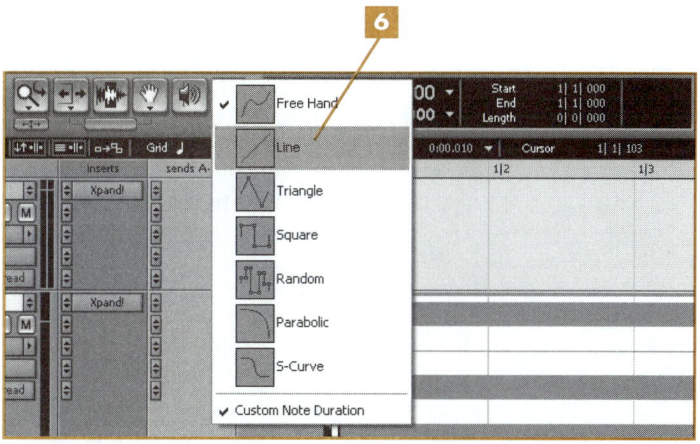

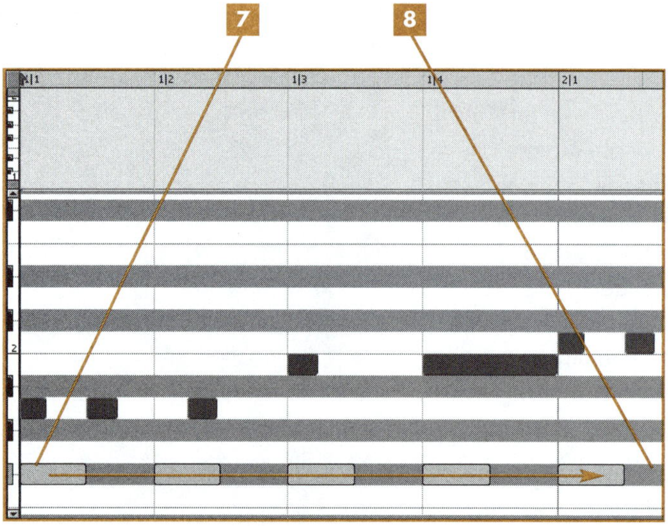

7 Now comes the fun part: Click and hold with your Pencil tool at the point that you want to begin entering new MIDI note data.

8 Drag the Pencil cursor horizontally (left or right) to create a string of notes. Note that in this example, the duration of each note is an eighth note (based upon the Custom Note Duration), and the spacing is every quarter note (based upon the grid value).

The Power of the Pencil Tool

The Pencil tool is great for quick MIDI editing—not only for its Pencil functions, but also for its other functions. If you click in the body of a preexisting note, the Pencil tool will take on the function of a Grabber. If you move the Pencil tool to either end of the note, it will become a Trim tool.

The MIDI Menu

In addition to editing with tools, you can also powerfully transform your MIDI with functions from the MIDI menu. (As of Pro Tools version 7, this menu has been moved under the Event menu.) Most of these features are commonly found in most MIDI sequencers and fall into the range of basic operations, but it is helpful to know where to find them and the specific layout of such windows.

Here's how you start the process:

1. **Select** the **group of notes** you want to process. The notes will be selected.
2. **Click** on **Event**. The Event menu will appear.
3. **Click** on **Event Operations**. A secondary menu will appear.
4. **Choose** the **process** you want to apply to the selection. There are a number of processes you can apply; the next few sections will explain these processes in more detail.

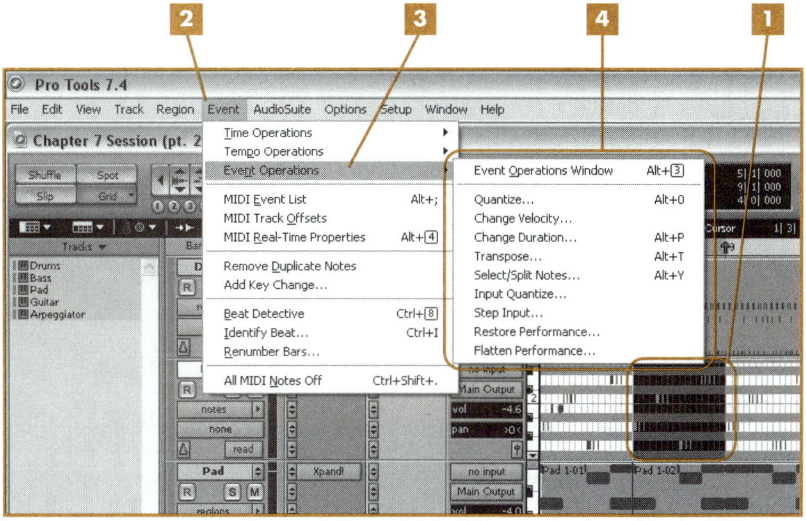

Grid/Groove Quantize

Basically, *quantize* is a MIDI function that aligns the timing of MIDI notes to a grid. It is commonly used to fix timing errors or create a mechanically timed track when the style of music calls for it. Pro Tools' Event Operations dialog box for quantization includes all the basic parameters, in addition to Include Within and Exclude Within options, which allow you to set thresholds of notes to be quantized based upon the distance of given notes from the grid.

- The What to Quantize section allows you to individually choose which part of your note will be adjusted.

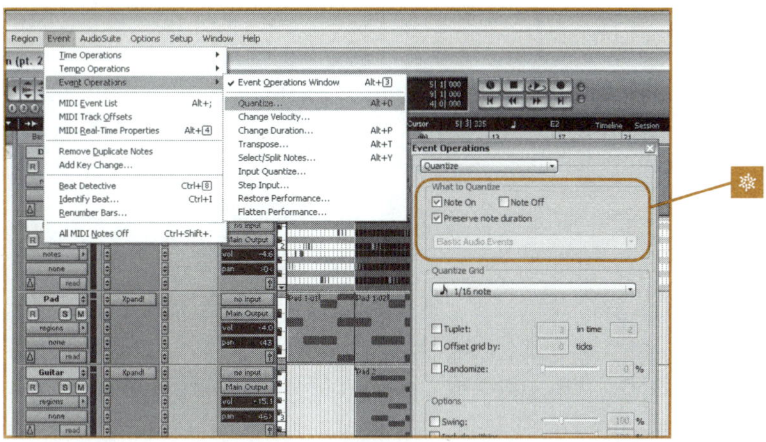

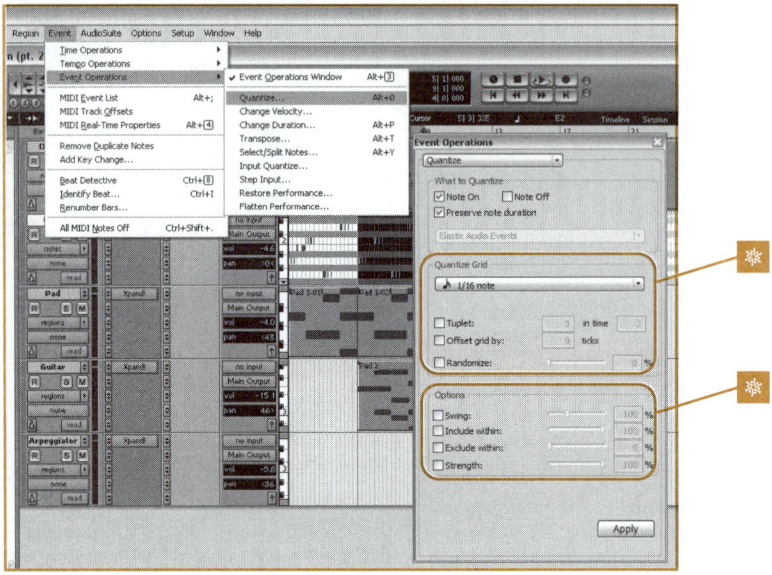

- The Quantize Grid section allows you to choose the resolution of your quantizing. This section also allows you to choose and define tuplet quantization, commonly used to create a triplet-style grid, with three quantize points in the space where there would normally be only two. Finally, there's a Randomize function, which will allow you to add a percentage of timing chaos. (See the note entitled "Advice on Randomizing" immediately following this section.)
- The Options section allows you to choose how your note data will respond to the quantization operation. Swing will add a triplet-style feel. The Include Within and Exclude Within parameters will allow you to choose which of your data will be affected. (Including 100% and excluding 0% will ensure that all of your MIDI data is quantized.) Strength will allow your quantize process to choose how much to correct your timings—for example, if your strength is set to 100%, your notes will be moved all the way to the nearest grid point, whereas at 50% strength they'll only be moved halfway to the nearest grid location.

Beyond basic grid quantizing, there's Groove Quantize. When you use Groove Quantize, you won't be moving your notes' timing to an equally spaced grid, but to a set of complex location points designed to emulate a certain musical feel. The good news is that groove quantizing is almost exactly the same as regular grid quantizing. Here's how it works:

1 Click the Quantize Grid button. A drop-down menu will appear.

- The first part of this list is a selection of musical note values. Choose the desired note value to change resolution when you are quantizing to a grid.
- Listed below are a number of musical grooves for you to quantize to. Choose the desired family of grooves, and a second drop-down menu will appear, allowing you to choose a specific stylistic feel.

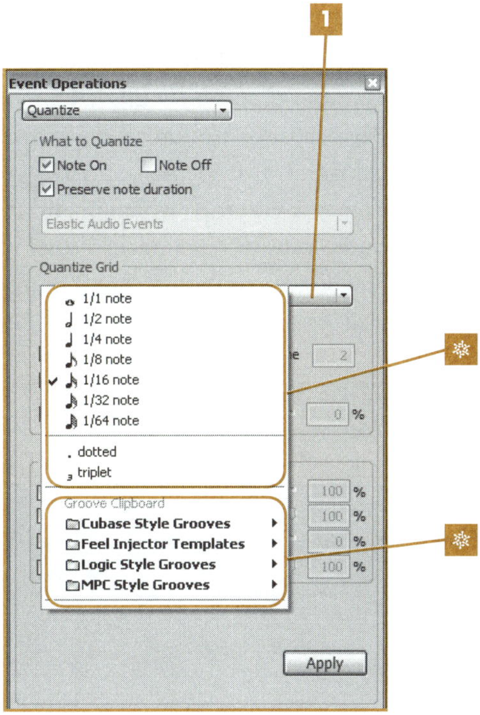

Beyond this difference, the Event Operations dialog box functions identically in either Grid or Groove Quantize mode.

Getting around in the Event Operations Window

You can change MIDI processes without going back to the MIDI menu. Simply click on the menu at the top of the Event Operations dialog box to reveal a menu of MIDI functions.

Advice on Randomizing

Users often apply the Randomize feature to a MIDI drum track in the hopes that it will "humanize" the track, but this commonly has a negative effect upon the groove. (Remember, a live drummer, though mathematically imperfect, is not playing in a random fashion!) However, used sparingly, the Randomize feature works well when you are dealing with a section of musical sounds (strings, brass, and so on)—it takes the edge off the mechanical accuracy sometimes associated with MIDI.

Restore Performance

Pro Tools' Restore Performance feature is a simple enough operation, but a powerful ally when you need it. Think of the Restore Performance option as an improved version of the Undo feature. Consider this: When you save your session, the Pro Tools' undo queue is cleared, which prohibits you from undoing things such as audio region edits and so on. What makes the Restore Performance function so special is that it extends *beyond* the last time you saved your session and the levels of undo that Pro Tools already has!

You can selectively restore specific aspects of your MIDI data (timing, duration, velocity, and pitch), so you're not locked into an all-or-nothing situation—you can choose what to recover and what to keep current. When you restore your performance, it will revert to the data's original state or the last time the performance was flattened (which we'll talk about next), whichever happened most recently.

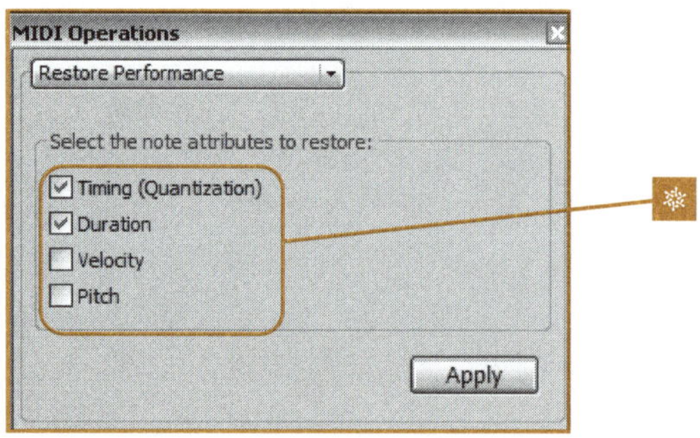

Flatten Performance

Suppose you've *perfected* your MIDI data, and you want to make sure you can easily recover this ideal state. When you choose the Flatten Performance option, you "print" your MIDI data to your session and remove the option to undo any previous edits that you've performed. If, in the future, you choose to restore the performance, it will revert to this new flattened state.

Just as with the Restore Performance option, you can selectively flatten specific aspects of your MIDI data. When you flatten your performance, you will effectively set a new restore point that you can recall at will, using the Restore Performance feature discussed in the preceding section.

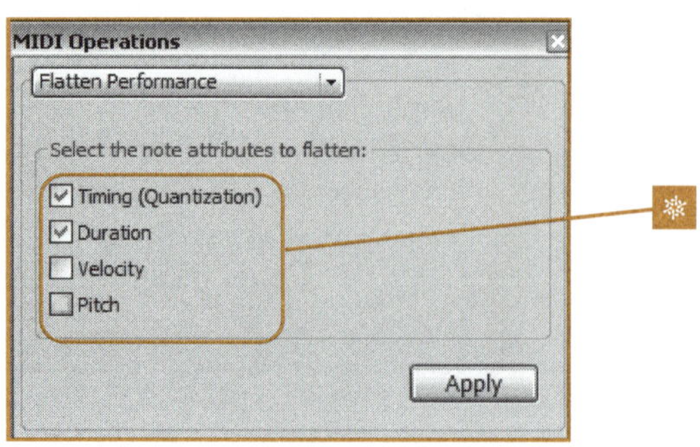

Change Velocity

The Change Velocity feature sports options with which you can manipulate MIDI velocity (how fast a key is pressed).

- The Set All To option assigns a single velocity value to all notes.
- You can directly increase or decrease the velocity value by a set amount using the Add or Subtract options.
- You can scale, or proportionally change, the velocity of a set of notes using the Scale By option.

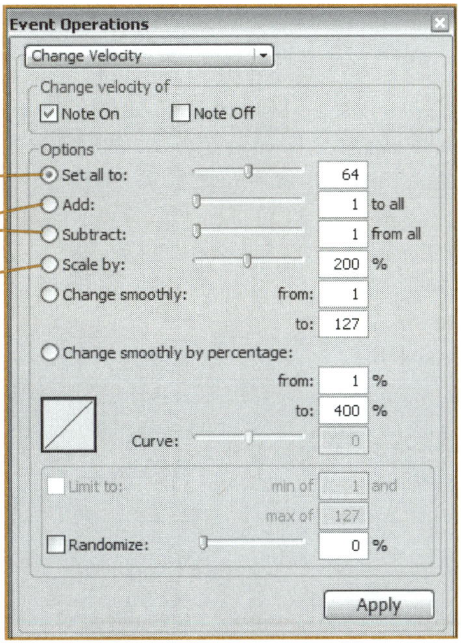

- Finally, you can use the Change Smoothly option to gradually change the velocity from the beginning of the selection to the end, resulting in an increase or decrease in intensity. By using the Change Smoothly by Percentage feature, you can even specify a smooth curve of change.

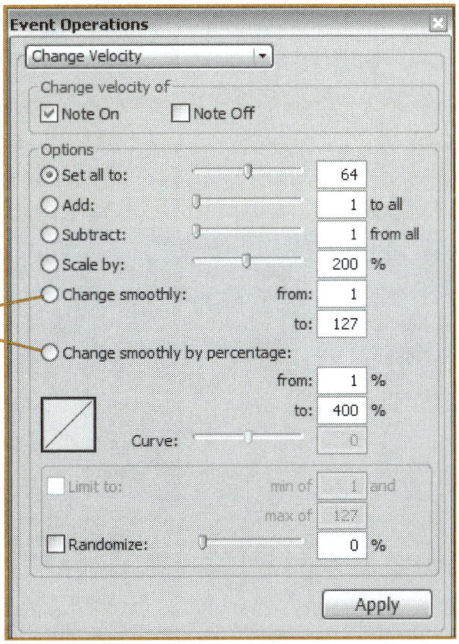

Change Duration

The Change Duration option is similar to the Change Velocity option, but the options affect the length of the selected notes.

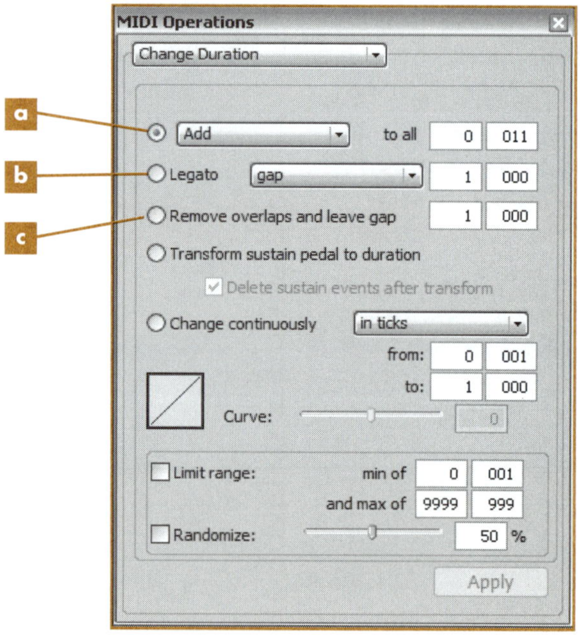

a Click here to set all durations to a single value or add/subtract a fixed value.

b The Legato option will allow you to extend the duration of the selected notes, and the drop-down menu to the right of the radio button will allow you to specify either an overlap or a gap between subsequent notes.

c This option can detect overlapping notes (which can be problematic in some circumstances) and change the duration to remove the overlap.

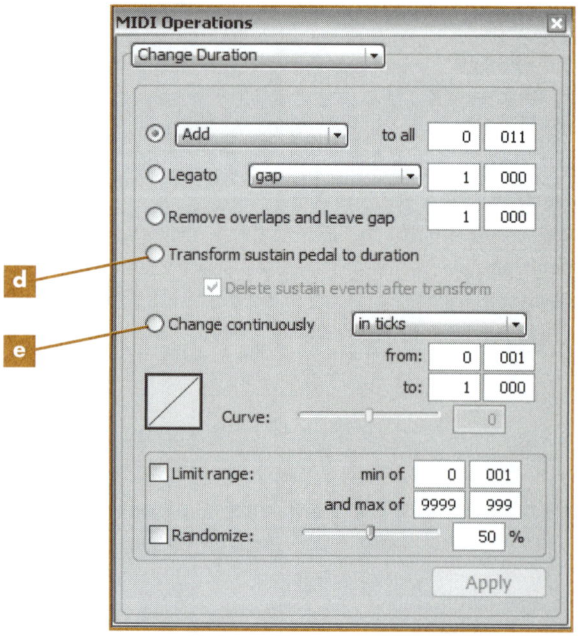

d The Transform Sustain Pedal to Duration radio button will detect pedal data and apply it to the durations of its associated notes.

e The Change Continuously option allows the user to change the durations over time, similar to the Change Continuously feature of the Change Velocity function.

Transpose

Transpose is a MIDI function that changes the note number of MIDI data, effectively changing the pitch of your MIDI music. The options for Pro Tools' Transpose function are very simple and straightforward:

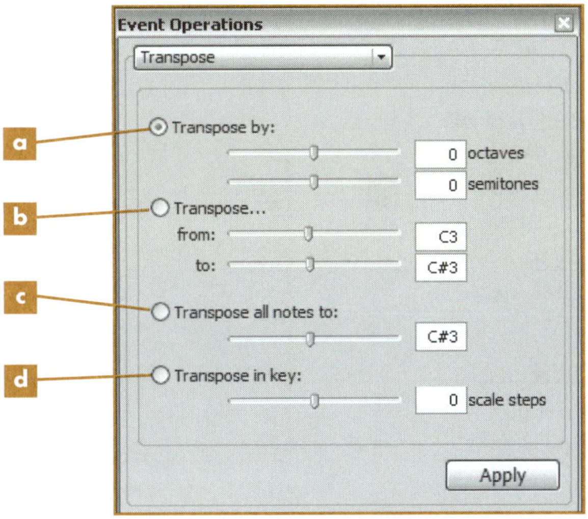

a You can adjust your music by octaves or semitones (also called *half steps*).

b You can transpose from one reference note to a target note.

c You can change all pitches to a single pitch (which is particularly useful for changing drum sounds).

d You can move notes up or down by scale steps in the key that is active in the Key Signatures ruler (which we'll discuss later in this chapter).

Be Careful with Your Drum Tracks!

Before you change the pitch of an entire section of a song, you might want to exclude your drum tracks from that transposition. Transposing drum kit patches tends to radically change the instrument assignments!

Select Notes/Split Notes

After you've selected notes using the Selector or Grabber tools, you can further logically select notes by setting certain criteria for them. Once you've selected those notes, you can then transform them with another process, or proceed to split the selected notes in a number of ways.

- For both the Select Notes and Split Notes options, you will select notes based on some sort of pitch value. You can set a range (using the Notes Between function) or you can pick out notes starting from the top or bottom of a chord.
- If you don't want to select your notes based upon pitch, you can choose to differentiate your notes based upon velocity, duration, or even the position (measured in beats|ticks) within the measure(s).
- If you choose to select notes for further editing, you're finished. You may, however, choose to split the notes.

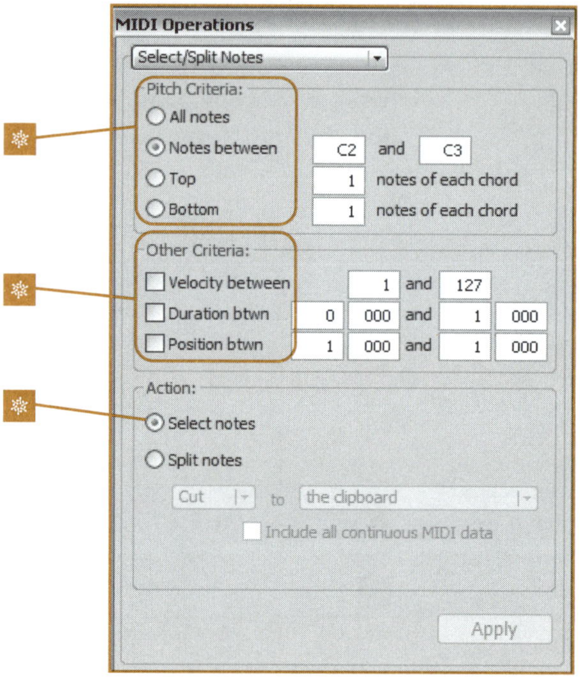

- You can choose to either cut or copy the notes by clicking the leftmost button.

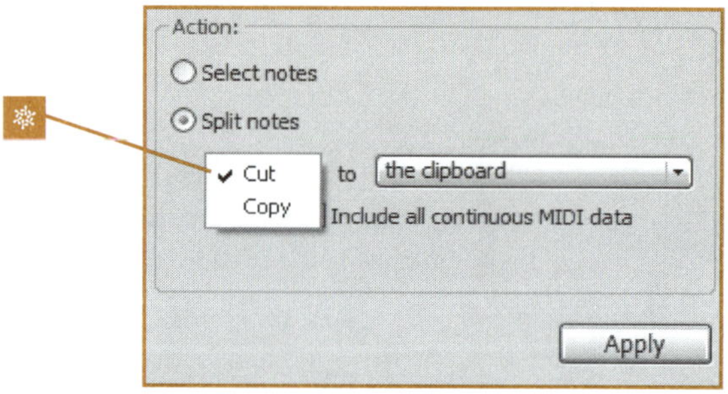

- You can choose to cut or copy your split notes to the clipboard (for later pasting) or paste the notes to a track, or series of tracks, based upon pitch (for example, if you split up a four-note chord, you could create four separate tracks, each with one note).

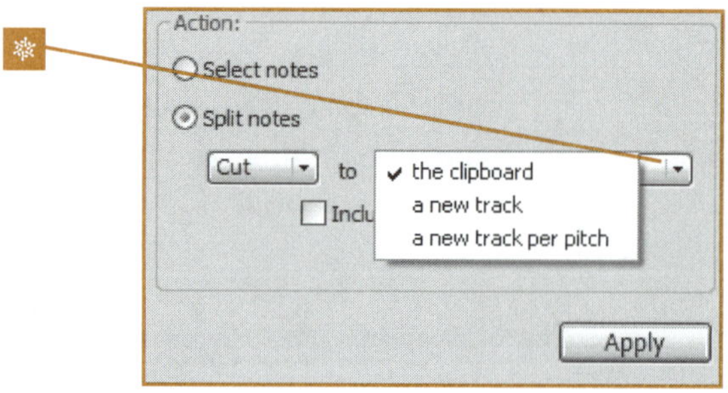

Input Quantize

The Input Quantize feature works exactly like the basic Quantize function except for one thing. Whereas Quantize is applied to MIDI data *after* it has been recorded, Input Quantize processes the audio as it is being played in the session. This feature is particularly nifty for technically challenged people like me because it fixes my timing as I play!

- Select the Enable Input Quantize check box to enable the Input Quantize feature. One thing to remember, though—Input Quantize will stay enabled until you turn it off!

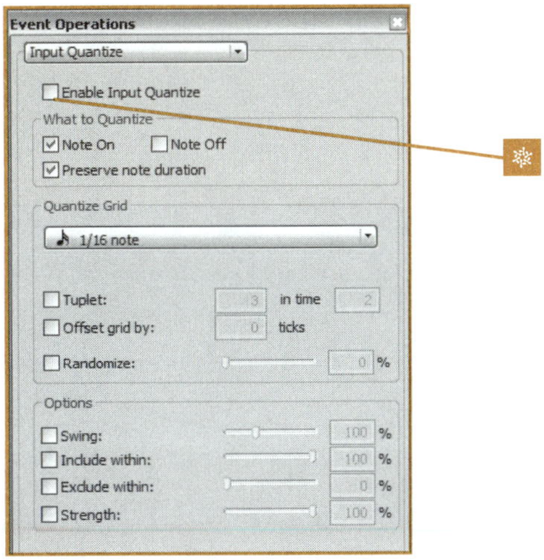

Getting the Most out of Input Quantize

You can have your Input Quantize use a groove template. Select a groove under the Input Quantize options in the MIDI Operations dialog box, just as you would for the regular Quantize options.

Step Input

If it can be said that MIDI can boost the performance of pedagogically challenged keyboardists (like yours truly), then it might well be said that Step Input is the ultimate expression of this aspect. Forget slowing down the tempo so that you can play a difficult passage slowly; why not play *completely* out of time instead? Recording in Step Input allows you to set a starting point and note value, and off you go! The really interesting thing about step recording is that you can play as fast or slow as you want, and notes will be sequentially created. Here's how:

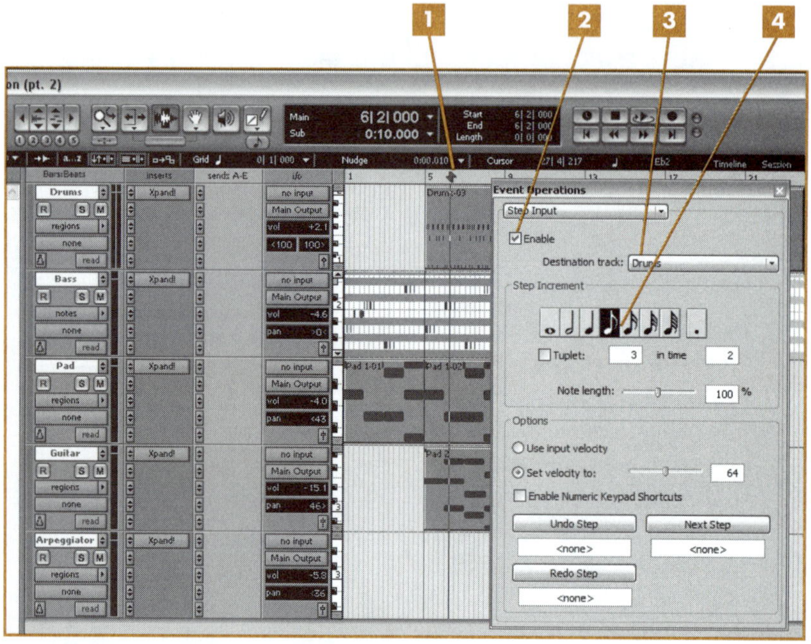

1. **Set** the session's **Timeline insertion** at the point at which you want to begin creating new data.
2. **Enable** the **Step Input options** in the Event Operations dialog box.
3. **Click** the **Destination Track button** to reveal a list of MIDI tracks in your session, and then choose the track upon which you want to write your data.
4. **Click** the **note value** that matches the value of the notes you want to create. The Note Length slider will allow you to change the duration of the note. (In this case, I've selected eighth notes as my step increment, and the 100% note duration specifies that each new note will be a full eighth note.)

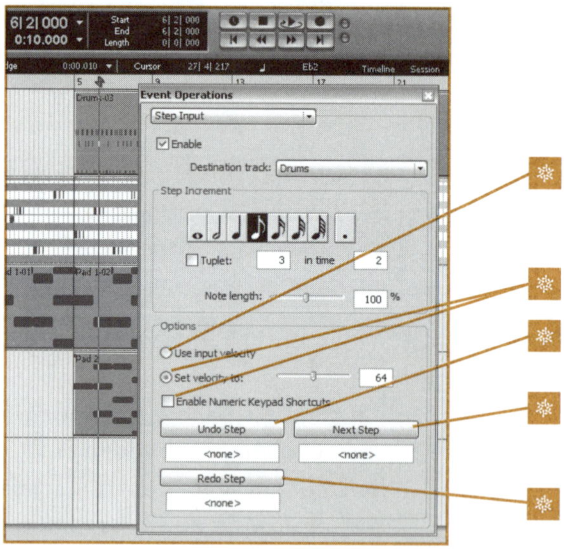

- You have a choice when it comes to note velocities: You can choose Use Input Velocity, which will record each note at the velocity at which it was played, or else Set Velocity To will assign all notes to a fixed velocity level.
- Click the Enable Numeric Keypad Shortcuts box to enable your keyboard's numeric keypad to change the step increment settings.
- The Undo Step button will clear your last note entry.
- Next Step will skip the current step and move you to the next increment, leaving a silent increment between notes (also called a *rest*).
- Finally, the Redo Step button will redo the most recently entered step.

Tempo Operations

As you learned in Chapter 6, your session's bars and beats time scale is actually a MIDI tempo map. You can control this tempo map quickly and easily from the Tempo ruler, or even enter values numerically.

For these sorts of tempo operations to work, you'll need to have the Tempo Ruler Enable button (or the "Conductor button") highlighted in the Transport window. You'll find this button in the lower-left corner of the MIDI section of the Transport window. (If your MIDI controls aren't showing, take a look back at Chapter 2 to learn how to reveal them.)

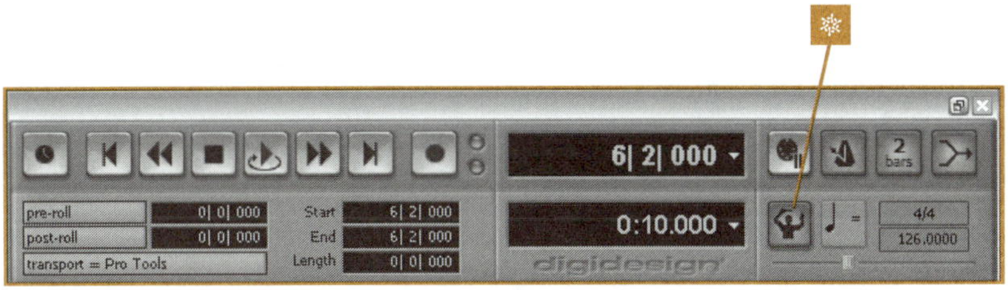

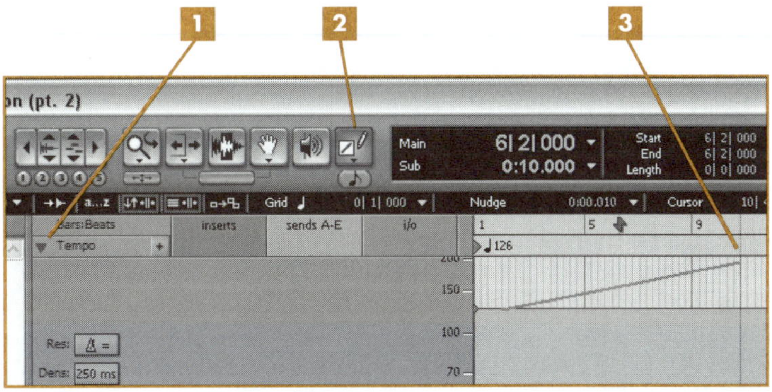

1. **Click** on the **Tempo down arrow** to reveal the expanded Tempo ruler. The horizontal line in the playback shows the tempo of your session over time. This flat line currently represents a static tempo of 126 beats per minute.
2. Changing tempo is very simple in this view. **Click** the **Pencil tool** (in this example, with the Line option selected).
3. Just **click and drag** to **create tempo change data**. Here's what you'll get:

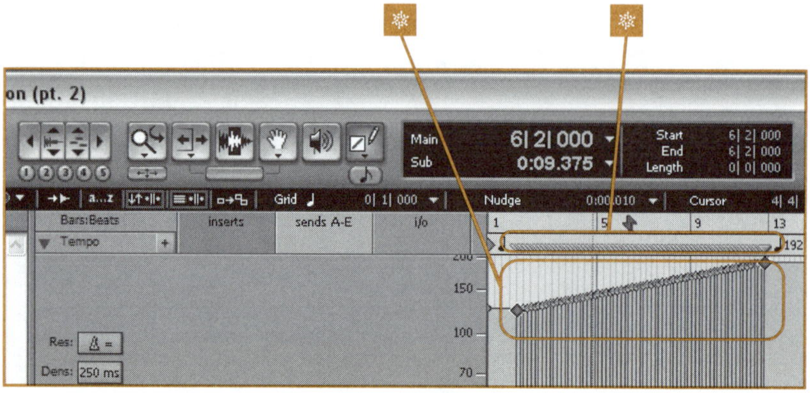

* The tempo change is represented as a straight ramp (because we were using the Pencil in Line mode), from 126 beats per minute up to 170 beats per minute. With the Pencil tool, you can write (and overwrite) tempo changes with the Freehand, Line, Parabolic, or S-Curve settings.
* The tempo changes that were created are also shown as a series of triangular value changes. These values can also be edited by clicking and dragging, or even double-clicking and typing a specific tempo value, though the more graphic tempo display as described previously is far easier for many Pro Tools LE users to work with.

Though using the Pencil tool will most likely be your easiest way to change tempo, it's not the only way. From the Event menu, then from the Tempo submenu, you can choose to create a tempo change with a Constant, Linear, Parabolic, or S-Curve shape (just as you saw with the Pencil tool). The process is generally similar regardless of the shape you've chosen:

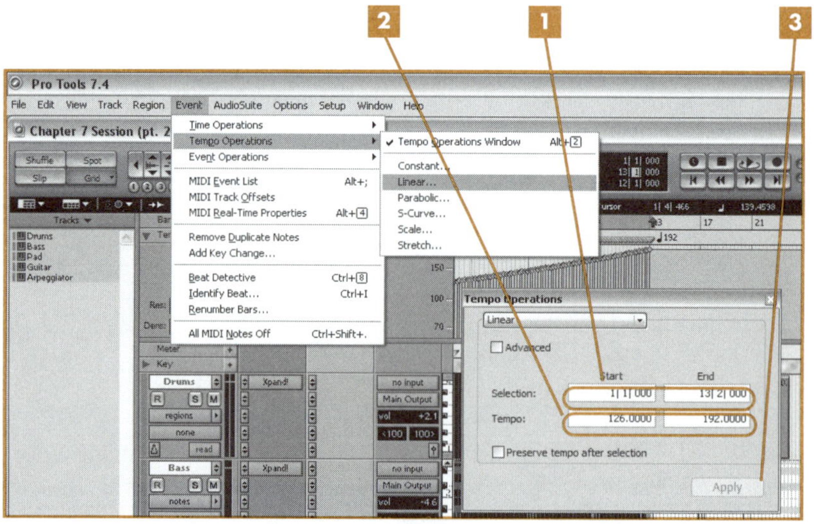

1. **Select** the **start** and **end points** of your tempo change.
2. **Select** the **starting** and **final tempos**.
3. When you're finished entering these values, **click** the **Apply button**, and your tempo change will be applied.

Beyond these easy ways of working with tempo, there are other ways to edit the MIDI tempo map as well.

Change Meter and Measures

The Change Meter options in the Time Operations dialog box are accessible from the Event menu and the Time submenu. Here are some of the key features that you will find useful:

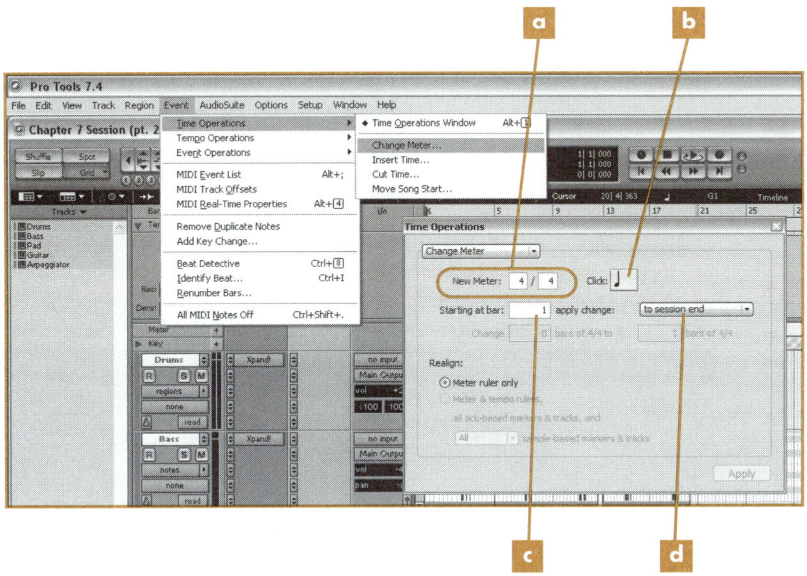

a Type your new meter here.

b You can change the resolution of your click track by clicking the Click selector button. For example, if you change your meter to 6/8 time, you would probably want to set your click up as eighth notes or dotted quarter notes.

c Type the starting measure of your meter change.

d The Apply Change button will allow you to choose the duration of your meter change. Clicking this button will allow you to choose To Session End, To Selected Range, or To Next Bar.

Renumbering the bars is even easier. . . .

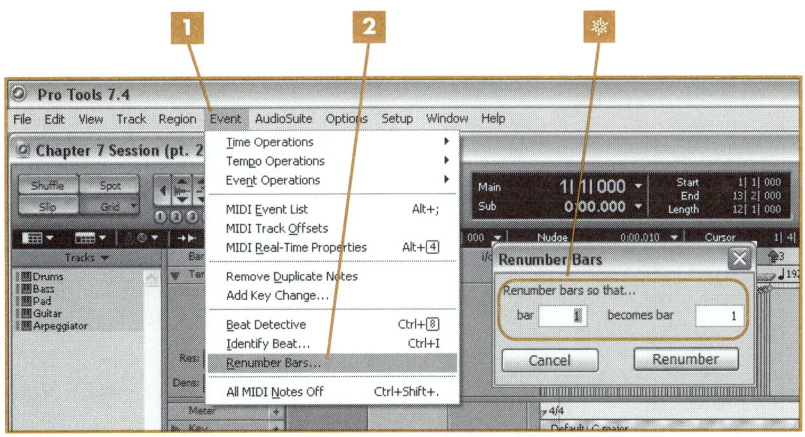

1 Click on **Event**. The Event menu will appear.

2 Click on **Renumber Bars**. The Renumber Bars dialog box will open.

- In this dialog box, you can transpose the number of the measures in your session. This doesn't change the way the session plays, but it does change the numbering of its bars and beats.

Changing the Song Start

Suppose you've written your song, only to find that you need to place some audio (or MIDI) *before* Bar 1. It's easy with Pro Tools' Move Song Start feature. As with most aspects of Pro Tools, there are a number of ways to access this tool:

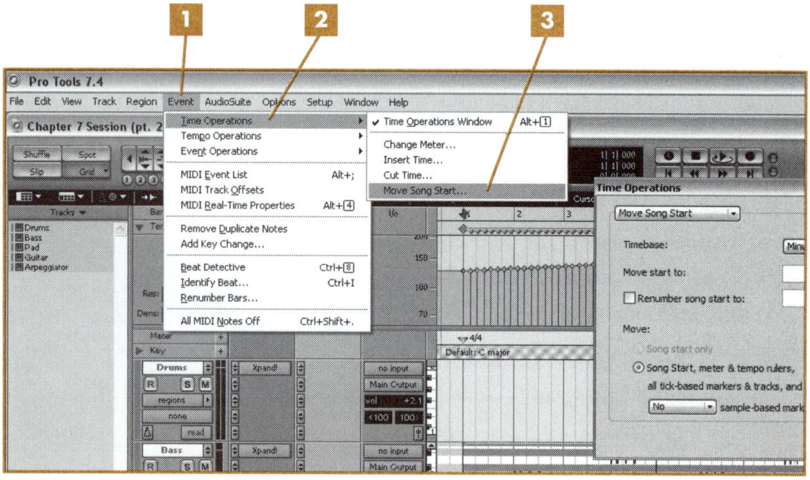

1. Click on Event. The Event menu will appear.
2. Click on Time Operations. A submenu will appear.
3. Click on the Move Song Start menu item. The Time Operations dialog box will open.

- The top section of the dialog box will allow you to type in a new location for your song start. The Timebase menu will allow you to chose different time scales for this choice. (Minutes and Seconds is shown here.)
- The bottom area will allow you to choose what aspects of your session will be affected by this choice. The top radio button—Song Start Only—will only affect your session's Tempo ruler and leave regions where they are. The bottom radio button will move the song start, Tempo ruler, and all tick-based tracks (by default, your MIDI and Instrument track regions), and it gives you the option of also moving sample-based tracks (by default, your audio regions). For more information on the distinction between tick-based and sample-based, refer to Chapter 6.

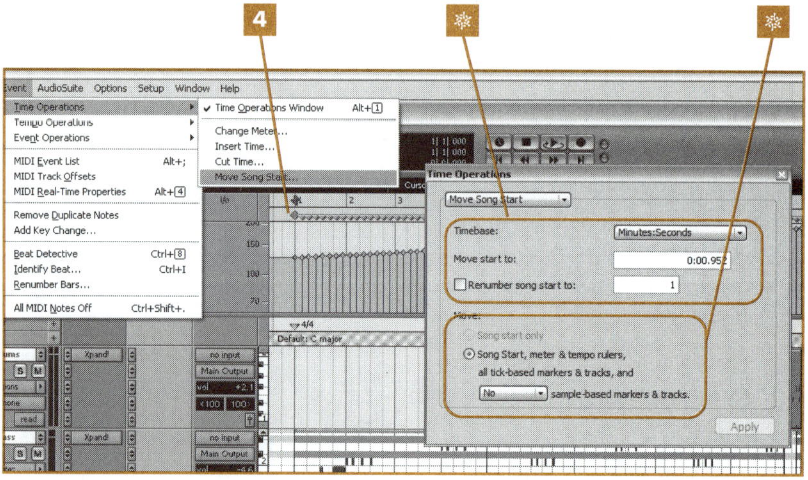

4. Here's perhaps an easier way: Just click and drag the first object on your Tempo ruler. (It will be slightly larger than the other tempo objects, and will be colored red.)

Cutting and Inserting Time

Though the nonlinear nature of the modern DAW is an undeniable advantage, sometimes you may long for the simplicity of the old tape-based cut-and-splice method. Pro Tools has just what the doctor ordered, in the form of the Cut Time and Insert Time operations. Pro Tools will go even further, though—not only moving your regions, but also "cutting" or "splicing" your MIDI Tempo ruler!

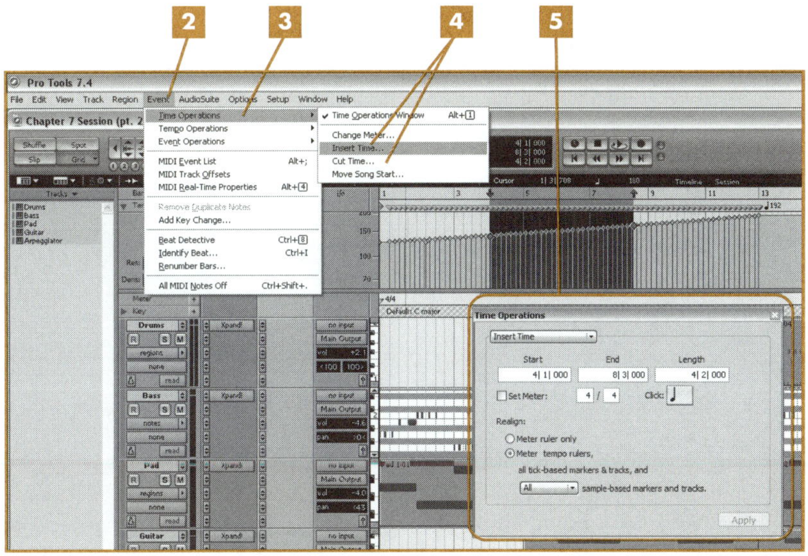

1. Though not strictly necessary, making a selection of what you want to cut or insert into your song will make the process easier.
2. Click on Event. The Event menu will appear.
3. Click on Time Operations. A submenu will appear.
4. Click on the Insert Time (shown here) or Cut Time menu item. The desired Time Operations dialog box will open.
5. You'll notice that this dialog box bears similarity to the Move Song Start window, with the main difference being that instead of shifting the Timeline, you're either adding to it or removing from it. If you've made a selection, you'll find these values reflected in the Start, End, and Length fields.

When either you insert time into or cut time from your session, you'll find that your regions, as well as your Tempo ruler, change accordingly.

More MIDI Tips

You will be using MIDI tracks side by side with Audio and Aux tracks in Pro Tools from this point on, but before we finish our focus on the wonderful world of MIDI, there are a few more key features to look at.

The Event List

MIDI tweakers rejoice! In addition to tools and drop-down menu processes, you can use the MIDI Event List window, a simple yet powerful window in which you can type the exact values you want! If you've used a MIDI sequencer before, you have probably seen this kind of window. Here's how to use it in Pro Tools:

1. Click on Event. The Event menu will appear.
2. Click on MIDI Event List. The MIDI Event List window will appear. The following list presents some highlights of the MIDI Event List window.

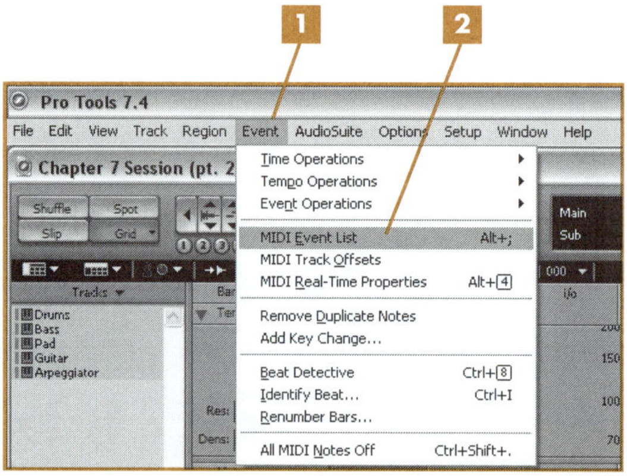

- This button shows the name of the MIDI track being viewed. Clicking this button will allow you to view a drop-down menu of all MIDI and Instrument tracks, where you can choose different tracks.
- You can click on Insert to create a new MIDI event.
- The Start column shows the beginning time for each event, listed sequentially.
- The Event column shows the type of data (note, pan, and so on) displayed by a small icon to the left of the column, as well as the value of that event.

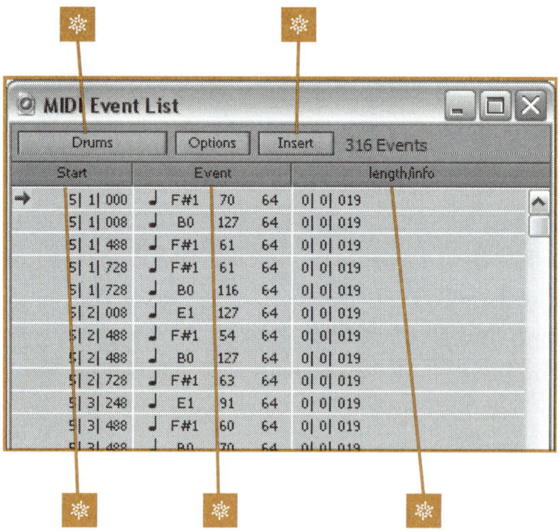

- The Length/Info column shows more specific information about each event.

  So how do you tweak this data? Easy—just double-click on the value you want to change, type the new value, and press the Enter key!

Removing Duplicate MIDI Notes

From time to time, a MIDI note can be doubly triggered. (In my experience, this has happened mostly with MIDI drum controllers.) Interestingly enough, this isn't the end of the world and will sometimes go completely unnoticed. Sometimes though, these duplicate notes can result in erratic behavior from your MIDI devices (notes being cut off prematurely and so on), so Pro Tools has added a new Remove Duplicate Notes command in Pro Tools 7.

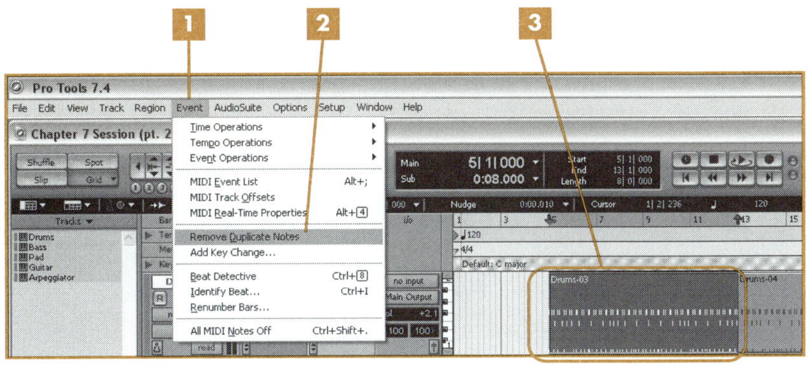

1. Select the MIDI data that you want to clean up through the removal of duplicate MIDI notes.
2. Click on Event. The Event menu will appear.
3. Click on Remove Duplicate Notes. The duplicate MIDI notes will be removed. That's it!

Viewing and Editing Non-Note Data

Of course, you can edit non-note data in the MIDI Event List, but can you edit non-note data (such as volume, velocity, or pan) on the track itself? Sure, but you've got to know how to view it before you can edit it.

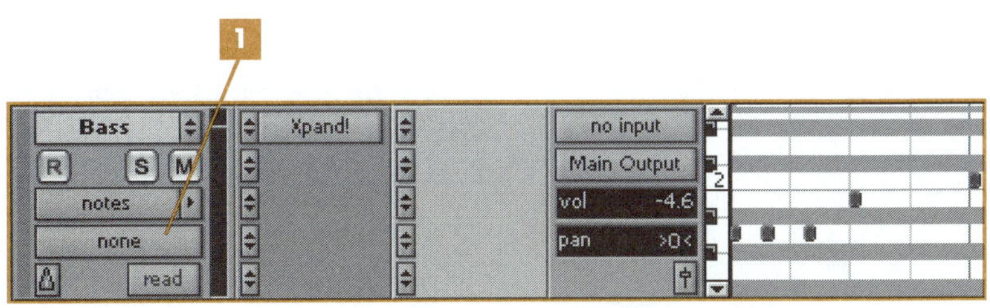

1. On this track, you're looking at (and thus able to edit) note data, as indicated by the label on the Track Display Format button. Click on the Track View Selector button. A menu of other MIDI data you can view will appear.

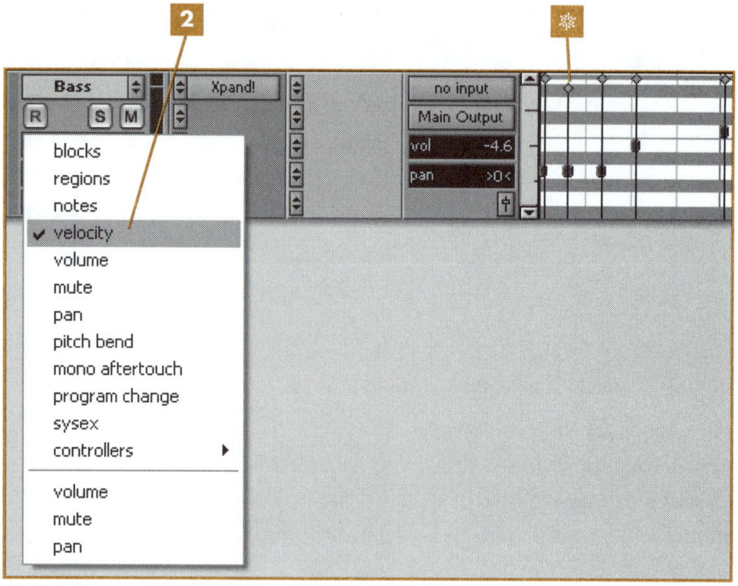

2. Select the kind of MIDI data with which you want to work. The track to the right will change to show the kind of data you selected.

- In this case, velocity data is shown. Although you can still see the notes in the background, you see velocity stems for each note event, and that's the only kind of data you can manipulate. It's easy from there because you can use the same tools you used for the note data (such as the Grabber, Trim, Selector, Pencil tools, and so on) to change these values.

MIDI Real-Time Properties

The MIDI Real-Time Properties feature is something new to Pro Tools 7 and is already promising to be one of my favorite additions to the DAW. What sets this feature apart from the rest of the MIDI processes we've discussed is that these Real-Time Properties, which are perhaps best described as real-time *processes*, only alter the data as it's being played and don't alter the recorded data in any permanent way.

The Chapter 7 session that I've used for the examples thus far has a bit of a problem that we can use the Real-Time Properties window to fix. The problem is some timing disagreement between the Pad 1 and Pad 2 tracks. Take a look.

1. **Select** the **region(s) or track(s)** that need to be fixed.
2. **Click** the **Event menu**. The Event menu will appear.
3. **Click** the **MIDI Real-Time Properties menu item**. The Real-Time Properties window will appear.

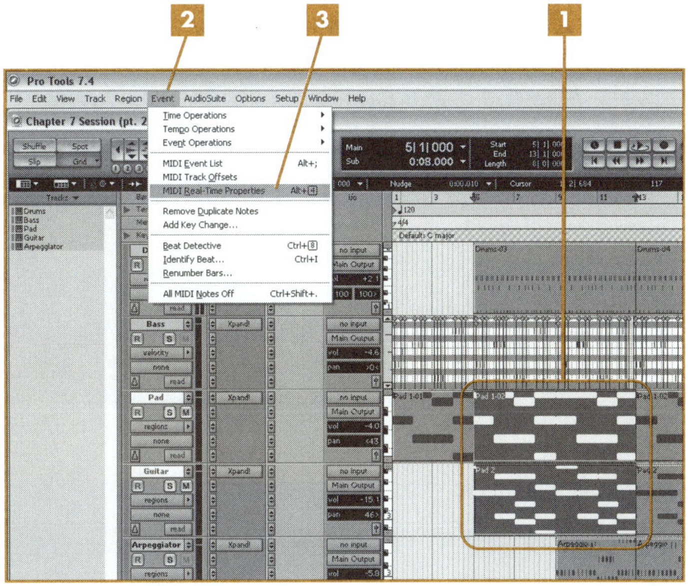

4. The first order of business is to choose what will be processed in real time. **Click** the **Apply To button**.

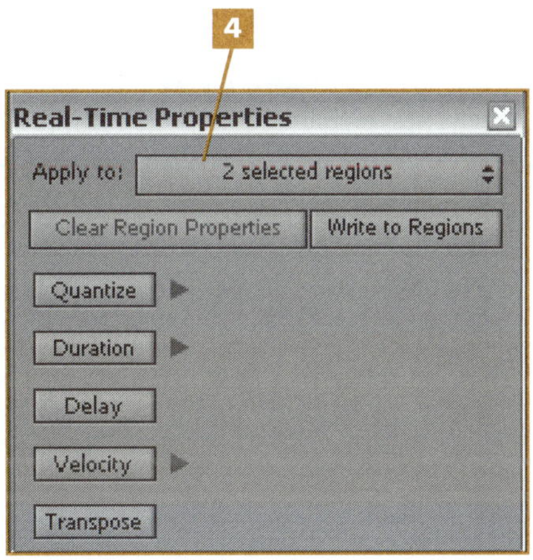

5 The application list will reflect your track and region selections. In this case, the Bass track is selected, as are two regions on the Pad 1 and Pad 2 tracks. For the purposes of this demonstration, choose 2 Selected Regions.

6 This next bit isn't an absolute necessity, but you'll hear the real-time effects better if you solo the tracks you want to hear.

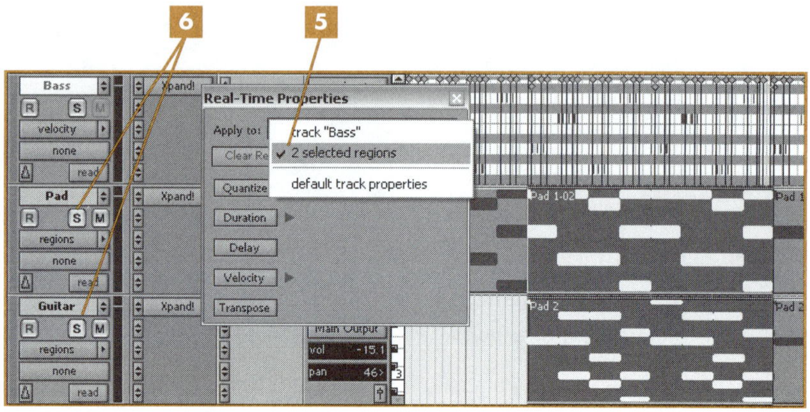

- The different processes that are available as Real-Time Properties are Quantize, Duration, Delay, Velocity, and Transpose. Each of these features is a reduced view of the Event Operations dialog boxes that we've discussed earlier in this chapter.
- The next column of buttons, next to each of these processes, is a tiny version of the main parameter(s) that you would otherwise have chosen in the Event Operations dialog boxes. This is followed by an extra area to the right that allows you to enter specific values relevant to the process(es) you've chosen.

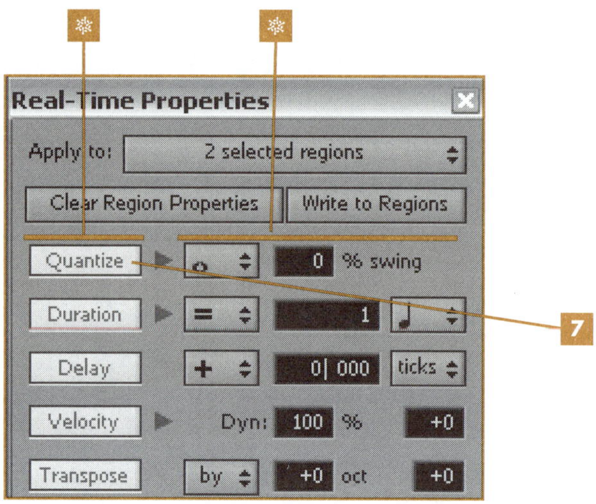

7 Click the Process Enable button to activate any of the available processes. In the window shown here, *all* of the processes are selected in order to show the complete layout of the window. In this example, we'll only need to apply Quantize, so make sure only the Quantize button is selected. Your window should look like this:

- In the figure shown here, Quantize is being applied in real time to the selected regions. The regions that are being processed will be marked by an R (for *Region-based*) in the upper-right corner of the region.
- Note that even though you will hear the benefit of quantization, the data itself will not be altered. (If you turn off the real-time process by clicking the Clear Region Properties button, you'll hear the timing problems come right back!)
- If you like the changes you're hearing, you can apply the changes to the data more permanently by clicking the Write to Regions button. Your MIDI data will be changed.

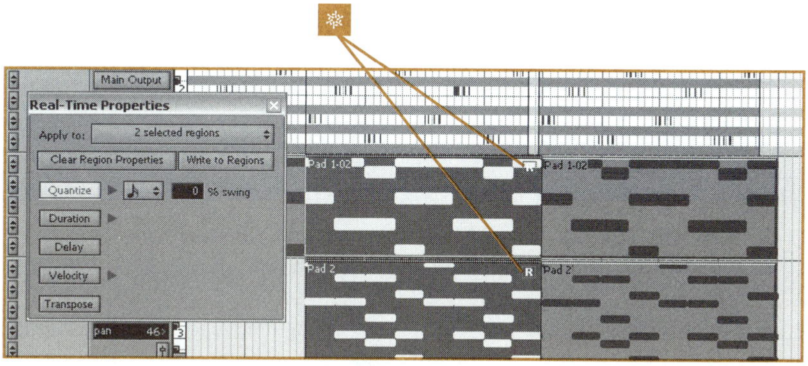

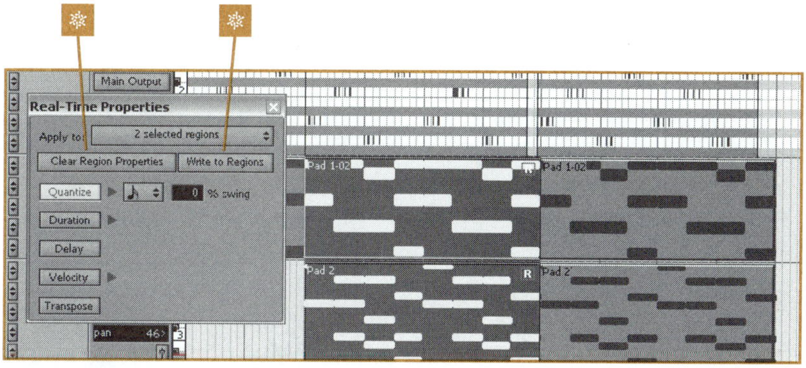

Although the Real-Time Properties floating window is the most flexible and comprehensive way to use this feature, there's another way that can be even easier under normal circumstances. For example, let's use Real-Time Properties in another way, to change the feel of the entire Drum track.

If You're Working with the Tutorial Session

So that you can easily hear the effect of what you're about to do, I recommend that you solo the Drum track and select the first region on the track. Putting yourself into loop playback will let you hear the drum beat continually.

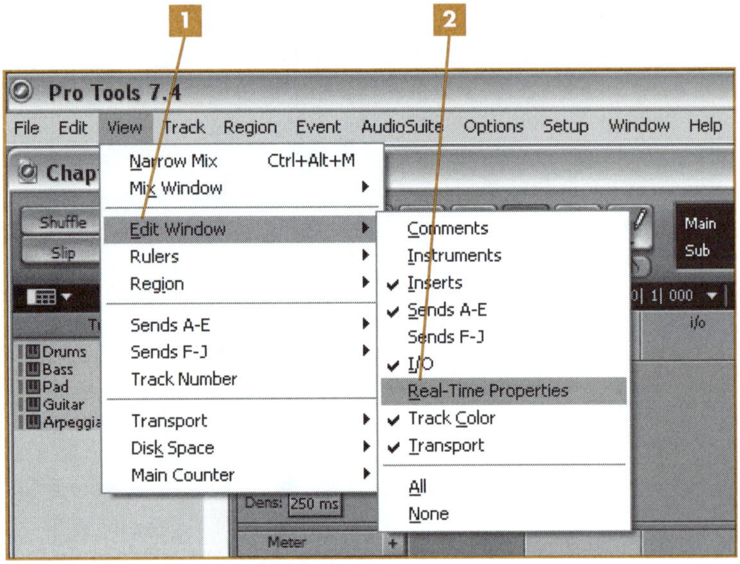

1. Instead of using the Real-Time Properties floating window, we're going to employ the Real-Time Properties Edit window column. Here's a way to show that column: From the View menu, choose Edit Window. A submenu will appear.

2. From the submenu, click the Real-Time Properties menu item (if it isn't already checked). The Real-Time Properties column will appear.

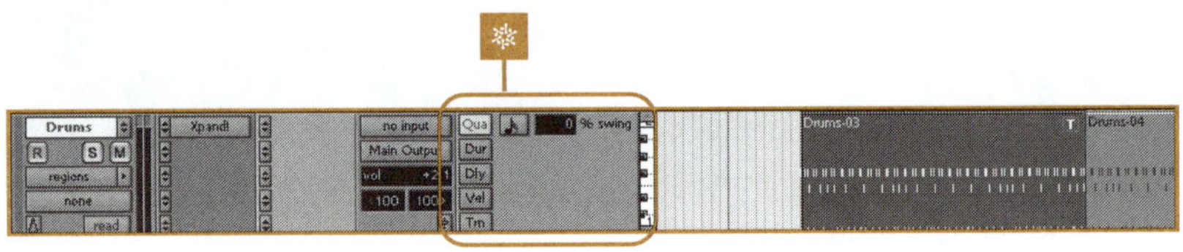

✻ You'll notice the familiar five buttons that you saw in the Real-Time Properties floating window (Quantize, Duration, Delay, Velocity, Transpose). Since this sort of data is pertinent only to MIDI data, you'll find that this column is blank for Audio, Aux, and Master Fader tracks.

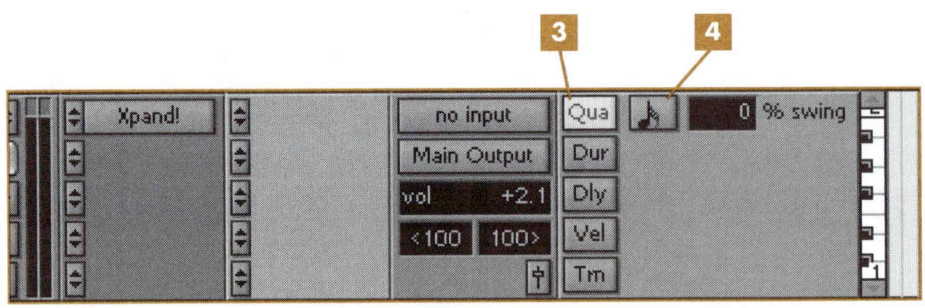

3. Because we're changing the feel of the drums, click the Quantize button. You'll immediately see that the regions on your track are marked with a T (for *Track-based* Real-Time Processes), and you'll hear the effect of your quantization.

4. As with the Real-Time Properties floating window, you can change the kind of quantize that you want to apply. Let's have some fun with some groove quantize. Click the button immediately to the right of the Qua button. A list will appear.

5 Choose the desired quantization—in this particular example, I've chosen FeelInjector_8th_shfl from the Feel Injector Templates folder, because it is a very different feel than the original beat. If you feel that this difference is an improvement, you're finished. If you don't like it, no sweat—you can choose any other kind of quantization you want, or you can choose not to quantize at all by clicking the Qua button and turning off Real-Time Properties. That's the beauty of this feature—nothing you've done is permanent!

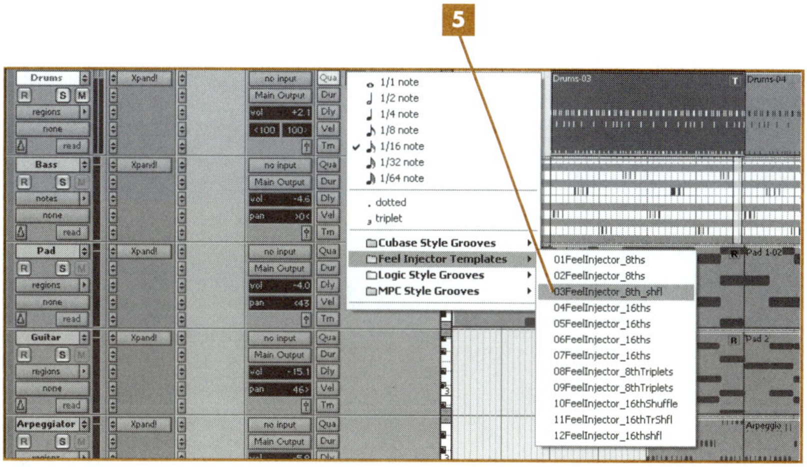

The fundamental difference between the Real-Time Properties floating window and the Real-Time Properties column is this: The floating window will allow you to modify any selected regions or tracks, and modified regions will continue to carry these changes to any track you may drag them to. The column on the other hand, only applies to tracks, and any regions that you drag onto those tracks will reflect these real-time changes (*unless* they have been changed previously using the floating window).

Panic!

Reality check: Sometimes things go wrong. Worse yet, sometimes the things that go wrong can be audible, as in the case of a "stuck" MIDI note that never ends. When that happens, the most important thing to do is stop the data! Whatever you do, don't forget this tip!

1 Click on Event. The Event menu will appear.

2 Click on All MIDI Notes Off (quickly!). A MIDI note-off command will be sent on all channels, on all ports of your MIDI interface, and through the four virtual MIDI connections.

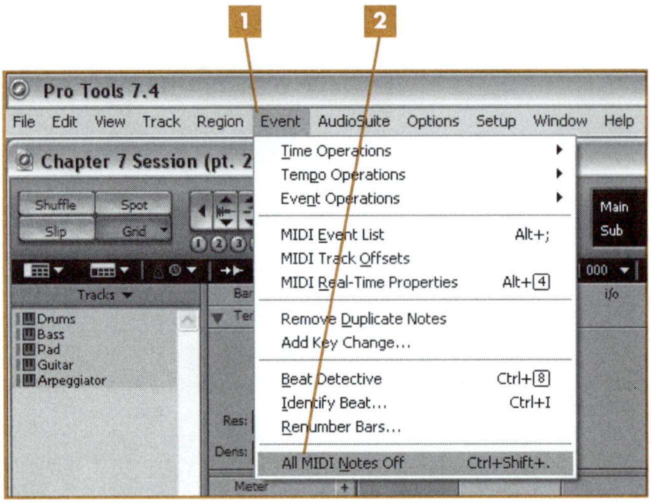

Panic Shortcut

The fastest way to trigger the All MIDI Notes Off function is to use the shortcut keys: Shift+Ctrl+. (period key) will do it on the PC, and Shift+⌘+. (period key) will do it on the Mac.

Importing and Exporting MIDI Data

One of MIDI's greatest advantages lies in its broad compatibility. Regardless of any proprietary file format, nearly every MIDI application can utilize the industry's SMF (*Standard MIDI File*) format. Pro Tools, although a relative newcomer to the world of MIDI, is no exception.

Importing MIDI Data from the File Menu

Just as you can import an audio file to an Audio track, you can import a standard MIDI file to one or more MIDI tracks in your session.

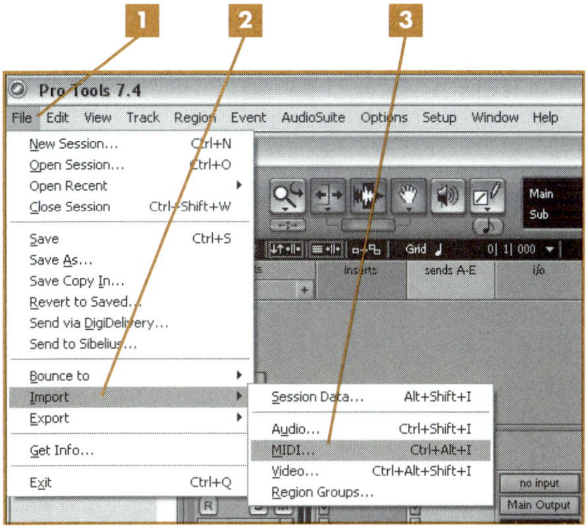

1 Click on File. The File menu will appear.

2 Select Import. A submenu will open.

3 Select the MIDI menu item. The Choose a MIDI File dialog box will open.

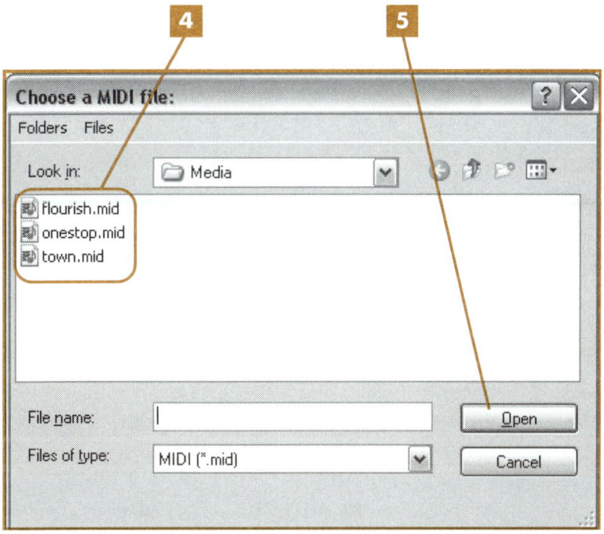

4 In this dialog box, select the MIDI file you want to import.

5 When you've selected the MIDI file you want, click Open. The MIDI Import Options dialog box will open.

- The Destination section of the MIDI Import Options dialog box will allow you to choose whether the imported MIDI will go to a new track or simply be added to the Regions list.
- The Location drop-down menu will let you choose *where* the region will be deposited on the Timeline. In this case, the new MIDI region will start at the beginning of the session, but you have the option of choosing the song start (if it is different than the session start), the beginning of a selected area, or a specific spot in your session. (The same Spot dialog box will open that you normally see when using Spot mode.)

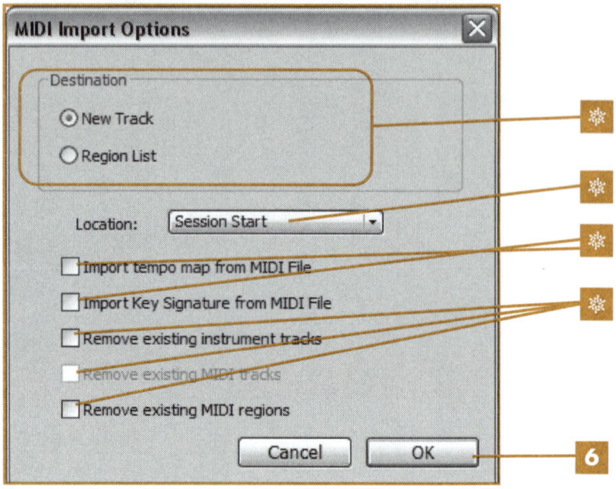

- You have the option of also importing that MIDI files tempo map (which will show up on your Tempo ruler) or key signatures (which will appear on the Key Signature ruler—something we'll talk about later in this chapter).
- Finally, you have the option of removing any MIDI regions, MIDI tracks, or Instrument tracks that may previously exist in your session.

6. When you've chosen the options that work best for you, click OK. The MIDI will be immediately imported into your session according to your settings.

Importing MIDI Data from the Workspace

Again, just as you can import audio from the Workspace window with ease, you can also import MIDI. With MIDI, though, the news gets even better, because you can import an entire song's worth of material with just a click and a drag. Here's how.

1 Click the Window menu.

2 Click the Workspace menu item. The Workspace window will open, as you've seen before in Chapter 3.

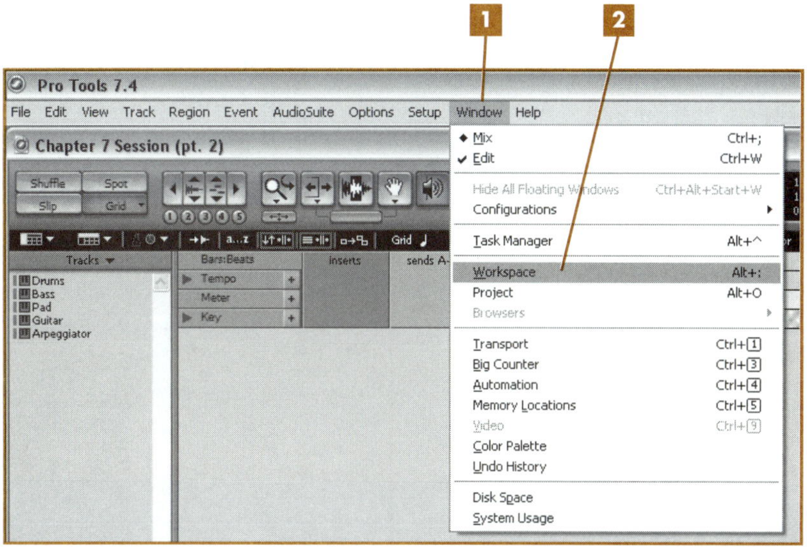

3 Drag the desired MIDI file into your Edit window's Timeline. When applicable, a window will appear, allowing you to replace MIDI tempo maps, tracks, and regions, as you've seen earlier in this section.

The individual MIDI tracks of the file will be created in your Edit window, and the appropriate regions will be created.

After You Import

Keep in mind that even after you import your MIDI data, you have to set your MIDI output and Aux track(s) before you can play and hear your MIDI data through the Pro Tools Mixer.

Exporting MIDI Data

When you save your session, your MIDI data will be saved in the session file. However, you can also save the MIDI data by itself as a standard MIDI file so you can open it in any MIDI sequencer.

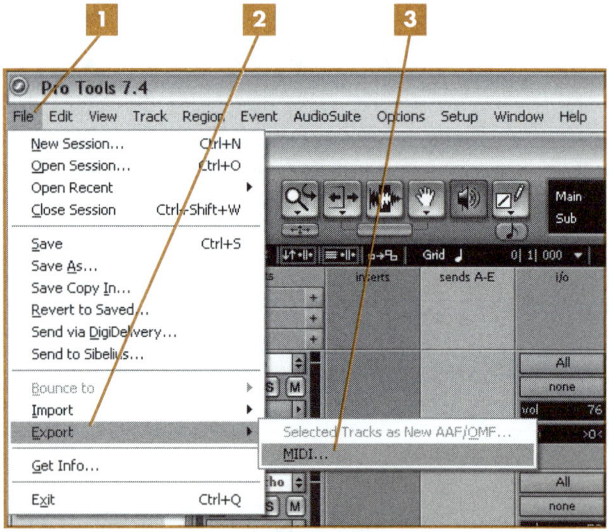

1. Click on File. The File menu will appear.
2. Click on Export. A second menu will appear.
3. Select MIDI. The Export MIDI Settings dialog box will open. This dialog box looks very similar to the Session Save window, and you will select your destination file and location in the same manner. However, before you get to that common window, you'll be able to make a few choices through the Export MIDI Settings dialog box.
4. Click the MIDI File Format button to reveal a list of saving options:
   - Select the 0 (Single-Track) option to save all of your data as one MIDI track, regardless of how many tracks you have in your session. (This is commonly used in multimedia applications.)
   - Select the 1 (Multi-Track) option to preserve the multitrack organization of your MIDI data. This is the type of Standard MIDI file most used in professional circles, and if you import it into a DAW, your tracks will be re-created.

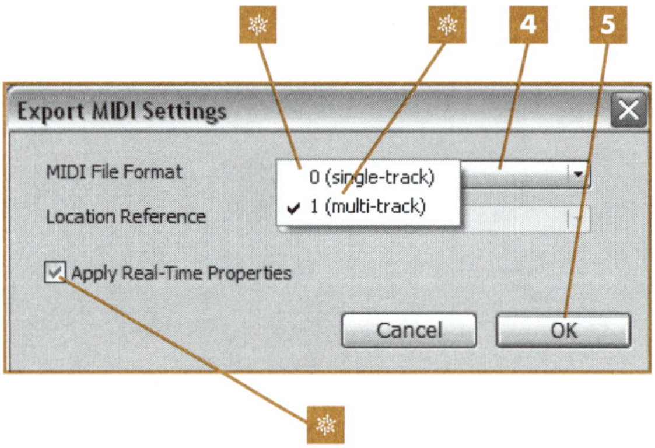

   - Click the Apply Real-Time Properties check box to "print" any real-time operations to your saved Standard MIDI file.
5. Click on OK. The MIDI data from your session will be saved to a Standard MIDI file, whose name and location you can determine according to your operating system.

A new feature in Pro Tools 7.3—here's another way to export MIDI on a track-by-track basis:

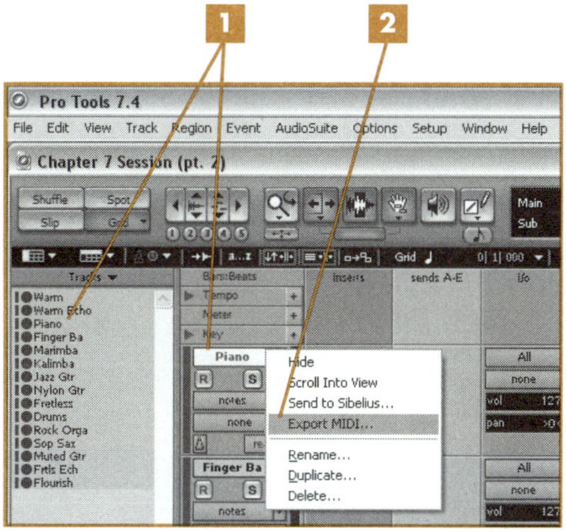

1. Right-click on the desired track name (in the Timeline area or in the Tracks list). A menu will appear.
2. Choose Export MIDI. The Export MIDI Settings dialog box will appear, just as you saw before. Make your choices, click the OK button, and you're set!

Send to Sibelius

For those of you who don't know the name "Sibelius" (other than the fact that Jean Sibelius was a famous Finnish composer), it's one of the leading notation programs on the market these days. Sibelius software is not only powerful and flexible, but it's also *fast*, which is making it an increasingly popular choice for musicians of all kinds.

Pro Tools can export MIDI data to Sibelius (if you have the program installed), allowing you to move your MIDI data from the Pro Tools production environment to a notation-based environment. It's easy:

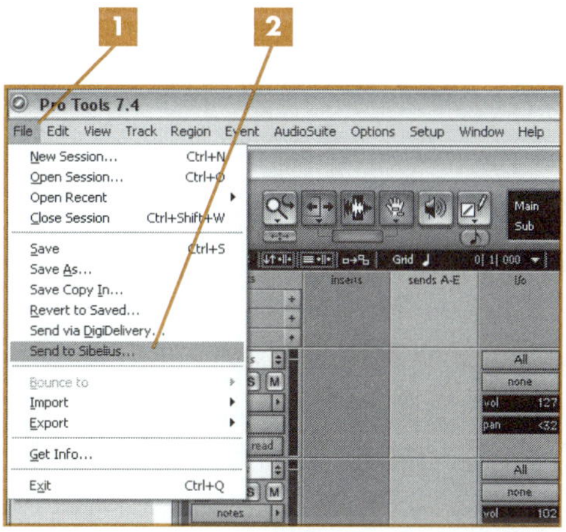

1. Click on File. The File menu will appear.
2. Click on Send to Sibelius. Immediately, the Sibelius application will be launched, and the MIDI data from your session will be exported to Sibelius, where you can work on it further.

Key Signatures

There's one more stop on our whirlwind tour through the world of MIDI in Pro Tools, and it's actually also related to notated music. Those of you who read traditional Western music notation know that a *key signature* is a notational device that tells the reader what the tonal structure, or *key*, the music is in. Keys are established at the beginning of a piece of music with a key signature, and can change during the course of a piece of music by inserting different key signatures.

Pro Tools now includes a Key Signature ruler to help you organize your music and keep track of what key you're in. In typical Pro Tools fashion, though, the functionality of key signatures goes beyond the basics. Let's take a quick look.

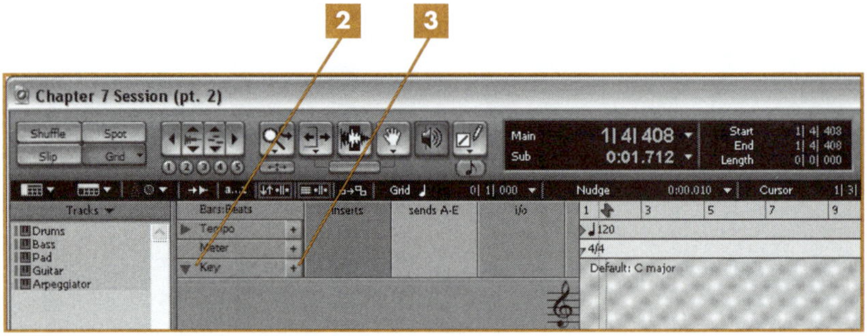

1. The Key Signature ruler can be shown just like any other ruler: Choose View, Rulers, Key Signatures.
2. To see an expanded display of the Key Signature ruler, click the triangle icon to the left of the word "Key."
3. Click the plus sign button to the right of the word "Key". The Key Change dialog box will open.

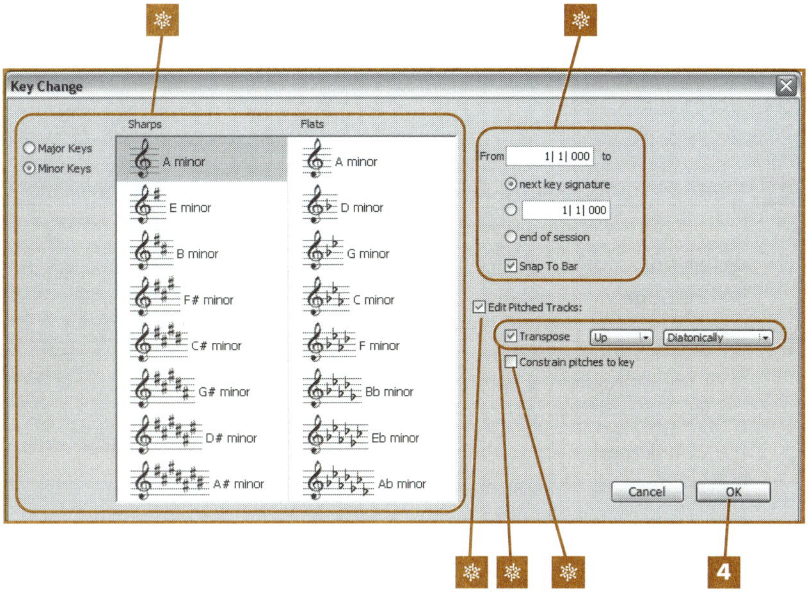

- You can choose either major or minor keys through the use of the radio buttons to the left of the window, and from there choose the specific key that you want to use.
- In the From field, you'll choose where your key change will be created, and the radio buttons below this field will let you determine where the key will end. Checking the Snap to Bar box will automatically set key changes to begin and end at the beginnings of bars (which is the most traditional way to use key signatures).
- You can choose to have your key signature simply be a visual marker for you, or you can have the key you choose affect your session's pitched tracks by clicking the Edit Pitched Tracks box. What is a "pitched" track, you ask? Patience—we'll get to that in just a second.
- If you decide to edit your pitched tracks, you can transpose them by clicking the Transpose check box. To the right of the box are two drop-down menus—the first will allow you to transpose your notes up or down. The second drop-down menu will allow you to transpose *chromatically* or *diatonically*. Chromatic transposition (the simplest form) will merely move your existing notes up or down by a set number of steps. Diatonic transposition will still move notes up or down, but will automatically adjust notes to fit the new tonality (major or minor). "Blue" notes and other non-scale tones will be maintained when transposing diatonically.
- Finally, the Constrain Pitches to Key check box will adjust all notes to fit the chosen key.

4. When you've made your choices, just click OK, and your new key signature will be created. You can create additional key signatures at any other point in your session.

There's only one more point to cover in connection with key signatures, and that's the idea of pitched tracks. MIDI regions (in MIDI and Instrument tracks) can either be pitched—in which case the actual pitches are tonal in nature and should therefore follow key changes—or unpitched, which deals with non-tonal sounds. Drum tracks, for example, are great examples of unpitched tracks.

If you want to work with key signatures, you'll want to set the drum track to *not* be a pitched track. Here's how:

1. Click the Playlist Selector button (to the immediate right of the track name). A menu will appear.
2. By default, all MIDI and Instrument tracks are set to be *pitched,* which is indicated by the check mark next to the word "Pitched." Because you don't want your drums to be pitched, just click this menu item to remove the check mark. You're all set!

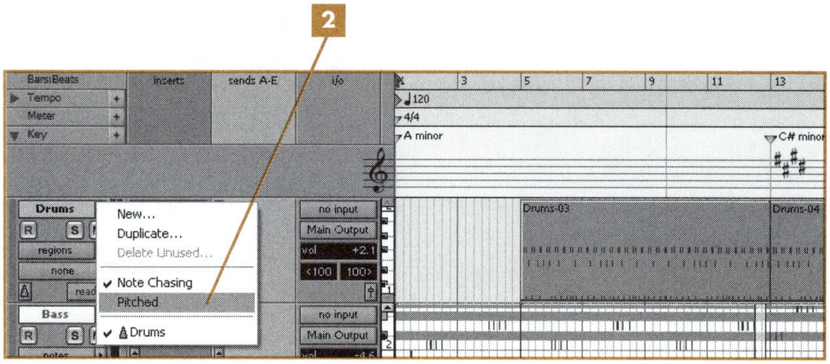

One more quick key signature tidbit: You can have pitched tracks follow key changes as a Real-Time Property.

1. In the Transpose section of the Real-Time Properties, you have three different modes, which you can show by clicking the button to the immediate right of the Trn button.
2. Choose the In mode to have the track automatically follow any key changes that you create.

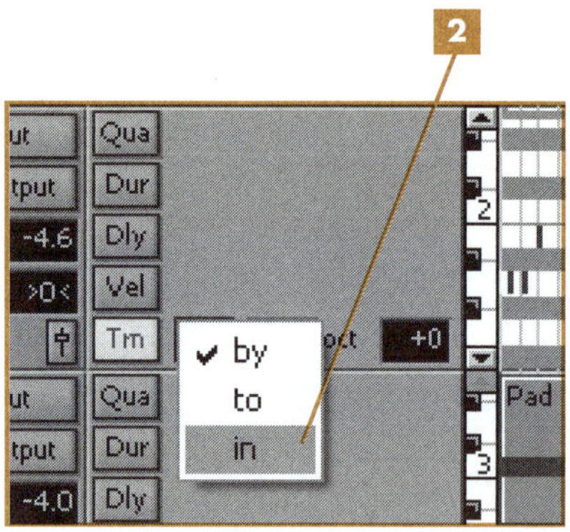

Next stop—mixing!

8 Basic Mixing

There are two schools of thought when it comes to Pro Tools mixing—mixing *inside* the box or *outside* the box. Mixing *inside* the box refers to when you use virtual mixer and virtual effects *within* the Pro Tools environment. At any given time, you will listen to the stereo output of your mix from your Pro Tools interface as all the required processing is performed by your computer (the "box"). Mixing *outside* the box refers to the practice of assigning individual tracks to individual outputs of your Pro Tools interface, and from there to the individual channels of a separate physical mixing board. The mixing and automation is performed by this external mixer, and Pro Tools is reduced to a recording, editing, and playback capacity only (which is still a critical role in any production workflow).

There is lively discussion (I'm being polite here) within the professional community regarding the virtues of mixing outside the box versus inside the box. For the end user, the debate boils down to an easy choice: If you've got a sweet-sounding, large-format, external mixing console (for example, an SSL) that you want to use, then by all means mix outside the box and use the board's circuitry to color the sound (kind of like an effect). If you don't have such a console at your disposal, or if you want to preserve the original sound of your tracks, you can feel confident in mixing inside the box. Rest assured, the math behind the Pro Tools mix engine ensures that the integrity of your mix will remain intact!

For the purposes of this book, you'll explore mixing inside the box (a method that has been used on countless professional projects). In this chapter, you'll learn how to:

- Work with the specific layout and function of the Mix window
- Use fader groups
- Use file-based and real-time effects
- Work with traditional mix routing
- Use basic automation techniques

On Mixing

Those of you who have some experience mixing with Pro Tools will notice some *big* differences between the way things used to be and the new world of mixing in Pro Tools. One of the most obvious that you'll find, as you go through this chapter, is that now you very rarely will have to stop playback to make changes to your mixer (things such as adding tracks, sends, plug-ins, and so on). Though such things necessitated stopping of playback in the past, now you can go ahead and make these changes as you continue playback.

There are two things to keep in mind, though: Depending upon what you're doing, you might hear a short gap of silence (as the mix engine reconfigures itself). Also, if you're recording audio, you *will* have to stop playback to make these sorts of changes (so that you don't interrupt the recorded audio).

Setting Things Up

For this section, please use Chapter 8 Session, included on the disc that came with your book. Remember, you'll want to copy the folder to a location on your computer's audio hard drive before working on it.

Exploring the Mix Window

You looked at the Mix window before (way back in Chapter 2). Now it's time to dig deeper.... If you're not looking at the Mix window already, the first thing to do is to switch over to the Mix window (which you also learned how to do in Chapter 2). Depending on how you left the Mix window last time, you might see the channel strips appearing rather narrow. Though the Narrow Mix view can certainly be useful in some situations, the Normal view will show you more information. Here's how to view the Mix window normally:

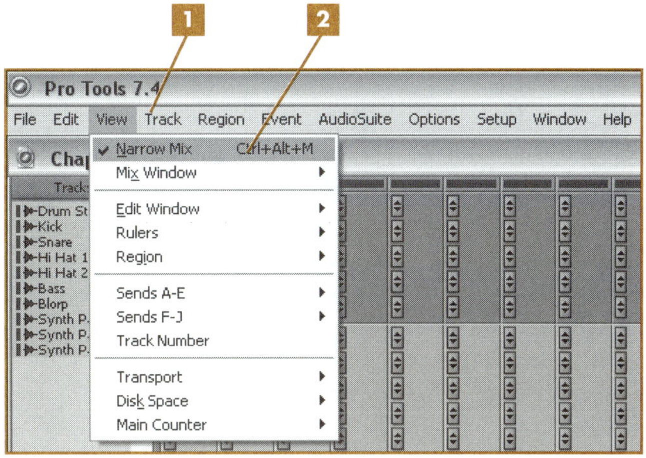

1 Click on View. The View menu will appear, in this case showing the Narrow Mix option checked.

2 Click on Narrow Mix to uncheck it. The channels will be shown in their normal mode.

When to Use Narrow Mix View

There are certainly times when the Narrow Mix mode is desirable. For example, when your session contains too many tracks to be normally displayed at once in the Mix window, switching to Narrow Mix mode will allow you to view more of your mix at once.

Basic Mixer Terminology

Just for a little reminder, this section reviews the basic layout of the Mix window.

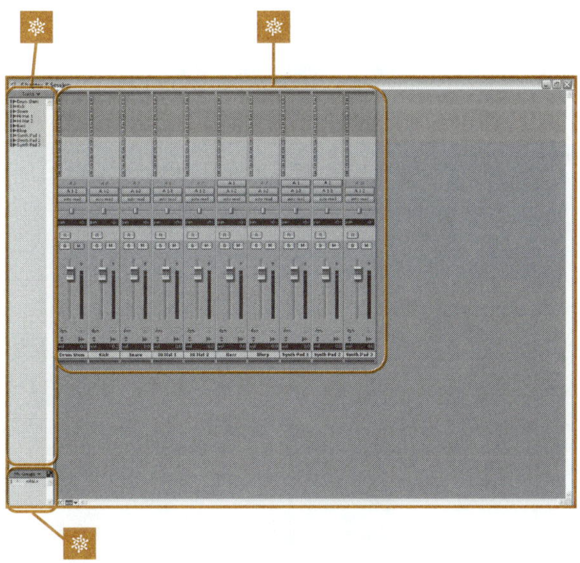

- Tracks list. As in the Edit window, highlighted tracks are displayed as channel strips.
- Groups list. You'll learn more about this in just a few pages.
- Channel strips. There is a separate channel strip for each track shown.

Now take a look at the different sections of each channel strip.

- At the top of the channel strips is the Inserts section. The important thing to remember is that any audio passing through that channel strip will be routed through the inserts first. You've got up to five inserts to use, and it is here that you will launch *plug-ins*, which can be virtual effect units or even virtual instruments.
- Next are the sends. With the introduction of Pro Tools 7, there are now ten sends for you to use (previous versions had only five), divided into two sections of five sends. You'll use sends to route a portion of your track's processed audio to another destination. Sends are commonly used in conjunction with other tracks to create more complex effect situations.

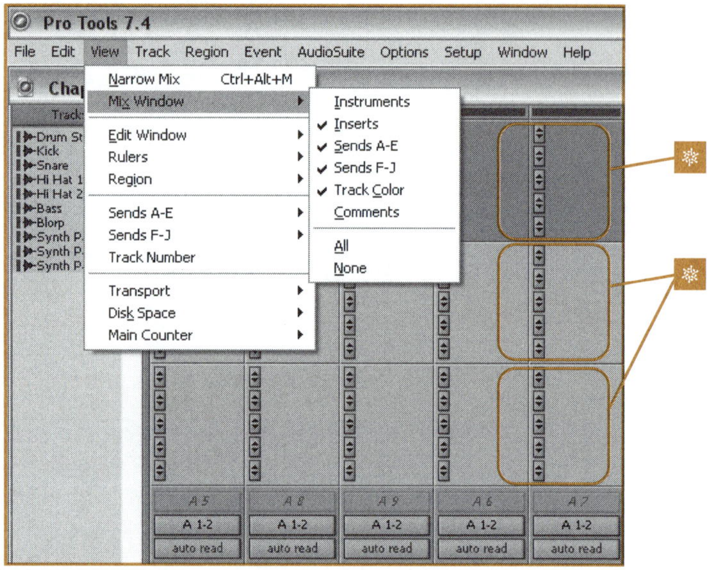

MIDI Track Signal Flow

MIDI tracks have no inserts or sends, as inserts and sends can route only audio data.

The next section looks and functions identically to the I/O column of a track in the Edit window. It consists of the following:

- Input button
- Output button
- Automation Mode button (covered later in this chapter . . . finally!)
- Pan slider
- Pan value

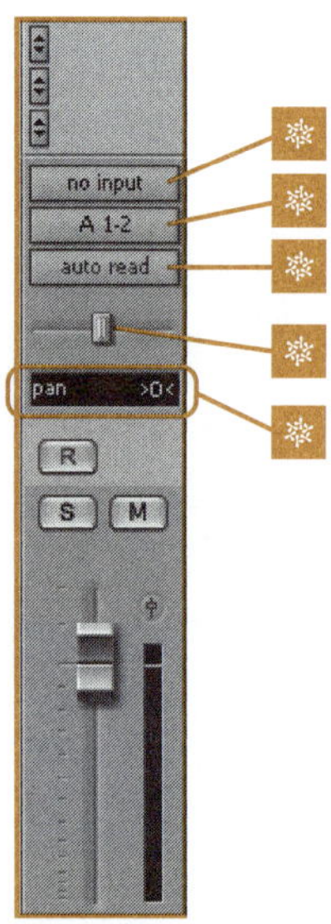

This section may not look much like anything you've seen in the Edit window, but these functions should be old hat by now.

- Record Arm button
- Solo button
- Mute button
- Volume fader
- Volume Level meter
- Track Type icon
- Volume value
- Track name

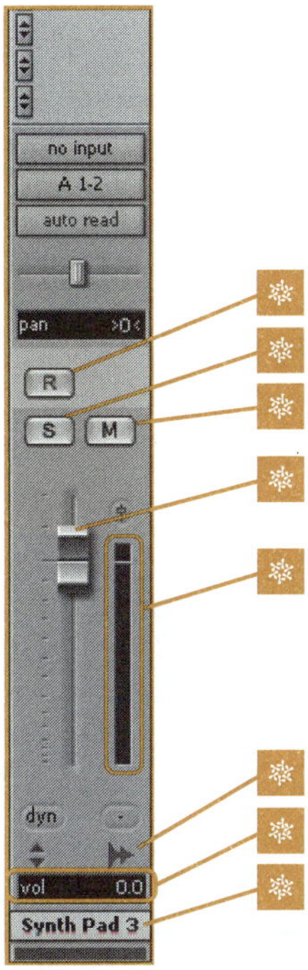

Track Type Icons

The icon at the bottom-right corner of each channel strip will let you know what type of track it is. A waveform indicates an Audio track; a MIDI plug indicates a MIDI track. An arrow signifies an Aux track, and a sigma marks a Master Fader. For Pro Tools 7's newest addition, Instrument tracks, a small keyboard symbol is used. The same icons can be found to the left of each track in the Tracks list.

Is It Mono or Stereo?

You can easily tell whether the track is stereo or mono by taking a look at the volume meters and pan sliders. One meter and pan signifies a mono track, and a stereo track will have two meters and pans. (The top pan is for the left side of the track, and the bottom pan is for the right side of the track.)

New Feature: Track Colors

If you take a look at the View menu, among the things you can look at in the Mix window you'll see that you can show track colors. You'll see that the track color is shown at the very top and bottom of each channel strip. Though their function is purely visual, you'll find that using track colors is pretty darn handy—let's use track colors to differentiate between the different kinds of tracks:

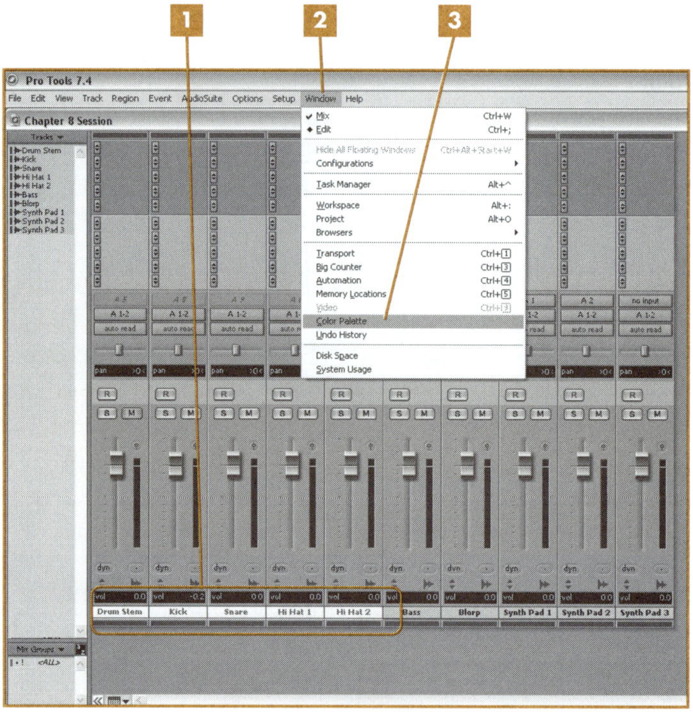

1. **Select** the **track(s)** that you want to recolor by clicking on the track name(s). Holding down the Shift key will allow you to select a block of tracks.
2. **Click** the **Window menu**.
3. **Choose** the **Color Palette menu item**. The Color Palette window will appear.

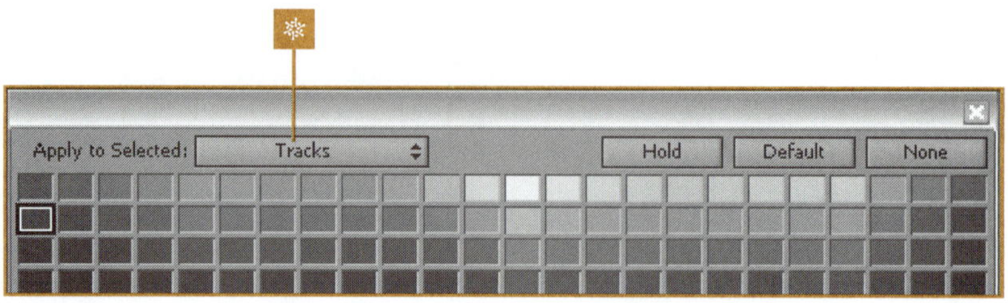

❋ The Apply to Selected drop-down menu will allow you to change the color of your selected tracks, regions, groups, or even markers.

4 If the button to the right of the words "Apply to Selected" does *not* read "Tracks," click the menu button and select Tracks from the menu that will appear.

5 Click the color that you want to assign to the selected tracks. In this case, I want my drum tracks to appear green. Once you click the desired color, the track's color code will change accordingly.

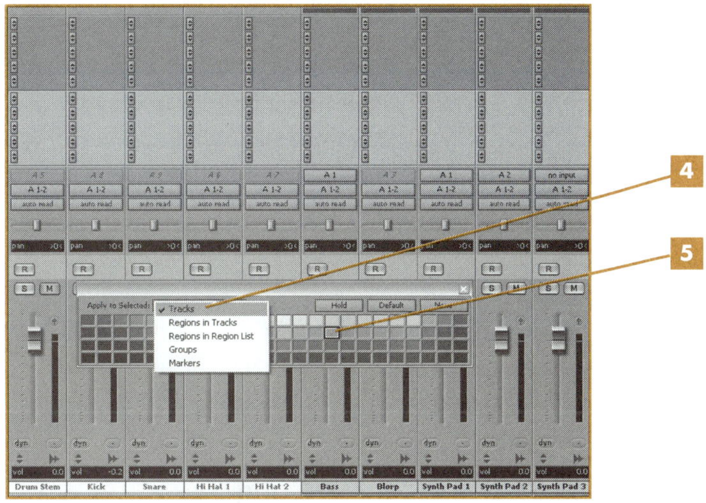

- If you're using Pro Tools 7.3, hold down Ctrl+Start+Alt (PC) or Control+Command+Option (Mac) and click and hold in the colored area of the Color Palette window. Without releasing your mouse, drag upward, and you'll notice that your tracks start to be colored according to their color code. The higher you drag, the stronger the coloring, and dragging downward will reduce the strength of the color. Release the mouse when your tracks get to the desired color level.
- If you're using Pro Tools 7.4, hold down Ctrl+Start+Alt (PC) or Control+Command+Option (Mac) and click in the colored area of the Color Palette window. Your tracks will be colored according to their color code. Clicking again will toggle the color off.

Usually, you'll repeat this process so that each track is colored according to whatever organizational method works for you. In this case, I've made my drum tracks green, my Bass and Blorp tracks red, and left the synth tracks blue (Pro Tools' default color code for Audio tracks). Now let's have a little fun and make the *whole* track follow this color code. The method of doing this varies slightly from version 7.3 to 7.4.

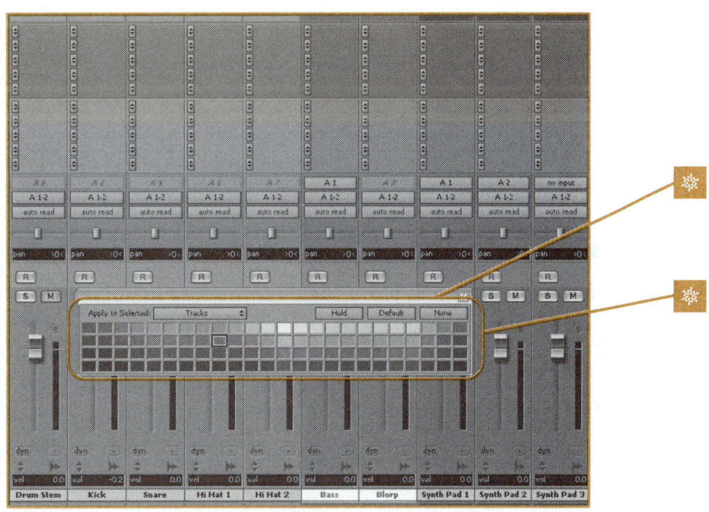

More Signal Flow

Whenever you talk about mixing, you're really talking about signal flow. The more complex your mix gets, the more complex the routing of that signal will be. The following list will go through the order of audio signal flow within a track.

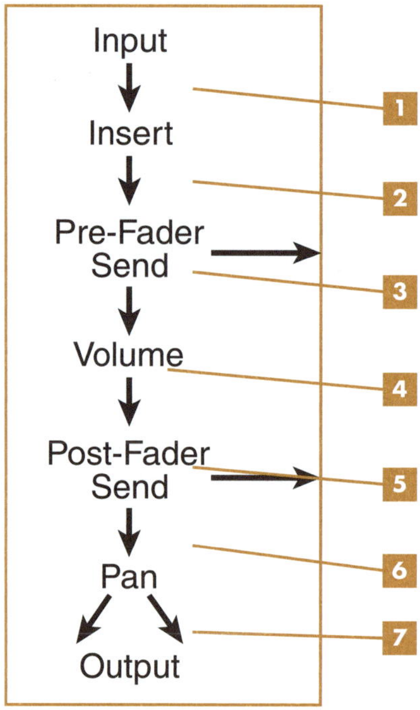

1. **Input.** On an Audio track, input can be from an interface input (if you're recording), from a bus, or from your hard drive. With Aux tracks, the input can only be from an interface input (although you can't record) or a bus.
2. **Insert.** One-hundred percent of your signal passes through your insert.
3. **Pre-fader send.** This type of send makes a copy before the signal hits your volume fader. The destination of this send can be an interface output or a bus.
4. **Volume fader.** This is where you control the output volume of the track.
5. **Post-fader send.** This kind of send makes a copy after the signal has been altered by the volume fader. As with a pre-fader send, the destination can be an interface output or a bus.
6. **Pan slider.** Panning comes next and allows the signal to be varied between a pair of outputs, usually left and right.

A Word about Faders

Keep in mind that the volume fader on your track *only* controls the output of that track. That means that the fader has absolutely no effect on the input coming to the track. The net effect is this: If you're recording audio and you see your levels clipping, turn down the output of the instrument. The fader in Pro Tools' Mix window cannot prevent clipping.

This is how you will create a stereo mix of several mono or stereo tracks. If you route your track to a singular output, no pan slider will be needed, and you won't see one in the channel strip.

7. **Output.** After all these stages are passed, the signal goes to the Pro Tools mix engine and out of an interface output pair.

Mix Groups

One neat thing about mixing in Pro Tools is that you can link faders together so that moving one fader will move a number of faders. This is particularly useful when you have a good relative blend between a number of tracks (for example, a nice balance between all the drums). By making a fader group of these tracks, you can adjust the volume within your entire mix, while maintaining the group's relative levels.

Those of you who have worked with previous versions of Pro Tools will find that Mix Groups have undergone a significant improvement beginning with Pro Tools version 7.3, and they give Pro Tools LE users more control over the mixing workflow than ever before. Now, not only can you group faders, but also other aspects of your mix, and in different ways. This might sound like Pro Tools is getting much more complex, but I think you'll find that the process remains pretty straightforward.

Before we dive in, though, you should get a feel for what a fader group can do. As luck would have it, Pro Tools automatically creates a group (named All) when a new session is created (and always includes all the tracks in your session). Take a look at what it does.

1. **Click** on the **All group name**. The group name will be highlighted, and the group, which includes all the tracks in your session, will be active.
2. **Click** on any **volume fader** and **drag it** to change the volume of the track. Because you're using the All group, all the tracks will move proportionally.

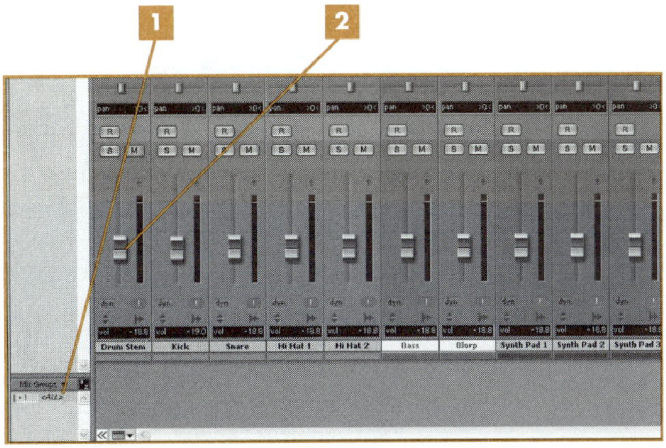

Group Icons

At the bottom-right of each channel strip is a small group icon. When a group is activated, the group's members will display a lit group icon.

Activating Groups

In a session that uses more than one group, you can highlight more than one group at a time, making multiple groups simultaneously active within your session. Simply click on any group you want to enable, and it will become active.

Creating a Fader Group

You can also set up a new group of your own. In this example, I've set up a blend of my Bass and Blorp volumes that I find pleasing, and I want to maintain their relative levels.

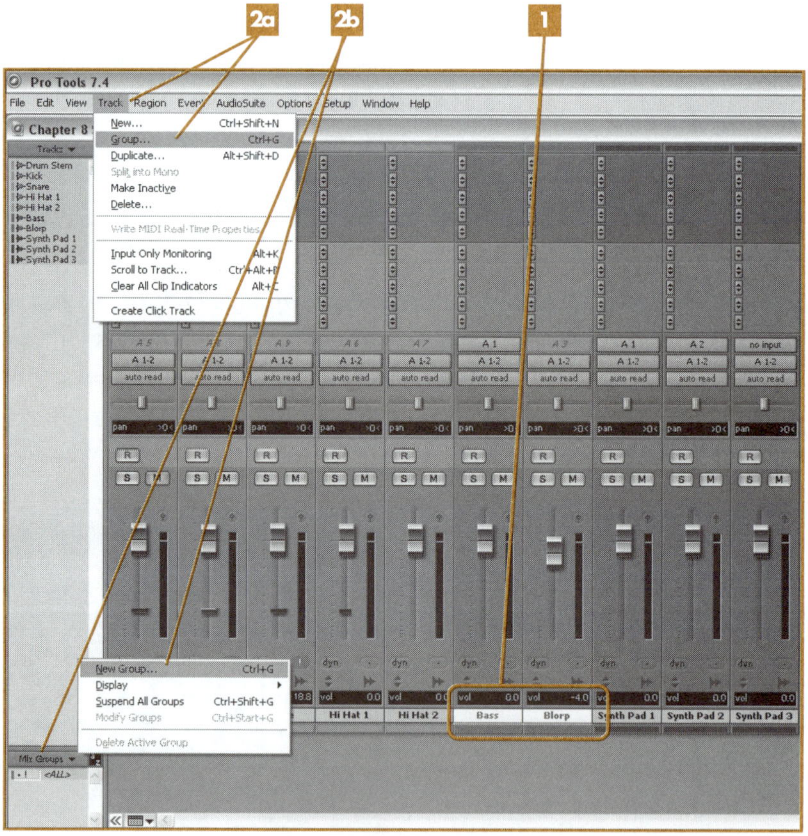

1. Though it's not strictly necessary at this point, selecting the tracks that you want to group together will make the process easier. (Hold the Shift key to select a block of tracks.) The tracks will be selected. Once that's done, you can open the New Group dialog box one of two different ways:

2a. Click on Track and select Group. The New Group dialog box will open.

OR

2b. Click on the Groups List menu button and select New Group from the menu that appears. The Create Group dialog box will open.

3 Type a name for your new group in the Name text box.

4 Click on a Group Type radio button to choose whether the group will exist in the Edit window (see Chapter 6 for more information on Edit Groups), the Mix window, or both. The option will be selected.

- Initially, your track selection will determine the tracks that will be part of the Currently in Group area. If you want to add more tracks to your group, just select the desired tracks in the Available area, then click the Add button. Incidentally, if you want to remove a track from the group, just select the track in the Currently in Group area, and then click the Remove button.

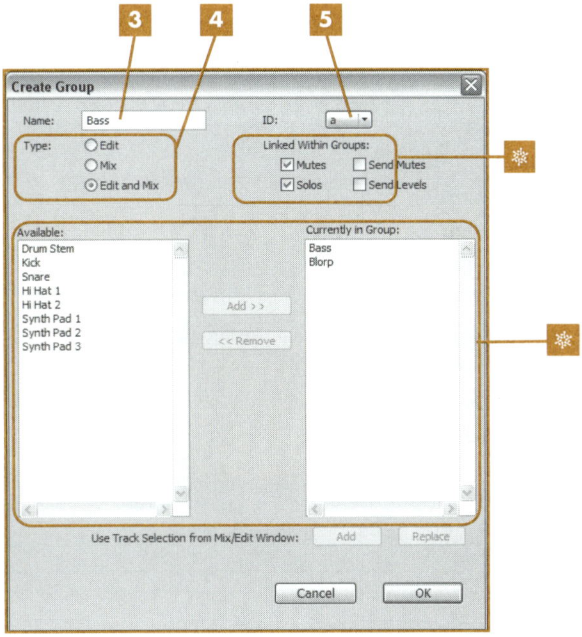

- Tracks that are grouped together in an active Mix Group are always grouped together as far as main volume faders are concerned, but starting with Pro Tools LE 7.3, you now have the ability to group other aspects together as well. Commonly, I like to have my track Mutes and Solos grouped together as well, so I've checked the appropriate boxes. Additionally, you can group your Send Levels and Send Mutes. (Using sends is something we'll talk about in the "Mixing Tips" section later in this chapter.)

5 Pro Tools will automatically assign a letter to your group for labeling purposes (in this case, it's currently assigned to group "a"), but there's a useful way to use group letters, so let's change that group ID assignment. Click on the ID button to select a different letter for the group. A submenu will appear.

6 With Pro Tools LE 7.3, you now have four banks of 26 group letters (for a grand total of 104 groups), as compared to a single bank of 26 group letters in pre-7.3 versions. From the ID submenu, choose the desired group letter. Since this is a group named Bass, I've chosen the "b" group letter from the first bank of letters.

7 Click on OK. Your settings will be saved, and the Create Group dialog box will close.

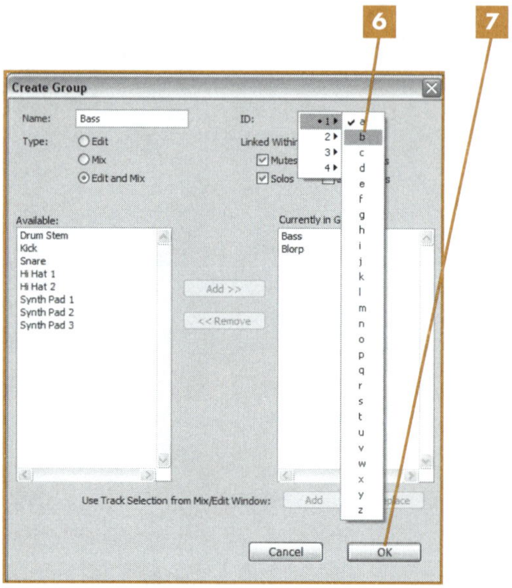

Nested Groups

Pro Tools allows tracks to be members of two groups at the same time. This can be very helpful, for instance, if you want to group your Tom-Tom tracks together and then group those tracks together with the rest of the drum kit. This is called a *nested group*.

In this example, I've duplicated the group creation process to also create a Drums group (which I've assigned to group ID letter "d"), and a Synths group (assigned to letter "s"). Here's what I've ended up with.

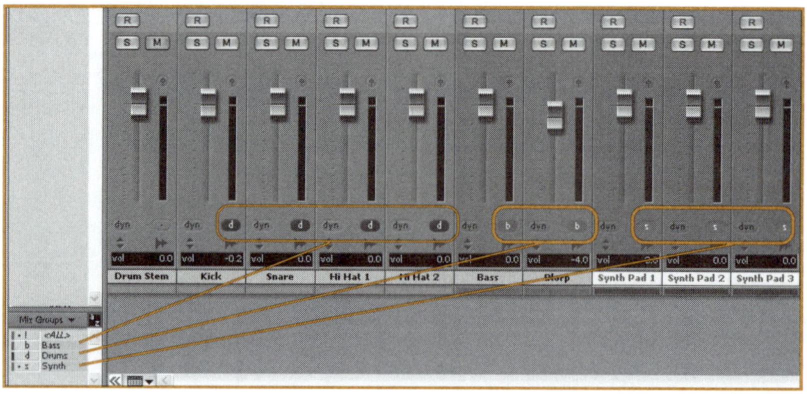

Active Mix Groups are shown by colored group indicators (showing the group ID letter) in each member track strip, and by highlighted group names in the Mix Groups list at the left of the Mix window. You can activate or deactivate by clicking the group name in the Mix Groups list. When a group is deactivated, you will be able to change individual track settings without changing the other members of the group.

Now here's where the care we took in choosing group ID letters is going to pay off: When you're in the Mix window, you can use your computer's keyboard to activate and deactivate groups by simply pressing the appropriate letter. The way we've set up our session in this example, you can now toggle the Bass group by just pressing the B key on your keyboard. (Pressing D will toggle the Drums group, and pressing S will toggle the Synths group.) I think you'll find that these shortcuts greatly speed up your mixing!

Shortcut Shortcoming

One limitation of these shortcuts is that they only work for the *first* bank of group letters. Groups in the other three banks can only be activated or deactivated by clicking the group name in the Mix Groups list.

Using Fader Groups

There's just a little more to learn about fader groups before you continue.

Since it's possible to have a fader group within another fader group (called a *nested fader group*), how do you know whether a given track is a member of more than one active group? In this case, I've created a group of my two Hi Hat tracks, but which track is also a member of my Drums group?

- A lowercase letter in a group icon (at the bottom-right of the channel strip) shows that the track is a member of only one active (highlighted) group.
- An uppercase letter means that the track is a member of more than one currently active group.
- You can click on the group icon to reveal a menu of all the active groups of which the track is a member.

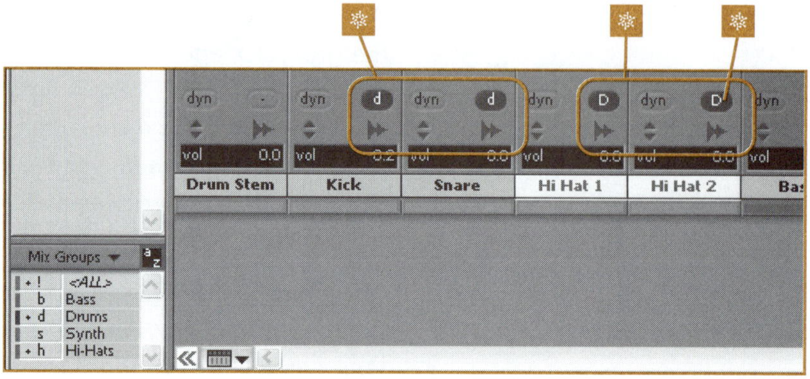

- In this example, the Hi Hat 2 track is a member of two active groups. If you move your mouse to either group, a submenu will be shown, which includes another submenu that will list all member tracks in that group.

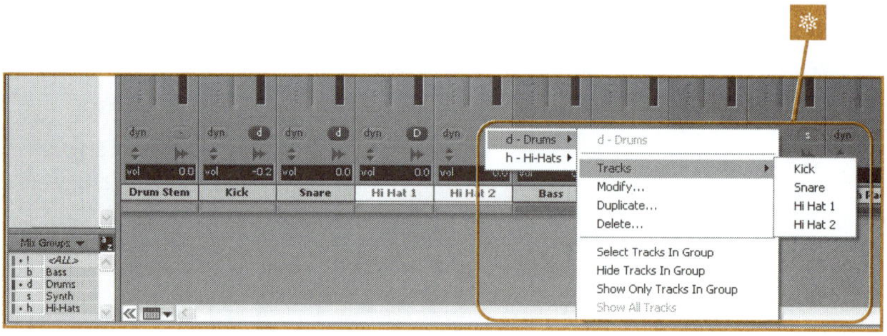

This group options menu is also a new feature released with Pro Tools LE 7.3, and it deserves a closer look. Not only can you call up this list by clicking on a track's group indicator, you can also see it by right-clicking a given group in the Mix Groups list. (This method also works for Edit Groups in the Edit window.) Here's how the different options behave:

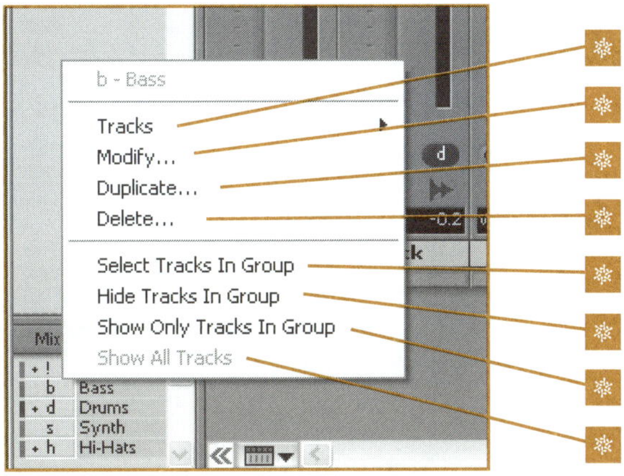

- Tracks displays a submenu showing all the member tracks of the group.
- Modify opens the Modify Group window, which is identical to the Create Group window. Here you can change any group attribute except group ID assignment.
- Duplicate opens the Create Group window, with settings identical to the selected group.
- Delete removes the group.
- Select Tracks in Group instantly selects all the tracks in the group. *Only* the group's member tracks will be selected.
- Hide/Show Tracks in Group will hide the group's tracks, if they are being shown. If the tracks are hidden, this command will show them.
- Show Only Tracks in Group shows the members of that group and hides all non-member tracks.
- Show All Tracks shows any hidden tracks in your session (whether or not they are members of a group).

Selecting Group Members

Another quick way to select all the members of a group is to click to the left of the group name in the Groups list.

There's one final list to take a look at before moving on: If you click on the Mix Groups list button, a menu will be shown, including:

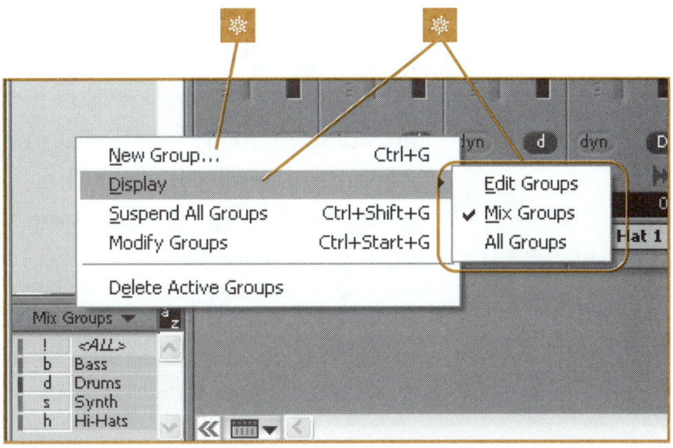

- New Group, which launches the Create Group window.
- Display, which shows a submenu, from which you can choose to see your session's Mix Groups, Edit Groups, or All Groups in the groups area of your Mix window.

- **Suspend All Groups**, which makes all groups become inactive, and group names are grayed out.
- **Modify Groups**, which opens the Modify Group window.
- **Delete Active Groups**, which removes all active groups in the list from your session.

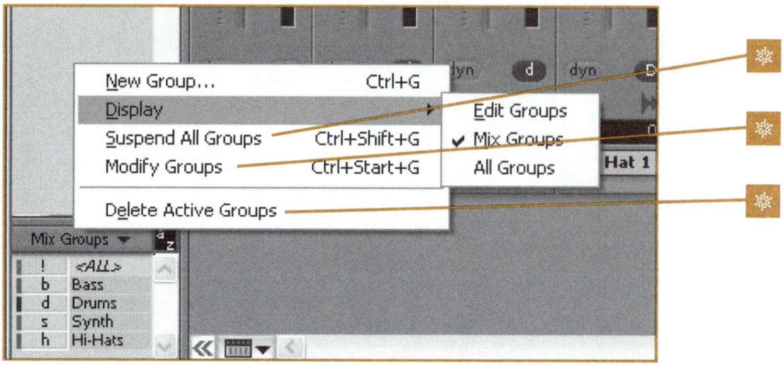

At this point, you've got a good sense of the layout of the Mix window, and you know how to set up your Mix Groups, which puts you in good shape to start doing a rough mix. Generally speaking, a first draft of a mix consists of volume and pan adjustments. You'll find that the Mix Groups that you create before you start this process will serve you well, especially with larger, more complex sessions.

If you're following along with the tutorial session, you should take some time to get a good rough mix. Once you've got a good blend of volume and pan, you'll probably find that you need to add some effects. Read on!

Using Effects

Many software applications use plug-ins—programs that run within programs. In word processors, plug-ins can be editing tools or macros; graphics applications have visual effect plug-ins; and so on. Pro Tools is no slouch when it comes to plug-ins. Pro Tools plug-ins include all manner of effects processors and even virtual instruments. Because they're software, they have all the benefits and flexibility of software, and they can even save you money and rack space in your project studio!

In a Pro Tools LE system, plug-ins fall into two families—file-based plug-ins (called *AudioSuite*) and real-time plug-ins (called *RTAS*, or *Real-Time AudioSuite*). First you will tackle AudioSuite.

AudioSuite

AudioSuite plug-ins are, generally speaking, the most basic of the Pro Tools arsenal of effects. They work directly with files (hence the name *file-based*), and this is *not* done in real-time as your session plays. This means that these plug-ins cannot be automated in your Pro Tools session. It also means that these plug-ins don't consume your session's valuable real-time resources, making AudioSuite a pretty powerful tool to work with. Here's how they work:

1. Select the region or selection you want to process. The region will be selected.
2. Click on the AudioSuite menu. A list of plug-in types will appear.
3. Click on the desired type of effect. A submenu will appear, showing all the specific plug-ins of that type.
4. Click on the desired plug-in. The plug-in's window will appear.

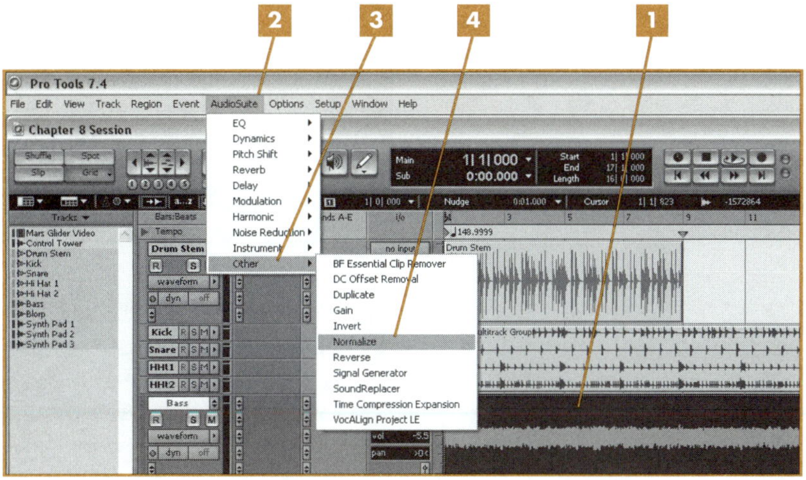

Normalize

The effect I've chosen is a handy little process called *Normalize*. This process is a semi-automatic level adjuster that will bring up your entire selection to the point where the loudest level is at its maximum without clipping. The simplicity of the effect window makes it an obvious choice for a book like this one.

Normalize can be very useful in some circumstances, but beware of overusing it! Though levels will be brought up, there can be minor damage done to the accuracy of your audio, and it will bring up ambient noise levels as well. The bottom line is to record at healthy levels, so you won't need to abuse normalization!

Although different effects have different appearances and parameters, they share some common elements.

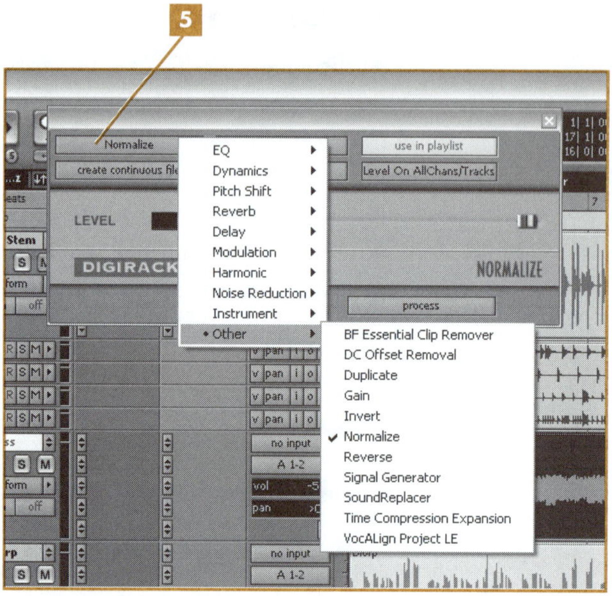

5 Click on the Plug-In Selector button (which will show the name of your current plug-in, such as Normalize). A list of available AudioSuite plug-ins will appear, from which you can change to another plug-in if necessary.

Getting around in the AudioSuite Plug-In Window

When taking a look at an AudioSuite plug-in window, it's important to make a distinction between the *function* of some of the buttons and the *labels* they may display at any given time. For example, in the figures above and below this note, the button discussed is used for Plug-In Selection, and the currently selected plug-in is Normalize. The buttons at the top of every AudioSuite window show their currently selected settings for quick visual reference.

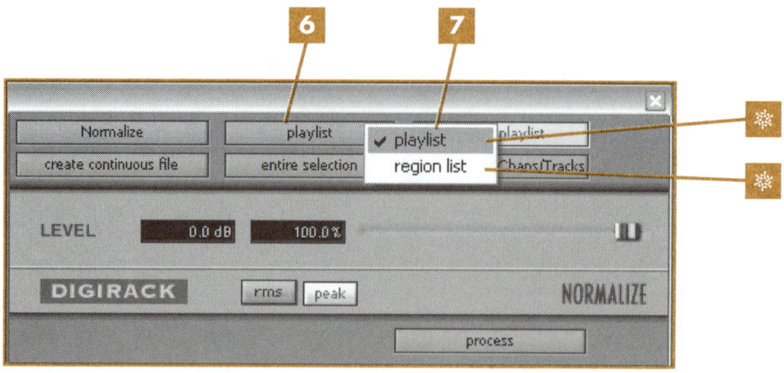

6 Click on the Selection Reference button (which reads "Playlist" in this image) to determine which selection will be processed. A menu with two options will appear.

- Playlist. The Playlist option will process the single selection in your track.
- Region List. The Region List option will process the currently selected regions in the Regions list and change all corresponding regions being used in your session.

7 Select Playlist if you want the processed audio to appear in your tracks and also in the Regions list. The button will be highlighted.

Use in Playlist

When the Use in Playlist button is not selected, the processed audio will only appear in the Regions list.

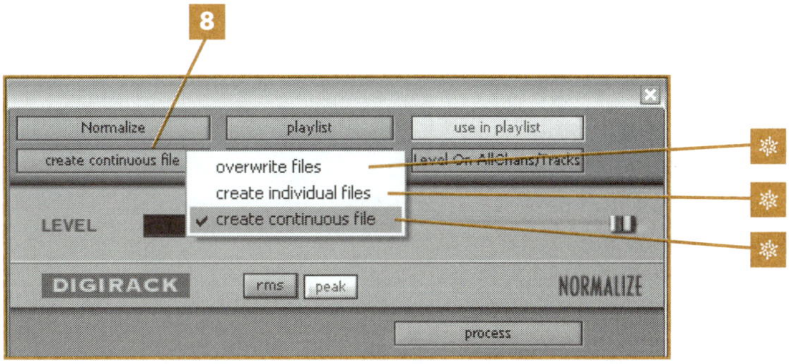

8 Click on the File Mode button (which presently reads "Create Continuous File" in this image) to determine how the audio will be processed. A menu will appear, showing three different processing options:

- Overwrite Files. This option processes the audio file directly and *destructively*. It *cannot* be undone.
- Create Individual Files. This option is nondestructive and creates separate audio files for each processed region if your selection includes more than one region.
- Create Continuous File. This option will process a selection nondestructively that includes more than one region and create a consolidated single file.

9 Click on the Process Mode button (which currently reads "Entire Selection" in this image) to determine how your regions will be analyzed prior to processing. A menu will appear, showing two options:

- Region by Region. This option will analyze individually each region within a selection.
- Entire Selection. This option will analyze multiple regions as a whole.

Region by Region and Normalize

The Region by Region option is commonly used when you are normalizing multiple regions of different volumes. With this mode enabled, each individual region within a larger selection will be analyzed and processed individually.

AudioSuite Variations

The controls discussed here are the basic AudioSuite settings common to all AudioSuite plug-ins. Different kinds of effects may have specific additional features relating to their function.

10 Click on Process to finally apply your effect. The effect will be rendered to a new audio file (or will overwrite your original file destructively if you have chosen the Overwrite Files option in Step 8). A progress window will appear, as shown here.

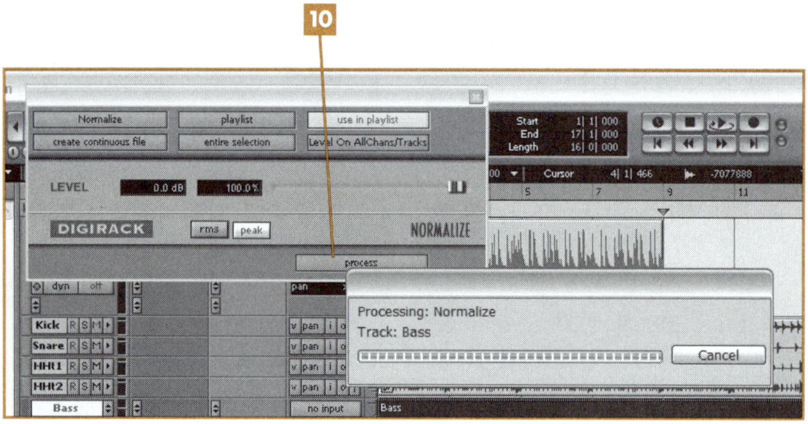

Here's what you'll end with:

- Since I've set up this AudioSuite process to use in a playlist (by highlighting the Use in Playlist button), a new region has been created to replace the previously selected region in the track.
- This new region has also been added to the Regions list and has been named Bass-NORM_01 to indicate that it has been processed by the Normalize AudioSuite plug-in.

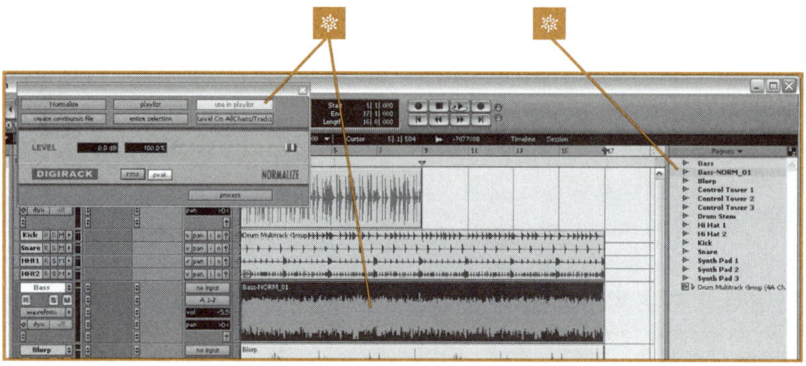

RTAS

The next evolutionary step in Pro Tools' plug-in effects is the RTAS (Real-Time AudioSuite) line. A number of RTAS plug-ins have AudioSuite counterparts (the EQs, for example), but the distinction between the two types is an important one. In the case of an RTAS plug-in, instead of processing audio on a file-by-file basis, the plug-in resides on a track's insert and processes the incoming signal as the session is played (in real time).

There are two huge benefits that come with using RTAS plug-ins. First, because the audio is being processed in real time, the audio files on your hard drive won't be changed as the audio plays, which allows you to experiment freely with different plug-ins and settings without worrying about filling your hard drive with tons of edited files. Also, as a result of RTAS's real-time qualities, you can automate the parameters of your plug-in (which we'll cover later in this chapter), meaning that your effects can change dynamically over time.

> If you've been using the Chapter 8 Session file, you might notice that a couple of tracks are hidden. Please un-hide the Control Tower track by clicking it in your Tracks list (it is the second track from the top) and un-mute it. There is also a video track in this session, and you can show it by going to the Window drop-down menu, and choosing Video. (A small video window will appear.)
>
> Incidentally, this video shows a space glider zooming over the Valles Marineris (a huge canyon on Mars). Thanks to Dave Oxenreider and Singularity Arts Inc. for providing this video!

Launching RTAS Plug-Ins

The following steps detail how to start using RTAS plug-ins in your session. In this particular example, I'm going to add some equalization (EQ) to the Control Tower track to make it sound like the voice is going over a radio transmission.

1 On an unused insert on the track you want to affect (in this case, the Control Tower track), click on the arrowed Insert button. A drop-down menu will appear.

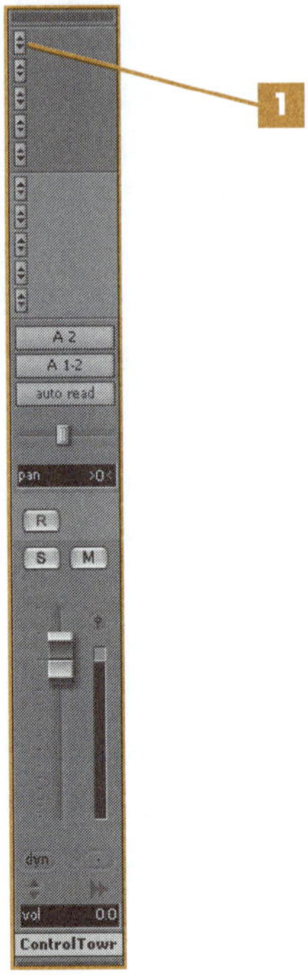

2 Click on Plug-In. The Plug-in menu will appear.

3 After choosing the type of plug-in you want (in this case, EQ), choose the specific plug-in that you want to launch (in this case, 7-Band EQ3). The effects window will open. This window will appear differently depending on the effect, but there are some common buttons that you should know.

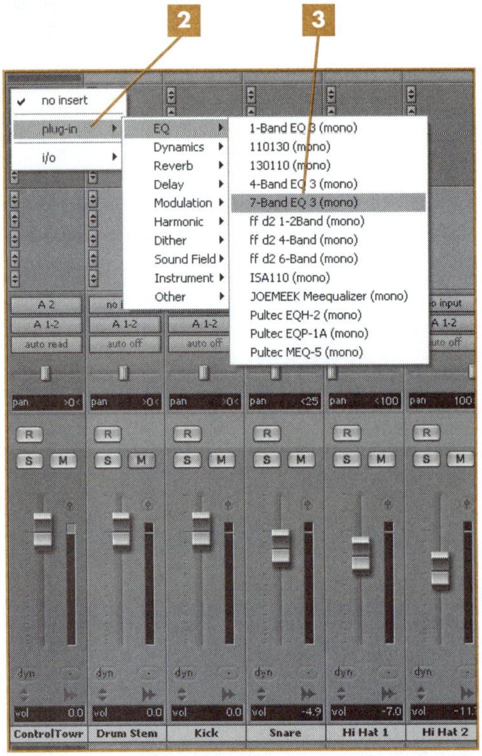

- If you click on the Track Selector button (which currently shows you the track you're working with), a list of available tracks will appear. From this list you can select another track and immediately open the Insert window for that track.
- The small lettered button to the right of the Track Selector button tells you what insert the effect is on. If you click on the Insert button, a list of all the inserts on the track will appear. From this list you can select any of the inserts for your track and jump to that insert immediately.
- Finally, the Plug-In Selector button (which currently shows you the plug-in you're using), will reveal the plug-in menu that you saw in Step 3.

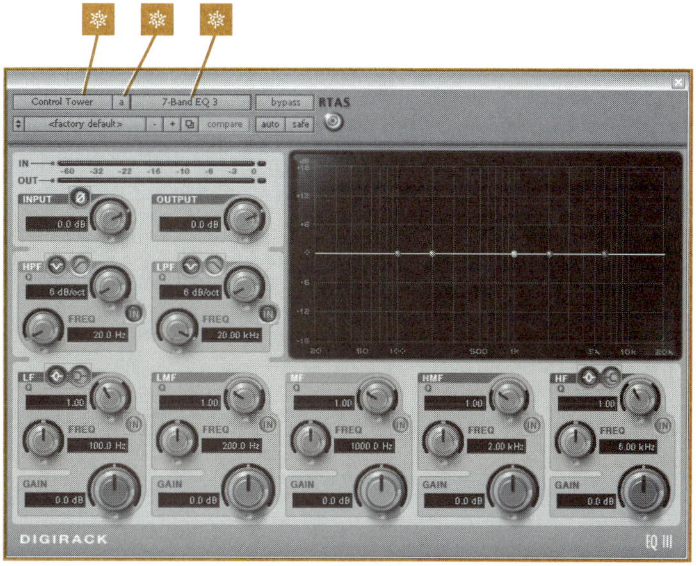

Advice on Inserts

Because inserts are processed in a series, from top to bottom, the order in which effects are placed in your tracks is indeed significant. For example, a virtual amplifier placed before a reverb will sound a good deal different than an amplifier placed after a reverb. The good news is that it's easy to change the order (or even the track assignment) of an RTAS plug-in simply by dragging and dropping the insert icon to a new location in your mixer.

Recalling Settings

In addition to setting and automating your plug-ins with ease, you can also recall previously created preset settings. This can work with both AudioSuite and RTAS—here's how we'll recall a good preset for the EQ we just launched:

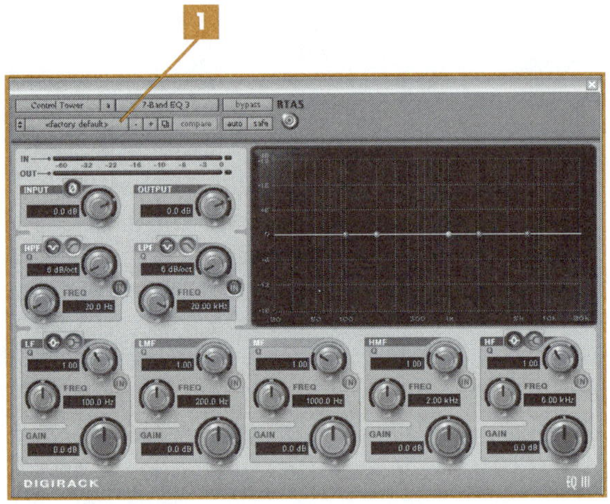

1 Click the Librarian button. (It will show the currently selected preset, like Factory Default in this case.) A list of available presets, specific to that particular plug-in, will be displayed. The location of the Librarian button is nearly identical for AudioSuite and RTAS.

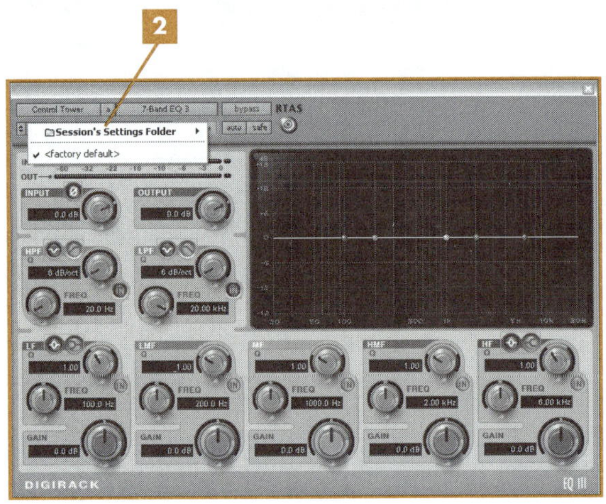

2 Any factory presets will be shown in this menu, plus any presets that are saved in your session's plug-in preset folder (something you'll learn about in Chapter 9, "Finishing Touches"). In this case, there are no factory presets to choose from, so click the Session's Settings Folder. A submenu will appear.

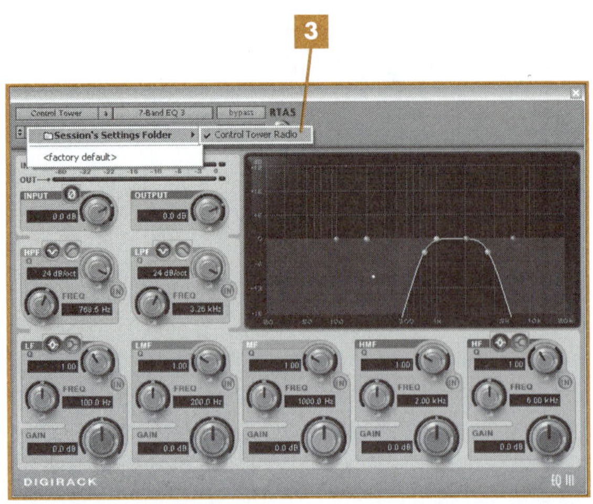

3 As it happens, there is a preset in the Session's Settings Folder—appropriately named Control Tower Radio, created by yours truly. Select this preset, and the parameters will be applied to your plug-in.

Notice that there are no factory presets associated with the 7-Band EQ3 plug-in. When there are presets listed (as with the Chorus in this example), there are a number of other ways that presets can be accessed. (Again, this works for both AudioSuite and RTAS.)

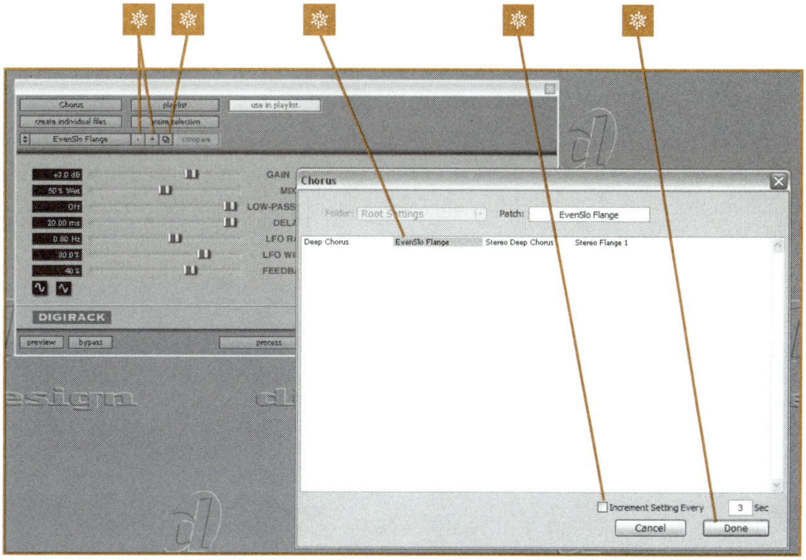

- Use the plus (+) and minus (-) buttons to increment or decrement through the available presets.
- Click the Plug-In Setting Select button to reveal the plug-in setting window, shown here.
- From the plug-in setting window, click the desired preset.
- Click the Increment Setting Every box (the box will appear checked) to automatically cycle through the available presets according to the value entered in the Sec box. In this case, the Chorus plug-in will cycle through all four of its presets, changing settings every three seconds. This is a handy way to choose the appropriate setting for your effect (especially when there are a large number of presets).
- When you settle upon the desired setting, click Done, and the setting will be applied to your effect.

Digging Deeper into RTAS

Okay, so far it's pretty straightforward, but things will get a little more complicated as you continue. For example, when you open a plug-in on a stereo track, you have a few more options. For this example, let's set up a multi-mono delay on a stereo Aux track.

SETTING THINGS UP

To follow along with these steps, you'll need to create a stereo Aux Input track.

1 On a stereo Aux track (in this case, named Delay Aux), click on an Insert button.

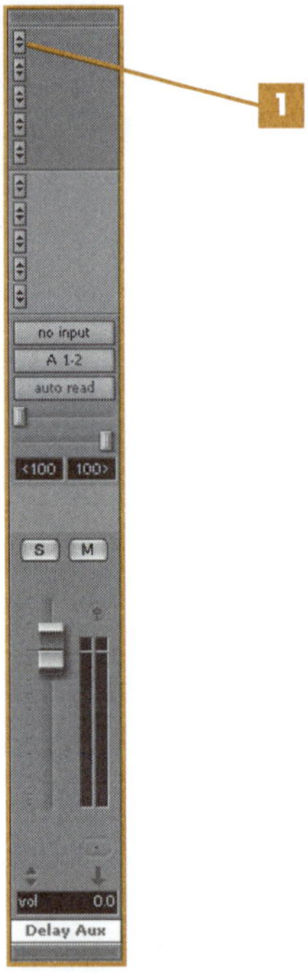

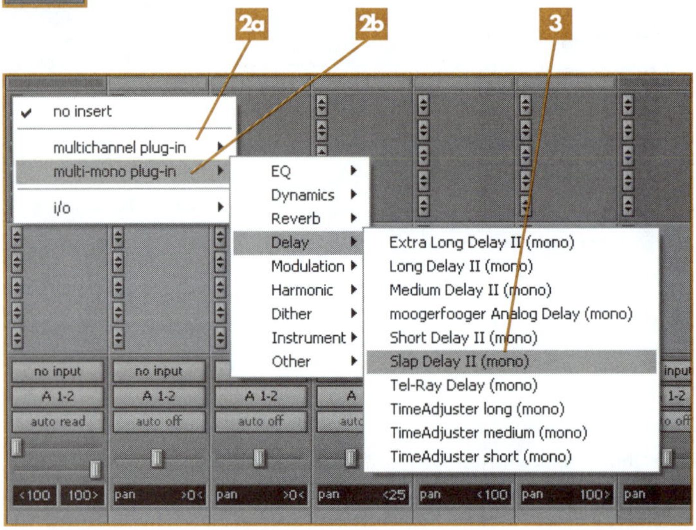

2a Click on Multichannel Plug-In. In the case of a stereo track, a list of stereo plug-ins will appear.

OR

2b Click on Multimono Plug-In. This option is available if you have tracks with more than one channel (such as stereo tracks). A list of mono plug-ins will appear. When you select a plug-in, it will be opened twice, although only one plug-in window will be shown. A multi-mono plug-in window has several unique features. For the purposes of our example, choose this option.

3 For the purposes of this example, choose Slap Delay II. The plug-in will be instantiated, and the plug-in window will open.

- The Channel Selector button will display either an L or an R to signify the side of the multi-mono plug-in you're presently viewing. When the link button is highlighted, both the left and right sides will appear identical.
- The Link button is unique to multi-mono plug-ins. When the button is highlighted, both instances (left and right) of the mono plug-in will share the same parameter settings. When the Link button is not highlighted, both sides are independently configurable.

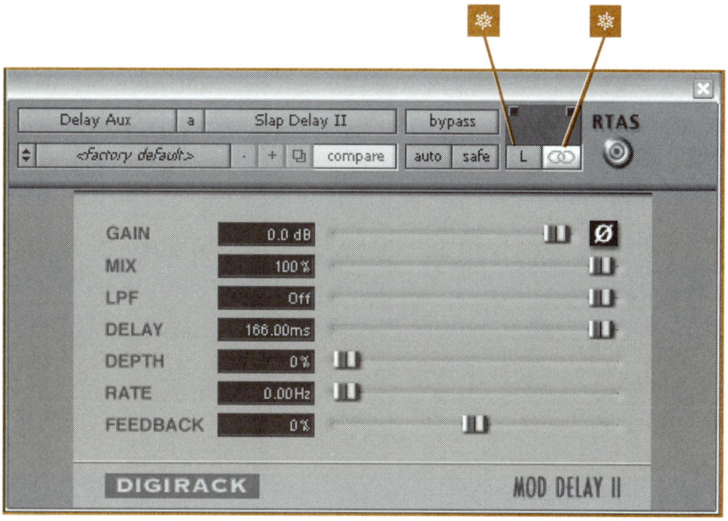

Re-Linking Multi-Mono Plug-Ins

If you unlink the two halves of a multi-mono effect and then choose to re-link them, the Relink dialog box will appear. This box is pretty self-explanatory. To re-link the two multi-mono plug-ins, you have to choose one side's parameters to be applied to the other side. Click on the Channel to Retain button to reveal a drop-down menu that contains both left and right sides. Once you've chosen which side's settings you want to keep, you can click on OK.

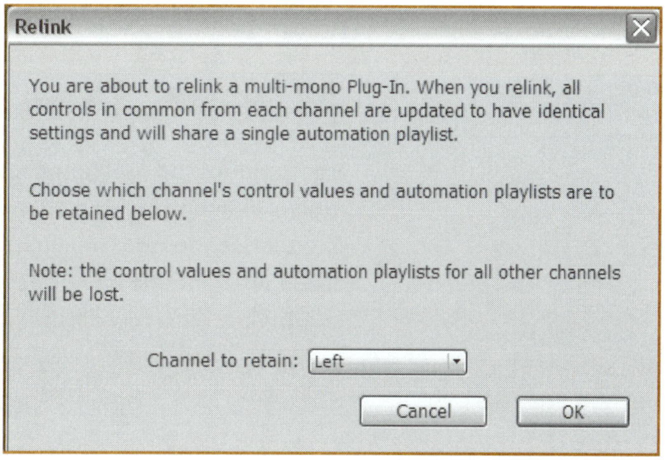

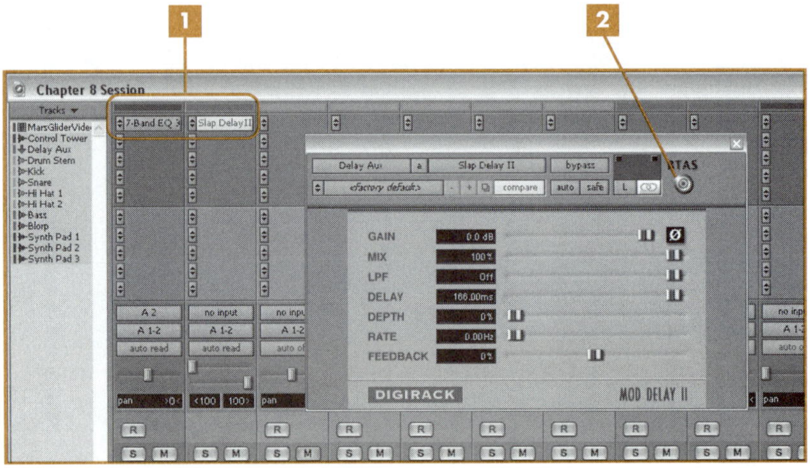

1. Each plug-in you launch (or instantiate, as Digidesign likes to say) will appear as a rectangular button next to its corresponding insert. Click on the desired button to reveal the effect window.

   You'll notice that by default, only one effect window can be open at a time. (Clicking on a new plug-in will replace the previous plug-in window with the new one.) So what if you want to view more than one plug-in window at a time? That's when the Target button comes into play.

2. The rule for the Target button is that there can only be one active target at a time. Click on the Target button to deselect it. You'll be able to open two (or more) effect windows at a time.

Targets and Control Surfaces

If you're using a control surface (a Digi 002 or Command|8, for instance), only the effect with the active Target button will be accessible from the surface's knobs and faders. Your mouse, however, will still manipulate all the open effect windows, regardless of the Target button's status.

Opening Multiple Plug-In Windows

You can also open more than one plug-in window at a time by holding down the Shift key while you click on a plug-in button on an insert. However, there can still be only one targeted effect at a time. (The first plug-in you opened will retain the active target.)

Mixing Tips

The point of the mixing process is to achieve just the right blend of audio elements in your session. Over the years, certain conventions have arisen to help mixing engineers work more efficiently, and these conventions have become something of a tradition. Let's start out by learning some traditional effects routing.

Using Dynamic-Based Effects

Traditional effects tend to fall into one of two categories—*dynamic*-based effects or *time*-based effects. Let's begin our discussion with dynamic effects. Dynamic-based effects change the volume level without changing its duration in any way. Some of the most common examples of dynamic effects are equalizers, compressors, and limiters.

Setting up a dynamic-based effect is very simple—in fact, you've done it once already with the Control Tower track if you've been following the examples shown in this chapter. Traditionally, you'll want these types of effects to process 100 percent of the track's audio, with little thought of creating a wet/dry kind of mix with these processes. Here's the traditional routing for dynamic effects.

New Free Plug-Ins!

For those readers who have until recently used Digidesign's EQ II and Dynamics II plug-ins, you're in for a treat with Pro Tools 7. The new free plug-ins that are included with Pro Tools 7 (1-band, 4-band, 7-band EQs, plus Compresser/Limiter, De-Esser, and Expander/Gate) aren't only better looking and easier to use, but they sound *much* better. Give them a try!

1. Click on an insert on the track you want to affect and select a dynamic-based effect (such as the EQ shown here). The plug-in window will appear.
2. Adjust the parameters of the effect to suit your mix's needs.

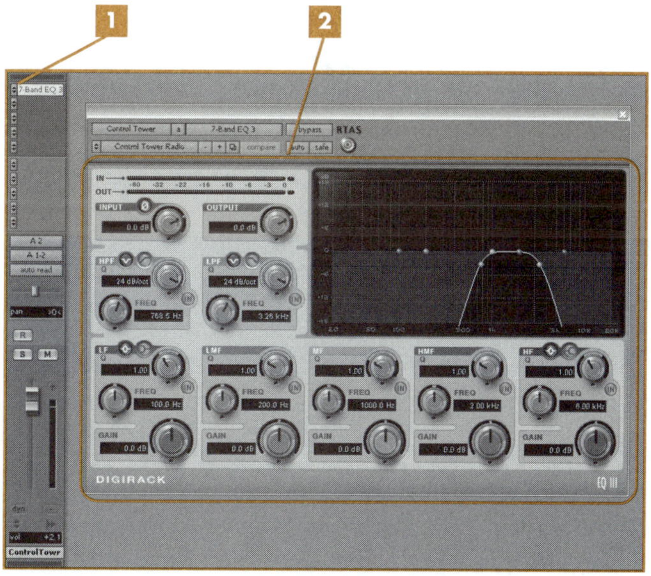

When you're finished tweaking the effect, you're finished with the routing. Although it is simple enough, this sort of routing works well with dynamic effects because 100 percent of the signal to the track first passes through the insert. This example shows a classic model—the entirety of a track's signal passing through an equalizer.

Using Time-Based Effects

Time-based effects *do* affect the duration of the sound beyond that of its original waveform. This family includes effects such as reverb, delay, and echo. In these cases, you generally will want to have some sort of a wet/dry mixing situation (*wet* meaning an affected signal and *dry* referring to an unaffected signal). The generally preferred way to mix these two signals is with two separate faders in your Mix window. Let's go through this process and add a little delay to the Control Tower track.

1. Create an Aux track and instantiate the time-based plug-in that you want to use (in this case, a delay). In this example, you can use the stereo Aux track (Delay Aux) that you created earlier in this chapter.
2. Click on a Send Selector button on the "dry" track. (In this case, let's use Synth Pad 3.) A drop-down menu will appear.

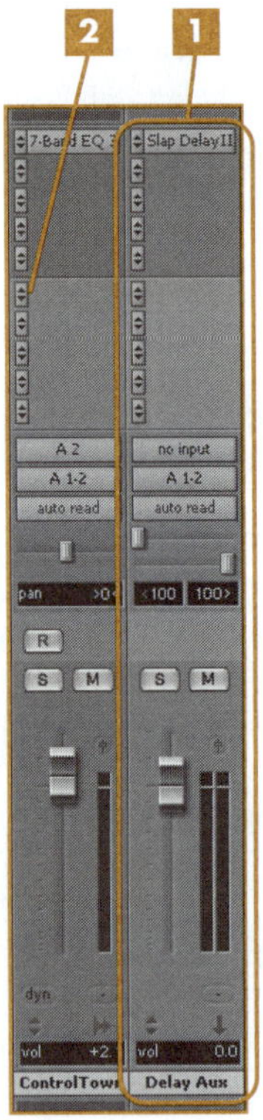

3 Because you'll be routing audio from one track to another within Pro Tools, you'll use a bus. Click on Bus from the drop-down menu.

4 Select an unused stereo bus. (We're using stereo busses because our Aux track is stereo in this case.) Busses already being used in the session will be shown in bold font.)

5 After you've sent a copy of your Audio track through a bus, you need to set the input of the Aux track. Set the input to match the same stereo bus you chose for your Audio track's send. The input will be set.

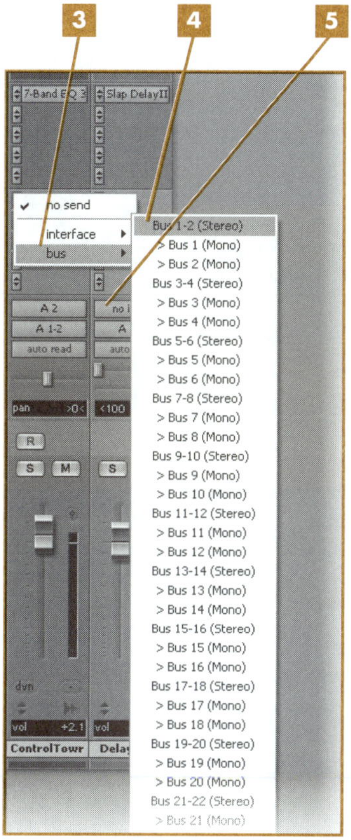

6 Drag the volume fader on the send's output window (if you're not seeing this window, just click on the send button) to increase the volume. The volume will be adjusted accordingly.

7 Play your session to test your connection. If you've routed the audio signal correctly so far, signal that is shown in the Audio track's meter will also be shown in the send's output window and the Aux track's meter.

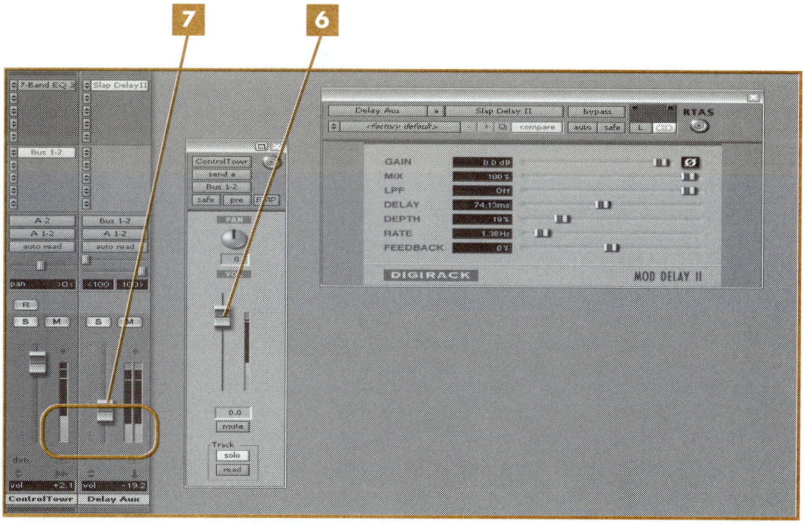

8 **Adjust** the initial **settings** for the plug-in.

9 **Click** the **volume display** on the destination Aux track, and **drag** the **volume slider** to the desired level. Keep in mind that the original Audio track is the "dry" part of the mix, whereas your Aux track is the "wet" part. (It is often useful to solo the appropriate tracks, as I have here.)

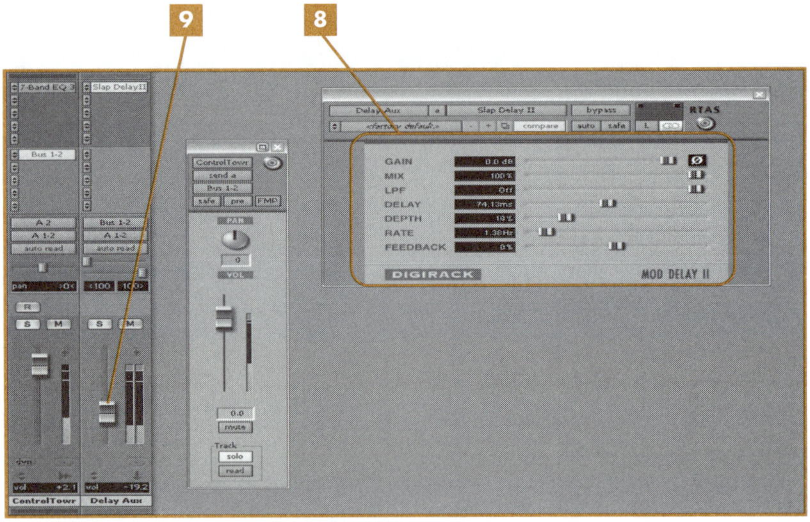

10 When the Pre button is highlighted on the send's output window, the send will be a pre-fader send, meaning that the output of the send will not be affected by the Audio track's volume fader. When the Pre button is not highlighted (the Pro Tools default mode), the send is a post-fader send, and the volume fader of the Audio track will affect the volume going out of the send, and from there to the Aux track.

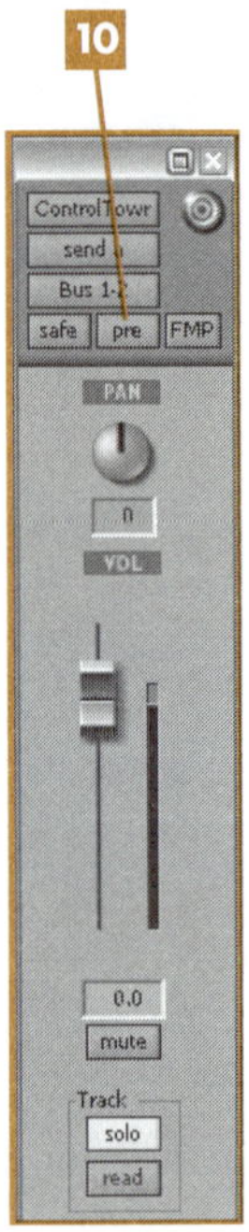

Pre- versus Post-Fader Sends

Although a post-fader send is generally more common (hence it is the default in Pro Tools), both pre- and post-fader sends have their uses. It all depends on the results you want. Choose post-fader if you want to have your dry track (the Audio track) and your wet track (the Aux Input) blend and then have the dry track's level affect the wet track's output. This way, when you raise and lower the volume fader on the dry track, you'll raise and lower the signal being routed to the Aux. If, however, you want the wet and dry tracks to be completely independent, use a pre-fader send. Because signal will be routed to the Aux track *before* the dry track's fader, a full signal will be sent to *both* faders. Experiment!

The Mix Parameter and Traditional Time-Based Routing

Most plug-in effects have a mix parameter that allows you to blend a dry and a wet signal. Often this setting defaults to 100-percent wet, but not always. Be sure to check your plug-in's mix parameter; in a mixing situation like this, you'll want the mix to be 100-percent wet.

11 One more button to talk about: The FMP button (which stands for *Follow Main Pan*) makes panning your sends much easier. Very commonly, it is preferable to have the pan's send mirror the panning of the track as a whole. That's just what FMP does. Just click the FMP button in the send output window, and the send's pan will follow the panning that you choose for your track's output. You can tell whether your send is set to follow the main panner by the lit FMP button and the grayed-out panner in the send output window.

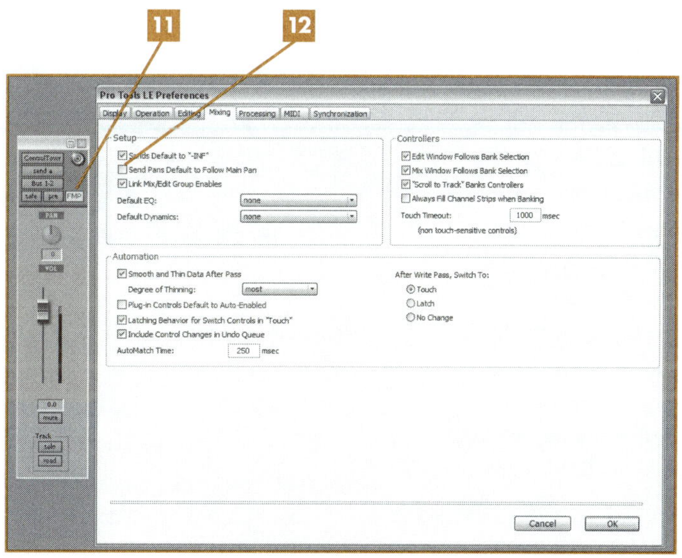

12 FMP can be automatically enabled on newly created tracks. From the Preferences window, go to the Mixing tab. Checking the Send Pans Default to Follow Main Pan box will do the trick.

Here's a variation on the previous workflow, and a way to make production much simpler and get more performance out of your DAW in the bargain.

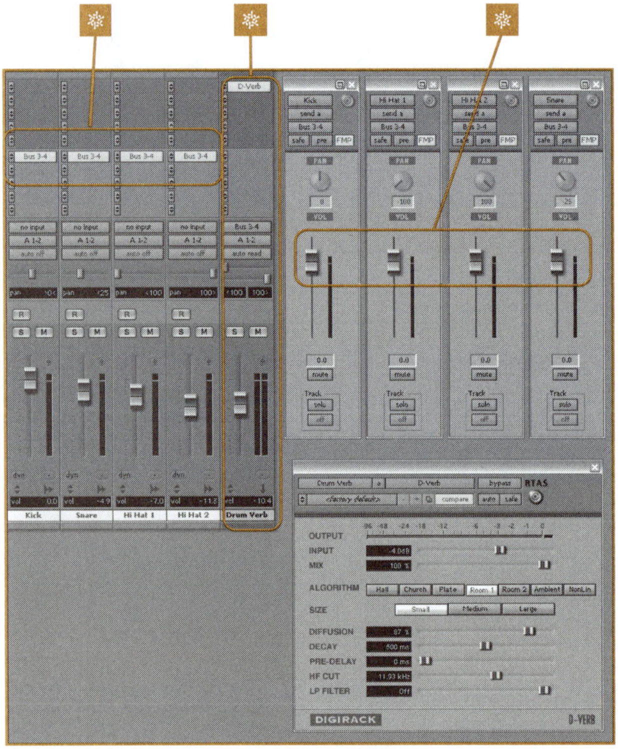

- You can have multiple sources and destinations for each bus in your system. That means you can create sends on a number of tracks and assign them all to the same bus(ses), as shown with the four individual drum tracks in the tutorial session.
- It's important to note that you can independently control the levels and panning of each of your sends, which will let you tailor the signal going to the Aux track.
- All of these signals will be combined and routed to a single Aux track, as shown here. Remember that you must set the input of the Aux track to match the busses you're using on your source tracks (in this case, busses 3 and 4). The Aux track will include the effect that you want to apply to your tracks (in this case, a reverb).

That's it! Now you have dry faders (the Audio tracks) and a wet track (the Aux track), and you can adjust the balance as you want. Remember, *all* of the parameters that you've just set up (send levels, Aux levels, plug-in parameters, and so on) are a starting point only, and you can tweak them to your heart's content.

Moving and Copying in the Mix Window

Pro Tools gives you even more power when it comes to inserts and sends. Want to move a plug-in or send from one track to another? No problem—just click on that plug-in or send button and drag it to any available track. To copy a plug-in or send, just hold down the Alt key (PC) or Option key (Mac) before you click and drag!

But wait, there's more. . . .

Automating Your Mix

Automation is truly one of the coolest things about mixing in Pro Tools. Automation basically refers to the ability to record parameter changes over time, to be recalled when you play your mix again. You'll find that the ability to control multiple volume and pan changes in real time as your session plays will be a huge advantage to your mix. Better still, not only can you automate faders and pans (features traditionally reserved for expensive mixing consoles), but you can even automate plug-in parameters!

Recording versus Writing

Before you start dealing with mix automation, you should get some terminology straight. Audio and MIDI data are *recorded*, and automation is *written*. This might seem like a matter of semantics, but you'll see the differences as you read on.

A New Way to Mix!

Those of you who have some experience mixing with older versions of Pro Tools (before 7.3) will notice a *big* difference between the way things used to be and the current state of automation in Pro Tools. You'll immediately note that when you write mix automation (which will be discussed later this chapter), your newly written automation will appear as a red line as you create the new automation. Though this is a definite improvement over the old paradigm (where you wouldn't see any visual feedback on the automation you were writing until after the automation pass was finished), it could come as a surprise—don't worry, all is well!

The Automation Modes

There are five automation modes, which determine the way your fader, pan, and other motions will be written into the session. Understanding the distinction between the modes is the best way to start working with automation.

1 You can find the Automation mode button for any track whether you're in the Mix window or the Edit window. Click on the Automation Mode button on the track you want to automate (which in this case reads "Auto Read"). A drop-down menu of the five automation modes will appear.

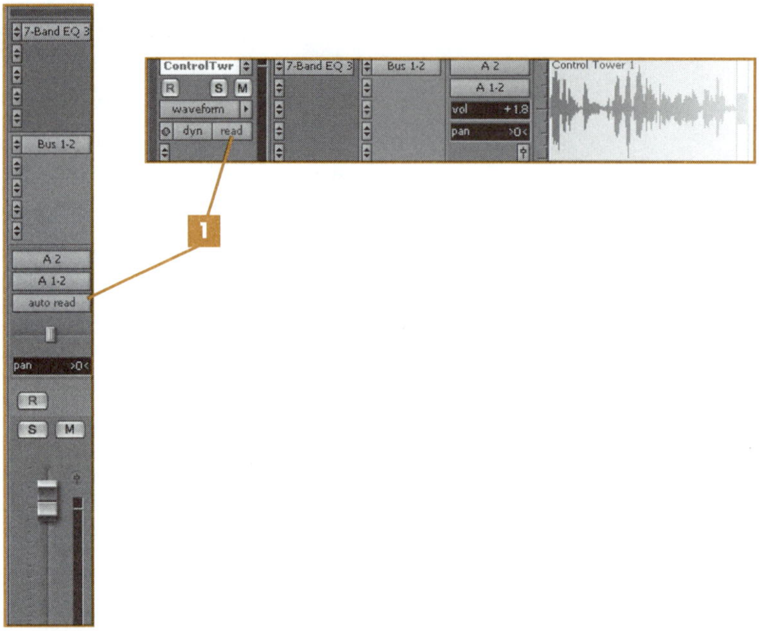

The modes are as follows:

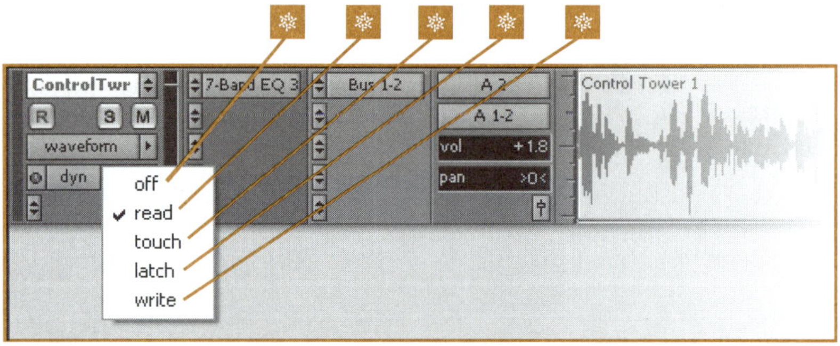

- Auto Off. In this mode, automation cannot be written or played back, even if automation has been previously written.
- Auto Read. Automation cannot be written in this mode, but previously written automation will be played back.
- Auto Touch. Only the parameter that is "touched" (by clicking with your mouse or using a control surface) will write automation. When the parameter is released, it will return to any previously written automation.
- Auto Latch. This mode is similar to Auto Touch—only the parameter that is "touched" will write automation. When the parameter is released in this mode, however, it will remain at the last value and continue to write automation at that position until you stop the transport.
- Auto Write. In this mode, automation will be written on all enabled parameters, regardless of whether the parameter is being touched.

A Word about Automation Workflow

With all of these modes, automation will be written during playback, and writing will stop when playback is stopped or, in the case of Auto Touch, when you let go of the parameter you are automating.

Here's an example of how to use the different automation modes. In this example, I want to work with Synth Pad 3 and change the track's volume over time.

Setting Things Up

You can (and often will) do all your automation in the Mix window, but for purposes of visualization, the screen shots in this section will be using the Edit window.

1 Click the Track View Selector button to change the graphical view of the parameter you want to automate.

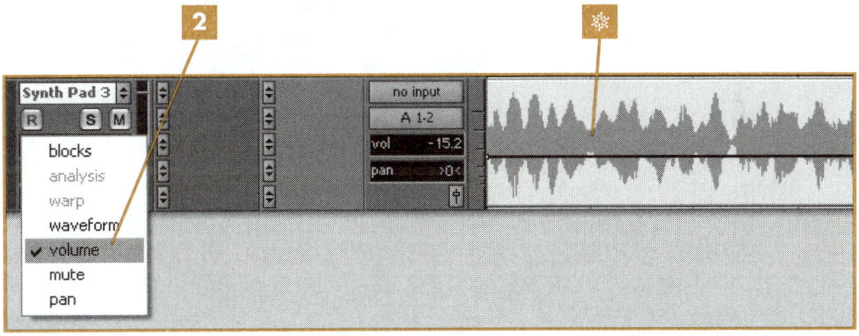

2 Choose the track parameter that you want to view. In this case, I've chosen Volume.

Note that when an automation parameter is selected, it is displayed in that track as a line.

3 Choose the Write automation mode from the Automation Mode button menu. You can access the menu either from the track itself or from the bottom of the output window. For the purposes of this example, let's start with Write mode, which will create new automation data for all automatable parameters.

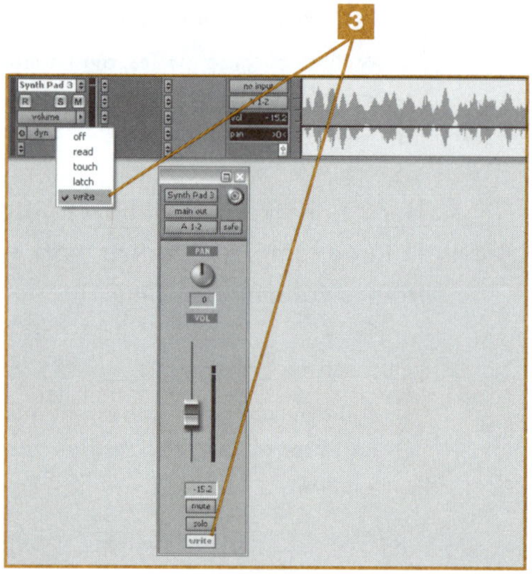

Automation on a Track-by-Track Basis

You can choose a different automation mode for each track.

4 Begin playback of your session.

5 Click on a mix parameter (such as volume or pan) and move it to create automation data.

6 When you're finished writing automation, stop your session's playback.

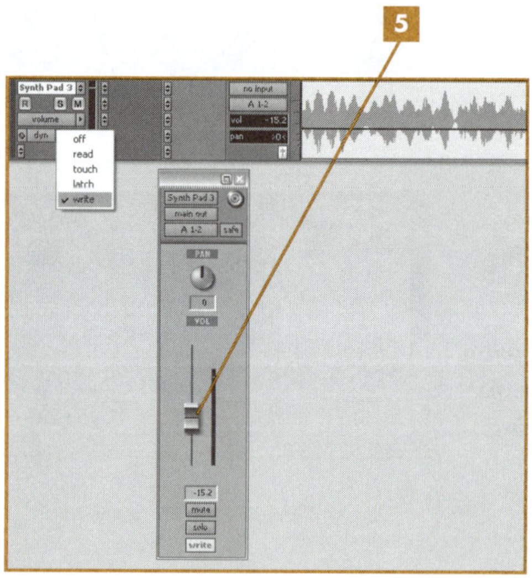

Auto Write Warning

Be careful of following an Auto Write pass with another Auto Write pass. Remember, this mode overwrites *all* enabled parameters (volume, pan, plug-ins, and so on) and will overwrite all these parameters at the same time. Auto Touch and Auto Latch, on the other hand, only operate on the specific parameter(s) being changed, and leave any others alone.

You'll note that new automation data has been written, such as the volume change that I created here. So what if you want to change things? That's where the "update" modes—Touch and Latch—come into play:

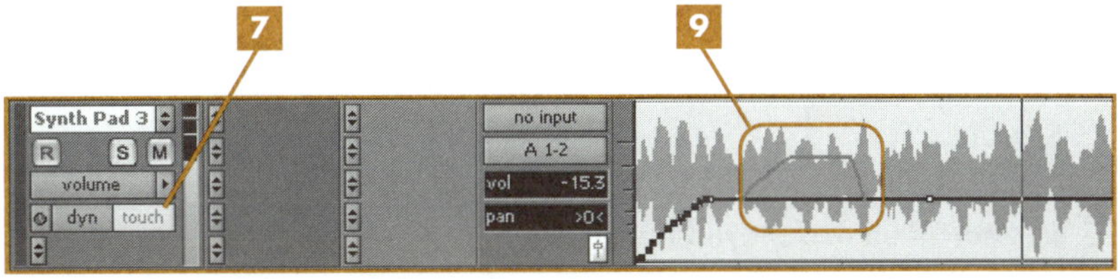

7. Select the Touch automation mode from the Automation Mode button menu.
8. Play your session. Your parameters will read back the automation you have just written, and the appropriate controls will move.
9. When you want to change your data, just click on the appropriate control and adjust it. Let go of the control when you want to return to the previously written automation, then stop playback.

As you write new automation, the newly created automation will be displayed as a red line during playback. When you stop playback, here's what you'll get:

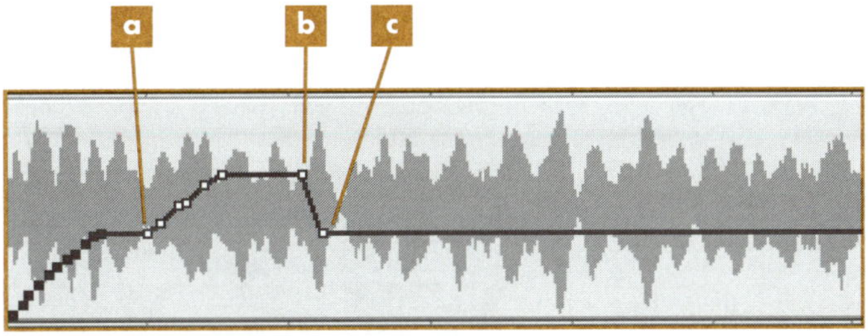

a. Automation was played back as originally written until this point, when I began moving the volume fader.
b. At this point, I released the fader. Because I was in Auto Touch mode, the fader began to move back to the previously written automation as soon as I let go of the fader.
c. Auto Touch mode will take a little time to go back to the previously written automation (a parameter called *AutoMatch time*).

The previous example shows Auto Touch as an update mode, but there is another update mode, Auto Latch, that is also available. Auto Latch works exactly the same way, except that the adjusted control won't go back as soon as it is released, but rather will retain its value until playback is stopped. Here's how a similar update pass would look with Auto Latch mode:

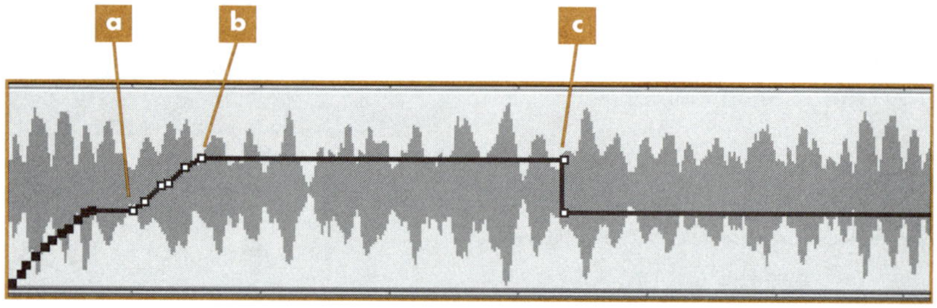

a Automation was played back as originally written until this point, when I began moving the volume fader.

b At this point, I released the fader. Since I was in Auto Latch mode this time, the fader stayed put when I let go of it.

c When playback is stopped, the automation will stop being written.

So how can you find out which mix parameters can be automated?

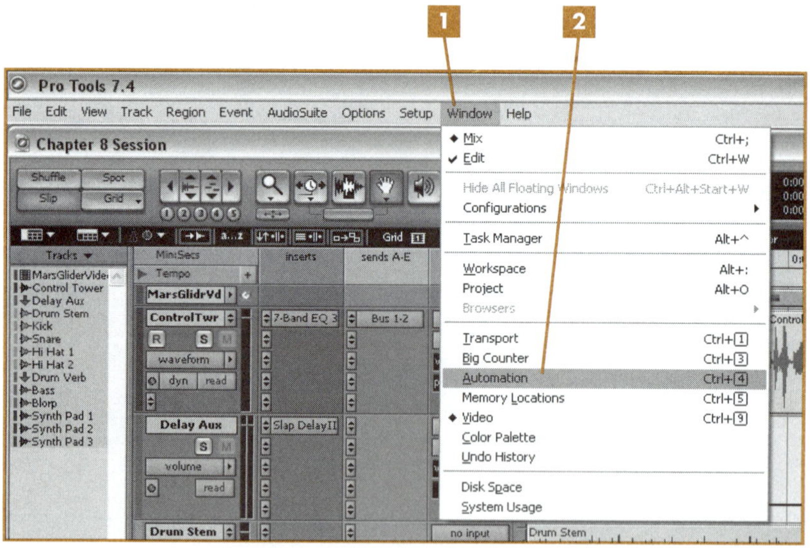

1 Click on Window. The Window menu will appear.

2 Click on Automation. The automation window will appear.

- The seven highlighted icons represent the automatable mix parameters—volume, pan, mute, plug-in, send volume, send pan, and send mute.
- If you click on an Auto Arm button (removing the highlighting), the parameter will be rendered unwritable.
- If you click on the Auto Suspend button, automation (writing and playback) will be disabled.

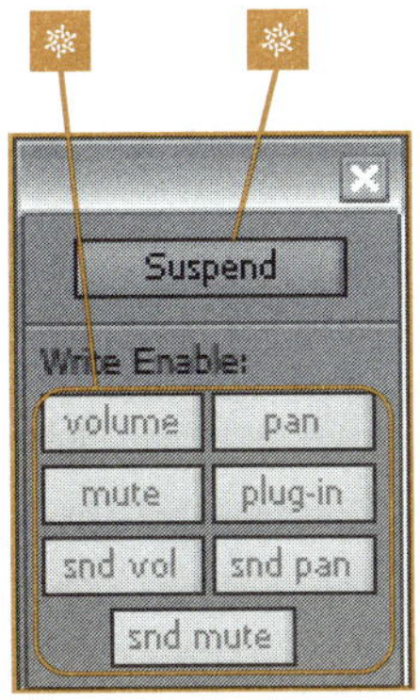

Automation Indicators

From time to time, you'll see your automation mode's font turn bold—what's up with that? Well, bold type in the Auto Enable window *or* a track's automation mode selector indicates that data is currently being written to it. The track's automation mode font will go bold when any kind of automation data is being written, and the individual parameters will be displayed in bold type in the Automation window. Write mode will always appear in bold type.

Plug-In Automation

Virtually every knob or button of a plug-in can be automated. There are two methods by which you can do this.

Working with the Tutorial Session

If you're following along with this chapter's tutorial session, there's a good example of plug-in automation in store for you—automating a frequency sweep on a drum loop. Solo the Drum Stem track and open the plug-in window on the track. (You'll find that there's a 1-Band EQ3 already instantiated for you.) You'll also notice that there is a very strong and very narrow frequency range being emphasized in the plug-in. Your job: Automate that frequency up and down.

Method One

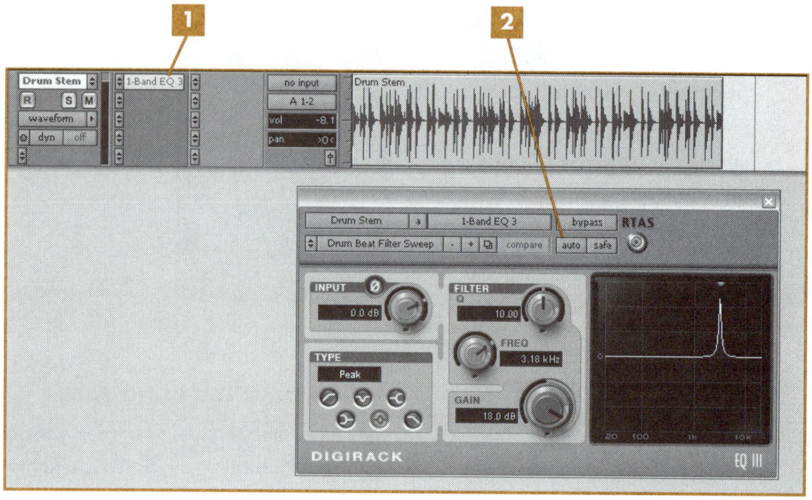

1 Click on the plug-in you want to automate (in this case, the 1-Band EQ3). The plug-in window will appear.

2 Click on the Auto button. The Plug-In Automation dialog box will open.

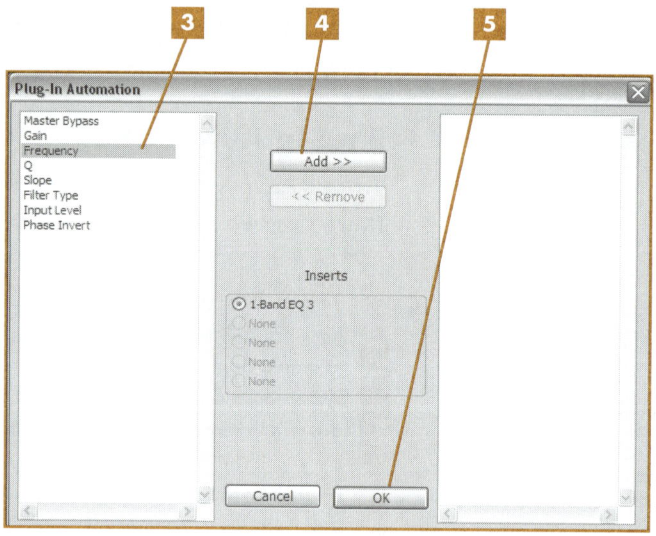

3 Highlight the effects parameters you want to automate (in this case, Frequency).

4 Click on the Add button. The selected parameters will be shown in the list to the right of the button.

5 When you're finished, click on OK. Your settings will be saved, and the Plug-In Automation dialog box will close.

Method Two

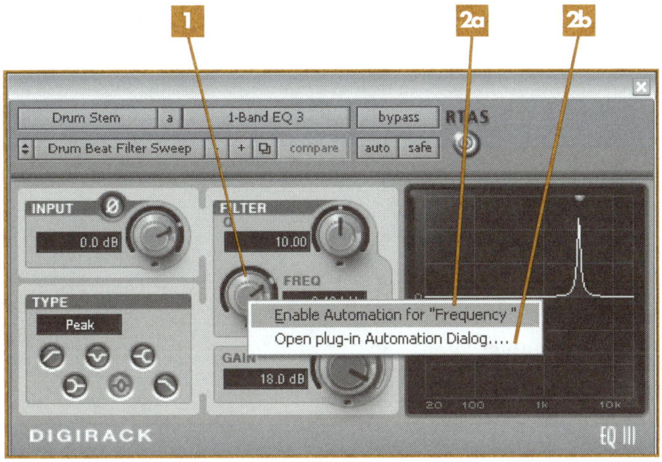

1 **Press and hold** the **Ctrl+Start+Alt** (PC) or **Control+Option+** (Mac) keys and **click** on the **parameter** you want to automate. A menu will appear.

2a **Click** on **Enable Automation for <parameter name>**. The parameter will be ready to be automated.

OR

2b **Click** on **Open Plug-In Automation Dialog**. The Plug-In Automation dialog box you saw in Method One will open. At this point you can follow Steps 3 through 5 from the "Method One" section.

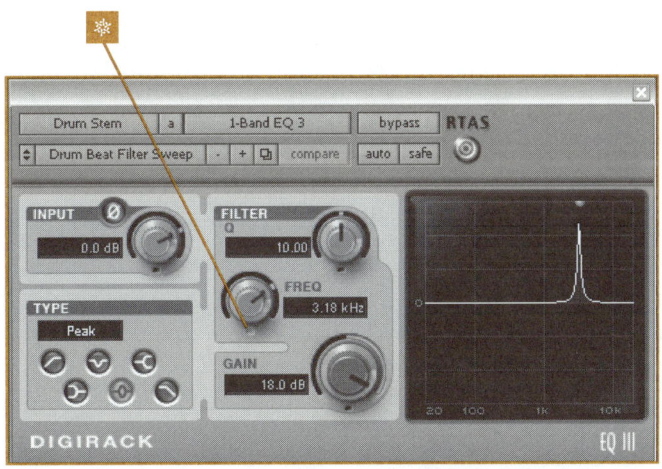

Parameters armed for automation will be identified with a color (sometimes it's an outline, a box, or in this case a small light beneath the parameter). In Auto Read mode, the label will be cool color such as green; in any of the Write modes, the box will be a warm color such as red.

Plug-In Automation Shortcut

Here's a quick way to enable all the parameters on a specific plug-in: Press and hold the Ctrl+Start+Alt (PC) or Control+Option+⌘ (Mac) keys and click the plug-in's Auto button.

You can also automatically enable all plug-in parameters for automation through the Preferences window. Just go to the Mixing tab, and click the Plug-In Controls Default to Auto-Enabled check box.

Once you've got the parameter(s) enabled for automation, writing plug-in automation is pretty much like any other kind of automation. Any plug-in parameters that you've enabled for automation will be added to the Track View menu, as shown here. Just begin playback in any automation mode you desire, and start writing plug-in automation!

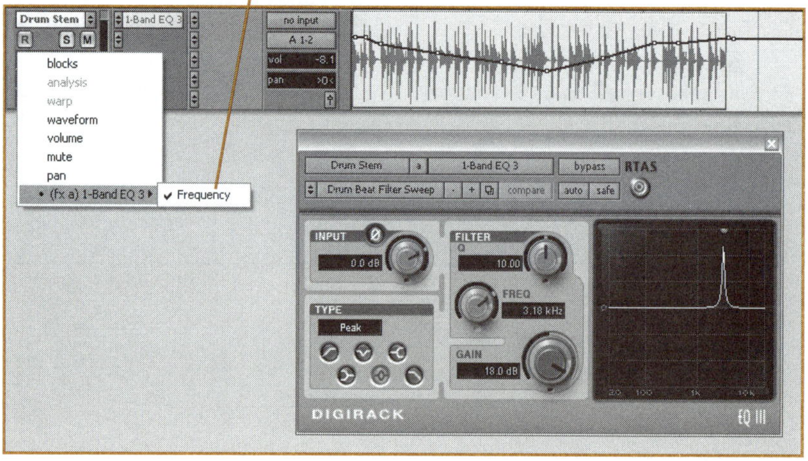

Checking Your Work

To see many of the steps we've gone over in this chapter, open the Chapter 8 Session-Finished session, included on your book's disc.

Next stop . . . the mixdown!

9 Finishing Touches

Almost done! Now that you're at the threshold of finishing your first project, it's interesting to look back at all you've accomplished to get here, from setting up your system to recording, and then editing (and more editing) to mixing. Now you're at the stage of creating a deliverable product—good job! Okay, enough reminiscing—break's over.

Before you can truly consider a project finished, there's usually some tweaking to be done. Then, when you're satisfied with the mix, it's time to mix it down to a file or a pair of files that you can actually listen to on something other than your Pro Tools rig, such as a CD player. Last but absolutely not least, there's the business of archiving your files. In this chapter, you'll learn how to:

- Tweak your mix automation in the Edit window
- Use subgroups and Master Fader tracks
- Bounce to disk in a CD-ready format

Using the Tutorial Sessions

For the purposes of this chapter's examples, you can launch the Chapter 9 Session file, which is included on the disc that came with your book. However, if you completed the tutorial exercises in Chapter 8 and you like your mix, you can continue working with that session as well!

More Fun with Mixing

Though you've certainly gotten a solid start with mixing in the previous chapters, there are a few more techniques that you might find useful.

More Fun with Plug-Ins

Learning more about managing your plug-in effects will save time and boost creativity!

Creating Presets

Suppose you created the *perfect* slap delay for the Delay Aux track, and you'd like to use the same settings in future projects. No problem—it's nearly as easy as recalling presets!

1 Adjust the settings for your effect until they're just right.

2 Click the Settings Menu button (the small arrow button immediately to the left of the Librarian button). The Settings menu will appear.

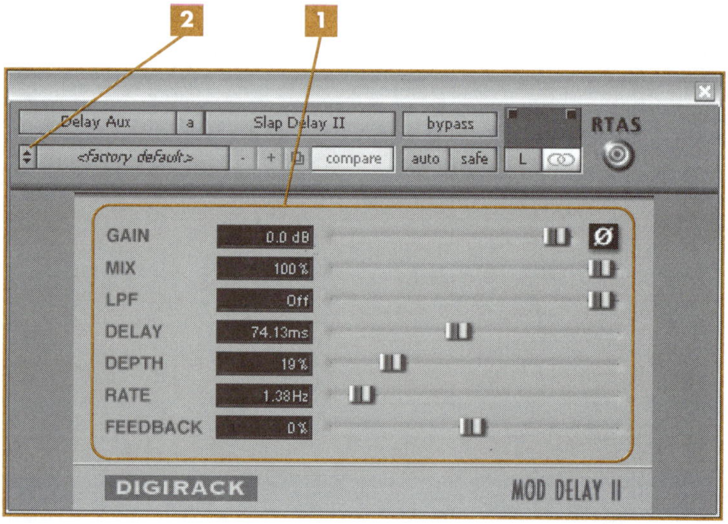

3. Before we go any further, there is a setting that you should check. Choose the Settings Preferences menu item. A submenu will appear.
4. Choose the Save Plug-In Settings To menu item. Another submenu will appear.
   - Choose Root Settings Folder to save your settings to your host computer's Root Settings folder. With this option selected, you'll be able to recall these settings with any other sessions you create or open on this computer.
   - Choose Session Folder to save your settings to a subfolder of the session in which you're currently working.
5. For the purposes of our example, choose Root Settings Folder.

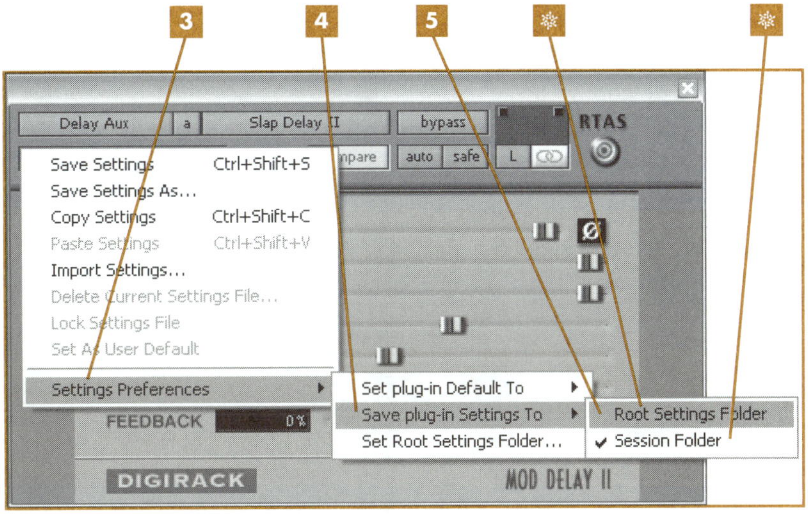

6. Click the Settings menu once more, then choose Save Settings As. The Save Effects Settings As dialog box will open.

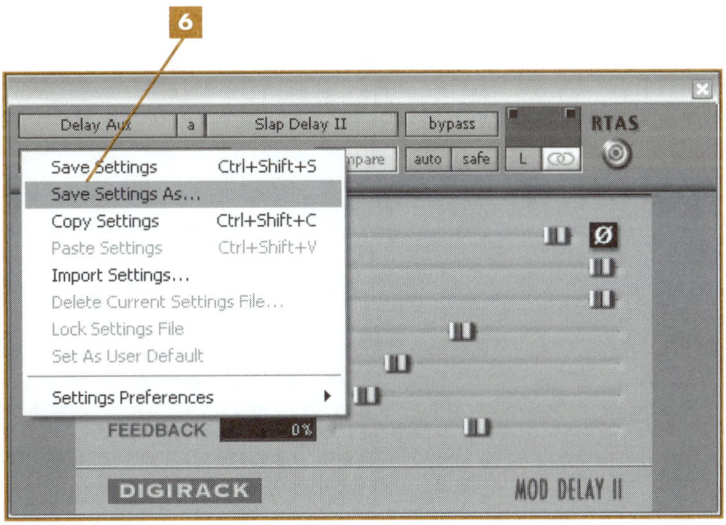

7 Type a descriptive name for your effect (such as "Control Tower Delay").

8 Click Save. The parameters will be saved, and the dialog box will close.

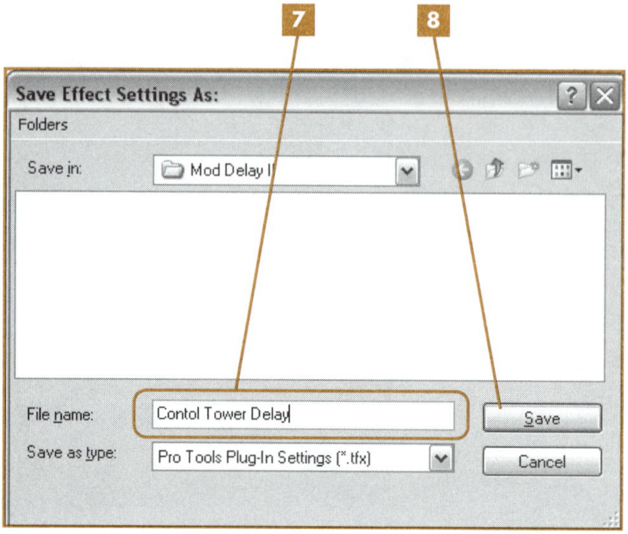

Here's what you'll end up with. You'll note that your saved preset will be added to the list of available presets. The more presets you save, the longer that list will become!

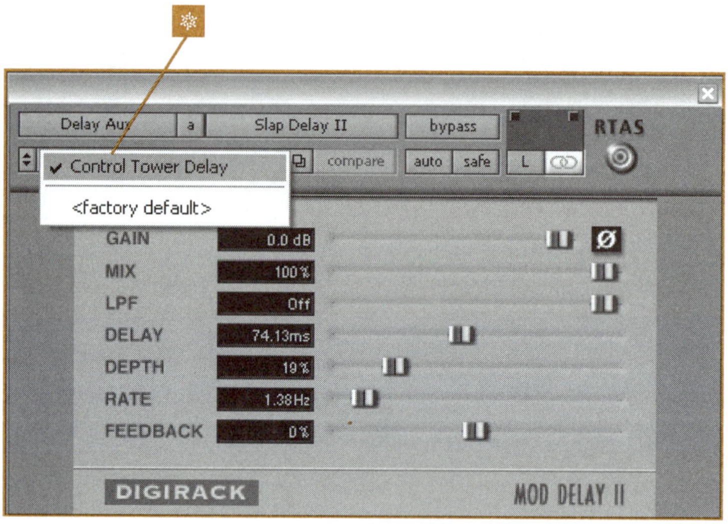

Setting Up Default Plug-ins

As you gain experience, you might find (as many do) that you have some favorite EQ and Dynamic effects that you use again and again. So how can you recall these preferred plug-ins quickly? Check this out:

1. Click the Setup menu.
2. Select the Preferences menu item. The Pro Tools LE Preferences window will appear.

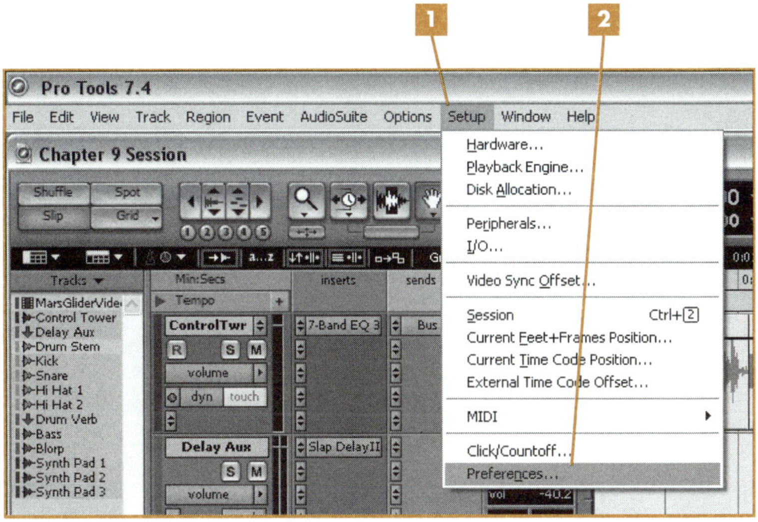

3. Click the Mixing tab of the Preferences window. The tab will move to the front.
4. You'll see two areas, where you can select Default EQ and Default Dynamics plug-ins. Start by choosing your favorite EQ—click the Default EQ menu button. A menu will be displayed, as shown here.
5. Select your favorite EQ plug-in. In this case, I've chosen the 7-Band EQ 3, which I found by clicking the Plug-In menu item, and then the 7-Band EQ 3 plug-in.

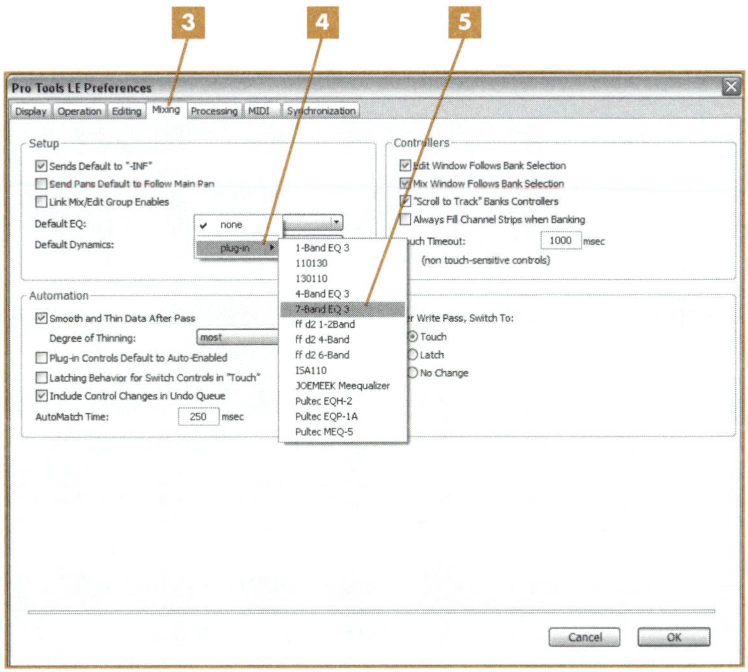

6 Now choose your default dynamic plug-in. Click the Default Dynamics menu button. A menu will be displayed, as shown here.

7 Select your favorite dynamics plug-in. In this case, I've chosen the Compressor/Limiter Dyn 3, which I found by clicking the Plug-In menu item, and then the Compressor/Limiter Dyn 3 plug-in.

8 When you've made your choices, click OK.

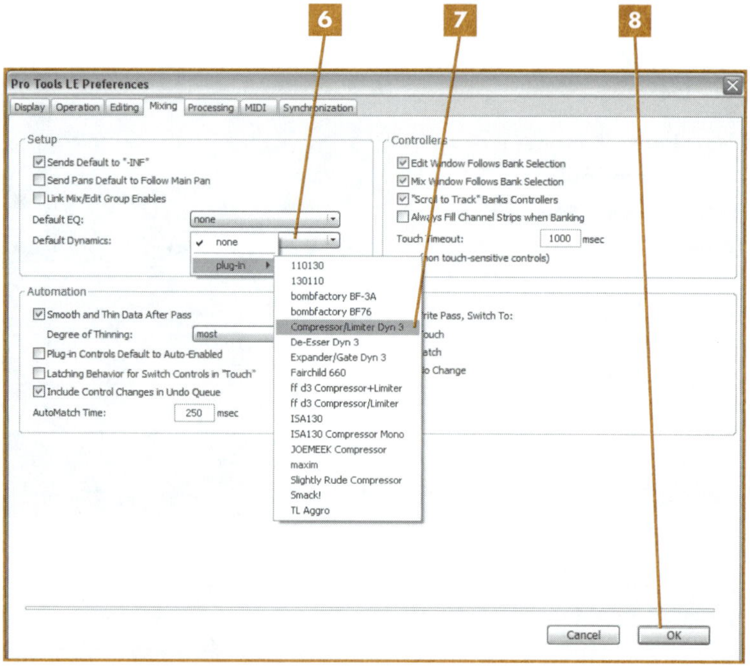

Here's what you've gained: Now, when you click any Insert Selector button, your default plug-ins will appear at the top of the list, easily accessible.

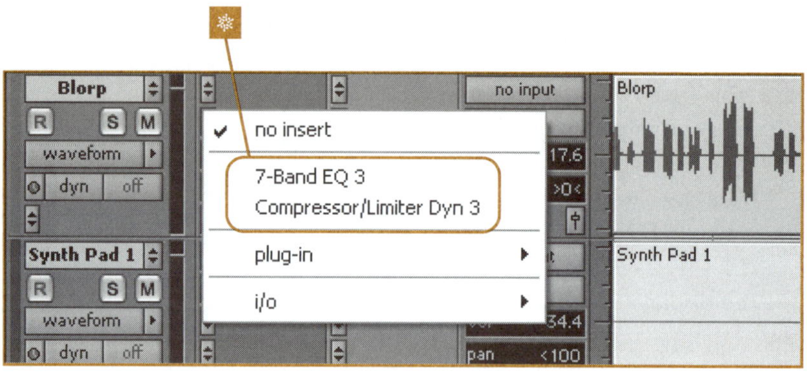

Using the Workspace Browser with Plug-Ins

You've looked at the Workspace Browser window and seen how easy it makes importing audio files. Starting with Pro Tools 7.3, you can now use the Workspace to import plug-in settings as well! There are two ways to make the Workspace work for you:

The first step (and probably the hardest in this overall easy process) is to locate your plug-in settings in the Workspace Browser. You'll find that by using the Search function (which you learned about back in Chapter 3), you can not only refine that search by typing in a descriptive name, but further refine that search by clicking the menu in the Kind column and choosing Plug-In Settings File.

Searching for Settings

If you *don't* type in a name, but you only search by plug-in settings file type, Pro Tools will search for *all* your plug-in settings files.

Plug-In Settings Files

The default location for your plug-in settings files is *boot drive* > Library > Application Support > Digidesign > plug-ins settings (Mac), or C:\Program Files\Common Files\Digidesign\DAE\Plug-In Settings (PC).

The only thing that you need to do is drag your desired plug-in settings file into the Inserts column. There are two ways to do it:

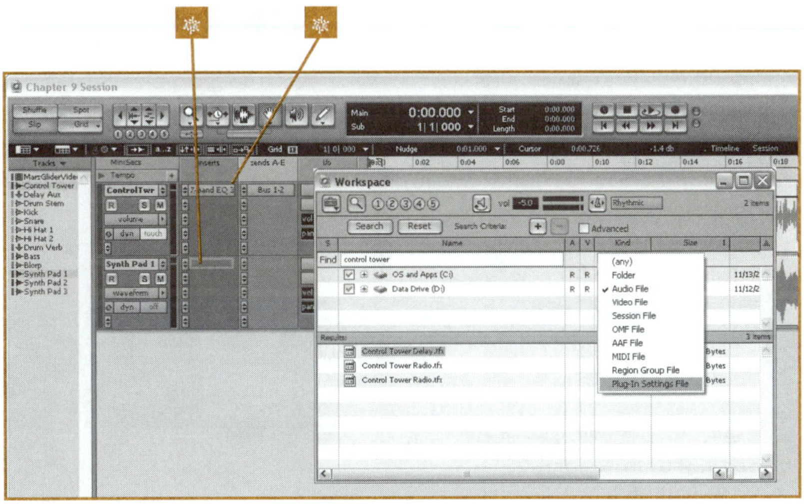

- If you drag the plug-in settings file onto an unused insert (a box will appear, as shown here), Pro Tools will instantiate the plug-in effect and load the preset. Job done!
- If you drag the plug-in settings file onto a used insert (making sure that the plug-in setting matches the type of plug-in that you're dragging to), the preset will be loaded in the plug-in.

More Fun with Automation

Creating mix automation by manipulating knobs, sliders, and faders with your mouse is a great feature, but it'll only take you so far. If you want to get really specific with your automation, sometimes the only place to do that is back in the Edit window.

1. If you're not already there, go to the Edit window. In this screen, you're looking at your regions, with waveform data inside. To edit your automation data, you have to see it first.

2. Click on the track display format button. (The button will display the currently selected display format for easy visual reference.) A drop-down menu will appear, displaying available data that can be shown.

3. Click on the data you want to edit. (For this example, let's take a look at volume.) The volume data will appear.

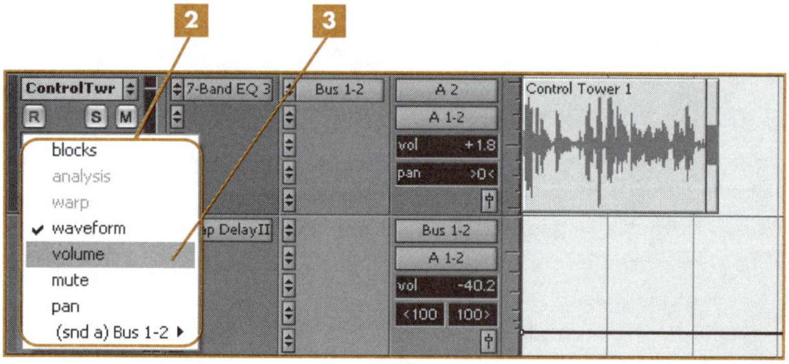

You can see a line that represents any movements that you wrote during any earlier automation sessions for the mix parameter you selected (in this case, volume)—if you haven't done any automation passes, the automation playlist will appear as a straight line. Note that you can still see your regions and waveforms in the background. Now, let's create some new automation data with the Pencil tool.

4 Click on the Pencil tool. The tool will be selected, and you will be able to write new automation or overwrite previously written automation.

5 For more options, click and hold the Pencil tool button. A drop-down menu will appear. Just like the Trim and Grabber tools, the Pencil has some interesting options. For example, suppose you want to change this automation from the curve that it is now into a straight linear ramp (which, when you're looking at volume automation, would be a linear increase in volume). The best version of the Pencil tool to do this would be the Line option.

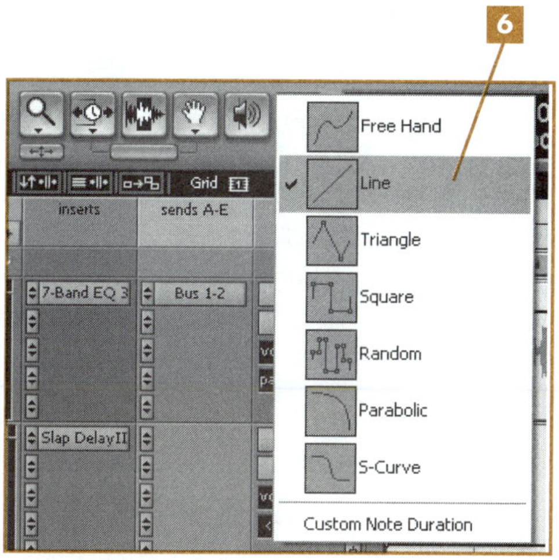

6 Click on the option you want to use. The option will be selected.

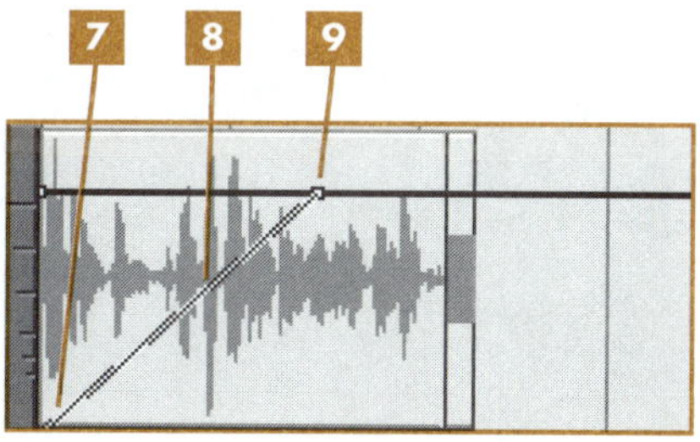

7 Click and hold the Pencil tool at the point where you want to begin writing new automation.

8 Drag the mouse to the place that you want to end writing automation. The Pencil tool will progressively write new automation over what was previously written. In this case, a straight line will be drawn because the Line option for the Pencil tool was chosen.

9 Release the mouse button. Your new automation line will be written.

Of course, you can write more than just volume automation in a straight line. Let's try some pan automation on the "Blorp" that ping-pongs from the left to the right side.

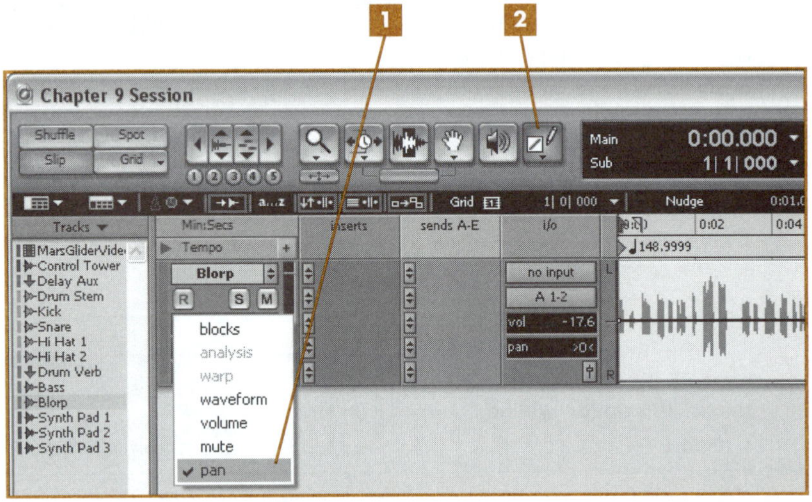

1. Click on the track display format button and choose Pan. The pan data will appear as a line along your track, looking a lot like volume automation. With pan, though, you're not getting louder and softer as your curve moves higher and lower—you're panning from right to left.
2. Although you *could* draw a straight line from left to right over and over again, there's an easier way to do it. Click and hold the Pencil tool button. A drop-down menu will appear.

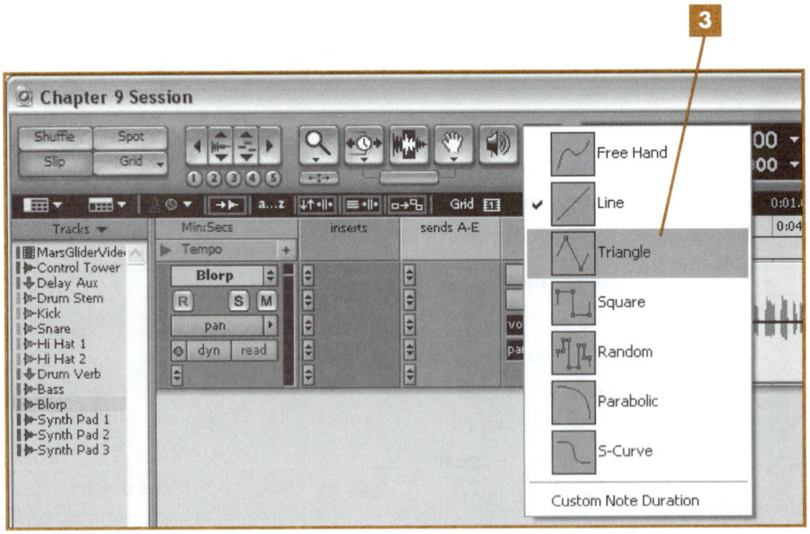

3. This time, click on the Triangle option. The option will be selected.

4 When you're dealing with the Triangle, Square, or Random Pencil options, the Grid setting will determine the frequency of the curve (even if you're not in Grid mode). In this case, you want to pan from side to side every measure, so choose 1 bar as your grid value.

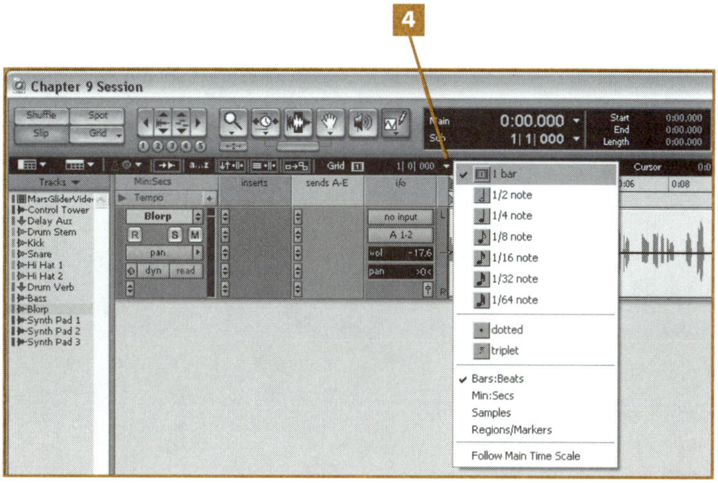

5 Click and hold the Pencil tool at the point where you want to begin writing automation. This time, as you drag to the right, a triangle wave will be drawn across the track. The frequency of your panning will be one measure, as set up in your Grid value. The severity of the ping-pong is determined by your cursor's height in the track. In the case of pan automation, a higher and lower triangle wave will translate into a more extreme pan from left to right.

6 When you're finished, release the mouse button. The pan automation will be written to your track.

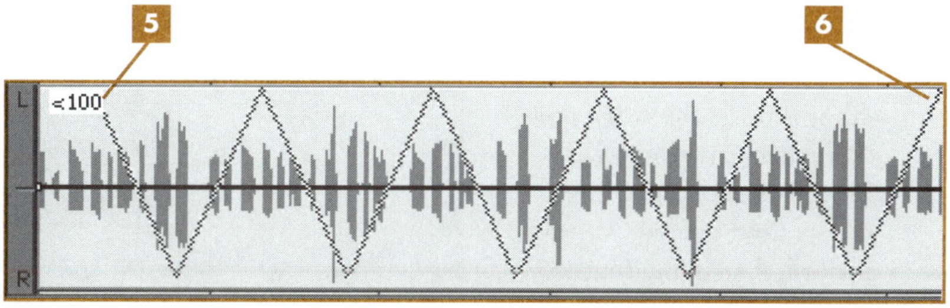

Automation and Grids

Although the triangle wave will change based upon the Grid value in any mode, if you want the apex of the triangle wave to fall on a grid line, you must be in Grid mode.

Copying and Pasting Automation

When you've got a segment of automation that you like, you can cut and paste that automation from one location to another. It's easy!

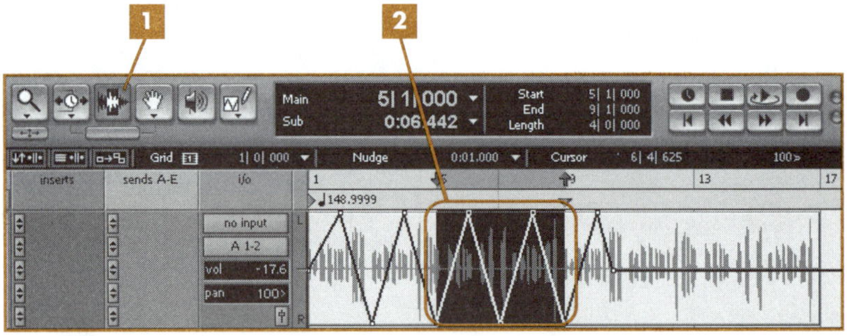

1. **Click** on the **Selector tool**. The tool will be selected.
2. **Select** the **area of automation** that you want to copy, just as if you were selecting a segment of audio. The area will be selected.

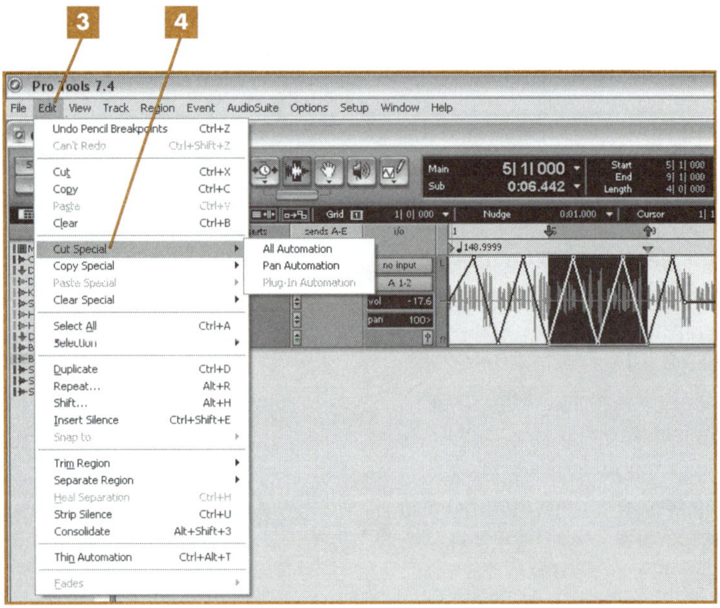

3. **Click** on the **Edit menu** and **choose** any of the **basic editing functions** (such as Cut, Copy, Paste, or Duplicate) you've used before. After you perform the editing functions, you'll be able to see that the automation curve has been edited. One thing to keep in mind, though: Regular editing that you do for a specific automation parameter (pan, for example) will not affect any audio or any other automation parameters; it will only affect the parameter you're looking at right now.
4. Choosing special editing, however (including Cut Special, Copy Special, Paste Special, and Clear Special) will reveal a submenu that will allow you to edit all automation, only pan automation, or all plug-in automation.

Shortcut Reminder

Remember, you can use the regular shortcut keys instead of clicking on the Edit menu.

Automation and Regions

With Pro Tools 7.3, you have a new level of control over the interaction between automation and regions. Let's take a quick look at some of the cool new things you can do with your automation editing.

If you move a region (using Block or Waveform view on your track), do you want the automation during that time follow the region, or will it stay put? Well, in different situations, you'll want different behaviors, and Pro Tools has you covered. Here's how you can set things up.

1. Click the Options menu.
2. The option we're looking for in this case is called Automation Follows Edit. Click this menu item to alternatively enable or disable this behavior. (If it is enabled, you'll see a check mark beside the option.) Here's a description of the two different options and how they behave:

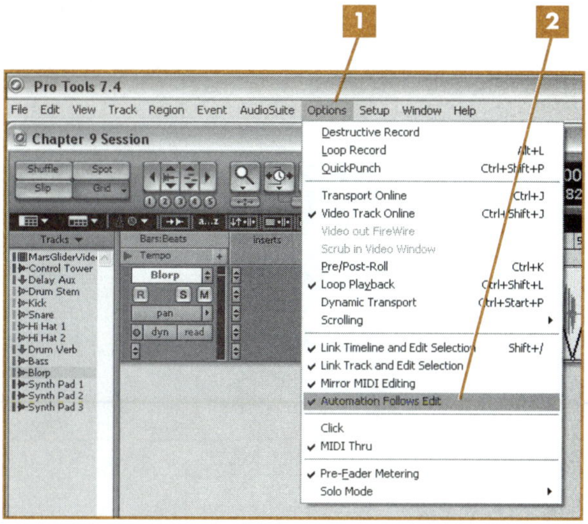

- This figure is a sort of before-and-after example. This first track shows the original position of the region and pan automation. Now, let's say that we go back into Block or Waveform view and move the region. What will happen to the automation?
- If Automation Follows Edit is enabled, the automation will be moved along with the region.

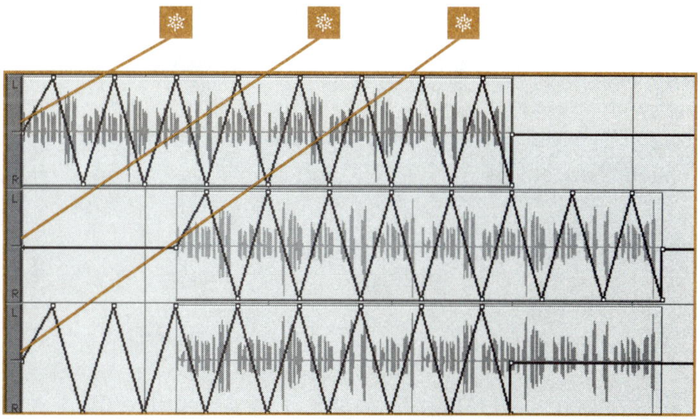

- If Automation Follows Edit is disabled, the automation will not be moved along with the region and will remain in its original position.

Here are a couple more things you can do with regions and automation:

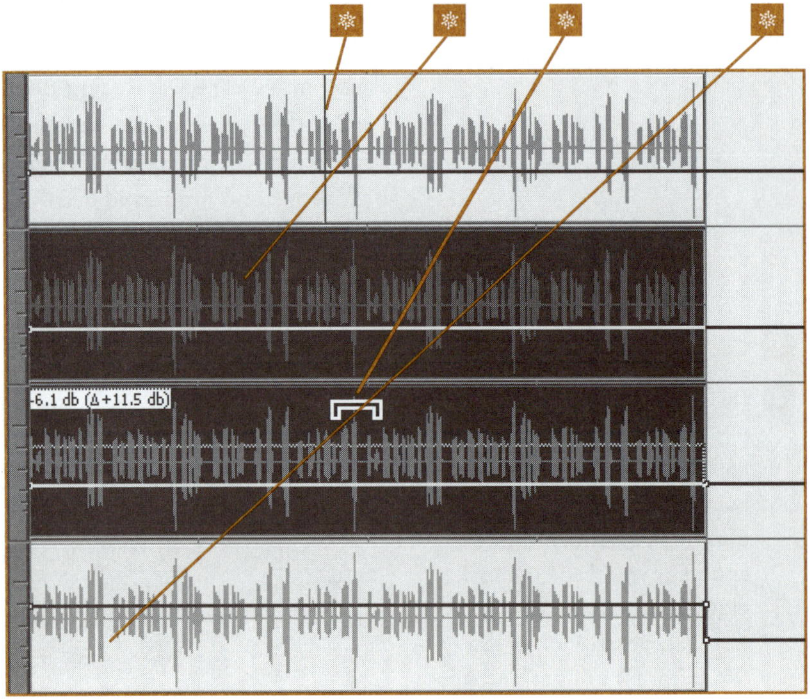

- If you want to separate a region, but you are currently in an automation view (in this example, we're looking at volume), it's no problem. Just use the Selector tool to place your cursor where you want to split the region, and separate the region as usual (using the processes you learned in Chapter 5).
- If you want to quickly select the area of a region, just double-click with the Selector tool. The time corresponding to your region will be selected.
- Once you've selected the area of a given region, here's a cool editing trick for you: Using the Trim tool, click and drag your mouse up and down to increase or decrease the level of the automation in that selected area. Note that when you use the Trim tool with automation, there will be a small box to the left that not only shows you the level of your new automation, but also a delta value (indicated here by a triangle), which lets you know the *amount* of change that you're applying.
- Here's what you'll get: The level of automation will be changed according to the amount you dragged with the Trim tool. This particular process is handy in setting levels for individual regions.

Momentary Switches and How to Use Them

Volume, pan, and plug-ins aren't the only parts of your mix that can be automated—switch-style aspects (those that have only an on or off state) can be automated as well. Common among them, things such as mute and bypass (for plug-in effects) are often automated in order to get even more control over you mix.

Typically, these controls "latch"—in other words, if you click the button once, it will change the state of the parameter until the button is clicked again, like a light switch. However, you might find that changing the behavior of these switches so that they *don't* latch (in other words, the state of the switch will only change when you press down on the mouse) opens new creative options.

Let's take a look at how you can use these in a real-world example. Here's the situation: If you take a look at your session, you'll see that you have a Region Group that includes four drum tracks (Kick, Snare, Hi-Hat 1, Hi-Hat 2). What I want to do is to add a *huge* reverb to every *other* snare hit. Here's how to do it using momentary (non-latching) switches:

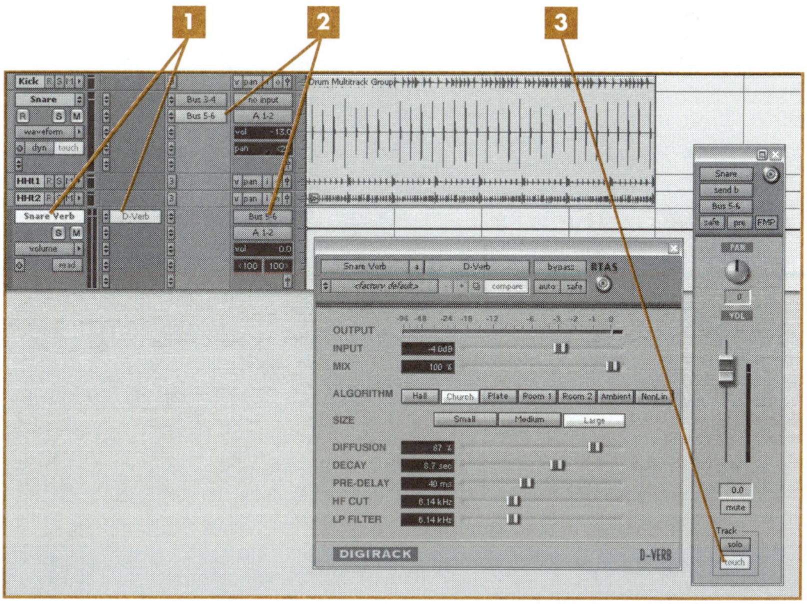

1. First, let's set things up (using the traditional time-based techniques we covered in Chapter 8). Create a stereo Aux track and instantiate a reverb plug-in on any available insert.

2. The next step is to route a copy of your snare track to this dedicated Aux track (which I've named Snare Verb). Assign the output of the send to an available pair of busses. (I've chosen Bus 5–6 in this case.) Set the input of the Aux track to the same busses.

3. Last but not least, put your Audio track in Touch automation mode and mute the send, since this is the state that you'll be starting off with.

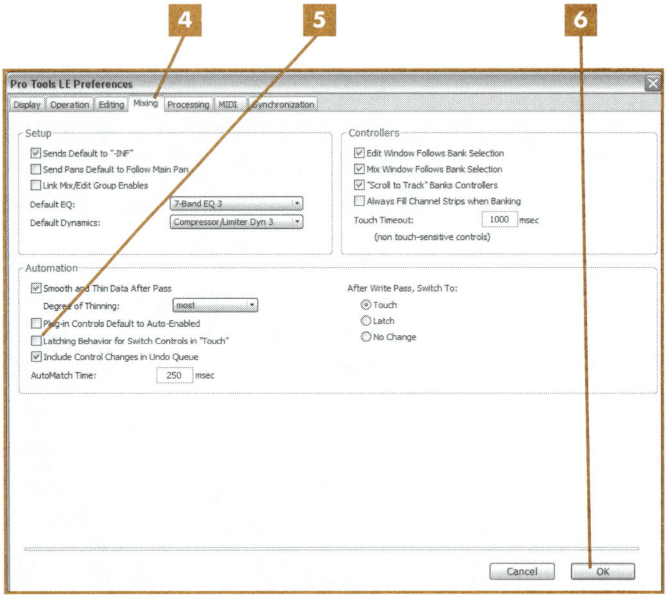

4 Now let's set up Pro Tools to treat switches as momentary. In the Preferences window, go to the Mixing tab.

5 By default, the Latching Behavior for Switch Controls in "Touch" box is checked. To make the switch momentary, click the box to remove the check mark.

6 Click OK.

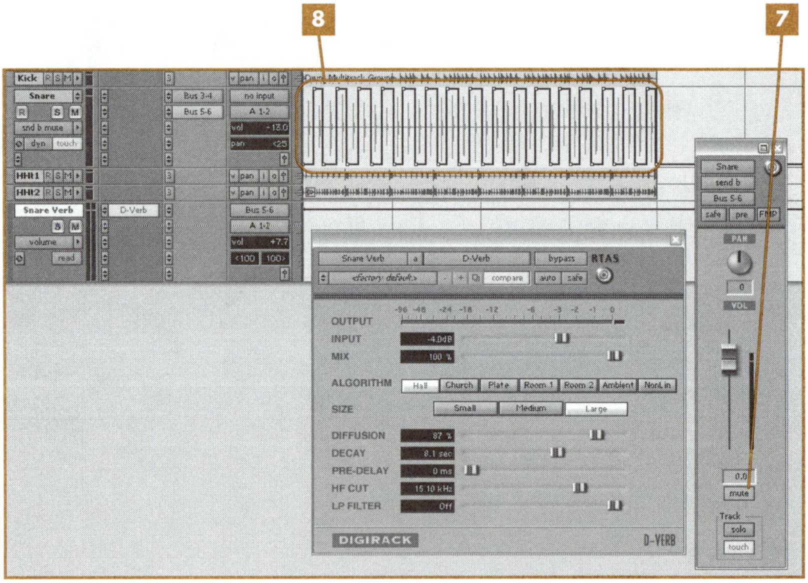

7 Now you're ready to rock. Here's what you'll do: After you start playback, click and hold on the Send Mute button (which you'll see in the Send Output window, as shown here) on every other snare hit. As soon as the snare hit is finished, release the button (which will effectively put the send into mute again). Basically, you're pressing the mouse to unmute the send when you want to hear the reverb.

8 Though it might take a couple attempts at first, this is what you should wind up with. If you look at your send's mute automation playlist, you will see your send alternately mute and unmute.

What you've created here is known in many circles as a *dub hit*, and it is used for every kind of track, from beats to vocals. Once you understand this process, you'll hear it in all sorts of modern music. The most obvious example is a vocal in which some individual words have reverbs (or echo or delay), but others are relatively dry.

Blue Breakpoints

Before we move on from the world of automation, there's one final detail you should be aware of. From time to time you might see an automation breakpoint (the small dots that make up an automation playlist) colored blue. This blue color indicates that the automation data has *overflowed* (think of it as automation "clipping"), and an automation value was attempted to be written that exceeds the limit of that parameter. This can sometimes happen when you are writing automation to grouped faders, and it should be avoided.

More Mixing Power with Subgroups

Subgroups can be a powerful ally when mixing, for a number of reasons. First, though, what's a subgroup? Simply put, a *subgroup* is an arrangement whereby the output of a number of tracks is routed to the input of a single track. This has the effect of "funneling" the audio through the single track, which can make levels and effects easier to manage. Take a look:

1. Create a track to be your subgroup master (in this case, I've chosen to create a stereo Aux track) and name it appropriately.
2. Because you'll be using internal routing for this sort of situation, choose an available bus for the input of the subgroup master. I've chosen Busses 7 and 8.

3 **Assign** the **outputs** of the tracks to be grouped (in this case, I've chosen the drum tracks in this session) to the same bus(es) as you've chosen for the input of your subgroup master.

4 Your subgroup master is now in control of the overall volumes of your subgrouped tracks. Note that the relative blend of the drums remains consistent and that the subgroup master controls the overall output.

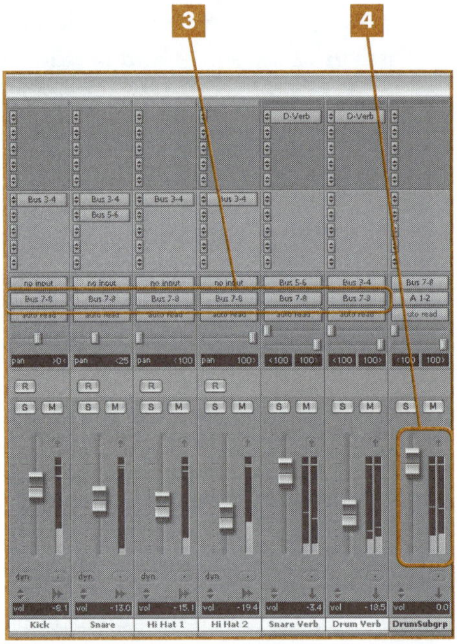

❄ In addition to making your levels more manageable, subgroups can also help you work intelligently with plug-ins. Suppose you want to apply a compressor to your drums (a very common thing to do). One way you could do this is to instantiate a compressor on each of the tracks, but that would be unwieldy to work with and wasteful of your limited processing resources. Instead, just launch *one* effect on an insert of the subgroup master. There's only one plug-in to adjust, and it's thrifty use of your CPU!

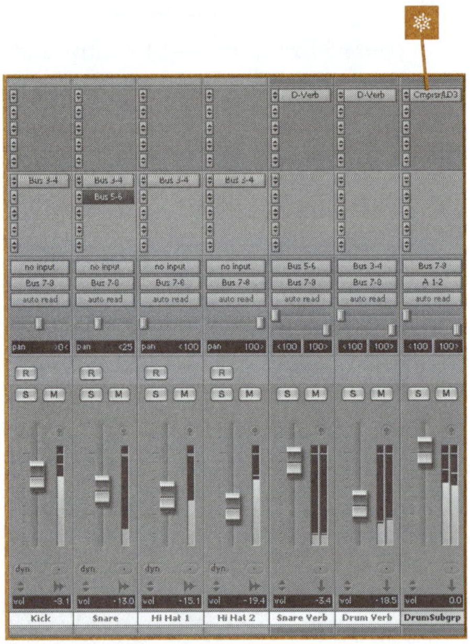

Using Master Faders

There's one kind of track we haven't touched on yet, called a *Master Fader*. Although it looks similar to an Audio track, its function is substantially different than anything you've seen up to this point.

A Master Fader is a way to control output. This output can be the signal of a bus, in the case of complex mixing, but most commonly, a Master Fader is used to control the output of an interface. With this simple but powerful track, you can control the level of your session globally. The following sections will show you how a Master Fader works.

Creating a Master Fader

First things first . . . you need to create a Master Fader.

1. Click on Track. The Track menu will appear.
2. Click on New. The New Tracks dialog box will open.

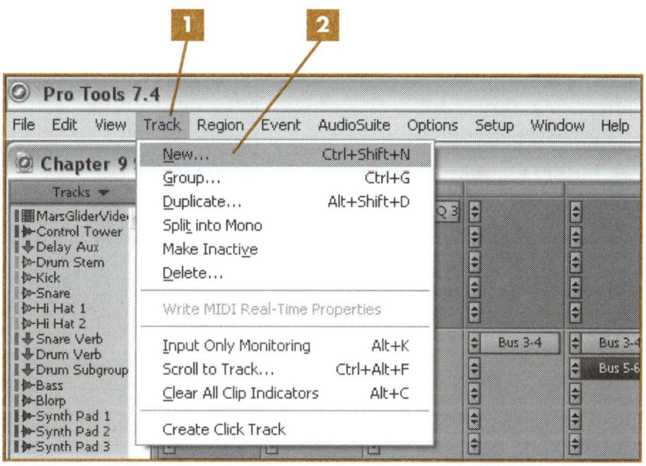

3. Create a stereo Master Fader. The new Master Fader will be created below the currently selected track. The Master Fader looks similar to any other track, but don't be fooled—it's significantly different!

- You'll notice that the position on the track that would normally display an Input button is conspicuously blank. That's because there is no input on a Master Fader; it is only a way to control an output.
- Notice also that there are no sends on a Master Fader. That's because a Master Fader is the last step in the signal path, so there's nowhere to send a signal to.
- You cannot place regions on this track (similar to an Aux track).

4 Click on the Output button and select the interface output you are using to listen to your mix. The interface output will be selected.

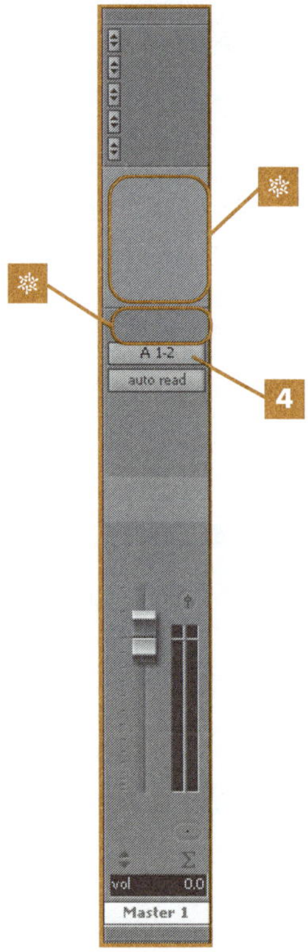

Controlling Your Mix with a Master Fader

Now you can use your Master Fader to control your entire mix. For example, the following steps will show you how to create a fade-out for your entire mix in one easy process.

Setting Things Up

For this section, switch to the Edit window if you're not there already.

1 **Select** the **Pencil tool** and **choose** the **Line option** to create a straight fade-out. The option will be selected.

2 **Write** the **automation** on the track as if you were editing prewritten automation. You'll hear a linear change in the volume of your entire mix, starting at the point where the Master Fader's automation begins.

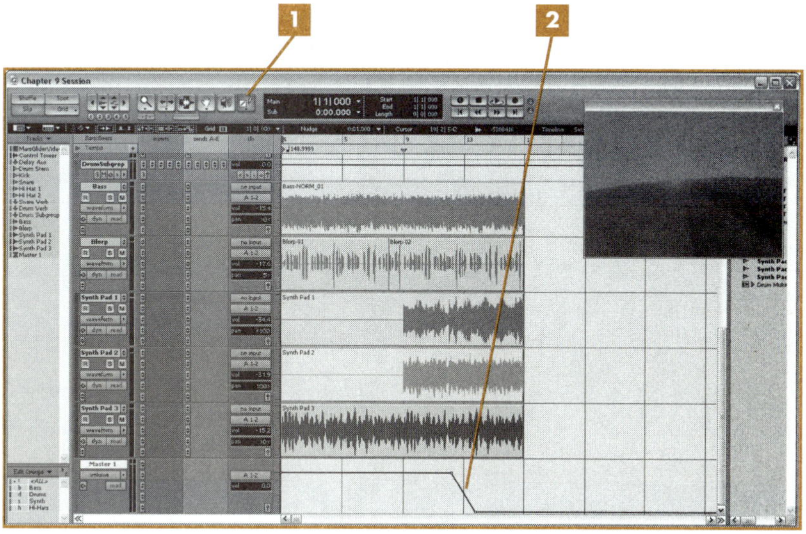

Automation and Master Faders

If you want to write automation onto your Master Fader in the Mix window, it's no problem. Simply write automation (in any of the automation modes) just as you would on any other type of track!

Basic Mastering Techniques Using a Master Fader

Mastering is a post-mix process that further refines a mix to a professional quality. It is such an exclusive and important process that there is an entire segment of the professional audio community dedicated to the specific task of mastering others' mixes. That being said, the task of professionally mastering a mix is certainly not recommended for the non-specialist.

You might, however, want to try your hand at a little basic mastering to punch up your mix for your own enjoyment or to make an evaluation mix a little more palatable for your client. That's where Master Faders really shine. You see, there's another interesting difference between a Master Fader and any other track—one that may not be initially apparent. This difference is in the area of signal flow, making the track more functional as a mastering device—the inserts are *after* the fader in the signal chain. Read on. . . .

Advice on Mastering

The discussion in this section relates to mastering a mix in your own studio (as opposed to having your mix professionally mastered). If or when you decide to have your mix professionally mastered, the mastering engineer will want to do this job himself, usually with highly specialized (and costly) gear specific to the process of mastering. It's always a good idea to consult your mastering engineer before submitting your mix so you can find out what he wants from a mix.

Adjusting Dither

Dither is a common mastering tool used to offset some of the negative sonic qualities of digital audio. In the simplest terms, it is a very low-level noise that may be added to your digital audio to combat distortion introduced in the signal when the bit depth is reduced. For example, if you're working in a 24-bit session but you will be creating a 16-bit file for an audio CD, you can improve the quality of your audio by applying a dither plug-in on a Master Fader. You can adjust the dither for your Master Fader by following these steps.

1. On the Master Fader's insert, select the POWr Dither (Stereo) option from the Multichannel Plug-In menu. The POWr Dither window will appear.

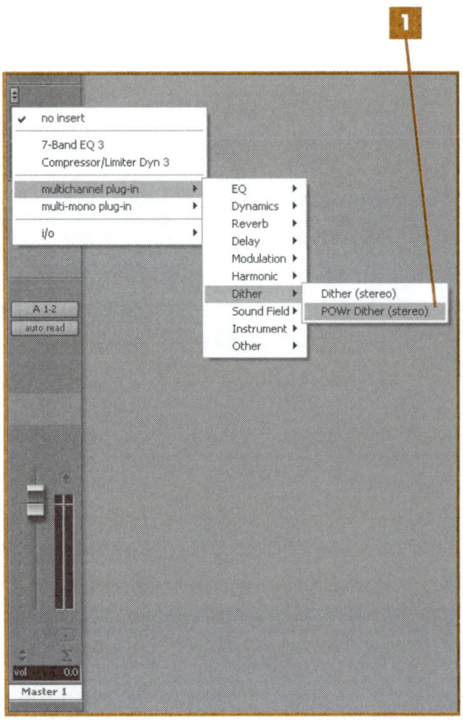

2 Click on the Bit Resolution button and choose the final resolution of your mix. For example, if you want to make an audio CD of the mix, you would choose the 16 bit option.

3 Noise shaping will help make the dither noise less audible. Select a Noise Shaping option. (For now, you can stick with the default shaping, but be sure to listen to different mixes with different noise shaping later.) The option will be selected.

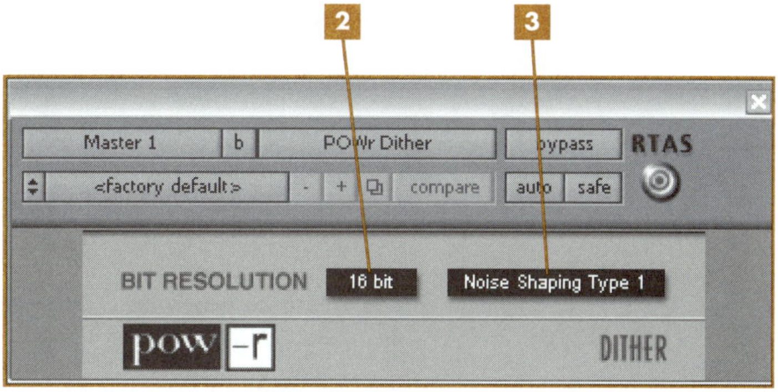

Punching Up Your Mix with Compression—Two Ways

Another common process in mastering is compression. Applying compression to a mix is a tried-and-true method employed to narrow the music's dynamic range, thereby maximizing the overall power of the audio. Give it a try in the following steps.

1 On your Master Fader, instantiate a compressor plug-in on an insert before (above) the one you used for dither. The Compressor plug-in window will appear.

2 Adjust your compressor's parameters to punch up your mix to suit your taste. It'll take some experimentation to find your ideal settings, of course. You can start with a preset configuration, like the one shown in this example.

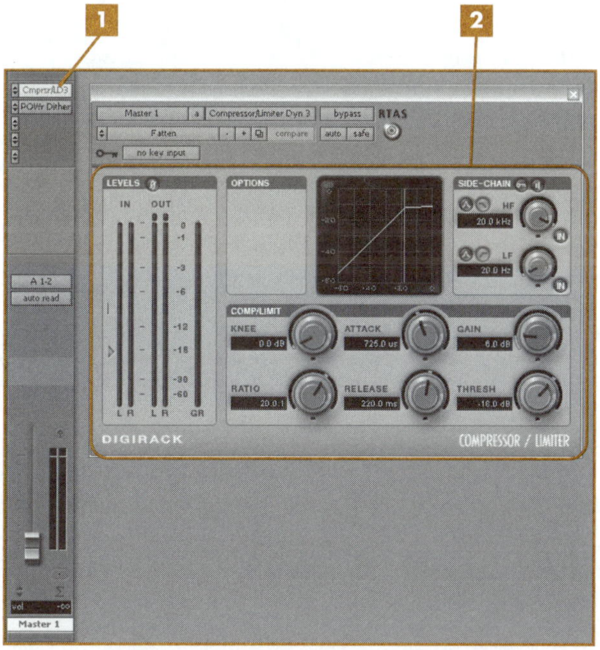

Compressors and Dither

If you're using dither *and* a compressor on a Master Fader, you'll want to arrange your inserts so that the dither is the last plug-in (on the lowest insert). Don't worry if your dither is currently on the top insert; you can just drag it down to a lower (and later in the insert's signal path) insert with your mouse, and then create your compressor above it.

Now, those of you with mixing experience might notice a problem with this sort of routing. You see, a compressor operates by attenuating (or reducing) any level above a certain threshold, which you set in your effect window. Any incoming signal that falls below that threshold will not be affected by a compressor. As long as you don't use your Master Fader for fade-ins or fade-outs, there's no problem with using a compressor on the Master Fader, but if you do use the Master Fader for such things, you'll hear your compressor kick in or out, depending on whether you're fading in or out. How do you get around this problem? I'm glad you asked!

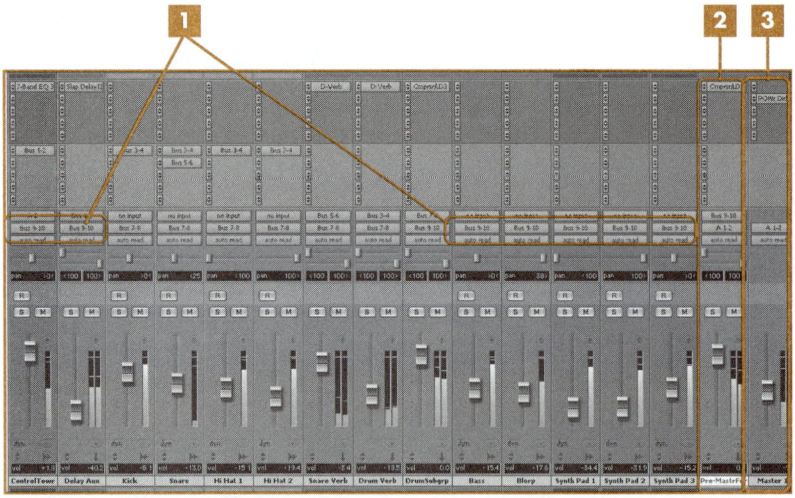

1 Reassign the output of all tracks previously assigned to Main Output to an available pair of busses (in this case, Busses 9 and 10). Your session will now be inaudible, but wait!

2 Create a stereo Aux track, assign the input to the same pair of busses (in this case, Busses 9 and 10), and drag the compressor plug-in to that track's insert.

3 The output of this Aux track, Main Output, will then be controlled by the Master Fader. Bear in mind that the inserts of the Aux track are *pre-fader*, and so the signal going to the compressor will be affected by neither the Master Fader volume level *nor* the Aux track's output level, meaning you can apply your global fade automation on either track. That's it!

There's one more very important use of a Master Fader track, one for which it is uniquely suited due to its post-fader inserts. Master Faders are great for monitoring the overall levels of your mix, and there are ways to view these levels in addition to the track's own level meters. A good example of these meters are the Bomb Factory Essential Meters (which include a Meter Bridge, Noise Meter, and Correlation Meter), shown here. (You'll find them in the Other category of Multichannel Plug-Ins menu.) Though you will rarely have to use *every* kind of meter in a given session, you'll find them a useful tool and an accurate picture of your total levels because of their post-fader position in the signal path.

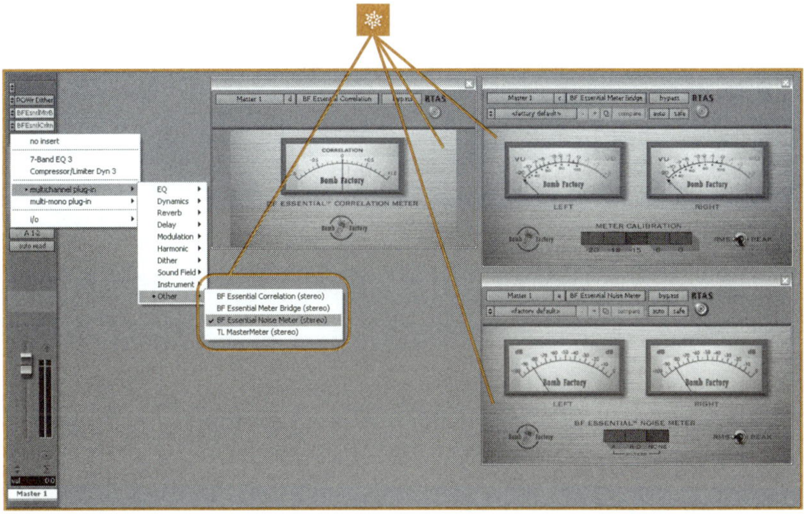

Bouncing to Disk

When you're working in a Pro Tools session, you're in a multitrack environment. Even though you're listening through stereo monitor speakers, you're hearing many component tracks, artfully mixed together by Pro Tools' software mix engine. From a production standpoint, it's a pretty cool way to work, but if you ever want to hear your song outside of the Pro Tools environment, you'll have to somehow render the mix down to a format that is compatible with the outside world.

The Bounce to Disk function is the right tool for this job. It will mix down your session as it plays in real time and create a new audio file of your entire mix. It's a simple process, but one that demands attention to detail to be done just right, so I'll go over all the steps carefully. For example, here's how to go about bouncing to disk so you can burn an audio CD (Red Book format) of your entire mix.

1. Using the Selector tool in the Rulers area, select the area of the session you want to bounce to disk. (In this case, I'll select from the beginning of my session to the end of my Master Fader's fade-out). The area will be selected.
2. Click on File. The File menu will appear.
3. Click on Bounce To. A submenu will be displayed.
4. Click on Disk. The Bounce dialog box will open.

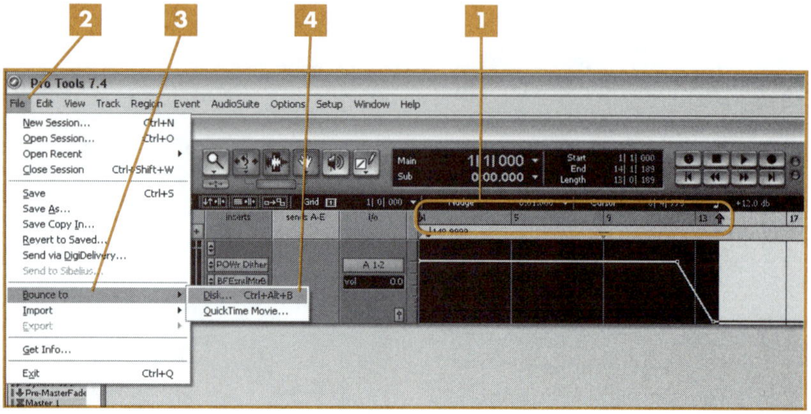

5. Select the output you are using to listen to this mix from the Bounce Source menu. This is perhaps the most important step in this process.
6. Click on the File Type down arrow. The File Type menu will appear, displaying a list of available formats for your mixdown.

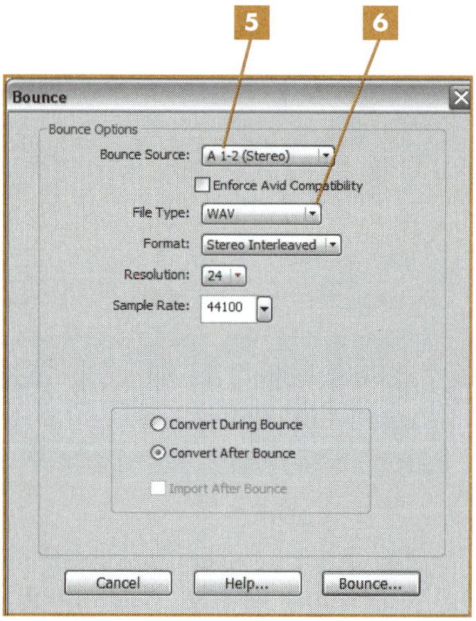

Bounce Troubleshooting

If you bounce to disk and then later find that your bounce is a silent audio file, you probably chose the wrong bounce source.

7 Choose the file type that suits your needs. The first three formats involve no data reduction, so they're well suited for tasks such as continued production or CD burning. The last three formats offer data reduction, which results in smaller file sizes.

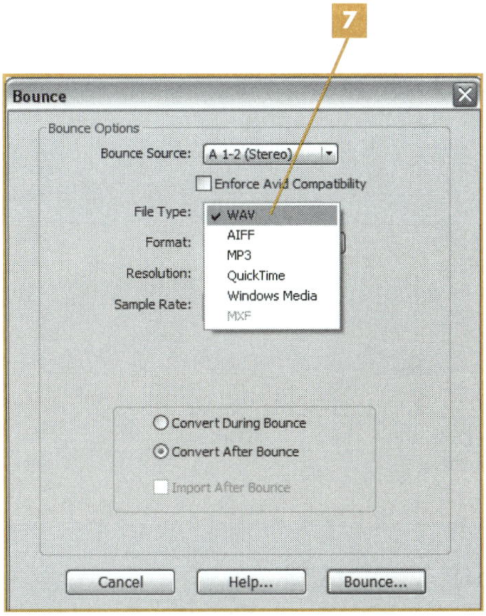

8 Click on the Format down arrow. The Format menu will appear.

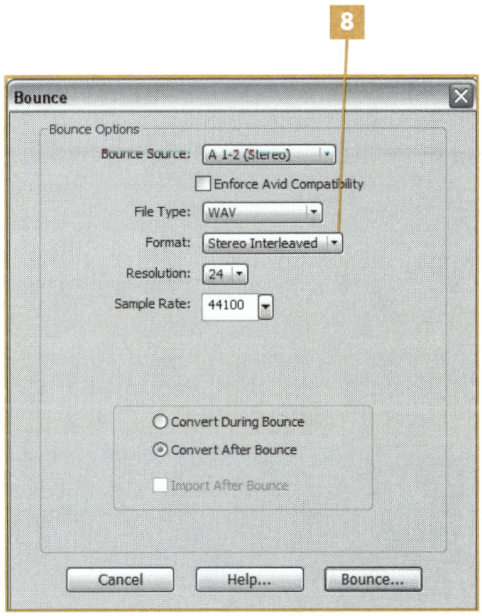

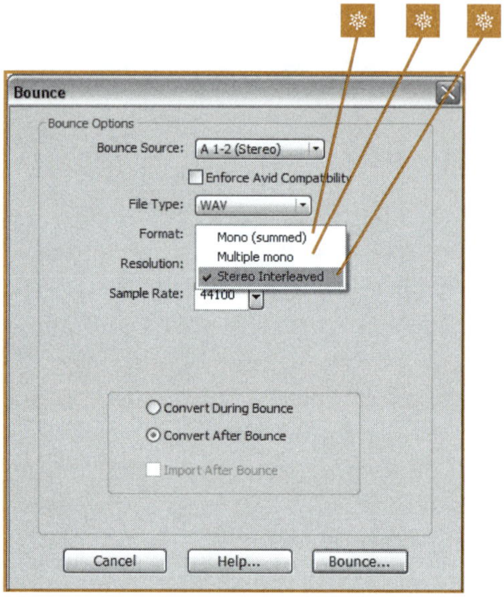

9 Select the file format that suits your purposes. Here's a brief rundown of the available formats:

- Mono (Summed). With this option, your mix, even if it is stereo, will be mixed down to a single mono file.
- Multiple Mono. With this option, your mix will be output to a pair of mono files—one for the left side (with a .l after the file name) and one for the right (with a .r after the file name). This is particularly useful for bounces that you intend to use in future Pro Tools sessions.
- Stereo Interleaved. Use this option for tracks destined for CD burning. Your mix will be rendered to a single stereo file.

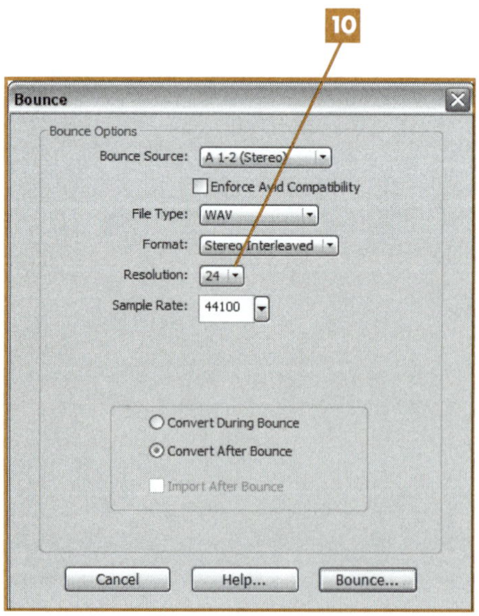

10 Click on the Resolution down arrow. The Resolution menu will appear, displaying the bit depths to which you can bounce.

11 Select the bit depth you want your bounced file to be. The bit depth will be selected.

12 Click on the Sample Rate arrow. The Sample Rate menu will appear, from which you can choose your bounce's sample rate.

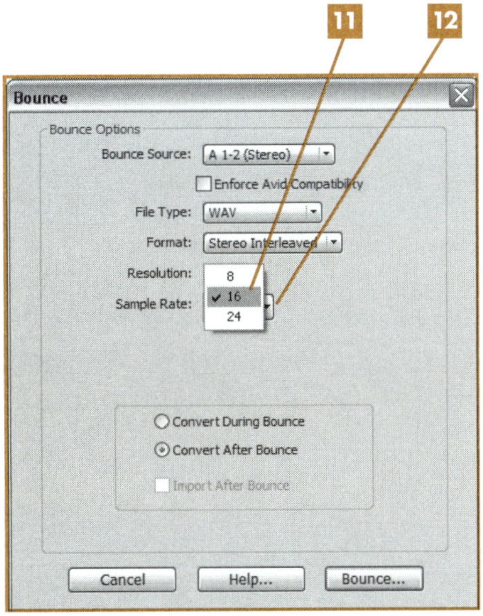

Red Book CD Bit Depth

For the purposes of CD burning, the bit depth must be 16.

13 Click on the desired sample rate for you mix.

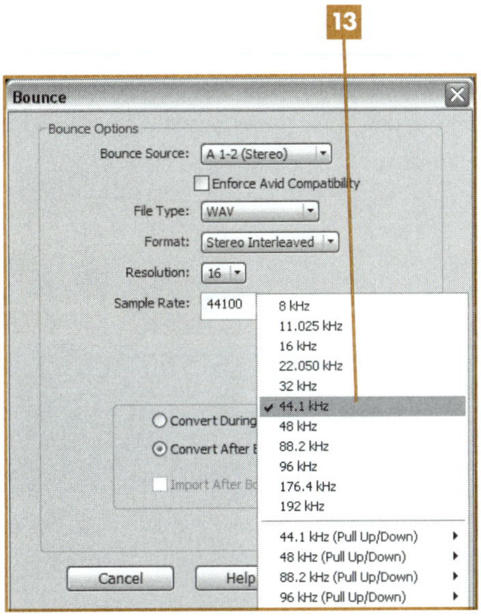

Red Book CD Sample Rate

For CD burning, the sample rate for your bounced file must be 44.1 kHz.

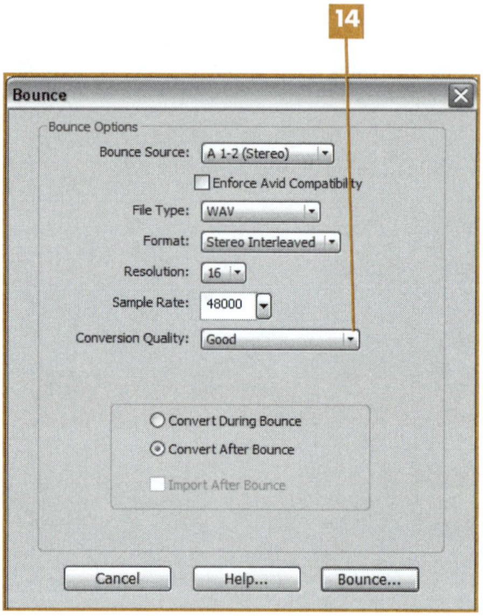

14 *If* the sample rate or bit depth you've chosen for your bounce file are different from those of your session, you will need to convert the bounce file. Click on the Conversion Quality down arrow. The Conversion Quality menu will appear.

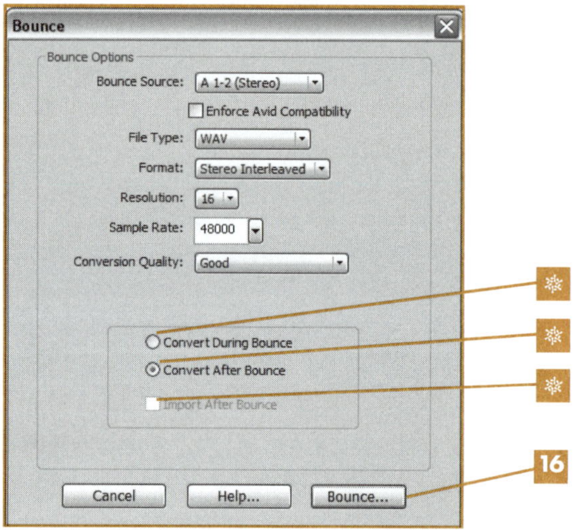

15 If you need to convert in any way, you have a few options:

- Convert During Bounce. This option allows you to convert during the bounce process (as your session plays).
- Convert After Bounce. This option allows you to convert after your bounce pass is completed.
- Import After Bounce. This option allows you to import your bounced file back into your session on an Audio track.

16 Click on Bounce. The Save Bounce As dialog box will open.

Some Advice on Bouncing

In some cases, the Convert During Bounce option can cause Pro Tools not to play back some types of automation (as a result of the extra burden of conversion while bouncing). For consistently good results, choose the Convert After Bounce option; it really won't take too long.

17 Save your file using the options in the Save Bounce As dialog box. You can save your file under any name you want, in any drive, and in any folder. For the purposes of illustration, I'll stick with the default location, which is within the session's Audio Files folder.

18 Click on Save. Your bounce will begin.

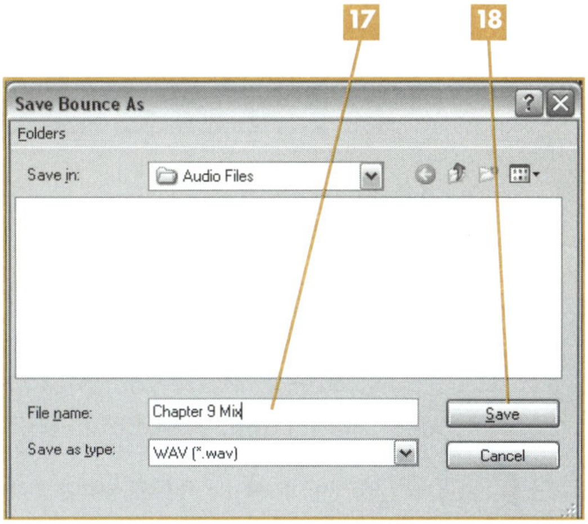

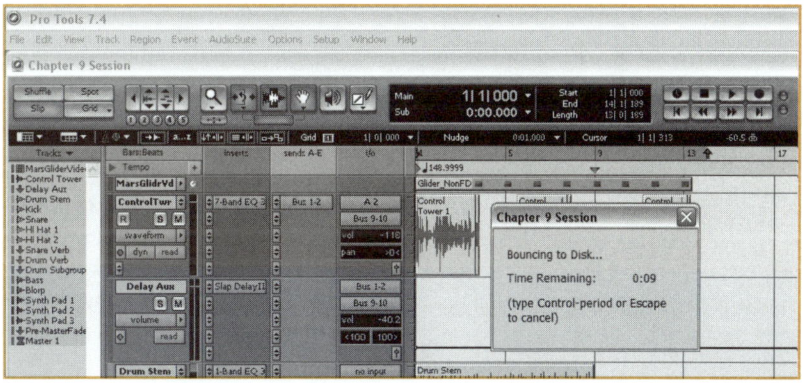

Your session will begin playing, and a small countdown window will indicate that bouncing is occurring.

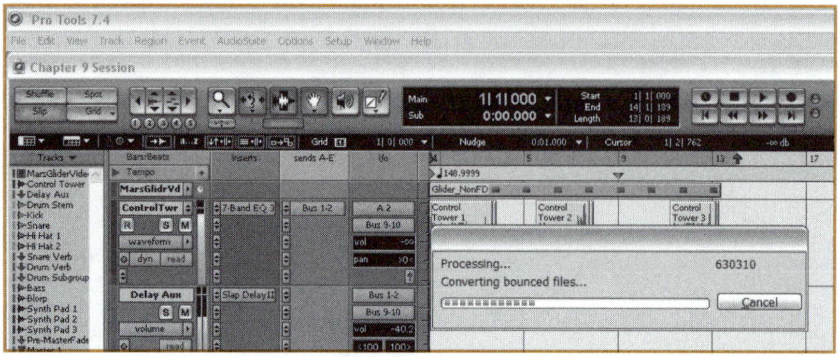

If conversion is necessary (and assuming you chose to convert *after* the bounce), you'll see a quick conversion process window after your session finishes the bounce.

Here's an example of what you'll end up with. It's important to know exactly where your files are created. If you followed the default location, your bounced file will be:

- In the hard drive that holds your session
- In any folders that house your session's folder
- In your session's folder
- In your session's Audio Files subfolder
- An audio file, with the name you created

The Importance of Good File Management

As you can see, your bounced file can get hidden quite well beneath layers of folders on any number of drives. The point I want to emphasize is that it is extremely important to know exactly where and under what name your files are saved. (This goes for session files and other audio files as well.) You can save your bounced file anywhere you choose in your system, but with this great flexibility comes the added responsibility of using this power wisely.

Because this session happens to have a video included in it, you also have the option of bouncing your work to a QuickTime movie file. The process is nearly identical to bouncing to disk.

1 Using the Selector tool in the Rulers area, select the area of the session you want to bounce to your movie. When you're bouncing to a QuickTime movie, a good rule of thumb is to select the length of the video track in your session. (We'll talk more about video tracks in the next chapter, but for the time being, just select the region in the top track of your session.) The area will be selected.

2 Click on File. The File menu will appear.

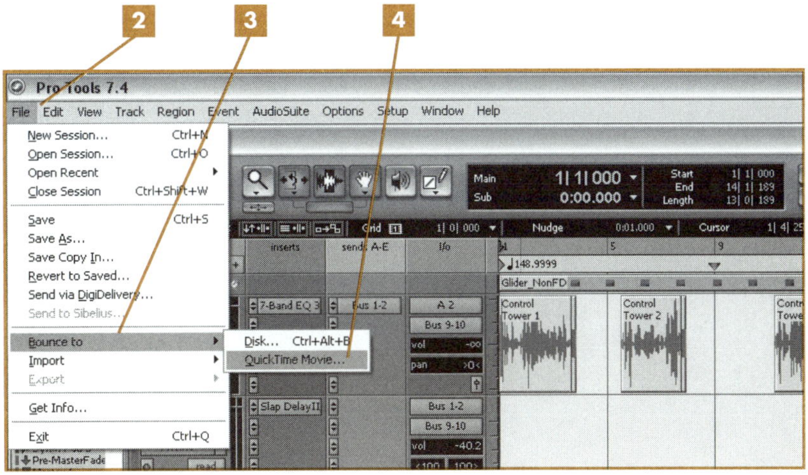

3 Click on Bounce To. A submenu will be displayed.

4 Click on QuickTime Movie. The Bounce dialog box will open.

5 The Bounce window that you'll see is nearly identical to the one you encountered when you bounced only your audio. The only difference is that you have fewer sample rate options—this is normal. When you've made your choices, click the Bounce button.

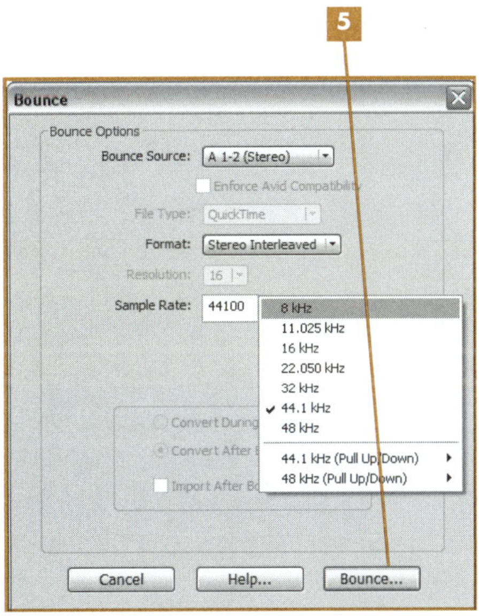

Enjoy your final mix—you've earned it!

10 Moving to the Next Level: Tips and Tricks

Pro Tools is a complex, professional application, and mastering it is a lifelong pursuit for industry professionals. This book is meant to provide you with a solid basic understanding of how to use this powerful product—a strong foundation upon which to build greater knowledge over time. The good news is that by mastering the previous chapters, you've attained that basic understanding.

Now, here's a laundry list of next-level functions, designed to allow you to be even more productive! In this chapter, you'll learn how to:

- Work more efficiently in the Edit and Mix windows
- View data more specifically
- Import and use movie files
- Boost your session's efficiency

> **Working with the Tutorial Session**
>
> To follow along with the examples shown in this chapter, launch the session named Chapter 10 Session. You'll note that the features are demonstrated through a series of memory locations. Also, you'll note that even though the session is extensive in its tracks and complexity, it's only using a few different audio files, keeping the overall session folder small!

Boosting Performance with Disk Allocation

When starting out with Pro Tools, most people don't set up a dedicated hard drive for recording audio files. (In fact, they usually record to their sole system drives.) Although this will work for relatively simple sessions, you may eventually find that a single hard drive—especially if it's your system drive—just doesn't cut it. Here are a few things that can happen in more complex sessions that can stress out a single hard drive:

- Audio track count.
- Higher-resolution audio and/or bit depth: Higher-quality audio requires a greater bit rate, which can quickly use up a single hard drive's limited bandwidth.
- Edit density: Each time you create a region boundary in a track, you require Pro Tools to access a specific location on your hard drive. In addition to just a lot of edits, other things can increase your edit density, including using Beat Detective and Strip Silence—two tools that we'll talk about later in this chapter.

The solution to this problem is to allocate different Audio tracks to different drives in your session, by going to the Disk Allocation window. But first, let's take a quick trip to the Workspace Browser to set up our different drives for different jobs.

- Immediately to the right of each drive name, you'll see a column with an A (for *audio*), which will allow you to set up how each drive deals with audio files and Pro Tools.
- Right next to the A column, you'll see a V (for *video*) column. This does the same thing as the A column, except that it's concerned with video files and Pro Tools.

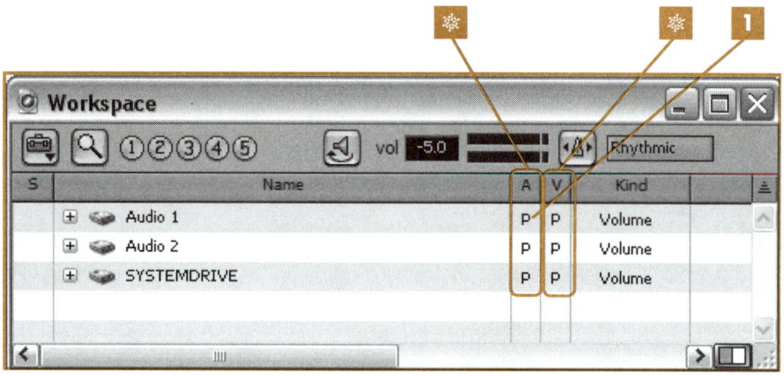

1 Let's start by setting up each drive's audio behavior. Just click the letter in the A column that corresponds to the drive you want to set up. A menu will appear.

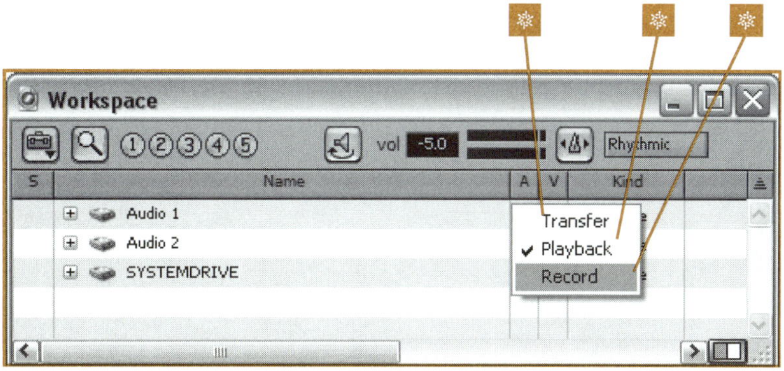

- If you set your drive up to be a transfer volume, you will not be able to record or play back audio from that drive. Essentially, the drive is off limits as far as Pro Tools audio is concerned. Very commonly, your system drive is set up as a transfer volume (assuming that you also have a dedicated hard drive for audio recording and/or playback).
- A playback volume will allow Pro Tools to play back audio, but you may not record new audio to this type of volume. This is a common setting for archival drives, allowing you to listen to your backed-up sessions, but not to inadvertently record to that hard drive.
- Finally, a record volume is fully functional for audio and Pro Tools, which means that you can record to it and play back from it. A typical audio drive is set up as a record volume.

The volume designations in the V column work just the same way, only for video files instead of audio files. You can (and should) set up each of your hard drive's operations with specific regard to audio and video files. Here's a common setup for a Pro Tools system with two dedicated audio hard drives:

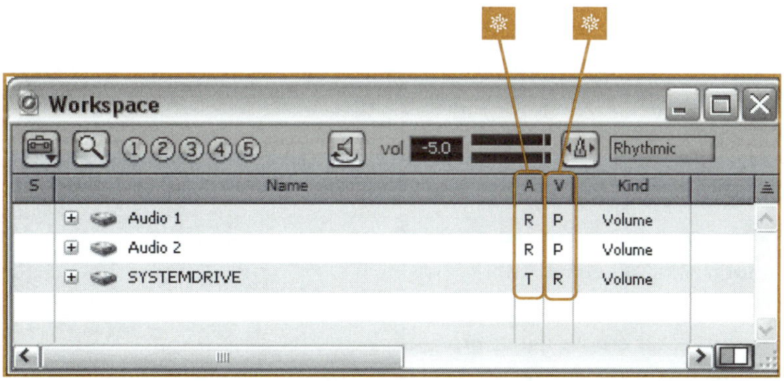

- As far as audio recording and playback are concerned, both the Audio 1 and Audio 2 drives can record and play back audio files. The system drive (cleverly named SYSTEMDRIVE) is set up as a transfer drive for audio, to keep it from getting filled up with audio files and to keep it running efficiently.
- With regard to video files, I've set up my audio files to be playback volumes, meaning that I can play back video files from those drives, but I can't record any video to these drives. On the rare occasion that I have to record video, I can record the files to my system drive.

When the behavior of the drives has been squared away, it's time to do some disk allocation. In this session, I've created 10 pretty generic tracks, and I'm almost ready to do some recording. This is just the time to set up disk allocation—*before* you record any new audio:

1. **Click** the **Setup menu**.
2. **Click** the **Disk Allocation menu item**. The Disk Allocation window will appear.

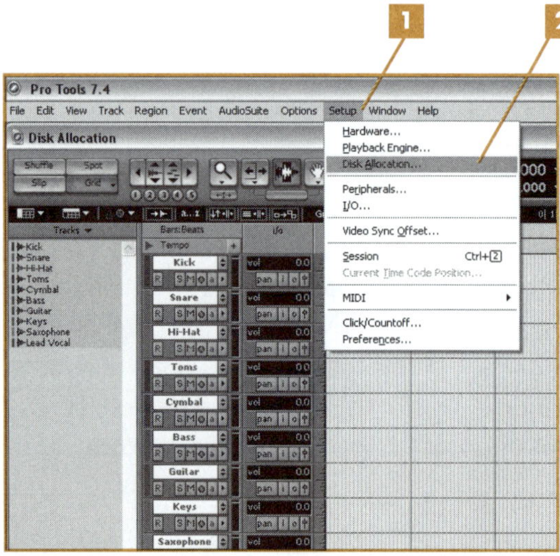

3. In the Disk Allocation window, you'll see a listing of all the Audio tracks in your session. From this window, you'll be able to assign your drives certain tracks on an individual basis. Just **click and hold** on the **Root Media Folder column** for the track you want to set up. A menu will be displayed.
4. From this menu, you'll be able to choose which drive will store the audio recorded on that track. You can either **choose** one of the **drives** and let Pro Tools create the appropriate folder for you, or **click** the **Select Folder option** to choose a preexisting folder or create a new folder of your own choosing.

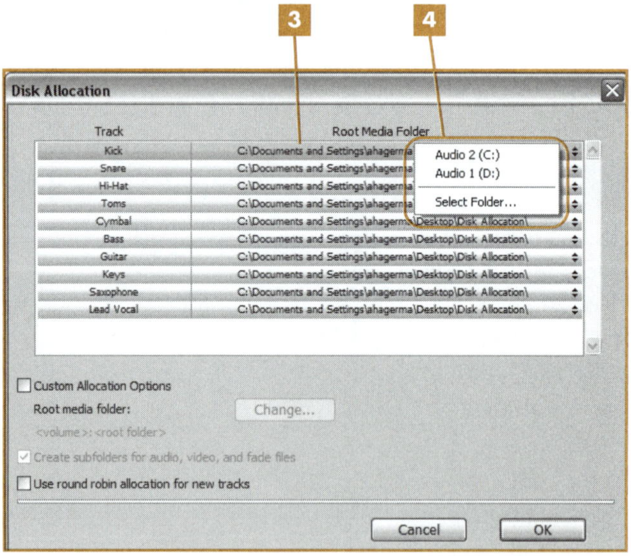

The general rule when setting up disk allocation is to balance the workload as evenly as possible between the audio drives that you have in your system, to ensure maximum performance. Here's what I've ended up with:

- In this particular case, I've alternated each track between the drives, so that of the ten tracks that I have in my session, only five of them are on any given audio drive.
- Here's a useful option: If you check the Use Round Robin Allocation for New Tracks option, Pro Tools will automatically cycle through all the record-enabled drives for your tracks as they are created.

5. Once you've set things up, click the OK button.

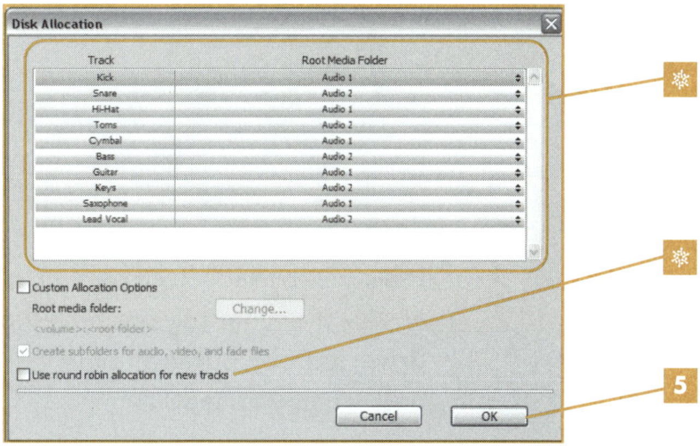

Drive Volumes and Round-Robin Allocation

Note that only the drives that you've designated as record volumes show up in the Assignment drop-down menu, and they will be the only drives that will be used when using round-robin allocation. By setting up your volume designations, you can make working in the Disk Allocation window easier and quicker.

Now you're ready to record as usual. When you're finished, you'll see regions created in your Regions list. But where have they been recorded to?

1. Click the Regions List button. A menu will appear.
2. Click the Show menu item. Yet another menu!
3. This menu will allow you to see different aspects of your regions in the Regions list. (You may find showing the full path very useful in tracking down individual files!) In this case, we want to see what disk they've been recorded to, so click the Disk Name menu item.

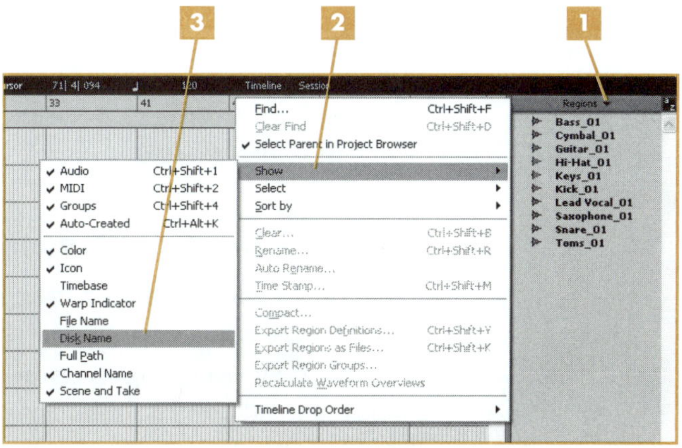

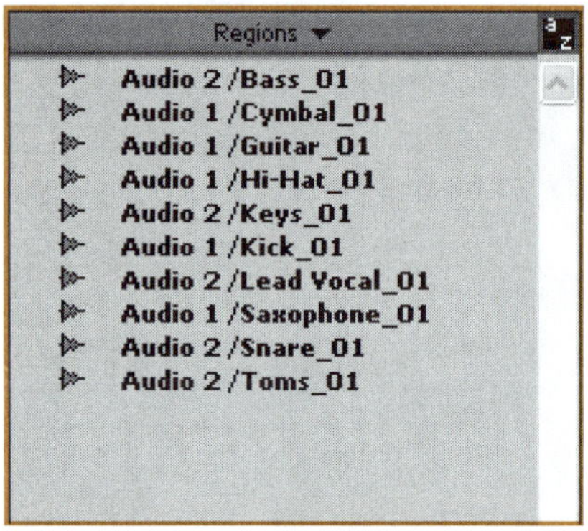

Here you can see confirmation of your carefully set up system. Notice that your regions have been recorded to the appropriate drive, thereby balancing the workload and giving you extra robustness when you need it.

> **When to Set Up Disk Allocation**
>
> Remember to set up your disk allocation *before* you start recording. Changing your disk allocation *after* your audio has been recorded (and your files have been created) will have no effect.

Making the Most of Editing

The follow sections detail processes that will make your editing even more efficient and fun!

> **Setting Things Up**
>
> To follow along with these first steps, go to Memory Location #1—Identify Beat. From the Window menu, open the Memory Location window, and simply click Location #1. (For more on how to use memory locations, please refer to Chapter 6.)

The Identify Beat Function

One of Pro Tools' greatest strengths is its ability to use MIDI and audio in the same environment. Before they'll work together, though, their tempos must agree. You can use the Identify Beat function to tell Pro Tools the tempo of your audio! This memory location (#1—Identify Beat) shows a great example of a very common dilemma. Listen to the region—sounds like eight full measures of drums, correct? Now look at the selection length *according to the Pro Tools Tempo ruler*—it says that the region is 6 measures, 1 beat, and 741 ticks! Obviously, your judgment is correct, and here's how to clue in Pro Tools!

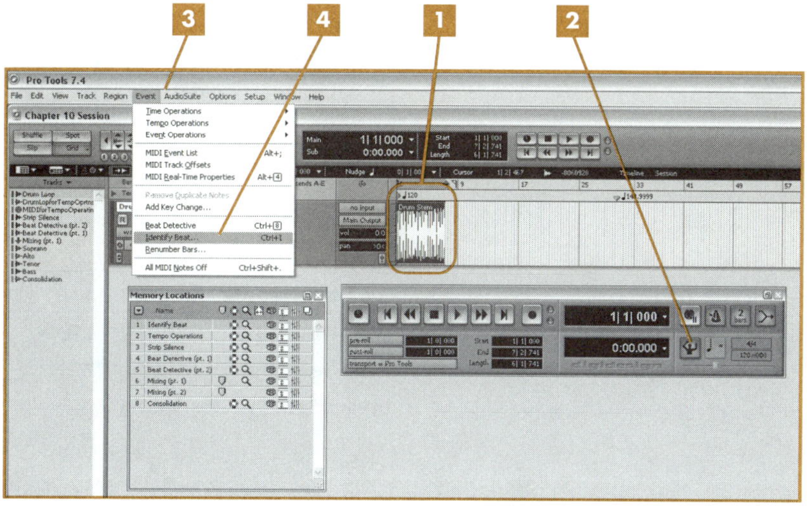

1 Make a selection of a specific musical length. (In this case, it's eight measures that loop perfectly.) Use your ears to make this loopable selection—*not* your MIDI tempo or session grid.

2 Select the Conductor icon if it isn't already lit. The icon will be selected.

3 Click on Event. The Event menu will appear.

4 Click on Identify Beat. The Add Bar | Beat Markers dialog box will open.

5 Type the location that your ears tell you is the beginning of the selection in the Location text box in the Start area.

6 Type the location that your ears tell you is the end of the selection in the Location text box in the End area. In this case, because you hear an eight-bar selection, it ends at the beginning of Bar 9 (9|1|000).

7 Click on OK. The Add Bar | Beat Markers dialog box will close, and your tempo will change to match your audio.

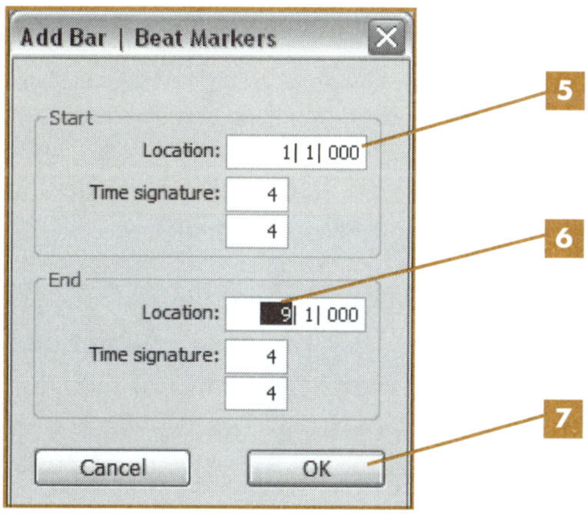

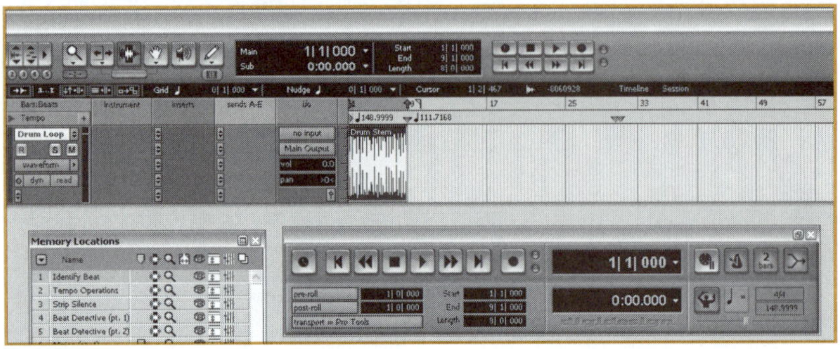

When you're finished, you'll see that your session and your ears are now in agreement about the tempo of the section of audio, as shown here. Now the grid lines will be aligned with the appropriate musical events (assuming that your grid scale is set to Bars:Beats), and the selection that you made will be correctly displayed in the Edit Selection display in the Edit window (assuming that your Main time scale is Bars:Beats).

Identify Beat Works Anywhere!

You can use the Identify Beat function at any point in a session. For example, if you have a live drummer who gets a little faster during the chorus, just select the chorus and enter your loopable selection in the Add Bar | Beat Markers dialog box.

Tips for the TCE Trim Tool

From time to time, you might hear some unpleasant side effects of using the TCE Trim tool—things such as noticeably degraded audio quality or audio artifacts.

The secret behind the TCE Trim tool is that it operates on the same software code as the AudioSuite Time Compress/Expand or Time Shift plug-in. Because of this, there are ways that you can customize its effectiveness and make the most of the TCE Trim tool. This is particularly easy to do because of the Time Shift plug-in's very useful presets—take a look:

1. To tweak the TCE Trim tool, you'll need to go to the Preferences window. From the Setup menu, choose the Preferences menu item. The Preferences window will appear.
2. Click on the Processing tab. The tab will move to the front.
3. The TC/E Plug-In area will display the AudioSuite plug-in currently used by the TCE Trim tool. These days, the default plug-in is Digidesign's Time Shift plug-in (though older versions will default to Digidesign TC/E). Click the TC/E Plug-In menu button (which in this case reads "Time Shift") to reveal a list of your other plug-in options.

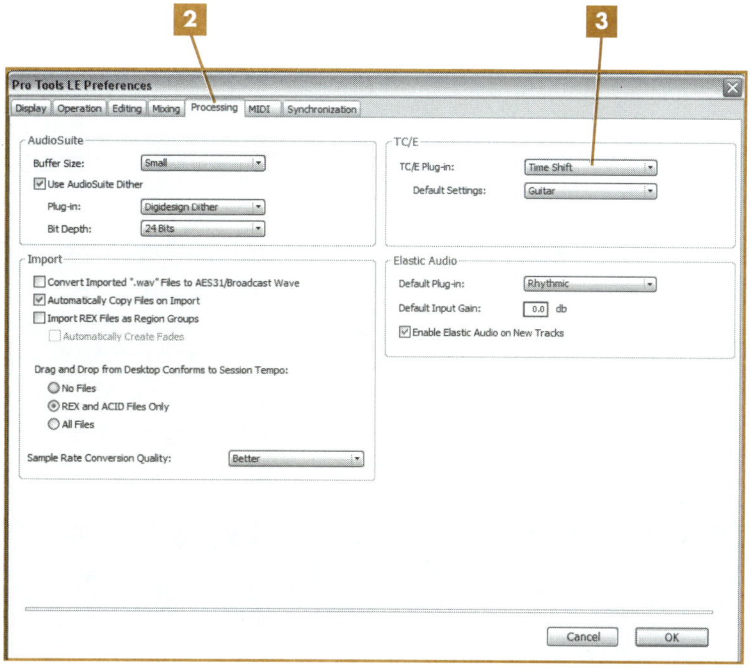

The list shown contains a number of options for your TCE trim tool, including third-party time compression/expansion plug-ins that are not included in a basic Pro Tools installation. Any plug-ins that you have installed on your system will appear in regular text and may be selected. Plug-ins that you have not installed on your system will be grayed out.

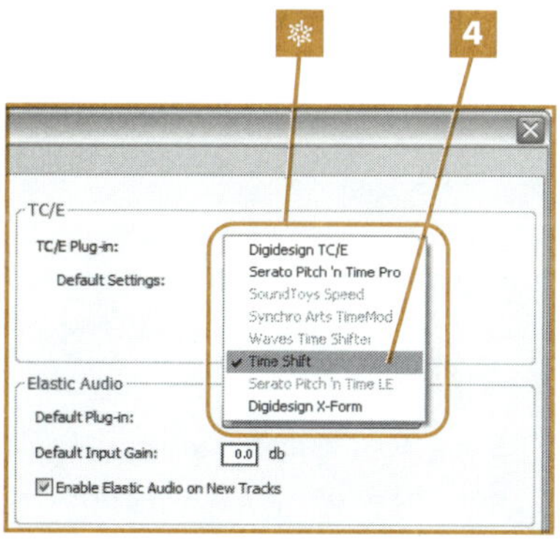

4. Click your preferred time compression/expansion plug-in. In this case, because it's included in a basic Pro Tools installation these days, I'll choose the Time Shift plug-in.

5 Click on the Default Settings down arrow. The Default Settings menu will appear.

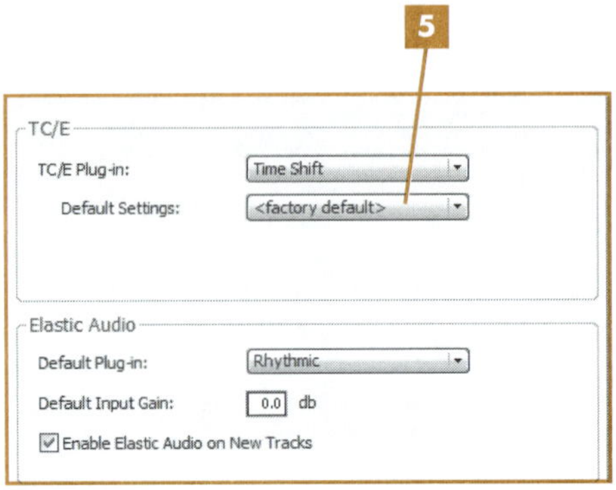

❊ You'll see all the available presets for the selected plug-in. Because it already has so many useful presets, Time Shift is a natural for this kind of job.

6 Click the desired preset. As the names might suggest, different presets are best suited for different jobs. For example, suppose you're working with drums. The Drums Rhythmic preset is probably a good choice, and it will help your drums sound as good as possible when using the TCE Trim tool.

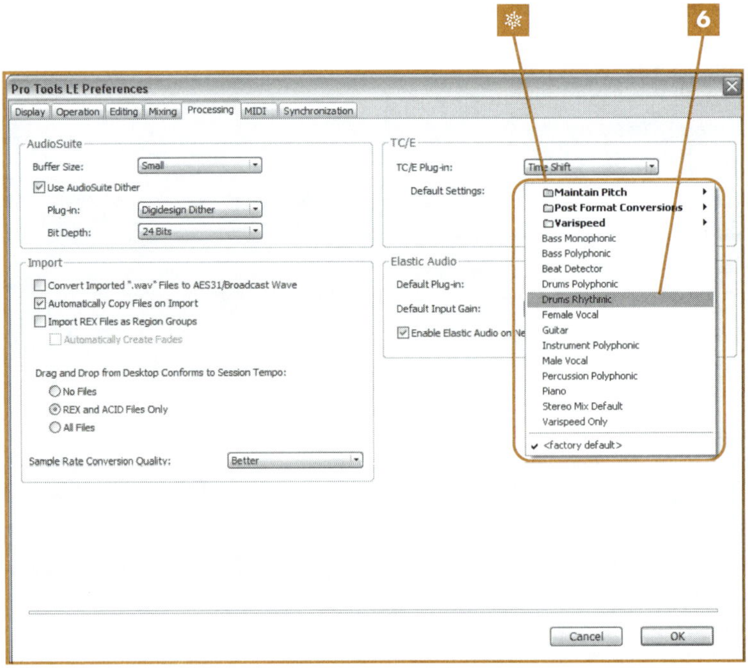

❊ TC/E Presets

Some AudioSuite plug-ins (such as the Digidesign TC/E plug-in, for example) don't have any preexisting presets, so before you can make the Preferences window work for you with those plug-ins, you'll need to create some presets. (You learned how to do this in Chapter 9.) Make sure you save your settings in the root settings folder. If you're not sure where you're saving your settings, click on the Settings menu (the arrow button to the left of the setting's name in the plug-in window) and click on the Settings Preferences option. From there, go to the Save Plug-In Settings To option and make sure Root Settings Folder is checked.

Edit versus Timeline Selection

Throughout this book, whenever you have made a selection on a track, that selection has been reflected in the Rulers area (or the Timeline) and vice versa. Normally this is the way to work, but these two selections don't *need* to be linked.

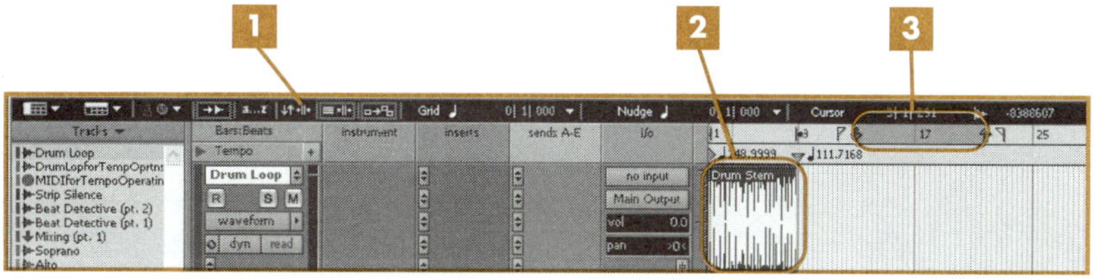

1. Click on the Link Timeline and Edit Selection button to deselect it. The button will be deselected.
2. Make a selection on any track.
3. Make a different selection in the Rulers area. Note that the two areas do not reflect each other.

It's important to take a moment to see just how Pro Tools acts in this situation. If you try to play back your selection, note how what plays back is your *Timeline* selection. In truth, this always has been the case, though most users don't make any distinctions between the edit selection and the Timeline selection, and they leave the linking enabled all the time.

Unlinking your edit and Timeline selections can be nifty when you want to hear a different part of your song than the part you're editing. For example, you want to hear a little *before* the region that you're working with, so unlink your edit and Timeline and make a Timeline selection that reflects what you want. Just be careful to *relink* when you're finished with this unusual mode of operation. You can either click on the Link Timeline and Edit Selection button again to reactivate it, or go into the Options menu.

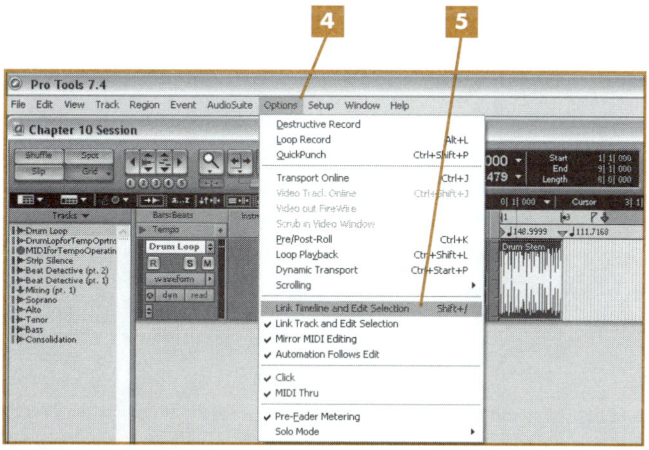

4. Click on Options. The Options menu will appear.
5. Click on the Link Timeline and Edit Selection option to re-enable it. The button will be enabled.

New Feature: Dynamic Transport

Beginning with Pro Tools LE 7.3, you now have yet another way to treat your selection and playback independently, through a feature called Dynamic Transport. Instead of unlinking your edit and Timeline selection (which can be a bit time consuming), Dynamic Transport gives you the power to start playback at any point in your session. Take a look:

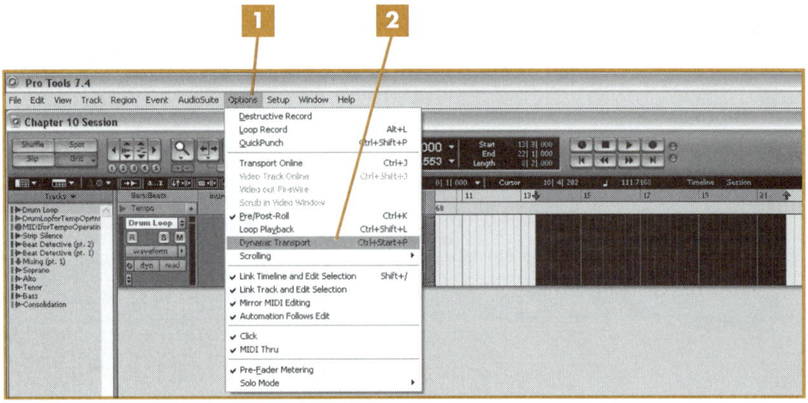

1. Before you can start using Dynamic Transport, you'll have to turn it on. Click the Options menu.
2. Choose the Dynamic Transport menu item.

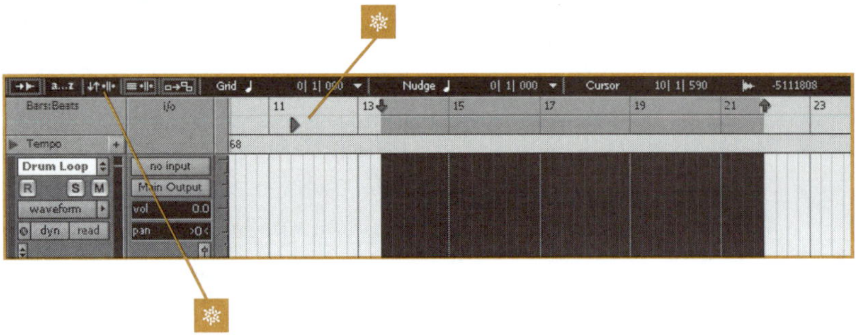

- You'll notice that your Timeline ruler has gotten twice as tall as any other ruler.
- In the bottom part of the Timeline ruler you'll see a right-facing blue triangle, which now indicates where your playback will begin. You can just click and drag the triangle to any place you like, and your session will play back from that point. This point can be before a selected area (as shown here), anywhere within a selection, or even after a selected area.
- You'll also notice that the Link Timeline and Edit Selection button is automatically deactivated when you turn on Dynamic Transport. (You can click Relink at any time.) When you turn off Dynamic Transport, Link Timeline and Edit Selection will be re-enabled.

Samples versus Ticks

You learned back in Chapter 6 about the advantages of tick-based Audio tracks, but there's a little more to the story! Let's take a look at Audio and MIDI track timing properties.

Setting Things Up

For this section, go to Memory Location #2—Tempo Operations.

Track Timings

Audio tracks, by default, are created as *sample-based* tracks, which means that each region is anchored to a specific sample location. This means that tempo changes and other MIDI functions will have no effect upon the regions of the track.

Instrument tracks and MIDI tracks, on the other hand, are created by default as *tick-based* tracks, which means that regions on this track *will* respond to tempo and meter changes. Speed up the MIDI tempo, and the MIDI notes will speed up accordingly.

Even though these are the *default* states for each kind of track, there are advantages to working unconventionally!

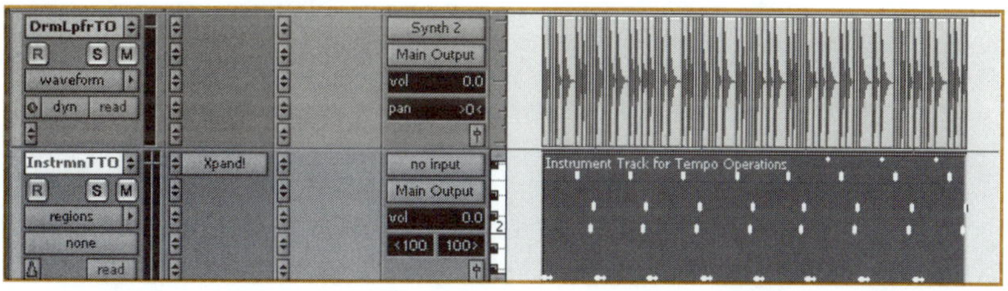

- As you saw in Chapter 6, changing an Audio track to tick-based timing (as shown by the Metronome icon) will allow you to put your region timing under the control of your MIDI tempo map. In this example, if you were to change the tempo of your session, your regions would move and change your drum audio's "tempo" as a result.
- Less common, but no less possible, is the practice of changing a MIDI track to sample-based timing, as shown here. To do it, just click the track's Time Base selector and choose Samples. In this mode, your MIDI track takes on a very interesting behavior, as your MIDI data will *not* change when you change tempo and meter in your session. You might ask, "Why would I want to do this, because MIDI is a musical tool?" Well, for starters, you might be using a MIDI note to trigger a sound effect that needs to be synched to video and is not being used in a musical way—this is a great way to keep that specific MIDI data in place!

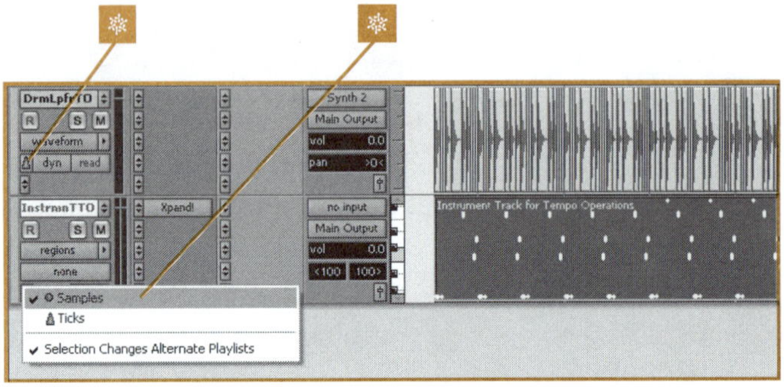

New Preference: Default Track Timebase

For some users, particularly those doing primarily music production, you might want *all* of your tracks to be tick-based. Beginning with Pro Tools LE 7.3, you have that option!

1. After opening the Preferences window (from the Setup drop-down menu), go to the Editing tab.
2. In the lower-left area of the Editing page, you'll see the New Tracks Default to Tick Timebase option. Just click the check box to make all your new tracks default to a tick timebase. A check mark will be displayed.
3. Click OK to exit the Preferences window.

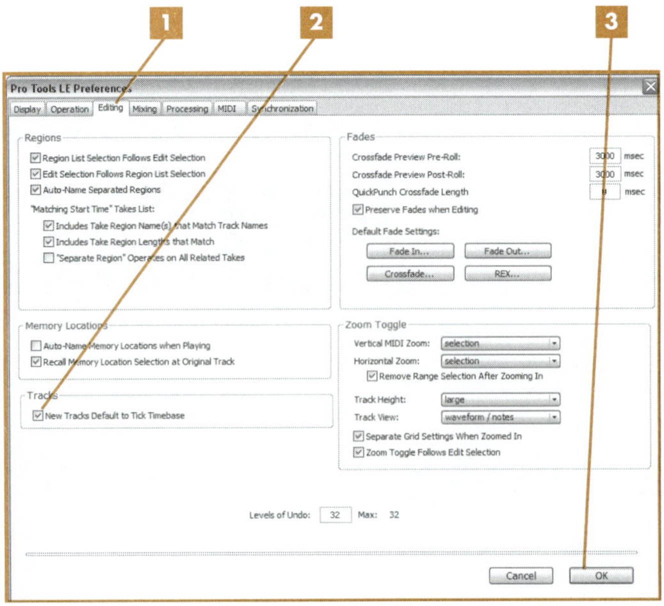

Session Linearity

This next bit can get a little tricky, so stick with me here. By default, the rulers of your sessions are evenly spaced (or *linear*) based upon real time, which can be broken down into hours, minutes, seconds, frames (for timecode use), and samples. This means that when you change tempo, a MIDI operation, your real-time display will remain evenly spaced, and your MIDI tempo spacing will expand or compress according to your tempo changes. Take a look:

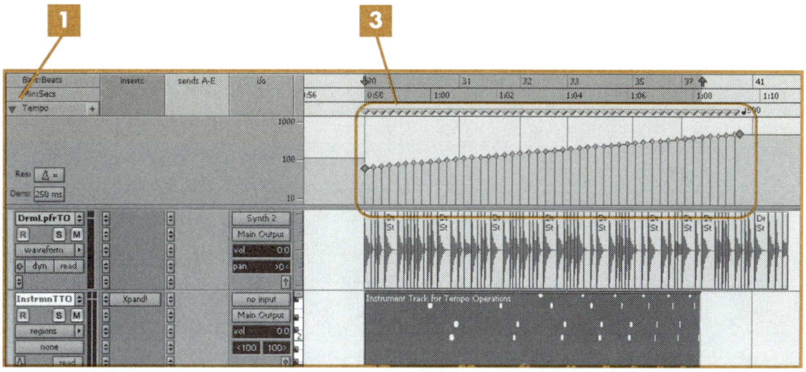

1. Click the Tempo Editor down arrow. Your Tempo ruler will expand to show you a graphic display of your tempo changes.
2. For the purpose of our example here, choose the Pencil tool with the Line option selected.
3. Draw a tempo change, starting from a lower tempo, then ramping up to a faster tempo. You'll notice a few things:

- Your sample-based tracks (in this case, an Audio track) will not react to the tempo change.
- Your tick-based tracks (in this case, MIDI) will change based upon your tempo change.
- Your real-time rulers will remain evenly spaced.
- Your Tempo ruler will change its spacing based upon your tempo changes.

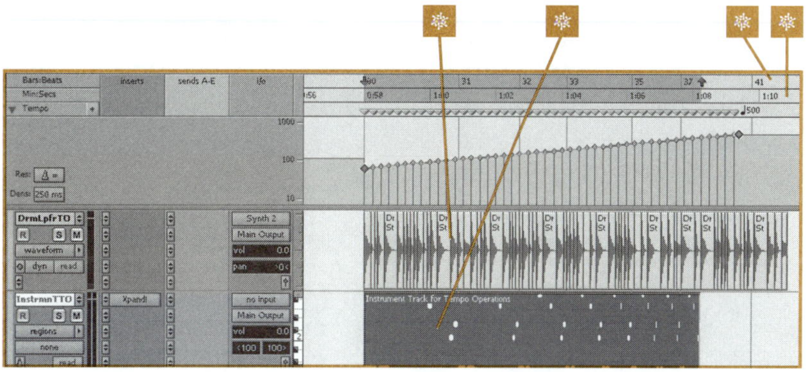

You'll also note that as a side effect of this tempo changed, the spacing of the notes has changed radically, and their appearance has really been altered. Often, this is a bit of an annoyance when working with MIDI data, and it's desirable to be able to see your note values displayed more consistently, regardless of tempo changes. It's very easy to do, and it makes quite a difference in your Edit window's view.

4 Click the Linearity Display Mode down arrow. A menu will appear.

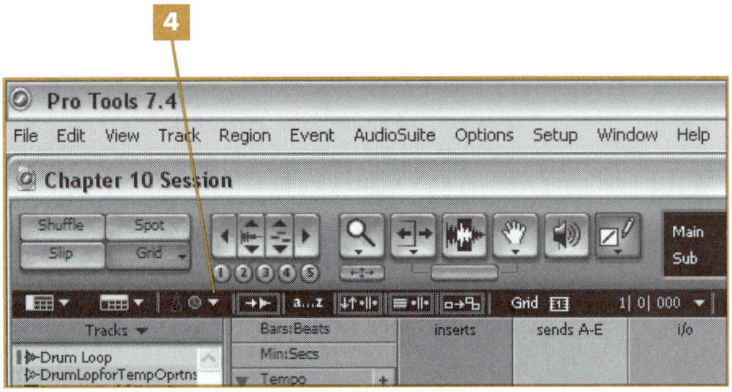

5 Click on Linear Tick Display. The Linearity icon will change from a blue clock to a green metronome. Notice how your screen changes (though the *sound* of your session does not—this is *only* a display change).

- Note that the spacing of both your Audio and MIDI tracks has changed. The timebase of each track hasn't changed, but the overall linear display of the session has been changed from real time to tempo linearity. Note that the sample-based Audio track is now not as evenly spaced as it once was, whereas the MIDI track (despite the tempo change) is perfectly spaced.

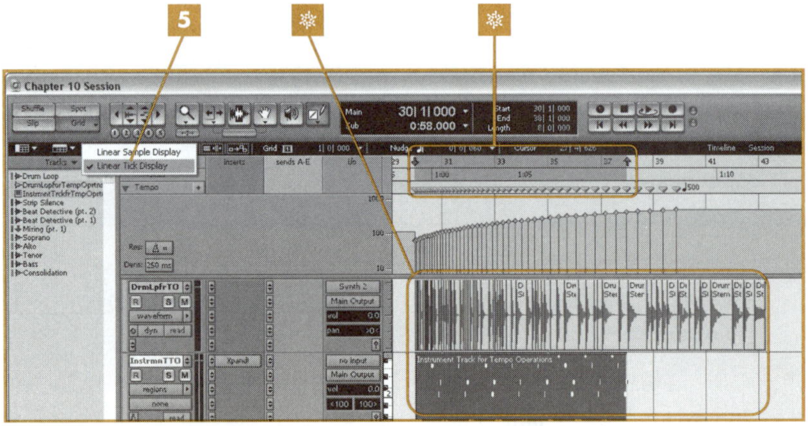

- Your rulers have also changed. Your Bars and Beats ruler (top) is now evenly spaced (again, despite the tempo change), and the Minutes:Seconds is now unevenly spaced. As you listen and watch the playback of your session, you'll see that the *only* change made to your session has been visual. This change in linearity is simply for your ease of use.

Cool Editing Tools

We've already covered a bunch of editing processes—here are a couple more for your bag of tricks!

New Ways to Spot Regions

Back in Chapter 5, we talked a little about the Spot edit mode, and how it can make placing regions at specific points in time a very easy proposition. Spot *mode*, however, is only really useful if you already know the specific numeric position to which you want your region to go. Many times, you'll want your region to go to a specific *selected* place in your session, and Pro Tools now makes this easy—especially if you have a mouse with a right-click button!

Setting Things Up

For this section, go to Memory Location #3—Spotting Regions.

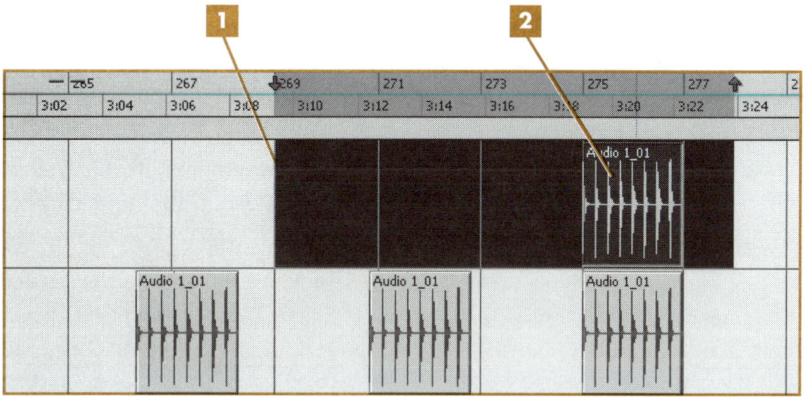

1. Using the Selector tool, make a selection or place your Timeline insertion cursor at the place where you want your region to move to.
2. Ctrl-right-click (PC) or Command-right-click (Mac) the region that you want to move. A box will appear around the region, and a menu will appear.

- Move Region Start to Selection Start will move the beginning of the region to the beginning of your selection or to the Timeline insertion cursor.
- Move Region Sync to Selection Start will move the region's sync point (if it has one) to the beginning of your selection or to the Timeline insertion cursor. (We'll quickly go through sync points later in this section of the chapter.)
- Move Region End to Selection Start will move the region's end point to the beginning of your selector or Timeline insertion cursor.

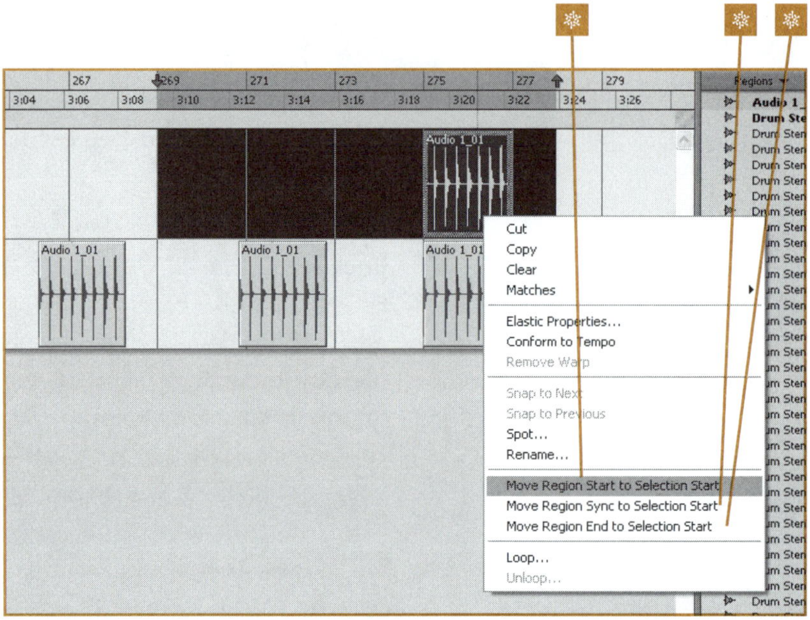

If you don't have a mouse with a right-click button, all is not lost. Here are some shortcuts for you to get the job done:

- To Move Region Start to Selection Start, hold the Start key (PC) or Control key (Mac) and click the region with the Grabber tool (*not* the Smart tool).
- To Move Region Sync to Selection Start, hold Shift+Start (PC) or Shift+Control (Mac) and click the region with the Grabber tool.
- To Move Region End to Selection Start, hold Ctrl+Start (PC) or Command+Control (Mac) and click the region with the Grabber tool.

Snapping Regions

Sometimes you'll want a region to move to the region either before it or after it. Again, the right-click comes to the rescue!

1 Select the region that you want to move.

2 Right-click the region. A menu will appear:

- Clicking Snap to Next will move the end of the selected region to the beginning of the region to the right.
- Clicking the Snap to Previous will move the beginning of the region to the end of the region to the left.

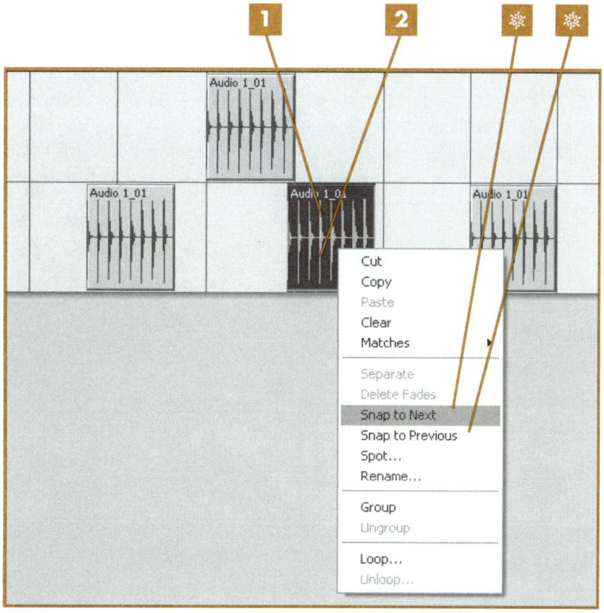

Spot

The menu item right below the Snap to Previous menu item, named Spot, will open the Spot Dialog window (the same window you would normally encounter in Spot mode).

Sync Points

So far, we've primarily focused on region boundaries (front and back) when talking about moving regions. However, it's important to remember that the really interesting part of a region might be somewhere *inside* the region. For example, within a drum beat, you might have a specific hit that you want to align with another region, or you might have a specific word in a dialog region that is particularly easy to spot. Sync points will help you mark these points of interest and move the region in different ways.

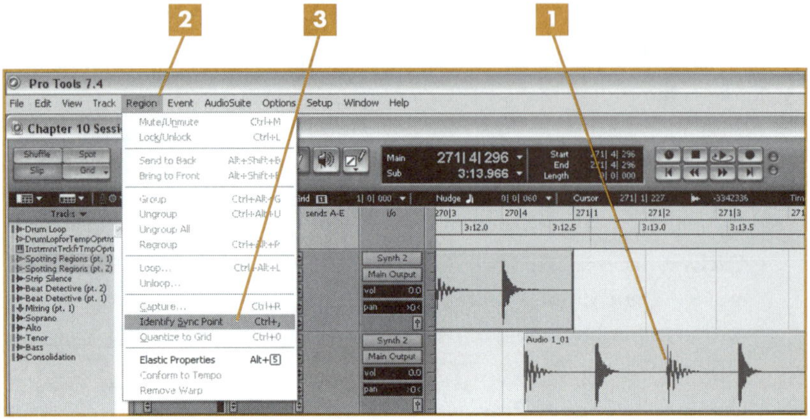

1. Using the Selector tool (or the Smart tool), place your Timeline insertion cursor at the point of interest within your region.
2. Click the Region menu.
3. Click the Identify Sync Point menu item. A small green triangle will appear at the bottom of the region at the point of interest.

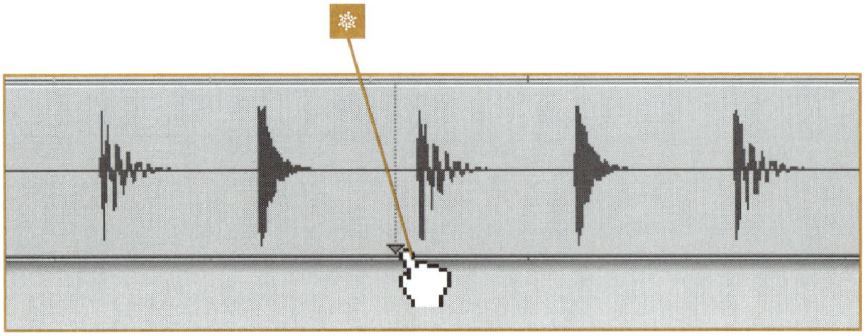

If you need to move your sync point once you've created it, the Grabber tool will let you move it. Just move your mouse close to the triangular sync point icon. When the Grabber tool turns into the "pointing hand," as shown here, you're ready to move the sync point—just drag and drop the sync point to its new location.

Now that you've created your sync point, you can utilize the right-click and shortcut commands described earlier in this section!

New Fade Functionality

Before we leave the region-moving section of this chapter, a last word on some region moving and nudging: With the advent of Pro Tools LE 7.3, you now have the ability to select fade regions (including crossfades) and move them with the Grabber tool or nudge them just as you would any normal region (using the +/– keys). As long as the fade region is the only region selected, the "parent" region will not be moved.

Using Strip Silence

Strip Silence is a nifty little editing tool that acts upon regions similar to how a noise gate acts upon audio. Simply stated, when you use the Strip Silence feature, any audio below a specified volume threshold will be removed from your selection, leaving discrete regions that you can move and edit separately.

Setting Things Up

Please go to Memory Location #4—Strip Silence.

1. **Click** on **Edit**. The Edit menu will appear.
2. **Click** on **Strip Silence**. The Strip Silence dialog box will open.

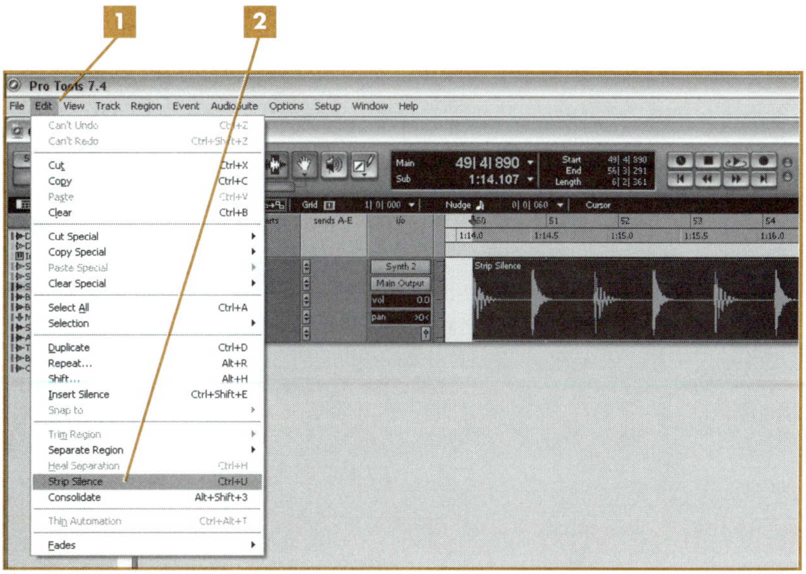

3. **Select** the **area** in your session that you would like to strip. The area will be selected.

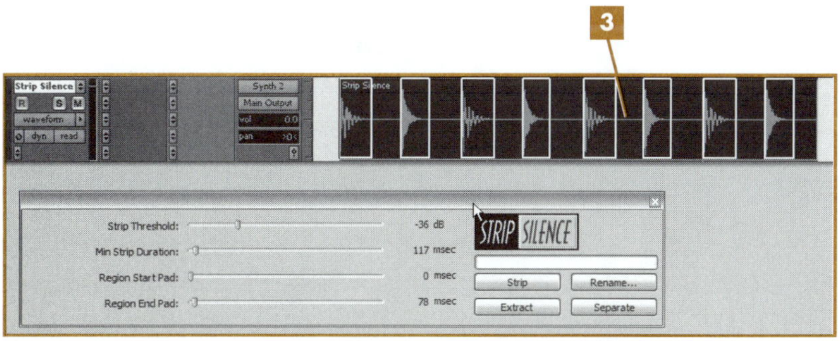

4 **Adjust** the **parameters** in the Strip Silence dialog box until you achieve the desired separation. (Before the regions are processed, you will see where new region boundaries will be created.) The available parameters include the following:

* **Strip Threshold.** Any volume level under the strip threshold will be removed from your selection.
* **Min Strip Duration.** This value determines the shortest region able to be created by Strip Silence.

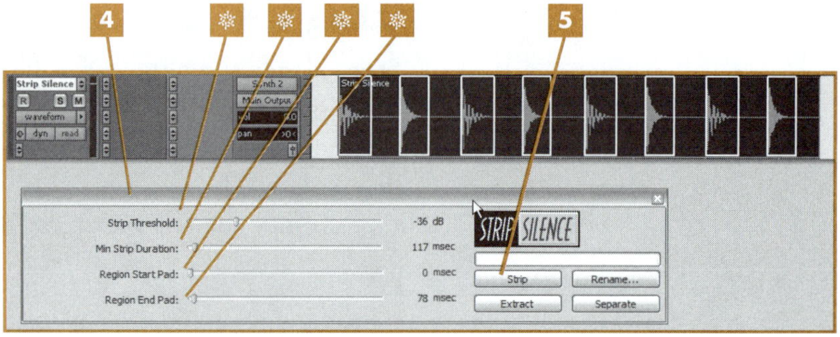

* **Region Start Pad.** This slider will move the front region boundaries earlier in time.
* **Region End Pad.** This slider will move the back region boundaries later in time.

5 **Click** on **Strip**. Your selection will be chopped into discrete regions, and the audio below your threshold value will be removed from the track altogether. These new regions will be shown in the Regions list.

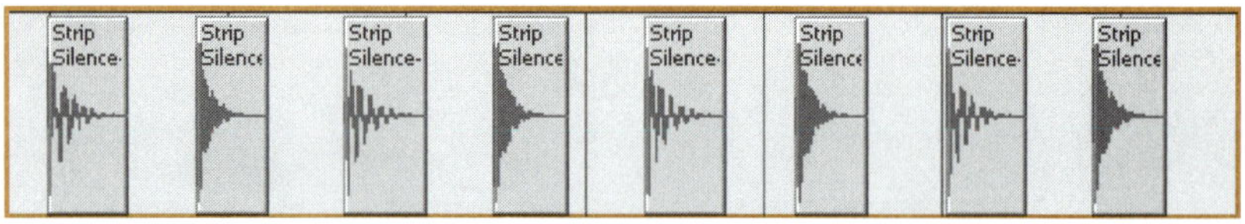

Don't worry; you haven't deleted any audio. In fact, you can use the Trim tool and drag any region boundary out to recover the audio that has been stripped. There are a few other options regarding the Strip Silence dialog box that are available to you:

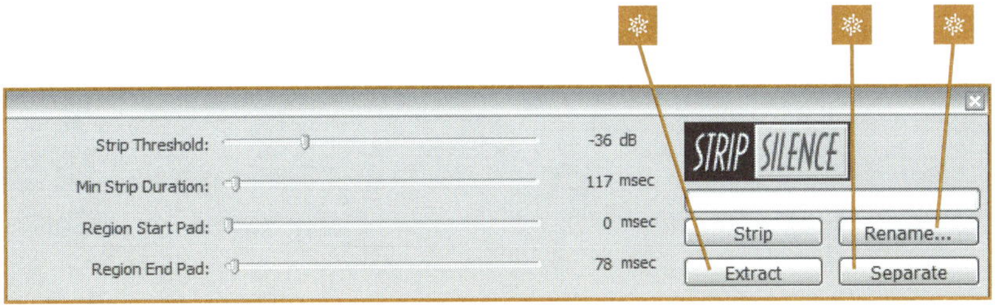

- **Extract.** This does the opposite of the Strip function and will leave only regions of silence.
- **Separate.** This mode will not actually strip any audio, but will leave regions of sound and silence, based on your settings.
- **Rename.** This option will allow you to custom name the regions that will be created when you strip. When you choose this option, the Rename Selected Regions dialog box will open:
  - The Name field will allow you to type a descriptive name for your selected regions.
  - You can choose a starting number for your regions as well. For example, in some situations, you might want to have the first region be numbered 0, and in other cases (such as the one shown here) you'll want to start your numbering with the number 1.

  - The Number of Places field will allow you to set the number of digits that will be used in your numbering. In this case, I've chosen three places, so my files will be numbered 001, 002, 003, and so on.
  - Finally, you may want to add a suffix to your file names. Commonly, these are used to record takes, dates, and other useful information.
  - When you've set up your names, click the OK button. In this case, your regions will be renamed Strip Silence001drum, Strip Silence002drum, and so on.

Beat Detective

One of the most interesting music production tools in Pro Tools' array is Beat Detective. Based on the same technology that makes the Tab to Transient feature work so well, this process has different kinds of applications. Generally speaking, it is used in conjunction with drum tracks, but it can be applied to any audio with clearly defined transients (or MIDI).

The first of these applications is based on the idea that a musical groove (from swing to rock to polka and everything in between!) is by definition *not* mathematically uniform. This "human" element is in opposition to the mathematical precision of a static MIDI tempo. What this means is that in order to get your audio and MIDI to groove together, you'll have to create a more complex MIDI tempo map, which is exactly what Beat Detective does!

Setting Things Up

For the first part of our Beat Detective discussion, go to Memory Location #5—Beat Detective (pt.1).

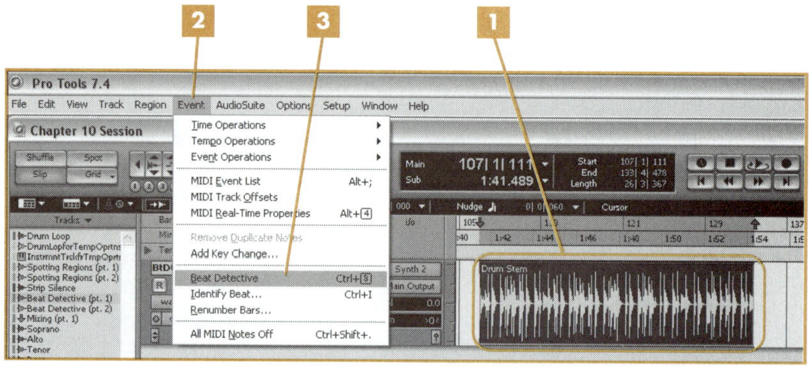

1. Select the segment of drums that you want to analyze.
2. Click on Event. The menu will appear.
3. Click on Beat Detective. The Beat Detective window will appear.

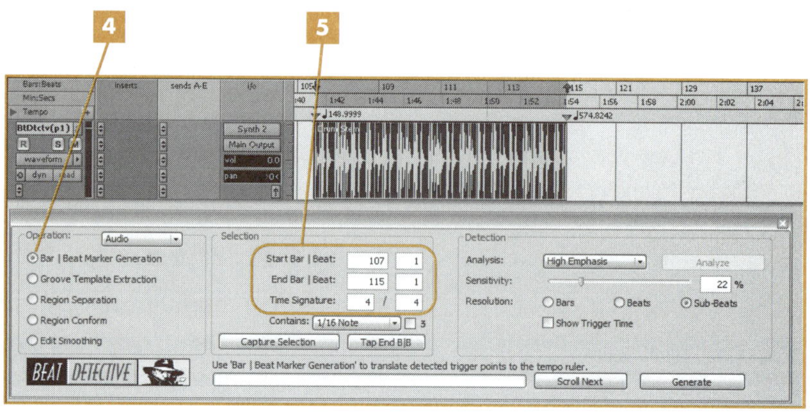

4. The mode for this sort of operation is Bar|Beat Marker Generation. Click its radio button to enter this mode.
5. This step is *very* important: Make sure that your values in Beat Detective's Selection area correctly reflect the same selections in your session.

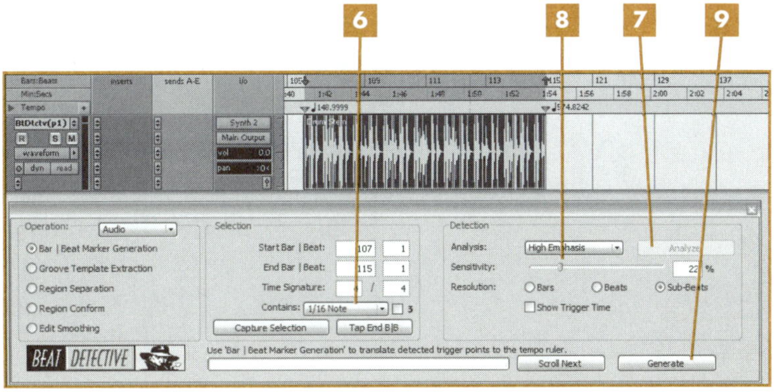

6 Choose the smallest musical note value of your audio (in this case, sixteenth notes) from the Contains button.

7 Click Analyze. Your audio will be examined by Beat Detective, which will look to detect transients.

8 Slowly raise the Sensitivity slider from zero. You will notice that as your sensitivity increases, you will see vertical lines intersecting the transients of your audio. Once you are satisfied that the important transients have been marked (and no others), stop moving the slider.

9 Click Generate. The Realign Session dialog box will open.

Using Capture Selection

Assuming that your selection is known to be in general agreement with the MIDI tempo, you can click the Capture Selection button in the Selection area of Beat Detective. This is an easy way to go with audio in which the beat has already been identified.

Thankfully, this dialog box is fairly self-explanatory. Basically, in the next step a very complex tempo map will be created, which, as you have learned, will have no effect on sample-based tracks, but which can have a *big* effect on tick-based tracks.

- If you have tick-based data (such as a drum part on a MIDI track), and you want the timing of that data to move to match the timing of this Audio track (which is usually the case with this workflow), choose Preserve Tick Position (Move).
- If you have tick-based data that doesn't need to be conformed to the groove of this audio, choose Preserve Sample Position (Don't Move).

10 In this example, where we have no other tracks, either option is fine. Click OK.

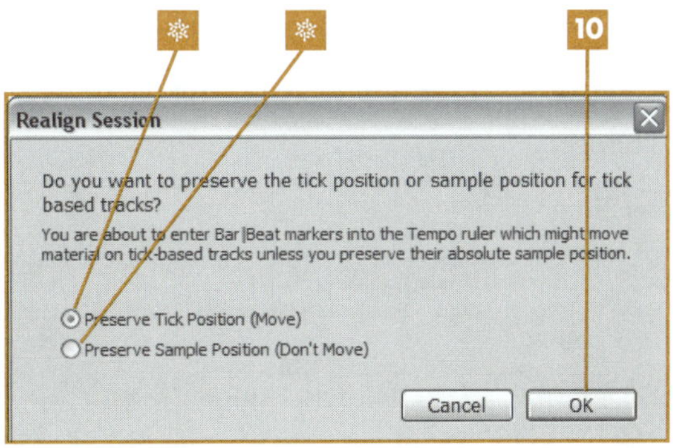

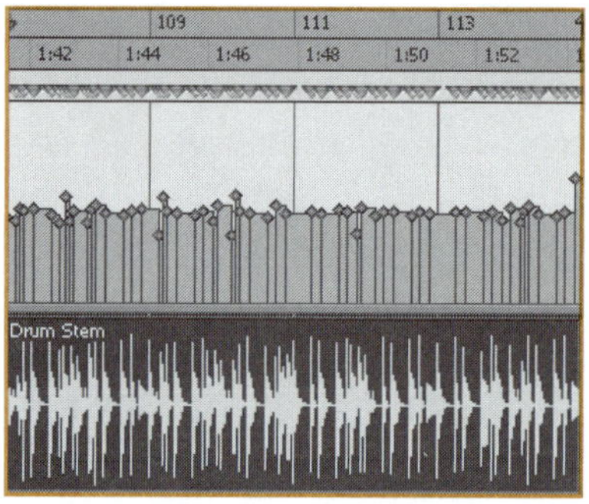

You will see now that a great number of small tempo changes have been added to your Tempo ruler (each shown as a blue triangle in the collapsed Tempo ruler, or as tempo events in the expanded Tempo ruler). What you've done is create a tempo map that changes constantly to match the groove of the drum audio, which has effectively created a MIDI *grid* that also reflects these changes. Because things like Grid mode and MIDI Quantize rely on this grid for their timing, you can now conform any additional MIDI and audio to this original drum beat, and they will all groove together!

Here's a variation on that same sort of logic.

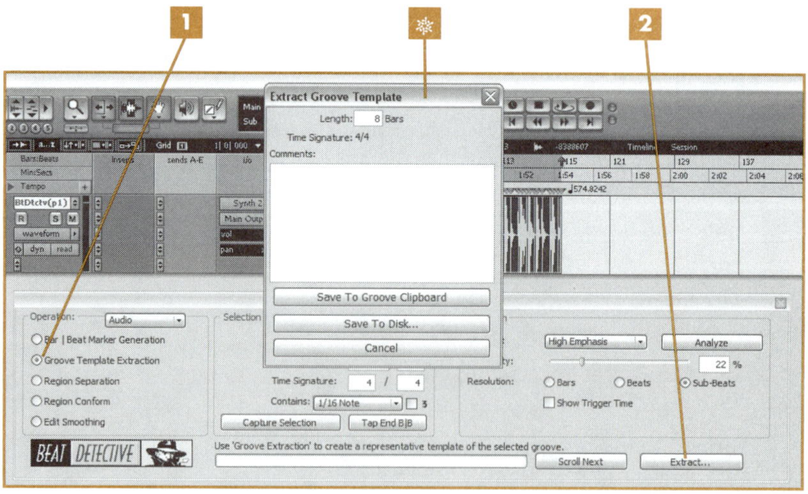

1. Click the Groove Template Extraction radio button.
2. After going through the same selection and analysis process that you used earlier in Steps 5 through 8, click the Extract button. The Extract Groove Template window will appear.

* In this window, you can either save to a clipboard for immediate use or to disk for more long-term use. What are you saving? Well, what you have extracted is the same sort of timing information that you used in Bar|Beat Marker Generation, except that by extracting this information you've added it to your list of usable MIDI Groove Quantize options. More simply put, you will now have the option to quantize future MIDI data to have the same feel as these drums here!

But that's not all Beat Detective can do—not by a long shot. Let's reverse the equation: Let's say that instead of creating a new tempo map so that the rest of your session can conform to my drum audio, you want to conform your audio to the current tempo of the session. Beat Detective can do that, too. In this example, we'll take our familiar Drum region and conform it to the mathematically static tempo of the session.

Setting Things Up

Please go to Memory Location #6—Beat Detective (pt. 2).

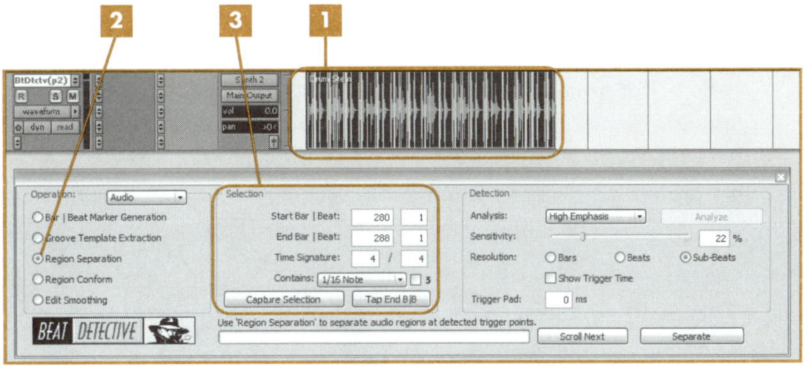

1. **Select** the **segment of drums** that you want to analyze.
2. The mode for this sort of operation is Region Separation. **Click** its **radio button** to enter this mode.
3. Again, **make sure** that your **values** in Beat Detective's Selection area correctly reflect the actual selections in your session. Be careful—Beat Detective does not automatically update its selection values, and this memory location is at a different section of your session!

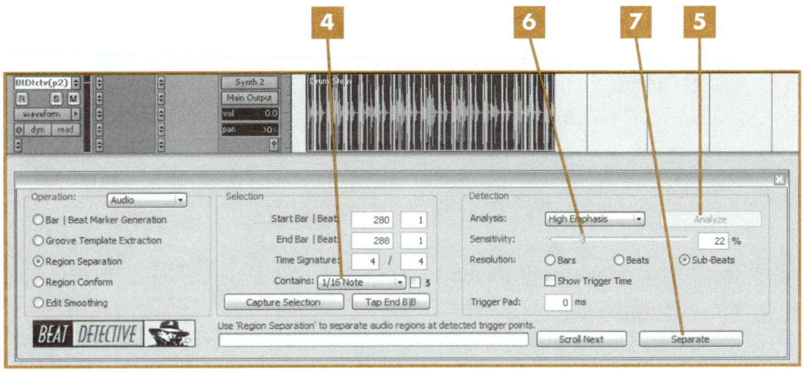

4. **Choose** the smallest **musical note value** of your audio (in this case, sixteenth notes) from the Contains menu button.
5. **Click Analyze**. Your audio will be examined by Beat Detective, which will look to detect transients.
6. Slowly **raise** the **Sensitivity slider** from zero. You will notice as your sensitivity increases, you will see vertical lines intersecting the transients of your audio. Once you are satisfied that the important transients have been marked (and no others), stop moving the slider.
7. **Click Separate**. Your region will be separated into a number of smaller regions.

8 Now that you've chopped up your larger region, it's time to get the smaller regions in line: Click the Region Conform radio button.

9 If you click on the Conform button at the top, you'll see that you can conform your regions in a standard way, or through Groove Conform (which will allow you to use the groove templates included with Pro Tools *in addition to* any grooves you may have extracted). For our purposes, choose the Standard mode.

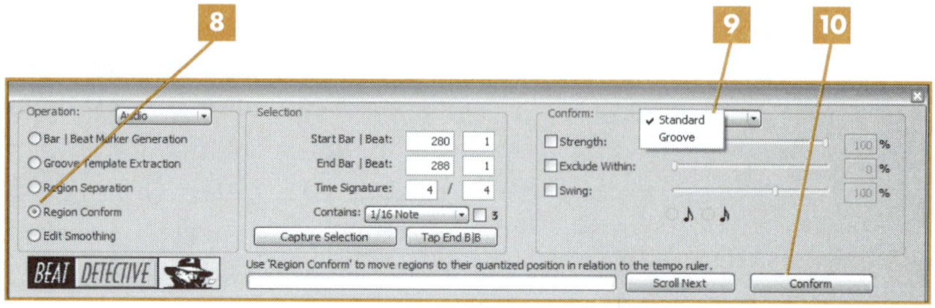

10 Click the Conform button. The regions will move subtly to match the existing tempo. Listen to the region, and you will hear a slight change in the feel.

11 As a byproduct of the conforming process, some gaps will be produced between the regions, and commonly there will be some clicks and pops (as you will hear in this example). That's where the final mode comes in: Click the Edit Smoothing radio button.

12 This last mode is very straightforward—it will eliminate the gaps between regions. If there is no problem with clicks or pops, click the Fill Gaps radio button. If there *are* clicks and pops (as there are in this example), a small crossfade between regions will fix the problem. Set the Crossfade Length to a reasonable amount (this will change from situation to situation—in this case, 3 ms sounds good), then click the Fill and Crossfade radio button.

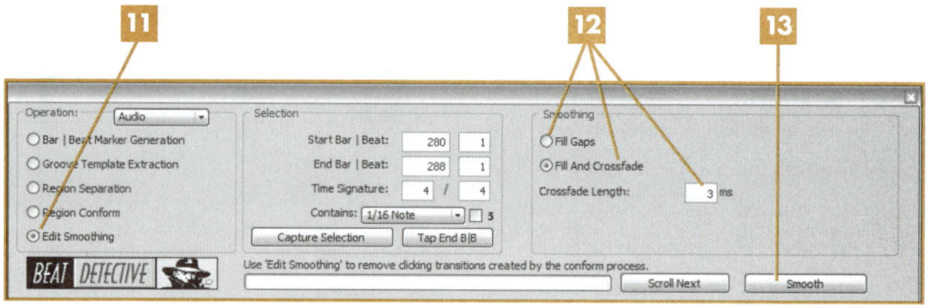

13 Click the Smooth button.

Your audio will now have a significantly different feel and no gaps!

MIDI Detective

Beat Detective can also analyze MIDI data and perform similar operations—a new addition to the Beat Detective process. To use Beat Detective with MIDI, just click the Audio button in the upper-left corner of the Beat Detective window. Some subtle changes in the window will be shown, but the general workflow is the same.

For More Information...

Even from this general description of Beat Detective, you've probably got a sense that it can be a very useful and complex tool. The implications of Beat Detective go beyond the scope of an introductory book like this one. If you want to go through every button in Beat Detective, you might want to check out *Working with Beats in Pro Tools: Skill Pack*, written by yours truly and published by Thomson Course Technology PTR (2007).

A Good Shortcut for Editing

Before I close the discussion on editing, I want to show you a useful shortcut. On either a Mac or a PC, hold the Shift key and press the spacebar to play back your session at half of real-time speed. This feature comes in particularly handy when you're setting punch-in or punch-out points for a particularly tight spot. (Just make sure not to record that way, or your audio will be twice as high in pitch!)

New Feature: Elastic Time!

As of this writing, Pro Tools 7.4 has only been available to the public for about a week, and already the rave reviews about Pro Tools' new Elastic Time feature (which has also been called *Elastic Audio* in some cases) are pouring in.

On the surface, Elastic Time might appear to be simply a nondestructive form of time compression and expansion, with some interesting options. In fact, if that's as far as Elastic Time went, it would be a significant upgrade, but the control and flexibility that you have with Elastic Time go far beyond that and give you the same control over your audio's timing that you might expect to have over MIDI!

Like any powerful new feature in Pro Tools, users will be discovering new tricks and workflows that can be done with Elastic Time for years, but even the obvious processes are very exciting. Let's take a look at the way Elastic Time works and some ways to use it, just to get you started!

Setting Things Up

Please go to Memory Location #7—Elastic Time.

Basic Operation

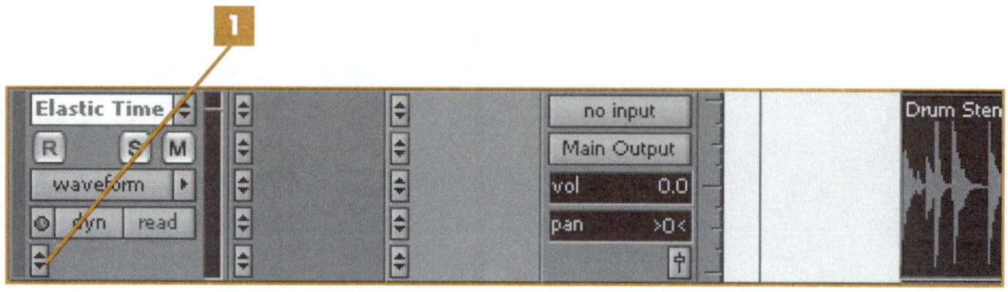

1 You can enable, disable, and configure Elastic Time on tracks on an individual basis. In this image, the track is currently *dis*abled for Elastic Time. Let's change that—click the Elastic Audio Plug-in Selector button. A menu will appear.

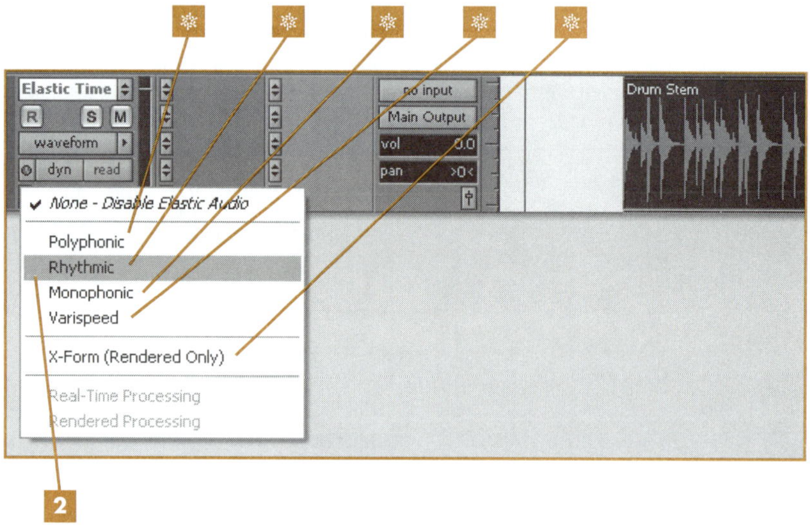

From this list you can choose the appropriate plug-in algorithm for the job. Here are your options:

- Polyphonic mode is a good general choice, and well suited to audio with multiple pitches being played simultaneously.
- Rhythmic mode is a good choice for your drum tracks and other percussive audio.
- Monophonic is great for Audio tracks in which only one note is being played at a time (for example, wind instruments or vocals).
- Varispeed is fundamentally different from the other plug-ins. The other algorithms will maintain the original pitches of your audio regardless of the speed of the audio being played. Varispeed mode, on the other hand, will lower the pitch of your audio when it is being played lower than normal, or raise the pitch when it's being played faster. This is particularly handy for turntable or tape-type effects.
- X-Form (Rendered Only) is a relatively higher-quality algorithm overall, but it is available in rendered form only. (We will discuss the difference between real-time and rendered in a moment.)

2 Click the desired algorithm. In this case, because the track is a drum loop, I'll choose Rhythmic.

You'll notice that once you make a choice, a button showing your choice will be displayed. Next to the name of the algorithm (in this case, Rhythmic), you'll see a rectangular area, which may either be dark or lit with a green color. This will tell you whether your Elastic Time is being provided to you in real time or in a rendered form.

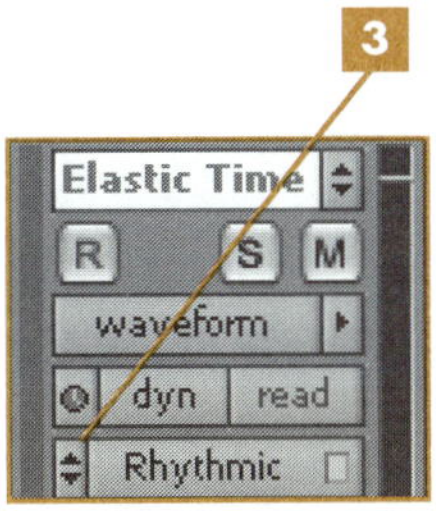

3 Click the Elastic Audio Plug-in Selector button once more, so we can take a closer look at real time versus rendered and discuss the difference between the two.

- Selecting Real-Time Processing will give you the quickest performance, and any changes that you make to your audio will be applied immediately. That being said, Elastic Time can be a bit demanding on a computer's CPU, particularly if your computer is not especially powerful.
- Selecting Rendered Processing will mean that your changes will not be immediately applied, but rather will take some amount of time (depending upon the speed of your computer) to apply the change. During that rendering time, the track will not be audible. Your changes will be rendered to files that are saved in your session's Rendered Files subfolder.

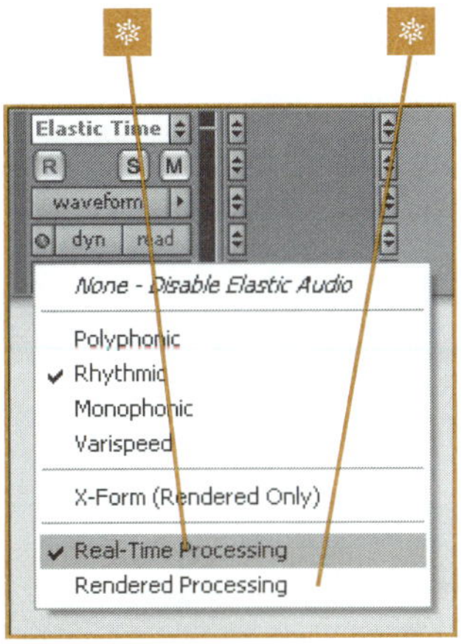

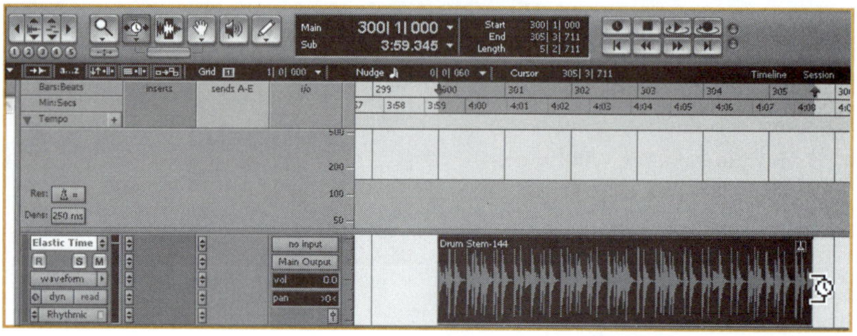

The first thing that you'll notice when you make a track Elastic is that the TCE Trim tool works a little differently. Instead of creating a new file and region each time you use the TCE Trim tool, your audio will simply be time compressed or expanded immediately. If you're using real-time processing, additional audio files won't even be created! In addition to the speed and convenience you gain, you will notice that as you use the TCE Trim tool multiple times on the same region, the audio quality won't degrade (something that can happen with non-Elastic Audio tracks).

But the party's just getting started, so let's set up our track to follow tempo changes:

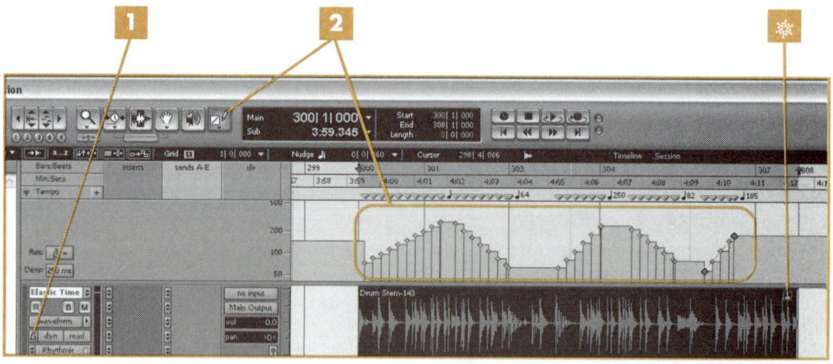

1. Change the Audio track from *sample*-based to *tick*-based. (For a refresher on how to do this, take a look at Chapter 6.)
2. Using the Pencil tool, draw some tempo change events onto the expanded Tempo ruler.

* If you listen to your audio, you'll hear that it follows your session's tempo changes.

You'll also notice a small icon in the upper-right corner of the region, indicating that it has been "warped" (something we'll talk about in just a moment).

Drawing tempo changes like this—with the Pencil tool—isn't always the best way to work. Let's undo the tempo changes that you just made with the Pencil tool and quantize the audio just as if it was MIDI!

1. Click the Event menu.
2. Select the Event Operations menu item. A submenu will appear.
3. Click the Quantize menu item. The Quantize window will appear.

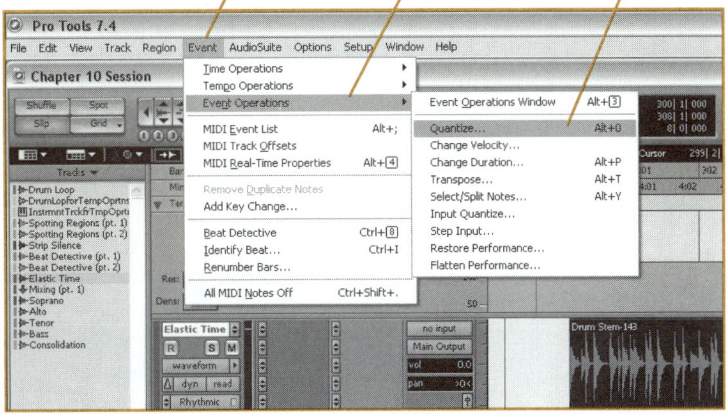

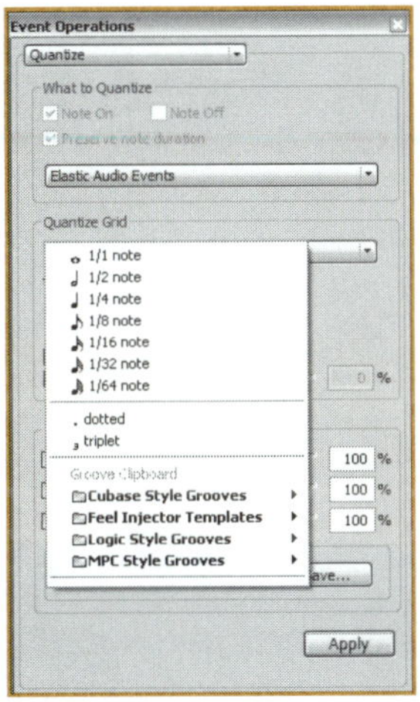

You'll notice that now that you've selected an Elastic Audio region (which contains Elastic Audio events, which we'll cover next), you have the option of quantizing this drum region, almost as if it was MIDI! If you click the Quantize Grid drop-down menu, you'll find that you can quantize to either a set value (such as sixteenth notes) or grooves (which you'll see at the bottom of the list). Once you quantize the audio (using the same method that you learned when quantizing MIDI in Chapter 7), you can hear the changes that you've made.

COMBINING TOOLS

Now that you've got two great tools like Beat Detective and Elastic Time under your belt, let's look at a possible way to get them to work together. Here's a scenario: Suppose you've got two drum regions that you want to have the same feel. Here's one way to go—choose the drum region whose feel you prefer, and use Beat Detective's Bar|Beat Marker Generation mode to change your session's tempo map. Your other tick-based Elastic tracks will adjust to match the new tempo map.

Event and Warp Markers (and How to Use Them)

With the addition of Elastic Time, longtime users of Pro Tools will notice that two new track views are available to you—Analysis and Warp. Both of these new views have their parts to play with regard to Elastic Audio. Let's take a look at these views one by one.

1 Click the Track View Selector button (which in this case currently reads Waveform). The Track View menu will appear.

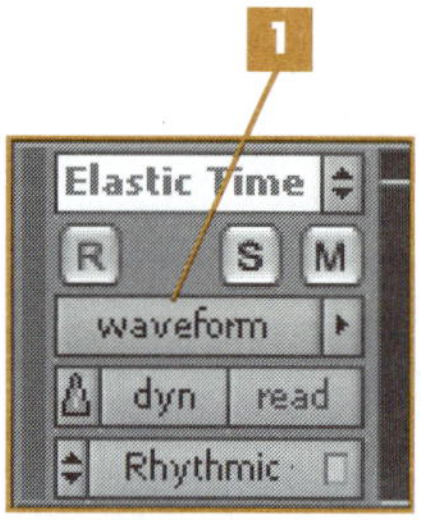

2 Choose Analysis from the list of view options.

You'll immediately note that there are markings at each transient of the region. Each of these markers is called an Event Marker. Let's take a closer look:

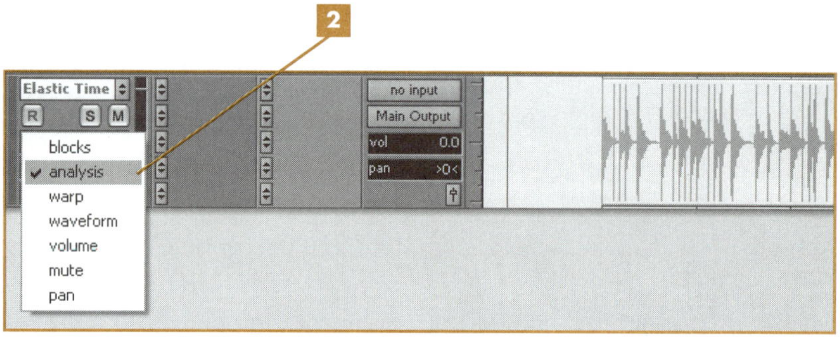

- Event Markers in this view are loosely analogous to the beat markers that you saw earlier in this chapter when you worked with Beat Detective. These markers determine the parts of the audio that are moved when the audio follows changes in the Tempo ruler, or when quantizing it, as we did earlier.

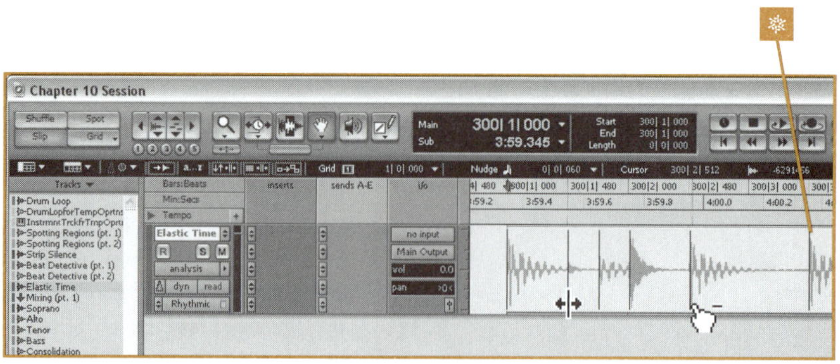

- From time to time, you may decide to change or remove Event Markers. The Grabber tool will help you with this:
  - When using the Grabber tool, move your cursor over an existing Event Marker. Your cursor will change to the double-arrow shown here, and you will be able to click and drag the Event Marker to a new location.

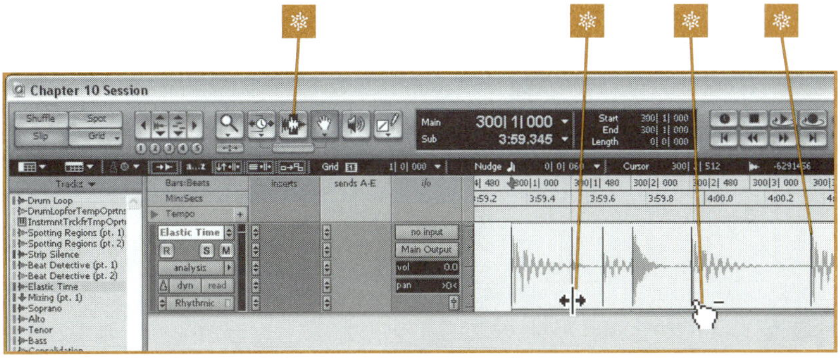

- If you hold down the Alt (PC) or Option (Mac) key while using the Grabber tool, you will see your cursor turn into the pointing hand (with a minus sign next to it). Click on any existing Event Marker to delete it.
- If you want to create a new Event Marker, just double-click where you want to create it!

3. Now, let's move on to the Warp view. Click the Track View Selector button and choose Warp from the list of options. Warp Markers go beyond Event Markers, and they allow you to take direct control over individual segments of your audio.

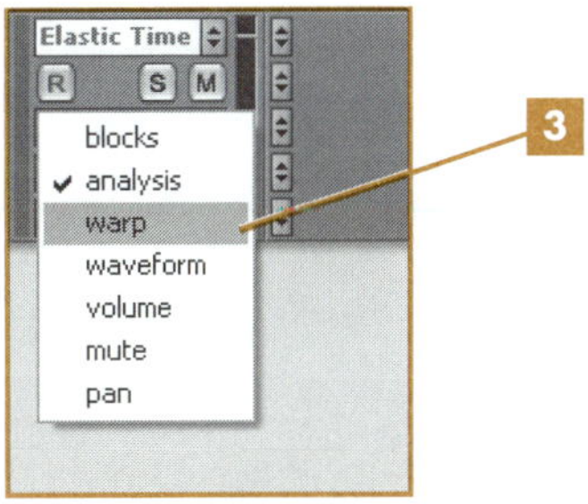

4. Here again, your Grabber tool will be your greatest ally. Move your mouse over any Event Marker (yes, you can still see your Event Markers, even though you're in Warp view. The cursor will turn into the icon shown here, indicating that you're ready to use the Telescoping Warp. Just click and drag to the left or the right to proportionally compress or expand the entire region.

5 Here's a powerful use of Elastic Time: Hold down the Shift key and move your mouse over an existing Event Marker. The cursor shown here is called Individual Warp.

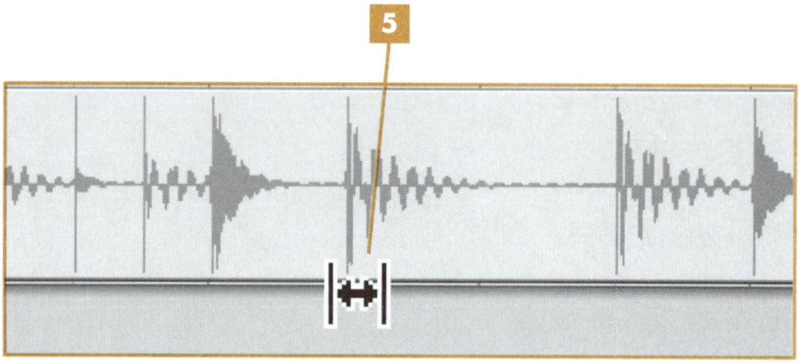

6 Click on the Event Marker. Here's what you get:

- You'll notice that not only has the marker you clicked changed, but also the markers immediately next to it. These are Warp Markers and can be identified by their darker color and the small blue triangle at the base of the marker. Think of Warp Markers as being "handles" that you can grab and stretch your audio.

7 Click and drag the center Warp Marker left or right.

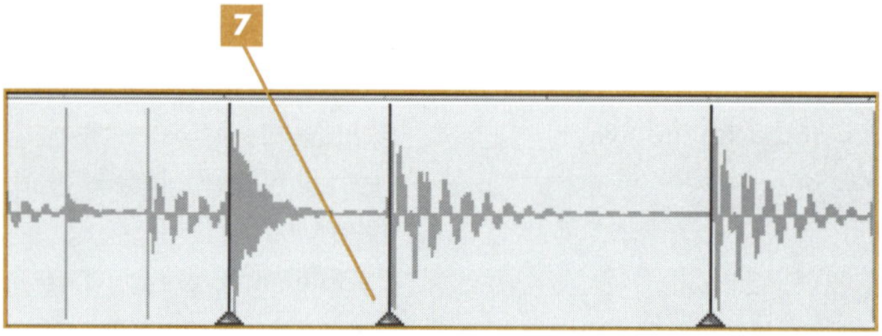

You'll immediately see that the audio is being pulled like taffy, giving you control over minute aspects of your audio region. The Warp Marker can be dragged smoothly if you're in Slip, Shuffle, or Spot modes—if you're in Grid mode, you'll see that your marker snaps according to your grid resolution.

8 In this particular case, I've moved the Warp Marker far enough from its original location that some aural side effects occur. That's not a problem, because I can tweak the plug-in a bit and fix it. Click the Elastic Audio Plug-In button. The plug-in window will appear.

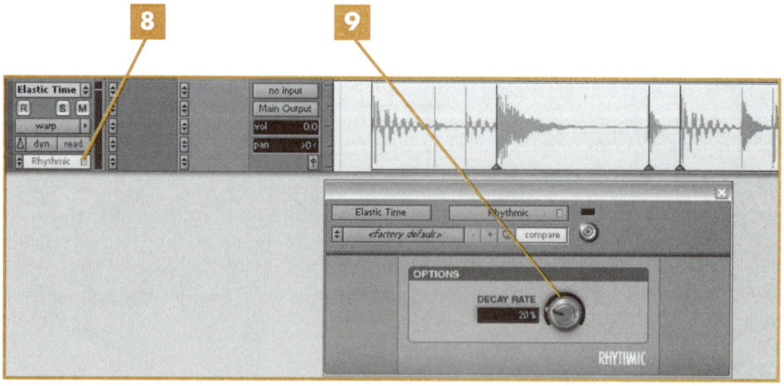

9 This window will appear differently for each kind of Elastic Audio plug-in, allowing you to adjust the parameter that is most relevant. In the case of the Rhythmic plug-in, you can just bring down the decay rate a bit and remove the unwanted audio.

Though the Individual Warp method shown here will work in many situations, you might want to create single Warp Markers. Again using the Grabber tool, there are two ways you can do it:

- Double-click an existing Event Marker to change it into a Warp Marker.
- If there's no marker in the place that you want to create a new Warp Marker, no problem—just double-click where you want to create one!

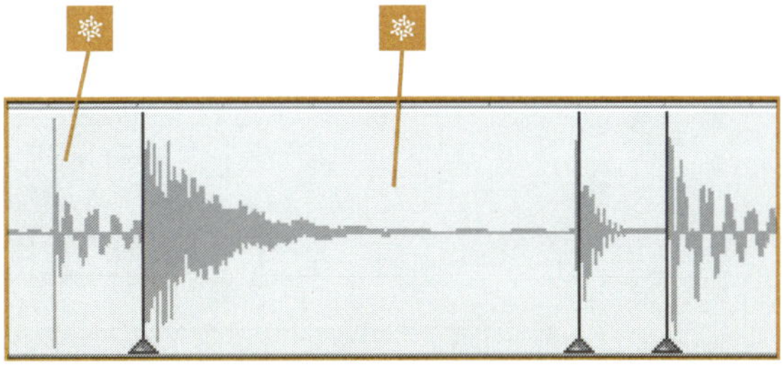

10 If you want to quickly look at (and change) some general information about a region, just right-click the region. A menu will appear.

11 Select Elastic Properties. The Elastic Properties window will open.

12 The Elastic Properties window will show you some overall information about the region, including length, tempo, meter, and so on. If you want to enter new information here, you can type your values into any of the dark areas. The Event Sensitivity value works in much the same way as the Sensitivity slider in Beat Detective.

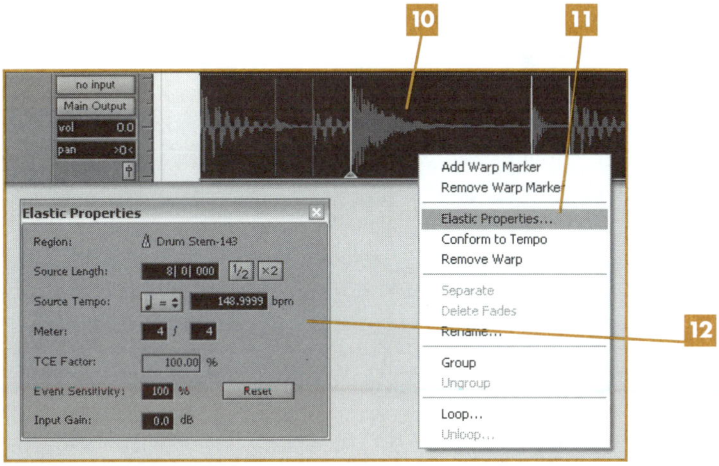

Elastic Audio and the Workspace

There have been a few new additions to the Workspace window, which will improve the way you preview and import your audio.

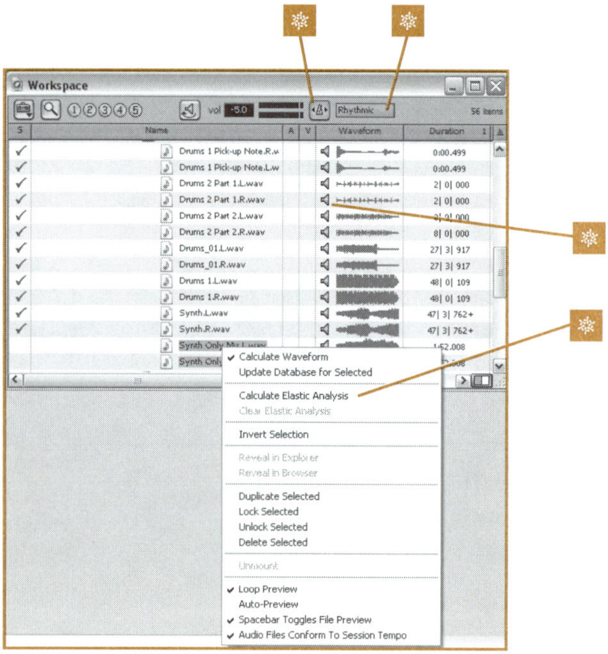

- At the top of the Workspace window, you'll see the green Audio Files Conform to Session Tempo button. When you click this button, your audio files will play at your session's tempo (rather than their original tempo) when previewed. Before this can happen, the audio must be analyzed for Elastic Time. Files that are analyzed will be indicated by a check mark in the S column.
- Clicking the button to the immediate right of the Audio Files Conform to Session Tempo button will display a list of all the real-time Elastic Time plug-in options, and you can choose the algorithm that sounds best to you.
- Just click the speaker icon by the region waveform that you want to preview; as long as the Audio Files Conform to Session Tempo feature is enabled, you'll hear the audio at the session's tempo. If there is no check mark by a given audio file in the S column, the audio will automatically be analyzed (a check mark will appear) before the region plays back.
- You can also manually analyze individual audio files by right-clicking the file name, and then choosing Calculate Elastic Analysis from the list that appears.

Elastic audio files can be dragged to the Timeline, Regions list, or Tracks list just like any other kind of audio file. When you import to the Tracks list or Timeline, a new Elastic track (tick-based) will be created, and the same plug-in algorithm that you had in your Workspace window will be applied. (You can change algorithms at any time by clicking the track's Elastic Audio Plug-in Selector button and choosing another plug-in from the list.)

Making the Most of Elastic Time

Because it's being done in real time, Elastic Time will consume some of your CPU's power, and you might run into some performance issues. As we've discussed earlier, choosing Rendered Processing instead of Real-Time Processing will give your CPU a break. You can also coax more power out of your computer by going to the Playback Engine window.

1. Click the Setup menu.
2. Click the Playback Engine menu item. The Playback Engine window will open.

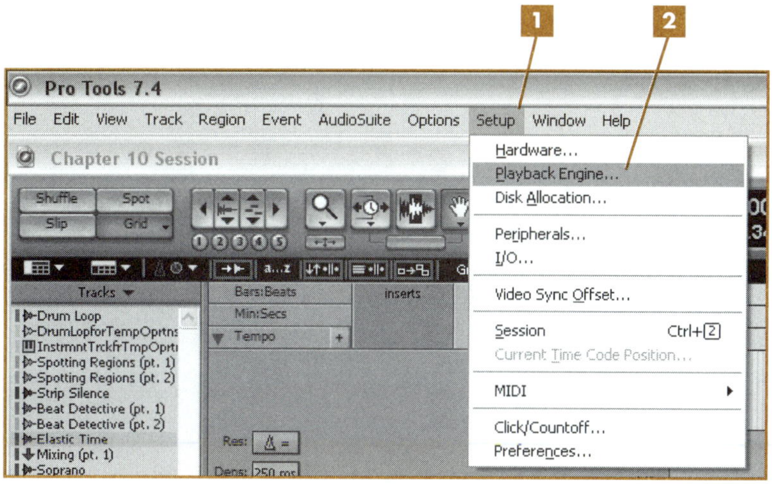

3. The Cache Size button will allow you to choose how much memory will be exclusively allocated to the playback of Elastic Audio regions. When you click the Cache Size menu button, you'll see that you've got three options:

- Minimum (reduces memory use)
- Normal
- Large (improves performance)

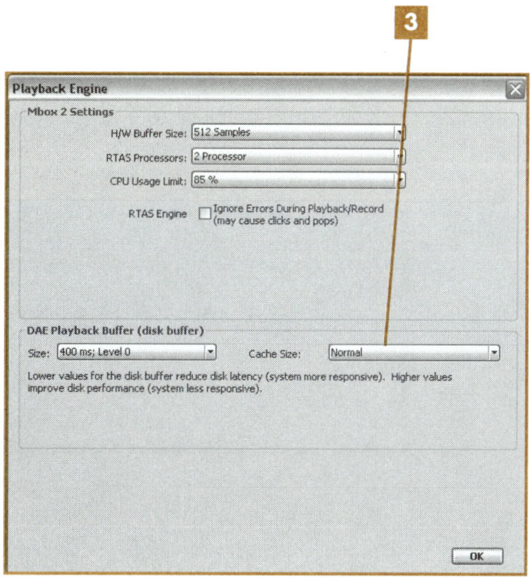

You can also control the behavior of your session with regard to Elastic Time through the Preferences window.

1. Click the Setup menu.
2. Click the Preferences menu item. The Preferences window will open.

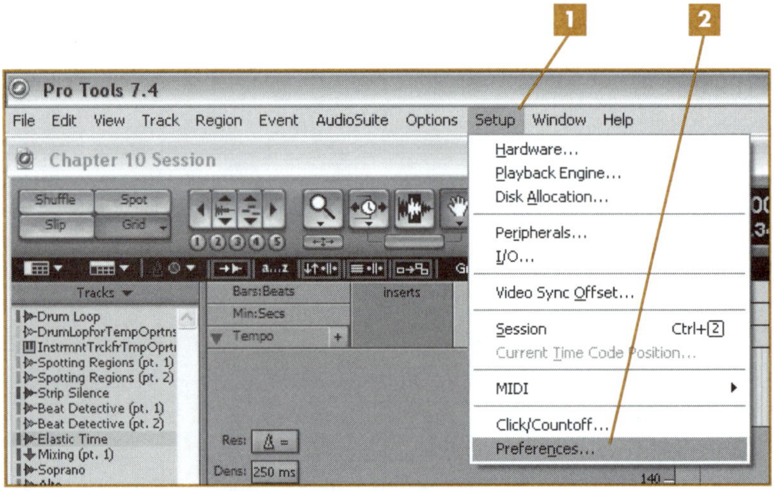

3. Click the Processing tab. In the Elastic Audio section of this page, you'll see three useful options:
   - Default Plug-in. Here you can choose the initial plug-in you'll use in the Workspace window, as well as the plug-in that is initially used when new tracks are created as Elastic Audio tracks.
   - Default Input Gain. This will allow you to automatically reduce the volume of Elastic regions.
   - Enable Elastic Audio on New Tracks. When this box is checked, new Audio tracks will be created with Elastic Time enabled.

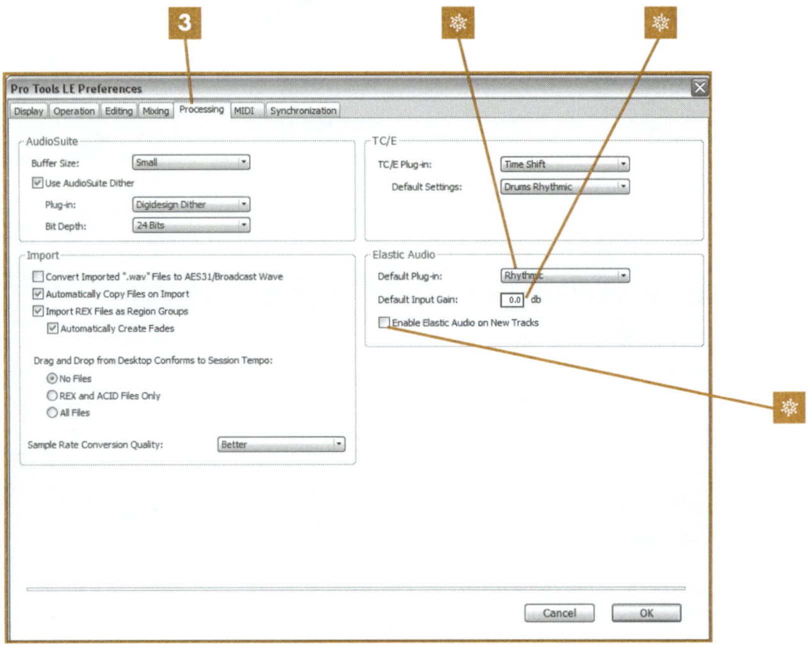

Elastic Warnings

One more thing: From time to time, you might see sections of your audio turn red when dragging Warp Markers. Not too worry—Pro Tools is just letting you know that you've applied a good deal of time compression or expansion. Technically speaking, you've gone beyond Pro Tool's recommended limits, but if it sounds good to your ears, go for it!

Making the Most of Mixing

Here are a couple of tips to make your mixes rock!

Using the Edit Tools

So far, you've only used the Pencil tool to edit your automation. This section will show you how to use a couple other tools.

Setting Things Up

Please go to Memory Location #8—Mixing (pt. 1).

1. Click on the Grabber tool. The tool will be selected.
2. Click on the automation line. A new breakpoint will be created. From that point, you can drag the breakpoint to the desired location.

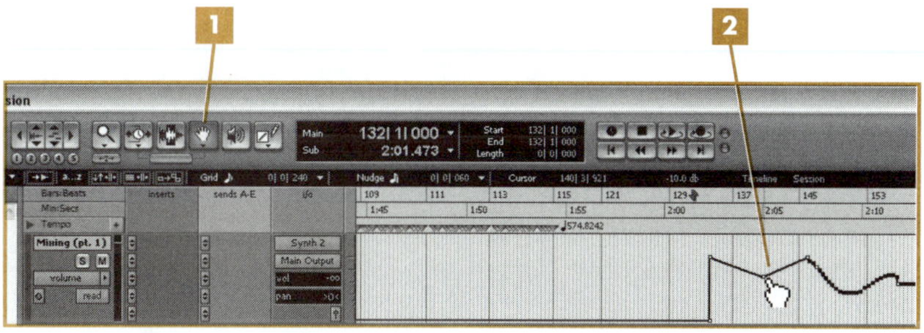

Deleting Automation Breakpoints

Hold the Option key (Mac) or the Alt key (PC) and click on a previously written breakpoint to remove it.

1. Make a selection on a track you want to change (using the Selector tool).
2. Click on the Trim tool. The tool will be selected.
3. Move the Trim tool into the selected area. The Trim icon will appear on its side.
4. Click and drag your mouse up or down to change any prewritten automation proportionally.

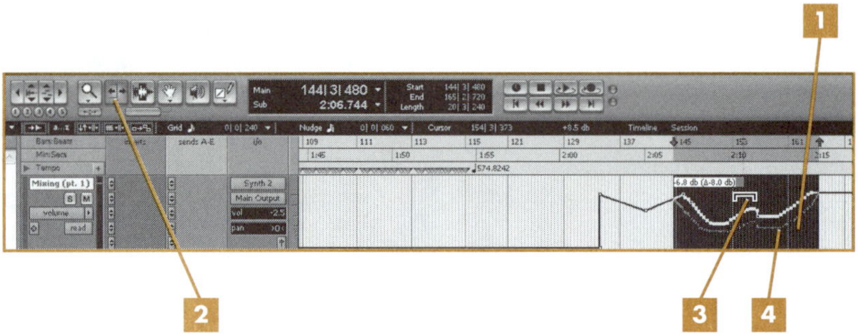

The amount of change effected upon your automation will be shown in the delta value.

5. Release the mouse button. The automation will be proportionally changed in the selected area.

Toggling Groups

This section will show you how you can temporarily suspend fader groups so you can quickly change the balance of the fader group.

Setting Things Up

For this section, please go to Memory Location #9—Mixing (pt. 2) and switch to the Mix window.

In this example, we've got four vocal parts that are grouped together. Here's a way to change the balance of the group without the hassle of deactivating the Mix group!

1. Press and hold the Start (Windows) key (PC) or the Control key (Mac), and then click and drag the fader you want to change. You can change the volume of a track without affecting other tracks in the group.
2. Release the key. Your group will be re-enabled.

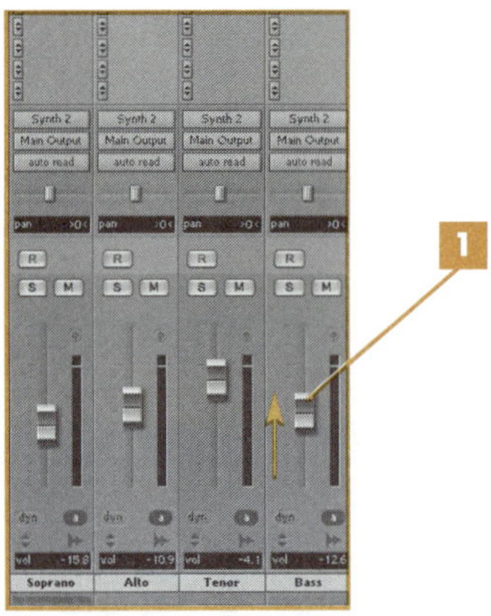

My Favorite Mix Window Shortcut

Here's a useful tip, especially for those complex sessions with many groups: To quickly show *only* the tracks in a given group, hold down the Start key (PC) or the Control key (Mac) and click the group that you want to see in the groups list. All tracks that are not members of that group will be hidden. This is particularly useful when working in the Mix window, giving you a sort of "layered" mixer view!

Getting the Most out of Your Mix

Before you leave the task of mixing, here's one more tip for your consideration. Remember when you used a send from a dry Audio track to a wet Aux track back in Chapter 8? Guess what? You can send from multiple tracks to a single Aux. Just create identical sends on each track you want to route to a single Aux, assigning each send to the same bus. This method is commonly used for assigning many tracks (such as drums, for example) to a single reverb. It's a simple and convenient way to work, and it conserves your CPU's resources as well!

Advanced Resource Management

This section includes yet more ways to view and manage your data!

Inactive Elements

There's a difference between an element that's offline and one that's inactive in your session. An *offline region* occurs when source media is not found when you open a session. When that happens, the region will appear on a track, but the region will be empty, with the region name in *italics*. *Inactive elements* are deliberately disabled by the Pro Tools user. There are many good reasons to make a track or a plug-in inactive. Making tracks inactive allows you to create and work with tracks beyond the 32-voice limitation of a Pro Tools LE system. An inactive plug-in will free up valuable CPU resources while maintaining automation and preset settings.

First take a look at a new window—the System Usage window:

1. Click on Window. The Window menu will appear.
2. Click on System Usage. The System Usage window will appear.

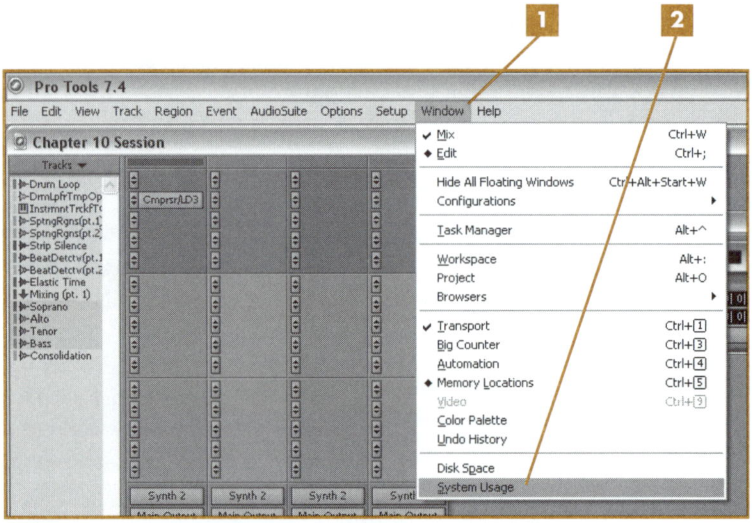

* The most important graph in the System Usage window is the CPU graph because your computer's CPU is assigned the task of processing your plug-ins.

3. Press and hold the Ctrl+Start keys (PC) or the ⌘+Control keys (Mac) and click on the effect you want to disable.

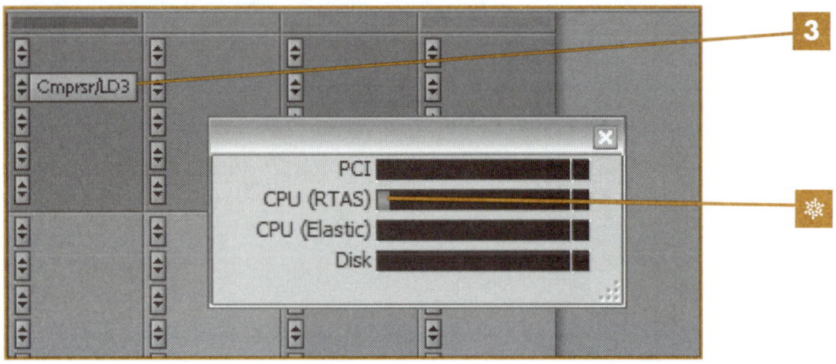

* The label for the plug-in will switch to italicized text, indicating that it is inactive. Also, the plug-in window will change to the Plug-In Inactive window.
* For every effect you disable, your CPU gauge will decrease, leaving more processing room for new effects.

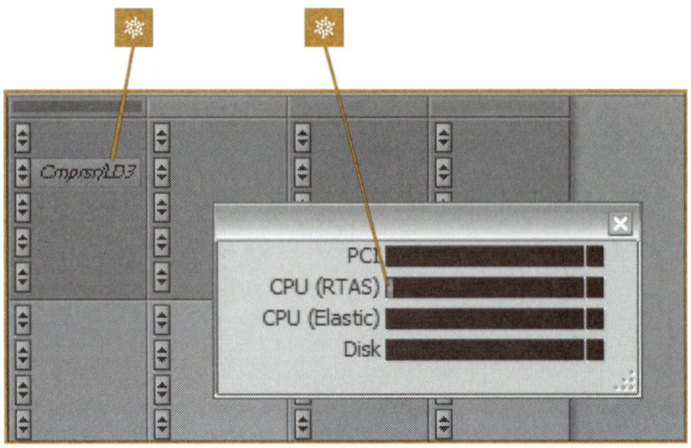

You can make an entire track (including all associated plug-ins) inactive by Ctrl+Start-clicking (PC) or ⌘+Control-clicking (Mac) on the small icon in the lower-right corner of the channel strip. The track's channel strip will be grayed out, and the track's voice will be freed up for use by another track.

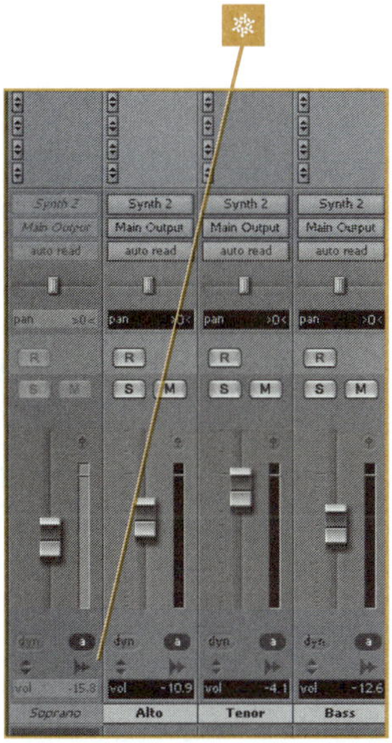

Working with HD Sessions

When you open a session created or used on an HD system, any voices above 32 will open deactivated. You can still use them by deactivating any of the first tracks to free up a voice, and then activating what you want to work on above 32.

How to Consolidate (and Why)

One way to increase the efficiency of your system is to minimize its edit density. *Edit density* refers to the number of times your system must acquire data from your hard drive during playback. If you have many small regions (such as drum loops, for example), it can increase your edit density. In extreme cases, high edit density can cause playback errors.

The trick is to decrease the number of regions without changing the sound of your session, and the Consolidate function is the key.

Setting Things Up

For this demonstration, go to Memory Location #10—Consolidation. You'll see a section of drums to which Beat Detective has been applied to conform it to an even grid—*lots* of regions!

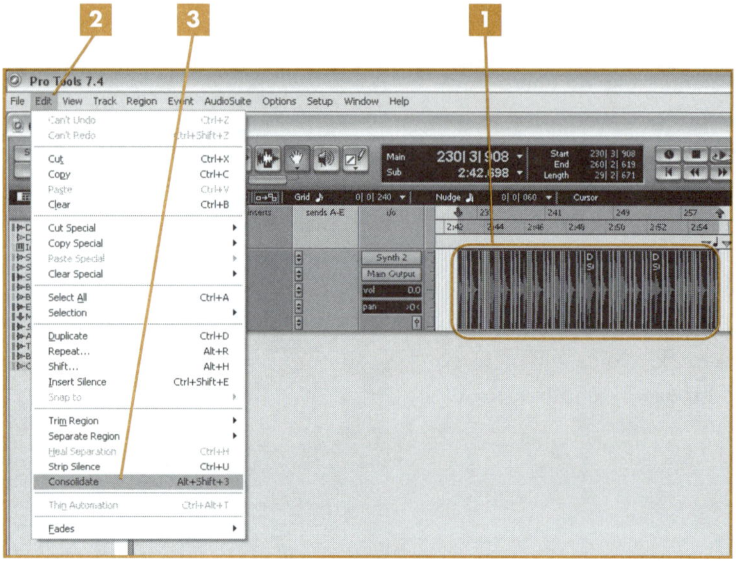

1. Select a section of your session that is particularly dense with regions. (This has been done for you in this example.)
2. Click on Edit. The Edit menu will appear.
3. Click on Consolidate. Your selection of multiple regions will be rendered into a single region.

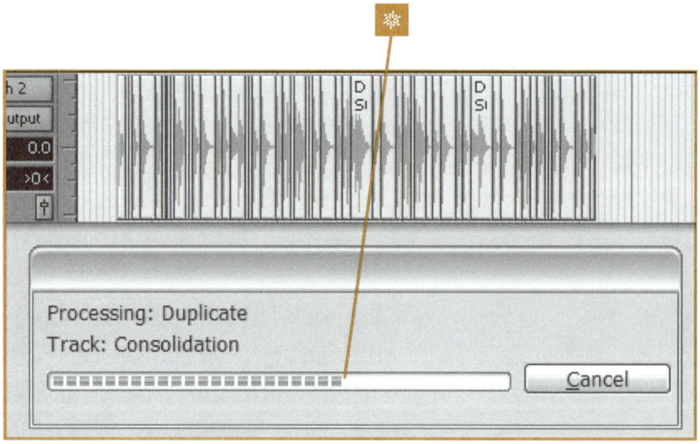

- A window will display the progress of the rendering process.

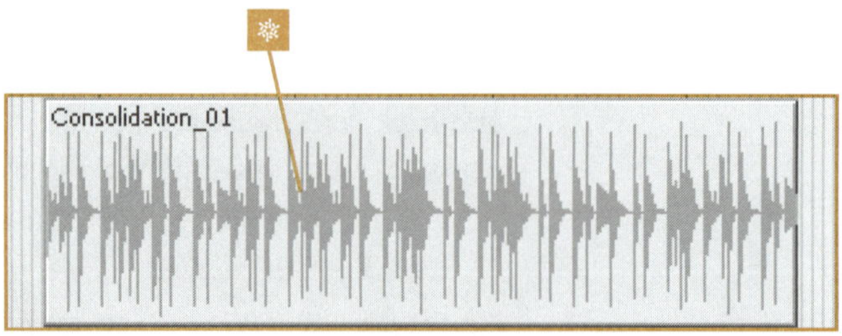

- Your selection will be replaced by a single region that sounds identical to the original selection.

Consolidating Silence?

When you consolidate, any selected space that is not occupied by a region will be rendered as silent audio, as will any gaps in between regions in your selection.

Working with Movies

Although Pro Tools is certainly an audio-oriented program, there is a degree of support for incorporating video into your session. Let's have a look at the process of importing a QuickTime movie, which couldn't be easier.

DV Toolkit 2

For the purposes of this book, we'll focus on the basic use of video files, rather than more advanced video workflows, such as digitizing analog video to the Pro Tools Timeline via a video interface (such as the Avid Mojo, for example).

For those of you who are in need of these more advanced features, there is a software addition to Pro Tools called the DV Toolkit 2, which not only gives you additional video power within Pro Tools, but also adds video-related features. You can learn more about the DV Toolkit 2 and what it offers by visiting Digidesign's website (www.digidesign.com) and going to the Products page.

1. Click on File. The File menu will appear.
2. Click on Import, and another menu will appear.
3. Click on Video. The Select Video File to Import dialog box will open.

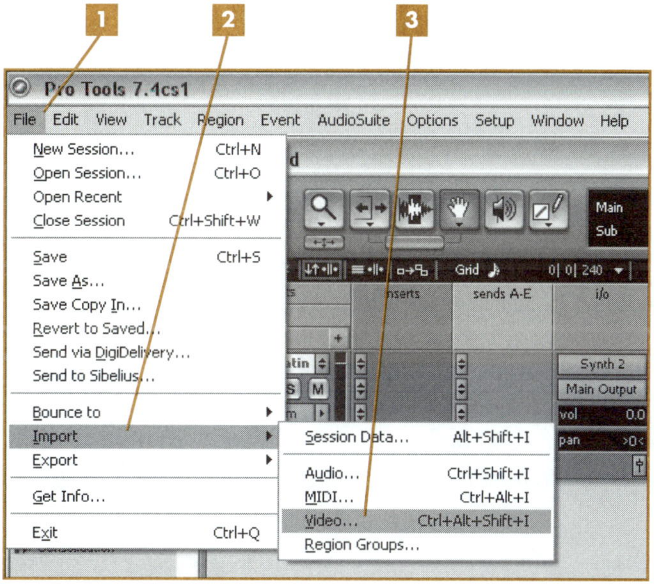

4 Navigate to the file you want to use and click on Open. The Video Import Options dialog box will open.

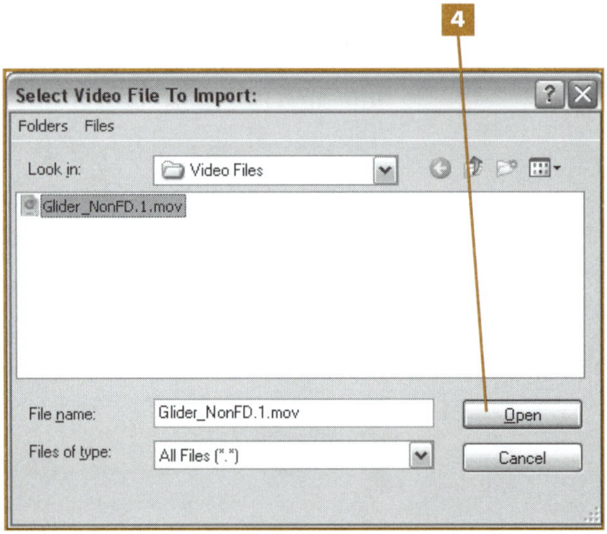

Don't Have Any Video Files? No Problem!

If you don't have any other video file to import, you can import the video file from the Chapter 8 session. Just go into the Chapter 8 Session folder, and then open the Video Files folder.

5 In the Video Import Options dialog box, the Location drop-down will give you a number of placement options. Just click on the Location menu button, which in this case reads "Session Start," to select the desired option. Here's what you have to choose from:

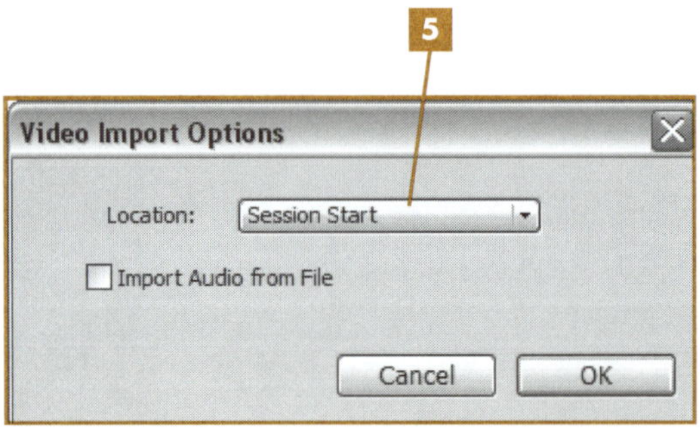

- Session Start. This will place the audio region at the very beginning of the track.
- Song Start. You can set your song to start at a place other than the beginning of a track (which we covered in Chapter 6). If you have done this, the option to place your audio at the song start will be available.
- Selection. Choosing this option will place your audio at the beginning of any selected area.
- Spot. The term *spot* is used (usually in a video context) to describe the placement of audio at a specific point in time. Choosing this option will open the Spot dialog box, where you can type a specific time location for your audio.

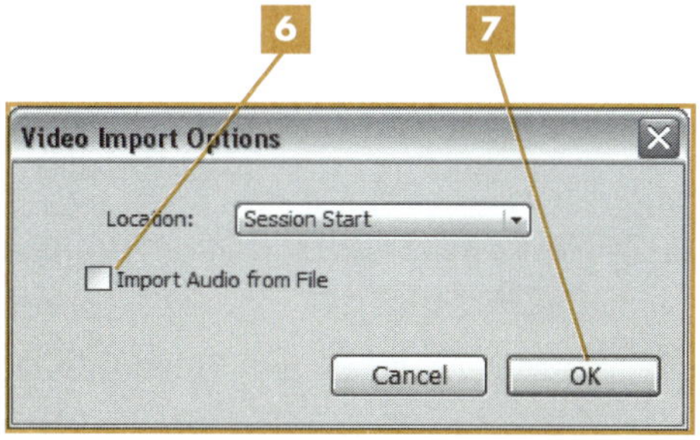

6 If you click the Import Audio from File check box, any audio that is included with the video will be imported to a new Audio track.

7 To import the video into your session, click OK. A new video track will be created in your session.

Although a video track isn't an Audio track, you'll see it displayed in your Edit window and in the Track Show/Hide list. You can arrange the track in your session just as you would any other track, and you can move and separate the video region just as you would any audio region. Additionally, a video window will appear.

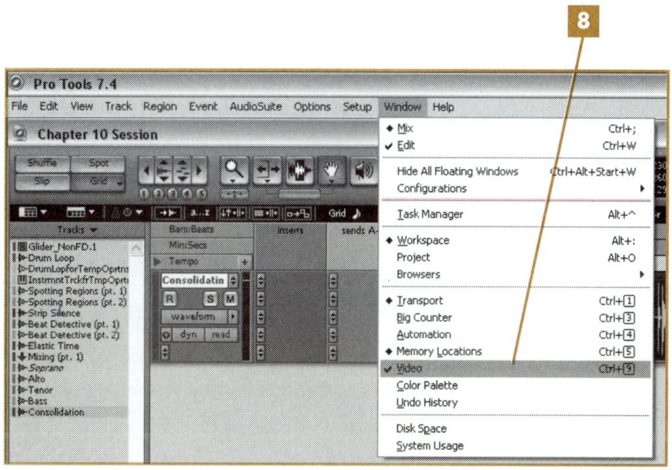

8 If your movie window doesn't appear, click on Video from the Window menu. The Video window will appear.

Resizable Video

Longtime users of Pro Tools might not be aware of this: The Video window is *resizable*! Just move your cursor to any of the window's boundaries and click and drag the window to the desired size. If you want the Video window to fill your entire screen, just right-click in the Video window and choose Fit Screen from the list of sizing options that will appear.

Checking Your Work

To see this chapter's steps in their completed form, check out the Chapter 10 Session-Finished session.

Interoperability: Making Shared Sessions Work

Perhaps the most compelling reason to learn and use Pro Tools is the fact that it is a global standard in the DAW world. From bedroom studios to multimillion-dollar studios, Pro Tools allows greater mobility for amateurs and professionals alike than perhaps any other application. Take your humble author, for example—I wrote a good portion of this book in airports with an Mbox 2 Mini LE system, and I could easily open the exact same work in any pro studio with a minimum of muss and fuss!

The best way to maximize the interoperability of Pro Tools is to make every effort to ensure that your session can be opened and heard properly on every system and that collaborators can easily get around in your work. Here are some recommendations on how to make this happen:

- Name all tracks *before* recording, and name them in a way that anyone can understand.
- Use your comments. The Comments column of every track and the Comment field of markers are valuable sources of information to others.
- Use your memory locations. Identify each section of your work and descriptively name it so that anybody can understand the overall layout of your work.
- Internally record (using a bus) all your virtual Instrument tracks to Audio tracks. This ensures that even if your collaborator doesn't have your virtual instruments in his system, he will still be able to hear them.
- Use AudioSuite when appropriate. Just as with internal recording, this will create a new file that can be played back in any Pro Tools situation, even if the actual plug-ins don't exist on the other system.
- Use a click track. Recording a great beat is all well and good, but if you're not in sync with the MIDI tempo of your session, operations such as Quantize, Beat Detective, and Grid mode will do more harm than good!

- Before you archive your session, or whenever moving it from one system to another, do a Save Copy of your session and click all appropriate options for saving. This will ensure that all your audio, video, and plug-in settings will be saved in one central location. *That's* the file you should archive or move to another system for further work. Incidentally, you can also use the Save Copy feature to save your session as an older version of Pro Tools (if you're collaborating with a user of an older version of Pro Tools).

Good Luck!

Congratulations—you made it! You've gone through a solid introductory tour of Pro Tools' basic operations and features. And although this discussion of Pro Tools is certainly not a comprehensive listing of *everything* that Pro Tools can do, you can rest assured that your creative journey has started well. Over time, you'll not only learn more about Pro Tools, but undoubtedly you will find your own working style—a process that will be constantly refined as you gain experience and speed.

Still Want More Shortcuts?

Over the course of this book we've covered a good number of useful shortcuts, but there are still many more for you to discover. Fortunately, there's a resource for your shortcut-browsing pleasure—the Digidesign support page. Just go to the Digidesign website (www.digidesign.com) and go to the Support page. From there, search "shortcuts" in the Technical Documents category. From the resultant page, you'll be able to download PDF documents of the latest shortcuts.

As your skills grow, you may crave more in-depth knowledge. Fortunately Digidesign has an excellent training program, which they offer through their worldwide network of training partner schools. Digidesign's Training and Education Program is a constantly evolving curriculum that can take you from where you are now all the way up to an elite Expert Certification, complete with worldwide listing! For more information, visit www.digidesign.com/training.

You've begun a great exploration and a worthwhile endeavor, in my humble opinion. I personally believe that artistic pursuits nourish the soul of not only the patron, but of the artist as well. It's my wish that this product and the technology to come inspire you to push the limits of your creativity. Good luck!

Index

Numbers

A

B

C

D

E

F

G

H

I

K

L

M

N

O

P

Q

R

S

T

U

V

Z

License Agreement/Notice of Limited Warranty

By opening the sealed disc container in this book, you agree to the following terms and conditions. If, upon reading the following license agreement and notice of limited warranty, you cannot agree to the terms and conditions set forth, return the unused book with unopened disc to the place where you purchased it for a refund.

License:

The enclosed software is copyrighted by the copyright holder(s) indicated on the software disc. You are licensed to copy the software onto a single computer for use by a single user and to a backup disc. You may not reproduce, make copies, or distribute copies or rent or lease the software in whole or in part, except with written permission of the copyright holder(s). You may transfer the enclosed disc only together with this license, and only if you destroy all other copies of the software and the transferee agrees to the terms of the license. You may not decompile, reverse assemble, or reverse engineer the software.

Notice of Limited Warranty:

The enclosed disc is warranted by Course Technology to be free of physical defects in materials and workmanship for a period of sixty (60) days from end user's purchase of the book/disc combination. During the sixty-day term of the limited warranty, Course Technology will provide a replacement disc upon the return of a defective disc.

Limited Liability:

THE SOLE REMEDY FOR BREACH OF THIS LIMITED WARRANTY SHALL CONSIST ENTIRELY OF REPLACEMENT OF THE DEFECTIVE DISC. IN NO EVENT SHALL COURSE TECHNOLOGY OR THE AUTHOR BE LIABLE FOR ANY OTHER DAMAGES, INCLUDING LOSS OR CORRUPTION OF DATA, CHANGES IN THE FUNCTIONAL CHARACTERISTICS OF THE HARDWARE OR OPERATING SYSTEM, DELETERIOUS INTERACTION WITH OTHER SOFTWARE, OR ANY OTHER SPECIAL, INCIDENTAL, OR CONSEQUENTIAL DAMAGES THAT MAY ARISE, EVEN IF COURSE TECHNOLOGY AND/OR THE AUTHOR HAS PREVIOUSLY BEEN NOTIFIED THAT THE POSSIBILITY OF SUCH DAMAGES EXISTS.

Disclaimer of Warranties:

COURSE TECHNOLOGY AND THE AUTHOR SPECIFICALLY DISCLAIM ANY AND ALL OTHER WARRANTIES, EITHER EXPRESS OR IMPLIED, INCLUDING WARRANTIES OF MERCHANTABILITY, SUITABILITY TO A PARTICULAR TASK OR PURPOSE, OR FREEDOM FROM ERRORS. SOME STATES DO NOT ALLOW FOR EXCLUSION OF IMPLIED WARRANTIES OR LIMITATION OF INCIDENTAL OR CONSEQUENTIAL DAMAGES, SO THESE LIMITATIONS MIGHT NOT APPLY TO YOU.

Other:

This Agreement is governed by the laws of the State of Massachusetts without regard to choice of law principles. The United Convention of Contracts for the International Sale of Goods is specifically disclaimed. This Agreement constitutes the entire agreement between you and Course Technology regarding use of the software.